CW00969242

EUROPEAN TORT LAW

European Tort Law

CEES VAN DAM

Professorial Fellow
British Institute of International and Comparative Law
London

*

Professor of Private Law
Vrije Universiteit Amsterdam

OXFORD
UNIVERSITY PRESS

OXFORD

UNIVERSITY PRESS

Great Clarendon Street, Oxford OX2 6DP

Oxford University Press is a department of the University of Oxford.
It furthers the University's objective of excellence in research, scholarship,
and education by publishing worldwide in

Oxford New York

Auckland Cape Town Dar es Salaam Hong Kong Karachi
Kuala Lumpur Madrid Melbourne Mexico City Nairobi
New Delhi Shanghai Taipei Toronto

With offices in

Argentina Austria Brazil Chile Czech Republic France Greece
Guatemala Hungary Italy Japan Poland Portugal Singapore
South Korea Switzerland Thailand Turkey Ukraine Vietnam

Oxford is a registered trade mark of Oxford University Press
in the UK and in certain other countries

Published in the United States
by Oxford University Press Inc., New York

© C. van Dam, 2006

The moral rights of the author have been asserted
Database right Oxford University Press (maker)

Crown copyright material is reproduced under Class Licence
Number C01P0000148 with the permission of OPSI
and the Queen's Printer for Scotland

First published 2006

All rights reserved. No part of this publication may be reproduced,
stored in a retrieval system, or transmitted, in any form or by any means,
without the prior permission in writing of Oxford University Press,
or as expressly permitted by law, or under terms agreed with the appropriate
reprographics rights organization. Enquiries concerning reproduction
outside the scope of the above should be sent to the Rights Department,
Oxford University Press, at the address above

You must not circulate this book in any other binding or cover
and you must impose the same condition on any acquirer

British Library Cataloguing in Publication Data

Data available

Library of Congress Cataloging in Publication Data

Dam, Cees van.
European tort law / Cees van Dam.
p. cm.
Includes bibliographical references and index.
ISBN-13: 978–0–19–929071–0 (alk. paper)
ISBN-10: 0–19–929071–7 (hardback : alk. paper)
1. Torts—Europe. 2. Liability (Law)—Europe. 3. Damages—Europe. I. Title.
KJC1640.D36 2006
346.2403—dc22
2006005022

Typeset by Newgen Imaging Systems (P) Ltd., Chennai, India
Printed in Great Britain
on acid-free paper by
Biddles Ltd., King's Lynn

ISBN 0–19–929071–7   978–0–19–929071–0

1 3 5 7 9 10 8 6 4 2

To Reinoud Hesper

Preface

A preface is not destined to give an overview, only to emphasize what is essential in the prefacer's view. That is, in my view, the way in which the author searches, in chapter 6, the significance of a European *ius commune*, as it emerges from his examination of three major European liability systems, the English, the French, and the German. The concept goes back to the 12th century and was based mainly in Roman law. In the Middle Ages it was not conceived of as a system of rules enacted for a specific territory. This traditional *ius commune* disintegrated, however, with the rise of rationalism and nationalism in the 18th century during which some rulers wanted the identity of the nation supported by a national codification (at 602). Currently, harmonization and the search for a new *ius commune* are at the very heart of the European private law discourse. Sometimes, the author observes, the discussion seems to have divided the European academic world into believers and heathen. Unfortunately, in this discussion the question whether harmonization is desirable and for what purpose is less debated (at 603-2) as are the differences in attitude towards the codification phenomenon and the level of systematization in the various legal systems, and the academic involvement in it (at 607-1).

In light of these differences, the author examines basic issues in common and codified legal systems, such as the predominance of the judiciary over the legislator (607-2), as well as the characteristics of legal cultures behind the laws (608): the German fondness for legal order, the English fondness for traditions, and the French fondness for *grands principes* He also examines the policy approaches of these systems based in diverging concepts of justice, *i.e.*, on what is considered to be just, fair and reasonable: English tort law is primarily about corrective justice and regulating conduct (609-2), French tort law is less focused on how someone should behave than on how someone can get damages whereas German law takes an intermediate position but being closer to French law in that both systems regard equality and solidarity, and victim protection, as the main concerns of tort law (609-3).

In this context the role of European law is a functional and fragmentised approach, in so far as harmonisation is needed for the functioning of the internal market, even although the European Parliament and the Commission tend to favour a more systematic approach (at 611). However, is such a systematic harmonisation feasible and desirable? The answer of the author, focused on tort law, is that the case for harmonisation of tort laws is not (yet) made (at 612): '[T]he focus should not be on a Europe united in unity with pan-European rules but rather on a Europe united in diversity with harmonised rules where needed and diversity where possible' (at 613). That does not mean that the quest for a

European *ius commune* should be abandoned. Quite the contrary: 'it has lifted academic discussions on private law to a European level. It has paved the way for a truly European legal scholarship rather than a national one. Comparative research has become core business and this has strongly stimulated the trans-boundary dissemination of information . . . The issue is to organize and stimulate this dynamic process but not to force it to provide results unless necessary. The results will need to be flexible and will therefore [depending on the area] to be diverse . . .' (ibid.). As the undersigned has written – a statement that is endorsed by the author: '. . . convergence of the minds of practitioners, judges, professors and future lawyers is at least as important as convergence of laws . . .' (ibid.).

Convergence of minds can be achieved in many ways: through national and supranational courts comparing notes and learning from each other, through national regulators spreading good practices amongst themselves, through academics providing teaching and reading materials that can be used in universities and by practitioners throughout the Union. Surely, to promote convergence may take more time than to harmonize laws and will, undoubtedly, be less spectacular than to prepare comprehensive codification (for which there is no legal basis, though, in the European treaties). But, in the long run, convergence may present a more solid basis in order for European integration to take root in the Member States' legal systems, than codification that is not supported by a sufficient convergence of the minds, will ever be able to do. However, as the author points out (at 613), to make convergence succeed in the area of tort laws, there is a pressing need for a general discourse on policy issues in European tort law in order to explore dividing issues. Issues such as: what are the driving forces and prevailing ideas behind tort law, how much protection victims and potential tortfeasors need, and should the emphasis be on the freedom to act, or on protecting interests, on corrective justice or on distributive justice? The present book is an excellent start to encourage such a policy discourse and to make it fruitful. From that angle, it is excellent reading for a large audience of academics and practitioners, students and teachers within the European Union and beyond.

Walter van Gerven

Leuven, December 2005

Acknowledgements

At the end of the day I wrote this book, the time has come to acknowledge the contributions of the people who supported me in various ways.

First of all, I feel very honoured that *Walter van Gerven*, Emeritus Professor at the Katholieke Universiteit Leuven, and former Advocate-General at the Court of Justice of the European Communities, wrote the preface to this book. I am inspired by the leitmotivs of his research that a European *ius commune* is already present but that we should continuously engage in uncovering it, guided by the vision that the law is not so much a technique but an instrument to build society.

I am very grateful to those who kindly and voluntarily offered to read drafts and to provide me with all kinds of useful suggestions and comments. My special thanks go to the interns at the British Institute of International and Comparative Law in London: *Mahir Gul* (University of Surrey), *Daniel Lons-dorfer* (Westfälische Wilhelms Universität Münster), *Henrik Schmidt-Horix* (Universitetet i Tromsø), and most particularly to *Changez Khan* (Université Paris 1, Panthéon-Sorbonne and King's College London) and *Michael Riegner* (Universität Passau).

I also received highly appreciated comments from *Gerrit Betlem* (Professor of European Law, University of Southampton), *Philippe Delebecque* (Professeur à l'Université Paris 1, Panthéon-Sorbonne), *Ken Oliphant* (Senior Lecturer, Cardiff University), and Professor Dr. *Gerhard Wagner* (Rheinische Friedrich-Wilhelms-Universität Bonn), as well as from anonymous Oxford University Press reviewers. All remaining mistakes in the book are mine.

Professor Dr. *Helmut Koziol*, Executive Director of the European Centre of Tort and Insurance Law in Vienna, kindly provided me with the proofs of the European Tort Law Yearbook 2004.

Karuna Herrmann, student at the School of Oriental and African Studies in London, took meticulous care for the case law references and the case law index. If any error has remained, it was mine.

I would also like to express my sincere gratitude to:

- the Law Faculty of the *Vrije Universiteit* in Amsterdam, which I joined in 1992 as a professor of private law; in 2002 its *Board* kindly and generously granted me a research year without which this book would never have seen the light of day;
- the *British Institute of International and Comparative Law* in London and its then director Dr. *Mads Adenas*, for the hospitality provided in 2002 and 2003 when I was writing the first drafts of the book;
- the *Max Planck Institut für ausländisches und internationales Privatrecht* in Hamburg and its directors Professor Dr. Dr. h.c. *Jürgen Basedow* and Professor Dr. Dr.

h.c. mult. *Reinhard Zimmermann*, for the hospitality I enjoyed and for providing me the opportunity to use the best library in the area of comparative private law during the rainy spring of 2002 and the twelve subsequent days of golden sunshine in the autumn of 2005.

Finally, I would like to thank my lovely colleagues at the *Vrije Universiteit* in Amsterdam and at the *British Institute of International and Comparative Law* in London for their invaluable support.

This book has been updated until 1 July 2005. Exceptionally, further developments have been incorporated.

London,
December 2005

Summary Contents

Contents

III. CATEGORIES OF LIABILITY

Contents

Contents

Contents

List of Abbreviations

A	Atlantic Reporter
ABR	Australian Bar Review
AC	Appeal Cases
AcP	Archiv für die civilistische Praxis
AG	Advocate General
AJCL	American Journal of Comparative Law
AJDA	Les actualités juridiques—Droit administratif
al.	alinéa
All ER	All England Reports
ALR	Australian Law Reports
App. Cas.	Law Reports Appeal Cases, House of Lords
Ass. plén.	Assemblée pléniaire de la Cour de Cassation
B & Ad	Barnewall & Adolphus' King's Bench Reports
BAG	Bundesarbeitsgericht
BGB	Bürgerliches Gesetzbuch
BGH	Bundesgerichtshof
BGHZ	Entscheidungen des Bundesgerichtshofes in Zivilsachen
BIICL	British Institute of International and Comparative Law
Bull. ass. plén.	Bulletin des arrêts de la Cour de cassation, assemblée plénaire
Bull. civ.	Bulletin des arrêts de la Cour de cassation, chambres civiles
Bull. crim.	Bulletin des arrêts de la Cour de cassation, chambre criminelle
BVerfG	Bundesverfassungsgericht
BVerfGE	Entscheidungen des Bundesverfassungsgerichtes
BVerwG	Bundesverwaltungsgericht
BVerwGE	Entscheidungen des Bundesverwaltungsgericht
BW	Burgerlijk Wetboek
C	Chronique
CA	Court of Appeal
Cal.	California Reporter
Cam LJ	Cambridge Law Journal
CC	Code civil
CE	Conseil d'État
CFI	Court of First Instance
Ch	Official Law Reports (Chancery Division)

Ch. mixte	Chambre mixte de la Cour de cassation
Ch. réun.	Chambres réunies de la Cour de cassation
Civ.	Cour de cassation (chambre civile)
CLR	Commonwealth law reports
CMLR	Common Market Law Review
CMR	Convention on the Contract for the International Carriage of Goods by Road
COM	Document of the European Commission
Com.	Chambre commerciale de la Cour de cassation
comm.	comments
Cons. const.	Conseil constitutionnel
CP	Common Pleas (Law Reports)
Crim.	Chambre criminelle de la Cour de cassation
D	Recueil Dalloz et Sirey
DAR	Deutsches Autorecht
DC	Recueil critique Dalloz
DDR	Deutsche Demokratische Republik
DH	Dalloz Hebdomadaire
DLR	Dominion Law Reports
DM	Deutschmark
DP	Recueil périodique et critique Dalloz
E & B	Ellis & Blackburn's Queen's Bench Reports
EC	European Community
	Treaty establishing the European Community
ECC	Draft for a European Civil Code (Von Bar Group) (nr 603–1)
ECHR	European Convention on Human Rights
ECJ	Court of Justice of the European Communities
ECR	Reports of Cases before the Court of Justice of the European Communities and the Court of First Instance
ECSC	European Coal and Steel Community
ECtHR	European Court of Human Rights
ECU	European Currency Unit
EEA	European Economic Area
EEC	European Economic Community
EFTA	European Free Trade Association
ELJ	European Law Journal
ELR	European Law Review
EMLR	Entertainment and Media Law Reports
ER	English Reports

ERPL	European Review of Private Law
ETL	Yearbook on European Tort Law (see Bibliography)
EU	European Union
EWCA Civ.	England and Wales Court of Appeal (Civil Division)
Ex	Court of Exchequer
F	Federal Reporter
Fam	Official Law Reports: Family Division
FamRZ	Zeitschrift für das gesamte Familienrecht
FLR	Family Law Reports
FRF	Franc français
FSR	Fleet Street Reports
Gaz. Pal.	Gazette du Palais
GDR	German Democratic Republic
GG	Grundgesetz
GmbH	Gesellschaft mit beschränkter Haftung
GmbHG	Gesetz betreffend die Gesellschaften mit beschränkter Haftung
GMO	Genetically Modified Organism
Harvard LR	Harvard Law Review
HL	Judicial Committee of the House of Lords
HPflG	Haftpflichtgesetz
HR	Hoge Raad
ICCPR	International Covenant on Civil and Political Rights
ICLQ	International and Comparative Law Quarterly
ICR	Industrial Cases Reports
IR	Informations rapides
ITL	Italian Lire
JCP	Juris-Classeur périodique (also: Semaine Juridique)
JW	Juristische Wochenschrift
JZ	Juristenzeitung
KB	King's Bench
KG	Kammergericht
LG	Landesgericht
LGR	Local Government Reports
LJ	Lord Justice

Lloyd's Rep.	Lloyd's List Law Reports
LQR	Law Quarterly Review
LR	Law Reports
LT	Law Times
LuftVG	Luftverkehrsgesetz
MDR	Monatschrift für Deutsches Recht
Mod. Rep.	Modern Reports
Mod LR	Modern Law Review
N	Randnummer
NE	North Eastern Reporter
NJ	Nederlandse Jurisprudentie
NJW	Neue Juristische Wochenschrift
NJW-RR	NJW-Rechtsprechungsreport Zivilrecht
NPC	New Practice Cases
NZLR	New Zealand Law Reports
obs.	observation
OJ	Official Journal of the European Communities
OJ C	Official Journal of the European Communities, Cases
OJ L	Official Journal of the European Communities, Legislation
OJLS	Oxford Journal of Legal Studies
OLG	Oberlandesgericht
P	Pacific Reporter
PACS	Pacte civil de solidarité
PC	Judicial Committee of the Privy Council
PETL	Principles of European Tort Law (Vienna Group) (nr 603–1)
PIBD	Propriété industrielle, Bulletin documentaire
PIQR	Personal Injuries and Quantum Reports
PNLR	Professional Negligence and Liability Reports
QB	Queen's Bench
QBD	Queen's Bench Division
RabelsZ	Rabels Zeitschrift
rapp.	rapporteur
Rb.	Rechtbank
Rec. CE	Recueil des décisions du Conseil d'État (also: Recueil Lebon)
Rec. cons. const.	Recueil des décisions du Conseil constitutionnel

Req.	Chambre des requêtes de la Cour de cassation
Resp. civ. et ass.	Responsabilité civile et assurances
RG	Reichsgericht
RGAR	Revue générale des assurances et des responsabilités
RGZ	Entscheidungen des Reichsgerichtes
RIDC	Revue de droit international et de droit comparé
RJDA	Revue de jurisprudence du droit des affaires
RM Themis	Rechtsgeleerd Magazijn Themis
RPC	Reports of Patent, Design and Trade Mark Cases
RTD civ.	Revue trimestrielle de droit civil
RTD pub.	Revue trimestrielle de droit public
RTR	Road Traffic Reports
RvdW	Rechtspraak van de Week
S	Recueil Sirey
SC	Session Cases
SI	Statutory Instrument
SLT	Scottish Law Times
SO	Southern Reporter
Soc.	Chambre sociale de la Cour de cassation
Somm.	Sommaires
StGB	Strafgesetzbuch
StVG	Straßenverkehrsgesetz
TBBR	Tijdschrift voor Belgisch Burgerlijk Recht
TC	Tribunal des Conflits
TGI	Tribunal de grande instance
TLR	Times Law Reports
Tulane LR	Tulane Law Review
UK	United Kingdom
UKHL	House of Lords (United Kingdom)
UmweltHG	Umwelthaftungsgesetz
UWG	Gesetz gegen unlauteren Wettbewerb
VAT	Value Added Tax
VersR	Versicherungsrecht
VLR	Victorian Law Reports
VR	Verkeersrecht
	Victorian Reports

List of Abbreviations

WAM	Wet Aansprakelijkheidsverzekering Motorrijtuigen
WHG	Wasserhaushaltsgesetz
WLR	Weekly Law Reports
Yale LJ	Yale Law Journal
ZEuP	Zeitschrift für Europäisches Privatrecht
ZfS	Zeitschrift für Schadensrecht
ZGB	Zivilgesetzbuch
ZIP	Zeitschrift für Wirtschaftsrecht und Insolvenzpraxis
ZPO	Zivilprozessordnung

Table of Cases

Table of Cases

Table of Cases

Table of Cases

EUROPEAN COURT OF HUMAN RIGHTS

Table of Cases

FRANCE

Bundesgerichtshof

Table of Cases

Other courts

Table of Cases

ENGLAND, WALES AND SCOTLAND

Table of Cases

Table of Cases

COMMONWEALTH COUNTRIES

UNITED STATES OF AMERICA

BELGIUM

THE NETHERLANDS

PART I

SYSTEMS OF LIABILITY

1

Introduction

101 Europe, European tort law, and international tort law

101-1 *Europe*

The contemporary political concept of a united Europe was born from the ruins of World War II. Visionary European leaders aimed to reconcile the former enemies, to prevent new conflicts, and to build a strong unity as a protection against the Soviet Union and the Eastern European Communist countries. Two of the major institutions with which these goals were pursued are the Council of Europe (nr 202) and the European Coal and Steel Community, later transformed into the European Union (nr 203). In the course of the years after the end of the Cold War in 1989 former Communist countries joined both these institutions.

Over the years visions on 'Europe' have varied from the idea of a federal Europe run by a European government and a European president to a economic cooperation only in order to achieve a common (internal) market. It is not surprising that the current political situation in Europe is somewhere in between these two extremes and that it is not entirely clear in which direction things will develop.[1]

Initially, the unity of the Member States was endorsed by the existence of a common enemy in Eastern Europe. After the Cold War, however, this changed and at the same time the Union was substantially extended eastward. Whereas it all started with 6 countries in 1952, this number was doubled to 12 in 1986 and doubled again to 25 in 2005. This growth raised concerns as to how the European Union could take the necessary and effective legislative measures to reach its goals, if only for the obvious reason that it was easier to compromise with 6 than it is with 25 parties. The Constitution for Europe was aimed to provide the necessary tools to make the European Union better 'manageable'. However, the rejection of this Constitution in referenda in France and the Netherlands in 2005 has put this reform in jeopardy. At the same time, this rejection is also considered to be a sign of concern and discontent with the steadily growing

---

[1] See about the legal, historical and political aspects of the European Union: Walter van Gerven, *The European Union. A Polity of States and Peoples* (Oxford: Hart, 2005).

ambitions of the European Union. It revealed that further European integration is no longer self-evident.

In the shadow of these major historic developments common European tort law came into being. Halfway through the 20th century European tort law was varied and only consisted of ever so many national habitats. By then, a *common* European tort law was without form, and void. At the beginning of the 21st century, however, it has got some substance and shape. Features of a common habitat have been developed—albeit cautiously and unsteadily (nr 101-2).

The ideas about the political future of Europe differ and so do the visions on the way ahead for European tort law. They vary from the vision of a full-fledged codification of European tort law as part of a European Civil Code to the idea that harmonization should only take place inasmuch as this is required for a proper functioning of the internal market. It is not surprising that the current situation in European tort law is somewhere in between these two extremes and that it is not entirely clear in which direction things will develop. There are various intertwined developments. The European Court of Justice has developed case law on the basis of the general principles common to the laws of the Member States; the European Commission has taken a new step into the direction of harmonization by proposing to develop a so-called Common Frame of References, and national courts and legislators are becoming more prepared to look at developments in other countries.

101-2 *European tort law*

Today, 'European tort law' is mentioned at many occasions and discussed at various levels—thus it exists. However, the concept as such is not strictly defined and European tort law has become the umbrella term for a number of various features concerning tort law in Europe. Two preliminary remarks have to be made as regards the terminology of European tort law: one about the word 'European' and one about the words 'tort law'.

As regards the latter, this book uses the terminology of 'tort' rather than 'delict' or 'extra-contractual liability'. This is not self-evident. 'Tort' is a typical common law term which does not have a proper parallel in the continental legal systems. However, a number of important European comparative law books on extra-contractual liability currently use the 'tort' terminology and this now has become common parlance. Certainly, 'European extra-contractual liability law excluding agency without authority and unjust enrichment' would have been a more accurate title but it would be also unnecessarily confusing to choose a deviating terminology that means the same.

Also the word 'European' in 'European tort law' needs further clarification although it is not intended to be a very clearly defined concept. It rather points at various 'Europes': the European continent, the Contracting States of the European Convention on Human Rights and the European Union. In fact three tiers of European tort law can be distinguished.

The upper tier is the binding European tort law: on the one hand the legislation of the European Union in the area of tort law, particularly a number of Directives, and the case law of the ECJ in Luxembourg, and on the other hand the case law of the European Court of Human Rights in Strasbourg based on the European Convention on Human Rights. The most prominent example of Community tort law is the so-called *Francovich* case law of the ECJ concerning liability for breach of Community law, which is linked with Article 288 EC regarding the extra-contractual liability of Community Institutions (nr 200). The case law of the European Court of Human Rights only addresses the Contracting states and is applied in the interest of individuals, particularly as regards their safety, health, privacy, and family life (nr 202).

The lower tier of European tort law consists of the various national tort laws. As Europe is still diverse in many ways so is this lower tier of European tort law. Whereas in medieval times the Western European legal landscape was characterized by a *ius commune* based on Roman law, the rise of the nation state in the 18th century has more or less eroded this harmony. However, due to increasingly permeable borders and border crossing information, these national laws become increasingly influenced by other national and supranational systems.

The link between the upper and lower tier is comparative law: the art of comparing and analysing the various European legal systems and discussing the desirability and feasibility of a dreamed European tort law, a European *ius commune*. These discussions are currently mainly concentrated in the academic area. Some have culminated in specific proposals for principles or rules such as, for example, the Principles of European Tort Law or the Principles of European Law of the Study Group on a European Civil Code (nr 603-1). Different from the supranational sources of the first tier, these principles and comparative law in general are not binding at all. They, however, provide a method of interpretation, both for supranational as for national law. The Commission aims to bring a small part of this discussion to a more practical level by its initiative to develop a so-called Common Frame of Reference which should bring more consistency and coherence in the terminology of Community legislation (nr 611).

The three tiers can be distinguished but they cannot be separated. Comparative law influences the legislation of the European Union and the case law of the European Court of Justice (nr 201-1). The case law of the European Court of Justice is influenced by the case law of the European Court of Human Rights (nr 202). And national legislation and case law are influenced by the law of the European Union, the European Convention on Human Rights, and sometimes by comparative law (nr 201-2). These developments are illustrative of the end of the so-called 'billiard ball state' and the emergence of a multilayered international order.

The three tiers also demonstrate that 'European tort law' does not necessarily imply unification, harmonization, or even convergence. Though a convergent tendency is apparent at some points, it is also clear that differences between the Member States remain substantial. This is not only the case as regards the contents of tort law but also as regards the differences in procedure, in legal culture, and in social, economic, and political backgrounds. European tort law is not only about a slowly growing harmony in certain respects but also about a rich diversity in many other (nr 608–610). Hence, European tort law does not automatically imply a *common* European tort law. This book could therefore also have been entitled 'The European law of *torts*'.

101-3 *International tort law*

Various aspects of tort law are also regulated in international treaties. Some of these treaties are not exclusively European and they also apply outside Europe; other treaties only bind a number of European states.

Examples of treaties that have considerably contributed to unification of tort law, sometimes also on a more global basis, are the treaties concerning civil liability for nuclear activities,[2] for oil pollution at sea,[3] the Convention on the Liability of Hotelkeepers Concerning the Property of their Guests 1962, and treaties concerning transport law including the liability of the carrier, such as the Convention for the Unification of Certain Rules Relating to International Carriage by Air (Warsaw Convention 1929), the Convention on the Contract for the International Carriage of Goods by Road 1956 (CMR), and the European Convention on Compulsory Insurance Against Civil Liability in Respect of Motor Vehicles 1959. Some aspects of these treaties will be described in nr 1405–2 and 1415–2.

Other treaties do not concern substantive matters, but only matters of private international law as regards the competent court and the applicable law in cases with an international aspect. Examples are the The Hague Convention on the Law Applicable to Products Liability 1973 (nr 1407–1), the The Hague Convention on the Law Applicable to Traffic Accidents 1971 (nr 1405–1),[4] and the Rome Convention (Rome II) on the applicable law concerning non-contractual obligations.[5]

102 Focus of the book

102-1 *Aim of the book*

The aim of this book is to introduce the reader to the main features of European tort law in a textbook format. References will be made to other comparative

---

[2] Paris Convention on Third Party Liability in the Field of Nuclear Energy (1960); Brussels Convention Supplementary to the Paris Convention (1963); Vienna Convention on Civil Liability for Nuclear Damage (1963); Protocol Amending the latter Convention (1997); Convention on Supplementary Compensation for Nuclear Damage (1997).

[3] International Convention on Civil Liability for Oil Pollution Damage (1969).

[4] See for the text, the entering into force, and the parties to these Conventions the website of the Hague Conference on Private International Law: www.hcch.net.

[5] The European Commission has proposed to adopt and broaden the Convention in a Regulation; see the Proposal for a European Parliament and Council Regulation of 22 July 2003 on the

books in the area of European tort law, particularly Christian von Bar's *The Common European Law of Torts*, Walter van Gerven's *Tort Law*, Basil Markesinis' *The German Law of Torts*, and the *Unification of Tort Law Series* of the European Centre for Tort and Insurance Law.[6]

This book will show the crucial basics of European tort law by illustrating: (a) that similar factual problems arise throughout the tort law systems; (b) from high in the sky the solutions for these problems do not seem to be very different; (c) a closer look down at the surface does not only confirm these similarities but will also show some striking differences in the way the problems are being solved; (d) digging below ground level may reveal the roots for the differences: the various historical and cultural backgrounds and the various policy views as to what can be considered to be fair, just, and reasonable solutions in tort law cases. The emphasis in this book will be on basics (a)–(c). Chapter 6 will go into some aspects as regards basic (d); see nr 608–610.

To learn and understand these basics no more than three national tort law systems are needed: in this book France, Germany, and England (nr 102-2). The choice of only three national systems is mainly a practical one. A survey of more than three legal systems would certainly provide a more precise and advanced picture of European tort law, but only to the detriment of conciseness and the ability to retain an the overview.[7] It goes without saying that there are dozens of tort law systems in Europe, and that a book like this cannot give a complete picture of European tort law (if ever such a picture were possible).

Given these limitations, it cannot be the aim of this book to make the case for a common European tort law (provided such a common law is desirable) or to look for common denominators throughout Europe. There are other, more extensive, comparative studies dealing with this topic, to which throughout this book references will be made, particularly the draft of a European Civil Code and the Principles of European Tort Law (nr 603-1).

102-2 *Three national systems*

The choice to limit the national tort law systems to those of France, Germany, and England is based on a number of considerations.

Firstly, France, Germany, and England represent three major legal traditions which have influenced a considerable number of other legal systems in the European Union. Common law has influenced the law of Cyprus, Ireland, and

---

law applicable to non-contractual obligations ('Rome II'), COM(2003) 427 final. See for a brief overview Bernhard A. Koch, ETL 2003, 435–439.

  [6] Christian von Bar, *The Common European Law of Torts*, Volume 1 and 2 (1998–2000); Walter van Gerven, Jeremy Lever and Pierre Larouche, *Tort Law* (2000); and the *Unification of Tort Law Series*, published by the European Centre of Tort and Insurance Law, all with further references.
  [7] Compare Konrad Zweigert and Hein Kötz, *Introduction to Comparative Law*, 3rd edn. (Oxford: Oxford University Press, 1998), 44.

Malta. French tort law has left roots in Belgium, Italy, the Netherlands, Poland, and Spain, whereas German tort law is linked to Austrian, Greek, and Portuguese law. In the end, European tort law is about more tort law systems than there are countries, since some countries comprise more than one legal and thus tort law system. For example, the United Kingdom does not possess a single national tort law but three regional tort law systems: the law of England and Wales, of Scotland, and of Northern Ireland.

Secondly, France and England represent two opposite policy approaches to tort law. Whereas French tort law primarily focuses on compensation and the principle of distributive justice (strict liability), the predominant focus of English tort law is on conduct regulation and the principle of corrective justice (fault liability). These differences are particularly, though not solely, recognizable in the area of accident law and in the way that liability of public authorities is dealt with. German tort law takes a somewhat intermediate position: on the one hand it formally and dogmatically often applies the tools of conduct regulation (fault liability), but at a policy level it is strongly inspired by the principle of distributive justice. The additional value of German tort law is that it is the most elaborated and systematized tort law system in Europe, and probably in the world, which makes it an important source for legal questions and answers to these questions.

Thirdly, from an economic, political, and demographic point of view France, Germany, and England basically represent the main powers in the EU. They comprise a substantial part of the European population, representing almost half of the EU citizens and producing more than half of the EU's gross national income.[8] Even though these three countries are far from having a majority vote in the European Council, they have a politically dominant position in the Union. Points of difference and conflict between these countries, including those on harmonizing European private law and tort law, will be of major importance for bringing the European discussion forward.

The downside of this choice of the 'big three' is that many interesting developments in other countries will not be mentioned. This goes not only for the Scandinavian and Eastern European countries, but also for countries like Spain, Italy, and the Netherlands which, though rooted in the French *Code civil*, have developed their own characteristic national tort laws.

103 Plan and structure of the book

103-1 *Introduction*

In order to deal with the broad topic of European tort law, this book first provides in *Part I* an analysis of the main tort law issues in three important

---

[8] www.worldbank.org.

European legal systems (France, Germany, and England). These analyses are preceded by an introduction to the European Court of Human Rights and the tort law system of the European Union and they are followed by a concluding chapter on common European tort law.

Subsequently, *Part II* provides a structured discussion of the requirements for liability: the protected interests, intention and negligence, violation of a statutory rule, strict liability, causation, and damage and damages.

Finally, it will be shown in *Part III* how the rules are applied in various categories of liability: liability for damage caused by movable things, by immovable things and by other persons, liability for not providing help in emergency cases and, finally, liability of public authorities.

The book provides a framework for structuring the discussion on European tort law. It brings together comparative law, Community law, and human rights law. The structure is open and flexible and is intended to be friendly to the particular features of the various national systems. It is meant to be an aid to comparison and to discussion, not a quasi draft for a European legal system. Since the framework is not akin to any of the national legal systems it will be important to familiarize oneself with it.

103-2 *Part I: Systems of liability*

The first part of this book discusses the main features of the national tort laws as well as supranational tort law.

Chapter 2 will deal with 'Europe' and starts with introductions to comparative law and to the European Court of Human Rights and the European Convention on Human Rights. The main part of the chapter is devoted to the tort law of the European Union. It will provide a brief overview of the history and judiciary of the European Union and will then set out the sources of liability in Community law. Firstly, the focus will be on relevant EU legislation, such as Article 288 on the liability of Community institutions and the important instrument of the Directive. Secondly, the case law of the European Court of Justice, particularly the development of the so-called *Francovich* case law on the liability of Member States and individuals for breach of Community law will be pointed out.

In the following three chapters the main features of the national tort law systems will be described. Additionally, information on the history of the legal system, its structure (codification or common), the judiciary, and the legal literature will be provided.

French tort law (*Chapter 3*) is characterized by its broad general principles and its general lack of detail. There are only a few rules regarding extra-contractual liability and these are laid down in the Napoleonic *Code civil* of 1804 which is still in force. The two main rules are article 1382 CC (liability for *faute*, liability for personal negligence) and article 1384 al. 1 CC (strict liability for damage caused by a thing, *responsabilité du fait des choses*). This latter rule of strict liability has been developed by the *Cour de cassation*. The *Cour de cassation* also developed a general strict liability rule for damage caused by other people. This rule supplements the more specific strict liability rules for parents (for damage caused by their children) and for employers (for damage caused by their employees). Hence, in France, in cases of personal injury and property loss strict liability is the rule and fault liability the exception.

German tort law (*Chapter 4*) is characterized by its systematic approach and its many subtle distinctions. Probably the most characteristic feature of German tort law is judge-made in order to fill lacunae in the *Bürgerliches Gesetzbuch* (BGB, Civil Code) of 1900. In the early 20th century the *Reichsgericht* created the so-called *Verkehrspflichten*. These are safety duties based on negligence but generally they require a very high level of care. The proper place of these *Verkehrspflichten* in the legal system is strongly debated in the legal literature, in which systematic aspects are generally considered to be of great importance even if their practical impact is not always clear.

English tort law (*Chapter 5*) is characterized by its traditional approach. English common law has its roots in medieval times but it has also been said that it has been there since time immemorial. In the area of non-contractual liability there are no rules but only torts. These torts provide a remedy (for example, damages) if something has gone wrong in a particular way. The most important and most general tort is the *tort of negligence*. This tort imposes liability on someone who has not acted carefully but only if this person owed the other person a duty of care. This latter aspect is the most characteristic feature of English tort law and in a number of tort law areas it still serves as an important obstacle for liability. The standard of care is generally not as high as in German tort law.

Chapter 6 will go into the possibilities and impossibilities of a European *ius commune*, a common European law, particularly in the area of tort law. With the increased cooperation in Europe after World War II and the extension of cooperation after the Cold War, there has been strong support for discussing the harmonization of national private laws, including the national tort laws. A number of initiatives have been taken and currently two important sets of principles of European tort law are on the table. This chapter will go into the thresholds for harmonizing the national laws, for example the fact that they hold different approaches to tort law. In France, the main goal is compensation of the victim and distributive justice (featured by the major general strict liability rule for things), whereas in England tort law is mainly about regulating conduct and corrective justice (embodied in the tort of negligence). In Germany, the approach focuses formally on regulating conduct (symbolized by the *Verkehrspflichten*) but this happens in a strict way which means that, in fact, distributive justice is the leading principle. From this perspective, doubts will be cast on the desirability and feasibility of European harmonization and an agenda for further debate will be proposed.

103-3 *Part II: Requirements of liability*

The second part of the book analyses and compares the different requirements for liability in the three national legal systems aforementioned and in supranational European tort law.

The national requirements of fault liability are dealt with as follows. The aspects of the French *faute* requirement in article 1382 CC will be analysed in Chapters 7, 8, and 9. The aspects of the English tort of negligence will be described in Chapter 7 (*duty of care*) and Chapter 8 (*breach of duty*), and the aspects of the German *unerlaubte Handlung* will be dealt with in Chapter 7 (*Tatbestand* and *Rechtswidrigkeit*), Chapter 8 (*Verschulden*), and Chapter 9 (*Schutzgesetzverstoß*).

An important difference between the legal systems is that liability for damage caused by 'pure' intentional or negligent conduct (Chapter 8) is not accepted in English and German law. Something more is required, namely that the conduct was legally wrong. In English law this aspect is embodied in the requirement of the *duty of care* in the tort of negligence, and in German law in the requirements of *Tatbestand* and *Rechtswidrigkeit*, whereas in French law the aspect of wrongfulness (*illicéité*) is acknowledged but in a rather concealed way. Chapter 7 will deal with both these aspects from the perspective of the legally protected interests.

Chapter 7 will firstly deal with protection of the person, not only of his or her life, bodily integrity, physical health, and mental health, but also of what has become known as someone's personality rights, particularly the protection of the right to privacy. As regards this latter aspect, the case law of the European Court of Human Rights is of particular importance. Personality rights also include the right to family life, and it will be considered what role this right plays in cases which have become known as wrongful birth (wrongful conception) and wrongful life (prenatal harm). Secondly, the chapter will analyse the protection of property, which is particularly relevant in German and English law. Here the question will be answered as to whether property interests represent only the value of a damaged object or also the value of using it. Finally, the focus will be on the protection of economic (commercial) interests. These interests are less protected than personal and property interests. In England particularly it is feared that a general rule to compensate pure economic loss would lead to a cascade of claims and would make tort law unsustainable. In France, however, tort law has survived such a general rule.

In *Chapter 8* the two aspects of fault—intention and negligence—will be further analysed. What these qualifications of personal conduct mean and which role they play in tort law will be described. Sometimes, particularly in English law, someone can only be liable if he acted intentionally. In most situations, however, liability requires that someone has acted negligently and this is where the gravity of the chapter lies. Courts establish negligence by balancing the defendant's freedom to act and the claimant's right to be protected against harm. This balancing technique, which results in so called unwritten rules, will be extensively illustrated.

Liability cannot only be based on the violation of an unwritten rule but also on the violation of written, statutory, rule. This will be the topic of *Chapter 9*. This chapter will show the intertwinement between criminal and administrative law (public law) on the one hand and tort law on the other. If a nursery uses banned pesticides, or an engineer installs wires contrary to health and safety rules, or someone builds house without proper licences, they violate statutory duties. In principle, such a violation gives rise to liability for the damage caused which means that, in all their variety, statutory rules are an important basis for establishing liability. However, the legal systems deal with this basis for liability in different ways.

Liability without fault is generally known as strict liability. These rules of strict liability in the various legal systems will be illustrated in detail in Part III of the book. In *Chapter 10* the *concept* of strict liability will be analysed. It will be shown that the difference between fault and strict liability is a gradual rather than a principle one. When finding rules, courts and legislators in all jurisdictions use different elements from both categories to achieve the best mix. However, what is considered to be the best mix differs throughout the legal systems. The French prefer it with many elements of strict liability whereas the English prefer it with a huge amount of negligence elements.

Chapter 11 focuses on the question of whether a causal connection can be established between the tortfeasor's conduct or the cause for which he is strictly liable on the one hand and the damage on the other. Particular problems arise if it is hard to establish who caused the damage or if there is more than one possible legal cause for the damage. In matters of causation of harm to health, it is pivotal and often decisive who has the burden of proof. If someone receives a vaccination against a certain disease and he subsequently suffers severe health problems, does he have to prove that there was a causal connection or does the doctor or the hospital have to prove that there was none? A general difference in causation matters is that the English and the French approach this requirement in a rather practical way, whereas the Germans have developed detailed theories in order to get to grips with the concept of causation.

Damage and damages, including contributory negligence, are the topic of *Chapter 12*. In this chapter the emphasis will first be on the functions of damages: these are not only paid to compensate the claimant but also to provide him with recognition of his rights and to deter the tortfeasor and other potential wrongdoers. The rights to compensation of the victim for personal injury differ substantially from system to system, particularly in the area of non-pecuniary loss. Differences are also apparent if someone gets injured or dies as the consequence of an accident, in which case his relatives will also suffer harm: pecuniary harm for the loss of maintenance and non-pecuniary harm for the loss of a beloved one (damages for bereavement or for grief and sorrow). Finally, this chapter will analyse the rules applying to the victim's contributory negligence. This defence generally leads to a lower amount of compensation and in extraordinary circumstances may lead to a reduction of the compensation to zero. Whereas England, and particularly Germany, are reluctant in attributing contributory negligence to children, the French approach is remarkably less advantageous for children.

103-4 *Part III: Categories of liability*

The final part of the book also assumes a comparative and a supranational point of view and deals with a number of categories of liability. Most of these categories are related to someone's quality as a supervisor over persons or things. *Chapter 13* introduces this part of the book by setting out the different ways such a supervisor is indicated, both on the basis of strict and fault liability. Subsequently, this chapter will briefly touch upon the topic of liability for information, both as regards situations in which someone is obliged to provide information (for example a doctor or a bank), and in which voluntarily provided information (for example in a book or on a website) has to be correct and reliable.

Movable objects often play an important role when someone causes personal injury or property damage to someone else. For this category even France holds a general strict liability rule. *Chapter 14* will cover liability for damage caused by animals, products, motor vehicles, and dangerous substances. Whereas liability for the first two categories shows a number of similarities in the various legal systems, liability in the two latter categories deviates strongly. For example, in England liability for motor vehicles is still based on fault, whereas France holds a system of almost absolute liability. The efforts of the European Commission to bring more harmony in liability for road traffic accidents and for damage caused to the environment have almost entirely failed. Even in the most harmonized area, that of liability for defective products, important differences remain throughout the legal systems.

Liability for damage caused on premises, grounds, and roads is the topic of *Chapter 15*. This chapter will deal with damage caused by, for example, falling roof-tiles and collapsing buildings, unsafe swimming pools and stadiums, and accidents caused by badly maintained roads. Stricter liability rules in this category apply to collapsing buildings, and in France the general strict liability rule for things also applies to immovable objects. In other circumstances liability has to be based on rules of fault liability, for example on the German *Verkehrspflichten* or on the English Occupier's Liability Acts. Specific attention will be paid to liability of the highway authorities for unsafe roads.

In addition to liability for damage caused by movable and immovable objects someone can also be liable for damage caused by another person with whom he has a special relationship. The most obvious examples are the responsibility of parents for children and that of employers for employees. These are the topics of *Chapter 16*. Liability of the employer for damage caused by the employee differs between the legal systems, in that England and France provide for strict liability and Germany for a liability for rebuttable negligence. The case law in Germany, however, has limited the employer's defences and has also provided ways around his liability which make the differences with English and French law negligible. Liability for children shows more differences, with France providing for the parents' strict liability, Germany for a liability for rebuttable negligence, and England for a traditional fault liability regime.

An extraordinary category concerns the liability in cases of emergency. *Chapter 17* will go into the question of whether someone can be liable for damage he causes (or rather did not prevent from happening) for failing to rescue a person from a dangerous situation. Is someone who sees another person in danger of drowning obliged to come to his rescue? The legal systems, again, provide different answers. A subsequent question is that, if someone undertakes a rescue, what are his duties? Is he required to be successful or is he only obliged not to make the victim's position worse?

Finally, *Chapter 18* might very well be the *pièce de résistance* of this book. It deals with one of the most disputed topics in tort law: liability of public authorities. In this chapter the link with public law is the most obvious complicated factor, combined with the role of discretion when assessing public authorities' liability. Also, the case law of the two supranational courts, the European Court of Justice and the European Court of Human Rights, is of increasing influence in shaping the requirements for liability of public authorities. The tendency is towards limiting the discretion of public authorities and this is particularly due to the influence of human rights.

2

Europe

201 Comparative law and *ius commune*

201-1 *Influences on Community law*

Initially, comparative law was considered to be a useful instrument to get to know other legal systems and to put one's own system in an international perspective. The fruits of comparative law studies have long and mainly been of academic interest: they were considered to be ' . . . difficult and, surely, very interesting; beautiful to know something about, but not immediately relevant to the daily life of the law.'[1]

Over the last decades comparative law has lost its innocence. It is becoming an important source for legislators, judges, and lawyers, not only on a national but also on a European level.

This evolution may be influenced by the process of European integration; it may also just result from the fact that we are living closer together (the 'global village' situation); it may, finally, be an autonomous process, occasioned by the lawyer's search for fresh perspectives, in particular when completely new legal problems are to be solved.[2]

In Community institutions, ' . . . such as the Council, the Commission and the Court—where lawyers from all Member States work closely together—"law making" and "solution finding" are unavoidably activities in which all national legal backgrounds play a role.'[3] According to Baron Mertens de Wilmars, a former president of the European Court of Justice, recourse to comparative law is essentially a method of interpretation of Community law itself.[4]

Although this remains mainly unnoticed by the outer world, the offices of the European Courts in Luxembourg accommodate the biggest comparative law

---

[1] T. Koopmans, 'Comparative Law and the Courts', *ICLQ* 45 (1996), 545.

[2] T. Koopmans, 'Comparative Law and the Courts', *ICLQ* 45 (1996), 545.

[3] Walter van Gerven, 'The Emergence of a Common European Law in the Area of Tort Law: the EU Contribution', in Duncan Fairgrieve, Mads Andenas and John Bell (eds.), *Tort Liability of Public Authorities in Comparative Perspective*, (London: BIICL, 2002), 138.

[4] Josse Mertens de Wilmars, 'Le droit comparé dans la jurisprudence de la Cour de justice des Communautés européennes', *Journal des Tribunaux* (1991), 37; see also Walter van Gerven, 'Comparative Law in a Regionally Integrated Europe', in Andrew Harding and Esin Örücü (eds.), *Comparative Law in the 21ˢᵗ Century, WG Hart Legal Workshop Series*, Volume 4, (London, New York: Kluwer International, 2002), 155.

research centre in Europe. It is beyond doubt that the courts intensively use the available knowledge when developing Community law though this remains very implicit. Usually the courts confine themselves to general expressions like 'legal principles common to all or several Member States.'[5]

The Opinions of the Advocates-General, however, regularly contain comparative analyses. An important example in the area of liability for breach of Community law is the Opinion of Advocate-General Tesauro in *Brasserie du Pêcheur and Factortame*. In this case the ECJ further elaborated the *Francovich* case law on the principle of Member State liability for loss or damage caused to individuals as a result of a breach of Community law (nr 205-1). In his Opinion the Advocate-General pointed out that in all legal traditions liability for legislative acts was subject to various limitations. In line with this common concept the ECJ ruled that a Member State will only be held liable where a sufficiently serious breach of a superior rule of law which intends to confer rights on individuals is established.[6]

In order to acknowledge the existence of a general principle of law, the ECJ does not require that the rule be a feature of all the national legal systems. Similarly, the fact that the scope and the conditions of application of the rule vary from one Member State to another is not material. The Court merely finds that the principle is generally acknowledged and that, beyond the divergences, the domestic laws of the Member States show the existence of common criteria.[7]

201-2 *Influences on national laws*

Comparative law can be used to look at the structure of foreign rules and decisions but it makes more sense to look at the outcome of the rules and the policy reasons given by the legislator and the courts. Lord Bingham said: 'In a shrinking world there must be some virtue in uniformity of outcome whatever the diversity of approach in reaching that outcome.'[8] Particularly in milestone cases, the highest national courts show an increasing interest in and need for comparative information in order to answer difficult questions. Here, comparative law is the mirror for national law and an instrument to avoid gaps between

---

[5] See extensively Koen Lennaerts, 'Interlocking Legal Orders in the European Union and Comparative Law', *ICLQ* 52 (2003), 873–906.

[6] ECJ 5 March 1996, Joined cases C-46/93 and C-48/93, ECR 1996, I-1029 (*Brasserie du Pêcheur and Factortame III*), paras 47–55, about which nr 206-2; see also ECJ 15 June 2000, Case C-237/98, ECR 2000, I-4549 (*Dorsch Consult v Council and Commission*) about liability for lawful acts in which implicitly reference was made to French and German principles. See also Opinion AG Léger before ECJ 30 September 2003, C-224/01, ECR 2003, I-1023 (*Gerhard Köbler v Austria*), paras 77–85 as regards liability for wrongful judicial decisions. See about the tasks and the role of the Advocate-General at the European Court of Justice nr 203-2.

[7] Opinion AG Léger before ECJ 30 September 2003, C-224/01 (*Gerhard Köbler v Austria*), para. 85 with further reference.

[8] *Fairchild v Glenhaven Funeral Services Ltd & Others* [2002] 3 All ER 305, nr 32, per Lord Bingham of Cornhill.

legal systems to grow and perhaps sometimes to provide support to make the gaps smaller. Because differences in structure will linger on, the interesting issues are about the substance of the law.[9]

English courts are very experienced with making use of comparative materials, particularly from other legal systems of the Commonwealth countries. This is, of course, facilitated by the common language. But recent English case law also gives examples of explicit use of comparative law in a European context. One may particularly think of the speeches of Lord Goff of Chieveley in *White v Jones*[10] and of Lord Bingham of Cornhill in *Fairchild v Glenhaven Funeral Services Ltd & Others*.[11] In the latter case, the claimants tried to get compensation for the damage they suffered from an asbestos-related occupational disease (mesothelioma). They had worked for two employers, each of whom was in breach of its duty to protect its employees from inhaling asbestos dust. The victims could not prove whether their illness was caused by the first or the second employer, or by both. For this reason the Court of Appeal dismissed the claims. In the House of Lords, Lord Bingham of Cornhill paid attention to the way other jurisdictions had dealt with this issue.[12] He said:

Development of the law in this country cannot of course depend on a head-count of decisions and codes adopted in other countries around the world, often against a background of different rules and traditions. The law must be developed coherently, in accordance with principle, so as to serve, even-handedly, the ends of justice. If, however, a decision is given in this country which offends one's basic sense of justice, and if consideration of international sources suggests that a different and more acceptable decision would be given in most other jurisdictions, whatever their legal tradition, this must prompt anxious review of the decision in question.[13]

Partially on the basis of this comparative approach the House of Lords set aside the 'but for' causation test, shifted the burden of proof to the employers, reversed the judgment of the Court of Appeal, and found for the claimants.[14]

German case law also provides examples of the use of comparative law. One may particularly think of the case in which the *Bundesgerichtshof* rejected a

---

[9] See extensively Guy Canivet, Mads Andenas and Duncan Fairgrieve (eds.), *Comparative Law before the Courts*, (London: BIICL, 2004); Basil Markesinis, 'Case Law and Comparative Law: Any Wider Lessons?', *ERPL* 11/6 (2003), 717–734.

[10] Lord Goff in *White v Jones* [1995] 1 All ER 691, 710, about which Van Gerven (2000), 219–224 and Markesinis and Unberath (2002), 338–348; see nr 714-2.

[11] *Fairchild v Glenhaven Funeral Services Ltd & Others* [2002] 3 All ER 305, about which nr 1107-3.

[12] He particularly referred to Von Bar's *The Common European Law of Torts*, Van Gerven's *Casebook on Tort Law*, Markesinis and Unberath's *The German Law of Torts*, and Spier's *Unification of Tort Law: Causation*.

[13] *Fairchild v Glenhaven Funeral Services Ltd & Others* [2002] 3 All ER 305, nr 32, per Lord Bingham of Cornhill.

[14] See for an overview of recent cases in which English courts made use of comparative law Unberath, Hannes, 'The German Courts', in Guy Canivet, Mads Andenas and Duncan Fairgrieve (eds.), *Comparative Law Before the Courts*, (London: BIICL, 2004), 313, note 35.

wrongful life claim referring to the then recent approach adopted by the English Court of Appeal in *McKay v Essex Health Authority*.[15]

The French *Cour de cassation* never refers to foreign national law. It is, however, interesting to note that in *Perruche*, also a wrongful life case, the *Cour* asked the French Comparative Law Institute to issue a research report which was then notified to the parties for use before the court.[16]

Comparative law is not only interesting from a converging but also from a diverging point of view. In this sense it can illustrate how legal cultures, legal structures, legal reasoning, and legal thinking differ. If these differences are obstacles for a common European market, this can be a reason to remove them. The same goes for areas in which the differences are not acceptable from a human rights or safety point of view. But there are other fields of tort law where no direct need exists to eliminate the differences and where differences in legal cultures, structures, reasoning, and thinking may linger on and can flourish (nr 600).

202 European Convention on Human Rights

The main goal of the Convention for the Protection of Human Rights and Fundamental Freedoms (usually referred to as the European Convention on Human Rights, ECHR) is to protect individuals, businesses, and organizations against infringement of their human rights by the Contracting States.[17] This Convention is the 'constitution' of the Council of Europe, an intergovernmental organization established in 1949, and not to be confused with the European Union. The Council of Europe comprises 46 Member States and includes all 25 European Union Member States.[18] Its headquarters are in the *Palais de l'Europe*

---

[15] BGH 18 January 1983, BGHZ 86, 241, referring to *McKay v Essex Health Authority* [1982] 2 All ER 771 (CA), about which nr 707-2. See also BGH 27 June 1995, NJW 1995, 2407 (wrongful birth), about which nr 700 and BGH 5 November 1974, BGHZ 63, 140 (reference to French law in a case as regards liability for sports injuries).

[16] Guy Canivet, 'The French Private Law Courts', in Guy Canivet, Mads Andenas and Duncan Fairgrieve (eds.), *Comparative Law Before the Courts*, (London: BIICL, 2004), 191, referring to Ass. plén. 17 November 2000, D. 2001. 332, note Denis Mazeaud and Patrice Jourdain. See also Conseil d'État 29 October 2003, Droit Administratif 2004, 32, with reference to an English High Court decision.

[17] See for instance Robin White and Clare Ovey, *Jacobs and White, the European Convention on Human Rights*, 3rd edn., (Oxford: Oxford University Press, 2002); Stephen Livingstone, *The European Convention on Human Rights*, (Oxford: Oxford University Press, 2000).

[18] Since 1949: Belgium, Denmark, France, Greece, Ireland, Italy, Luxembourg, Netherlands, Norway, Sweden, Turkey, United Kingdom; 1950: Germany, Iceland; 1956: Austria; 1961: Cyprus; 1963: Switzerland; 1965: Malta; 1976: Portugal; 1977: Spain; 1978: Liechtenstein; 1988: San Marino; 1989: Finland; 1990: Hungary; 1991: Poland; 1992: Bulgaria; 1993: Czech Republic, Estonia, Lithuania, Romania, Slovakia, Slovenia; 1994: Andorra; 1995: Albania, Latvia, Moldova, Former Yugoslav Republic of Macedonia, Ukraine; 1996: Croatia, Russian Federation; 1999: Georgia; 2001: Armenia, Azerbaijan; 2002: Bosnia & Herzegovina; 2003: Serbia and Montenegro; 2004: Monaco.

in Strasbourg (France). The European Convention is applied by the European Court of Human Rights (ECtHR) which has its seat in the same palace.

The aims of the Council of Europe are to protect human rights, pluralist democracy, and the rule of law. The ECHR was signed in Rome on 4 November 1950 and entered into force in September 1953. The starting point for the Convention was the Universal Declaration of Human Rights, adopted by the General Assembly of the United Nations on 10 December 1948.[19] The Convention represents the first steps for the enforcement of a number of the rights set out in the Universal Declaration.

Initially, the European Commission of Human Rights and the European Court of Human Rights were responsible for the enforcement of the obligations entered into by the Contracting States to the Convention. The 11th Protocol to the Convention, which entered into force in 1998, replaced the part-time Court and Commission by a single, full-time Court.

The Court consists of 46 judges, a number equal to that of the Contracting Parties to the Convention (Article 20). The Court sits in committees of three judges, in Chambers of seven judges and in a Grand Chamber of seventeen judges (Article 27). Committees decide on the admissibility of a claim (Article 28, see about the criteria Article 35), Chambers decide on the merits of the application (Article 29), whereas serious questions affecting the interpretation of the Convention or the Protocols hereto are decided by a Grand Chamber (Article 30). A judgment of a Chamber may be open to appeal before the Grand Chamber (Articles 43 and 44).

The Court decides by a majority vote. Judges who 'sit' on the case are entitled to append a separate opinion to the judgment. This can be a concurring or dissenting opinion, or a bare statement of dissent (Article 45 s. 2).

The execution of the Court's judgments is supervised by the Committee of Ministers (Article 46). If a State has violated the Convention or the Protocols hereto, the Committee will see whether the State has taken adequate remedial measures to comply with the obligations arising out of the Court's judgment. The Court can afford just satisfaction to the injured party if the internal law of the Contracting Party concerned allows only partial reparation to be made (Article 41). This provision presupposes that a violation of the Convention obliges the Contracting Party to fully repair the loss of the injured party. This will primarily be a *restitutio in integrum* (re-establishment of the situation prior to the violation) but, if this is not possible, it can also imply the obligation to pay compensation (nr 1202-6).[20]

Articles 2–18 ECHR define the rights and freedoms secured by the Contracting Parties within their jurisdiction. There are a dozen additional Protocols

---

[19] See for the text of this Declaration http://www.un.org/Overview/rights.html.

[20] See Tom Barkhuysen, Michiel Leonard van Emmerik and Piet Hans van Kempen (eds.), *The Execution of Strasbourg and Geneva Human Rights Decisions in the National Legal Order*, (The Hague, London: Martinus Nijhoff, 1999).

to the Convention which only apply to the States for which the Protocols have entered into force. The case law of the ECtHR has considerably influenced the accountability and liability of Contracting States for the infringement of fundamental rights and tort law in particular.[21] In the framework of tort law one may particularly think of the application of Article 2 (the right to life, nr 1807), Article 3 (protection against torture or inhuman or degrading treatment or punishment, nr 1808-1), Article 5 (the right to liberty and security), Article 6 (fair trial and access to justice, nr 1804-3), Article 8 (nr 1808-2), Article 10 (freedom of expression), Article 13 (the right to an effective remedy), Article 14 (prohibition of discrimination), and Article 1 of the First Protocol to the Convention as regards the protection of property.

203 European Union

203-1 *History and structure*

Soon after World War II a great political need to achieve reconciliation between the enemies of the war and to create conditions for a long-lasting peace in Europe became apparent. In September 1946 Winston Churchill, the legendary British Prime Minister during the war, delivered a remarkable speech in Zurich, saying: 'We must build a kind of United States of Europe'. Similar thoughts were expressed by other politicians. It is not surprising that these ideas encountered opposition since for many people the wounds of the war were too deep. But despite those concerns the political train of European integration had started running. It was run by train drivers who not only had a vision of sustainable European cooperation but also were aware of the necessity of a strong counterpart to the Soviet Union and the Eastern European countries. After the establishment of the Council of Europe in 1949 (nr 202) the sight was set on economic cooperation.

In 1950, in a speech inspired by Jean Monnet, Robert Schuman, the French Foreign Minister, proposed that France and Germany and any other European country wishing to join them would pool their coal and steel resources. This so-called 'Schuman Declaration' was subscribed to by Belgium, France, Luxembourg, Italy, the Netherlands, and Germany. In 1952 these six countries founded the European Coal and Steel Community (ECSC), and in 1958 the European Economic Community (EEC). These institutions marked the coming into being of what has now become the European Union.[22]

Since then, five waves of accessions can be distinguished: Denmark, Ireland, and the United Kingdom entered 'Europe' in 1973, Greece in 1981, Spain and Portugal in 1986, and Austria, Finland, and Sweden in 1995. In 2004 the

---

[21] See for example, Jane Wright, *Tort Law & Human Rights*, (Oxford: Hart, 2001).

[22] See about the legal, historical and political aspects of the European Union: Walter van Gerven, *The European Union. A Polity of States and Peoples* (Oxford: Hart, 2005).

15 Member States got the company of 10 new Member States: Cyprus, Czech Republic, Estonia, Hungary, Latvia, Lithuania, Malta, Poland, Slovenia, and Slovakia, 8 of them members of the former Eastern bloc. The accession of Bulgaria and Romania is foreseen for 2007.[23]

The European integration is based on four major treaties. The Treaty establishing the ECSC entered into force in 1952 and expired in 2002. The Treaty of Rome established the EEC in 1957, entered into force in 1958 and aimed to abolish tariffs and trade restrictions between member countries. The Treaty establishing the European Atomic Energy Community (Euratom) entered into force in 1958, and the Treaty on European Union (Maastricht Treaty) entered into force in 1993. The Maastricht Treaty also changed the name of the European Economic Community to 'the European Community'.[24] Finally, the Constitution for Europe was supposed to bring further changes by improving the division of competences, the instruments of action, as well as democracy, transparency, and efficiency of the European Union.[25] After the rejection of the Constitution by France and the Netherlands, however, it is unlikely that the Constitution will enter into force in its present shape.

The EU is run by five institutions, which each play a specific role: the European Parliament (elected by the peoples of the Member States), the Council of the Union (composed of the governments of the Member States), the European Commission (the driving force and executive body of the Union appointed by the Council and Parliament), the Court of Auditors (responsible for a sound and lawful management of the EU budget), and the Court of Justice (see about the latter nr 203-2).[26]

203-2 *Judiciary*

The Court of Justice of the European Communities (ECJ) comprises 25 judges and 8 Advocates-General. The judges and Advocates-General are appointed by the governments of the Member States for a renewable term of six years. The Advocates-General assist the Court in its task. The institution of Advocate-General is akin to and obviously inspired by the French system (nr 301-3). The Advocate-General provides, in open court and with complete impartiality and independence, reasoned Opinions (*Schlußanträge, Conclusions*) on cases brought before the Court (Articles 221–223 EC).

[23] OJ L 157/3, 22 February 2005: Commission Opinion on the applications for accession to the European Union by the Republic of Bulgaria and Romania.
[24] The founding treaties have been amended on several occasions. The Merger Treaty (1967) provided for a Single Commission and a Single Council of the then three European Communities. Adaptations for the achievement of the Internal market were provided by the Single European Act (1987). The Amsterdam Treaty (1999) amended and renumbered the EU and EC Treaties and the Nice Treaty (2003) merged the former Treaty of the EU and the Treaty of the EC into one consolidated version; see Craig and De Búrca (2003), 10–53.
[25] See about the Constitution http://europa.eu.int/comm/press_room/presspacks/constit/index_en.htm. [26] Craig and De Búrca (2003), 54–110.

In 1994 the Court of First Instance (CFI) was established. In the framework of tort law the CFI has jurisdiction to hear and decide on actions for annulment, for failure to act, and for damages which are brought by natural and legal persons (Articles 224–225a). The action for damages concerns the reparation of damage caused by an unlawful act of or a failure to act by a Community institution such as the Commission or the Council. Appeals can be brought before the Court of Justice but on points of law only and not on the facts (Article 225(1)).[27]

The ECJ gives preliminary rulings and hears various types of action. In the framework of tort law one may particularly think of the ECJ's competence to establish liability of the Community for damage caused by Community institutions or civil servants in the performance of their duties; this is the action for damages (nr 204-5). Other competences of the Court are to determine whether a Member State has fulfilled its obligations under Community law (actions may be brought by the Commission—as is practically always the case—or by another Member State, see Articles 226–228) and to review the legality of the acts of the Community institutions (actions may be brought by a Member State, the Council, the Commission and, in certain circumstances, Parliament; individuals may seek the annulment of a legal measure which is of direct and individual concern to them, Articles 230–233).

It is the task of the ECJ and the CFI to ensure that the law is observed in the interpretation and applications of the Treaties establishing the European Communities and of the provisions laid down by the Community institutions (Article 220(1)). The ECJ has carried out its task with great strength.

The ECJ is generally perceived to have pursued a vigorous policy of legal integration over the years, and in particular in the early decades of the Community's history. It is seen as having undertaken the task of giving flesh and substance to an 'outline' Treaty, and as having developed a particular vision of the kind of Europe it sought to promote. The primary concern of the Court has probably been to enhance the effectiveness of Community law and to promote its integration into national legal systems.[28]

Next to the ECJ and the CFI also the national courts of the Member States are empowered to apply Community law. They have jurisdiction to review the administrative implementation of Community law and have to uphold individual rights on nationals of Member States conferred by Community law. In order to ensure that Community law is interpreted and applied uniformly throughout the Community a national court may, and sometimes must, seek a preliminary ruling from the Court if it is in doubt as to the interpretation or validity of that law (Article 234). The national courts are encouraged to do so by the ECJ's *Köbler* decision, a case about liability of a Member State for breach of Community law by the national judiciary (nr 205-4).

---

[27] See about the Court of Justice: Lionel Neville Brown and Tom Kennedy, *The Court of Justice of the European Communities*, 5th edn., (London: Sweet & Maxwell, 2000), 175. See more generally Christiaan Timmermans, 'The European Union's Judicial System', *CMLR* 41/2 (2004), 393–405.
[28] Craig and De Búrca (2003), 87.

What is the role of fundamental rights in the framework of the European Union and how does this relate to the case law of the European Court of Human Rights (nr 202)? The European Court of Justice has long acknowledged that fundamental rights form part of the general principles of Community law.[29] Article F(2) of the Treaty on European Union (Maastricht Treaty) explicitly provides that the Union shall respect fundamental rights as guaranteed by the Convention as general principles of Community law.[30]

The current situation was elegantly summarized by Advocate-General Jacobs:

Although the Community itself is not a party to the Convention (. . .) and although the Convention may not be formally binding upon the Community, nevertheless for practical purposes the Convention can be regarded as part of Community law and can be invoked as such both in this Court and in national courts where Community law is in issue. (. . .). Community law cannot release Member States from their obligations under the Convention on this.[31]

204 Vicinity of liability for breach of Community law

204-1 *Legislation and case law*

The legal framework of the European Union consists of the treaties, Regulations, Directives and case law. In the area of tort law, a number of rules can be found in tort law Directives (this section).[32] Liability can also be based on the violation of Community provisions having so-called direct effect. The issue of direct effect and of the consequences thereof will be dealt with in the following sections. The explicitly regulated liability of Community institutions in Article 288 EC will be the subject of nr 204-5. Finally, the development of a general principle of liability for breach of Community law in the so-called *Francovich* case law of the ECJ will be pointed out in nr 205.[33]

[29] ECJ 17 December 1970, Case 11/70, ECR 1970, 1125 (*Internationale Handelsgesellschaft mbH v Einfuhr- und Vorratsstelle für Getreide und Futtermittel*), § 4.

[30] The Constitution for Europe (nr 203-1) contained the Charter of Fundamental Rights of the European Union which to a great extent were identical with the provisions of the ECHR. See Craig and De Búrca (2003), 358–363; Jacqueline Dutheil de la Rochère, 'The EU and the Individual: Fundamental Rights in the Draft Constitutional Treaty', *CMLR* 41/2 (2004), 345–354.

[31] Advocate-General Jacobs before ECJ 30 July 1996, Case 84/95, ECR 1996, I-3953 (*Bosphorus Hava Yollari Turizm ve Ticaret v Minister for Transport, Energy and Communications, Ireland and the Attorney General*). This case eventually landed at the ECtHR and illustrates interesting aspects of the concurrence of two supranational jurisdictions over the same facts: ECtHR 30 June 2005, case 45036/98 (*Bosphorus Hava Yollari Turizm ve Ticaret v Ireland*). See also Craig and De Búrca (2003), 365–368.

[32] See Peter-Christian Müller-Graf, 'EC Directives as a Means of Private Law Unification', in Hartkamp et al. (eds.), *Towards a European Civil Code* (New York: Aspen Publishers, 2004), 77–100.

[33] Walter van Gerven, 'The ECJ-Case law as a Means of Unification of Private Law?', in Hartkamp et al. (eds.), *Towards a European Civil Code* (New York: Aspen Publishers, 2004), 101–123.

The most well known Directive in the area of tort law is the Product Liability Directive, issued in 1985 and harmonizing the law on liability for defective products.[34] This is a so-called 'maximum harmonisation Directive' which means that Member States are not allowed to deviate from it, for instance by providing a higher level of consumer protection. However, differences remain between the Member States, not only because of a number of options but also because the Directive hardly touches upon the law of damages which varies considerably in the Member States (nr 1202–1211). The Product Liability Directive has given rise to interesting cases before the ECJ and to a number of cases before the national courts. See nr 1406–1411.

As a sequel to the Product Liability Directive, the European Commission in 1990 proposed a Directive concerning Liability for Defective Services. This would provide for a liability regime covering a huge range of services. Although the Directive was intended to be an instrument of minimum harmonization only, it met strong opposition in the Council and in 1994 the Commission decided to withdraw its proposal.[35]

Since 1995 European law has also provided for legislation as regards misleading advertising.[36] These 'minimum harmonisation Directives' only provide a general framework and have not brought the Member States' legislation to a similar level. The main harmonizing effect was that most Member States copied the definitions of advertising and misleading advertising (Article 2). Article 3 only contains a very general clause, providing that 'In determining whether advertising is misleading, account shall be taken of all its features, and in particular of any information it contains', followed by a number of relevant circumstances like the characteristics of goods or services, the price or the manner in which the price is calculated, and the conditions on which the goods are supplied or the services provided.

The Directive concerning Liability for Damage Caused to the Environment focuses on competences of governmental authorities as regards prevention and reparation of environmental damage. The Directive only provides for a right to compensation for public authorities and not for private parties. See nr 1415-3.

The most recent example of European legislation in the area of tort law is the Directive on Unfair Commercial Practices, providing a general prohibition of such practices and a list of specific practices that are deemed to be unfair.[37] A business-to-consumer practice is 'any act, omission, course of conduct or representation, commercial communication including advertising and marketing, by a trader, directly connected with the promotion, sale or supply of a product to

---

[34] Directive 85/374/EEC.   [35] OJ C 12/8, 18 January 1991, COM (94) 260.

[36] 1984/450/EEC (Misleading Advertising) and 1997/55/EEC (Comparative Advertising), amended by Directive 2005/29/EC of 11 May 2005 on Unfair Commercial Practices (see below).

[37] Directive 2005/29/EC of 11 May 2005 concerning unfair business-to-consumer commercial practices in the internal market. See also Hugh Collins (ed.), *The Forthcoming EC Directive on Unfair Commercial Practices* (The Hague, London, New York: Kluwer Law International, 2004).

consumers.' Misleading and aggressive practices are the main targets of the Directive. Misleading practices include the hiding of material information or providing it in an 'unclear, unintelligible, ambiguous or untimely manner', thus preventing the consumer from taking an informed decision (Articles 6–7).[38] Aggressive commercial practices by the trader include harassment, coercion, and undue influence (Article 8). It is claimed that the Directive does not deal with contract law matters but in most Member States it will be hard to implement the Directive without affecting national contract law provisions. The Directive provides for maximum harmonization which means that the Member States are not allowed to deviate from it. The Member States are, however, allowed to continue to apply national provisions that are more restrictive or prescriptive for six years from 12 June 2007, the date by which the Directive must have been implemented.[39]

204-2 *Vertical direct effect*

The Community instrument of the Directive is quite often used in private law matters.[40] As distinct from the Treaty and Regulations, however, a Directive is not suitable to *unify* the laws of the Member States. Article 249 (ex Article 189) provides that a Directive 'shall be binding as to the result to be achieved, upon each Member State to which it is addressed, but shall leave to national authorities the choice of form and methods.' Hence, Directives generally only *harmonize* the laws.

In principle, rules in Directives only apply as from the time and in as much as the national legislator has transposed them into national law. However, a Directive and more generally other Community law provisions may have direct effect. In a broad sense, direct effect of EC law means that 'provisions of binding EC Law which are clear, precise and unconditional enough to be considered justiciable can be invoked and relied on by individuals before national courts.'[41]

This definition is derived from the famous *Van Gend en Loos* case.[42] Van Gend en Loos imported chemical products from Germany into the Netherlands and had to pay 5 per cent increased customs and excise charge and an import duty. It alleged that these charges and import duty infringed Article 12 (now Article 25) EC and the question was whether this provision has direct effect within the territory of a Member State; in other words whether nationals of such a State can invoke individual rights which the courts must

[38] The drafting of this wording could have been inspired by the communication style of some governmental authorities.
[39] The provisions have to be applied as from 12 December 2007.
[40] See extensively Sacha Prechal, *Directives in European Community Law* (Oxford: Oxford University Press, 1995). [41] Craig and De Búrca (2003), 178.
[42] ECJ 5 February 1963, Case 26/62, ECR 1963, 1, 12 (*Van Gend en Loos v Nederlandse Administratie der Belastingen*).

protect.[43] The ECJ held

... that the Community constitutes a new legal order of international law for the benefit of which the states have limited their sovereign rights, albeit within limited fields, and subjects of which comprise not only Member States but also their nationals. Independently of the legislation of Member States, Community law therefore not only imposes obligations on individuals but is also intended to confer upon them rights which become part of their legal heritage.[44]

The ECJ concluded:

The wording of Article 12 contains a clear and unconditional prohibition which is not a positive but a negative obligation. (...). The very nature of this prohibition makes it ideally adapted to produce direct effects in the legal relationship between Member States and their subjects. (...) Article 12 must be interpreted as producing direct effects and creating individual rights which national courts must protect.[45]

Though uncertainty remains about the exact meaning and scope of direct effect, the main requirements are that a provision of EC law is clear, precise and unconditional. The latter requirement implies that the provision does not leave the implementing Member State any margin of discretion.[46]

An example of a Directive provision having direct effect can be found in the case of *Van Duyn v Home Office*. Van Duyn, a Dutch national, was refused leave to enter the UK to work for the Church of Scientology because the British Government regarded this church as socially harmful. However, no legal restrictions were placed upon its practice. Van Duyn alleged that the refusal was, *inter alia*, an infringement of Directive 64/221, regulating the free movement of workers within the Community. The ECJ held:

It would be incompatible with the binding effect attributed to a directive ... to exclude, in principle, the possibility that the obligation which it imposes may be invoked by those concerned. In particular, where the Community authorities have, by directive, imposed on Member States the obligation to pursue a particular course of conduct, the useful effect of such an act would be weakened if individuals were prevented from relying on it before their national courts.[47]

204-3 *Horizontal direct effect*

In addition to this rule of vertical direct effect (an individual invokes a right against a Member State), provisions can also have 'horizontal direct effect', which means that an individual may bring an action against another individual for infringing a rule of Community law. In *Defrenne v Sabena* (1976) a Belgian air

---

[43] Craig and De Búrca (2003), 183.
[44] ECJ 5 February 1963, Case 26/62, ECR 1963, 1, 12 (*Van Gend en Loos v Nederlandse Administratie der Belastingen*).
[45] ECJ 5 February 1963, Case 26/62, ECR 1963, 1, 13 (*Van Gend en Loos v Nederlandse Administratie der Belastingen*).   [46] Craig and De Búrca (2003), 178–189.
[47] ECJ 4 December 1974, Case 41/74, ECR 1974, 1337, 1348, para. 12 (*Van Duyn v Home Office*).

hostess alleged that she received lower wages than her colleague male stewards who did the same job, this being an infringement of the equal treatment provision of Article 141. The ECJ held that this provision could be relied upon not only against the State but also against other individuals. 'In fact, since Article [141] is mandatory in nature, the prohibition on discrimination between men and women applies not only to the action of public authorities, but also extends to all agreements which are intended to regulate paid labour collectively, as well as to contracts between individuals.'[48] Other examples of Treaty provisions having direct horizontal effect are Articles 81 and 82 (competition law), 28 and 29 (prohibition of quantitative restrictions on import and export), 39 (freedom of movement for workers) and 49 (prohibition of restrictions on freedom of services).

Provisions of a Directive do not have direct horizontal effect: an individual cannot invoke provisions of a Directive against another individual. This follows from *Marshall (No. 1)*, a decision handed down in 1986. A UK health authority required female employees to retire at 60 and male employees at 65. Helen Marshall argued that her dismissal at the age of 60 violated the 1976 Equal Treatment Directive. The ECJ held:

With regard to the argument that a directive may not be relied upon against an individual, it must be emphasized that according to Article 189 of the EEC Treaty, the binding nature of a directive, which constitutes the basis for the possibility of relying on the directive before a national court, exists only in relation to 'each Member State to which it is addressed'. It follows that a directive may not of itself impose obligations on an individual and that a provision of a directive may not be relied upon as such against such a person.[49]

In this case, however, the health authority was considered to be a public authority and Helen Marshall was entitled to invoke the rights provided by the Directive against the health authority.[50]

The ECJ confirmed this decision in 1994 in the *Dori* case which was about the late implementation by Italy of a Directive concerning protection of the consumer in respect of contracts negotiated away from business premises such as door-to-door selling. Dori therefore could not invoke the rights conferred by this Directive and argued that the Directive provision had direct horizontal effect.[51] The ECJ, however, considered that

... in the absence of measures transposing the directive within the prescribed time-limit, consumers cannot derive from the directive itself a right of cancellation as against

[48] ECJ 8 April 1976, Case 43/75, ECR 1976, 455, 476 (*Defrenne v Sabena*)

[49] ECJ 26 February 1986, Case 152/84, ECR 1986, 723, 749 para. 48 (*Marshall v Southampton and South-West Hampshire AHA (Marshall (No. 1))*. See also Craig and De Búrca (2003), 207.

[50] See about direct effect of decisions of the European courts ECJ 6 October 1970, Case 9/70, ECR 1970, 825 (*Franz Grad v Finanzamt Traunstein*) and about direct effect of provisions in international agreements ECJ 26 October 1982, Case 104/81, ECR 1982, 3641 (*Hauptzollamt Mainz v Kupferberg*). See also Craig and De Búrca (2003), 193.

[51] Directive 85/577/EEC, OJ 1985 L 372, 31.

traders with whom they have concluded a contract or enforce such a right in a national court.[52]

This decision has been fiercely criticized by academics. Also a number of Advocates-General have pleaded in favour of full direct horizontal effect.[53]

204-4 *Purposive interpretation (horizontal indirect effect)*

There is, however, an alternative to direct horizontal effect of Directive provisions in order to contribute to the effectiveness of Community law. This is the instrument of purposive or consistent interpretation (also called indirect horizontal effect) which the ECJ introduced in *Von Colson*.[54] This means that the national court is obliged to interpret domestic law in the light of the (not or wrongly transposed) Directive. In *Pfeiffer*, twenty years after *Von Colson*, the ECJ held that the ' . . . requirement for national law to be interpreted in conformity with Community law is inherent in the system of the Treaty.'[55] *Pfeiffer* was about emergency workers claiming that German legislation providing for weekly working time in excess of 48 hours was in breach of EC Directives concerning employees' health and safety and working times. The ECJ held that the national court had to interpret national law in the light of the Directive:

. . . when hearing a case between individuals, a national court is required, when applying the provisions of domestic law adopted for the purpose of transposing obligations laid down by a directive, to consider the whole body of rules of national law and to interpret them, so far as possible, in the light of the wording and purpose of the directive in order to achieve an outcome consistent with the objective pursued by the directive. In the main proceedings, the national court must thus do whatever lies within its jurisdiction to ensure that the maximum period of weekly working time, which is set at 48 hours (. . .), is not exceeded.[56]

Even if a claimant can invoke the direct or indirect effect of a rule, this will not always help him since he may have suffered damage which cannot be repaired in this way. This means that the enforcement of Community rights conferred on individuals is not fully guaranteed by the direct or indirect effect of Community rules. Therefore, it was necessary for the Court to provide additional enforcement instruments by creating the principle of liability of Member States for breach of Community law. This happened in a range of cases starting with *Francovich* in

[52] ECJ 14 July 1994, Case C-91/92, ECR 1994, I-3325 (*Dori v Recreb Srl*), para. 25.
[53] Craig and De Búrca (2003), 209–210.
[54] ECJ 10 April 1984, Case 14/83, ECR 1984, 1891 (*Von Colson and Kamann v Nordrhein-Westfalen*); see also Sara Drake, 'Twenty Years after Von Colson', *ELR* 30 (2005), 329–348.
[55] ECJ 5 October 2004, Joined Cases 397–403/01, ECR 2004, I-8835 (*Pfeiffer and others v Deutsches Rotes Kreuz*), para. 114. See also ECJ 16 June 2005, Case 105/03, (*Pupino*) [2005] 2 CMLR 63 (ECJ), as regards the role of consistent interpretation in the context of the EU as opposed to the EC Treaty.
[56] ECJ 5 October 2004, Joined Cases 397-403/01, ECR 2004, I-8835 (*Pfeiffer and others v Deutsches Rotes Kreuz*), para. 119, with reference to ECJ 13 November 1990, Case 106/89 ECR 1990, I-4135 (*Marleasing v La Comercial Internacional de Alimentación*).

1991. In this case the ECJ acknowledged that this principle of liability of Member States is inherent in the system of the EC Treaty (nr 205-1). In other words, both the principle of purposive interpretation and the principle of liability form part and parcel of the Treaty even though they are not explicitly mentioned therein. These are two great examples of how the ECJ 'finds' Community law and thus considerably contributes to its development by creating principles that aim to ensure the application and effectiveness of Community law.

Before dealing with the principle of Member State liability the ECJ created in its *Francovich* case law, attention needs to be paid to the liability of Community institutions which is explicitly regulated in the Treaty. In nr 205 it will be pointed out how these two sets of liability rules relate to each other.

204-5 *Article 288 EC: liability of Community institutions*

Article 288 EC provides a rule for liability of Community institutions for damage caused by the breach of Community law. The relevant sections of this provision read as follows:

(. . .).
(2) In the case of non-contractual liability, the Community shall, in accordance with the general principles common to the laws of the Member States, make good any damage caused by its institutions or by its servants in the performance of their duties.
(. . .).
(4) The personal liability of its servants towards the Community shall be governed by the provisions laid down in their Staff Regulations or in the Conditions of employment applicable to them.

Article 288(2) EC does not give a precise liability rule but refers to 'the general principles common to the laws of the Member States'. A difficulty that immediately rises is, that ' . . . there does not exist within the (. . .) countries of the Communities a common corpus of legal principles governing State liability in tort.'[57] Neither does Article 288(2) mean

. . . that the Community judicature must search for a solution favoured by a majority of the Member States or for some sort of arithmetic mean, still less that it has to apply the lowest common denominator. It means simply that the Community judicature must look to the national systems for inspiration in divising a régime of non-contractual liability adapted to the specific circumstances of the Community.[58]

According to Van Gerven,

. . . no one holds the view that, for a principle to be 'common', it must exist in all of the Member States. (. . .). 'Common' means in this context, I would think, that the principle

[57] Lionel Neville Brown and Tom Kennedy, *The Court of Justice of the European Communities*, 5th edn., (London: Sweet & Maxwell, 2000), 175.
[58] Anthony Arnull, 'Liability for Legislative Acts under Article 215(2) EC', in Ton Heukels and Alison McDonnell, *The Action for Damages in Community Law*, (The Hague, London, Boston: Aspen Publishers, 1997), 129–130.

is accepted (by a prevailing opinion) in a sufficiently large number of Member States in which the issue concerned has arisen in similar terms. Furthermore, the notion of 'principle' does not refer to precise rules but to maxims or concepts with a considerable degree of abstraction which, in concrete cases, may nonetheless result in similar solutions. In some States such principles may have been reduced to writing, in others they may find support in legislation or in case law.[59]

The search for these common maxims or concepts is not an easy one but it is to be preferred to looking for common precise rules. Even at this more abstract level difficulties remain, because not only the legal frameworks, structures, and rules in the Member States differ but also the policy-oriented principles (nr 608-610). Therefore it is sometimes inevitable for the ECJ to pave its own way and to impose principles and concepts which are not really common to the laws of the Member States or which are even disputed or rejected by a number of them. An important example is the fact that it is doubtful whether it is a common principle in the laws of the Member States that breaches of Community law attributable to a national legislator or a national court are to give rise to liability (the *Francovich* rule, see nr 205-1).[60] Indeed, the ECJ did not only refer to principles common to the laws of the Member States but also to principles of international law.[61]

The ECJ used the general principles to which Article 288 refers as a basis to develop a remedy in compensation for individuals who suffered damage because of the violation of Community law by a Member State (including local authorities) and individuals (nr 205).

Four stages can be distinguished on the road to this comprehensive Community law liability principle: (i) recognition of liability of the Community in Article 288 EC (see below); (ii) recognition of liability of a Member State for violation of Community law in *Francovich* (nr 205-1); (iii) recognition of the direct relation between these two kinds of liability in *Brasserie du Pêcheur and Factortame* and its common set of requirements in *Bergaderm* (nr 205-2) and (iv) recognition in the *Courage* case that the general liability principle of Community law also applies to private persons (nr 205-3).[62] This case law is one of the forces for developing European tort law.

---

[59] Walter van Gerven, 'A Common European Law in the Area of Tort Law', in Fairgrieve, Andenas and Bell (eds.), *Tort Liability of Public Authorities in Comparative Perspective*, (London: BIICL, 2002), 135.   [60] Van Gerven (2000), 391–392.
   [61] ECJ 5 March 1996, Joined cases C-46/93 and C-48/93, ECR 1996, I-1029 (*Brasserie du Pêcheur and Factortame III*), para. 34:
... in international law a State whose liability for breach of an international commitment is in issue will be viewed as a single entity, irrespective of whether the breach which gave rise to the damage is attributable to the legislature, the judiciary or the executive. This must apply *a fortiori* in the Community legal order.
   [62] See already R.H.G. Hesper, 'Op weg naar Europeesrechtelijke aansprakelijkheid voor schade bij schending van Europees kartelrecht', *RM Themis* 1999/4, 143–162.

205 General principle of liability for breach of Community law

205-1 *Member State liability for breach of Community law*

The second stage in the development of Community tort law is heralded with the *Francovich* case, handed down by the ECJ in 1991. In this decision the ECJ acknowledged liability of the Member States towards individuals for violation of Community law as being inherent in the system of the Treaty and being necessary for the effectiveness of Community law.[63] The case was about employees of an Italian company that went bankrupt and therefore was not able to pay the wages. At that time the Italian legislator had wrongfully not yet implemented in its national law European Directive 80/987 on the protection of employees in case of insolvency of the employer. This was a violation of Article 249 s. 3 (ex 189 s. 3) EC. The Italian court asked preliminary questions to the ECJ.

Firstly, the ECJ decided that Directive 80/987 did not have direct (vertical) effect; this meant that Francovich did not have the right to invoke direct protection on the basis of that Directive (para. 27). Generally, the conditions for direct effect are that the provision has to be clear, precise and unconditional and this was not the case in the applicable Directive (nr 204-2).

Subsequently the ECJ took up the issue of whether a Member State could be liable for damage caused by the violation of a duty which is imposed upon it by Community law. The EC Treaty did not provide a direct basis for this new principle but the Court considered it to be inherent in the Treaty's system. This implied that the Court had competence to decide the case and that it did not have to wait for the European legislature to develop new rules. The landmark consideration of the ECJ was '... that it is a principle of Community law that the Member States are obliged to make good loss and damage caused to individuals by breaches of Community law for which they can be held responsible' (para. 37). The ECJ based this principle on the more general principle of the effectiveness of Community law and the corresponding need that the rules of Community law take full effect and that the rights which they confer on individuals must be protected (para. 32). Against this background the Court concluded that the principle of liability is inherent in the system of the Treaty (para. 35).

On the basis of the general principles to which Article 288 refers, the ECJ developed three requirements for liability: (i) the rule of law infringed must be intended to confer rights on individuals; (ii) the breach must be sufficiently serious; (iii) there must be a direct causal link between the breach of the obligation resting on the State and the damage sustained by the injured parties.[64]

---

[63] ECJ 19 November 1991, Joined cases C-6/90 and C-9/90, ECR 1991, I-5357 (*Francovich and Bonifaci v Italy*).

[64] ECJ 19 November 1991, Joined cases C-6/90 and C-9/90, ECR 1991, I-5357 (*Francovich and Bonifaci v Italy*), paras 40–41; ECJ 5 March 1996, Joined cases C-46/93 and C-48/93, ECR

The fulfilment of these requirements is sufficient for a right to compensation, which is directly based in Community law.[65]

If these conditions are met, it is on the basis of rules of national law on liability that the State must make reparation for the consequences of the loss and damage caused. However, the conditions for reparation of loss and damage laid down by the national legislation must not be less favourable than those relating to similar domestic claims and must not be so framed as to make it in practice impossible or excessively difficult to obtain reparation.[66]

The result of *Francovich* was that an effective remedy was made available to enhance the effectiveness of unimplemented Directives next to the right of the Commission to enforce the Member State's obligations in this respect. But the importance of *Francovich* is not restricted to not (timely) implemented Directives. The principle applies to all breaches of Community law. See nr 1805.

At an individual level, the *Francovich* case ended rather disappointingly because Signore Francovich did not benefit from the case law that had provided him with everlasting fame within the European legal world. In a later judgment, the ECJ held that Francovich's claim did not come within the scope of application of the Directive because Francovich's insolvent employer was not one against whom a collective procedure on behalf of the creditors could be brought under Italian law.[67]

205-2 *Link between Member State liability and Article 288 EC*

The third stage was reached in the decision of the ECJ in *Brasserie du Pêcheur* and *Factortame* in 1996.[68] In this decision the Court made a direct link between liability of the Community based on Article 288 II EC (nr 204-5), and liability of a Member State based on the *Francovich* case law (nr 205-1). *Brasserie du Pêcheur* was about a French brewer whose distribution contract with a German importer was terminated because the German authorities did not allow the import and sale of French beer that did not meet the production requirements of

1996, I-1029 (*Brasserie du Pêcheur and Factortame III*), paras 50–51; ECJ 26 March 1996, Case C-392/93, ECR 1996, I-1631 (*The Queen v HM Treasury, ex parte British Telecommunications*), paras 39–40; ECJ 23 May 1996, Case C-5/94, ECR 1996, I-2553 (*The Queen v Ministry of Agriculture, Fisheries and Food, ex parte Hedley Lomas (Ireland) Ltd*), paras 25–26; ECJ 8 October 1996, Joined cases C-178/94, C-179/94, C-188/94, C-189/94 and C-190/94, ECR 1996, I-4845 (*Dillenkofer and Others v Germany*), para. 21.

[65] ECJ 8 October 1996, Joined cases C-178/94, C-179/94, C-188/94, C-189/94 and C-190/94, ECR 1996, I-4845 (*Dillenkofer and Others v Germany*), para. 27: '. . . no other conditions need be taken in consideration'.

[66] ECJ 19 November 1991, Joined cases C-6/90 and C-9/90, ECR 1991, I-5357 (*Francovich and Bonifaci v Italy*), paras 41–43; ECJ 2 April 1998, Case C-127/95, ECR 1998, I-1531 (*Norbrook Laboratories Ltd v Ministry of Agriculture, Fisheries and Food*), para. 111.

[67] ECJ 9 November 1993, Case C-479/93, ECR I-3313 (*Francovich v Italy*), paras 21–22. See also Walter van Gerven, 'State Liability for Breach of EC Law', *ICLQ* 45 (1996), 516–517.

[68] ECJ 5 March 1996, Joined cases C-46/93 and C-48/93, ECR 1996, I-1029 (*Brasserie du Pêcheur and Factortame III*).

the so-called *Reinheitsgebot* (purity requirement). This German regulation on the purity of beer is one of the oldest food regulations and was issued by Elector Wilhelm IV of Bavaria in 1516. It allows only malted corn, hops, yeast, and water to be used as ingredients for beer. In 1987, the ECJ had decided that the appliance of the *Reinheitsgebot* to French beer was a violation of the prohibition to impede the free movements of goods in the Community.[69] This prohibition can be found in Article 28 EC and has direct effect (see about direct effect nr 205-2).

Factortame III was a case of Spanish fishermen against the UK government. In *Factortame II* the Court had decided that the UK had breached Article 43 EC by setting statutory conditions for registration as a British vessel.[70] Article 43 prohibits restrictions on the freedom of establishment of nationals of a Member State in the territory of another Member State. This prohibition also applies to restrictions on the setting-up of agencies, branches, or subsidiaries by nationals of any Member State established in the territory of any Member State.

In the combined cases of *Brasserie du Pêcheur* and *Factortame* the ECJ decided firstly that, if a Member State breaches a directly effective provision of Community law, a claim for damages is possible, which until then was controversial. The Court subsequently considered that the right of individuals to rely on the directly effective provisions of the Treaty ensures that provisions of Community law prevail over national provisions, but it

... cannot, in every case, secure for individuals the benefit of the rights conferred on them by Community law and, in particular, avoid their sustaining damage as a result of a breach of Community law attributable to a Member State. As appears from paragraph 33 of the judgment in *Francovich and Others*, the full effectiveness of Community law would be impaired if individuals were unable to obtain redress when their rights were infringed by a breach of Community law (...) the right to reparation is the necessary corollary of the direct effect of the Community provision whose breach caused the damage sustained. (paras 20 and 22).

In other words, the instrument of direct effect is not sufficient to guarantee the effectiveness of Community law. Hence, a Community right to compensation is the necessary complement of direct effect.

The recognition of the liability of a Member State for the violation of an indirectly effective provision in *Francovich* and the violation of a directly effective provision in *Brasserie du Pêcheur and Factortame* implied a general principle of liability of the Member States. The Court made it clear that liability does not depend on the character or nature of the violated Treaty provision. The decision in *Brasserie du Pêcheur and Factortame* therefore made it clear that the principle of liability is 'inherent in the system of the Treaty'.[71]

[69] ECJ 18 September 1986, Case C-178/84, ECR 1987, I-1227 (*Commission v Germany*).

[70] ECJ 25 July 1991, Case C-221/89, ECR 1991, I-3905 (*Factortame II*).

[71] ECJ 19 November 1991, Joined cases C-6/90 and C-9/90, ECR 1991, I-5357 (*Francovich and Bonifaci v Italy*), para. 35, referred to in ECJ 5 March 1996, Joined cases C-46/93 and

The importance of the principle was furthermore confirmed by the fact that in *Brasserie du Pêcheur and Factortame* the ECJ directly linked its decision to Article 288 EC, which applies to the non-contractual liability of the Community (nr 204-5). The ECJ considered that this provision ' . . . is simply an expression of the general principle familiar to the legal systems of the Member States that an unlawful act or omission gives rise to an obligation to make good the damage caused'.[72] The Court added that the protection of the rights which individuals derive from Community law cannot vary depending on whether a national authority or a Community authority is responsible for the damage, unless there is a particular justification for a different regime.[73]

In *Bergaderm* the ECJ confirmed the parallels between the liability of Member States (*Francovich* case law) and the liability of Community institutions (Article 288). It summarized the three conditions for liability under Community law:

. . . Community law confers a right to reparation where three conditions are met: the rule of law infringed must be intended to confer rights on individuals; the breach must be sufficiently serious; and there must be a direct causal link between the breach of the obligation resting on the State and the damage sustained by the injured parties.[74] As to the second condition, as regards both Community liability under Article 215 [288] of the Treaty and Member State liability for breaches of Community law, the decisive test for finding that a breach of Community law is sufficiently serious is whether the Member State or the Community institution concerned manifestly and gravely disregarded the limits on its discretion.[75] Where the Member State or the institution in question has only considerably reduced, or even no, discretion, the mere infringement of Community law may be sufficient to establish the existence of a sufficiently serious breach.[76]

Despite this very general and almost soothing statement, several questions remain as regards differences in detail between Member State liability on the one

C-48/93, ECR 1996, I-1029 (*Brasserie du Pêcheur and Factortame III*), para. 31; ECJ 26 March 1996, Case C-392/93, ECR 1996, I-1631 (*The Queen v HM Treasury ex parte British Tele-communications*), para. 38; ECJ 23 May 1996, Case C-5/94, ECR 1996, I-2553 (*The Queen v Ministry of Agriculture, Fisheries and Food, ex parte Hedley Lomas (Ireland) Ltd*), para. 24; ECJ 8 October 1996, Joined cases C-178/94, C-179/94, C-188/94, C-189/94 and C-190/94, ECR 1996, I-4845 (*Dillenkofer and Others v Germany*), para. 20; ECJ 2 April 1998, Case C-127/95, ECR 1998, I-1531 (*Norbrook Laboratories Ltd v Ministry of Agriculture, Fisheries and Food*), para. 106; ECJ 4 July 2000, Case C 424/97, ECR 2000, I-5123 (*Salomone Haim v Kassenzahnärztliche Vereinigung Nordrhein*), para. 27.

[72] ECJ 5 March 1996, Joined cases C-46/93 and C-48/93, ECR 1996, I-1029 (*Brasserie du Pêcheur and Factortame III*), para. 42.

[73] ECJ 5 March 1996, Joined cases C-46/93 and C-48/93, ECR 1996, I-1029 (*Brasserie du Pêcheur and Factortame III*), para. 29 and 42.

[74] ECJ 4 July 2000, Case 352/98, ECR 2000, I-5291 (*Laboratoires Pharmaceutique Bergaderm SA and Gouplin v Commission*), paras 42–44. The Court referred to ECJ 5 March 1996, Joined cases C-46/93 and C-48/93, ECR 1996, I-1029 (*Brasserie du Pêcheur and Factortame III*), para. 51.

[75] ECJ 5 March 1996, Joined cases C-46/93 and C-48/93, ECR 1996, I-1029 (*Brasserie du Pêcheur and Factortame III*), para. 55; ECJ 8 October 1996, Joined cases C-178/94, C-179/94, C-188/94, C-189/94 and C-190/94, ECR 1996, I-4845 (*Dillenkofer and Others v Germany*), para. 25.

[76] ECJ 23 May 1996, Case C-5/94, ECR 1996, I-2553 (*The Queen v Ministry of Agriculture, Fisheries and Food, ex parte Hedley Lomas (Ireland) Ltd*), para. 28.

hand and liability of Community institutions on the basis of Article 288 II on the other (see nr 1809-1811).

Liability for breach of Community law is mainly but not solely governed by these Community rules. The ECJ only refers to national law after formulating the European liability principle and the requirements for European liability.[77] Only inasmuch as Community law does not provide a rule, the case has to be decided on the basis of national law. However, even if this is the case, national law has to be applied within the limiting conditions of non-discrimination and effectiveness.[78]

205-3 *Liability of individuals for breach of Community law*

The latest stage in the development of Community tort law was reached in *Courage v Crehan* in which the Court acknowledged the possibility of Community liability of private persons, particularly for breach of Article 81 EC.[79] Some authors had already predicted this decision on the basis of the general wordings of the decisions of the ECJ in *Brasserie du Pêcheur and Factortame*. In this case the Court considered that someone is liable if he causes damage by breaching a rule of Community law. It was also predicted that this general rule could be particularly applied in the field of competition law.[80]

The case was about Inntrepreneur Estates Limited (IEL), jointly owned by Courage Limited and Grand Metropolitan plc, which had entered into two 20 year leases with Mr Crehan. The trade tie was not negotiable and Mr Crehan had to purchase a fixed minimum quantity of beers at prices stated in Courage's price list. Courage Limited sued Mr Crehan for £15,266 for unpaid beer deliveries. Mr Crehan argued that the claim was contrary to Article 81 EC and that he was entitled to damages, contending that Courage sold its beers to independent pub tenants at considerably lower prices. English law did not allow a party to an illegal agreement to claim damages from the other party, so that even if the defendant's defence were upheld, his claim for damages would be barred as a matter of English law. The Court of Appeal referred issues arising to the European Court.

The Court considered it to follow from the automatic nullity provision in Article 81(2) and the fact that Article 81(1) had direct effect that any individual, even a party to a contract that was liable to restrict or distort competition within Article 81(1), could rely before a national court on the breach of that provision.

[77] ECJ 19 November 1991, Joined cases C-6/90 and C-9/90, ECR 1991, I-5357 (*Francovich and Bonifaci v Italy*), paras 41–43.
[78] ECJ 16 December 1976, Case C-33/76, ECR 1976, I-1989 (*Rewe-Zentralfinanz eG et Rewe-Zentral AG v Landwirtschafiskammer für das Saarland*) and ECJ 16 December 1976, Case C-45/76, ECR 1976, I-2043 (*Comet BV v Produktschap voor Siergewassen*).
[79] ECJ 20 September 2001, Case C-453/99, ECR 2001, I-6297 (*Courage v Crehan*).
[80] W. van Gerven, Opinion of 27 October 1993, para. 36 ff. for ECJ 13 April 1994, Case C-128/92, ECR 1994, I-1209 (*Banks v British Coal*) and furthermore Van Gerven, *ICLQ* 45 (1996), 530–532; see also R.H.G. Hesper, *RM Themis*, 1999/4 143–162.

Since it was the duty of national courts effectively to protect rights conferred on individuals by Community law, such a party could in principle claim damages for loss caused to him by the contract. The Court considered:

The full effectiveness of Article [81] of the Treaty and, in particular, the practical effect of the prohibition laid down in Article [81(1)] would be put at risk if it were not open to any individual to claim damages for loss caused to him by a contract or by conduct liable to restrict or distort competition. Indeed, the existence of such a right strengthens the working of the Community competition rules and discourages agreements or practices, which are frequently covert, which are liable to restrict or distort competition. From that point of view, actions for damages before the national courts can make a significant contribution to the maintenance of effective competition in the Community. There should not therefore be any absolute bar to such an action being brought by a party to a contract which would be held to violate the competition rules.[81]

The Court continued that, in the light of the general principle that a litigant should not benefit from his own unlawful conduct, Community law did not prevent national law from refusing relief to a party who was found to have borne significant responsibility for the distortion of competition. Matters that were to be taken into account for that purpose included whether one party to the contract was in a markedly stronger position than the other, and so, *inter alia*, was in a position to impose terms on the other. See about contributory negligence 12 D.

It remains to be seen how effective the action for damages will be in enforcing rules of competition law. This is particularly relevant since the revised rules for the enforcement of competition law give a great deal of prominence to private law enforcement and the expectations seem to be high.[82] The practical problem, however, is that individuals and companies negatively affected by an infringement of Articles 81 or 82 have to take high hurdles before liability can be established. Though it is conceivable that they may be enabled to rely on the assistance of competition authorities to prove the existence of a restrictive agreement or a concerted practice, or of an abuse of dominant position, this will not be the case for the proof of causation or the quantification of loss sustained. It will be particularly difficult to prove that the infringement has caused damage to the individual person or company and if so, how much.[83] Hence, additional Community legislation might be necessary to ease the claimant's burden of proof. One may think of legal presumptions or defendant's obligations to disclose information about their business practices.[84] This issue is the topic of the

---

[81] ECJ 20 September 2001, Case C-453/99, ECR 2001, I-6297 (*Courage v Crehan*), paras 26–28.   [82] Regulation 2003/1, OJ L 001, 4 January 2003, 1–25.

[83] See C.D. Ehlermann and I. Atanasiu (eds.), *European Competition Law Annual 2001: Effective Private Enforcement of EC Antitrust Law* (Oxford: Hart, 2003). See also nr 1106 and 1202-4 about causation and damage.

[84] Jürgen Basedow, 'Private Enforcement of Article 81 EC: a German View', in C.D. Ehlermann and I. Atanasiu (eds.), *European Competition Law Annual 2001: Effective Private Enforcement of EC Antitrust Law* (Oxford: Hart, 2003), 137–145.

Commission's Green Paper on damages actions for the infringement of EC competition law as laid down in Articles 81 and 82 (nr 1217).

Liability of individuals and companies for breach of Community law will not only play a role in Article 81 and 82 cases. One may also think of Article 141 as regards equal treatment,[85] and the free movement Articles 39 and 49.[86] However, up until now, the straight question of liability for breach of a Treaty provision has not yet been addressed to the European Courts. The same issues arise, for example, as regards obligations imposed on individuals in Regulations. The Court has given more guidance in the *Muñoz* case.[87] This case will be dealt with in Chapter 12 in the framework of remedies in Community law in combination with the European Commission's plans to enhance the possibilities for private enforcement of competition law (nr 1217).

205-4 *Member State liability for judicial decisions*

After the ECJ's decisions on liability of Member States for breach of Community law it was almost inevitable that the Court would have to decide on Member State liability for decisions of national courts which were in breach of Community law. This happened in 2003 in *Köbler*.[88]

The case was about an Austrian university professor who had applied under Article 50a *Gehaltsgesetz* (Law on Salaries) for the special length-of-service increment for university professors. This increment was, however, only available for university professors having worked at least 15 years at Austrian universities. The duration of positions at universities of other Member States was not taken into account. Köbler claimed that this amounted to indirect discrimination unjustified under Community law. The Austrian *Verwaltungsgerichtshof* (Administrative Court) dismissed the claim on the ground that the increment was a loyalty bonus which justified derogation from the Community law provisions on freedom of movement for workers. Subsequently, Köbler filed a claim for damages against Austria, maintaining that the Austrian Administrative Court had infringed directly applicable provisions of Community law. The Austrian *Landesgericht* (Court of First Instance) referred to the Court for a preliminary ruling under Article 234 EC questions on the interpretation of Article 39 EC (freedom of movement for workers) and on the application of the *Francovich* case law on acts of the judiciary.

---

[85] ECJ 8 April 1976, Case 43/75, ECR 1976, 455, 476 (*Defrenne v Sabena*), para. 39.

[86] ECJ 12 December 1974, Case 36/74, ECR 1974, 1405 (*Walrave and Koch v Association Union Cycliste Internationale and Others*), para. 17; ECJ 6 June 2000, Case 281/98, ECR 2000-I, 4139 (*Roman Angonese v Cassa di Risparmio di Bolzano SpA*), paras 31–36.

[87] ECJ 17 September 2002, Case C-253/00, ECR 2002, I-7289 (*Antonio Muñoz y Cia SA and Superior Fruiticola SA v Frumar Ltd and Redbridge Produce Marketing Ltd*), about which see Andrea Biondi, *CML Rev*, 40 (2003), 1243–1250.

[88] ECJ 30 September 2003, C-224/01 (*Gerhard Köbler v Austria*).

In its decision the Court acknowledged that the principle for breach of Community law (nr 205-1) does not only apply if the infringement stems from a decision of a national legislator or a national executive power, but also if it stems from a decision of a national court adjudicating at last instance. Exempting the national judiciary from liability for breach of Community law would call in question the full effectiveness of Community rules.[89]

The ECJ rejected several objections. Firstly, liability for wrongful judicial decisions does not affect the principle of *res judicata* because the action for damages does not require revision of the decision. Secondly, there is no risk of a diminution of the authority of a court adjudicating at last instance to the contrary: liability for '. . . an erroneous judicial decision could also be regarded as enhancing the quality of a legal system and thus in the long run the authority of the judiciary.' Thirdly, application of the principle cannot be compromised by the absence of a competent court. Finally, referring to the Advocate-General's Opinion, it stated that the principle of liability for judicial decision was not unknown in most of the Member States.[90]

As to the requirements for liability, the Court reiterated that they are threefold: conferment of rights on individuals, sufficiently serious breach, and a direct causal link between breach and damage (nr 205-1). As to the second requirement, the Court explicitly stated that in case of a judicial decision Member State liability '. . . can be incurred only in the exceptional case where the court has manifestly infringed the applicable law.' Relevant factors are:

. . . in particular, the degree of clarity and precision of the rule infringed, whether the infringement was intentional, whether the error of law was excusable or inexcusable, the position taken, where applicable, by a Community institution and non-compliance by the court in question with its obligation to make a reference for a preliminary ruling under the third paragraph of Article 234 EC. In any event, an infringement of Community law will be sufficiently serious where the decision concerned was made in manifest breach of the case-law of the Court in the matter.[91]

As to the case, the ECJ considered that Article 39 EC is intended to confer rights on individuals, securing the freedom of movement for workers, and prohibiting any discrimination based on nationality as between the workers of

---

[89] ECJ 30 September 2003, C-224/01, ECR 2003, I-10239 (*Gerhard Köbler v Austria*), paras 50 and 33.

[90] ECJ 30 September 2003, C-224/01, ECR 2003, I-10239 (*Gerhard Köbler v Austria*), paras 39–48. Opinion Advocate-General Léger before ECJ 30 September 2003, C-224/01 (*Gerhard Köbler v Austria*), paras 77–85. See particularly the Belgium *Anca* case: Cass. 19 December 1991, Journal des Tribunaux, 1991, 141 (*Anca*), about which Van Gerven (2000), 385–388 and the commentaries in *ERPL*, 2/2 (1994), 111–140.

[91] ECJ 30 September 2003, C-224/01, ECR 2003, I-10239 (*Gerhard Köbler v Austria*), paras 53–56. In the same sense as regards Member State liability for breach of Community law in general: ECJ 5 March 1996, Joined Cases C-46 and 48/93, ECR 1996, I-1029 (*Brasserie du Pêcheur and Factortame III*), para. 57.

the Member States. Article 50a *Gehaltgesetz* could not be justified by a pressing public interest reason.[92]

As regards the requirement of a sufficiently serious breach, the ECJ said that the Austrian *Verwaltungsgerichtshof* had infringed Community law by deciding that the special length-of-service increment was a loyalty bonus which justified derogation from the Community law provisions on freedom of movement for workers. However, the ECJ did not consider this breach as being manifest in nature and thus as sufficiently serious. Firstly, Community law had not expressly covered this point. Secondly, the Austrian court had withdrawn its request for a preliminary ruling on the view that the answer had been given in *Schöning-Kougebetopoulou*[93] but this was based on incorrect reading of the judgment.[94] It is important to note that AG Léger had argued in favour of state liability by taking the more convincing view that it was '... difficult to accept that the *Verwaltungsgerichtshof* made an excusable error'. He also doubted '... that the supreme court was in fact convinced... that the application—even if correct—of Community law was so obvious as to leave no scope for any reasonable doubt'.[95]

A national court against whose decisions there is no judicial remedy under national law has to request the ECJ for a preliminary ruling (Article 234(3) EC) if it is in doubt about the interpretation of Community law.[96] The *Köbler* case shows that an infringement of this obligation does not amount to a sufficiently serious breach if the national court has only incorrectly read or interpreted the ECJ's case law. Apparently, a more serious mistake is needed for liability, namely a manifest mistake.

At the end of the day Köbler must have had mixed feelings. Though his name, like that of Francovich (nr 205-1), is now in the hall of fame of European law, the end of the matter was that he lost the case.

206 Requirements for liability for breach of Community law

Liability of Member States for breach of Community law is to a certain extent 'communitarized' but national law may still be decisive in this respect because the *Francovich* case law does not exclude the application of national law provided its conditions for liability are less restrictive. The principle of non-discrimination even requires the application of these more favourable rules, such as the

---

[92] ECJ 30 September 2003, C-224/01, ECR 2003, I-10239 (*Gerhard Köbler v Austria*), para. 87.
[93] ECJ 15 January 1998, C-15/96, ECR 1998, I-47 (*Schöning-Kougebetopoulou v Hamburg*).
[94] ECJ 30 September 2003, C-224/01, ECR 2003, I-10239 (*Gerhard Köbler v Austria*), paras 121–124.
[95] Opinion Advocate-General Léger before ECJ 30 September 2003, C-224/01 (*Gerhard Köbler v Austria*), paras 170 and 173.
[96] ECJ 6 October 1982, C-283/81, ECR 1982, 3415 (*CILFIT and Others v Ministry of Health*).

possibility to award exemplary damages in English law (nr 1202-3). This means that the *Francovich* case law in fact provides for minimum harmonization.

As has been pointed out in nr 205-2 the ECJ has held in *Bergaderm* that the Community law action for damages requires the fulfilment of three conditions: (i) the violated rule must confer rights on individuals, (ii) the breach of the rule must be sufficiently serious, and (iii) there must be consequential damage. These conditions apply to all potentially liable parties, be it a Community Institution, a Member State, a company, or an individual.

The three requirements of this Community liability rule will be analysed in more detail later in this book. The first requirement—the violated rule must confer rights on individuals—will be discussed in the chapter on breach of statutory duty (nr 905). The second requirement—the breach of the rule must be sufficiently serious—will be dealt with in the chapter on liability of public authorities (nr 1805). Finally, the not yet well-elaborated requirements of causation and damage will be touched upon in nr 1106 and nr 1202.

It has taken the ECJ about a decade to develop the principle of liability for breach of Community law. In this period decisions were not always presented in a consistent way. One may, for example, think of the many changes in the meaning of the concept of 'sufficiently serious breach' (nr 1805). Although these difficulties are inevitable to a certain extent, some of them may also be due to the system of the European Community Courts with its judge-rapporteur, with the differences in composition of the chamber in subsequent cases, and with a less strong emphasis on central direction than in continental courts, particularly as regards the precise wording and references to cases.

Of more substantive concern is that, in all cases of State liability, the standard for a sufficiently serious breach now depends on a catalogue of circumstances. This makes the outcome of a case rather unpredictable (nr 1805). Another cause for concern is the *Peter Paul* case, in which the ECJ complicated the first requirement that the violated rule must confer rights on individuals. This decision seems to have lowered the chances of a damages remedy in Community law in a more than sufficiently serious way (nr 905).

The value of the principle of liability for breach of Community law lies in its practical application and in practice the claimant has many hurdles to take. This means that the barking of the principle does not necessarily lead to biting. Although they are not necessarily representative, it is remarkable that, in many of the above-mentioned cases in which the principle of liability for breach of Community law was established or elaborated, the claimant entered the hall of fame but lost the case. It is one thing to have a principle of liability to ensure the application and effectiveness of Community law but it is another thing to see what it achieves in practice.

3

France

301 Introduction

301-1 *History*

Before the enactment of the *Code civil* in 1804 France had already been a centralized country for centuries. Until the end of the 17th century French law was a mixture of Roman law, canon law, and local laws and customs but from then on influential lawyers like Domat, Pothier, and Bourjon contributed to the development of French law as a harmonized national system. In contrast to the German BGB (nr 401-1) the French *Code civil* confirmed rather than created legal unity. Its main goal was to proclaim the ideas of the French revolution: *liberté, égalité et fraternité* (liberty, equality and brotherhood).[1]

The most cataclysmic event of the past one thousand years in France was the Revolution at the end of the 18th century. In 1789, this Revolution brought to an end the absolute *Ancien Régime*, which was by then personalized by King Louis XVI and Queen Marie-Antoinette. The Revolution also carried the fruits of the Age of Enlightenment, primarily marked by the Declaration of Rights of Men and Citizens (*la Déclaration des droits de l'homme et du citoyen*). This Declaration proclaimed all citizens to be equal before the law and was intended to bring to an end the class-based justice system.

When Napoleon Bonaparte came into power in 1799, he set up a commission featuring the four best civil lawyers of the country to produce a draft Civil Code. One of them was the famous lawyer Portalis. Napoleon himself was actively engaged in the preparatory work for this *Code civil des français* which relied heavily on the works of Domat, Pothier, and Bourjon. Soon after its adoption in 1804 a number of other Codes followed: the Code of Civil Procedure (*Code de procédure civil*) in 1806, the Commercial Code (*Code de commerce*) in 1807, and the Criminal Code (*Code pénal*) in 1810. Most of these codes have since been

---

[1] Viney, Introduction (1995), nr 14. English language books on French law are: John Bell, Sophie Boyron and Simon Whittaker, *Principles of French Law*, (Oxford: Oxford University Press, 1998); John Bell, *French Legal Cultures* 2nd edn., (London: Butterworths, 2001); Catherine Elliott and Catherine Vernon, *French Legal System*, (Harlow: Longman, 2000); Andrew West et al., *The French Legal System*, 2nd edn., (London: Butterworths, 1998).

altered but the heart of the *Code civil*, the law of obligations, has remained largely unchanged.

301-2 *Code civil*

The *Code civil* is one of the monuments of the French nation. It is called the civil constitution of France (*la Constitution civile de la France*), the memorial place of the nation (*le lieu de mémoire de la Nation*), the flower of French culture (*la fleur de la culture française*), and the grammar of our law (*le grammaire de notre droit*).[2] The bicentennial of the *Code civil* in 2004 was extensively celebrated.[3]

Despite this love and admiration, Napoleon's legacy seems to be in jeopardy. The Minister of Justice (*le Garde des Sceaux*) has asked the advice of a commission about a reform of the law of obligations, including the law of tort. The *Rapport Catala* was published in 2005 and holds, *inter alia*, a proposal to codify recent judicial developments and redraft articles 1382–1386 *Code civil*.[4]

The structure of French tort law is rather simple. The drafters of the Civil Code only gave a few very brief and general provisions in articles 1382–1386. Generally, three categories of liability are distinguished: liability for one's own act (*la responsabilité du fait personnel*), strict liability for things (*la responsabilité du fait des choses*), and strict liability for acts of other persons (*la responsabilité du fait d'autrui*).

Liability for one's own act is governed by two general provisions, articles 1382–1383, which only require damage, causation, and a *faute*. These requirements basically imply that negligent conduct which causes damage is sufficient for liability (nr 302). Though this basic rule of fault liability still plays an important role, it has, in many ways, lost ground to the growing number of strict liability rules. Particularly in cases of death, personal injury, and damage to property, fault liability is the exception rather than the rule.

The Civil Code of 1804 holds a number of specific rules of strict liability in articles 1384–1386, such as strict liabilities for children, employees, buildings, and animals. However, the highest civil and criminal court in France, the *Cour de cassation*, has made important generalizations on this point. In 1896 it called into being a general strict liability for *things*, which was based on article 1384 al. 1 (nr 303). Almost a century later, in 1991, the *Cour de cassation* decided to establish a general strict liability for *persons*, based on the same words of article 1384 (nr 305).

One of the few contributions of the contemporary legislator to tort law is the *loi Badinter*, holding a regime of strict (in fact almost absolute) liability for

---

[2] See Bénédicte Fauvarque-Cosson, 'Faut-il un Code civil européen?', *RTD civ.* 2002, 464.

[3] See http://www.bicentenaireducodecivil.fr.

[4] *Avant projet de réforme du droit des obligations (Articles 1101 à 1386 du Code civil) et du droit de la prescription (Articles 2234 à 2281 du Code civil)* (Rapport Catala). See www.justice.gouv.fr and the interview with Pierre Catala, 'Il est temps de rendre au Code civil son role de droit commun des contrats', *JCP* w2005. I. 170.

damage caused by motor vehicles in road traffic accidents. This Act entered into force in 1985 (nr 1404-1). Another example of legislative action, though pointing in a different direction, was the legislative ban on wrongful life claims, which were initially acknowledged by the *Cour de cassation* (see nr 707-2).

Articles 1382–1386 are still of great importance. The general character of these provisions implied that the legislator only gave the rough guidelines and left the interpretation of these provisions to the courts, particularly the *Cour de cassation*. It also implied that the French courts were able to keep the provisions up to date over the centuries in a completely changed society. According to the famous French legal writer Henri Mazeaud, the French could consider themselves lucky with these provisions, because they have enabled the judge to answer liability questions of all times.[5]

The *Code civil* has influenced the civil law of many countries. When Napoleon reached the end of his glory in his defeat at Waterloo, a number of the previously occupied countries retained and accepted the Civil Code for their own use. Other countries adopted the Code because of its exemplariness. Hence, the *Code civil* served as a basis for the civil laws of, *inter alia*, Belgium, Italy, the Netherlands, Poland, Portugal, and Spain. Outside Europe the *Code civil* gained a firm foothold in a number of African countries. Though all these countries have since then made their own choices in many ways, it can be said that in the area of civil law Napoleon has not yet met his Waterloo.

301-3 *Judiciary*

The highest civil and criminal court in France is the *Cour de cassation*.[6] It sits in the *Palais de Justice* in Paris and has jurisdiction to review all decisions of lower criminal and civil courts. The court only deals with questions of law and does not decide questions of fact: unifying the interpretation of the law is one of its main tasks.[7] The court consists of three civil chambers, a commercial, a social and a criminal chamber. Each of these chambers has its own chief judge known as a *Président*. In total, the *Cour de cassation* comprises almost one hundred judges (*conseillers*).

When the merits of a case are clear, three judges decide civil appeals; otherwise, the matter may be sent to a five-judge panel. Sometimes the *Cour* also decides cases in a Mixed Chamber or in a Full Assembly. Review in the Mixed Chamber (*Chambre mixte*) takes place when two or more chambers need to share

[5] Mazeaud-Tunc (1965), nr 16: '... les rédacteurs du Code n'ont posé que quelques règles très brèves, le plus souvent d'allure générale; encore doit-on s'en féliciter, puisque c'est avec elles qu'il faut résoudre les questions les plus modernes.'

[6] See about the following, *inter alia*, Jacques Boré, *La cassation en matière civile*, 3rd edn. (Paris: Dalloz, 2003); A. Perdriau, 'La chambre mixte et l'assemblée plénière de la Cour de cassation', *JCP* 1994. I. 3798; Bicentenaire de la Cour de cassation, Paris 1991; www.courdecassation.fr.

[7] Compare the German approach as regards the BGB where the emphasis was on finding unity by way of drafting precise statutory provisions. See nr 401-1.

an equal voice on an issue of law. Review by the Full Assembly (*Assemblée pléniére*)—comprising at least one judge of each chamber—is required for certain repeat appeals in the same case and is permitted for appeals on issues where case law may diverge. This is the highest level of review at the court.

If a Chamber of the *Cour de cassation* rejects an appeal, the lower court's decision becomes final. If the Chamber quashes the decision of the lower court, it can refer the case to a different lower court with remand for further review of factual issues in light of the decided law. However, this court is not bound by the Chamber's decision. If the court disagrees with the Chamber, an appeal may be sought before the Full Assembly of the *Cour de cassation*. The Full Assembly may reject the appeal, in which case the first remand court's decision becomes final. The Full Assembly may annul the lower court's decision and send it to a third and different lower court known as the 'second remand court'. This court may review the facts but it has to adhere to the principles of law as they have been set out by the Full Assembly.

The main features of the *Cour de cassation's* decisions are its concise wording, its apodictic way of reasoning, and often the lack of reasoning at all. Decisions are generally not more than one page long and therefore they are not always crystal clear. The *Cour* does not discuss opinions of legal writers (as is the case in Germany), nor does it make any reference to its earlier decisions (as is the case in English, German, and European cases). French civil procedure law maintains a strict principle of anonymity which prohibits the divulgation of individual diverging or dissenting opinions of named judges. Compromises are enabled because there is no elaboration of the reasoning behind a decision—judges may reach the same conclusion albeit by different routes. A single judgment focusing on a narrowly formulated *ratio* and containing no *obiter dicta* is considered essential in ensuring a uniform interpretation and coherence of the law. This means that in decisions of the *Cour de cassation* the law appears to be self-evident. In this sense the interpretation of Napoleon's Civil Code is still determined by Montesquieu's maxim that the judge is the mouth of the law (*le juge est la bouche de la loi*).[8] Hence, when reading a judgment of the *Cour de cassation* one may hear the mumbling of Napoleon himself.

A special role is played by the *Procureur Général* of the *Cour de cassation*. Not only is he the highest ranked prosecutor in France but he also advises the *Cour de cassation* in criminal and civil law cases. The opinions contain important information on the content and the legal background of the case to be decided by the court. He is assisted by a *premier avocat général* and about 22 *avocats généraux*. This system has been adopted by the European Court of Justice (nr 203-2).

The courts of first instance are the *Tribunal d'instance*, the *Tribunal de grande instance* and the *Tribunal de commerce*, and the *Conseil des Prud'hommes* (labour law). Decisions of these courts can be brought before the *Cours d'appel* (Courts

---

[8] Hein Kötz, *Die Begründung höchstrichterlicher Urteile* (Deventer: Kluwer, 1982), 8–9.

of Appeal). These lower courts generally use a more accessible style than the *Cour de cassation* in reasoning and explaining their decisions.

The lower courts are neither bound by the decisions of the *Cour de cassation* nor by their own decisions. Hence, courts will never make references to other court decisions. But in fact they take other case law into consideration and deviate only occasionally from the decisions of the *Cour de cassation*. To put it briefly: though the *Cour's* decisions are not precedents, they have strong authoritative power.[9]

Cases of liability of public authorities do not belong to the competence of the civil courts but the administrative courts. The highest administrative court is the *Conseil d'État* (the State Council), sitting in the *Palais Royale* in Paris. Administrative courts hear all cases against public bodies such as the state, departments, state-owned companies, and institutions such as hospitals. As creative as the *Cour de cassation*, the *Conseil d'État* has developed a full-fledged body of case law as regards liability of public authorities. This implies, for example, that different rules apply to medical negligence cases, depending on whether a private or a public hospital is at stake. It goes without saying that the division of competences between the *Conseil d'État* and the *Cour de cassation* has not been without complications and it is the very *raison d'être* of the *Tribunal des conflits* to resolve these issues. See nr 1802-1.

301-4 *Doctrine*

The French doctrine plays an important role in analysing, explaining and interpreting the decisions of the *Cour de cassation*. This is very useful because, as has been pointed out (nr 301-3), these decisions are very concise and apodictic and therefore not always crystal clear. The legal writers are in fact the priests serving the legal mass, mediating between the highest judge and *le peuple*, and whose sermons teach the congregation how to behave. This might explain why the legal authors, mostly academics, generally stand in high esteem, not only in the legal world but also amongst the general public. This is comparable to the German situation (nr 401-4) but slightly different from the English approach where the judges have descended from their high seat, have learned to talk everyday language, and thus have made legal academic mediators less needed (nr 501-5).

Generally, the approach of the French legal writers is practical rather than theoretical. Long commentaries, such as produced in Germany (nr 401-4), are rare but in the area of tort law Philippe Le Tourneau *Droit de la responsabilité et des contrats* comes close to it. Important textbooks are Mazeaud-Chabas' *Leçons de droit civil* and Geneviève Viney and Patrice Jourdain's volumes in Jacques Ghestin's *Traité de droit civil*. More concise textbooks are Jean Carbonnier's

[9] Andrew West et al., *The French Legal System*, 2nd edn., (London: Butterworths, 1998), 55 ff.; John Bell, *French Legal Cultures*, 2nd edn. (London: Butterworths, 2001), 66 ff.

Droit civil (volume IV on obligations), the volume on obligations in the Dalloz series by Terré, Simler and Lequette, and Flour and Aubert's *Les obligations*.[10] In addition to handbooks and monographs there are several encyclopaedias, for instance the famous *Répertoire Dalloz*.

302 Fault liability (arts. 1382 and 1383 *Code civil*)

302-1 *General observations*

Article 1382 of the *Code civil* is one of the most general tort provisions ever drafted. It reads: 'Any act whatever of man, which causes damage to another, obliges the one by whose "faute" it occurred, to compensate it.'[11] Subsequently, article 1383 CC holds: 'Everyone is liable for the damage he causes not only by his act, but also by his negligence or by his imprudence.'[12] These two very general and concise rules apply to all areas of liability, such as personal injury, nuisance, and deceit, for each of which for instance English law holds a separate tort. In theory, article 1382 applies to acts and article 1383 to omissions, but in practice this distinction has lost its significance.[13]

Articles 1382 and 1383 do not have an exclusive domain of application. In practice, there is a common area of overlap between the material domains of the strict liability of article 1384 al. 1 and the fault liability of articles 1382–1383: indeed it can be said that the former has absorbed much of the latter (nr 300). However, if no other provision applies, articles 1382–1383 retain their utility as malleable 'safety net' dispositions. Courts have applied them even in complex cases on unfair competition and, where the claimant has unsuccessfully invoked article 1384 al. 1 alone, a trial judge can validly consider the application of articles 1382–1383 *ex officio*.

Liability based on articles 1382 and 1383 (*faute*) has an extremely simple structure: to establish liability it is sufficient to prove intention or negligence

---

[10] Philippe le Tourneau, *Droit de la responsabilité et des contrats*, 8th edn. (Paris: Dalloz, 2004–2005); Henri Mazeaud et al., *Leçons de droit civil*, part II, volume 1, *Obligations, théorie générale*, 9th edn. by François Chabas, (Paris: Montchrestien, 1998), Geneviève Viney, *Introduction à la responsabilité*, 2nd edn., (Paris: LGDJ, 1995); Geneviève Viney and Patrice Jourdain, *Les conditions de la responsabilité*, 2nd edn. (Paris: LGDJ, 1998); Geneviève Viney and Patrice Jourdain, *Les effets de la responsabilité*, 2nd edn. (Paris: LGDJ, 2001); Jean Carbonnier, *Droit civil*, volume IV: *Les obligations*, 22nd edn. (Paris: PUF, 2000); François Terré, Philippe Simler and Yves Lequette, *Droit civil: les obligations*, 8th edn. (Paris: Dalloz, 2002); Jacques Flour, Jean-Luc Aubert and Eric Savaux, *Les obligations*, volume II, 10th edn. (Paris: Colin, 2003). A somewhat outdated but still excellent textbook is Henri Mazeaud, Léon Mazeaud and André Tunc, *Traité théorique et pratique de la responsabilité civile: délictuelle et contractuelle*, (Paris: Montchrestien, 1965).

[11] 'Tout fait quelconque de l'homme, qui cause à autrui un dommage, oblige celui par la faute duquel il est arrivé, à le réparer.'

[12] 'Chacun est responsable du dommage qu'il a causé non seulement par son fait, mais encore par sa négligence ou par son imprudence.'

[13] Charles Aubry, Charles Frédéric Rau and Noël Dejean de la Bâtie, *Droit civil français*, 8th edn., (Paris: Librairie Techniques, 1989), nr 9; Terré-Simler-Lequette (2002), nr 679.

(*faute*), damage (*dommage*), and causation (*lien de causalité*). See about causation nr 1100 and about damage nr 1105 and 1202-1.

In most cases *faute* means that someone has not observed a certain standard of care. Hence, *faute* liability mainly implies negligence liability. *Faute* does not imply the notion of the duty of care. Basically any relationship can give rise to liability. In principle, it is sufficient that negligent conduct caused damage. There are several ways to establish a *faute*.

Firstly, a person commits a *faute* if he violates a statutory rule (*violation d'un devoir légal*). It is not necessary to establish that the statutory duty intended to protect the victim from the damage he suffered. Each statutory rule is considered to have an absolute scope in the sense that it protects each person who suffers damage which is caused by the violation of the statutory rule. See nr 904.

Secondly, a *faute* can be established on the basis of the breach of an unwritten pre-existing duty. Unwritten duties can be derived from regulations, morals, customs, and technical standards. In most situations, however, the courts use a standard of reference: this implies that someone commits a *faute* if he does not meet the standard of the *le bon père de famille*, a creature also known as the *bonus pater familias* (the good family father), *l'homme droit et avisé* (the just and cautious man), or *le bon professional* (the good professional). This standard of reference has been elaborated thoroughly in legal literature and it is applied in all areas of fault liability. See nr 812.

Thirdly, a non-intentional criminal *faute* automatically implies a civil *faute*. This means that the commission of a criminal offence causing harm to another person is considered to be a *faute* in the sense of article 1382 CC. Until 2000 this rule had the drawback that no right to compensation existed if the defendant had been found not guilty by a criminal court, but a reform of the Code of Criminal Procedure has to a limited extent dissociated the civil *faute* from the non-intentional criminal *faute*. This means that the absence of non-intentional criminal liability does not bar an action based on article 1382 provided civil liability under that article can be established on the basis of a civil *faute*.[14]

Finally, someone also commits a *faute* if he abuses his right (*abus de droit*). This is, in principle, the case if he acted intentionally (*intention de nuire*). See nr 302-2.

Initially, a subjective element of *faute* was also distinguished. This element mainly related to culpability and it played a role as regards liability of children and mentally disabled persons. However, for some decades French tort law has abandoned the view that culpability is a necessary element of a *faute*, neither does it have a moral content: it is a social concept.[15] There is no separate test that

[14] Act No. 2000-647 of 10 July 2000. See also Civ. 2e 16 September 2003, D. 2004. 721. comm. Bonfils, *ETL* 2003, 170 (Lafay, Moréteau and Pellerin-Rugliano).

[15] Le Tourneau (2004), nr 6706 : 'La faute, violation d'une norme de conduite, est un comportement anormal. Ainsi entendue, la faute s'écarte considérablement de la faute morale. C'est un concept *social*.'

applies to children or disabled persons: an objective test applies to everyone. Children are judged by the objective standard of an adult person. It is not required that they have understood that they were at fault (nr 813-2).

The vague notions of *faute, dommage*, and *lien de causalité* have caused controversy and contradiction in the various ways they have been interpreted by the doctrine and the courts. In 1948 Rabut counted 23 different definitions of *faute* in the legal literature.[16] In this sense the *liberté* provided by the legislator has not contributed to much *égalité* and *fraternité* in the courts and the doctrine.

302-2 Abus de droit *(abuse of rights)*

If someone abuses his right this constitutes a *faute* under articles 1382–1383 CC. Provided that the outstanding conditions of damage and causality are established, the defendant may be liable to pay damages (monetary reparation) or, where necessary, to reparation in kind, for example demolishing a structure (reparation in kind which in practice has a similar effect to an injunction).[17]

The origins of the theory of *abus de droit* may be found in well-established case law on the abuse of freedoms (*abus des libertés*), which is itself inspired by Article 4 of the Declaration of the Rights of Man and the Citizen 1789 which provides: 'Freedom means to be able to do all that does not harm others'.[18] This essentially negative definition of a freedom has allowed the *Cour de cassation* to limit not only fundamental liberties (such as freedom of expression[19] and freedom to participate in commerce),[20] but also the exercise of subjective rights.

The starting point is that the exercise of a subjective right *per se* does not give rise to liability. What is at issue is the defendant's *manner* of exercise. So the question becomes: when does the valid exercise of a subjective right (something which is enjoined by law) degenerate into abuse (an act which gives rise to liability)? Though the position of the *Cour de cassation* is not entirely clear, the courts often makes reference made to the intention to harm (*intention de nuire*),[21] to fraudulent fault (*faute dolosive*),[22] or to more attenuated forms of moral guilt, such as the defendant's bad faith (*mauvaise foi*),[23] or culpable levity of conduct (*légèreté blamable*).[24] Hence, in this area *faute* implies intentional conduct or acting in bad faith. In certain cases, however, there is not a great

---

[16] Albert Rabut, *De la notion de faute en droit privé* (Paris: Libr. Gén. de Droit et de Jurspr., 1948), 199–200. See also Paul Esmein, 'La faute et sa place dans la responsabilité civile', *RTD civ.* 1949, 481–490.

[17] Req. 3 August 1915, DP 1917. 1. 79 (*Coquerel c. Clément-Bayard*).

[18] 'La liberté consiste à pouvoir faire tout ce qui ne nuit pas à autrui'.

[19] Ass. plén. 12 July 2000, Bull. ass. plén., no 8.

[20] Com. 5 July 1994, Bull. civ. IV, no 258, JCP.1994. II. 22323, comm. Léonnet, RTD civ. 1995, 119, obs. Jourdain. [21] Civ. 3e 12 October 1971, Bull. civ. III, no 480.

[22] Civ. 2e 11 January 1973, Gaz. Pal. 1973. 2. 710.

[23] Civ. 2e 11 January 1973, Gaz. Pal. 1973. 2. 710.

[24] Com. 22 February 1994, Bull. civ. IV, no 79.

difference with the way *faute* is generally established: what is decisive is whether the defendant's conduct was different from that of a reasonable man.[25]

Perhaps the most striking application of the abuse of rights theory was in the *Clément-Bayard* case.[26] It involved two neighbouring landowners, one of whom was frustrated with the other's enthusiasm for flying hot air balloons. Taking extreme measures, the former went out of his way to erect a 16m fence surmounted by metal spikes which served no purpose other than to damage those of his neighbour's balloons which might stray over onto his land. Unsurprisingly, it was held that there was an abuse of property rights. Although there has since been a wealth of case law limiting property rights in a similar fashion,[27] such disputes are now resolved on the firmer footing of neighbourhood laws (*trouble de voisinage*) which provide for a form of stricter liability (nr 1413-3).

The *Cour de cassation* also applies the abuse of rights theory in other cases, especially in situations where the defendant is able to unilaterally modify a legal situation to the detriment of an interested third party. For example, the abrupt, capricious, and humiliating retraction by a fiancé after an engagement,[28] the refusal of a Jewish husband to deliver the *gueth* needed by his divorced wife in order to remarry,[29] and the filing of a claim by a vexatious litigant.[30] The variety of examples in case law illustrates the broad application and the elasticity of the concept of *abus de droit*.[31]

303 General rule of strict liability for things (art. 1384 al. 1 *Code civil*)

303-1 *History and background*

One of the most characteristic features of French law is the dominant position of rules of strict liability. Though there are a number of more specific rules of strict liability, such as for animals, motor vehicles, products, buildings, minors, and employees (nr 304 and 306), French law holds two general rules of strict

[25] Aubry and Rau-Dejean de la Bathie (1989), nr 49: 'En certains cas il n'est pas douteux que l'abus de droit s'analyse simplement, selon le critère ordinaire de la faute, comme un comportement différent de celui d'un homme raisonnable.'

[26] Req. 3 August 1915, DP 1917. 1. 79 (*Coquerel c. Clément-Bayard*).

[27] Civ. 3e 30 October 1972, Bull. civ. III, no 576, D. 1973. Somm. 43: the construction of a wall for no reason other than to obstruct light and perspective of neighbouring land.

[28] There is an abundance of case law on this question despite the fact that an engagement ('*fiançailles*') does not create any legal obligation to get married under French law: Civ 1re 3 March 1964, Gaz. Pal. 1964. 2. 83, RTD civ. 1964, 707, obs. Desbois; Civ. 1re 30 June 1992, Bull. civ. I, no 204; Resp. civ. et assur. 1994.

[29] Civ 2e 5 June 1985, JCP 1985. II. 20728, comm. Agostini; Civ. 2e 15 July 1988, Bull. civ. II, no 146, 78, D. 1998, IR 191, RTD civ. 1988, 770, obs. Jourdain; Civ. 2e 21 November 1990, D. 1991. 435, note Agostini, JCP 1991. IV. 26.

[30] Comm. 11 May 1999, Bull. civ. IV, no 101; Civ. 1re 10 December 1968, D. 1969, 165.

[31] Terré-Simler-Lequette (2002), nr 712.

liability: one for damage caused by another person (nr 1305) and one for damage caused by a thing. The latter rules are judge-made and were derived from the introductory words of article 1384 al. 1: liability for things at the end of the 19th century and liability for persons about a century later.

By the end of the 19th century, industrialization had caused a great increase in the number of casualties at the workplace. Employees who suffered damage had a very weak legal position for getting compensation, since they had to prove that the employer had committed a *faute*. In practice, this was often very difficult or impossible. Hence, in the *Teffaine* decision in 1896, the *Cour de cassation* read article 1384 al. 1 in a new light. The provision holds that a person is liable not only for the damage he causes by his own act, but also for that which is caused by the acts of persons for whom he is responsible, or by things which are in his custody.[32] Though the Civil Code's fathers intended these words to be only an introduction to the subsequent specific rules of strict liability for persons and not a liability rule as such, the *Cour de cassation* initially used the provision to create a liability regime for rebuttable *faute* for damage caused by a *chose* (thing).[33] This implied that the custodian of a thing (*le gardien de la chose*), for instance the employer owning a dangerous machine, was liable for the damage caused by the thing, unless he could prove that he did not commit a *faute*.[34] In *Jand'heur II* in 1930 the *Cour de cassation* took a second step by turning the liability for a rebuttable *faute* into a real strict liability.[35]

Since then *le gardien de la chose* (the custodian of a thing) is liable for the damage caused by *le fait de la chose* (the act of the thing). He has only two defences. Firstly, the custodian may invoke the victim's contributory negligence (*faute de la victime*) which, if successful, reduces the amount of compensation. Secondly, he can prove an unforeseeable and unavoidable external cause of the damage (*un cause étrangère imprévisible et irrésistible*). Such an external cause can be a case of *force majeure*, an act of a third party (*fait d'un tiers*), or the act of the victim (*fait de la victime*). This defence is generally very hard to prove; there are few examples in which courts have accepted it.[36]

Of all modern legal systems, article 1384 al. 1 is probably the most general strict liability rule and it is certainly the most important landmark of French tort

[32] 'On est responsable non seulement du dommage que l'on cause par son propre fait, mais encore de celui qui est cause par le fait des personnes dont on doit répondre, ou des choses que l'on a sous sa garde.'

[33] Civ. 16 June 1896, S. 1897. I. 17, comm. Esmein (*Teffaine*); Terré-Simler-Lequette (2002), nr 746.

[34] Two years later, the legislator introduced an Act on damages for industrial accidents. This Act provided employees with a social security right on compensation, which was independent of liability. Though this system has been changed in the course of time, it is still in force today; Terré-Simler-Lequette (2002), nr 910–928; Viney-Jourdain (1998), nr 628–629. Currently, art. 1384 al. 1 does not apply any more to industrial accidents.

[35] Ch. réun. 13 February 1930, DP 1930. I. 57, comm. Ripert, S. 1930. I. 121, comm. Esmein (*Jand'heur II*); Terré-Simler-Lequette (2002), nr 758.

[36] Terré-Simler-Lequette (2002), nr 796-803; Carbonnier (2000), § 258, 465; Le Tourneau (2004), 7921.

law. The best way to understand the concepts of this rule (*fait de la chose, gardien*) is to keep in mind that it is instrumental for providing compensation to the victim of an accident in which a thing is involved. The defendant's conduct is generally not relevant and the focus is completely on strengthening the claimant's position to get damages.

The development of strict liability was based on the so-called '*théorie du risque*', designed by Saleilles at the end of the 19th century and further developed by Josserand, two of the leading law professors of their time. The main idea of this theory is that the person who benefits from an activity that involves a risk (an employer, a driver) should bear the burden of the damage caused by that risk.[37] Halfway through the 20th century, Boris Starck developed '*la théorie de la garantie*' which puts the emphasis on the fact that the person who is insured should bear the risk and the costs of the accident.[38] Both theories funded and strengthened the legal practice to provide victims with a stronger position by creating rules of strict liability. They reflect the idea of *solidarité* and can be linked to one of the keys of the French Revolution: *la fraternité*.

This development has raised the question of what role was left for article 1382 since in very many cases a thing is instrumental for causing harm. Ripert stated: 'It would . . . be necessary to imagine a collision between two persons practising nudism before article 1382 would apply.'[39] Indeed, article 1382 does not play an important role in the area of liability for accidents but it does apply if there is no strict rule applicable, for instance in certain cases of omissions and of negligent misrepresentations.

303-2 Fait de la chose *(fact of the thing)*

Liability on the basis of article 1384 al. 1 requires the act of a thing (*fait de la chose*). This implies that a *chose* must have contributed to the realization of the damage.

A thing (*chose*) includes all inanimate objects (*choses inanimées*), irrespective of whether they are defective or not, natural or artificial, dangerous or not dangerous, and movable or immovable. The *Cour de cassation* applied article 1384 al. 1 for the first time to an immovable thing in 1928, in a case in which someone suffered damage as the consequence of an accident with a lift. Later the court also applied the provision to other immovable things like a falling tree, a landslide, a burst dyke, and an accident on an escalator.[40]

---

[37] Le Tourneau (2004), nr 51: 'Toute activité faisant naître un risque pour autrui rend son auteur responsable du préjudice qu'elle peut causer, sans qu'il y ait à prouver une faute à son origine.'
[38] B. Starck, *Essai d'une théorie générale de la responsabilité civile considerée en sa double fonction de garantie et de peine privée* (Paris: Rodstein, 1947).
[39] Cited by Brice Dickson, *Introduction to French Law*, (London: Pitman, 1994), 161.
[40] Req. 6 March 1928, DP 1928. 1. 97, comm. Josserand, S. 1928. 1. 225, comm. Hugueney (lift); Civ. 30 April 1952, D. 1952. 471, JCP 1952. II. 7111, comm. Blaevoet (tree); Civ. 2e

Snow is not a thing, at least not if there is no-one who has it in his custody. Neither is the human body considered as a thing as long as it is still alive.[41]

The act of a thing (*fait de la chose*) can be established in different ways.[42] Firstly, if there has been contact between the claimant or his property and a moving thing, a *fait de la chose* is easy to establish. In such a case it is assumed that the *chose* has contributed to the realization of the damage. One may think of a rolling stone and a falling tree. It is not necessary that the custodian has in any way contributed to the action of the *chose*.[43]

Secondly, if there has been contact between the claimant or his property and a non-moving thing then the claimant has to prove that one way or another the thing has been instrumental in causing the damage, that it has played an active role (*un rôle actif*).[44] This can particularly be the case if a *comportement anormal de la chose* (abnormal behaviour of the thing) can be established. One may think of a defective thing or a situation where a thing is put at a wrong place.[45] For example, when someone fell through an open door in a lift shaft, it was decided that the harm was caused by the fact of the thing.[46] An older case concerned Mme Cadé, who fell in the changing room of a swimming pool after she suffered a fit. When she lay unconscious on the ground her arm rested on a heating pipe and she suffered injury. The *Cour d'Appel* in Colmar dismissed her claim because the swimming pool had not committed a *faute*. The *Cour de cassation* quashed this decision and held that the appeal court should also have established whether liability could have been based on article 1384 al. 1.[47] But on this basis Mme Cadé was not successful either because the court held that the heating installation was installed in a normal way.[48] Neither was someone who slipped on snowy stairs in a ski resort successful. Slippery snowy stairs are normal in a ski resort and the *Cour de cassation* concluded that there was no *fait de la chose*. The custodian of the stairs was not liable for the damage.[49]

Thirdly, if there has been no contact between the claimant or his property and the thing, article 1384 al. 1 can apply but here the claimant also has to prove that

12 May 1966, D. 1966. 700, comm. Azard (tree); Civ. 25 June 1952, D. 1952. 614, JCP. 1952. II. 7338, comm. Esmein (landslide); Civ. 2e 26 April 1990, JCP 1990. IV. 235 (burst dyke); Civ. 2e 2 April 1997, D. 1997. IR. 105 (escalator); see also about the latter case nr 1505).

[41] Terré-Simler-Lequette (2002), nr 763–776; Viney-Jourdain (1998), nr 635; Carbonnier (2000), § 257, 463–464.

[42] Civ. 19 February 1941, D.C. 1941. 85, note Flour; Terré-Simler-Lequette (2002), nr 772–775; Carbonnier (2000), § 257, 463–464. Compare the word *implication* in the liability for motor vehicles according to the *loi Badiner* nr 1404-1.   [43] Le Tourneau (2004), nr 7786.

[44] Civ. 2e 5 May 1993, Bull. civ. II, no 168: '...que la chose a été, en quelque manière, l'instrument du dommage'. See also Civ. 2e 2 April 1997, Bull. civ. II, no 110.

[45] Le Tourneau (2004), nr 7805.

[46] Civ. 2e 29 May 1996, Bull. civ. II, no 117, D. 1996. IR. 156. See also Civ. 2e, 19 February 2004, Bull. civ. II, no 75, ETL 2004, 287 (*Cannarsa and Others*), concerning a successful claim for damage sustained by a glass panel shattering in a shopping mall after the claimant had bumped into it.

[47] Civ. 19 February 1941, D.C. 1941. 85, comm. Flour.

[48] Civ. 19 February 1941, D.C. 1941. 85, comm. Flour; in the same sense Civ. 19 November 1964, D. 1965. 93.   [49] Civ. 2e 15 March 1978, D. 1978. IR. 406.

the *chose* was the cause of his damage.[50] The 'easy' cases are those in which there is contact but not with the *chose* of the liable custodian. One may think of a car which is hit by another car which in its turn is pushed by a third car, and the custodian of the third car is held liable.[51] More difficult and radical are cases in which there is no contact whatsoever between the custodian's *chose* and the claimant. Examples are situations in which someone tries to avoid an obstacle or another person, such as the driver swerving to avoid an abandoned vehicle or the glider touching the ground in an effort to avoid another plane. One may also think of someone who is dazzled by the lights of another car.[52] More generally, the provision applies to situations of psychological causation in which a *chose* by its sole presence and in an abnormal way makes another person commit a harmful act from fear or lack of skill.[53]

303-3 *Gardien (custodian): general observations*

The liable person is *le gardien* (the custodian). This is the person who, at the time of the accident, has the power to use, to direct, and to control the thing.[54] The owner is assumed to be the custodian but this is no longer the case if the thing has been stolen from him. This, however, does not exclude the possibility to file a claim against the owner on the basis of article 1382 if he has been negligent in taking precautionary measures against theft.[55]

Many people other than the owner can be *gardien* of a thing, because the concept of *gardien* is a factual rather than a legal one. A striking example is the child who kicked a bottle abandoned on the street. He was deemed, for that split second, to have become the bottle's custodian.[56] The concept of custodianship is instrumental to the idea of enabling claimants to easily identify the liable person without having to deal with the legal relationship someone has with the thing.

It is generally accepted that persons with a mental disorder and young children can be *gardien* of a thing.[57] For example, the *Cour de cassation* regarded a three

---

[50] Le Tourneau (2004), nr 7789.   [51] Civ. 2e 4 October 1961, D. 1961. 755, comm. Esmein.
[52] Besançon 15 April 1986, Gaz. Pal. 1987. 1. Somm. 139 (vehicle); civ. 2e 26 February 1970, Bull. civ. II, no 345 (glider); Civ. 28 March 1974, Bull. civ. II, no 115 (lights).
[53] Le Tourneau (2004), nr 7788.
[54] Ch. réun. 2 December 1941, D 1942. 25, comm. Ripert (*Franck c. Connot*) ('le pouvoir d'usage, de direction et de contrôle'). See also Civ. 2e 22 January 1970, D. 1970. 228, RTD civ. 1971, 150, obs. Durry; Civ. 2e 16 May 1984, RTD Civ. 1985, 585, obs. Huet; Viney-Jourdain (1998), nr 677–681; Terré-Simler-Lequette (2002), nr 786–792; Carbonnier (2000), § 257, 463–464.
[55] Ch. réun. 2 December 1941, D. 1942. 25, comm. Ripert, (*Franck c. Connot*); Civ. 2e 5 April 1965, D. 1965. 737; Carbonnier (2000), § 257, 463–464; Viney-Jourdain (1998), nr 676.
[56] Civ 2e 10 February 1982, JCP 1983.II.20069, comm. Coeuret.
[57] Civ. 2e 18 December 1964, D. 1965. 191, comm. Esmein, Gaz. Pal. 1965. 1. 202, RTD civ. 1965, 351, obs. Rodière (Trichard). Terré-Simler-Lequette (2002), nr 791; Viney-Jourdain (1998), nr 583 and 685.

year old child, who fell out of a swing with a stick in its hand, injuring another child, as the custodian of the stick.[58]

Parties to a contract cannot invoke article 1384 al. 1. Also, an employee cannot be custodian of his employer's things because the qualities of employee and custodian are considered to be mutually exclusive.[59] This may be explained by the idea that there is an incompatibility between the hierarchical relationship of subordination to which (by definition) the employee is subject *vis-à-vis* his employer, on the one hand, and the need for a custodian to have the control and direction over the thing belonging to his employer, on the other hand.

If the *gardien* of a thing is a public body article 1384 al. 1 does not apply. In such cases the administrative courts are competent and these have developed a separate liability system for public bodies. The rules applying to damage caused by public things are less strict than the rules developed under article 1384 al. 1 (nr 1508 and 1802).

An important distinction is made between *garde du comportement* (custody of the thing's conduct) and *garde de la structure* (custody of the thing's structure or composition). In most cases these two aspects will be in one hand: usually that of the owner. In other cases, however, the two aspects can be distinguished: transporters or keepers can be liable for the *garde du comportement* whilst the *garde de la structure* stays with the owner. Also, the manufacturer stays *gardien de la structure* after having put his product onto the market and he can be liable if the product's structure appears to be defective.[60] An example is a claim by a lung cancer patient against a cigarette manufacturer in which the *Cour de cassation* held that the manufacturer was the *gardien de la structure* of the cigarettes. However, the smoker's claim was dismissed because the court also held that there was no indication that the structure of the cigarettes was defective.[61]

Independent from this basis for liability, the *Cour de cassation* has developed a more direct way to deal with liability for defective products by imposing *obligations de sécurité* (security obligations) on manufacturers and sellers. See nr 1407-2.

303-4 *Garde commun (common custodianship); transfer of custodianship*

In certain circumstances several persons can simultaneously have the quality of custodian if they have similar powers over the thing (*garde commune*). One may think of co-proprietors in respect of their land[62] and tennis players in relation

---

[58] Ass. plén. 9 May 1984, JCP 1984. II. 20255, comm. Dejean de la Bathie, D. 1984. 525, comm. Chabas, RTD civ. 1984, 509, obs. Huet. Terré-Simler-Lequette (2002), nr 791.

[59] Civ. 30 December 1936, DP 1937.1.5, comm. Savatier; Civ. 2e 20 October 1971, D. 1972. 414; Carbonnier (2000), § 265, 477–478.

[60] Carbonnier (2000), § 265, 477–478; Viney-Jourdain (1998), nr 691–701; Le Tourneau (2004), nr 7873–7881.

[61] Civ. 2e 20 November 2003, JCP 2003. J. 589, ETL 2003, 161 (Lafay, Moréteau and Pellerin-Rugliano).   [62] Civ. 2e 3 January 1963, S.1963.161, comm. Plancquéel.

to the tennis balls.[63] However, there is no *garde commune* between two paddlers in a canoe since it is the rear paddler alone who retains sole control over the steering (and thus the direction of movement) of the vessel.[64] Where there is a plurality of co-custodians, each can be held liable individually to compensate the full extent of the damage caused.[65]

If someone has personally participated in the custodianship of the thing himself, he is estopped from invoking article 1384 al. 1 as against his co-custodians.[66] As far as competition games are concerned a claim would also fail on the basis of assumption of risks (*l'acceptation des risques*) (nr 809-2). Outside competition games, for example training or individual exercise, the individual player is regarded to be custodian of the ball and article 1384 al. 1 applies.[67] This also applies if the ball is played with a racket and someone is hit by the ball: the racket is considered to be the *chose* causing the damage and the keeper of the racket is considered to be the *gardien*.[68]

The defendant will be exonerated if he is able to show that, at the time the damage occurred, he was in fact divested of the custodianship of the thing, which was thus transferred to a third party. A simple illustration of this defense is provided by the case where a child who threw back a snowball initially thrown at him was deemed to have become the recipient of the custodianship.[69] The burden of proof is always on the defendant to show that a transfer of custodianship actually took place.[70] Additionally, it helps if he can show a transfer of control over the thing by virtue of a legal agreement: for example, proof that he had rented the thing out to another person.[71] However, he also has to demonstrate that the transfer of custodianship was real and effective: the third party must have had *de facto* (and not just legal) control over the thing.[72] For example, a hunter who leaves a minor child to look after his gun while relieving himself does not divest himself of custodianship. Transfer of custodianship often implies a duty upon the defendant to inform the recipient of the custodianship of the risks of handling the thing and the ability of the new custodian to prevent the damage.[73]

[63] Civ. 2e 20 November 1968, Bull. civ. II, no 277, 194, RTD civ., 1969.335, obs. Durry.
[64] Bordeaux 18 January 1996: Juris-Data no 040097.
[65] Civ. 2e 7 November 1988, Bull. civ. II, no 214.
[66] Civ. 2e 20 November 1968, Bull. civ. II, no 277, 194, RTD civ. 1968.335, obs. Durry.
[67] Le Tourneau (2004), nr 7735; Viney-Jourdain (1998), nr 643. Civ. 2e 21 February 1979, Bull. civ. II, no 58, RTD civ. 1979, 615, obs. Durry (basketball training). See particularly Civ. 2e 4 July 2002, D. 2003. 519 and comparative case comments in *ERPL* 12/1 (2004), 111–132: during a training session a young goalkeeper was injured by a ball thrown at her by the supervising trainer. The *Cour de cassation* held that the fact that the child was participating in a pedagogical activity under the authority and supervision of a trainer excluded the assumption of risk.
[68] Civ. 2e 28 March 2002, D. 2002, 3237, ETL 2002, 198 (Brun).
[69] Civ. 2e 6 October 1982, Gaz. Pal. 1983. 1. Somm. 80, obs. Chabas.
[70] Civ. 2e 22 January 1970, D. 1970. 228, RTD civ. 1971.150, obs. G Durry.
[71] Ch. mixte 26 March 1971, JCP 1972. II. 16057, comm. Dejean de la Batie; also, in relation to the transfer by a ship owner of his vessel to a professional skipper charged with an official mission, see Nancy 6 June 1991, Juris-Data no 049700.   [72] Civ. 2e 9 October 1996, Resp. civ. et ass. 1996, 380.
[73] Civ. 1re 9 June 1993, JCP 1994. II. 22202, comm. Viney, RTD civ. 1993, 833 obs. Jourdain: there was no transfer of custodianship over factory waste in favour of a waste disposal company,

The rules of attribution, combination, dissociation, and transfer of custodianship may in some cases seem rather fictitious. This in turn reflects how article 1384 al. 1, and particularly the notion of *gardien*, is instrumental for reaching the goal of better protection of the victim's position to get compensation.

304 Specific rules of strict liability for things

Article 1385 holds a strict liability for damage caused by an animal in that the owner of an animal, or whoever is making use of it, while it is being so used, is liable for the damage caused by the animal, whether the animal was under his control or whether it had got lost or escaped.[74] This rule has been absorbed by the case law based on article 1384 al. 1 which means that the custodian of an animal is liable for the damage caused by 'the fact of the animal' and that the custodian can only invoke an external cause and contributory negligence of the victim (nr 1402).

According to article 1386, the owner of a building is liable for the damage caused by its collapse, provided that this collapse is due to a lack of maintenance or to a defect in its construction.[75] Although this provision also has to compete with the general rule of article 1384 al. 1, there is some space left for an autonomous application. It should be kept in mind that claims against the architect or the contractor of a building have to be based on article 1382 since articles 1384 and 1386 only apply to the custodian and the owner. Though a contractor may qualify as a custodian during the construction of the building he will not be a custodian after its completion (nr 1502).

Articles 1386-1 ff. contain the implementation of the European Directive on the liability for damage caused by defective products. In 1998 France was the last of the Member States to transpose the Directive into national law (Loi no. 98-389). In product liability cases the law on the sale of goods also provides protection, perhaps even more than the implemented Directive. This was an important reason for the delay in implementing the Directive and it is still a source of dispute between France and the European Union (nr 1407-2).

A strict, in fact almost absolute, liability regime for damage caused by motor vehicles was launched in 1985 in the French *loi Badinter*, named after the Minister of Justice (*Garde des Sceaux*) who was politically responsible for this Act. The main rule in this Act is that pedestrians, cyclists, and passengers can claim damages from the driver or the custodian of the vehicle, unless the victim acted voluntarily and committed an inexcusable *faute* (nr 1404-1).

since the owner of the waste had failed to inform the company of its potential risks of environmental pollution.

[74] 'Le propriétaire d'un animal, ou celui qui s'en sert, pendant qu'il est à son usage, est responsable du dommage que l'animal a causé, soit que l'animal fut sous sa garde, soit qu'il fut égaré ou échappé.'

[75] 'Le propriétaire d'un bâtiment est responsable du dommage causé par sa ruine, lorsqu'elle est arrivée par une suite du défaut d'entretien ou par le vice de sa construction.'

Mention can also be made of two important Acts. Firstly, Act 1991-1406 of 31 December 1991, which created a special fund for persons infected with HIV as a result of blood transfusions. The Act was a reaction to the blood transfusion scandal of the 1980s. About 4,000 people were given blood infected with HIV; most received transfusions before the link between HIV and blood was fully understood. Politicians were accused of delaying the introduction of a US blood-screening test in France until a rival French product was ready to go on the market. Most of the politicians were acquitted on charges relating to the deaths of five people and the contamination of two others during a key period in 1985. Victims of this scandal are entitled to get compensation from the afore-mentioned fund but they can also lodge claims for damages on the basis of tort law.[76]

Secondly, Act 2002-303 of 4 March 2002, as regards the law on the rights of sick people and the quality of the health care system (*Loi sur les droits des malades et la qualité du système de santé*), the so-called *loi Kouchner*. In addition to the retained liability system, this Act provides a special compensation fund for victims of medical accidents (unusual consequences of medical treatment), iatrogenic illnesses (for example infections by blood transfusions), and nosocomial infections (hospital infections), or who are suffering from unusual consequences of medical treatment, provided the damage is sufficiently serious, which means that the resultant incapacity needs to be at least 25 per cent. The Act was also supposed to put an end to the disputed case law as regards prenatal harm (wrongful life) implied by the *Perruche* case (nr 707-2).[77]

305 General rule of strict liability for persons (art. 1384 al. 1 *Code civil*)

After its *Teffaine* decision in 1896, in which it introduced a general rule of strict liability for *things* (nr 303-1), it seemed to be only a matter of time before the *Cour de cassation* would also recognize a general rule of strict liability for *persons*.[78] However, it took the court almost a century to take that step in its famous *Blieck* decision.

[76] Le Tourneau (2004), nr 8502–8561; Van Gerven (2000), 629–630. See for instance Cour d'appel de Paris 7 July 1989, Gaz. Pal. 1989. 752, about which Van Gerven (2000), 122–123: a woman got infected with HIV when she was treated in a hospital for injuries following a car accident. The court of appeal held that the liable driver also had to pay for the damage caused by the HIV infection. It was up to him to hold the doctor, the hospital, the blood transfusion centre, and the state liable for the same damage. See Y. Lambert-Faivre, 'L'indemnisation des victimes post-transfusionnelles du SIDA: hier, aujourd'hui et demain . . .', *RTD civ.* 1993, 17 ff. See also nr 1100 about multiple causes.

[77] See about this legislation for instance Simon Taylor, 'Clinical Negligence Reform: Lessons from France?', *ICLQ* 52 (2003), 737–748 and Philippe Brun, 'France', in *ETL*, 2002, 179–194; Le Tourneau (2004), nr 8562–8577.

[78] This was for instance supported by René Savatier, 'La responsabilité générale du fait des choses que l'on a sous sa garde a-t-elle pour pendant une responsabilité générale du fait des personnes dont on doit répondre', *DH* 1933, 81–84, but rejected by Mazeaud-Tunc (1965), nr 712 ff.

The case was about Joel Weevauters who was put under the care of an institution for mentally disabled persons. During working hours, when he had full freedom of movement, the boy set on fire a wood which was possessed by Blieck. Though the boy was liable, the damage could not be recovered from him, so Blieck filed a claim for damages against the institution. The *Cour de cassation* held that the institution was liable on the basis of article 1384 al. 1, because it had accepted the charge of organizing and controlling the life of this mentally disabled person.[79]

Since this decision, a general rule of strict liability for acts of third persons has applied to organizations which have a permanent or temporary duty to organize, direct, and control the conduct of other persons, particularly minors and disabled people. In support of a *principe general* of liability for other persons, it has been noted that article 1384 al. 1 must be interpreted coherently in respect of both things and persons; in both areas the social risk they expose is equally relevant.[80]

The exact scope of the rule is still not perfectly clear and the decision has received considerable criticism. Decisions following *Blieck* have clarified that application of the new rule is not restricted to institutions supervising mentally or physically disabled persons. The rule applies to all institutions charged with the task of organizing, controlling, and directing other persons' conduct. It has for instance been applied to a football club for damage which one of its members had caused to another player during a football match,[81] to a municipal centre for the homeless,[82] a crèche, a holiday camp for children, and a recreation resort.[83]

An example of the consequences of *Blieck* is the case of three teenage girls who had been placed in the Foyer Notre-Dame des Flots care centre (article 375 CC) during which they committed a series of thefts. One of the victims claimed damages from the care centre for his stolen car. *The Cour de cassation* considered that the Foyer was entrusted with the custody and care of the girls, that it was in charge of controlling and organizing their life on a permanent basis, and that therefore it was liable on the basis of article 1384 al. 1 without the need to prove a *faute* on its part.[84]

The conduct of the supervised does not need to be potentially dangerous. During a majorettes' parade one of the majorettes was hit by a twirling stick used

[79] Ass. plén. 29 March 1991, D. 1991. 324, comm. Larroumet, JCP 1991. II. 21673 (*Blieck*): . . . que l'association avait accepté la charge d'organiser et de contrôler, à titre permanent, le mode de vie de ce handicapé, la cour d'appel a décidé, à bon droit, qu'elle devait répondre de celui-ci, au sens de l'article 1384, alinéa 1er, du code civil, et qu'elle était tenue réparer les dommages qu'il avait causés.

[80] Terré-Simler-Lequette (2002), nr 855.
[81] Civ. 2e 22 May 1995, JCP 1995. II. 22550, comm. Mouly, JCP 1995. I. 3893, nr 5 ff., obs. Viney, RTD civ. 1995, 899, obs. Jourdain. Terré-Simler-Lequette (2002), nr 853.
[82] Civ. 2e 22 May 1995, D. 1996. 453 (municipal centre for the homeless).
[83] Viney-Jourdain (1998), nr 789-20.
[84] Crim. 26 March 1997, Bull. crim. 1997. 124, no 2, JCP 1997. II. 22868, D. 1997. 496, comm. Jourdain, about which Van Gerven (2000), 520–521.

by another majorette. The organizing communal association was held liable because it was in charge of organizing, directing, and controlling the conduct of the members during the parade, regardless of the potential dangerousness of the activity.[85]

Generally, it does not seem to be necessary to establish a *faute* of the supervised person. This follows from the *Blieck* case[86] and is consonant with the *Cour de cassation's* case law on the liability of parents for damage caused by their children for which a *faute* of the child is not a prerequisite (nr 1602-1). An exception to this rule is the liability of a sporting club for damage caused by a member in the course of a game. During training a rugby player was injured when he tried to make a tackle which was evaded by his opponent. He claimed damages from his club (and its insurance company) for the injuries sustained. The *Cour de cassation* held that liability on the basis of article 1384 al. 1 requires a *faute caractérisée* (an established fault) and such a *faute* was not committed in this case. The rugby player's claim was dismissed.[87] This case law is in line with the rules for liability for injuries caused during sports activities (nr 809).

The general strict liability rule is only applicable to legal bodies and not to persons, except for the tutor.[88] Neither are grandparents affected by the general rule. Their liability has to be based on article 1382 CC, which requires the proof of a *faute* (*de surveillance*).[89] This reluctance of courts to adopt such an expansive approach may be explained by policy reasons: namely, the fact that such defendants are uninsured, non-professional carers often acting out of their own benevolence.[90]

The conduct of the supervised person does not have to amount to a *faute*. It is sufficient for liability on the basis of article 1384 al. 1 that the conduct of the supervised person was the direct cause of the damage the victim has suffered (*un acte qui soit la cause directe du dommage invoqué par la victime*). See about this more general principle nr 1603-1.[91] This illustrates that the liability of the supervisor under article 1384 al. 1 is not derived from or dependent upon that of the person that he supervises.

Liability can only be escaped by proving *force majeure* or the victim's contributory negligence.[92]

---

[85] Civ. 2e 12 December 2002, ETL 2002, 201 (Brun). In the same sense Civ. 2e 22 May 1995, JCP 1995. II. 22550, comm. Mouly, JCP 1995. I. 3893, nr 5 ff., obs. Viney, Gaz. Pal. 1996. 1. 16, obs. Chabas, RTD civ. 1995, 899, obs. Jourdain and Civ. 2e 3 February 2000, Bull. civ. II, no 26.

[86] Ass. plén. 29 March 1991, D. 1991. 324, note Larroumet, JCP 1991. II. 21673 (*Blieck*).

[87] Civ. 2e, 21 October 2004, Bull. civ. II, no 202, ETL 2005, 282 (*Cannarsa and Others*).

[88] Civ. 2e 25 February 1998, Bull. civ. II, no 62, D. 1998. 315, RTD Civ. 1998, 388, obs. Jourdain; Carbonnier (2000), § 235, 426–427.

[89] Civ. 2e 18 March 2004, JCP 2004. II. 10123, comm. Moisdon-Châtaigner, ETL 2004, 285 (*Cannarsa and Others*).   [90] Terré-Simler-Lequette (2002), nr 852.

[91] Ass. plén. 13 December 2002, D. 2003. 231, comm. Jourdain, ETL 2002, 199 (Brun), about which nr 1602-1.

[92] Crim. 26 March 1997, Bull. crim. 1997. 124, no 2, JCP 1997. II. 22868, D. 1997. 496, comm. Jourdain, about which Van Gerven (2000), 520–521.

306 Specific rules of strict liability for persons

Article 1384, al. 2–7 contain a number of stricter rules of liability for persons with a more specific content. These provisions have kept their significance in addition to the above-mentioned general strict liability rule.

Article 1384 s. 4 holds that the father and mother, in so far as they exercise 'parental authority', are jointly and severally liable for damage caused by their minor children who live with them.[93] The parents only have the defences of an external cause and contributory negligence of the victim. Previously, parents could also prove that they had sufficiently educated and supervised the child. This was in fact a liability with a rebuttable presumption of negligence. The *Cour de cassation* struck out this defence in 1997, thus creating a parallel with the general strict liability for persons. This move is clearly not consonant with article 1384 s. 7 which holds: 'The above liability exists, unless the father and mother (. . .) prove that they could not prevent the act which gives rise to that liability.'[94] This again illustrates the freedom and authority with which the *Cour de cassation* contributes to the development of French tort law. Since this liability is only reasonable if it can be insured, this case law has also stimulated the development of liability insurance. See nr 1602-1.

Article 1384 s. 5 holds masters and employers liable for the damage caused by their servants and employees in the functions for which they have been employed.[95] Masters and employers are strictly liable without any defence whatsoever apart from contributory negligence of the victim. See nr 1606-3.

Teachers and craftsmen are liable for the damage caused by their pupils and apprentices during the time when they are under their supervision (article 1384 s. 6).[96] Craftsmen are not liable if they can prove they could not have prevented the act that gave rise to liability (article 1384 s. 7, see above). As regards teachers, a negligence liability regime applies because article 1384 s. 8 holds that the claimant has to prove that the damaging act was caused by the teacher's fault, imprudence, or negligent conduct.[97] A teacher at a public school (ie a school run by the State or the municipality) cannot be personally liable for damage caused by one of his pupils.[98] Only the school is liable towards the victim. See nr 1603.

---

[93] 'Le père et la mère, en tant qu'ils exercent l'autorité parentale, sont solidairement responsables du dommage causé par leurs enfants mineurs habitant avec eux.'
[94] 'La responsabilité ci-dessus a lieu, à moins que les père et mère (. . .) ne preuvent qu'ils n'ont pu empêcher le fait qui donne lieu à cette responsabilité.'
[95] ' . . . les maîtres et les commettants, du dommage causé par leurs domestiques et préposés dans les fonctions auxquelles ils les ont employés'.
[96] ' . . . les instituteurs et les artisans, du dommage causé par leurs élèves et apprentis pendant le temps qu'ils sont sous leur surveillance.'
[97] 'En ce qui concerne les instituteurs, les fautes, imprudences ou négligences invoquées contre eux comme ayant causé le fait dommageable, devront être prouvées, conformément aux droit commun, par le demandeur à l'instance.'
[98] Carbonnier (2000), § 239, 433–435; Le Tourneau (2004), nr 7592.

4

Germany

401 Introduction

401-1 *History*

The German Civil Code, *das Bürgerliche Gesetzbuch (BGB)*, entered into force on 1 January 1900. The Code was intended to unify the patchy legal landscape of the young German empire that was established in 1871 on the merger of the North German Federation and the South German States. It is considered to be the political masterpiece of statesman Otto von Bismarck (1815–1898) to transform a loose collection of small states into the strongest industrialized nation in continental Europe.

The BGB was supposed to be one of the symbols of the new German unity. However, the codification was also an economic necessity since the second half of the 19th century saw an expanding economy increasingly operating on a supra regional level.[1]

After World War II the western part of Germany was transformed into the Federal Republic of Germany and retained the BGB. In the eastern part of the country the German Democratic Republic (GDR) was established, and in 1976 it replaced the BGB by its own Civil Code, *das Zivilgesetzbuch* (ZGB).[2] In 1989 the GDR said goodbye to Lenin and the following year the two Germanies were re-united, the eastern part of Germany exchanging the ZGB for the good old BGB.

Germany is a federal state composed of lands (*Länder*), including city-states like Berlin, Hamburg, and Bremen. Compared to the powers of the federal government, the powers of the lands are limited. This is expressed by saying that Germany is a *Bundesstaat* (federal state) and not a *Staatenbund* (federation of

---

[1] See about the history of the BGB: Reinhard Zimmermann, 'An Introduction to German Legal Culture', in Werner F. Ebke and Matthew W. Finkin (eds.), *Introduction to German Law* (The Hague, London, Munich: Kluwer Law International, 1996). The English language book on German tort law is Basil S. Markesinis and Hannes Unberath, *The German Law of Torts, A Comparative Treatise*, 4th edn., (Oxford: Oxford University Press, 2002).

[2] Instead of the 2,358 paragraphs of the BGB, the ZGB contained only 480. See Klaus Westen (ed.), *Das neue Zivilrecht der DDR nach dem Zivilgesetzbuch von 1975* (Baden-Baden: Nomos Verlag, 1977).

states). Though the lands have autonomy in a number of areas, civil law is mainly the competence of the federal government.

It took 26 years to draft the BGB, this monument of 19th century legal scholarship.[3] The main work was done by a commission of judges, officials, and professors and it is not surprising that the draft was criticized as being too abstract, pedantic, and doctrinaire. According to Zimmermann, the BGB ' . . . is marked by a degree of conceptual abstraction that has caused, and continues to cause, both admiration and consternation. (. . .). The internal logic (. . .) is usually quite magnificent, but it does not promote the code's comprehensibility.'[4]

Generally, the abstract level of the BGB provisions has contributed to its flexibility and lasting practicability and it has given the courts sufficient space to develop the law as was desirable from a social and economic point of view. In cases in which provisions lacked the flexibility to deal properly with social and economic needs, the highest courts of appeal, the *Reichsgericht* and the *Bundesgerichtshof* (nr 401-3), did not hesitate to create additional judicial rules, *inter alia* in the area of tort law (nr 403).

401-2 *Bürgerliches Gesetzbuch (Civil Code)*

Like most other German Acts the BGB does not consist of articles but of paragraphs which are indicated with the § symbol, whereas sections are usually indicated with a Roman number, for example § 823 I.[5] On a federal level only the Constitution or Basic Law (*Grundgesetz*, GG) is subdivided into articles.

The BGB comprises five books, and most provisions relevant to establishing liability and damages can be found in the second book on the law of obligations (*Recht der Schuldverhältnisse*: § 241–853).

Part of the rules relating to the law of damages is codified at the beginning of the second book where the most general rules on obligations can be found (§ 241–304). These rules apply to contractual and non-contractual liability alike. The most important general rules on damages are § 249–253. In this part of the second book, definitions of fault and negligence (§ 276) and contributory negligence (§ 276) have also found a place.

The rules as regards torts (*unerlaubte Handlungen*) are incorporated in § 823 ff., in the 25th title of the part on particular obligations (*einzelne Schuldverhältnisse*). This title contains not only the general and specific liability rules, including liability rules for minors and mentally handicapped (§ 827–829), and for officials (§ 839–841), but also special rules for the compensation of damage

---

[3] Münchener Kommentar-Wagner (2004), Vor § 823, N 7–15.
[4] Reinhard Zimmermann, 'An Introduction to German Legal Culture', in Werner F. Ebke and Matthew W. Finkin (eds.) *Introduction to German Law* (Dordrecht: Kluwer Law International, 1996), 9.
[5] See for an English translation of the BGB provisions Markesinis and Unberath (2002), 14–18.

which only apply in tort law cases (§ 842–851). Furthermore, the BGB holds one rule of strict liability in §833 (strict liability for animals, nr 1402) and a number of liability rules for rebuttable negligence (§ 831–838). Since 1900 a considerable number of rules of strict liability have been issued by the legislator, but they all have been embodied in separate Acts and not in the BGB in order to keep the cherished Code free from too many systematic disturbances (nr 405).

These amendments have kept German tort law up to date with the social and economic developments during its existence. However, the patchwork caused by these changes as well as the abundant case law of the BGH has also disturbed the tort law system. More than once this disturbance has tempted the minds of the legislator and of academics to try to restore systematic clearness. A number of major inquiries into the possibilities of a comprehensive reform have been carried out, particularly a reform of the law of obligations (*Schuldrechtsreform*). The first one was published in 1940 (rather unfortunately timed), the second in 1967 (the *Referentenentwurf*), and the third one in 1981 (*Gutachten und Vorschläge zur Überarbeitung des Schuldrechts*).[6] Despite the high level of these reports most of the proposals have disappeared in a filing cabinet of the *Bundesjustizministerium* (Federal Ministry of Justice).

A partial reform of the law of obligations, particularly in the area of limitation and breach of contract, was enacted in 2001. This is the so-called *Schuldrechtsreform*.[7] In the same year a number of new provisions in the law of damages were introduced. This is called the *Schadensersatzrechtsreform* (nr 1202-2).

A reform of the BGB system as such could be welcomed on systematic grounds but there is no urgent factual need.[8] To most questions the judge can find reasonable answers even though the way in which he has to operate is not always very elegant and transparent. German lawyers are familiar with their rather complicated legal system. Many of them cherish the peculiarities of its application and prefer specific and precise rules over general rules, as they are not afraid to use complicated reasoning. Some even seem to feel uneasy and unsatisfied with giving simple answers to legal questions. For a foreign lawyer this may be sometimes confusing, particularly because authors are sometimes inclined to design various and rather complicated reasons for reaching the same answers.

401-3 *Judiciary*

Until the end of World War II the *Reichsgericht* (RG) was Germany's highest civil and criminal court. Its successor in the Federal Republic of Germany, the *Bundesgerichtshof* (BGH), was established in 1950. Both courts have played an

---

6 See the overview in Münchener Kommentar-Wagner (2004), Vor § 823, N 77–80.
7 See for a clear overview Jörg Fedtke, 'Germany', *ETL* 2001, 229–252.
8 Münchener Kommentar-Wagner (2004), Vor § 823, N 80.

important role in the development of civil law in general, and tort law in particular (nr 403–404).

The decisions of the BGH usually contain a comprehensive discussion of the legal problems raised by the facts of the case. Furthermore, case law and academic literature are thoroughly considered. 'A German decision, at the regional appellate or Federal Supreme Court level, addresses itself as much to the scholarly legal community as to the parties of the individual case.'[9] In this sense most decisions of the BGH contain small academic papers as regards the state of affairs in the area of the law at stake. And the BGH refers not only to authors who are in agreement with its line of reasoning but also to those who are of a different opinion. So, the 'correct ones' and the 'wanderers' have equal chances to appear in the case law.

Hence, academics play an equally important role in developing civil law as the courts. However, decisions of the BGH may be sometimes easier to read and understand than books and articles of legal writers. The decisions are much more informative than the French court decisions but they are not as juicy as the personal opinions of English judges. German decisions are written in an objective style and dissenting opinions are not allowed, except in decisions of the *Bundesverfassungsgericht* (Constitutional Court).[10]

The fundamental rights in the *Grundgesetz* (Constitution or Basic Law) have considerably influenced the law in general and also tort law.[11] Respect for human dignity and the right to personal freedom, mentioned in the first two articles of the *Grundgesetz*, are interests which are also protected by tort law. In this respect the case law of the *Bundesverfassungsgericht* (Federal Constitutional Court) is relevant and will be referred to when appropriate. The Court was established in 1951 and sits in Karlsruhe. It guards the observance of the *Grundgesetz* and is entitled to abolish legislative, executive, and judicial acts as unconstitutional, either for formal violations, eg of prescribed procedures, or for material conflicts, eg because of the encroachment of human rights.

The German tendency to go to court rather readily has produced a large amount of extensively and well-reasoned court decisions. In published decisions the parties appear anonymous; instead of names the words *Kläger* (claimant) and *Beklagte* (defendant) are used. The sad consequence is that most German cases have dull numbers. Only in special cases are they baptised with proper names, for instance *Herrenreiter* (Jockey) or *Hühnerpest* (Chicken plague).[12]

The *Bundesgerichtshof* is seated in Karlsruhe, in the former Palace of the Hereditary Grand Duke Friedrich II. The court consists of twelve Senates each

---

[9] Reinhard Zimmermann, 'An Introduction to German Legal Culture', in *Introduction to German Law* (1996), 22.

[10] Zimmermann, op. cit., 21–22; Markesinis and Unberath (2002), 8–14.

[11] Münchener Kommentar-Wagner (2004), Vor § 823, N 57–60.

[12] Hein Kötz, *Die Begründung höchstrichterlicher Urteile*, Preadvies Nederlandse Vereniging voor Rechtsvergelijking, (Deventer: Kluwer, 1982), 12–14.

having its own area of competence. According to §132 *Gerichtsverfassungsgesetz* (Act on the Organization of the Judiciary) disputes between the Senates are decided by the *großer Senat* (Great Senate).

The BGH's position as the highest appellate court in civil and criminal cases implies that it has to guarantee justice in individual cases and to ensure the uniform application and the development of the law. The BGH reviews decisions of the lower courts of appeal in the *Länder*, the *Oberlandesgerichte* (higher regional courts), and certain divisions of the *Landgerichte* (regional courts). The *Oberlandesgerichte* are the highest courts in the *Länder* and mainly hear appeals from the first instance courts, the *Amtsgerichte* (local courts), and some sections of the *Landgerichte*. The *Landgerichte* are both first instance courts for more important cases and courts of appeal for certain cases from the *Amtsgerichte*.[13]

401-4 *Doctrine*

The extensive German doctrine on the law of torts (*unerlaubte Handlungen*) is a rich source of information and inspiration, also for foreign lawyers. It produces an abundant number of commentaries, handbooks, monographs, and theses. In this respect the German doctrine is unique in the world. The commentaries (*Kommentare*), especially, are masterpieces of detailed analyses of legal provisions. The BGB has inspired academics and practitioners to write major commentaries, such as the *Staudinger*, the *Münchener Kommentar* and the *Soergel*,[14] as well as a number of more concise ones, such as the classical *Palandt* and the *Jauernig*.[15]

In addition to these commentaries on the German Civil Code, there are a number of textbooks in the area of tort law, the so called *Lehrbücher*, for instance the classic *Schuldrecht* by Karl Larenz, continued by Claus-Wilhelm Canaris, and the also classic but less traditional *Schuldrecht* by Josef Esser, continued by Eike Schmidt and Hans-Leo Weyers.[16] The most elegant and accessible German textbook in the area of tort law is *Deliktsrecht* by Hein Kötz and Gerhard Wagner.

A downside of this major force of legal writing is that the practical interest of the discussions is not always crystal clear. In the area of tort law one may, for instance, think of controversies about the relationship between the requirements *Rechtswidrigkeit* and *Verschulden* (nr 402-2) and quarrels about the place of the

---

[13] Markesinis and Unberath (2002), 1–8.

[14] *Münchener Kommentar zum Bürgerlichen Gesetzbuch*, 4th edn., (München, 2000 ff.); Julius von Staudinger, *Kommentar zum Bürgerlichen Gesetzbuch mit Einführungsgesetz und Nebengesetzen*, (Berlin, 2000 ff.); Soergel, Hans Th. (ed.), *Bürgerliches Gesetzbuch, mit Einführungsgesetz und Nebengesetzen*, 12th edn., (Stuttgart: Kohlhammer, 1987 ff.).

[15] Otto Palandt, *Bürgerliches Gesetzbuch*, 64th edn., (München: Beck, 2005); Othmar Jauernig, *Bürgerliches Gesetzbuch*, 11th edn., (München: Beck, 2004).

[16] Josef Esser, *Schuldrecht. Ein Lehrbuch* (Heidelberg: Mueller). Particularly relevant as regards tort law and damages are Band 1, Teilband 2: *Durchführungshindernisse und Vertragshaftung. Schadensausgleich und Mehrseitigkeit beim Schuldverhältnis*, 8th edn., by Eike Schmidt (2000) and Band 2, Teilband 2: *Gesetzliche Schuldverhältnisse*, 8th edn., by Hans-Leo Weyers (2000).

Verkehrspflichten in the legal system (nr 403-1). More generally, there is a strong tendency within the German doctrine to try frantically to reconcile the pragmatic approach of the BGH with the BGB system which, despite its flaws, is still considered to be the cornerstone of German civil law. Kötz speaks of the spilling of ink by his fellow countrymen which in his view is due to the strongly developed German passion to reflect on legal controversies and to the fact that these kinds of questions undoubtedly possess high theoretical attraction.[17]

The flip side of this coin is that almost all problems of tort law are conveniently mapped by authors who love to systematize the law and to divide detailed legal questions into dozens of even more detailed sub-questions, whereas cases are classified in detailed layer categories, the so-called *aufgegliederte Fallgruppen*. If anywhere in the world a legal question arises, there is a considerable chance that a German author has already thought about it, has identified the different aspects of the problem, and has produced a proper detailed analysis.

402 Fault liability: the BGB provisions

402-1 *General rules*

The traditional distinction in German tort law is between *Verschuldenshaftung* and *Gefährdungshaftung*. The latter term is here translated as strict liability, whereas the former will be referred to as fault liability. *Verschuldenshaftung* includes liability for intentional as well as negligent conduct (nr 402-2). However, apart from liability based on § 826 BGB (nr 402-4), intentional conduct is not a necessary condition for liability: in all cases negligent conduct will do provided the other requirements for liability (*Tatbestand, Rechtswidrigkeit*) are met.

The first draft of the BGB contained two very general rules for fault liability but this was much criticized at the time of its presentation in 1888. It was considered that a general rule would leave the courts too much freedom and this was not consonant with the urge for unity. The need and desire to strengthen the unity of the young German empire (nr 401-1) led to the conclusion that the BGB had to deviate from the French Civil Code with its sole general rule for fault liability (nr 302). A general rule would lead to uncertainties and doubts and particularly to lack of boundaries.[18] This position was possibly not only fuelled by legal-technical reasons since the main drafting of the BGB took place in the wake of the

---

[17] Kötz-Wagner (2001), N 99: 'Wenn gleichwohl in der deutschen juristischen Literatur zu dieser Frage ganze Ströme von Tinte vergossen worden sind, so liegt das einmal an dem hierzulande stark ausgebildeten Hang zum Durchleiden rechtswissenschaftlicher Kontroversen, zum anderen daran, daß das in Rede stehende Problem fraglos von hohem theoretischem Reiz ist.'

[18] Ernst von Caemmerer, *Wandlungen des Deliktrechts*, (Karlsruhe: Mueller, 1960), 471: the drafters feared '... die Unsicherheiten und Zweifel, zu denen eine solche Generalklausel führen könnte. Man fürchtete insbesondere die Uferlosigkeit.' See also Christian Katzenmeier, Zur neueren dogmengeschichtlichen Entwicklung der Deliktsrechtstatbestände, *AcP* 203 (2003), 80–118.

Franco-German war (1870–1871), in an era of growing national self-consciousness. During the preparatory work it was even said that: '. . . the German legal conscience which alone is relevant has no room for the notions of the *code civil*.'[19]

On the other hand, it was also considered to be impracticable to draft only specific rules as was the position in English law (nr 502). Hence, an intermediate way was chosen by designing three general rules with a restricted scope of application. However, for several reasons this way appeared to be not completely satisfactory either (nr 403–404).[20] Though currently German tort law in fact operates on the basis of a general fault rule,[21] the text of the old BGB provisions still gives rise to a number of technical peculiarities and complications.

The three general rules with the restricted fields of application are called *Grundtatbestände* and can be found in § 823 I, § 823 II, and § 826 BGB. Each of these provisions contains five requirements for liability: a *Tatbestand* (the violation of a codified normative rule), *Rechtswidrigkeit* (unlawfulness), *Verschulden* (intention or negligence), causation (*Kausalität*), and damage (*Schaden*).

The *Tatbestand* restricts the field of application of the general rules: application of § 823 I requires the infringement of a right such as life, body, health, freedom, and property, § 823 II the violation of a statutory rule (*Schutzgesetzverstoß*), and § 826 intentional unethical conduct, also known as intentional infliction of damage *contra bonos mores* (*sittenwidrige vorsätzliche Schädigung*). These *Tatbestand* requirements imply that it is not possible to lodge a claim for damages on the sole basis of intention or negligence: the violation of a *Tatbestand*, a codified normative rule, has to be established as well.

The BGB contains not only three general rules but also three specific rules which are called *Einzeltatbestände*: § 824 about financial and economic trustworthiness (*Kreditgefährdung*), § 825 about the infringement of sexual integrity (*sexuelle Selbstbestimmung*), and § 839 about the breach of an official duty (*Amtspflichtverletzung*, see about this provision nr 1803-2). In addition to causation and damage both the general and specific rules require a *Tatbestand*, *Rechtswidrigkeit*, and *Verschulden*. Together with the three *Grundtatbestände* these three *Einzeltatbestände* are the core of German fault liability (*Verschuldenshaftung*).

402-2 *Requirements for fault liability*

The first requirement for fault liability is the fulfilment of a *Tatbestand*. This means that it has to be established that someone infringed another person's

---

[19] Protokolle der Kommission für die zweite Lesung des Entwurfs des Bürgerlichen Gesetzbuch. II, 603, cited in von Bar (1998), N 186.

[20] Müchener Kommentar-Wagner (2004), Vor § 823 N 15.

[21] See Ernst von Caemmerer, *Wandlungen des Deliktrechts*, (Karlsruhe: Mueller, 1960), p. 526: 'Sieht man sich die Fälle an, die als "bloße Vermögensschädigungen" noch offenbleiben, so sind es solche, in denen auch in den Rechten mit allgemeinem Deliktstatbestand Widerrechtlichkeit oder "faute" verneint oder festgestellt wird, daß eine "duty" dem Betroffenen gegenüber nicht verletzt ist.'

protected right (§ 823 I, nr 402-3), that he intentionally inflicted damage *contra bonos mores* (§ 826, nr 402-4), or that he violated a statutory rule (§ 823 II, nr 903). This *Tatbestand* requirement aims to limit the scope of fault liability.

If someone has fulfilled such a *Tatbestand*, this is an important indication for unlawfulness (*Rechtswidrigkeit*). This means that someone's conduct is in principle unlawful (*rechtswidrig*) if it infringes another person's protected right (§ 823 I), if it violates a statutory rule (§ 823 II), or if he has intentionally inflicted damage *contra bonos mores* (§ 826). Fulfilling a *Tatbestand* does not amount to unlawfulness if the defendant can invoke a ground of justification (*Rechtfertigungsgrund*), for example self-defence (*Notwehr*, § 227), necessity (*defensiver Notstand* in § 228 and *agressiver Notstand* in § 904), and self-help (*Selbsthilfe* in § 229 and 859).

In addition to *Tatbestand* and *Rechtswidrigkeit*, the third requirement for liability is *Verschulden* (§ 276 BGB). This requirement is fulfilled if the wrongdoer acted intentionally (*vorsätzlich*) or negligently (*fahrlässig*). Conduct is deemed to be negligent if it is contrary to the care required in society.[22] See about *Verschulden* nr 802-2.

For example, sawing down a tree which hits a bystander fulfils the *Tatbestand* of § 823 I since it infringes the victim's right to bodily integrity. The fulfilment of the *Tatbestand* amounts to *Rechtswidrigkeit*, unless there was a ground of justification, such as self-defence. If no such ground can be invoked, it has to be assessed whether the defendant's conduct was intentional or negligent (*Verschulden*). In these cases of a direct infringement (*unmittelbare Verletzung*) the system is reasonably clear.

However, the system is less clear if the infringement has not been direct but indirect (*mittelbare Verletzung*), for example, if a rotten tree falls onto a road and a car collides with the tree.[23] The above-mentioned system would lead to the conclusion that the sole fact that the car owner's right to property is infringed amounts to unlawfulness unless a ground of justification applies. This is, of course, considered to be undesirable. For this reason the German courts have developed safety duties in all areas of accident law (*Verkehrspflichten*, see nr 403). In case of an indirect infringement the breach of such a safety duty determines unlawfulness. Hence, the applicable rule for unlawfulness differs: in cases of direct infringement (the flowerpot on the head), this sole fact will do for unlawfulness, and in cases of indirect infringement (the fallen tree on the road), the breach of a safety duty is decisive.

These different ways to establish unlawfulness also have an impact on the role of negligence (as one of the elements of *Verschulden* as well as intention) and this has given rise to thorough discussions in the legal literature. In cases of direct

---

[22] § 276 I BGB: 'Der Schuldner hat, sofern nich ein anderes bestimmt ist, Vorsatz und Fahrlässigkeit zu vertreten. Fahrlässig handelt, wer die im Verkehr erforderliche Sorgfalt außer acht läßt.'

[23] Compare the similar distinction made in English law (nr 502-3) between trespass (directly caused harm) and trespass on the case (indirectly caused harm).

infringement the distinction between unlawfulness and negligence is not difficult to grasp, but in cases of an indirect infringement the difference between unlawfulness (breach of a safety duty) and negligence is not obvious. The BGH and the majority of the authors nevertheless want to maintain this system which means that, in practice, *Verschulden* hardly plays an independent role. Conversely, a minority of the authors advocate a straightforward system in which *Rechtswidrigkeit* is always established on the basis of negligent conduct, regardless of the character of the infringement.[24]

402-3 § 823 I: infringement of a right

§ 823 I protects *Rechtsgüter* (life, physical integrity, health, and personal liberty) and *Rechte* (property and 'another right'), the former being invariably attached to the person, whereas the latter can be transferred. If someone infringes such a protected right, he has fulfilled a *Tatbestand* and is deemed to have acted unlawfully (*rechtswidrig*). Provided he has also acted negligently (*fahrlässig*), he will be liable for the damage caused, not only for the physical damage but also for the consequential economic loss. This means that § 823 I applies to all cases of personal damage and property damage. It is in fact a general rule of fault liability for cases of death, personal injury, and loss of property.

In order to provide victims with proper access to damages and thus better protection, the courts are inclined to interpret the rights protecting against death and personal injury in a broad way.[25] Infringement of the right to bodily integrity and health will generally be caused by an accident but it can also be caused by a newspaper article which destroys someone's honour and reputation in such a way that his health is seriously affected too.[26] The infringement of the right to health has also been established in a case of HIV contamination although the victim did not yet have health complaints.[27] Finally, the right to health can also be infringed before birth: the driver who collided with a pregnant woman was also liable for the brain damage of the child.[28] See nr 707-1.

§ 823 I also protects 'another right' (*sonstiges Recht*). With this concept the legislator aimed to bring comparable rights within the ambit of this provision, such as rights regarding intellectual property (patents, trademarks, and copyrights), mortgage, name, portrait, and family law related rights such as the right to parental care. However, 'another right' was not supposed to serve as a general 'safety net' *Tatbestand*.[29]

---

[24] Münchener Kommentar-Wagner (2004), § 823 N 5–7; Markesinis and Unberath (2002), 79–83.   [25] Kötz-Wagner (2001), N 50.

[26] RG 20 June 1935, RGZ 148, 154.

[27] BGH 25 April 1991, BGHZ 114, 284 = NJW 1991, 1948.

[28] BGH 11 January 1972, BGHZ 58, 48 = NJW 1972, 1126 = JZ 1972, 363, about which Markesinis and Unberath (2002), 144–147. See also BGH 20 December 1952, BGHZ 8, 243 = NJW 1953, 416 = JZ 1953, 307, about which Van Gerven (2000), 80–81 and Markesinis and Unberath (2002), 147–149; Larenz-Canaris (1994), §76 II 1h, 385.

[29] Münchener Kommentar-Wagner (2004), § 823 N 136–166; Kötz-Wagner (2001), N 71–73.

Personal or obligational rights (*obligatorische Forderung*), particularly rights under a contract, are not protected under § 823 I. The provision of 'another right' does not aim to cover these rights.[30] Neither does provision this cover liability for pure economic loss, ie financial damage which is not caused by death, personal injury, or property loss. In order to get compensation for this kind of loss, a victim has to base his claim on other provisions, particularly § 823 II (nr 903) and § 826 (nr 402-4).

Psychological damage, for instance a shock after witnessing a serious accident, is also considered to be a health injury.[31] However, it is required that the psychological damage surpasses the normal reactions of pain, mourning, and sorrow. See nr 800.

The right to property (*Eigentumsrecht*) is also broadly interpreted. Of course, it applies to cases in which objects are being damaged or destroyed. But a property right can also be infringed (*Eigentumsverletzung*) if the object itself remains undamaged but cannot be used in a proper way any more. One may think of animals fed with toxic food and which cannot be sold any more[32] or of a motor ship that could not sail for months because of a negligently damaged quay wall.[33] Other examples of the infringement of a property right are the wrongful confiscation of a driving licence, the reprogramming of a computer, or the ransacking of an archive.[34] See in more detail about this issue nr 709.

402-4   § 826 BGB: intentional infliction of damage
contra bonos mores

§ 826 holds a person liable if he intentionally causes damage to another person in a manner *contra bonos mores*, which means contrary to ethical principles (*Sittenwidrigkeit*). This provision was especially intended for situations in which § 823 I (infringement of a right) and § 823 II (violation of a statutory rule) were not applicable.

In a classical sense acting *contra bonos mores* means acting contrary to the moral feelings of all good and right-thinking members of society (*ein Verstoß gegen das Anstandsgefühl aller billig und gerecht Denkenden*). However, the increasing divergence of moral convictions in society has cast doubt on the value of this definition. Moreover, the definition is apt to serve as a standard for proper economic conduct in economic competition or generally as regards commercial practices. Currently, the idea has become dominant that acting *contra bonos*

---

[30] Larenz-Canaris (1994), 392 ff.; Kötz-Wagner (2001), N 74; Münchener Kommentar-Wagner (2004), § 823 N 154–155.

[31] BGH 2 October 1990, NJW 1991, 747 = VersR 1991, 432; see also BGH 4 April 1989, NJW 1989, 2317, about which Markesinis and Unberath (2002), 119–122.

[32] BGH 25 October 1988, BGHZ 105, 346 = NJW 1989, 707 = VersR 1989, 91 = JZ 1989, 638 (*Fischfutter*).

[33] BGH 21 December 1970, BGHZ 55, 153 = NJW 1971, 886 = VersR 1971, 418 (*Motorschiff Christel*), about which Markesinis and Unberath (2002), 219–222.

[34] BGH 31 October 1974, BGHZ 63, 203; BGH 26 February 1980, BGHZ 76, 216.

mores implies conduct contrary to the existing economic and legal order or the *ordre public*.[35] Examples of economic conduct covered by § 826 are provoking a breach of contract, providing someone with incorrect information, abusing a right, and most kinds of unfair competition.

As regards conduct contrary to the legal and economic order, the courts increasingly refer to the Basic Rights enshrined in the *Grundgesetz*. This concept consists notably of the *objektive Werteordnung des Grundgesetzes* (objective value order of the constitution) and reflects the change from a 19th century free market state to a 20th century social state.[36] It implies that the constitutional human rights are increasingly considered as a benchmark for conduct not only in a vertical way between public authorities and citizens but also in a horizontal way among citizens.

The impact of § 826 is limited since it is required that the defendant acted intentionally. Notably intention is a high threshold, and it is not surprising that this requirement is broadly construed by the courts and criticized in the doctrine. The courts have mitigated the requirement in several ways. Firstly, they accept *dolus eventualis*, which implies that someone accepts the consequences of his conduct as inevitable even though he did not want them to happen. Hence, it is sufficient that the tortfeasor was aware that it was possible that damage would occur.[37] Secondly, intention must only be present with regard to the primary infringement of the victim's interest. The tortfeasor need not have intended all consequential damage resulting from the infringement, nor is it required that he even knew the person his conduct would harm.[38] For instance, if someone has intentionally induced the breach of a contract *contra bonos mores*, he will probably be liable for the resulting bankruptcy of the contractor even if he did not intend this. Finally, the courts sometimes also accept *Leichtfertigkeit*, ie a form of recklessness, notably in cases of information by auditors or expert witnesses. If the tortfeasor was aware that his conduct was reckless, the courts tend to deem this to be sufficient for *Vorsatz*. This has been criticized in the doctrine. An example is a doctor who declared a person mentally ill and advised that he should be put under guardianship. This diagnosis was entirely wrong and could have been avoided by a slightly more careful examination. Although the doctor did not intend the damage ensuing from the incapacitation, he was held liable for it due to his reckless conduct.[39]

The limited possibilities which the legal system provides to obtain compensation for pure economic loss have had two important consequences. Firstly,

---

[35] Kötz-Wagner (2001), N 191; Larenz-Canaris (1994), § 78 I 1b, 448; Markesinis and Unberath (2002), 889–890. An important contribution to this change was Konstantin Simitis, *Gute Sitten und ordre public. Ein kritischer Beitrag zur Anwendung des § 138 I BGB* (Marburg: Elwert, 1960). [36] Kötz-Wagner (2001) N 191.
[37] Münchener Kommentar-Wagner (2004), § 826 N 19–26; Kötz-Wagner (2001), N 187–188; Larenz-Canaris (1994), § 78 I 1b, 447–448.
[38] Münchener Kommentar-Wagner (2004), § 826 N 20f.
[39] Münchener Kommentar-Wagner (2004), § 826 N 25f.

the courts are inclined to rather easily establish the infringement of a protected right in the sense of § 823 I. If someone intentionally or negligently infringes one of the protected rights, he has to compensate all the consequential damage of this infringement, including economic loss, provided that there is a sufficient causal connection between the conduct and the harm. This means that, by broadening the concept of infringement of a right, the courts tighten the concept of pure economic loss and thus provide victims with more chances to get compensation for loss suffered. Secondly, in 1904 the *Reichsgericht* created the *Recht am Gewerbebetrieb* and other instruments to provide better ways to get compensation for pure economic loss on the basis of negligent rather than intentional conduct. See nr 404-1. Thirdly, an important legislative contribution to provide compensation for pure economic loss was the enactment of the *Gesetz gegen unlauteren Wettbewerb* (Unfair Competition Act) that protects against negligent infliction of pure economic loss through unfair competition.[40]

The gaps in the BGB became apparent not only in the area of pure economic loss. In 1902 the *Reichsgericht* had to create so-called *Verkehrssicherungspflichten* (safety duties of care) in order to cover liability for omissions (nr 403-1). And in 1954 the BGH called into being *das allgemeine Persönlichkeitsrecht* (the general personality right) for the better protection of a person's interests like privacy, honour, and reputation (nr 404-2).

403 Fault liability: judge-made safety duties (*Verkehrspflichten*)

403-1 *Origin, character, and place in the legal system*

The first lacuna in the BGB occurred in 1902 and was related to liability for omissions. The case was about someone who suffered damage when he was injured by a rotten tree that had fallen onto the highway. Hence, the damage was not caused by an act but by an omission, ie the owner of the tree had not removed the fallen tree. It was clear that the claimant had suffered personal injury and that his right to bodily integrity was infringed (§ 823 I BGB). One could therefore argue that a *Tatbestand* was fulfilled and that the owner of the road had acted unlawfully. This, however, did not seem to be a proper conclusion since it could very well be that the owner had behaved carefully, for example by regularly inspecting the road. The problem was that § 823 I primarily seemed to focus on liability for acts, and that the scope of § 823 II (violation of statutory rule) was not sufficient to deal with all the omissions.

The *Reichsgericht* therefore concluded that, in cases of omissions, unlawfulness (*Rechtswidrigkeit*) could not simply be based on the infringement of a protected right but had to be based on the breach of a safety duty. Therefore, the court

---

[40] § 9 I UWG in its reformed version of 2004. See for this and the foregoing Münchener Kommentar-Wagner (2004) § 826 N 3.

72

created unwritten safety duties, which were affirmative duties imposed on persons who had opened their roads, premises, or grounds to the general public to ensure the safety of the visitors.[41] A few months later the *Reichsgericht* confirmed its decision in a case about stairs that had become slippery owing to snow.[42] The *Reichsgericht* thus added a new and extremely important judicial rule to the legislative framework.[43] These safety duties were called *Verkehrssicherungspflichten* (literally societal safety duties). Later other areas were also covered by safety duties and these were simply called *Verkehrspflichten* (societal duties).[44] This is now mostly used as the generic term and includes the *Verkehrssicherungspflichten*.

The new judicial rule implied that if someone suffers personal injury or property loss as a result of someone's omission, the infringement of his right is not sufficient for unlawfulness. It is necessary to establish that the defendant has breached a safety duty (*Verkehrspflicht*). If someone operates a fair, a skating-rink, a swimming pool, a riding school, or a hotel, it is obvious that at a certain point an accident may occur. However, the fact that the operator has provided the general access to his premises and subsequently an accident occurs is not sufficient to establish unlawful conduct. Such a qualification requires that the operator has breached his safety duty by failing to take appropriate safety measures, such as preventing dangerous situations, providing safety materials, or placing warning signs for dangerous situations.[45]

Currently, safety duties are not restricted to duties to act but are related to the slightly broader field of indirectly caused damage (*mittelbare Verletzungen*). The German commentaries and handbooks on tort law are now packed with these *Verkehrspflichten* and there have been many idle efforts to categorize them in a proper way.[46]

The safety duties have provoked a profound dispute in the legal literature about the question of how these duties can be fitted into the legal system. This dispute has lasted until this day. The BGH holds, as does the prevailing opinion in the doctrine, that *Verkehrspflichten* have to be categorised in § 823 I because they protect against personal and physical loss. The BGH has agreed with this point of view.[47]

A minority of the doctrine, however, argues that *Verkehrspflichten* need to be subsumed under § 823 II because the scope of safety duties is to regulate people's

[41] RG 30 October 1902, RGZ 52, 373.   [42] RG 23 February 1903, RGZ 54, 53.
[43] Münchener Kommentar-Wagner (2004), § 823 N 220–247; Deutsch-Ahrens (2002), N 253.
[44] RG 23 February 1903, RGZ 54, 53, 59: '... daß derjenige, welcher sein Grundstück zum öffentlichen Verkehr bestimmt und einrichtet, verpflichtet ist, das in einer Weise zu tun, wie es den Anforderungen der Verkehrssicherheit entspricht.' See also BGH 15 June 1954, BGHZ 14, 83, NJW 1954,1403; BGH 30 January 1961, BGHZ 34, 206.   [45] Kötz-Wagner (2001), N 232.
[46] See Deutsch-Ahrens (2002), N 262–273 (brief) and Münchener Kommentar-Wagner (2004), § 823 N 407–546 (detailed).
[47] BGH 27 January 1987, NJW 1987, 2671, 2672 considers '... die Verkehrs(sicherungs)-pflichten allein als durch die Schutzgüter des § 823 I festgelegte, auf den sozialen Umgang bezogene Verhaltenspflichten.' It thus does not link the scope of application of the *Verkehrspflichten* to § 823 II. However, it does so for the burden of proof as regards negligence (*Verschulden*); see nr 903.

conduct rather than to protect people's interests. With this choice the restriction imposed by § 823 I as regards the limited number of protected interests no longer applies. This means that categorizing *Verkehrspflichten* under § 823 II opens the door to acknowledging that these duties also protect against pure economic loss. However, the BGH has not been convinced by these arguments and keeps the safety duties in the safe haven of § 823 I.[48]

Though the discussion in the doctrine is complicated, it is mainly of an academic character since, in the eyes of a foreign observer, *Verkehrspflichten* are simply unwritten duties of care (even though they are of major practical importance).[49] The discussion is a fine illustration of the fact that the German approach to (tort) law is strongly characterized by dogmatic and systematic issues (nr 401-4).

403-2 *Application*

The case law requires a very high level of care by the person who owes the *Verkehrspflicht*. This reflects the importance many Germans attach to safety. These duties are based in fault liability and it is decisive whether the harm could have been avoided by any reasonable precautionary measure of the defendant. In their practical application, however, the safety duties come close to a rule of strict liability although the BGH stresses that they do not amount to a warranty of the potential victim's safety.

The oldest category of safety duties applies to roads and premises. Apart from the examples mentioned in the previous section, one may think of the duty to safeguard passers-by from harm caused by snow falling off the slanted roof of a building. The building's possessor is obliged to take all measures a careful person in the same situation would take in order to protect pedestrians, cyclists, and drivers. Whether he needs to take measures and, if so, which measures (such as using warning signs or constructing small fences on the roof to prevent snow or ice falling down), depends on how steep the roof is, the frequency of heavy snowfall in the particular region, and the distance to the pavement or the road.[50] Similar considerations apply to the owner of a wood bordering on a street as regards the prevention of trees falling down[51] and to the owner of a graveyard to protect visitors against falling tombstones.[52] This category of *Verkehrspflichten* relating to immovable objects has a counterpart in § 836–838 BGB holding a liability for rebuttable negligence for collapsing buildings: see nr 1503.

---

[48] Von Bar, *Verkehrspflichten* (1980), 157 ff; Deutsch-Ahrens (2002), N 276. See for an overview Münchener Kommentar-Wagner (2004), §823 N 58 and 213–216.

[49] This practical importance can be illustrated with the fact that Münchener Kommentar-Wagner (2004) devotes almost half of his commentary on § 823 to the content of *Verkehrspflichten* in areas varying from gardens and swimmers, via water pipes and tour operators to manufacturers and doctors.   [50] BGH 8 December 1954, NJW 1955, 300.

[51] BGH 30 October 1973, MDR 1974, 217.

[52] BGH 30 January 1961, BGHZ 34, 206.

In the course of time the courts have extended the application of the safety duties to all other indirectly caused harm, for example by movable objects. For example, a chemist who sells highly explosive chemicals to a 15-year-old breaches his safety duty and is liable for the damage caused by the explosion of the chemicals.[53] And the keeper of a motor vehicle has to take precautionary measures to prevent his car from being stolen or used for joyriding, which has a high risk of causing damage to persons or property.[54] Most other safety duties as regards motor vehicles are hardly important any more because of the strict liability of § 7 StVG (nr 1404-2). Safety duties as regards products are still of great importance because, until recently, a claim based on strict liability (as is possible on the basis of the EC Product Liability Directive implemented in the *Produkthaftungsgesetz* (Product Liability Act) did not provide for the compensation of non-pecuniary loss (nr 1206 and 1409).

A final category of safety duties to be mentioned here relates to a variety of activities. One may think of someone who organizes a firework display,[55] operates a merry-go-round,[56] or carries out constructing activities.[57] Safety duties also apply to skiers: they have to take measures which in the circumstances are required to prevent unreasonable risks for other persons.[58] Medical activities (*Arzthaftung*) are also governed by safety duties.[59]

Safety duties are not owed to everybody. For example, someone who has illegally entered someone else's premises may not have a claim because he is outside the duty's scope of personal protection (*persönlicher Schutzbereich*). This will certainly be the case as regards a burglar; it will generally be the case for an adult trespasser but not necessarily for children. See about this issue nr 1506-3.

404 Fault liability: judge-made rights

404-1 *Right to business (Recht am Gewerbebetrieb)*

The second problem appearing soon after the entering into force of the BGB was the difficulty of granting damages for pure economic loss (*reiner Vermögensschaden*). This was only possible on the basis of § 823 II and § 826 or specific statutory provisions.[60] This lacuna was filled by the *Reichsgericht* in 1904 by calling into being *das Recht am eingerichteten und ausgeübten Gewerbebetrieb*, literally the right inherent in an established and exercised business. Nowadays

---

[53] Kötz-Wagner (2001), N 233.   [54] BGH 12 November 1963, VersR 1964, 300.
[55] BGH 22 February 1966, VersR 1966, 524.
[56] OLG Frankfurt 10 February 1961, MDR 1962, 477.
[57] BGH 30 June 1964, VersR 1964, 1082.   [58] BGH 11 January 1972, BGHZ 58, 40.
[59] Münchener Kommentar-Wagner (2004), § 823 N 642–750.
[60] Compensation for pure economic loss is generally allowed within the framework of governmental liability (§ 839): see nr 1803-2.

this right is also briefly called *das Recht am Unternehmen*: the right to business.[61] The BGH has continued this line and has, for example, applied this right in cases of unfair competition (eg using someone else's brand), statements which endanger the creditworthiness of a company (eg testing of consumer products), and strikes.[62]

The *Reichsgericht* categorized the right to business as 'another right' in the sense of § 823 I (nr 402-3). However, the character of the right to business differs considerably from that of the rights enumerated in §823 I BGB. In applying the right to business, the court has to balance the interests of the business and the interests of the infringing party. This implies, for instance, that the defendant's freedom of expression prevents the conclusion that the right to business is infringed.[63]

Though the drafters of the BGB were reluctant to provide general possibilities to compensate pure economic loss (nr 402-1), the *Reichsgericht* and later also the BGH have shown a remarkable creativity in finding legal basis to grant damages for this head of damage. See about this creativity and more generally about compensation for pure economic loss in German law, nr 713.

404-2 *General personality right (allgemeines Persönlichkeitsrecht)*

A third area in which the *Tatbestand* system of the BGB appeared to have gaps was the protection of privacy and other personality rights. The significance of this protection became clear after World War II, because of what had happened during the war and also because of the development of mass media and modern techniques. In 1954, 50 years after the birth of the right to business (*das Recht am Gewerbebetrieb*), the BGH created the general personality right (*das allgemeine Persönlichkeitsrecht*) in the famous *Dr. Schacht* case, thus providing a better protection of human dignity and the right of free development of one's personality.[64]

The general personality right has proved to be an excellent umbrella for protecting all kinds of aspects of the person. It has for instance been applied to protect against telephone-tapping and taping telephone calls, against disclosing medical data to third parties without the consent of the person involved, and against the use of photographs for commercial purposes.[65]

[61] RG 27 February 1904, RGZ 58, 24, about which Markesinis and Unberath (2002), 372–376; Deutsch-Ahrens (2002) N 197–201; Münchener Kommentar-Wagner (2004), § 823 N 179–212.
[62] BGH 11 November 1958, BGHZ 28, 320; BGH 9 December 1975, NJW 1976, 620; BAG 19 June 1973, NJW 1973, 1994. See the overview in Münchener Kommentar-Wagner (2004), §823 N 190–212.
[63] BGH 21 June 1966, BGHZ 45, 296 = NJW 1966, 1617 = JZ 1967, 174 (*Höllenfeuer*), about which Van Gerven (2000), 190–191.
[64] BGH 25 May 1954, BGHZ 13, 334 = NJW 1954, 1404 = JZ 1954, 698 (*Dr. Schacht*). See about this case also Markesinis and Unberath (2002), 412–415 and nr 705-2. Münchener Kommentar-Wagner (2004), § 823 N 171–175; Deutsch-Ahrens (2002), N 202–210.
[65] BGH 20 May 1958, BGHZ 27, 284; BGH 2 April 1957, BGHZ 24, 72; BGH 26 June 1981, BGHZ 81, 75. See also Kötz-Wagner (2001), N 626–636; Larenz-Canaris (1994), § 80 II, 498 ff.

The general personality right also plays a role in cases in which it is hard to establish the infringement of the right to bodily integrity or to health (§ 823 I, nr 402-3) but legal protection is nonetheless desirable. An example is the case of a 31 year old man who suffered from bladder cancer. Prior to an operation with the inherent risk that he would become infertile, he had his sperm frozen by a hospital. After the surgery the man indeed appeared to be infertile. Some time later the hospital destroyed the man's sperm without his consent. The BGH awarded him damages of DM 25,000 (€12,800), not for the infringement of his body or health but for the infringement of his general personality right.[66]

In long-standing case law the BGH has held that this general personality right has to be considered to be 'another right' in the sense of § 823 I. The character of this right, however, differs from that of the ones mentioned in this provision. The infringement of the general personality right cannot be easily factually established, as is the case with the infringement of the body or of property, but in most cases it requires balancing the interests of the claimant and the defendant. Particularly in cases of infringement by the media, the freedom of expression will be at stake on the part of the defendant.[67]

See also nr 705 about the general personality right in a comparative perspective, particularly as regards the way damages are used as a deterrent for potential infringements.

405 Rules of stricter liability

405-1 *General observations*

Rules of strict liability (*Gefährdungshaftung*) can be found outside the BGB in specific Acts. The only exception is the liability of the keeper of a luxury animal (*Luxustier*) which is governed by § 833 BGB (nr 1402). In strict liability regimes, dangerous devices or installations (*Anlagen)* or dangerous activities are generally the basis for liability. Hence, strict liability mainly applies to the specific risks caused by subsequent technological developments. This has resulted in a long list of extra BGB statutory strict liability rules for damage caused by railways (1838), motor vehicles (1909), aeroplanes (1922), water contamination (1957), and nuclear damage (1959).[68] They will be briefly described below. Some of them will be further analysed in Part III of this book. One of the more recent fruits of the legislative activity is a strict liability rule for damage caused by genetically modified organisms in the *Gentechnikgesetz*, which entered into force in 1993.

---

[66] BGH 9 November 1993, NJW 1994, 127 = JZ 1994, 464.
[67] Kötz-Wagner (2001), N 630–631.
[68] Josef Esser, *Grundlagen und Entwicklung der Gefährdungshaftung*, 2nd edn. (Munich: Beck, 1969), 97 ff, Hein Kötz, 'Gefährdungshaftung', in *Gutachten und Vorschläge zur Überarbeitung des Schuldrechts*, (Cologne: Bundesjustizministerium, 1981), 1779; Kötz-Wagner (2001), N 338.

The legislator enacted rules of strict liability in categories of cases in which fault liability (*Verschuldenshaftung*) did not lead to satisfactory results. The legislator did not dare to take too great a risk and often drafted specific rules with a limited scope. Hence, the German system of strict liability is quite patchy. Efforts to design a general strict liability rule for installations creating a specific risk (*Anlage von der eine besondere Gefahr ausgeht*) have failed because of differences of opinion as regards the wording and the scope of such a general rule (*Generalklausel*).[69]

One of the specific features of German strict liability rules was that they did not provide compensation for non-pecuniary loss (*Schmerzensgeld*), except for § 833 BGB (liability for animals, see nr 1402). This compelled victims to also base their claim on fault liability such as § 823 I. This restriction has been abolished by the reform of the law of damages in 2002 (*Schadensersatzrechtsreform*) (nr 1202-2).

Most rules of strict liability limit the amount of compensation to a certain maximum, except for § 22 *Wasserhaushaltsgesetz* (WHG, Water Resources Act), § 31 I 1 Atomgesetz, and § 833 BGB.[70] These maxima have been increased by the reform of the law of damages in 2002 but they have not been abolished. This implies that, in cases in which the victim suffers a big loss, he has to rely on the rules of fault liability in order to get full compensation. This system of compensation limits is adopted in the European Product Liability Directive as an option for Member States to limit the amount of compensation to be paid by the manufacturer of a defective product (nr 1407-1).

405-2 *Liability for things*

The most important strict liability rule for things is § 7 *Straßenverkehrsgesetz* (StVG) (Road Traffic Act). It holds the keeper of a motor vehicle strictly liable for physical and property damage to pedestrians, cyclists, passengers, and drivers caused by the so-called operational risk (*Betriebsgefahr*) of the vehicle. The keeper of the motor vehicle can only invoke an external cause (*höhere Gewalt*) with which he can escape liability, and contributory negligence with which he can lower the amount of damages. See nr 1404-2.[71]

A second important example of strict liability is § 1 I *Haftpflichtgesetz* (HPflG, Liability Act): the operator of a railway, a tramway, a hover track, or a ski lift (except ski tows) is strictly liable for the physical and property damage caused by the operational risk (*Betriebsgefahr*) of the means of conveyance. The operator's only defences are an external cause and contributory negligence. The restriction to operational risks implies for instance that the rule does not apply when someone slips on the platform of a railway station, because such an accident is

---

[69] Proposed by Hein Kötz, 'Gefährdungshaftung', in *Gutachten und Vorschläge zur Überarbeitung des Schuldrechts*, (Cologne: Bundesjustizministerium, 1981), 1785 ff.; see also Hans Stoll, *Richterliche Fortbildung und Überarbeitung des Deliktrechts*, (Heidelberg: Mueller, 1984), 19 ff.
[70] Deutsch-Ahrens (2002), N 365.   [71] Deutsch-Ahrens (2002) N 380–385.

not related to the operational risk of the railway. However, the rule does apply when someone suffers damage caused by the crowd of passengers ascending and descending from a train.[72]

§ 33 *Luftverkehssgesetz* (Air Traffic Act) establishes strict liability for the operator of an aeroplane. This rule also applies to damage caused by the noise of an aeroplane, for instance when the driver of a motor vehicle, distracted by the noise of a low-flying jet plane, collides with a tree.[73] See about this causation rule also nr 1103-2.

Furthermore, rules of strict liability apply to operators of electricity mains and pipelines (§ 2 I *Haftpflichtgesetz*, Liability Act), to operators of nuclear plants (§ 25 ff. *Atomgesetz*, Nuclear Act), to manufactures of defective products in general (*Produkthaftungsgesetz*, Product Liability Act), and of pharmaceutical products (§ 64 *Arzneimittelgesetz*, Drugs Act). See about product liability nr 1406-1411.

The strict liability rules in the *Umwelthaftungsgesetz* (Environmental Liability Act) and the *Wasserhaushaltsgesetz* (WHG) will be pointed out in nr 1414-1.

405-3 *Liability for persons*

The BGB only holds a few special rules as regards liability for damage caused by other persons. These are not rules of strict liability but they provide for liability with a rebuttable presumption of negligence (*Verschulden*).

§ 832 imposes liability on anyone who is statutory or contractually obliged to supervise another person. This provision does not only apply to parents for damage caused by their minor children, but also to supervisors of mentally or physically handicapped persons and to operators of crèches. The supervisor is liable for damage wrongfully caused by the minor or the handicapped person, unless he can prove that he complied with his supervisory duty or that the injury would also have occurred if that duty had been satisfied. The level of supervision depends on the age of the child (the younger the child, the more vigilant the supervisor has to be) or on the character of the handicap. See in more detail nr 1602–1605.

According to § 831 the employer is liable for damage caused by his employees unless he can prove that he was not negligent in selecting, instructing, and supervising the employee (*Haftung für den Verrichtungsgehilfen*). Such an escape route for the employer is not available in English and French law and the provision has been strongly criticized for being too employer-friendly. It is not surprising, that the BGH in its well-known masterly way has developed other ways for holding employers liable for damage caused by their employees in the framework of their business. This has in fact deprived the employer of the escape route which the legislator provided him in §831. It has also brought the German employer's liability in line with the rules in France and England; see nr 1606.

---

[72] Deutsch-Ahrens (2002) N 376–379.
[73] BGH 1 December 1981, NJW 1982, 1046 = VersR 1982, 243. Deutsch-Ahrens (2002) N 386–387.

5

England

501 Introduction

501-1 *Common law in England*

The United Kingdom, Member of the European Union, comprises Great Britain, which includes England, Wales and Scotland, and Northern Ireland. It contains three different legal systems of which English law is only one. This chapter will deal with English law, which includes the law of Wales. Scotland[1] and Northern Ireland[2] have their own legal systems, with many similarities but also important differences in comparison to English law. There are, however, no watertight borders between the systems: many of the most important 'English' tort decisions are in fact Scottish, for example the famous case of *Donoghue v Stevenson* (nr 503-1). This is because the House of Lords also hears appeals from the highest civil courts in Scotland (nr 501-3).

England does not have a civil code. The civil law has been mainly developed by the courts in their case law. This system is called common law and dates back to the 11th century, more particularly to the Norman Conquest of England by Duke William of Normandy in the famous Battle of Hastings in 1066. From then on, common law was meant to bring a unitary, national legal system under the auspices and control of a centralized power in the form of a sovereign king.[3] This medieval origin of the current English legal system implies that even today centuries-old cases may still be relevant for legal practice.

The common law system is not run by rules but by cases and precedents. When a common law judge is called to decide a case he will look for a comparable case rather than an applicable rule. Subsequently, he will try to find guidance in the decision given in the comparable case. In finding the rule in common law, the emphasis is on the comparison of the facts of the case and not, as is the case in most continental systems, on the application of an abstract standard. However, these differences between the common law and the

---

[1] See for example Derek Manson-Smith, *The Legal System of Scotland*, 2nd edn. (Edinburgh: Stationery Office, 2001); Joe Thomson, *Delictual Liability*, 3rd edn. (Edinburgh: Tottel, 2004).
[2] See for example Brice Dickson, *The Legal System of Northern Ireland*, 4th edn. (Belfast: SLS, 2001).
[3] Gary Slapper and David Kelly, *English Legal System*, 5th edn. (London: Cavendish, 2001), 3.

continental approach should not be exaggerated. The differences between common law and civil law seem to be on a policy rather than a systematic level (nr 609).

The doctrine of binding precedent refers to the fact that a decision of a higher court will be binding on a lower court.[4] Decisions of the House of Lords, the highest civil and criminal court in England, bind all other courts. The House of Lords was even bound by its own decisions until this rule was abolished by the Lord Chancellor on behalf of his fellow law lords in a Practice Statement in 1966.[5]

Despite the key role of the judge in developing common law, statutes have always played a role in correcting, adapting, or supplementing common law, and their importance seems to be growing. In the area of tort law one may think of the Occupier's Liability Act 1957 and the Occupier's Liability Act 1984 (nr 1504-1), the Highways Act 1980 (nr 1507), the Consumer Protection Act 1987 (nr 1406), the Animals Act 1971 (nr 1402), the Human Rights Act 1998 (nr 1804-3), and the Torts (Interference with Goods) Act 1977. In English law, breach of a statutory duty is considered to be a separate tort with its own rules.[6] See in more detail nr 902.

501-2 *Common law around the world*

Just like the benefits of cricket, the good news of common law has been proclaimed all over the former British Empire, of which the United States, Canada, Australia, and India are perhaps the most prominent examples. The Empire thus established the most extensive form of legal-cultural imperialism. The end of the British Empire did not bring common law in these countries to an end. The legal systems have been preserved after gaining independence and the establishment of the Commonwealth. The Judicial Committee of the Privy Council, whose decisions are also of importance for English law, is still the court of final appeal for a number of the Commonwealth countries. In many Commonwealth

[4] See about precedents Slapper and Kelly, *English Legal System* (2001), 62 ff.
[5] Practice Statements, [1966] 3 All ER 77:

Their Lordships . . . recognise that too rigid adherence to precedent may lead to injustice in a particular case and also unduly restrict the proper development of the law. They propose, therefore, to modify their present practice and, while treating former decisions of this House as normally binding, to depart from a previous decision when it appears to do so.

For instance, in the area of tort law, the House of Lords overruled *Anns v Merton London Borough Council* [1978] AC 728 in *Murphy v Brentwood District Council* [1991] AC 398 (HL). See about these cases nr 503-2.

[6] See Keith Stanton, Paul Skidmore and Jane Wright, *Statutory Torts*, (London: Sweet & Maxwell, 2003); F.A.R. Bennion, *Statutory Interpretation: A Code*, 4th edn., (London: Butterworths, 2002); Sir Rupert Cross, *Statutory Interpretation*, edited by John Bell and George Engel, 3rd edn., (London: Butterworths, 1995); K.M. Stanton, *Breach of Statutory Duty in Tort*, (London: Sweet & Maxwell, 1986).

countries, such as Canada, Australia, and New Zealand, national supreme courts are now established and do not refer to London to learn how to interpret the law. This development has created differences in application between common law countries.

The common roots of common law in so many countries and its common language have stimulated the exchange of information on national developments. In this sense comparative law has already existed for a long time for English lawyers and academics.[7]

It is not surprising that in the US, where traditions do not have the same status as in England, common law rules are applied in a less reluctant and less formal way (they play baseball, not cricket). The impartial French comparative lawyer André Tunc wrote:

The English judge is permanently restrained and may have great difficulty in finding his way toward the desirable solution through precedents which are deemed immovable. The American judge is more willing to bulldoze his way and apply his energy to going forward. This may not be dignified and does not always require great technical capacities, but it produces results.[8]

A paradox is, however, that American legal terminology seems sometimes to be more traditional than in England, especially in matters of procedure. Despite these differences, there are sufficient parallels between the legal systems on both sides the Atlantic to justify some references in this book to American cases and authors.

501-3 *Judiciary*

The highest civil and criminal court in England is the House of Lords.[9] It is the second chamber of Parliament but its judicial tasks are carried out by the independent Judicial Committee of the House of Lords. Since 1876 this committee has been entirely composed of professional people; they are also known as the Law Lords.[10] Thus, the House of Lords as a court was by then slightly removed from the House as a chamber of Parliament.[11]

---

[7] One of the famous examples of a comparative common law handbook on tort law is John G. Fleming, *Law of Torts*, 9th edn. (Sydney: Law Book Co, 1998).

[8] André Tunc, 'The Not So Common Law of England and the United States', *Mod LR* 47 (1984), 169. In the same sense Dobbs I (2001), §15, 28. See also Markesinis and Deakin (2003), 215–235 for a concise overview of American negligence law. See furthermore for instance George Edward White, *Tort Law in America: An Intellectual History*, expanded edn. (New York: Oxford University Press, 2003).

[9] The House of Lords also hears appeals from the Court of Session in Scotland in civil matters. The other 'highest' court is the Judicial Committee of the Privy Council which is the court of final appeal for some of the Commonwealth countries; see nr 501-1.

[10] See Max Barrett, *The Law Lords: An Account of the Workings of Britain's Highest Judicial Body and the Men Who Preside Over It*, (Basingstoke: Macmillan, 2000).

[11] In 2003 the government proposed to make the separation complete and visible by creating a Supreme Court. This proposal, however, received criticism and does not seem to have a high priority for the government any more.

The House of Lords acts as the final court on points of law for the whole of the United Kingdom, except in criminal cases for Scotland.

Usually five Law Lords sit on a case. All of them may deliver a speech to explain the reasons for their decision (appeal allowed or appeal dismissed). The case itself is decided by the majority of the votes of the Lords who sit on the case. This system gives an excellent insight in the way the decision is taken and the speeches of the Law Lords are mostly very eloquent, expressing opinions as regards the legal, practical, cultural, and policy aspects of the case and regularly with a trademark English sense of humour.

However, a downside of the system is that the Law Lords can decide a case on different grounds. It is then hard to establish in which direction the law subsequently will develop. Another downside is that lawyers who want to keep updated with the case law of the House of Lords need to have time at their disposal to read the small monographs of each decision. This is compensated for by the fact that the number of cases before the House of Lords is much smaller than those before the German *Bundesgerichtshof* or the French *Cour de cassation*. The latter courts also comprise a much higher number of judges.

In the majority of civil cases the court of first instance is the local county court.[12] Depending on the value of the claim, the case may also go to the High Court in London and certain large cities. Its work is handled by three divisions, notably the Queen's Bench Division of the High Court deals with contract, tort, and commercial matters. The Divisional Court of the High Court hears appeals from most county courts. Appeals from the High Court, and in certain cases from the county court, have to be brought before the Court of Appeal in England and Wales of which the senior judge is the Master of the Rolls.[13] Appeals from the Court of Appeal are heard by the House of Lords.[14] The issues involved must be of general and public rather than of individual importance, and questions of law rather than questions of fact must be at issue. The lower court may grant leave to appeal to the House of Lords but, if the lower court refuses this leave, a party may seek leave to appeal from the House itself. If the appeal is allowed either by the court below or by the House of Lords itself, the case will be heard by five (sometimes seven) Law Lords. The average duration of a hearing is more than two and a half days.

A special feature is the strike out procedure. This procedure allows a defendant to request the court to dismiss a claim without hearing the facts. In a

---

[12] See for the following also www.publications.parliament.uk and www.dca.gov.uk.

[13] The most famous judge in recent British history, Lord Denning, was Master of the Rolls for many years. He was happier with that post than a post in the more senior House of Lords. He quipped: 'To most lawyers on the bench, the House of Lords is like heaven. You want to get there someday—but not while there is any life in you'.

[14] The rules for civil appeals are laid down in the Appellate Jurisdiction Act 1876 and the Administration of Justice (Appeals) Act 1934. Certain kinds of civil cases may also be brought directly from the High Court to the House of Lords under what is known as the 'leapfrog' procedure, regulated in the Administration of Justice Act 1969.

strike out procedure the court can decide beforehand that the claimant does not have a case even if he can prove the facts he alleges. This procedure is regarded as an important efficiency tool since in English civil procedure the emphasis is on the time-consuming and expensive trial where the case, pleaded by barristers, is heard by the judge. Trials can take many days or weeks and, in complicated cases, even months.[15]

In particular, the existence of a duty of care in the tort of negligence has been challenged in strike out procedures. And in many cases the courts have indeed struck out such claims on the basis that the defendant did not owe the claimant a duty of care, even if the claimant could prove the facts he alleged. This has principally happened in claims for pure economic loss and claims against public authorities. Since the strike out procedure came under fire from the European Court of Human Rights, the House of Lords seems to be inclined to be more cautious with striking out claims against public authorities (nr 1804-4).

The old rules put a heavy burden on the defendant to satisfy the court that the claim was 'frivolous and vexatious' and ought to be struck out. In the new Civil Procedures Rules, rule 24.2 now provides that the court may give summary judgment in favour of a defendant if it considers that 'the claimant has no real prospect of succeeding on the claim.' This new procedure should enable the courts to deal summarily and more easily with truly vexatious proceedings and '... to dispose of weak claims without a full trial in a manner which satisfies the requirements of Article 6 [ECHR].'[16]

Finally, the 'Glorious Revolution' of the 20th century in the United Kingdom has been the Human Rights Act 1998 which entered into force in 2000. This Act, the fruit of Labour coming into power in 1997, obliges the courts to take account of the rights under the European Convention on Human Rights when interpreting the common law. As a consequence of this direct binding effect of the Convention, the development of common law has gained new grounds, particularly in the area of protection of privacy (nr 705-4) and the duty of care of public authorities (nr 1804-4). Before the entering into force of the Human Rights Act in 2000, the European Convention on Human Rights was not incorporated into United Kingdom law and could not be invoked before UK courts. Only an appeal to the European Court and Commission on Human Rights was possible.

501-4 *Legislation and judiciary*

English statutory provisions are in most cases very specific and detailed and rarely contain broader notions or general principles. This has to do with the delicate

---

[15] This contrasts with the mainly written civil procedures on the continent which are generally less costly.

[16] Winfield and Jolowicz (2002), para. 5.3. See also Lord Woolf MR in *Swain v Hillman*, The Times, 4 November 1999, Court of Appeal; Lord Hoffmann in *Arthur JS Hall & Co (a firm) v Simons* [2002] 1 AC 615 at 691; *S v Gloucestershire County Council* [2001] 2 WLR 909, at 935–937. See about Article 6 ECHR and the duty of care of public authorities nr 1804-3.

relationship between legislature and judiciary. The judiciary's capacity to develop common law is limited by Parliament's ability to pass statutes. The narrower and more specific the wording of a statute, the less freedom Parliament leaves for the courts' own interpretation. 'This doctrine of parliamentary sovereignty thus asserts a hierarchical relationship between the judiciary and Parliament in which the judiciary are the inferior body.'[17] But the hierarchy between Parliament and the judiciary is less black and white than the previous remarks suggest.

Firstly, statutes have to be interpreted and their wording is hardly ever crystal clear, all the more given the increase in the quantity of statute law. Though literal interpretation of statutes is the rule, the current opinion has slightly moved away from this starting point. Lord Blackburn added his golden rule to the rule of literal interpretation:

[W]e are to take the whole statute together, and construe it all together, giving the words their ordinary signification, unless when so applied they produce an inconsistency, or an absurdity or inconvenience so great as to convince the Court that the intention could not have been to use them in their ordinary signification, and to justify the Court in putting them in some other signification, which, though less proper, is one which the Court thinks the words will bear.[18]

The courts can go even further in the direction of a purposive approach on the basis of the so-called 'Mischief rule', which strangely enough goes back to the 16th century. In this rule the emphasis is on the purpose of the statute and the intention of the legislator rather than on the words of the statute. However, the Mischief rule is merely applied in cases in which the wording of the statute and the statutory rule are clearly inconsistent or worse.[19]

Secondly, the relationship between the judicial and legislative powers has to find a new equilibrium after the entering into force of the Human Rights Act 1998. Section 3 of this Act requires all legislation to be read so far as possible to give effect to the rights provided under the Convention. Section 2 of the Act requires courts to take into account any previous decision of the European Court of Human Rights. These provisions may invalidate previously accepted interpretations of statutes and in this sense the legislator has provided substantial powers to the judiciary.[20]

On the other hand, the fact that the courts are obliged to take the Strasbourg case law into account has also restricted the courts' freedom to interpret

---

[17] Fiona Cownie, Anthony Bradney and Mandy Burton, *English Legal System in Context*, 3rd edn., (London: LexisNexis UK, 2003), 109. Lord Woolf, 'Droit Public—English Style', *Public Law*, 57 (1995), 67–69, has argued that Parliamentary sovereignty is subservient to the doctrine of the rule of law.   [18] Lord Blackburn in *River Wear Comrs v Adamson* [1977] 2 AC 743, 764–765.
[19] *Davis v Johnson* [1979] AC 264. In *Pepper v Hart* [1993] 1 All ER 42, the House of Lords allowed the courts to use Hansard, in which the House of Commons debates are recorded. See also *Donaghey v Boulton & Paul Ltd* [1968] AC 1, about which Van Gerven (2000), 415–416, in which Lord Reid applied the Mischief rule. See nr 906-1.
[20] Before the entering into force of the Human Rights Act in 2000, the European Convention on Human Rights was not incorporated into United Kingdom law and could not be invoked before UK courts. Only an appeal to the European Court and Commission on Human Rights was possible.

legislation as they wish. This case law directly influences the way the common law is being applied and developed. An example is the way in which Article 8 ECHR (protection of the right to private life) is playing a pivotal role in developing the tort of breach of confidence (nr 705-4). In a more indirect way, the case law on Articles 3 (inhuman treatment) and 6 (access to justice) ECHR has influenced the interpretation of the duty of care in the framework of the tort of negligence (nr 1800).

501-5 *Doctrine*

Academic authors do not play a predominant role in the legal discourse. The main task for academics is considered to be teaching students and doing research. This research, however, was hardly cited by the courts and generally academics stood in somewhat lower esteem than their continental colleagues. This backward position can be explained on historic grounds since common law has been mainly developed by practitioners. Although their position has improved in recent years, academics only play a modest role, much more modest than their German and French counterparts who were involved in the creation of the major civil codes.

The restricted role of the academics prevented the development of more general concepts and formulations, let alone building a logical and comprehensive legal system. Common law has been developed in practice during almost a millennium. Hence, it is not surprising that it is very patchy and fragmented. Still, academics do not seem to be inclined to do construction work in this respect. There is some logic in this because such work is hardly satisfactory in a country with a legal tradition in which conceptual and academic thinking has never been of the utmost importance.

Given the common law system in which cases rather than rules provide the guidelines, it is not surprising that casebooks, the ultimate example of a non-conceptual book, are still very popular throughout the common law world. These case books compile cases under rather broad themes and quote large parts of the decisions, often introduced or followed by brief comments. However, there are also many examples of more conceptually orientated handbooks. The classics are *Salmond and Heuston on the Law of Torts* and *Winfield and Jolowicz on Tort*. A more recent handbook but already classic is *Markesinis and Deakin's Tort Law*. The two latter books also contain comparative analyses with continental legal systems. John Fleming's *The Law of Torts* is the most authoritative comparative handbook in the common law world. The most teachable and thought-provoking books in this area are Tony Weir's *Tort Law* and his *A Casebook on Tort*.[21] Finally, English tort law also has detailed and practice-oriented

---

[21] Tony Weir, *Tort Law* (Oxford: Oxford University Press, 2002); Tony Weir, *A Casebook on Tort*, 10th edn. (London: Sweet & Maxwell, 2004).

commentaries such as *Clerk and Lindsell on Torts* and *Charlesworth and Percy on Negligence*.[22]

In the United States the last edition of the classic *Prosser and Keeton on the Law of Torts* was published in 1984. In 2001 it got a successor in Dan Dobbs' *The Law of Torts*.

502 Origins of tort law

502-1 *Writs*

The three main sources of liability in English law are contracts, unjust enrichment, and torts.[23] A tort provides requirements for liability in a certain factual situation. There are many torts, all with their own field of application and specific requirements. Hence, it is quite common to speak about the *law of torts*, although some authors suggest an emerging generalization of this area of the law and speak about the *law of tort*.

The origin of the tort law system (rather the lack of system) can be found in old English procedural law. To file an action in court one needed a writ, which could only be obtained from the head of the judiciary, the Lord Chancellor. 'Where there was no writ there was no right.'[24] The number of writs was restricted and the art of litigation was to have the applicable writ. Each writ had its own procedural rules and substantive requirements and, if the claimant used the wrong writ, the claim was dismissed even if it could have been awarded on the basis of another writ.

During the 14th century, when it became more and more difficult to gain access to the common law courts, the claimant sought relief from the King (in fact from his Lord Chancellor) in a direct plea. This was the beginning of the development of *equity*. In the course of time equity evolved into a new system with its own forms, rules, and peculiarities and its own category of wrongs, the most significant of which (for current purposes) is breach of confidence (nr 705-4). These equitable wrongs are only now coming to be regarded as torts.

The rigid systems were substantially relaxed by the Common Law Procedure Act of 1852. 'Today the claimant does not necessarily have to specify the particular tort on which he wishes to rely, for the issue is whether what he alleges (in traditional terminology) "discloses a cause of action", *i.e.* a set of facts for which there is a legal remedy.'[25]

---

[22] John Frederic Clerk, William Henry Barber Lindsell and Reginald Walter Michael Dias, *Clerk and Lindsell on Torts*, 18th edn. (London: Sweet & Maxwell, 2000); John Charlesworth and Rodney Algernon Percy, *Charlesworth and Percy on Negligence*, 10th edn., edited by Judge Walton, Roger Cooper and Simon E. Wood (London: Sweet & Maxwell, 2001).
[23] Peter Birks, *Unjust Enrichment*, (Oxford: Clarendon, 2003) See for a comparative perspective Jack Beatson and Eltjo Schrage (eds.), *Unjustified Enrichment*, (Oxford: Hart, 2003).
[24] Salmond and Heuston (1996), 1; Dobbs I (2001), §14, 25.
[25] Winfield and Jolowicz (2002), para. 2.4.

In the course of time the writs got their own names and the different torts with their own requirements came into being, such as assault, battery, nuisance, and negligence.[26] Sometimes they are named after a case, such as the *Rule in Rylands v Fletcher*. Other torts are living in anonymity and there are even wrongs of which it is not clear whether they are torts: 'Thus, as a family group, torts may be divided into those which received names soon after birth, those which seem to be awaiting baptism in their riper years and those whose paternity is uncertain enough to make it doubtful whether they ought to be included in the family at all.'[27] Family life has not always been easy, apparently not even for torts.

502-2 *Torts*

In Salmond and Heuston a tort is classically described as ' . . . a species of civil injury or wrong.(. . .). A civil wrong is one which gives rise to civil proceedings—proceedings, that is to say, which have as their purpose the enforcement of some right claimed by the plaintiff as against the defendant.'[28] The emphasis is on the procedural rights a tort provides. For American tort law, Dobbs gives the following definition: ' . . . a tort is conduct that amounts to a legal wrong and that causes harm for which courts will impose civil liability.'[29] This is more comparable to a continental approach while focusing on the wrongful conduct.

Most torts require either intention or negligence. Strict liability is very rare in English law (nr 506). Trespass to the person requires intention. If the claimant cannot prove intention he may try to file an action on the tort of negligence which, obviously, requires negligent conduct. However, this tort also requires the existence of a so-called duty of care as well as damage (nr 503).

Not every tort requires damage. This goes for different kinds of trespass: trespass to the person (assault, battery, false imprisonment), trespass to goods and trespass to land, and to certain other torts as well (eg libel). These torts are actionable *per se* (nr 504). This is useful when someone is bothered by the conduct of another person rather than by the damage caused and wants the court to issue an injunction in which the defendant is ordered to stop his conduct.

Torts also differ in the remedy provided. An injunction is for instance an equitable remedy (nr 1201-1). Furthermore, the limitation period for actions may differ under the Statute of Limitations: sometimes it may be too late for an injunction but not too late to recover damages.

Finally, the defendant's defences can differ. For instance the proof of self-defence would clear the defendant from liability not only in an action for assault and battery but also in an action for libel: the victim of a verbal attack has a right

---

[26] Salmond and Heuston (1996), 1; Winfield and Jolowicz (2002), para. 2.2.
[27] Winfield and Jolowicz (1994), 54; Dobbs I (2001), §1, 1.
[28] Salmond and Heuston (1996), 8.   [29] Dobbs I, (2001), §1, 1

to respond.[30] Acting in good faith is not a defence. In a case of assault the defendant may argue that his beating was prompted by good motives and that the claimant deserved it but it is not a proper defence. See about trespass to the person nr 504.

The case by case approach of tort law and the lack of generalization imply the risk of lacunae. Until quite recently one of these lacunae could be found in the protection of immaterial personal interests, particularly privacy. It may seem odd but, until the early 21st century, English law did not contain a general rule on the protection of privacy (nr 705-4).

502-3 *Trespass and case*

Initially, the most important writs were for trespass and trespass on the case (briefly: case). These two forms of action are in fact the ancestors of most torts.[31] The basic difference was that trespass required direct physical contact and that indirectly caused damage could only give rise to a claim on the basis of trespass on the case. The classical example was that there was trespass if someone threw a piece of wood and it hit someone; there was case if nobody was directly hit but later someone stumbled over the piece of wood. According to Salmond and Heuston, an

...injury is said to be direct when it follows so immediately upon the act of the defendant that it may be termed part of that act; it is consequential, on the other hand, when, by reason of some obvious and visible intervening cause, it is regarded, not as part of the defendant's act, but merely as a consequence of it.[32]

From this latter category of trespass on the case the tort of negligence has been developed (nr 503).

Initially, an action on trespass to the person only required that the claimant proved a 'direct injury caused by the act of the defendant'. If the claimant succeeded, the defendant was liable unless he could prove some defence, eg that the patient had given his consent for the surgery.[33] However, this rule did not apply to damage caused by traffic accidents: in such a case the claimant had to prove that the defendant had caused the damage intentionally or negligently.[34]

Since the 1960s an action on trespass to the person (also in cases other than traffic accidents) generally requires intention. The first step was taken in *Fowler*

[30] *Turner v Metro-Goldwyn-Mayer Pictures Ltd* [1950] 1 All ER 449, 470, per Lord Oaksey.
[31] John H. Baker, *An Introduction to English Legal History*, 4th edn. (London: Butterworths, 2002); David J. Ibbetson, *An Historical Introduction to the Law of Obligations*, (Oxford: Oxford University Press, 1999).
[32] Salmond and Heuston (1996), 5–6. See also Winfield and Jolowicz (2002), para. 2.3; Winfield, *The Province of the Law of Tort*, (Cambridge: Cambridge University Press, 1931), 11–14; Dobbs I, (2001), §14, 25–26; *Hutchins v Maugham* (1947) VLR 131, 133.
[33] Winfield and Jolowicz (2002), para. 4.26.
[34] *Holmes v Mather* (1875) LR 10 Ex 261; Winfield and Jolowicz (2002), para. 4.27.

v Lanning in which the claimant stated that he was injured by a shot from the
defendant but he did not mention whether this shooting was intentional or
negligent. His claim was dismissed and it was decided that in trespass to the
person the burden of proving fault was on the claimant. Diplock J went a step
further: 'Trespass to the person does not lie if the injury to the plaintiff, although
the direct consequence of the act of the defendant, was caused unintentionally
and without negligence on the defendant's part. Trespass to the person on the
highway does not differ in this respect from trespass to the person committed in
any other place.'[35]

Six years later the Court of Appeal adopted this opinion, holding that fault in
the framework of trespass to the person meant intention and not merely negligence. Frank Cooper, driving his Jaguar, hit the legs of Doreen Letang, while
she was sunbathing on a piece of grass near a hotel car park. More than three
years passed before Doreen issued a writ which meant that her negligence claim
had expired. She therefore relied on battery, for which the general limitation
period is six years. The Court decided that, not only in traffic cases but generally,
the rule was that in cases of trespass to the person the claimant had to prove
intention. Lord Denning said: ' . . . when the injury is not inflicted intentionally,
but negligently, I would say that the only cause of action is negligence and not
trespass.'[36] So, Doreen did not get compensation for her injured legs since her
claim for negligence was expired and her claim for battery was dismissed for lack
of intention on the part of the driver.

This decision effectively marked the end of liability in trespass for uninten-
tional personal injury. From this time on, the proper action was negligence. In
negligence, the claimant has to show that the defendant breached a duty of care,
but in trespass to the person he must prove that the defendant intentionally
inflicted direct injury.[37] See about the tort of negligence nr 503; see about
trespass nr 504.

503 Tort of negligence

503-1 *History*

Unlike the continental systems, English tort law did not start from a generalized
conception of liability for negligence. English tort law is still rather fragmented
and consists of many more or less specific liability rules each with their own fields

---

[35] *Fowler v Lanning* [1959] 1 QB 426, 439.

[36] *Letang v Cooper* [1965] 1 QB 232, 240; Markesinis and Deakin (2003), 414–415.

[37] Winfield and Jolowicz (2002), para. 4.26 ff. In the same sense Buckley LJ in *SCM (United Kingdom) Ltd v Whittall Ltd* [1971] 1 QB 337, 357 and Croom-Johnson LJ in *Wilson v Pringle* [1986] 3 WLR 1, 6. See also Dobbs I (2001), § 26, 50 and Salmond and Heuston (1996), 7.

of application. However, over the 20th century the courts have developed the tort of negligence into a general liability rule.

The tort of negligence springs from trespass on the case (nr 502-3). It required and still requires that the wrongdoer owed the victim a duty of care, which implies the existence of a relationship between the claimant and the defendant previous to the infliction of harm.[38] This duty of care is the most characteristic and most disputed element of the tort of negligence.

Initially there were only specific duty situations but in the 19th century judges attempted to formulate a general principle. For instance, Brett MR in *Heaven v Pender* said that if

... one person is by circumstances placed in such a position with regard to another that everyone of ordinary sense who did think would at once recognise that if he did not use ordinary care and skill in his own conduct with regard to those circumstances he would cause danger of injury to the person or property of the other, a duty arises to use ordinary care and skill to avoid such danger.[39]

The most famous generalization was made by Lord Atkin in *Donoghue v Stevenson* in 1932. A woman became ill after drinking ginger beer. It was alleged that the bottle had contained the decomposed remains of a snail which in its last moment must have slipped into the bottle. The woman claimed damages from the manufacturer of the ginger beer on the basis of the tort of negligence. The majority of the House of Lords decided that the manufacturer owed the consumer a duty of care. Lord Atkin looked further than the product liability case and said:

... in English law there must be, and is, some general conception of relations giving rise to a duty of care, of which the particular cases found in the books are but instances. (...). The rule that you are to love your neighbour becomes in law, you must not injure your neighbour; and the lawyer's question, Who is my neighbour? receives a restricted reply. You must take reasonable care to avoid acts or omissions which you can reasonably foresee would be likely to injure your neighbour. Who, then, in law is my neighbour? The answer seems to be—persons who are so closely and directly affected by my act that I ought reasonably to have them in contemplation as being so affected when I am directing my mind to the acts or omissions which are called in question.[40]

This *Atkinian neighbour principle* implies that someone owes a duty of care to everyone who, by negligent conduct, can suffer foreseeable damage provided there is sufficient proximity between the wrongdoer and the victim.

Initially, the courts considered Lord Atkin's speech as an *obiter dictum* and they restricted the scope of the decision to the special duties of manufacturers towards consumers. However, even in product liability cases the courts remained

---

[38] Percy H. Winfield, 'The History of Negligence in the Law of Torts', *LQR* 42 (1926), 184–201; Markesinis and Deakin (2003), 75–76; Dobbs I (2001), § 111, 259–263.

[39] Brett MR in *Heaven v Pender* (1883) 11 QB 503, 509.

[40] *Donoghue v Stevenson* [1932] AC 562, 580.

reluctant. It was, for instance, decided that the owner of a house did not owe a duty of care to someone who died in a bath because of a lack of oxygen, caused by the unsafe installation of a geyser.[41] Little by little this restricted view lost ground and in the 1970s the House of Lords stepped up the development of the duty of care and thus the tort of negligence.[42]

503-2 *Rise and fall of the neighbour principle*

In 1970 the speech of Lord Reid in *Home Office v Dorset Yacht Co Ltd* marked an important step in extending the scope of the general duty of care. He said that the time had come that the passage in Lord Atkin's speech about a general duty of care for foreseeable harm '. . . ought to apply unless there is some justification or valid explanation for its exclusion.'[43] In 1978 these words got the House of Lords approval in *Anns v Merton London Borough Council*. According to Lord Wilberforce the question whether there was a duty of care consisted of two parts:

First one has to ask whether, as between the alleged wrongdoer and the person who has suffered damage there is a sufficient relationship of proximity or neighbourhood such that, in the reasonable contemplation of the former, carelessness on his part may be likely to cause damage to the latter-in which case a prima facie duty of care arises. Secondly, if the first question is answered affirmatively, it is necessary to consider whether there are any considerations which ought to negative, or to reduce or limit the scope of the duty or the class of person to whom it is owed or the damages to which a breach of it may give rise.[44]

Lord Wilberforce's *two-stage principle* marked the summer of the duty of care[45] but soon clouds appeared and the House of Lords began to withdraw from its position. In 1986 in *The Aliakmon* the Law Lords unanimously agreed with Lord Brandon of Oakbrook, who said:

. . . that Lord Wilberforce was dealing, as is clear from what he said, with the approach to the questions of the existence and scope of a duty of care in a novel type of factual situation which was not analogous to any factual situation in which the existence of such a duty had already been held to exist. He was not, as I understand the passage, suggesting that the same approach should be adopted to the existence of a duty of care in a factual situation in which the existence of such a duty had repeatedly been held not to exist.[46]

---

[41] *Travers v Gloucester Corporation* [1947] KB 71.
[42] See also *London Graving Dock Co v Horton* [1951] AC 737, 757. Winfield and Jolowicz (2002), paras 5.5–5.6; Markesinis and Deakin (2003), 76–77.
[43] *Home Office v Dorset Yacht Co Ltd* [1970] AC 1004, 1027; see also *Central Asbestos Co Ltd v Dodd* [1973] AC 518. Winfield and Jolowicz (2002), para. 5.6.
[44] *Anns v Merton London Borough Council* [1978] AC 728, 751–752; see also *Arenson v Casson, Beckman, Rutley & Co* [1977] AC 405, 419.
[45] See also *Junior Books Ltd v Veitchi Co Ltd* [1983] AC 520 about which nr 710.
[46] Lord Brandon in *Leigh and Sillivan Ltd v Aliakmon Shipping Co Ltd* (*The Aliakmon*) [1986] AC 785, 815.

It is beyond doubt that this interpretation of the *Wilberforce principle* is contradictory to Lord Wilberforce's words and intention. As a result of the decision in *The Aliakmon*, *Anns* lost its meaning for the general duty of care, and in 1991 the Lords formally overruled *Anns* in *Murphy v Brentwood District Council*. The House of Lords could do this more easily considering that the Defective Premises Act 1972 imposed liability upon the builder of a dwelling transmissible from one owner to the other. Lord Bridge said: 'It would be remarkable to find that similar obligations... applicable to buildings of every kind and subject to no such limitations or exclusions as are imposed by the 1972 Act, could be derived from the builder's common law duty of care.'[47]

503-3 *Current situation*

Starting from a case by case approach the tort of negligence has, in the course of the 20th century, evolved to a general rule for liability for death, personal injury, and property loss. But the tort has not evolved into a general liability rule regardless of the harm suffered.

Currently, the duty of care is still a difficult hurdle to take in cases of pure economic loss (nr 714), mental harm (nr 704), damage caused by an omission (nr 808), and liability of public bodies (nr 1804).[48] In these and other novel situations the so-called *Caparo* test has to be passed. In the *Caparo* case the House of Lords created three hurdles to be taken before a duty of care can be established: (i) the harm must be reasonably foreseeable, (ii) there has to be proximity between the claimant and the defendant, and (iii) imposing a duty of care has to be fair, just, and reasonable.[49] Though these elements are most contested in the above-mentioned categories, even in cases of personal injury or property damage, policy considerations might lead to the ultimate conclusion that the existence of a duty of care has to be denied: '... it has been settled law that the elements of foreseeability and proximity as well as considerations of fairness, justice and reasonableness are relevant to all cases whatever the nature of the harm sustained by the plaintiff.'[50]

[47] *Murphy v Brentwood District Council* [1991] AC 398 at 480 (HL). This decision was strongly criticized, for instance by B.S. Markesinis and S. Deakin, 'The Random Element of their Lordships' Infallible Judgment: An Economic and Comparative Analysis of the Tort of Negligence from *Anns* to *Murphy*', *Mod LR*, 55 (1992), 619. See furthermore *Governors of the Peabody Donation Fund v Sir Lindsay Parkinson & Co Ltd* [1985] AC 210; *Investors in Industry Ltd v South Bedfordshire District Council* [1986] QB 1034; *Curran v Northern Ireland Co-Ownership Housing Association Ltd* [1987] 2 WLR 1043; *D & F Estates Ltd v Church Commissioners* [1988] 3 WLR 368.

[48] Winfield and Jolowicz (2002), paras 5.31–5.52.

[49] *Caparo Industries plc v Dickman* [1990] 2 AC 605, about which nr 714-1. According to the Privy Council in *Yuen Kun Yeu v Attorney General of Hong Kong* [1988] AC 175, 191 proximity means '... the whole concept of necessary relationship between the plaintiff and the defendant'. Winfield and Jolowicz (2002), para. 5.9; Salmond and Heuston (1996), 203; Markesinis and Deakin (2003), 87–91.

[50] Lord Steyn in *Marc Rich & Co AG v Bishop Rock Marine Co Ltd* [1996] 1 AC 211, [1995] 3 WLR 227, [1995] 3 All ER 307 (HL).

The difference with the *Wilberforce principle* is the change in approach: whereas Lord Wilberforce accepted a duty of care *unless* there was a good reason not to do so, since *Caparo* a duty of care is only accepted *if* there is a good reason to do so.[51]

Though the general approach is thus rather reluctant, there are also cases in which a new duty of care was accepted. For instance, in *Spring v Guardian Assurance plc*, the House of Lords held that the writer of a reference might be under a duty of care to the subject of the reference although until then it was assumed that liability in such a case could only be based on libel and malicious falsehood which required proof of malice.[52]

It is clear, then, that the seemingly objective criterion of the duty of care hides an important policy discussion: 'It is, I think, at bottom a matter of public policy which we, as judges, must resolve. This talk of "duty" or "no duty" is simply a way of limiting the range of liability for negligence.'[53] The House of Lords' reluctance seems to be inspired by a number of factors: fear to open the floodgate of claims, fear for far-reaching consequences of general concepts, a desire to return to traditional, small-scale categories of distinct and recognizable situations as guides to the existence of a duty of care. The common factor in these considerations is a policy approach which is, compared with the general approaches in France and Germany, conservative and free market oriented (nr 609).[54]

503-4 *Relationship between the requirements*

It is generally assumed that the tort of negligence consists of three elements: a duty of care, a breach of that duty and consequential damage. An authoritative definition of the tort of negligence can be found in Winfield and Jolowicz: 'Negligence as a tort is the breach of a legal duty to take care which results in damage to the claimant.'[55] See about causation and damage nr 1104 and 1202-3.[56]

---

[51] According to Markesinis and Deakin (2003), 88, the House of Lords

... stated that in 'novel' cases courts should not make a general assumption of prima-facie duty but should, instead, seek to develop the law 'incrementally and by analogy with established categories' of already decided cases. The courts thus turned their back on the broad formulations adopted in *Anns* and *Dorset Yacht* and confined *Donoghue v Stevenson* to cases of physical damage.

[52] *Spring v Guardian Assurance plc* [1995] 2 AC 296; see also *Perrett v Collins* [1998] 2 Lloyd's Rep 255 and the case law on liability of public bodies, about which nr 1804-4. Winfield and Jolowicz (2002), para. 5.13.

[53] Denning LJ in *Dorset Yacht Co Ltd v Home Office* [1969] 2 QB 412, 426. See also F.H. Lawson, 'The Duty of Care in Negligence: A Comparative Study', *Tulane LR*, 22 (1947), 113; Winfield and Jolowicz (2002), para. 5.6; Markesinis and Deakin (2003), 83–85; Salmond and Heuston (1996), 205–206.

[54] See for instance the excerpts of the main speeches in *Caparo Industries plc v Dickman* [1990] 2 AC 605, [1990] 1 All ER 568, in Van Gerven (2000), 51–52.

[55] Winfield and Jolowicz (2002), para. 5.1. See also Markesinis and Deakin (2003), 74–76; Salmond and Heuston (1996), 196.

[56] Dobbs I (2001), § 114, 269, divides the third requirement in 'causal connection' and 'proximate and actual damage'. In the same sense Markesinis and Deakin (2003), 74–76; Salmond and Heuston (1996), 218–222, consider the scope of the duty to be a separate requirement.

In this tort the requirement of negligence is embodied in the *breach of duty*. A person breaches his duty of care when he fails to act as a reasonable man would have acted (nr 804–805). However, as has been said, the establishment of damage caused by negligent conduct is not sufficient for liability. It is also required that the person who acted negligently owed the victim a duty of care. Lord Edmund Davies said: 'In most situations it is better to be careful than careless, but it is quite another thing to elevate all carelessness into a tort. Liability has to be based on a legal duty not to be careless.'[57]

The interrelationship between the different requirements for liability under the tort of negligence can be illustrated with the famous American case *Palsgraf v Long Island Railroad* from 1928. Employees of a railroad company helped a passenger to get onto the train but when doing so a packet fell out of the passenger's hands. The packet appeared to contain fireworks and it exploded. At a distance from the place of the accident, the air pressure caused some large scales to fall on a certain Ms. Palsgraf. She lodged a claim for damages against the railroad company but the New York Supreme Court dismissed her claim. Cardozo CJ said: 'The conduct of the defendant's guard, if a wrong in its relation to the holder of the package, was not a wrong in its relation to the plaintiff standing far away. Relative to her it was not negligence at all. Nothing in the situation gave notice that the falling package had in it the potency of peril to persons thus removed.'[58]

Opinions about how to classify this case diverge. Salmond and Heuston think it is a matter of scope of the duty, whereas Markesinis and Deakin consider the *Palsgraf* case as a matter of causation.[59] Winfield and Jolowicz consider:

In some cases there is no doubt whatever that the defendant's conduct was negligent towards someone; what is seriously in issue is whether the defendant was negligent towards the claimant and this is most conveniently considered in terms of duty; in other cases there is no doubt that if the defendant was negligent at all then he was negligent towards the claimant and these cases are most conveniently discussed in terms of breach. If there is a duty and a breach then the extent of the liability to *that claimant* will be considered as a matter of remoteness.[60]

Lord Denning said about the relationship between the three requirements: 'It seems to me that they are simply three different ways of looking at one and the same problem.'[61]

[57] Lord Edmund Davies in *Moorgate Mercantile Co Ltd v Twitchings* [1977] AC 890, 919. See also Salmond and Heuston (1996), 198; Dobbs I (2001), §226, 577–578.
[58] *Palsgraf v Long Island Railroad* (1928) 162 NE 99. The English equivalent is *Bourhill v Young* [1943] AC 92, about which nr 704.
[59] Salmond and Heuston (1996), 218–219; Markesinis and Deakin (2003), 208–210.
[60] Winfield and Jolowicz (2002), paras 5.17–5.18.
[61] Lord Denning in *Roe v Minister of Health* [1954] 2 QB 66, 85.

504 Intentional torts to the person

504-1 *Torts*

Trespass to the person involves direct and intentional interference with a person's body or liberty.[62] Torts in this field concern battery, assault, harassment (Protection from Harassment Act 1997), residuary trespass (*Rule in Wilkinson v Downton*), malicious prosecution, false imprisonment, defamation (libel and slander), and breach of confidence. Most of these torts are actionable *per se*, which means that the claimant does not have to prove damage; the proof of the committed tort is sufficient.[63] In such a case nominal damages can be awarded; these damages do not have to reflect the actual damage suffered (see nr 1202-3).

Battery is the intentional and direct application of force to another person, whereas assault is an act which causes the claimant reasonable apprehension of the infliction of a battery on him by the defendant.[64] These definitions imply that, for instance, driving a car at a person is an assault but driving it against him is a battery.[65] In the 18th century case of *Cole v Turner* it was held that even 'the least touching of another in anger is a battery'[66] but in *Collins v Wilcock* Goff LJ, the later Law Lord, said that:

... most of the physical contacts of ordinary life are not actionable because they are impliedly consented to by all who move in society and so expose themselves to the risk of bodily contact. So nobody can complain of the jostling which is inevitable from his presence in, for example, a supermarket, an underground station or a busy street; nor can a person who attends a party complain if his hand is seized in friendship, or even if his back is, within reason, slapped.[67]

However, this can be different in case of hostile touching or an unwanted kiss.[68]

Historically, assault required some bodily movements; threatening words alone were not accepted as an assault.[69] But in *R v Ireland & Burstowe* a different view was taken. Someone had made silent phone calls to several women. The women consequentially suffered from depressive illness. It was held that '... an assault might be committed by words or gestures alone, depending on the circumstances; and that where the making of a silent telephone call caused fear of immediate and unlawful violence, the caller would be guilty of an assault.'[70]

---

[62] Winfield and Jolowicz (2002), para. 4.1.

[63] Markesinis and Deakin (2003) 414; *Stanley v Powell* [1891] 1 QB 86.

[64] Winfield and Jolowicz (2002), para. 4.4.

[65] For other examples of these torts see Winfield and Jolowicz (2002), para. 4.4.

[66] *Cole v Turner* [1704] 6 Mod. Rep.149; see also Winfield and Jolowicz (2002), para. 4.6.

[67] *Collins v Wilcock* [1984] WLR 1172 at 1177; See also Winfield and Jolowicz (2002), para. 4.6.

[68] *Wilson v Pringle* [1987] QB 237; *R v Chief Constable of Devon and Cornwall* [1982] QB 458; Markesinis and Deakin (2003) 416–417; Winfield and Jolowicz (2002), para. 4.6.

[69] *R v Meade* (1823), 168 ER 1006; this case is also known as *Meade's & Belt's Case*; Winfield and Jolowicz (2002), para. 4.10.

[70] *R v Ireland & Burstowe* [1997] 3 WLR 534.

Today, s. 1(1)(2) of the Protection from Harassment Act 1997 may provide a firmer, statutory footing for such torts. The defendant must have pursued a 'course of conduct' (at least two material acts, including speech) which he knew or ought reasonably to have known amounted to harassment.

A defendant will be liable for *false imprisonment* if he has restricted the claimant's movement in every direction and irrespective of whether or not the claimant was aware of such a restriction.[71] It has been suggested that liability is strict.[72] Support for this view may be gleaned from a decision which holds that mistaken imprisonment is nonetheless false imprisonment,[73] as well as from the need to ensure the widest possible protection in law to individual liberty and from the notion that false imprisonment is actionable *per se*.

In order to successfully make out the tort of *malicious prosecution*, the claimant must show that the defendant had initiated an unsuccessful criminal prosecution against him.[74] Firstly, this requires that the defendant did not have an honest belief, based upon objective facts, as to the claimant's guilt.[75] Secondly, the defendant's initiation of the prosecution must have been inspired by a malicious personal motive, alien to any genuine desire to assist the police in the enforcement of justice; this is a question for the jury.[76] The tort is not actionable *per se*: the claimant must show that the proceedings had reached such a stage that they had caused him damage to his reputation, his person (imprisonment or the threat of imprisonment), or his property (costs and court expenses).[77]

There was no remedy for intentionally but indirectly caused damage to the person until such a remedy was established in the *Rule in Wilkinson v Downton* at the end of the 19th century. By way of a practical joke, a woman was told that her husband had broken his legs in an accident. This message caused her shock. The joker was held liable for intentionally indirectly caused damage.[78] This rule has also been applied in a case involving a stalker.[79]

Defamation encompasses the torts of libel (the defamatory statement was in permanent and visible form) and slander (a temporary and audible statement is sufficient for liability). The common backbone is that there was a defamatory statement referring to the claimant that was published by the defendant.[80] The defamatory nature of the statement is answered by the judge (is the statement

---

[71] *Bird v Jones* [1845] 7 QB 742; *Murray v Ministry of Defence* [1988] 1 WLR 692.

[72] Markesinis and Deakin (2003), 426–427.

[73] *R v Governor of Brockhill Prison, ex parte Evans* (No 2) [2001] 2 AC 19.

[74] *Martin v Watson* [1996] 1 AC 74.   [75] *Herniman v Smith* [1938] AC 305, 316.

[76] *Mitchell v Jenkins* (1835) 5 B & Ad 588; 110 ER 908.

[77] *Savill v Roberts* (1698) 5 Mod. Rep. 394; *Martin v Watson* [1996] 1 AC 74; *Rayson v South London Tramways Co* [1893] 2 QB 324.

[78] *Wilkinson v Downton* [1897] 2 QB 57. See about the low impact of this case Mark Lunney, 'Practical Joking and Its Penalty: *Wilkinson v Downtown* in Context', *Tort Law Review*, 10 (2002), 168 ff. See also *Wong v Parkside Health NHS Trust* [2001] EWCA Civ 1721; *Home Office v Wainwright* [2002] QB 1334.   [79] *Khorasandjian v Bush* [1993] QB 727.

[80] See *Newstead v London Express Newspaper Ltd* [1940] 1 KB 377: claimant shared the same name as the person mentioned in the statement.

capable of being defamatory in law?) and the jury (is the statement in fact defamatory in the circumstances?).[81] Examples of defamatory statements include allegations that the claimant had been raped, was 'insane', or simply that he was 'hideously ugly'.[82]

504-2 *Defences*

Several defences are available in the torts of assault and battery and an important one is consent. If, for example in medical treatment ' . . . there is consent to the contact there is no battery.'[83] Concerned by the need to protect doctors, courts have *de facto* reversed the burden of proof as compared with defences in general: it is for the patient to show lack of effective consent, this being analysed as a definitional element of the intentional tort.[84] A doctor who informs the patient 'in broad terms' of the nature of the procedure has a valid defence,[85] whereas fraud or misrepresentation by the doctor will vitiate any purported consent.[86] Non-disclosure by a doctor of the risks of an operation is treated by the courts as a claim in negligence and not battery.[87]

If there is no consent, the principle of necessity can be used as a 'fall back' defence, for instance as regards mentally disabled or unconscious patients who are incapable of giving a valid consent in law.[88] The defendant must show that there was a necessity to act without it being practicable to communicate with the victim, and that the defendant's intervention was in the 'best interests' of the victim.[89] The notion of 'best interests' has been construed widely by the courts in order to authorize the sterilization of a mentally incapable woman[90] and even the bone marrow transplant from a victim to her sister.[91] However, necessity remains essentially a tightly knit defence and the courts are reluctant to use it in respect of a victim of sound mind who expressly refuses her consent, for example to a Caesarean section.[92] The necessity defence must not encroach upon the victim's personal autonomy.

Closely connected to the defence of consent is the defence of *volenti non fit injuria* (no injury can be done to a willing person). It is often used as regards

---

[81] See Fox's Libel Act 1792 which has been followed in civil trials. See also *Lewis v Daily Telegraph* [1964] AC 234, at 259–260.
[82] See *Youssoupoff v Metro-Goldwyn-Mayer Pictures Ltd* (1934) 50 TLR 581; *Morgan v Lingen* (1863) 8 LT 800 and *Berkoff v Burchill* [1996] 4 All ER 1008 respectively.
[83] Winfield and Jolowicz (2002), para. 4.7.
[84] *Freeman v Home Office* (No 2) [1984] 1 QB 524, 537–9, 557.
[85] *Chatterton v Gerson* [1981] 1 QB 432, 443.
[86] *Sidaway v Board of Governors of the Bethlem Royal Hospital* [1984] 1 All ER 1018.
[87] Markesinis and Deakin (2003), 294–295.
[88] *Re T (Adult, Refusal of Treatment)* [1993] Fam. 95; Markesinis and Deakin (2003), 419; Winfield and Jolowicz (2002), para. 4.8.   [89] *Re F* [1990] 2 AC 1, per Goff LJ.
[90] *Re F* [1990] 2 AC 1, per Goff LJ.
[91] *Re Y (Mental Incapacity: Bone Marrow Transplant)* [1996] 2 FLR 787.
[92] *St George's Healthcare NHS Trust v S* [1998] 3 All ER 673.

sports and games: by accepting the rules of the game, players accept injuries that can occur during the game. An obvious example is the boxer who enters the boxing ring and hence accepts intentional hits from his opponent.

Statutory defences can also be used. For example the Criminal Law Act 1967, s. 3(1) states: 'A person may be use such force as is reasonable in the circumstances in the prevention of crime, or in effecting or assisting in the lawful arrest of offenders or suspected offenders or of persons unlawfully at large.' Thus there may also be the possibility for a defendant to plead self-defence, provided that there is a degree of proportionality between the threat and his reaction to it.[93]

The publisher of a defamatory statement may avail himself of several defences specific to the tort of defamation. For example, the defence of 'fair comment' is open to defendants who published a statement in good faith and thus 'genuinely believed the opinion they expressed'.[94] The role of the fair comment defence is essentially to protect the freedom of expression.[95] Next, it must be shown that the legal, moral, or social duty of the defendant to publish the statement is reciprocated by a legitimate interest in the public receiving it.[96] Hence, the burden of proof of reasonable conduct is thus reversed as compared with traditional negligence claims.[97] In the end, each case is essentially about trying to balance the freedom to disseminate and receive political information on the one hand, with the claimant's competing right to preserve his reputation on the other.[98]

505 Intentional interference with goods

505-1 *Trespass to land*

Torts in this area are trespass to land, trespass to goods, conversion, private nuisance, deceit, injurious falsehoods, and passing off.

Trespass to land is '. . . the name given to that form of trespass which is constituted by unjustifiable interference with the possession of land.'[99] An action for an injunction or for damages on the basis of trespass to land only requires that the trespasser acted voluntarily and caused the damage directly. There is trespass to land if someone sets foot on another person's land without permission, if he throws something on land that does not belong to him, or pastures his cattle on that land. In these cases the trespass implies liability; intention is not required.

The question of whether the damage was caused directly was at stake in *Southport Corporation v Esso Petroleum Co Ltd.* An oil tanker ran aground on

---

[93] *Lane v Holloway* [1968] 1 QB 379.
[94] *Branson v Bower* (No 2) [2002] 2 WLR 452 (paras 7 and 23–28).
[95] *Branson v Bower* (No 2) supra (paras 17–20).
[96] *Adam v Ward* [1917] AC 309, 334; *Loutchansky v Times Newspapers* (Nos 2, 3, 4 and 5) [2002] EMLR 14, paras 31, 32.   [97] Markesinis and Deakin (2003), 678–682.
[98] Markesinis and Deakin (2003), 678–682.
[99] Winfield and Jolowicz (2002), para. 13.1. See also Salmond and Heuston (1996), 40–41; Markesinis and Deakin (2003), 444–454.

a sandbank and in order to be able to get away the captain ordered the discharge of 400 tons of oil into the sea. The oil drifted ashore and polluted Southport beach. The majority of the judges decided that the damage was not caused directly but only after the oil had drifted ashore and they dismissed the trespass claim. The victim had to rely on the tort of negligence (nr 503) and private nuisance (nr 506-1).[100]

A person who uses the highway in an ordinary way of 'passing and repassing' does not commit a trespass against the private owner of the subsoil but he commits a trespass if he exceeds that purpose.[101] For example, in *Hickman v Maisey* it was held that the defendant had exceeded the ordinary and reasonable use of a highway by using it as a base from which to spy on the performance of race horses on the claimant's land.[102] However, in *DPP v Jones* it was held that it was not a trespass to participate in a peaceful assembly on the highway as long as it was reasonable and caused no obstruction.[103] This decision illustrates how the medieval concept of trespass has been adapted by human rights: the case was decided in line with Articles 10 (freedom of expression) and 11 (freedom of assembly) ECHR.[104]

A trespass can also be committed by entering into someone else's airspace. A leading case is *Kelsen v Imperial Tobacco Co*.[105] Defendants erected on their own property an advertising sign which extended about eight inches into the claimant's airspace. McNair J held that this created a trespass to land.[106] In *Bernstein of Leigh v Skyviews & General Ltd*,[107] it was held that it is not a trespass at common law if an aircraft flies several hundred feet above a house.[108] In this case the defendant took photographs of Lord Bernstein's residence from an aircraft. In his action before the court Lord Bernstein claimed that the maxim of *cujus est solum ejus est usque ad coelum* (the owner of the land owns the land from down up to the heaven) should be applied, but the court did not agree and dismissed the claim. Currently, s 76 of the Civil Aviation Act 1982 holds that if an aircraft flies at a reasonable height, this does not create a trespass into the airspace. However, if anything falls upon the land from an aircraft it is a trespass even if the aircraft was flying at a reasonable height. In such a case damage is compensable without proof of fault.[109]

In order to escape liability, the defendant may avail himself of several defences: permission (the claimant had granted him a licence to enter the land),

---

[100] *Southport Corporation v Esso Petroleum Co Ltd* [1956] AC 218.
[101] *Harrison v Duke of Rutland* [1893] 1 QB 142 at 158, per Kay LJ.
[102] *Hickman v Maisey* [1900] 1 QB 752; Markesinis and Deakin (2003), 446.
[103] *DPP v Jones* [1999] 2 AC 240; Winfield and Jolowicz (2002), para. 13.5; Markesinis and Deakin (2003), 446.   [104] Markesinis and Deakin (2003) 447.
[105] *Kelsen v Imperial Tobacco Co* [1957] 2 QB 334, 2 All ER 343.
[106] Winfield and Jolowicz (2002), para. 13.7; Markesinis and Deakin (2003), 445.
[107] *Bernstein of Leigh v Skyviews & General Ltd* [1978] QB 479.
[108] Winfield and Jolowicz (2002), para. 13.7.   [109] Markesinis and Deakin (2003), 445.

necessity (for example, the necessary destruction of a building to prevent a fire from spreading), and inevitable accident.[110]

The claimant has an action for recovery of the land (the so-called *Doe d. A v B action*)[111] and a supplementary action for damages in respect of loss (of profit) he suffered as a result of being kept out of possession.[112] He is also entitled to use reasonable force in order to eject a trespasser. This, however, does not include knocking him off a ladder.[113]

505-2 *Trespass to goods*

Section 1 of the Torts (Interference with Goods) Act 1977 provides for a statutory tort of 'wrongful interference with goods', including trespass and conversion in respect of chattels. Salmond and Heuston describe trespass to goods (also called trespass to chattels) as the tort consisting ' . . . in committing without lawful justification any act of direct physical interference with goods in the possession of another person'.[114] In this sense the main remedy is an injunction which enables an owner to stop unauthorized use of his properties or possessions. Intention or negligence is not required.[115]

As is the case in trespass to the person and land, trespass to goods is actionable *per se* but there is some authority to the effect that trespass to goods requires proof of some damage.[116] However, if the owner lodges a claim for damages he has to prove intention or negligence. *National Coal Board v JE Evans & Co (Cardiff) Ltd* was about Evans who damaged a cable while digging a ditch. He did not know nor ought he to have known where the cable was exactly located. This implied that negligence could not be established and according to the Court of Appeal this was an obstacle for liability based on trespass to goods. Since it was also an obstacle for an action on the tort of negligence, the claim was dismissed.[117]

If goods are not directly infringed, or if the claimant did not have possession of the goods at the date of the alleged meddling, the claim cannot be based on trespass but has to be grounded on *conversion*: 'A conversion is an act or complex series of acts, of wilful interference, without lawful justification, with any chattel in a manner inconsistent with the right of another, whereby that other is

---

[110] *Thomas v Sorrell* (1674) 124 ER 1098; *Re F* [1990] 2 AC 1, 74, per Goff LJ; *Southport Corp v Esso Petroleum Co Ltd* [1953] 2 All ER 1204, 1212 (Devlin J).
[111] Markesinis and Deakin (2003), 449.
[112] *Inverugie Investments Ltd v Hackett* [1995] 1 WLR 713.
[113] *Collins v Renison* (1754) 96 ER 830.
[114] Salmond and Heuston (1996), 94. See also Winfield and Jolowicz (2002), para. 17.3; Markesinis and Deakin (2003), 436–438. See furthermore the mainly procedural reform by the Torts (Interference with Goods) Act 1977 (SI 1977 No. 1910 and SI 1978 No. 579).
[115] See for instance *Wilson v Lombank* [1963] 1 WLR 1294.
[116] Winfield and Jolowicz (2002), para. 17.3; *Everitt v Martin* [1903] NZLR 29; see also Markesinis and Deakin (2003), 437.
[117] *National Coal Board v JE Evans & Co (Cardiff) Ltd* [1951] 2 KB 861.

deprived of the use and possession of it'.[118] Unlike trespass, which is founded on possession (a fact), the tort of conversion is founded on property—that is a denial of the claimant's legal title. Liability for conversion is strict: the defendant need only intend the voluntary act in question and not necessarily the consequences of this act for the claimant. For example, an auctioneer who sells the claimant's property in good faith on behalf of a client with no title cannot plead ignorance or mistake in order to escape liability.[119] A claimant's remedy lies in an action for damages representing the market value of the chattel as well as any special loss. However, it is also open to him to request the equitable remedy of specific restitution as well as an interlocutory order for delivery pending full trial.[120]

The tort of *deceit* is committed wherever a person knowingly makes a false statement of fact with the desired result that another person acts upon it to his detriment. False statements include walking into a shop dressed in an official dress which one is not entitled to wear, making a true statement which later becomes false, and even remaining silent when one was under a duty to correct a false impression.[121] The defendant must have been aware of this falsity or at least been subjectively reckless (that is to say personally indifferent) as to its correctness: mere negligence is not enough.[122] It must also be the case that the defendant intended to invite reliance by the claimant upon his false statement.[123] However, it is not necessary that the defendant's statement be the condition *sine qua non* which urged the claimant to act to his detriment: it is enough that it had influence him in some way, and the fact that the latter had sought independent advice does not amount to a *novus actus interveniens*.[124]

Injurious falsehood may be thought of as 'defamation against a person's goods'. There are, however, several differences as compared with the tort of defamation. The burden is on the claimant: to show the falsity of the statement (in defamation it is the defendant who must prove the veracity of the statement to avail himself of the 'truth' defence); to establish the defendant's malice (in the case of malicious falsehood);[125] and to show that he has suffered actual pecuniary loss (and not simply injury to feelings).[126] It is also significant that, whereas the claimant in a defamation action has an action only as against the defendant personally, the successful outcome of an action for injurious falsehood is a right against the defendant and his estate.[127]

---

[118] Salmond and Heuston (1996), 97–98. See also Winfield and Jolowicz (2002), para. 17.6; Markesinis and Deakin (2003), 438–443.   [119] *Consolidated Co v Curtis* [1892] 1 QB 495.

[120] Section 3(2)–(3) of the Torts (Interference with Goods) Act 1977.

[121] *R v Barnard* (1837) 173 ER 342; *Incledon v Watson* (1862) 175 ER 1312; *Schneider v Heath* (1813) 170 ER 1462.

[122] *Derry v Peek* (1889) 14 AC 337.   [123] *Peek v Gurney* (1873) LR 6 HL 377.

[124] *Downs v Chappell* [1997] 1 WLR 426 (per Hobhouse LJ).

[125] *Serville v Constance* [1954] 1 WLR 487, 490

[126] *Royal Baking Powder Co v Wright Crossley & Co* (1901) 18 RPC 95, 99

[127] Markesinis and Deakin (2003), 696.

506 Rules of stricter liability

506-1 *Public and private nuisance*

'Few words in the legal vocabulary are bedevilled with so much obscurity and confusion as "nuisance". Once tolerably precise and well understood, the concept has eventually become so amorphous as well nigh to defy rational exposition.'[128]

There is an important distinction between private and public nuisance:

Private nuisance traditionally was, and still is confined to invasions of the interest in the use and enjoyment of land, although occasionally an occupier may recover for incidental injury from a public nuisance sustained by him in the exercise of an interest in land, such as for illness caused by noxious gases from an adjoining factory. A *public* nuisance, in contrast, consisting in an interference with a public or common right, such as an obstruction of the highway, can confer a cause of action on a private individual, although no rights or privileges in land of his have been invaded at all.[129]

Private nuisance primarily covers damage to land and perhaps goods but no personal injury, whereas a public nuisance claim can also be for personal injury and economic loss.[130]

Both private and public nuisance are considered to be forms of strict liability since it is not required that the defendant knew about the risk.[131] However, in most cases the interests of the claimant and the defendant have to be balanced, which is comparable to what happens in the framework of establishing negligence (nr 805).

Private nuisance is an act which, without being trespass, interferes with a person in the enjoyment of his land or premises or a right which he has over the land of another person.[132] Examples of private nuisance are producing smoke, noise and smells, or causing crowds to assemble and thus preventing other persons from entering their land or premises. Private nuisance also plays an important role as regards liability for damage to the environment. The available remedies are the award of damages and an injunction, though the award of the latter is solely within the discretion of the court. See in more detail about private nuisance nr 1413-2.

---

[128] Fleming (1998), 457. See also Markesinis and Deakin (2003), 455; Dobbs II (2001), 1319–1320.

[129] Fleming (1998), 459–460. See also Winfield and Jolowicz (2002), para. 14.4: Private nuisance may be described as unlawful interference with a person's use or enjoyment of land, or some right over, or in connection with it.' [130] Markesinis and Deakin (2003), 490.

[131] It follows from *Cambridge Water Co v Eastern Counties Leather plc* [1994] 2 WLR 75, about which Van Gerven (2000), 172–175 and nr 1413-2 that the way the damage occurs needs to be foreseeable. [132] Winfield and Jolowicz (2002), para. 14.1 ff.

According to Lord Denning, *public nuisance* 'covers a multitude of sins, great and small'.[133] It is not only a tort but also a crime. There is public nuisance if an unlawful act or omission causes annoyance to the general public, such as failing to repair a highway, carrying on an offensive trade, keeping a disorderly house, selling food unfit for consumption, or holding an badly organized pop festival.[134]

A fine illustration of the distinction is *Tate & Lyle Industries Ltd v GLC*.[135] Defendants constructed ferry terminals in the Thames, which caused the landing stage of the claimant to get silted up. This compelled to perform dredging operations. His damages claim in private nuisance was rejected since the stage itself was not affected and the claimant did not have any property rights with regard to the riverbed. However, the claimant's costs were compensated on the basis of public nuisance, since the silting up had infringed the public right of navigation which was a right of the claimant and of all other users of the river.

A further requirement for public nuisance is that the damage is special ('particular' would be more accurate, see nr 1806),[136] which means that the damage is not related to general inconveniences: the damage has to be distinct from that of the general public.[137] The prevailing view is probably '... to allow the action whenever the claimant can show that the right he shares with others has been appreciably more affected by the defendant's behaviour.'[138] This is for instance the case if a passer-by is injured by the collapsing wall of a building. However, if this person had been in the building at the moment of the collapse, he would not have a claim on public nuisance, because in that case there is no infringement of a common right. The victim has to base his claim on the tort of negligence.[139]

Though this is not entirely clear, a claim for special damages based on public nuisance generally requires negligent conduct. However, negligence is presumed and it is up to the defendant to prove that he did not act negligently.[140] As regards falling natural projectiles, liability seems to be less strict (nr 1504-2).

The tort of public nuisance is a good illustration of the way in which common law has developed: 'The mess that public nuisance is in is partly due to the haphazard and piecemeal growth of a legal system developed solely by practitioners without the kind of doctrinal backing that universities provided to the law of the Continent of Europe.'[141] See more about public nuisance in nr 1504-2.

---

[133] Lord Denning LJ in *Southport Corporation v Esso Petroleum Co Ltd* [1954] 2 QB 182, 196.
[134] Winfield and Jolowicz (2002), para. 14.2.
[135] *Tate & Lyle Industries Ltd v Greater London Council* [1983] 2 AC 509. See also Stephen Tromans, 'A Tale of Sugar and Silt, or, Muddy Waters in the House of Lords', *CLJ* (1984), 21–23. See furthermore *Jan de Nul (UK) v AXA Royale Belge SA* [2002] 1 Lloyd's Rep 583 (CA).
[136] Markesinis and Deakin (2003), 491.
[137] Winfield and Jolowicz (2002), para. 14.3; Fleming (1998), 461.
[138] Markesinis and Deakin (2003), 491.   [139] Fleming (1998), 461–462.
[140] Markesinis and Deakin (2003), 490.
[141] Markesinis and Deakin (2003), 489. See also Von Bar (1998), N 269: '... why should it not be possible simply to replace these diffuse and ill-defined categories with interests protected by the general duty of care in negligence?'

506-2 *Other rules of stricter liability*

More than other legal systems, English tort law is based on negligence. Rules of strict liability have not gained a firm foothold. Even liability for road traffic accidents is still exclusively based on negligence. In this area, strict liability based on trespass to the person has already been abolished in the early days of motoring (nr 502-3).

Apart from private and public nuisance, covered in the previous section, strict liability rules only apply to liability for damage caused by animals (nr 1402) and employees (nr 1606-4), though based on different rules. Initially, the *Rule in Rylands v Fletcher* was also strict but it has been toned down into a rule in which negligence plays a more dominant role. Despite its legacy as one of the famous rules in English law, the rule has not been successfully invoked in the past 60 years (nr 1414-2).

The only strict liability rule of the 20th century came from Brussels: the European Directive as regards liability for damage caused by a defective product has been transposed into English law in the Consumer Protection Act 1987 (nr 1406).

Breach of statutory duty is often considered to be a form of strict liability but whether this is the case depends upon the wording of the statute: it may be strict or negligence-based, or somewhere in between. Important categories of strict statutory provisions concern the regulation of health and safety at the workplace (determining the employer's liability towards his employee) and the regulation of road traffic. See about these specific rules of strict liability nr 902-4. Hence, though *common law* has only a few general strict liability rules, *statutory provisions* can also provide for strict liability. A rather general rule in this respect, at least to English standards, can be found in the Environmental Protection Act 1990, holding the polluter of land strictly liable for the damage caused (nr 1414-2).

6

Ius Commune

A INTRODUCTION

601 Overview

The foregoing chapters have shown interesting similarities and differences between the various tort law systems. In fact, the European picture is even more complicated since only three national tort law systems have been dealt with. It is now time to draw together the lines of the previous chapters.

Twenty years ago this chapter would have been called *Comparative observations*. Nowadays, it needs to be called *ius commune* in order to reflect the search for a common European private law, including a common European tort law (nr 201). Indeed, at certain levels and in certain areas there is enough common ground between the legal systems to discuss further harmonization. However, in other areas and on a policy level, important differences remain between the various national approaches and this will make it more difficult to find common ground.

In this chapter first of all the quest for a European *ius commune* in tort law will be pursued. The idea of a European *ius commune* based on Roman law fundaments goes back to medieval times but did not survive the rise of the national states (nr 602). When the drawbacks of too much nationalism became apparent after two World Wars, the increasing European cooperation endorsed the idea of a revival of a European *ius commune* (nr 603).

A number of differences between the legal systems deserve attention in order to put the quest for harmonization into perspective. Firstly, the tort law systems will be compared on the level of rules: fault and strict liability rules (nr 604–606) as well as the differences between codification and common law, and the pivotal role of the courts in developing tort law (nr 607). Secondly, a comparison will be carried out on the level of the differences behind the rules, ie legal-cultural differences, differences in policy approach and differences in the role of rights (nr 608–610).

In some European academic bedrooms, dreams are dreamed not only of a European *ius commune* but also of a European Civil Code. However, the question is whether such an ambitions project would be feasible. For this reason the positions of the European Commission and European Parliament will be explained (nr 611). Subsequently, the case for harmonization and codification will be discussed (nr 612), and finally, an agenda for further research and discussion will be proposed (nr 613).

B THE QUEST FOR A EUROPEAN *IUS COMMUNE*

602 From old to new *ius commune*

Wisdom teaches us that there is new nothing under the sun.[1] This wisdom also applies to the idea of a European *ius commune*, more particularly to the discussion of whether European private law systems are converging or ought to converge. This idea of a *ius commune* received a firm backing in the framework of European integration in the second half of the 20th century.

The concept goes back to the *ius commune* that was applied throughout Europe from the 12th century onward, and which was mainly based on Roman law.

Roman legal learning soon formed a major component of what has come to be known as the Roman-Canon *ius commune*. Law, in the Middle Ages, was not conceived of as a system of rules enacted for, and exclusively applicable within, a specific territory, and thus the *ius commune* provided the cornerstone for the emergence of an essentially unified, European legal tradition.[2]

The traditional *ius commune* disintegrated in the 18th century with the rise of rationalism and nationalism. The new rulers wanted the identity of the nation to be supported by a national codification, starting with Prussia in 1794, France in 1804 (nr 301-2) and Austria in 1811. This was the beginning of a process of nationalization of the rules of private law. In the course of the next centuries it encouraged the rules to start diverging.[3]

[1] Ecclesiastes, Chapter 1:9.
[2] Reinhard Zimmermann, 'An Introduction to German Legal Culture' in Wener F. Ebke and Matthew Finkin (eds.), *Introduction to German Law*, (The Hague, London: Kluwer International; München: Beck, 1996), 2–3. See also Reinhard Zimmermann, 'Savigny's Legacy: Legal History, Comparative Law, and the Emergence of a European Legal Science', *LQR*, 112 (1996), 557 ff.
[3] See also Reinhard Zimmermann, 'Roman Law and the Harmonisation of Private Law in Europe', in *Towards a European Civil Code* (2004), 21–42; Konrad Zweigert and Hein Kötz, *Introduction to Comparative Law*, 3rd edn., (Oxford: Clarendon Press; New York: Oxford University Press, 1998), 138 ff. and 163 ff.

After the First and Second World Wars, the drawbacks of extreme nationalism became obvious, and the need for cooperation instead of pursuing national interests was strongly emphasized. A major European cooperation process was launched with the founding of the Council of Europe (nr 202) and the establishment of what later became the European Union (nr 203). Combined with the globalization of trade, this political development has boosted the internationalization of private law. Talks in the private law village also got a European and an intercontinental dimension.

It was against this political background that the search for a new European *ius commune* began.[4] For some, this search ought to culminate in a new symbol of unity and identity: a European Civil Code. It is thought that such a Code could build bridges between Member States and support a common European identity. The question, however, is whether such a Code is feasible and desirable (nr 612).

603 Search for harmonization

603-1 *Publications and principles*

Since the late 1980s the discourse on a common European private law—which includes the discussion on a common European tort law—has grown extensively. This is not the place to set out this development in detail but two headlines will be mentioned: publications and harmonization initiatives.

Though they do not deal specifically with European private law or European tort law, the Torts section in *The International Encyclopaedia of Comparative Law* and Konrad Zweigert and Hein Kötz's *Introduction to Comparative Law*, the first German edition of which was published in 1969–1971 are nevertheless of major importance.[5] Of similar importance from a historic perspective is Reinhard Zimmermann's *The Law of Obligations. Roman Foundations of the Civilian Tradition*, published in 1990.[6] Another outstanding comparative book in this area is Basil Markesinis' *The German Law of Torts*, the first edition of which was published in 1986.[7]

---

[4] See for an early example Walter Hallstein, 'Angleichung des Privat- und Prozessrechts in der Europäischen Wirtschaftsgemeinschaft', *RabelsZ* 28 (1964), 211–231.
[5] Konrad Zweigert and Hein Kötz, *Introduction to Comparative Law*, 3rd edn., translated into English by Tony Weir (Oxford: Clarendon Press, 1998).
[6] Reinhard Zimmermann, *The Law of Obligations. Roman Foundations of the Civilian Tradition* (Cape Town: Juta, 1990).
[7] Basil S. Markesinis and Hannes Unberath, *The German Law of Torts: a Comparative Treatise*, 4th edn. (Oxford: Hart, 2002). See also Basil S. Markesinis, Werner Lorenz and Gerhard Danneman, *The German Law of Obligations* (Oxford: Clarendon Press, 1997); Gert Brüggemeier, *Common Principles of Tort Law: A Pre-Statement of Law* (London: British Institute of International and Comparative Law, 2004).

One of the first overarching books of modern time in the area of European private law, though primarily from a historic point of view, is Helmut Coing's *Europäisches Privatrecht*.[8] A more future-oriented approach can be found in *Towards a European Civil Code*, the first edition of which was published in 1994.[9]

Since the mid 1990s it has been hard to keep track of the ever-growing amount of publications in this area. In 1996 and 1999 Christian von Bar published his two encyclopaedic volumes on *Gemeineuropäisches Deliktsrecht*. The English translation of these volumes was published in 1998 and 2000 as *The Common European Law of Torts*. In 2000 Walter van Gerven published his *Cases, Materals and Text on National, Supranational and International Tort Law*. As from the late 1990s the European Group on Tort Law, headed by Jaap Spier and Helmut Koziol started to publish a series of books under the (ambitious) title *Unification of Tort Law*.[10] A number of journals are devoted to the topic of European private law, such as the *European Review of Private Law* and the *Zeitschrift für europäisches Privatrecht* (also with articles in English) but articles on this topic are, of course, also published in other law journals and reviews. A major source of information on European tort law, *inter alia* many translated French and German statutes and cases, can be found on the website of Basil Markesinis' Institute of Global Law of University College London.[11] Finally, to complete this incomplete list: regular overviews of publications on European Private Law are provided by Ewoud Hondius,[12] whereas the *European Tort Law Yearbooks*, edited by Helmut Koziol, provide concise overviews of recent tort law developments in most European countries.[13]

In addition to these publications a number of initiatives were taken up in order to study the possibilities to harmonize European private law and to come up with recommendations.[14] One of the best known and most fundamental

---

[8] Helmut Coing, *Europäisches Privatrecht*, 1st vol. (Munich: Beck, 1985) and Helmut Coing, *Europäisches Privatrecht*, 2nd vol. (Munich: Beck, 1989).

[9] Arthur Hartkamp et al. (eds.), *Towards a European Civil Code*, 3rd edn. (The Hague: Kluwer Law International, 2004); See furthermore P.-C. Müller-Graf (ed.), *Gemeinsames Privatrecht in der Europäischen Gemeinschaft* (1993); Jan Smits, *The Making of European Private Law*, (Antwerp: Intersentia, 2002); Wolfgang Wurmnest, *Grundzüge eines europäischen Haftungsrechts* (Tübingen: Mohr, 2003); Nils Jansen, 'Auf dem Weg zu einem europäischen Haftungsrecht', *ZEuP* 2001, 30–65, all with further references

[10] In the series *Unification of Tort Law* (The Hague, London, New York: Kluwer Law International): H. Koziol (ed.), *Wrongfulness* (1998); J. Spier (ed.), *Causation* (2000); U. Magnus (ed.), *Damages* (2001); B.A. Koch and H. Koziol (eds.), *Strict Liability* (2002); U. Magnus and M. Martin-Casals (eds.), *Contributory Negligence* (2004); W.V. Horton Rogers (ed.), *Multiple Tortfeasors* (2004). [11] http://www.ucl.ac.uk/laws/global_law.

[12] Ewoud Hondius, 'European Private Law—Survey 1998–2000', *ERPL*, 8 (2000), 385–416; idem, 'European Private Law—Survey 2000–2002', *ERPL* 10 (2002), 865–900; idem, 'European Private Law—Survey 2002–2004', *ERPL* 12 (2004), 855–899.

[13] Helmut Koziol and Barbara C. Steininger (eds.), *European Tort Law 2002–2004* (Vienna, New York: Springer, 2003–2005).

[14] There may be about a dozen initiatives in this area: Wolfgang Wurmnest, 'Common Core, Grundregeln, Kodifikationsentwürfe, Acquis-Grundsätze—Ansätze internationaler Wissenschaftlergruppen zur Privatrechtsvereinheitlichung in Europa', *ZEuP* 2003, 714–744.

initiatives is the *Lando Commission on European contract law*, named after its Danish founder and chairman Ole Lando. This Commission has completed and published its *Principles of European Contract Law*.[15]

The *Study Group on a European Civil Code* was founded in 1998 by Christian von Bar. It considers itself as the successor of the Lando Commission and aims to deal with the other areas of private law. In 2005 this Group published a draft on *Non-Contractual Liability Arising out of Damage Caused to Another*. At various places in this book reference will be made to this draft.[16]

The University of Trento has set up a project on *The Common Core of European Private Law*. In this framework two working groups are dealing with topics like pecuniary loss and no fault liability.[17]

Last but not least, the *European Group on Tort Law* (formerly known as the Tilburg Group) was founded in 1993 by Jaap Spier and Helmut Koziol. In 2005 this group, currently based in Vienna, published its draft *Principles of European Tort Law* accompanied by an extensive commentary.[18]

These headlines show that the area of European private law generally and European tort law in particular is buzzing with activity. Academic bees are busy collecting the honey of the national flowers and bringing it to the European honeycomb where the queen-bee of European harmony is watching the work with approval.

The various study groups and their respective proposals are private initiatives and do not have an official status. Naturally, the groups primarily consist of academics who are sympathetic towards the idea of harmonization or think that harmonization is in some way desirable. Indeed, the groups have representatives from England and France although these countries are generally not well-known for their keenness to achieve more European harmonization in the area of private law. Also, the final proposals are, of course, a matter of give and take but it is questionable whether the members of these study groups can be considered to have the authority to give and take on behalf of their national legal systems. This is particularly the case when it comes to policy-related matters of which tort law contains quite a few. Hence, the principles are intermediate points for discussion—and excellent ones—rather than the final result of the discussion. See also nr 611–613.

---

[15] Ole Lando and Hugh Beale (eds.) *Principles of European Contract Law—Parts I and II*, (The Hague, London: Kluwer Law International, 2000); Ole Lando (ed.), *Principles of European Contract Law—Part III*, (The Hague, London: Kluwer Law International, 2003).

[16] www.sgecc.net. See Christian von Bar, 'Konturen des Deliktsrechtkonzeptes der Study Group on a European Civil Code', *ZEuP* 2001, 515 ff.; John W.G. Blackie, 'Tort/Delict in the Work of the European Civil Code Project of the Study Group on a European Civil Code', in Zimmermann (ed.), *Grundstrukturen des europäischen Deliktsrecht* (2002), 133–146.

[17] M. Bussani and U. Mattei (eds.), *The Common Core of European Private Law* (The Hague, London, New York: Kluwer Law International, 2003).

[18] www.egtl.org. European Group on Tort Law: *Principles of European Tort Law* (Vienna, New York: Springer, 2005). See Helmut Koziol, 'Die "Principles of European Tort Law" der "European Group on Tort Law"', *ZEuP* 2004, 234–259.

603-2 *Background of the discussion*

Harmonization and the search for a new *ius commune* are at the very heart of the current European private law discourse. However, the preliminary question of whether harmonization is desirable is less discussed. Sometimes it seems that the discussion about a European *ius commune* has divided the academic private law world into believers and unbelievers. The former believe in a new and unified European private law to come, whereas the latter refuse to believe that differences and division will or should be overcome. For many authors, the quest for a new *ius commune* seems to be self-evident. It is understandable, particularly after the end of the Cold War, that the emphasis has been on commonalities and similarities. It was in 1989 that Francis Fukuyama wrote his article on 'the end of history': 'We may be witnessing the end of history as such: that is, the end point of mankind's ideological evolution and the universilation of Western liberal democracy as the final form of human government.' He further argued that the future would be devoted to resolving mundane economic and technical problems.[19] It was against this background that optimism about a united Europe dominated the agenda. Nothing seemed to be more appropriate than to set out to find the holy grail of Europe's *ius commune*.

In addition to this, there is a widespread belief that Europe's national legal systems are converging. This is for instance strongly advocated by Markesinis who argues that there is

... a convergence of solutions in the area of private law as the problems faced by courts and legislators acquire a common and international flavour; there is a convergence in the sources of our law since nowadays case law *de facto* if not *de jure* forms a major source of law in both common and civil law countries; there is a slow convergence in procedural matters as the oral and written types of trials borrow from each other and are slowly moving to occupy a middle position; there may be a greater convergence in drafting techniques than has commonly been appreciated ... ; there is a growing rapprochement in judicial views.[20]

One of the few authors who explicitly dared to advocate against harmonization is Legrand who considers particularly the differences between common law and civil law to be unbridgeable:

... if one insists on the cognitive structure of the common law world as it differs from that of the civil law world (...) one must see that, in addition to being rudimentary, the analysis of European legal integration at the level of posited law suggesting a convergence of legal systems is misleading. Indeed, if one forgoes a surface examination at the level of

---

[19] Francis Fukuyama, 'The End of History', *The National Interest*, 16 (1989), 4, 18.
[20] B.S. Markesinis, 'Learning from Europe and Learning in Europe, in B.S. Markesinis, *The Gradual Convergence*', (1994), 30. See also James Gordley, 'Common law und civil law: eine überholte Unterscheidung', *ZEuP* 1993, 498–518; Jan Smits, *The Making of European Private Law*, (Antwerp: Intersentia, 2002), 73–105.

rules and concepts to conduct a deep examination in terms of legal *mentalités*, one must come to the conclusion that legal systems, despite their adjacence within the European Community, have not been converging, are not converging and will not be converging (. . .) law as rules must have a sense of its limits: cultural integration or convergence is a promise that law is simply ontologically incapable of fulfilling.[21]

The discussion on this topic is very diverse, and opinions are expressed in all kinds of shades between the two singled out above. This discussion on convergence and divergence seems to be an empirical question (*Sein*), the answer to which requires extensive research into case law and legislation in Europe over a number of years. However, the discussion also has a strong policy angle (*Sollen*). In other words, the debate is not just about what is desirable for Europe(an private law): harmony or diversity? Rather, the arguments put forward in this discussion are expressions of legal-political visions about the direction Europe and national laws should take.[22]

In this respect there is also a difference in the way harmonization is supported in the three legal systems. Whereas France and England are generally reluctant, Germany seems to be the most supportive country in the harmonization quest. The reasons for this are threefold.

Firstly, from a systematic point of view, many German authors love to draft legal texts and to systematize the law. This interest fuels the motor of harmonization.[23] The French are generally less interested in drafting structured and detailed codification because their Civil Code, at least in the area of tort law, is a code of general principles rather than rules, let alone detailed rules. And the English never had a codification. Though they are interested in details, they are generally less inclined to think about systematizing the law.

Secondly, from an interest point of view, Germany is at the heart of Europe and is perhaps the country with the greatest interest in European cooperation. The French strongly support the European idea but seem to be less convinced when European interests do not run parallel with French interests (see also nr 1407-2 about the French reactions to an ECJ decision on product liability). Also, a European Civil Code will probably deviate strongly from the French *Code civil*. Finally, in England the continent is still called *Europe* as if it is something to which it does not belong to. Although the United Kingdom is one of the most cooperative and loyal Member States, for example when it comes to implementation of Directives, its general approach to Europe is practical rather than a matter of principle.

---

[21] Pierre Legrand, 'European Legal Systems are not Converging', *ICLQ*, 45 (1996), 63–64. See also Pierre Legrand, 'A Diabolical Idea', in *Towards a European Civil Code* (2004), 245–272.

[22] See for instance Pierre Legrand, 'European Legal Systems are not Converging', *ICLQ*, 45 (1996), 64: 'I wish to argue that such convergence, even if it were thought desirable (which, in my view, it is *not*), is impossible on account of the fact that the differences arising (. . .) are irreducible' (emphasis original).

[23] The Germans found supporters in Dutch academics who became familiar with drafting techniques and discussions surrounding them in the 45 years they worked on their Civil Code of 1992.

Finally, there is the political argument. If English and French law are supposed to be at the opposite ends of the European tort law continuum (nr 609), German law takes a kind of middle position. Though German tort law is closer to the French system, a European Civil Code would, in fact, preserve most of its national features and allow it to gain much greater influence in Europe.

C VARIOUS LEGAL RULES

604 Fault liability

604-1 *Requirements*

There is a striking variety in the number of requirements for liability based on negligent conduct in each country: one in France *(faute)*, two in England *(duty of care* and *breach of duty)* and three in Germany *(Tatbestand, Rechtswidrigkeit*, and *Verschulden)*. At first glance, one could assume that a French victim is better off than a German victim since the latter has to prove two more requirements than his French fellow-sufferer.

A closer look reveals that to a certain extent the total of formal requirements in the different systems is the same: the French *faute* is comparable to the English combined concepts of *duty of care* and *breach of duty* and to the German combination of *Tatbestand, Rechtswidrigkeit*, and *Verschulden*. In fact, in all systems the basic requirement for fault liability is intentional or negligent conduct. The main difference is that English and German law contain additional requirements which imply that not every kind of misconduct is sufficient for liability. These requirements are aimed at restricting the scope of application of the rule, but they do not play an important role in cases of personal injury and property damage caused by the wrongdoer's active conduct. However, it has to be stressed that precisely in these areas French tort law mainly applies rules of strict liability (nr 303–304). In other words: although the theoretical differences in the framework of fault are small, in practice a French claimant has a much higher chance of obtaining compensation than an English or—to a somewhat lesser extent—German claimant, because he can rely more often on rules of strict liability.

The ECJ has set two conditions as regards liability for breach of Community law: the conferment of rights on individuals and a sufficiently serious breach (nr 207). Whereas the latter requirement generally refers to a kind of unlawful or negligent conduct, the former requirement is also known within the tort of breach of statutory duty and aims to restrict the scope of application of the liability rule (nr 905).

604-2 *Casuism and conceptualism*

In the area of fault liability two systems can be distinguished. Casuistic systems, like the ones in Germany and England, limit the scope of application of fault liability beforehand by specific requirements established by tradition or designed by the legislator. These specific requirements are the German *Tatbestand* (nr 402) and the English *duty of care* (nr 503). German and English tort law are called casuistic systems since the extra requirements both relate to certain categories of cases.

Conceptualistic systems, like the French one, depart from a general rule and leave it to the courts to set the limits of application, for instance by using the requirement of causation. The basis of conceptualism in French law is the general rule for fault liability, embodied in articles 1382 and 1383 CC. These rules apply to all cases in which someone's conduct causes damage to another person. The requirements as such (*faute, dommage, lien de causalité*) do not restrict the field of application.

The Belgian comparatist Limpens wrote that casuistic systems tend to formulate a definite but necessarily incomplete list, whereas conceptualistic systems adopt a less precise notion which tends to cover a wider area and to be more akin to reality.[24] In other words: in the casuistic model the reasoning of the judge tends to be inductive; in the conceptualistic model it tends to be deductive.[25]

In practice, the differences between casuism and conceptualism are not as big as they seem to be from a theoretical point of view. Particularly in the area of personal injury and property damage, the German § 823 BGB and the English tort of negligence both lean in the direction of a general liability rule. The obstacles erected by the English tort law system and by the German legislator have not held back the courts in either country from setting the hurdles aside if they deemed this to be necessary.[26]

The systems set out from opposite positions, concept versus case, but they meet somewhere in the middle. According to Limpens the function of the law has always been to distinguish in social matters between shadow and light. But between these two there are uncertain cases, bathed by an indistinct light. The casuistic technique,

---

[24] Limpens, 'De la faute et de l'acte illicite en droit comparé', in *Mélanges en l'honneur de Jean Dabin* (Brussels: Bruylant, 1963), volume II, 723–741, nr 33: 'L'une tend à dresser une liste *sûre*, mais forcément incomplète. L'autre adopte une *notion moins précise*, mais susceptible de couvrir un champ plus vaste et de mieux "coller" à la réalité.'

[25] *The International Encyclopaedia of Comparative Law* (1983), Chapter 2, nr 4, distinguishes between the *single-rule approach* (France), *restricted pluralism* (Germany), and *unrestricted pluralism* (England). This distinction focuses on the number of negligence rules. The distinction between casuism and conceptualism focuses on the character of the rules. Both distinctions run mainly parallel since the single-rule approach has a conceptualistic character and the pluralistic approaches have a casuistic character.

[26] See for Germany E. von Caemmerer, *Wandlungen des Deliktsrecht* (Karlsruhe: Mueller, 1960), 526: 'Der Rechtsschutz der gewährt wird, ist heute nicht weniger umfassend als in den Rechten des allgemeinen Deliktstatbestandes.'

presumptuously, confines itself to encompassing the zone of light and ignores the less well defined cases. The conceptualistic technique, on the other hand, penetrates more deeply into the half-lit zone and gives the judge the power to discern the peaks that deserve interest in his view.[27]

604-3 *Unlawfulness and fault*

The scope of application of fault liability needs to be limited since it is undesirable that each kind of loss or harm and each kind of harmful negligent conduct can give rise to liability. Casuistic systems like England and Germany capture the necessary restrictions in specific requirements, whereas conceptualistic systems like France had to develop restrictions in the case law.

Though the concept of unlawfulness or wrongfulness is at the heart of each tort law system, only Germans dare to speak openly about this mystery. The fact that not all harmful conduct should lead to liability is in Germany embodied in the requirement of unlawfulness (*Rechtswidrigkeit*). If someone's conduct fulfils a *Tatbestand*, his conduct is, in principle, unlawful unless the defendant can invoke a ground of justification. This concept is, however, also very problematic in that it has caused a subtle and complicated discussion on direct and indirect infringements on the one hand, and on the relation between *Rechtswidrigkeit* (unlawfulness) and *Verschulden* (intention and negligence) on the other (nr 402). This is certainly not a discussion to be transplanted to a European level.[28]

The concept of unlawfulness has also gained some foothold in the French doctrine (*fait illicite*), particularly as regards liability for omissions, but it has not greatly restricted the scope of fault liability.[29] In France, the control mechanism to prevent infinite liability is neither the *faute* (nr 302) nor damage (*dommage*) (nr 1202-1), but causation (*lien de causalité*) (nr 1105).

In English law, unlawfulness does not play an explicit role in establishing liability but ' . . . it is at the foundation of it. The law of torts is, after all, the law of 'civil wrongs'. But from another point of view the concept is almost

---

[27] Limpens, 'De la faute et l'acte illicite en droit comparé', in *Mélanges en l'honneur de Jean Dabin*, volume II (Brussels: Bruylant, 1963), volume II, 723–741, nr 33:

L'office de la loi a été de tout temps de distinguer dans la matière sociale les zones d'ombre et de lumière. Mais entre les deux il y les cas incertains, baignés d'une lumière imprécise. La technique casuiste, présomptueusement, se borne à cerner la zone de lumière et ignore les cas mal précisés. La technique conceptualiste, au contraire, pénètre plus avant dans la zone de pénombre, et donne au juge le pouvoir de discerner les sommets qui lui paraissent dignes d'intérêt.

[28] Gerhard Wagner, in Zimmermann (ed.), *Grundstrukturen des europäischen Deliktsrecht* (2002), 215 ff. speaks about the backwardness of the German unlawfulness doctrine (*Rückständigkeit der deutschen Rechtswidrigkeitslehre*).

[29] See for instance Le Tourneau (2004), nr 6705 : 'La faute est un comportement illicite qui contrevient à une obligation ou à un devoir imposé par la loi ou par la coutume.'

meaningless since 'wrong'/ 'wrongfulness' may be regarded as merely a short-hand description of the situations in which tort liability is imposed.'.[30]

In this book most of the issues dealt with by the concept of unlawfulness will be described in Chapter 7 in which chapter it will be investigated which limitations the law has set to 'pure' fault liability, particularly as regards the interests to be protected by tort law. In this respect, each system grapples or has grappled one way or another with liability for pure economic loss (nr 711–714), liability for psychological damage (nr 704 and 1211), damage caused by omissions (nr 808), and liability of public bodies (Chapter 18).[31]

605 Stricter liability

The structure of fault liability may vary in the legal systems; this goes even more for the structure of strict liability. Although initially rules of strict liability were considered to be exceptions to the rule of fault liability, they have gained a firm foothold in continental tort law during the 20th century.[32] French tort law contains several general provisions and German tort law holds a high number of specific provisions. In England, rules of strict liability are rare, although specific statutory rules may provide for micro strict liability rules within the framework of breach of statutory duty. There is a tendency to consider negligence to be the only sound basis for liability. The development of the *Rule in Rylands v Fletcher*, which was born as a rule of strict liability but in later life lost most of its strict faculties, is a good illustration (nr 1414-2).

The distinction between conceptualism and casuism (nr 604-2) also applies to strict liability. The legal system with the most general rule for fault liability (France) contains two general rules of strict liability, whereas the country with limited fault liability rules (England) only has a few general rules of strict liability and a high number of specific statutory strict provisions. The general approach in France is considered to be an exception in Europe.[33]

---

[30] Rogers, in Koziol (ed.), *Unification of Tort Law: Wrongfulness* (1998), 39. See also David Howarth, 'The General Conditions of Unlawfulness', in *Towards a European Civil Code* (2004), 607–644.

[31] Konrad Zweigert and Hein Kötz, *Introduction to Comparative Law*, 3rd edn., translated from the German by Tony Weir, (Oxford: Clarendon Press; New York: Oxford University Press, 1998), 596–628. See also E. von Caemmerer, *Wandlungen des Deliktrechts*, (Karlsruhe: Mueller, 1960), 526.

[32] See also Konrad Zweigert and Hein Kötz, *Introduction to Comparative Law*, 3rd edn., (Oxford: Clarendon Press; New York: Oxford University Press, 1998), 646–684.

[33] Koch and Koziol, in *Unification of Tort Law: Strict Liability* (The Hague, London, New York: Kluwer Law International, 2002), 395. The drafters of the PETL have proposed a sophisticated general rule of strict liability for abnormally dangerous activities in art. 5:101:

(1) A person who carries on an abnormally dangerous activity is strictly liable for damage characteristic to the risk presented by the activity and resulting from it. (2) An activity is abnormally

Strict liability has reached its peak in France with general strict liability rules for things and for persons. The courts derived these rules, though contrary to the intention of the legislator, from article 1384 s. 1 CC. These rules establish liability unless the defendant can prove a kind of *force majeure*, whereas contributory negligence of the victim may lower the amount of compensation to be paid (nr 303–305).[34] These defences are not even allowed as regards the almost absolute liability for damage caused in road traffic accidents (nr 1404-1).

German law does not have a general strict liability for defective goods or for dangerous substances. The many specific rules of strict liability are almost all embodied in special Acts. The adoption of these rules was mainly dictated by the practical needs of the time. Their history illustrates from which time particular risks were considered to need deterrence by a rule of strict liability. For instance, in the 19th century strict rules were imposed on the operators of railways; and strict liability for environmental harm was enacted in the second half of the 20th century. The rules of strict liability are characterized by low abstraction and many details. Liability for persons is not strict but established with a rebuttable presumption of negligence (nr 404).

English law only has strict liability for damage caused by defective products (the European Directive), by animals, and by employees. In England the development of a more general strict liability rule on the basis of the *Rule in Rylands v Fletcher* was brought to a halt in the 1940s in *Read v Lyons* by allowing negligence and foreseeability to play a more important role. Fleming said that the most damaging effect of this decision was that ' . . . it prematurely stunted the development of a general theory of strict liability.'[35] Indeed, since World War II it has never been successfully invoked by claimants (nr 1414-2). No rule of strict liability applies to the compensation of damage caused in road traffic accidents. The risks of the 20th century have occurred without being noticed by the English legislator. There are, however, specific strict statutory provisions that apply to road traffic accidents and employer's liability for damage suffered by his employee (nr 902-4).

It is a remarkable course of history that the modern French rule of strict liability for things (nr 303) is quite similar to the old English rule of trespass (nr 504). In both rules the fact that damage is directly caused is, in principle, sufficient for liability to arise unless the defendant can prove *force majeure*. One may wonder which of the two approaches is the 'modern' one and which is the 'old fashioned'.

---

dangerous if a) it creates a foreseeable and highly significant risk of damage even when all due care is exercised in its management and b) it is not a matter of common usage. (3) A risk of damage may be significant having regard to the seriousness or the likelihood of the damage. (4) This Article does not apply to an activity which is specifically subjected to strict liability by any other provision of these Principles or any other national law or international convention.

This provision is less broad than the French general strict liability rule and according to section 4 only supplementary to existing provisions.

[34] Von Bar (1998), N 106–116.   [35] Fleming (1998), 383.

Whereas English law treats strict liability as an outcast on which one should rely in exceptional circumstances only (nr 506), it has assumed great power in France where it reigns as a Sun King, at least in the area of liability for death, personal injury, and property damage (nr 303–306). The general strict liability rule for things is a creation that is to a great extent instrumental in providing compensation to victims of accidents. The different roles which strict liability rules play in the various legal systems reflect important policy differences (nr 609).

See Chapter 10 for more detail about stricter liability.

606 The basic liability rules in the Principles

Both the draft ECC and the PETL hold a basic rule for liability. Article 1:101(1) ECC reads as follows: 'A person who suffers legally relevant damage has a right to reparation from a person who caused the damage intentionally or negligently or is otherwise accountable for the causation of the damage.'

Article 1:101 PETL states:

(1) A person to whom damage to another is legally attributed is liable to compensate that damage. (2) Damage may be attributed in particular to the person a) whose conduct constituting fault has caused it; or b) whose abnormally dangerous activity has caused it; or c) whose auxiliary has caused it within the scope of his functions.

These rules reflect what is supposed to be the basic rule in European *ius commune*, but they do not say much more than that someone can be liable for fault and that he can be strictly liable. This is indeed so basic that one can hardly disagree with such a rule. However, the picture is different if one looks at the current basic rules in the three systems in the area of personal injury law. Approached from this angle the systems have less in common.

The basic rule for the English judge in personal injury law is the tort of negligence. A duty of care will only be assumed in cases of actively caused damage and breach of this duty will be based on the lack of care (nr 503). The German judge, however, will have § 823 I BGB in mind when it comes to the basic rule in his tort law system. This implies either the direct infringement of a right or the breach of an unwritten safety duty (*Verkehrspflicht*, nr 403). This does not only lead to procedural advantages for the claimant; the German courts are also inclined to apply a higher standard of care than the English courts. Finally, in personal injury cases the French judge will hardly be interested in fault liability, and for his basic rule will immediately jump to the strict liability rule of article 1384 al. 1 CC (*responsabilité du fait des choses*) (nr 303).

Another example is liability of public authorities. In England a claim has to pass the test that imposing a duty of care on a public authority is fair, just, and reasonable. In many cases the House of Lords has argued that this was not the case. In German law a normal liability regime for fault applies in which no such barrier as a duty of care exists. The same goes for France, although in this country liability for damage can also be based on strict liability, ie if the damage is caused contrary to the equality principle. These differences reflect the various visions on the role of the State, particularly the difference between an individualistic and a solidarity approach (nr 1811).

One may conclude that on one hand the *structure* of fault liability does not differ considerably, or at least not that much that the differences would be irreconcilable. On the other hand, the *areas* in which fault liability is applied and the level of care do differ strongly. These latter differences seem to be of more importance and seem to be harder to reconcile because of the policy and political aspects involved. In this respect it will not be easy to change ingrained national traditions (nr 608).

607 Common law and codified law

607-1 *Different views on systematization*

Friedmann has described the differences between common law and civil law systems '... as one between logical and empirical methods, between deductive and inductive thinking, between the rule of reason and the rule of experience.'[36] Indeed, major differences seem to exist between systems with a codification (France and Germany) and systems without (England and the European Union). In the former systems, the tort law rules are laid down by the legislator in a more or less structured and general framework, whereas in the latter systems the rules have been fleshed out by the courts in a step-by-step approach which has resulted in a rather fragmented phenomenon. Tony Weir wrote:

One can find principles common to the different legal systems in Europe and offshore islands, but that does not amount to much. One might as well say that all religions are the same in having a God with strikingly common features, characteristically power and duration—though perhaps one might distinguish the legal systems that have only one God, a Code, from those that hearken to a range of voices.[37]

Indeed, an outsider to common law may sometimes find himself lost in fragmentation.

However, it would be an exaggeration to simply juxtapose civil law and common law. The starting point for the English judge may be to look for comparable cases but, according to Lord Denning, he '... proceeds, in our English fashion, from case to case until the principle emerges.'[38] For the civil law judge, on the other hand, the general principles of the continental systems do not

[36] W. Friedmann, '*Stare Decisis* at Common Law and Under the Civil Code of Quebec', *Canadian Law Review*, 31 (1953), 724.
[37] Tony Weir, 'The Timing of Decisions', *ZEuP* 2001, 684.
[38] *Chic Fashions (West Wales) Ltd v Jones* [1968] 2 QB 299, 312, 313.

give the judge much information to go by. Hence, the civil law judge had to build up a body of case law and will thus, just like the common law judge, look for comparable cases to find a basis for his decision.

The common law has been developed over centuries, mainly by practitioners. In contrast to the codifications on the continent, at least until rather recently, academic writing and thinking was hardly relied on by the judiciary. 'The Englishman is naturally pragmatic, more concerned with result than method, function than shape, effectiveness than style; he has little talent for producing intellectual order and little interest in the finer points of taxonomy.'[39] There is concern for the negative consequences of systematic thinking: ' . . . the common law of England has not always developed on strictly logical lines, and where logic leads down a path that is beset with practical difficulties the courts have not been frightened to turn aside and seek the pragmatic solutions that will best serve the needs of society.'[40]

This concern is, however, not so different from that of the German Reichsgericht and BGH, the highest courts in the most system-loving country, when they had to deal with the undesirable consequences of the system the legislator provided in the BGB. The German courts were not afraid to seek pragmatic solutions that could best serve the needs of society (nr 403–404). The lacunae in the legislative system were filled in order to be able to do justice by creating rights and remedies.

Hence, the contrast between common law and codified law is not so much between the courts' approaches (these are generally focused on finding pragmatic solutions, not bound by systematic hurdles but by ideas of justice) but between the level of systematization and the different levels of academic involvement in the development of private law. Whereas the BGB is known as *Professorenrecht* (law made by professors) and the BGH in its decisions extensively discusses opinions of legal authors, English law is still very much practitioners' law. It is true that in the past decades academic publications are increasingly cited or referred to in speeches by the members of the House of Lords. This is not surprising since most judges are now academically educated and not just vocationally trained. However, this does not mean that there is a growing desire to systematize the common law, let alone to codify it. Not by coincidence are casebooks still a popular species of law book in the common law world.

607-2 *Predominance of judiciary over legislator*

Not only is there a difference between common law and codified law, but the legislative approaches on the continent also differ. The tort law provisions of the

---

[39] Tony Weir, 'The Common Legal System', in *International Encyclopedia of Comparative Law*, Volume II: *The Legal Systems of the World: Their Comparison and Unification*, Chapter 2: 'Structure and the Divisions of the Law', René David (ed.), nr 82, 77.
[40] *Ex parte King* [1984] 3 All ER 897, 903 (CA) per Griffiths LJ.

French *Code civil* are very general and loose, and were supposed to be interpreted by the courts in the spirit of the ideas of the French Revolution. The tort law provisions of the German *Bürgerliches Gesetzbuch* are more structured and detailed. The BGB legislator designed the *Tatbestand* system to limit the freedom of the courts and to secure unity in application of the provisions. But this system showed gaps in the requisite protection of interests (omissions, pure economic loss) and was a barrier to adjusting the law to new social and technical developments (protection of personality rights). Therefore, the *Reichsgericht* and the *Bundesgerichtshof* had to knock down the hurdles the legislator had erected and to supplement the statutory liability rules with judicial ones (nr 403–404).

This all shows that tort law is mainly case law which implies that the power of developing this part of the law has been with the courts rather than with the legislator. According to Tunc, the content of tort law historically has been determined by the judges; this continues to evolve even faster because of the desire to respond to social needs.[41] It is impossible for a legislator to draft specific rules that cover all tort law aspects of every day life. Therefore, its starting point can only be to provide general rules and leave the main part of the development of tort law to the courts. In addition to this he can provide legislation in specific areas which he considers needs apposition, either to restrict the protection the case law provides or to enlarge it, for instance by creating rules of strict liability. In this respect important lessons can be learned for the idea of harmonizing private law and tort law by enacting a European Civil Code. The power to create harmony lies not so much with the legislator as with the judiciary.

The pivotal role of the judiciary may also be illustrated with the position of the European Court of Justice. This court increasingly recognizes the benefits of establishing a body of case law which is best illustrated in the *Francovich* case law regarding liability of Member States and individuals for breach of Community law (nr 205). This case law has been developed on the basis of general principles of Community law and an analogous interpretation of the statutory provision as regards liability of the Community institutions (Article 288). As well as this development, however, Community law is strongly fragmented by Brussels' piecemeal approach of Directives regulating small areas using inconsistent terminology. Here, the role of the ECJ is a very modest one. It interprets Directives in isolation from other Directives[42] and does not consider it to be its task to bring more harmony in this area (which would be an impossible task anyway).

It can be concluded that in tort law the differences between a codified system and a common law system are not very great from a systematic point of view.

---

[41] Tunc, *La responsabilité civile* (1981), nr 15: 'Le contenu de la responsabilité civile a été historiquement déterminé par les juges; il continue à évoluer, assez rapidement même, par suite de leur désir de répondre aux besoins sociaux.'. See also Josef Esser, 'Responsabilité et garantie dans la nouvelle doctrine allemande des actes illicites', *RIDC* 1961, 481 and E. von Caemmerer, *Wandlungen des Deliktrechts*, (Karlsruhe: Mueller, 1960), 478–479.

[42] ECJ 12 March 2002, C-168/00, [2002] ECR I-2631 (*Simone Leitner v TUI Germany*).

At least they can be overcome by a pragmatic and benevolent judiciary. More important differences between codified systems and common law are to be found at a deeper level: that of the legal cultures (nr 608) and policy backgrounds (nr 609).

D VARIOUS SCENES BEHIND THE RULES

608 Legal cultures

608-1 *Germany*

German legal culture is best characterized by its fondness for the legal order (*Rechtsordnung*) which is embodied in the BGB and profoundly elaborated by the legal literature.[43] Reading one of the German commentaries is like descending a pyramid: firstly, a rule is presented, then this rule is divided into sub-rules, and these are again divided into sub-sub-rules and so on for many stages.

This pyramid structure also reflects the German approach to legal reasoning on a more general level, especially the technique used to construe a statute (*Auslegung*). When applying the abstract wording of a statutory provision to a particular case, the German lawyer first seeks meticulously to define the elements of the provision (*Tatbestandsmerkmale*) and then find further sub-definitions if necessary. If the abstract provision has been boiled down to a pyramid of (sub-)definitions, the facts of the specific case are applied to or subsumed under these definitions. As in other pyramid-research this not infrequently leads to interesting discoveries. However, it also creates the risk of losing sight of what happens in the outside world. Hence it should be stressed that the German judge will equally look for rulings in similar cases to help him to construe a statutory provision in the way described above.

It has been said, somewhat exaggeratedly, that

German private law is a meticulous piece of legal engineering which, by use of concepts, attributes legal solutions to legal problems as precisely and mercilessly as a Swiss chronometer ticks away the years, hours, and seconds of a human life from the cradle to the grave. German law, it has been suggested, is forever prepared to sacrifice notions of justice on the altar of the concept.[44]

---

[43] An excellent recent example of high level German scholarship in the area of tort law is Nils Jansen, *Die Struktur des Haftungsrecht. Geschichte, Theorie und Dogmatik außervertragliche Ansprüche auf Schadensersatz* (Tübingen: Mohr, 2003).

[44] Basil S. Markesinis, Werner Lorenz and Gerhard Dannemann, *The German Law of Obligations. Vol. 1, The Law of Contracts and Restitution: A Comparative Introduction*, (Oxford: Clarendon Press, 1997), 26–27.

However, it has already been said by Von Jhering, one of the great German lawyers of the 19th century, that: 'Life is not there for the sake of legal terms, but legal terms serve for the sake of life.'[45]

608-2 *England*

English legal culture is strongly characterized by its fondness for traditions: '... we tend to cling to long-standing habits of thought and even to pass them on after they have become unnecessary.'[46] English tort law forms part of the common law which is considered to have no beginning. The assumption that the common law is not created but that it has to be found adds to its quasi theological character. Precedents are discoveries of what already has been there from time immemorial. '... a precedent is not only the antecedent of a judicial decision but also the consequence of a political decision to make custom the pre-eminent value in a given legal culture.'[47]

The judges, particularly the Law Lords, serve as high priests who are called upon to find the precedent and, if appropriate, to distinguish it. Such a system inevitably tends to a static rather than a dynamic approach. On the other hand, the sharp end of this principle has been softened by the House of Lords' ability not just to discover the law that is already there but also to create law by deviating from existing precedents (nr 501-3). This is, indeed, a Lord's rather than a high priest's job.

Part of the tradition is also that the common lawyer thinks in actions and remedies rather than in wrongful or negligent conduct. In 1909 Maitland wrote: 'The forms of action we have buried, but they still rule us from their graves'.[48] But Lord Atkin replied in 1941: 'When these ghosts of the past stand in the path of justice clanking their mediaeval chains the proper course for the judge is to pass through them undeterred'.[49] Not every English judge has proved to be as courageous as Lord Atkin and it can still be said that English tort law is prepared to sacrifice notions of justice on the altar of tradition out of fear of the ghosts of the past.[50] The course of history has fragmented tort law but the result is cherished rather than despised. English law is considered to be too pragmatic to

---

[45] Rudolf von Jhering, *Der Geist des römischen Rechts auf den verschiedenen Stufen seiner Entwicklung*, 4th edn. (Lepizig: Breitkopf und Härtel, 1878), Part III, § 59 321.

[46] W.V. Horton Rogers, 'Liability for Damage Caused by Others under English Law', in J. Spier (ed.), *Unification of Tort Law: Liability for Damage Caused by Others* (The Hague, London, New York: Kluwer Law International, 2003), 66.

[47] Pierre Legrand, 'European Legal Systems are not Converging', *ICLQ*, 45 (1996), 72.

[48] Frederic William Maitland, *Equity. Also the Forms of Action at Common Law*, edited by Alfred Henry Chaytor and William Joseph Whittaker, 1st edn. (Cambridge: University Press, 1909), 296.

[49] Lord Atkin in *United Australia Ltd v Barclays Bank Ltd* [1941] AC 1, 29.

[50] Basil S. Markesinis, Werner Lorenz and Gerhard Dannemann, *The German Law of Obligations. Vol. 1, The Law of Contracts and Restitution: A Comparative Introduction*, (Oxford: Clarendon Press, 1997), 26–27.

develop it to a higher level of abstraction (the French principles)[51] or to develop it to a more logical and coherent system (the German legal order).[52]

608-3 *France*

An important feature of French legal culture is the use of *grands principes* which are the basis of general concepts and general rules. This forms part of a more general fondness for '*grands*' things. The French nation has its '*Grands hommes de la patrie*' (a French person is only a real '*Grand homme de la patrie*' if his or her body has been interred in the *Panthéon*), the *Président de la République* has his '*Grands projets*' and the main decisions of the *Cour de cassation* are, of course, published under the title: '*Les grands arrêts de la Cour de cassation*'.

In this field of the law the basic legislation stems from the times of Napoleon and it holds a lot of vague notions, such as *faute* (intention or negligence), *chose* (thing), and *dommage* (damage). The legislator left the interpretation of these general notions to the courts, especially to the *Cour de cassation*. Its decisions are usually very brief, apodictic and hardly specific (nr 301-3). Therefore, it is not always clear what the practical consequences of a general concept are but this does not seem to bother the French very much.

Where the Germans keep digging and thinking to find out the truth, the French seem to be more able to live with a certain lack of clarity and certainty. In contrast to the English and German courts the French *Cour de cassation* does not seem to bother too much about the facts of the case which are only very briefly mentioned. The short and apodictic decisions suggest unity—the *Cour de cassation* being the '*gardien de l'unité de droit*'—and this unity is maintained by keeping the considerations and motivations at a high abstract level. More concreteness would only be possible to the detriment of unity.

608-4 *Europe*

The EU approach to private law matters is functional and fragmented. The approach is functional because it is only supposed to regulate matters which are relevant to achieve Community goals. Initially, this was the creation of an internal market but in the course of its existence the number of goals has increased and will probably further increase in the future. According to Article I-1 of the Draft European Constitution the competences of the Union would

[51] Tony Weir, 'The Staggering March of Negligence' in Peter Cane and Jane Stapleton, *The Law of Obligations: Essays in Celebration of John Fleming*, (Oxford: Clarendon Press; New York: Oxford University Press, 1998), 98: '...the intellectual appeal of the abstract may prove pragmatically unhelpful.'
[52] *Ex parte King* [1984] 3 All ER 897, 903 (CA) per Griffiths LJ: '...where logic leads down a path that is beset with practical difficulties the courts have not been frightened to turn aside and seek the pragmatic solutions that will best serve the needs of society.'

even expand to objectives which the Member States have 'in common'. This functional approach leads to fragmentation. There are currently various 'Community torts' (such as the *Francovich* case law, Articles 81 and 82 EC and the Product Liability Directive) but they do not have much in common on a more conceptual level. They are solely created to provide remedies for an effective functioning of Community law in a certain area. In this respect there are some commonalities with the way English tort law was 'born' (nr 502). The plans by the Commission to develop a Common Frame of References could lead to more consistency and coherence but it remains to be seen whether this ambitious goal can be achieved. More consistency and coherence can be achieved on a high abstract level and this means that discretion needs to be left to the national courts which will interpret the broad harmonized concepts from their own national perspective. More guidance could be given by confining the rules to well-defined smaller areas, making them more specific and less abstract.

Legal systems differ in their legal culture, ie in their ways of thinking, reasoning, and applying rules. Where French believe in their general principles (*les grands principes*), Germans love their legal order and its details (*die Rechtsordnung*), and English cherish their traditions (*the precedents*). This is, of course, a simplified map of reality which omits many things, distorts some things, and obscures others but it allows us to indicate the various starting points of thinking in the different tort systems.[53]

It may be concluded from this section that a European *ius commune* may need the identification and development of a European culture. Such a culture would be a proper and fertile basis for a European Civil Code. However, this is not something that will develop overnight, particularly not in a continually extending Union. It will also invoke the rather intriguing question what can be identified as a European culture in this respect.[54]

609 Policy approaches

609-1 *Introduction*

Tort law is not just a system. It is about balancing the interests of individuals, private, and public bodies. It distributes rights, duties, and money. In this sense

---

[53] See also David Howarth, 'The General Conditions of Unlawfulness', in *Towards a European Civil Code* (2004), 607–644; H. Patrick Glenn, 'La tradition juridique nationale', *RIDC* 2003, 263–278; Hugh Collins, 'European Private Law and the Cultural Identity of States', *ERPL*, 3 (1995), 353.

[54] See for example Bénédicte Fauvarque-Cosson, 'Faut-il un Code civil européen?', *RTD civ.* 2002, 480: 'L'unité juridique en Europe suppose une adhésion forte des gouvernements et de citoyens. Elle se fera, à condition de reposer, non sur la force, mais sur une culture européenne qui reste à construire. Elle se fera, à condition de lui en laisser le temps.' See also David Howarth, 'The General Conditions of Unlawfulness', in *Towards a European Civil Code* (2004), 643.

tort law has a high policy impact and it goes without saying that there are diverging views on this topic throughout Europe.

In deciding cases the courts are not just guided by the formal requirements for liability but they are also—probably and hopefully ultimately even more strongly—driven by their sense of justice. Within the limits of their legal system they are inclined to look for a proper solution of the case, rather than just applying formal requirements with the help of a kind of ready formula. The question, however, is what reasonableness and justice in this respect means. This does not only differ from judge to judge and from country to country but also within legal systems. In this chapter national accents are being indicated but this, of course, does not imply that everyone in a country takes the same or a similar view.

The differences in policy approach between the legal systems are reflected in a number of features, such as the difference in importance of strict liability (nr 605), the difference in treatment of public authorities (nr 1809–1811), and, on a more general level, the difference in the function of tort law and the kind of justice that is pursued (nr 609). These differences all indicate that the concept of what is just, fair, and reasonable differs substantially, particularly between England on the one hand and Germany and France on the other.

It is sometimes thought that the formal common law requirements are due to the differences with the civil law systems and to the general reluctance raising the level of care or creating rules of strict liability. However, a much better explanation is the difference in policy approach.[55] As has been demonstrated in the previous chapters, courts throughout the systems have been able and prepared to knock down systematic hurdles if there was a social or economic need to do so (see for France the creation of the general strict liability rule for things, nr 303, and for Germany the creation of the safety duties and the protection of the general personality right, nr 403–404). A striking English example concerns the rise and fall of the tort of negligence in the second half of the 20th century. In the 1970s and 1980s the House of Lords *broadened* the concept of the duty of care, in order to develop the tort of negligence into a general rule for negligently caused pure economic loss. But in the late 1980s the political wind changed and the duty of care was used as a tool to *restrict* the scope of the tort of negligence (nr 503-2).

609-2 *England*

The above-mentioned differences boil down to the difference in the kind of justice that is pursued: corrective or distributive justice. Corrective justice is making good a wrong without taking into consideration the needs, the character,

---

[55] This also follows from the fact that many other common law countries take different and often more progressive views than England.

or the worth of the parties concerned: '... private law looks neither to the litigants individually nor to the interests of the community as a whole, but to a bipolar relationship of liability.'[56] Distributive justice is concerned with the distribution of goods in society as a whole, taking into consideration every person's need and desire.[57]

The rough picture here is that English tort law is mainly about corrective justice and regulating conduct. This is, for example, expressed in the fact that fault liability generally does not require more than is humanly possible, that English law puts a strong emphasis on the foreseeability of the loss (nr 1104), and that it provides the possibility to award exemplary damages (nr 1202-3).

One of the few examples in which distributive justice was used as an argument to provide compensation was Lord Dennings' speech in *Nettleship v Weston* in which a learner driver caused an accident and his lack of skills was not accepted as an excuse to escape liability.[58] This different approach to motor vehicle accidents is not surprising since this also goes for the other legal systems. Due to compulsory liability insurance, the hurdles for liability are substantially lower than in other areas. Still, even in this area English law sticks to its fault liability regime.

Another example of the use of the idea of distributive justice in English courts was striking enough to dismiss a tort claim. In *McFarlane v Tayside Health Board*, a wrongful birth case, the House of Lords held that damages were not recoverable for the maintenance of a healthy child born following a negligently performed vasectomy operation on her father. Lord Steyn held that the parents' claim for the cost of bringing up the child must succeed on the basis of corrective justice. However, he preferred to dismiss the claim on arguments of distributive justice, guessing that his 'fellow travellers on the London Underground' would 'instinctively' consider '... that the law of tort has no business to provide legal remedies consequent upon the birth of a healthy child, which all of us regard as a valuable and good thing.'[59] Lord Steyn's striking knowledge of what an ordinary traveller on the London Underground would consider aside, his argument illustrates that the concept of distributive justice can also be applied to dismiss a claim.

The English reluctance towards rules of strict liability is related to the concern for unfathomed economic consequences for society. Markesinis, one of the authors who strongly criticizes this reluctance, describes the courts' fears for strict

[56] Ernest J. Weinrib, *The Idea of Private Law* (Cambridge, Mass: Harvard University Press, 1995), 1.
[57] Peter Cane, 'Corrective Justice and Correlativity in Private Law', *OJLS*, 16 (1996), 471; Tony Honoré, *Responsibility and Fault* (Oxford: Hart, 1999), 80–87.
[58] *Nettleship v Weston* [1971] 2 QB 691.
[59] *McFarlane v Tayside Health Board* [1999] 3 WLR 1301 at 1318, per Lord Steyn. This unprecedented imputation of authority to the ordinary man invoked Thomson to rightly argue that Lord Steyn thus abandoned not only the law of delict but also the law itself: J. Thomson, 'Abandoning the Law of Delict?', 2000 *SLT (News)* 43, 44. See about this case also nr 706-1.

liability as follows. 'More precisely it would mean that the cost of damage resulting from such operations would have to be absorbed as part of the overheads of the relevant business rather than be borne (where there is no negligence) by the injured person or his insurance.'[60] Indeed, it seems to be very much the fear of hampering business and disturbing the free market economy that prevents the development of a stronger position for victims. Moreover, there is even reluctance as to too broad a principle of liability for negligent conduct: 'The House of Lords has warned against the danger of extending the ambit of negligence so as to supplant or supplement other torts, contractual obligations, statutory duties or equitable rules in relation to every kind of damage including economic loss'.[61]

This reluctance is directly related to the absence in England of a general liability of public authorities for lawful conduct. In France and Germany such a strict liability is based on the principle of equality before the public burdens: if an activity of the State causes disproportionate damage to one or more particular citizens, it has to compensate them in order to prevent the public burdens weighing more heavily on some than on others (nr 1811). Strict liability for private actors is nothing more than the expression of the same idea: if socially beneficial activities cause damage (like motor vehicles and mass production), and they cause disproportionate damage to one or more particular citizens, these persons have to be compensated in order to prevent the burdens of these useful activities weighing more heavily on some than on others.

609-3 *France and Germany*

Whereas the English approach to tort law is reluctant and focuses primarily on how someone should behave, French approach is primarily focused on the question of how someone can get damages. Most liability rules in the area of death, personal injury, and property damage are strict; fault rules hardly play a role in this area. The whole system is intended to provide distributive justice.[62] Article 1384 al. 1 is an excellent example of how a provision has been made instrumental to provide damages for victims (nr 303). The idea is that, whereas everyone takes more or less advantage of the increased welfare, the materialization of the risks is highly arbitrary: disadvantages only strike a small number of individuals. It is, therefore, argued that the costs of contemporary risks should not be borne by the individual victim but that, in principle, they have to be borne by society. This is impregnated into French law by the values of solidarity

---

[60] Markesinis and Deakin (2003), 545.
[61] *Downsview Nominees v First City Corporation* [1993] 3 All ER 637 (PC) by Lord Templeman.
[62] Le Tourneau (2004), nr 51: 'L'indemnisation de la victime en est grandement facilitée. Mais cela au prix d'une perversion de la responsabilité qui n'est plus commutative (comme elle devrait l'être) mais distributive.'

and equality.[63] This idea has strongly influenced the development of rules of strict liability (nr 1002). In this approach tort law has a different function: it has become an instrument to establish who has to bear the costs of the accident. In this area, tort law has become a system of risk attribution. Sometimes even the line between tort law and social security is blurred. A striking example is the French *loi Badinter* providing liability rules for damage caused in road traffic accidents (nr 1404-1).

German tort law takes a somewhat intermediate position though it is closer to the French than the English ideas of justice. German tort law strongly focuses on regulating conduct but stretches the requirements as much as possible within the existing framework. This system is complemented by detailed rules of strict liability with a limited scope of application. It is, in the end, mainly focused on distributive justice.

In other words, the German and the French systems are mainly based on notions of equality and solidarity and are more inclined to apply the neighbourhood principle that made Lord Atkin famous in England. The approach in France and Germany is determined by a mix of free market and social policy with a strong emphasis on victim protection, whereas the English approach is predominantly free market oriented with an emphasis on the protection of freedom. In 2003, Jane Stapleton published an article in which she argued that protection of the vulnerable is a core moral concern of common law tort law.[64] By then such an article could not have been published in France or Germany because it would only discuss what is obvious and self-evident in these legal systems.

610 The role of rights

Another important difference in approach between the legal systems is the role of rights. The relationship of common law with rights is considered to be awkward because it is focused on remedies rather than rights. The roots for this go back to the fact that English tort law was born from the medieval writ system. A writ had to be obtained from the Lord Chancellor and provided for a remedy in certain factual situations (nr 502-1). The focus on a remedy implies a focus is on a solution of the problem. Samuels writes that litigants in the English legal system

... can certainly assert that they have in such or such a situation an action against some public or private body—and they can probably assert that they have a 'legitimate interest'

---

[63] Le Tourneau (2004), nr 51: 'La théorie du risque, imprégnée par la valeur morale de la *solidarité*, paraît surtout inspire par *l'équité*: Par son activité, l'homme peut se procurer un profit (ou, a tout le moins, un plaisir). Il est juste (equitable) qu'en contrepartie il répare les dommages qu'elle provoque.'

[64] Jane Stapleton, 'The Golden Thread at the Heart of Tort Law: Protection of the Vulnerable' (2003) *ABR* 29.

or 'expectation'. What they cannot claim is a right to the actual substance, or object, of the action itself—they cannot claim a right, as a citizen, to succeed.[65]

This, and the absence of an entrenched written constitution, do not mean that citizens' rights have been unprotected in the United Kingdom but, according to Lord Bingham, ' . . . it has inevitably meant that protection, where it exists, has been piecemeal and ad hoc.'[66]

The relationship between rights and English law can also be illustrated by the fact that in English law the European Convention on Human Rights did not get direct effect any earlier than 2000 with the entering into force of the Human Rights Act 1998. Even after 2000 the courts have shown reluctance in confirming that someone has a 'right' to something. An example is the way the House of Lords has conducted the implementation of the right to respect for private life embodied in Article 8 ECHR. It did not develop a right to privacy but chose to re-interpret the equitable wrong of 'breach of confidence' in the light of the requirements following from Article 8 (nr 705-4). This way of bringing the right to privacy home in English law is not only disguising the right as a duty for others, it is also a remarkable turn of history since in medieval times remedies for equitable wrongs were granted by the King's grace (nr 502-4). Hence, the emphasis remains on the availability of a cause of action providing for a remedy. Rights only exist if they are protected by a cause of action. This focus on duties and remedies causes the landscape of rights to be patchy.[67]

There are, however, other developments also indicating the acknowledgements of rights. For example, one may think of the conventional sum awarded to the parents in cases of wrongful conception (nr 706-2) and the *Chester v Afshar* case about the patient's right to be informed about the risk inherent in a surgery (nr 1107-3). Both decisions seem to be inspired by the acknowledgement of the right to family life and the patient's right to self-determination respectively.

Though there are signs that the gap is starting to narrow, the contrast with French and German law remains. The main German tort law provision, § 823 I, lists the citizen's private law rights in, particularly, the right to life, physical integrity, health, personal liberty, and property. For the courts these rights are the starting point for deciding on a claim for compensation (nr 402-3) and this starting point has strongly influenced the BGH's case law in providing protection for victims of accidents.

French tort law does not take rights as its starting point but it is implied in the way the *Cour de cassation* has interpreted the few provisions of the *Code civil* applying to liability. The many strict liability rules, some of a very general

    [65] Geoffrey Samuel, ' "Le droit subjectif" and English Law', (1987) *Cam LJ* 264, 286.
    [66] Lord Bingham of Cornhill, 'Tort and Human Rights' in Peter Cane and Jane Stapleton, *The Law of Obligations: Essays in Celebration of John Fleming*, (Oxford: Clarendon Press; New York: Oxford University Press, 1998), 2.
    [67] See also Nils Jansen, 'Duties and Rights in Negligence. A Comparative and Historical Perspective on the European Law of Extracontractual Liability', *OJLS*, 24/3 (2004), 443–469.

character, embody the right to safety and security, whereas the application of the principle of 'equality before the public burdens' in liability of public authorities is based on the right of equal treatment of citizens. In the second part of the 20th century French law has codified the right to protection of privacy.

Whereas French and German law both focus on rights protecting a person's life and good, English law takes a different starting point by protecting the freedom to act. Indeed, in common law the protection of the freedom to act is often mentioned as an important consideration in deciding liability matters. This preference is related, particularly in the area of personal injury and property damage, to the principle of corrective justice in English law and of distributive justice in German and French law (nr 609).

It is inevitable that the different starting points in English law on the one hand, and German and French law on the other, as regards the role of citizen's rights, have consequences for the outcome of cases. The difference is, however, not only of a constitutional or conceptual character as regards the approach to rights but also based on a different vision on society and rights in general.

E THE WAY AHEAD

611 Role of the Community institutions

Where *ius commune* can be considered to be an experimental botanic garden, Community law is an inescapable natural phenomenon. In Lord Denning's famous words: 'When it comes to matters with a European element, the Treaty is like an incoming tide. It flows into the estuaries and up the rivers. It cannot be held back.'[68] There is, however, important interaction between European law and *ius commune*. The reference to common general principles in Article 288 EC implies that the *ius commune* approach and the European law approach are two sides of the same coin (nr 201-1). As Van Gerven has put it: 'To say it paraphrasing *Lord Denning's* famous statement: Time has come for the incoming tide of Community law to be reversed. That is to say it in warrior's terms of the past: Time has come for the Community invader to be invaded by the legal orders of the Member States.'[69]

Up until now the EU legislator has approached private law on an ad hoc basis only. It has looked at private law from a functional rather than a formal, and from a fragmented rather than a systematic, point of view. It has regulated areas which it deemed to be necessary in order to create the internal market,

---

[68] Lord Denning in *Bulmer Ltd v Bollinger SA* [1974] 2 All ER 1226, 1231.
[69] Walter van Gerven, 'The Invader Invaded', in Rodriguez Iglesias et al. (eds.), *Mélanges en hommage à Fernand Schockweiler*, (Baden-Baden: Nomos, 1999), 593, 598.

particularly competition law, company law, and the law of obligations. As regards the latter, in the past decades more than a dozen Directives have been adopted, mainly in the field of contract law. Significant Directives regarding tort law are the Product Liability Directive (nr 1406–1411), the E-Commerce Directive (nr 1302), the Directives on Misleading and Comparative Advertising, and the Unfair Commercial Practices Directive (nr 204-1).

In 1989 the European Parliament adopted a resolution in which it called for a start to be made ' . . . on the necessary preparatory work on drawing up a common European Code of Private Law.'[70] This resolution was followed by a similar one in 1994 though here reference was made to a Common European Code of Private Law.[71] In a third resolution on this subject in 2000 the EP stated ' . . . that greater harmonisation of civil law has become essential in the internal market and calls on the Commission to draw up a study in this area'.[72]

By this time the issue had also been taken up by the European Council. Its conclusions of the summit held in Tampere in 1999 were quite cautious, requesting 'as regards substantive law an overall study on the need to approximate Member State's legislation in civil matters in order to eliminate obstacles to the good functioning of civil proceedings'.[73] A first step towards implementation of these conclusions was the Commission's *Communication on European Contract Law*, which was intended to gather information on the need for farther-reaching EC action in the area of contract law, in particular to the extent that the case-by-case approach might not be able to solve all the problems which might arise.[74]

In 2003 this Communication was followed by the *Action Plan on European Contract Law* in which the Commission proposes to establish a Common Frame of Reference, which should contain common rules and terminology in the area of European contract law. The Commission aims to use this document, where possible and appropriate, to integrate relevant definitions and common rules when reviewing the existing *acquis communautaire* and submitting new proposals. According to the Commission, this document could serve as a basis for an optional instrument to be adopted by parties to a contract. This implies that an 'optional' European Code of Contract Law is also still in the mind of the Commission.[75] The

[70] European Parliament Resolution on Action to Bring into Line the Private Law of the Member States [1989] OJ C 158/400, 26.6.1989.
[71] European Parliament Resolution on the Harmonisation of Certain Sectors of the Private Law of the Member States [1994] OJ C 205/518, 25.7.1994.
[72] European Parliament Resolution on the Commission's Annual Legislative Programme for 2000 [2000] OJ C 377/326, point 28, 29.12.2000.
[73] Communication of the European Commission to the Council and the European Parliament. *On European contract law*, COM (2001) 398 final, OJ C 255/4, 13.9.2001.
[74] Communication of the European Commission to the Council and the European Parliament. *On European contract law*, COM (2001) 398 final, OJ C 255/2, 13.9.2001.
[75] Communication of the Commission to the European Parliament and the Council. *A more coherent European contract law. An Action plan*, COM (2003) 68 final, OJ C 63, 15.3.2003, nr 92. See also Dirk Staudenmayer, 'The Way Forward in European Contract Law', *ERPL*, 13/2 (2005), 95–104.

2004 Communication on *European contract law and the revision of the acquis: the way forward* confirms the Commission's aim to develop a Common Frame of Reference.[76] In the framework of this book, the development of common concepts of 'damage' and 'damages' may be especially important (see nr 1200). It remains to be seen, however, whether such a concept will be general enough to provide flexibility, and detailed enough to provide legal certainty.

612 The case for harmonization

Despite these actions, there is still the preliminary question of whether harmonization is feasible and desirable, particularly in the area of tort law. [77] Is there a case for harmonizing European tort law? Most probably the answer is no. This may sound awkward, for harmonization

> ... is a delightful notion. How could one possibly be so unsophisticated as to oppose it? Surely everything in Europe, not only private law, would sound so much better if it were brought into harmony? (...) More than that, it would vividly demonstrate the common commitments undertaken by European States which have a bloody history of living in disharmony.[78]

However, harmonization is not as self-evident as it seems to be at first sight. To confine the question to tort law matters: why should England enact rules of strict liability and lose its focus on corrective justice just because other countries in Europe have strict liability rules and use tort law to pursue solidarity? And why should France and Germany lose their focus on distributive justice and tone down their rules of strict liability just because the 'European average' asks for it?

Harmonization (of tort law) does not only need a formal legal basis but also a substantial justification.[79] This may be obvious but such a justification has not been subject of an intense political or academic debate, at least not until recently. The need for harmonization seemed to be self-evident to a great extent because the idea was that differences between the Member States were an obstacle to the achievement of an internal market. Skipping over this matter of principle, the emphasis was put on the technocratic work: drafting rules for a European Civil Code and Principles of European Tort Law. However, there are many

[76] Communication of the Commission to the European Parliament and the Council. *European contract law and the revision of the acquis: the way forward*, COM (2004) 651 final, OJ C 242, 11.10.2004.
[77] See also, *inter alia*, with further references, Gerhard Wagner, 'The Project of Harmonizing European Tort Law', *CMLR*, 42 (2005), 1269–1312.
[78] Stephen Weatherill, 'Why Object to the Harmonization of Private Law by the EC?', *ERPL* 11/5 (2004), 633.
[79] See also Walter van Gerven, 'Harmonization of Private Law: Do We Need it?', *CMLR* 41 (2004), 505.

preliminary questions to be answered before the stage of drafting sustainable rules is reached (see about this nr 608–610).[80]

There is an interesting parallel with the self-evidence with which the European Community has extended its competence over the past decades. Even though the EC cannot do more than the Treaty permits (Article 5), the interpretation of the EC's competences has been flexible.[81] This self-evident growth has been challenged before the ECJ in the *Tobacco Advertising* case. More specifically, Germany had challenged the legal basis of Directive 98/43 on the advertising of tobacco products, a Directive issued on the basis of, *inter alia*, Article 95 EC as a measure of harmonization directed at integrating goods and services markets.

The ECJ annulled the Directive because it did not meet the requirements arising from Article 95. The Court pointed out that Article 95 does not provide a general basis for regulating the internal market. Neither is it a sufficient ground for issuing a measure of harmonization that there are differences between national rules and that this may in the abstract lead to distortions. According to the ECJ a measure of harmonization must actually contribute to improving the establishment and functioning of the internal market. This should happen by eliminating obstacles to the free movement of goods and services or to removing appreciable distortions of competition. In other words, a harmonizing measure has to make clear on a factual basis not just what the differences between the national laws are, but also which distortions follow from these differences and how the proposed measure aims to prevent these distortions.[82] This decision will also be the benchmark for harmonizing measures by the European Community in the area of private law in general and tort law in particular.

Of course, there are obvious differences between the national tort laws. The foregoing chapters have made this clear and it will be further demonstrated in the following chapters. It is, however, a different matter whether these differences provide obstacles for the free movement of goods and services or the distortion of competition. Diversity is not synonymous with distortion. Of course, differences impose extra compliance costs on industry to calculate the impact of these differences. There is, however, no empirical evidence that this leads to market problems. Indeed, there are many examples of economic market integration with differentiated legal systems.[83] In addition to this, legal practice does not seem to

[80] See for example Guy Canivet and Horatia Muir Watt, 'Européanisation du droit privé et justice sociale', *ZEuP* 3 (2005), 518: '... il nous semble que l'européanisation du droit privé exige un débat approfondi sur de très nombreuses questions qui se posent préalablement à celle du seul choix de la technique legislative adequate'.

[81] Stephen Weatherill, 'Why Object to the Harmonization of Private Law by the EC?' *ERPL*, 11/5 (2004), 634–640.

[82] ECJ 5 October 2000, Case C-376/98, ECR 2000 I-8419 (*Germany v European Parliament and Council*).

[83] Michael Faure, 'Economic Analysis of Tort Law and the European Civil Code', in *Towards a European Civil Code* (2004), 672–673.

134

be so much concerned about the diversity of the private law systems as about the fragmentation and inconsistency of Community legislation.[84]

The case for harmonization of the national tort laws is not (yet) made. Of course, this does not rule out that in specific areas distortions occur which need to be redressed by harmonization measures. In such cases the advantages of these measures need to be balanced with the costs involved: the transaction cost savings of harmonization need to outweigh the costs of differentiated legal rules. This is, however, not self-evident.[85] Harmonizing measures also entail compliance costs. Moreover, at first new rules are usually unclear and may be applied differently throughout the internal market. The EC Directive on Liability for Defective Products provides an illustration of how long it may take before the meaning of the various provisions is fleshed out (nr 1406–1411).

Two final observations can be made which may further question the desirability and feasibility of the harmonization of tort law. Firstly, real harmonization of tort law is hard to achieve without taking into account other compensation systems, such as private insurance and social security systems. It is widely acknowledged that these systems are strongly interconnected and it seems undesirable to harmonize tort law and to leave insurance law and social security law untouched.[86]

Secondly, real harmonization of tort law would also need harmonization of administrative and criminal law. Most legal systems acknowledge the possibility to be liable for damage caused by the violation of a statutory duty, albeit with different variations (Chapter 9). Hence, if one would harmonize the rules for breach of statutory duty one should also harmonize the statutory rules that can be invoked as a basis for this tort. Even though many of the statutory rules are now issued by Brussels rather than by the national legislators, this seems to be an impossible task.

613 The need for a European policy discourse

It is clear from the foregoing that the focus should not be on a Europe united in unity with pan-European rules, but rather on a Europe united in diversity with

---

[84] See the responses to the Communication of the Commission to the Council and the European Parliament, COM (2001) 398 final (OJ C 255, 13.9.2001) and the Communication of the Commission to the European Parliament and the Council. *A more coherent European contract law. An Action plan*, COM (2003) 68 final (OJ C 63, 15.3.2003) at http://europa.eu.int/comm/consumers.

[85] Michael Faure, 'Economic Analysis of Tort Law and the European Civil Code', in *Towards a European Civil Code* (2004), 666–668. U. Mattei, 'A transaction cost approach to the European Code', *ERPL* 5 (1997), 537; Hein Kötz, 'Rechtsvereinheitlichung—Nutzen, Kosten, Methoden, Ziele', *RabelsZ* 186 (1986), 1–18.

[86] See for instance Ulrich Magnus (ed.), *The Impact of Social Security Law on Tort Law*, (Vienna, New York: Springer, 2003).

harmonized rules where needed and diversity where possible. What then, apart from situations in which harmonization is indicated to achieve an integrated market, is the agenda for the discussion on a European *ius commune* in tort law?

Firstly, perhaps the most important result so far of the quest for a European *ius commune* is that it has lifted academic discussions on private law issues to a European level. It has paved the way for a truly European legal scholarship rather than a national one. Comparative research has become core business and this has strongly stimulated the transboundary dissemination of information. This information has created mirrors for national legal systems, first of all for students who are provided with an ever richer choice of courses of European private law of some kind. More and more students are being educated about various other legal systems, so that lawyers will increasingly have not only knowledge of their own system but also some knowledge of 'foreign' ones.[87] Also, legislature and judiciary are increasingly making use of the information provided and they also conduct comparative research themselves. This does not necessarily mean that national legislatures and judiciaries choose solutions which tend towards harmonization, but they will probably try to make their solution 'look good' in a European context.

Secondly, the old *ius commune* disintegrated more than two centuries ago (nr 602) and it would be far too optimistic to build a new *ius commune* in the short term—results are to be expected in decades rather than years. The issue is to organize and stimulate this dynamic process but not to force it to provide results unless necessary. The results need to be flexible and will therefore be diverse. In some areas, legislation by the European Community will be needed, whereas in other areas a Common Frame of Reference (nr 611) or a kind of non-binding Restatements following the American example could be helpful.[88] And, no doubt, there will be areas where we will get nowhere. It is important to leave the ends of the discussion open in order to let a common European habitat freely develop.

In this respect, the current proposals for principles of European tort law are extremely useful in further developing restatements in certain areas. However, a lot of water needs to flow down the European rivers to provide a restatement with sufficient authority. This needs not only input from all European countries but also discussion at a policy rather than a systematic level. And finally, as Walter van Gerven has rightly said:

> ... convergence of the minds of practitioners, judges, professors and future lawyers is at least as important as convergence of laws. Learning about each other's legal mentalities, and ways of solving concrete legal problems, is therefore of crucial importance—which

---

[87] See for example Michael Faure, Jan Smits and Hildegard Schneider (eds.), *Towards a European Ius Commune in Legal Education and Research* (Antwerp: Intersentia, 2002).

[88] See about the US Restatements for instance Whitmore Gray, 'E pluribus unum? A Bicentennial Report of Unification of Law in the United States', *RabelsZ* 50 (1986), 111–159.

means that it is also of the utmost importance to make available teaching materials for lawyers, young and old, who want to familiarise themselves with growing convergence between the EU Member States' legal systems.[89]

In this respect, insurers and practitioners, for example the Pan-European Organization of Personal Injury Lawyers (PEOPIL), may also play an important role in this dynamic process of convergence.

Thirdly, this voluntary convergence is limited by what national legislators and judiciaries consider to be the limits of their own legal system. Lord Bingham said:

Development of the law in this country cannot of course depend on a head-count of decisions and codes adopted in other countries around the world, often against a background of different rules and traditions. The law must be developed coherently, in accordance with principle, so as to serve, even-handedly, the ends of justice.[90]

Even though he and his learned and noble friends and courts in other countries are prepared to make use of comparative materials in order to decide a case (see nr 201-2), they only do so as far as their national law allows them to do so. Where the limits of national laws lie is not so much a matter of legal system as of policy approach.

Finally, what is very much needed is a general discourse on the policy issues in European tort law. This is one of the most dividing issues in tort law and perhaps generally in European private law (nr 609). What are the driving forces behind tort law? What are the prevailing ideas of what are fair, just, and reasonable decisions as regards liability matters? How much protection do we want to provide to victims? And how much to potential tortfeasors? What is the role of rights in tort law? How much free-market protection and how much solidarity do we want in Europe?

To put it in an informal way, more emphasis should be put on the question 'Who gets what, when and how?' In the end, this question is about what kind of Europe is to be preferred and pursued: should the emphasis be on the freedom to act, on corrective justice and regulating conduct, or should it be on protecting interests, on distributive justice and equality before the public and private burdens? Though this is certainly too strong a simplification of the discussion, it reflects the dimensions of a European tort law debate and echoes a more general debate on the future of Europe.

Just as in the European Parliament, a debate on tort law should not be one conducted between countries but between policy opinions because policy issues are genuinely transboundary. Indeed, not all English lawyers are happy with the

[89] Walter van Gerven, 'The ECJ-Case law as a Means of Unification of Private Law?' in *Towards a European Civil Code* (2004), 123.
[90] Joined Cases of *Fairchild v Glenhaven Funeral Services Ltd and others* [2002] 3 All ER 305 at 334, per Lord Bingham.

path taken by the House of Lords and they may find common ground with lawyers in Germany. And French representatives being unhappy with the approach of the *Cour de cassation* may find allies in Germany or England. The challenge of a real sustainable European discussion on tort law is to raise it to a policy level in which discussants do not 'represent' their country but their policy preferences.[91]

[91] See for a similar discussion in contract law, *inter alia*, Gert Brüggemeier et al., 'Social Justice in European Contract Law: A Manifesto', *ELJ*, 10 (2004), 653–674; Martijn W. Hesselink, 'The Politics of a European Civil Code', *ELJ* 10 (2004), 675–697; H. Collins and D. Campbell, 'Discovering the Implicit Dimensions of Contracts', in D. Campbell, H. Collins and J. Wightman (eds.), *Implicit Dimension of Contract: Discrete, Relational and Network Contracts* (Oxford: Hart, 2003); Guy Canivet and Horatia Muir Watt, 'Européanisation du droit privé et justice sociale', *ZEuP* 3 (2005), 517–522.

PART II
REQUIREMENTS OF LIABILITY

7

Protected Interests

A INTRODUCTION

701 Overview

701-1 *Protected interests in the framework of torts and damages*

As has been pointed out, in German and English tort law fault liability is subject to certain formal limitations. German law requires unlawfulness (*Rechtswidrigkeit*) (nr 402-2), whereas the English tort of negligence requires a duty of care (nr 503). Before embarking on the requirements of intention and negligence in Chapter 8, it is therefore necessary to deal with the limitations provided for in German and English law. This will be done by discussing the interests protected by tort law.

The approach of this chapter reflects the German system of § 823 I BGB, but the issue of protected interests can also be recognised in the English requirement of the duty of care (protecting personal injury and property but pure economic loss only in a very limited way) and—to a lesser extent—in the French requirement of *faute*. It all boils down to the fact that negligent conduct must be legally wrong or that the damage needs to be legally relevant.[1] These are usually two sides of the same coin (nr 715).

A variety of rights and interests may deserve protection in tort law, such as personal interests (life, physical integrity, mental and physical health, and privacy), property interests, and economic interests. This chapter will analyse which interests are protected in the different legal systems and to what extent.[2]

Section B will focus on protection of the person, particularly his life, bodily integrity, mental and physical health, and his personality rights, as well as the disputed issues of wrongful conception and wrongful life. Section C will deal with protection of property, both movable and immovable property. Finally,

---

[1] This is the key requirement by which the draft for a European Civil Code avoids using the term 'unlawfulness'.

[2] See for a comparative view Helmut Koziol (ed.), *Unification of Tort Law: Wrongfulness*, (The Hague, London, Boston: Kluwer, 1998); Van Gerven (2000), 77–277; David Howarth, 'The General Conditions of Unlawfulness', in *Towards a European Civil Code* (2004), 607–644.

section D will analyse the protection of economic interests. This mainly concerns the problem of pure economic loss and particularly its lower level of protection.

Intellectual property rights, such as copyrights, trademarks, patents, and the like, usually protect both personal and economic interests involved in someone's creative abilities. They will not be dealt with in this book as they are considered to be a separate part of tort law, or rather an independent part of private law which is strongly influenced by international conventions, particularly because of the need for cross-border protection.

Infringement of a protected right or interest as such does not give rise to liability. This is only the case if the defendant also acted negligently (Chapter 8), violated a statutory rule (Chapter 9), or if a rule of strict liability applies (Chapter 10).

The topic of this chapter is related to most of the other chapters in this second part of the book. The link between protected interests and negligence is that the required level of care corresponds with the value of the infringed right or interest. A highly valuable interest justifies greater care than an interest that is worth less to protect (nr 806).

In statutory provisions rules are laid down as to how one ought to behave. It is often also implicitly or explicitly indicated which rights and interests are particularly protected by these rules (nr 906).

Strict liability protects rights and interests in the best way by holding someone liable for the damage he caused, unless he can invoke *force majeure* or a similar limited defence. Hence, rules of strict liability generally aim to protect highly valued rights such as personal and property interests (nr 1002).

Protected interests are also closely connected to damage and damages. In this chapter the emphasis will be on the protected rights and interests as such, whereas Chapter 12 will go into the financial consequences of the infringement. For instance, a collision with a car infringes a property right (this chapter). The damage following from this infringement is the reduction in value of the car or the costs of repairing it (Chapter 12).

701-2 *Protected interests in the framework of the legal systems*

In the legal systems the question of protected interests arises in different ways. In Germany § 823 I BGB contains a number of protected rights: life, body, health, freedom, property, or other another right. The legislator intended this list to be of a limitative character but the list appeared to be too small. Hence, *das Recht am Gewerbebetrieb* (the right to business) and *das allgemeine Persönlichkeitsrecht* (the general personality right) were called into being (nr 404).

The English system has grappled with similar problems but in a different way. Torts generally do not focus on the protection of interests (let alone rights) but they approach the issue from the opposite side, namely whether the law provides a remedy. In the framework of the tort of negligence, the emphasis is on the question of whether the defendant owed the victim a duty of care. From the claimant's point of view the emphasis is on the question of whether he has an action in tort. However, the question of which interest is infringed is relevant in a number of torts, not least in the tort of negligence. This tort protects life and goods but provides a rather hazardous way to obtain compensation for pure economic loss (nr 503).

French law does not provide an *a priori* limitation as to protected interests. It has been up to the courts to decide which interests are to be protected and which not, solely on the basis of the word *dommage* in article 1382 CC. The concept of protected interest has nevertheless gained foothold in French tort law, for instance in the *droit à la sécurité corporelle* (the right to bodily safety) embodied in the many rules of strict liability, in the contractual safety obligations (*obligations de sécurité*, nr 1407-2), and in the right to privacy codified in article 9 CC (nr 705-3).

In European Union law, Article 288 EC and the case law of the European Court of Justice do not make a distinction between the various heads of loss (nr 1202-5). However, the Directive on Liability for Defective Products does make such a distinction. It only covers damage caused by death or by personal injuries and damage to property other than the defective product itself. Thus the Directive distinguishes between (covered) material loss as a consequence of personal injury and property loss on the one hand, and (not covered) pure economic loss and non-pecuniary loss on the other (nr 1409). Other Directives contain different definitions of recoverable loss and this does not make it easy to find a common policy in this respect. A Common Frame of References might be eligible to tackle these kind of problems (nr 611).

B PROTECTION OF THE PERSON

702 Life

The right to life is the most fundamental human right. Article 2(1) ECHR provides that everyone's right to life shall be protected by law. Though this provision suggests that a Contracting State is only obliged to protect against active infringement, the European Court of Human Rights has extended the scope of Article 2 by imposing positive obligations on the State to protect citizens against fatal injuries caused by third parties, be it intentionally or negligently. Hence, State liability does not only apply to acts but also to omissions (see about this distinction nr 808-1). Though this positive obligation to protect life is of increasing importance in the European Court's case law, the consequences for the States remain quite modest. See more extensively nr 1807–1808.

At first sight tort law seems to protect a person's life in a more effective way. Establishing liability of someone who caused another person's death will be relatively easily. In France this liability will be often strict (nr 303–306),[3] whereas in Germany it will be either based on a strict rule, on the negligent infringement of a protected right, or on the breach of a statutory duty (nr 402–406). English law protects life with the tort of negligence (nr 503) and the tort of breach of a statutory duty, which can sometimes lead to mini rules of strict liability (nr 902), and with several torts based on intentional conduct (nr 504).

Despite this low threshold as regards establishing liability, the protection of the right to life is limited. The loss of someone's life, the loss of the reasonably expected years he could have enjoyed life, the value of his person for his family and for society—this damage is not recoverable, neither by the deceased person who does not exist any more as a legal subject, nor by members of his family.[4] This means that legal systems do not protect the right to life as such.

Though the loss of life as such does not cause a recoverable loss in tort law, all systems provide relatives (mainly his life partner and children) under certain conditions with a right to claim loss of livelihood. Some legal systems provide the employer of the deceased with a right to claim financial losses from the tortfeasor and in most systems the costs of the funeral or cremation of the deceased person are also recoverable; see nr 1208.

However, in a number of fatal accidents there will be no dependant relatives or other third parties who suffer a recoverable loss. One may think of situations in which a child or a student dies as the consequence of an event for which someone else is liable.

In England and France next of kin can also claim damages for non-pecuniary loss but the amount of these damages is generally modest. The reason is that the amount does not reflect the value of human life but, only in a rather symbolic way, the sorrow of the next of kin (nr 1210).

Considering that the amount of damages in a case of a fatal accident is generally much lower than if a person is injured, it has been cynically concluded that it is cheaper to kill than to maim.[5] This implies that rates of liability insurance for motor vehicles do not reflect the highest risk involved in driving, which is killing someone. In this respect motoring does not pay its way because it is, in fact, 'subsidized' by those who die in traffic accidents and their relatives.

---

[3] The French law on liability for damage caused by traffic accidents (*loi Badinter*) even imposes an almost absolute liability on the driver and the custodian of a motor vehicle; see nr 1404-1.

[4] Portuguese law is still an exception to this rule: von Bar (2000), N 47. In English law the loss of expectation of life as such was acknowledged until the enactment of the Administration of Justice Act 1982; see nr 1206.

[5] See for instance Dan Barrett, *Cheaper to Kill Than to Maim. A Patient's Guide to Medical Malpractice in Texas*, edited by Larry Upshaw (Chicago: Independent Publishers Group, 2002). In the same sense Viney-Jourdain (1998), nr 254: '. . . un accident mortel subi par un enfant pourrait, à la limite, ne rien "coûter" au responsable, alors que de simples blessures jusitifieraient une lourde condamnation destinée à compenser les frais de soins et l'incapacité de travail définitive.'

703 Physical integrity and physical health

The right to *physical integrity* is perhaps the best protected right in tort law. When someone is physically injured, liability will be generally rather easy to establish: in many cases either a rule of strict liability will apply or the wrongdoer has not acted with due care. Usually it will not be difficult to find the wrongdoer and to prove the causal connection between the wrongful conduct and the damage.

This position does not differ from the protection of the right to life. However, compensation for damage caused by the infringement of the right to physical integrity is much more adequate than in cases where someone has died: in case of injury the pecuniary loss, particularly medical expenses and loss of income, is compensable as is non-pecuniary loss, particularly for pain and suffering. The amounts for the latter can be rather substantial (nr 1206).

An exception to the strong protection of bodily integrity can be found in sports cases. If someone suffers physical injury in the course of a game, he may have more difficulty in getting compensation if risks to bodily integrity are inherent in the sport. One may think of a footballer who is injured because of a tackle by his opponent, or a tennis player who gets a ball in his eye during a game. In these cases, the fact that bodily injury is caused does not bring the victim close to the successful claim he may have had if the same injury had happened outside the sports arena. It also has to be established that the opponent acted in a way that the claimant did not need to expect within the framework of the game (nr 809). This illustrates that the level of protection of a right or interest depends on the character of the activity that caused the damage (nr 715).

The right to *physical health* protects people against the consequences of diseases, for instance cancer (mesothelioma), AIDS or legionnaire's disease. An infection, for instance with HIV, can also be considered to be an interference with health because it is an impairment of the normal bodily functioning, even if no pain is suffered or no marked change is apparent.[6]

Though health is globally considered to be of the utmost importance and stands at the same level as the right to bodily integrity, effective protection by tort law depends mainly on the possibility of proving causation between the negligent conduct and the damage. In health cases this causal connection often has to be diagnosed by medical experts. In the course of the 20th century medical science has proved able to establish causal connections better and better in a

---

[6] Germany: BGH 30 April 1991, NJW 1991, 1948 (contaminated blood transfusion), about which Van Gerven (2000), 84–85. France: Cour d'appel de Paris 7 July 1989, Gaz. Pal. 1989. 752, about which Van Gerven (2000), 122–123 and the Act 91-1406 of 31 December 1991 *pour l'indemnisation des victimes contaminées par le virus de l'immuniodéficience humaine*, creating a special fund for persons who were infected with HIV as a result of blood transfusions; see Van Gerven (2000), 629–630; Le Tourneau (2004), nr 8502–8561.

general sense.[7] In individual cases, however, it can still be impossible to establish a causal connection.

A good example is the English *Fairchild* case, a case about someone who was exposed to asbestos.[8] Exposure to asbestos increases the risk of several illnesses, of which the most serious is mesothelioma, a lethal form of lung cancer caused by the inhalation of asbestos fibres. This disease has an incubation period of 20–40 years. Technically it is impossible to establish where and when the patient inhaled the fatal asbestos fibres. Hence, such cases will be decided by the question of who has to prove the causal connection. Basically the burden of proof for causation is on the claimant but, in order to ensure a reasonable protection of the claimant's health interests, courts are under certain circumstances inclined to shift the burden of proof to the defendant and this was exactly what the House of Lords did, referring to similar decisions in other European jurisdictions.

Though for instance German tort law differentiates between the right to bodily integrity and the right to health (§ 823 I BGB, see nr 402-3), there is no reason to elaborate the difference or to look for strict definitions. 'It is generally accepted that most types of damage to a person's body commonly also constitute an impairment of his health'.[9] Article 10:202 (1) PETL quite rightly uses the words 'bodily health'. The rights cannot be separated but the distinction illustrates the practical difficulty of protecting the right to health compared with the protection of the right to bodily integrity. This is, however, not a matter of principle: it is due to the fact that it is harder to factually prove infringement and causation in health cases than in cases of bodily integrity.

704 Mental health

People can not only suffer physical harm by other people's conduct but they can also be affected in their mental well-being. One may think of feelings of discomfort and irritation, grief and sorrow, pain and suffering, unconsciousness, and serious psychiatric problems, such as a post traumatic stress disorder (PTSD), neuroses, and psychoses. Psychiatric diagnoses are categorized by the 4th edition of the *Diagnostic and Statistical Manual of Mental Disorders*, published by the American Psychiatric Association in 1994. Better known as DSM-IV, this manual covers all mental health disorders and also lists known causes of these disorders and statistics in terms of sex and age.

In daily life, people often suffer feelings of discomfort caused by other persons but these are not compensable. 'Just as some harm to the body is negligible,

---

[7] One may for instance think of the increased chance of developing a certain type of cancer if living in the neighbourhood of a nuclear plant.
[8] *Fairchild v Glenhaven Funeral Services Ltd & Others* [2002] 3 All ER 305, about which also nr 201-2 and 1107-3.   [9] Von Bar (2000), N 57.

eg pushing and shoving on the underground, or noise, or dirt on the skin, and does not constitute 'injury', negligible impairments of a person's psyche are equally insufficient bases for action.'[10]

The question is, therefore, from which level of mental harm can compensation be granted? French law does not require a mental illness but the damage has to be direct and certain. All kinds of mental harm caused by the death or severe injury of another person, including natural grief, are eligible for compensation.[11]

In Germany mental harm only gives rise to a right to compensation if the feelings amount to mental illness and thus can be considered to be an infringement of health. The harm must have surpassed the normal reactions of pain, mourning, and sorrow (nr 402-3 and 704). For example, a couple had to cancel a cruise after their son died in a car accident. They claimed compensation for the cancellation costs from the liable person, asserting that these were caused by the grief and disturbance on hearing of the death of their son. The BGH dismissed the claim for lack of an infringement of the right to health.[12]

It has to be foreseeable that someone would suffer some kind of mental illness as the consequence of the accident. This implies that an extreme reaction to an accident can be unforeseeable, even though it exceeds the normal degree of suffering and amounts to a mental illness. For example, the BGH considered that it was not foreseeable that a woman whose husband died in a traffic accident would suffer from ' . . . a serious mental shock resulting in character changes manifesting themselves as depression, uncontrollable fits of crying, extreme excitability, insomnia, and nervous trembling at the slightest sign of excitement.'[13]

English law requires that the victim suffered a mental illness and that such a shock was foreseeable. A mental illness can be a nervous shock but the House of Lords has also held that, for example, dyslexia may constitute an impairment of a person's mental condition. In particular, the negligent failure to ameliorate the consequences of dyslexia by appropriate teaching may be said to prolong the injury, giving rise to an action for personal injury.[14]

In the case of a secondary victim (for example a relative of the primary victim) a foreseeable mental illness is sufficient: it is also required that the illness occurred as a consequence of witnessing the fatal accident or its immediate aftermath.[15] This implies that the English control mechanism is not just the

[10] Von Bar (2000), N 60.
[11] Civ. 2e 22 February 1995, D. 1996. 69, comm. Chartier and Cour d'appel Paris 10 November 1983, D. 1984. 214, about which Van Gerven (2000), 118–119.
[12] BGH 4 April 1989, NJW 1989, 2317, about which Van Gerven (2000), 87–89 and Markesinis and Unberath (2002), 119–122.
[13] BGH 11 May 1971, BGHZ 56, 163 = NJW 1971, 1883 = VersR 1971, 905, about which Markesinis and Unberath (2002), 115–119; translation derived from von Bar (2000), N 65.
[14] *Adams v Bracknell Forest Borough Council* [2004] UKHL 47. See also *Phelps v Hillingdon London Borough Council* [2001] 2 AC 619, in which it was held that a school was vicariously liable for the failure of its educational psychologist to diagnose dyslexia in a pupil with special educational needs, about which nr 1804-4.
[15] Markesinis and Deakin (2003), 96–111; Winfield and Jolowicz (2002), para. 5.47.

seriousness of the harm but also the way the harm has occurred. Fleming wrote that in this respect, '... the law is short on principle and predictability. It is a compound of compassion and fear of opening the floodgates of indeterminate liability.'[16]

Foreseeability of a nervous shock implies that a person with normal sensibility would have got a shock in the same situation. 'I think, a reasonably normal condition, if medical evidence is capable of defining it, would be the standard.'[17] In *Bourhill v Young* a speeding motorcyclist collided with a car when, close to the place of the accident, a pregnant woman got off a tram. She did not see the accident but got a nervous shock when hearing the crash; a month later her child was stillborn. The House of Lords deemed the harm not to be foreseeable and concluded that the motorcyclist did not owe the woman a duty of care.[18] See in more detail about the witness requirement nr 1211.

Things are different if the mental harm is suffered by the primary rather than the secondary victim, the latter being the person witnessing someone else's accident as in the above-mentioned cases. One example of mental harm suffered by a primary victim is *Page v Smith*, in which the claimant was involved in a car accident but did not suffer physical damage. Three hours later, however, he felt exhausted and the exhaustion continued. Compensation for this psychosomatic illness was granted. The claimant had been in the so-called zone of danger. In such a case foreseeability of the harm is assumed, be it physical or mental harm (nr 1112).[19] Another example of harm suffered by a primary victim concerns the employee's stress at work. In such a case the employer's duty of care is taken for granted though difficulties will arise as regards the breach of that duty and causation.[20]

A mental illness, as is required in German and English law, will be generally for an expert to assess and to advise the court about. Though psychology and psychiatry have made progress in the course of the 20th century, there are still many uncertainties as to the assessment of psychological harm. It is also well known that certain psychological problems can be simulated or exaggerated. Though this may be true, it cannot be decisive. Problems of simulation and exaggeration also occur in cases of physical harm, for instance as regards back injuries, and this argument is never used to dismiss a claim for damages for this kind of injury.

Pain and suffering, loss of amenities, sorrow, and grief can affect someone's mental well-being. However, these feelings only give a right to compensation for non-pecuniary loss for which a mental illness is not a prerequisite (nr 1206).

---

[16] Fleming, *The Law of Torts* (1998), 178. See also the Law Commission, Consultation Paper no. 137 (1995), para. 5.6 and Law Commission, Report no. 249 (1998), paras 6.5–6.9.

[17] Lord Wright in *Bourhill v Young* [1943] AC 92, 110. Salmond and Heuston (1996), 215; Markesinis and Deakin (2003), 100–101.

[18] *Bourhill v Young* [1943] AC 92; see also *The Wagon Mound (No. 1)* [1961] AC 388, about which nr 1104.

[19] *Page v Smith* [1996] AC 155, about which Van Gerven (2000), 103–105.

[20] See for example *Hatton v Sutherland* [2002] 2 All ER 1, ETL 2002, 155 (Oliphant); *Rahman v Arearose Ltd* [2001] QB 351. See also Winfield and Jolowicz (2002), para. 5.50.

Other kinds of interference with mental health can also be thought of. Anxiety cases are an important category in this respect. Anxiety for things that may, but not necessarily will, happen is a kind of mental suffering. An example is anxiety caused by the possibility of being infected with HIV, for instance because of a blood transfusion, a rape, or a bite. In such a case the victim has to wait several months to know for certain whether or not he is infected. In this respect the courts take different approaches as to whether to grant compensation for anxiety as a kind of mental harm. Tort law protection against the consequences of serious anxiety is only at the beginning of its development.[21]

This matter is closely related to grief and mental harm suffered by relatives of someone who has died in an accident for which someone else was liable. This issue will be discussed more extensively in nr 1211.

705 Personality rights

705-1 *Introduction*

People need protection not only of their life, body, and health but also of aspects of their personality, for example their privacy, honour and reputation, and their freedom to move.[22] Talking about these kinds of personality rights means entering 'a shimmering, systematically and factually still very unsettled world.'[23] Particularly in this area, differences between the legal systems and the legal cultures reinforce each other. This makes comparison a far from easy task (nr 705).

In the 1950s the German BGH acknowledged the general personality right (*das allgemeine Persönlichkeitsrecht*) and this right has appeared to be a strong driving force for the protection of a wide range of aspects of the person. French tort law explicitly protects a number of specific personality rights. English law, however, does not acknowledge a general personality right. Claimants and courts have to struggle with the pigeonhole system of available actions.

One of the most well-known aspects of the protection of the person is the protection of his privacy. This right to privacy is considered to be one of the cornerstones of the life of a human being. It was mentioned for the first time in 1890 in a famous essay by Warren and Brandeis.[24] Its importance gained

---

[21] Von Bar (2000), N 61 with further examples including *Wilkinson v Downton* [1897] 2 QB 57 about which nr 504-1.

[22] As regards the freedom to move, reference can be made to the four economic freedoms of the European Union. The free movement of goods, persons, capital, and services can be considered as rights created for the benefit of every person and legal body in the European Union. See Craig and De Búrca (2003), 580 ff.   [23] Von Bar (2000), N 81.

[24] S.D. Warren and L.D. Brandeis, 'The right to privacy. The implicit made explicit', *Harvard LR*, 4 (1890), 193. It is remarkable that Warren and Brandeis made their case for a right to privacy on the basis of the English wrong of breach of confidence and the English case of *Albert v Strange* (1849) 64 ER 293. Their argument decisively influenced American tort law but left English tort law unaffected for more than a century.

momentum after World War II, and it is a remarkable course of history that in Germany privacy is now protected on the basis of the general personality right, whereas in England, one of the allies that liberated the continent from the totalitarian Nazi regime, it underlies a number of legal remedies but it is not in itself a principle of the common law. In this respect the Human Rights Act 1998 is considered to be a substantial gap filler.[25] In France the statutory right to privacy seems to be a heritage of the 1960s movement rather than of World War II: in 1970 the right to privacy was inserted in article 9 CC even though by then a high level of protection had already been achieved on the basis of article 1382 CC.

An important hurdle for properly comparing the different legal systems is that it is not easy to categorize the area of personality rights. Various aspects of the personality overlap each other and are strongly interwoven. The BGH has rightly concluded that even the right to bodily integrity is merely yet another aspect of the general personality right.[26] Important categories of personality rights are the weakening and distortion of the profile of an individual in society (which includes exploiting and damaging someone else's reputation or name) and the wrongful disclosure to the public (including the violation of the right to one's own image, passing on confidential information, and interference with the private and intimate sphere of others), but these categories are not exhaustive nor can they always be clearly distinguished.[27]

Despite the systematic and cultural differences, there are also converging developments, particularly in the area of the protection of private life. The most important one is beyond doubt the case law of the European Court of Human Rights on Article 8 ECHR. This provision protects the right to private and family life. It is not just a shield against the state (vertical effect) but indirectly also against fellow citizens, companies, and especially the media (horizontal effect) (nr 705-5).

In line with the latest European developments, Article 2:205 ECC provides: Loss caused to a person as a result of the communication of information which, either from its nature or the circumstances in which it was obtained, the person communicating the information knows or ought to know is confidential to the person suffering the loss is legally relevant damage.[28]

705-2 *Germany*

Shortly after World War II the German BGH created the general personality right (*das allgemeine Persönlichkeitsrecht*) (nr 404-2). This happened in the

---

[25] *Wainwright v Home Office* UKHL [2003] 53, ETL 2003, 137 (Oliphant), § 33–34 per Lord Hoffmann.

[26] BGH 9 November 1993, BGHZ 124, 53, 54. See also ECtHR 24 February 1998, Case 21439/93 (*Botta v Italy*), § 32 (no facilities for the disabled at private beaches in Italy): in which the ECtHR has set out that private life in the sense of Article 8 includes a person's physical and psychological integrity. In so far as this provision is related to Articles 2 and 3 ECHR, see nr 1807–1808.

[27] Von Bar (2000), N 82–104.

[28] The PETL do not hold a provision regarding this issue.

Schacht case. A magazine published an article about the establishment of a bank by Dr. Schacht, who had been Minister of Economic Affairs and Director of the National Bank during the Hitler regime. On behalf of his client, Dr. Schacht's lawyer sent corrections and comments to the magazine, demanding a counter-declaration under the Press Act, but the newspaper published the letter in the 'letters to the editor' column. This suggested that the lawyer personally defended the interests of Dr. Schacht. The lawyer claimed rectification and the BGH awarded his claim because the publication created a wrong image of his personality.

The BGH did not just decide the case but, in an unprecedented step, it created the general personality right (*das allgemeine Persönlichkeitsrecht*) as a protected right within the framework of § 823 I. In doing so it referred to the Articles 1 and 2 I *Grundgesetz* (Basic Law) protecting the right to human dignity (*das Recht des Menschen auf Achtung seiner Würde*) and the right to free development of one's personality (*das Recht auf freie Entfaltung der Persönlichkeit*).[29]

With the general personality right the BGH thus created a home for more specific rights, such as the right to privacy and to honour and reputation.[30] In order to provide more vigorous and effective protection, the BGH later decided that in cases of a serious infringement of the general personality right the victim is entitled to claim damages for non-pecuniary loss (nr 1202-2).[31] However, in order not to open the floodgate to claims, no protection is provided in cases of insignificant injuries (*Bagatellschaden*). In many of these cases the courts must balance the claimant's general personality right and the defendant's freedom of expression. A similar infringement (eg publication of private letters) may then lead to a different outcome depending on the interest involved in the freedom of expression: be it to reveal someone's secret love life or his involvement in a political scandal. See about this balancing act also nr 715.

In Germany personality rights are also protected by statutory provisions and consequently by § 823 II (nr 903): one may think of provisions in § 201 ff StGB (Criminal Code) regarding the protection of the home or the private sphere, oral and written communications, personal data, and confidential information.

---

[29] BGH 25 May 1954, BGHZ 13, 334, 338 = NJW 1954, 1404 = JZ 1954, 698 (*Dr. Schacht*): Nachdem nunmehr das Grundgesetz das Recht des Menschen auf Achtung seiner Würde (Art. 1 GrundG) und das Recht auf freie Entfaltung seiner Persönlichkeit auch als privates, von jedermann zu achtendes Recht anerkennt (...), muß das allgemeine Persönlichkeitsrecht als ein verfassungsmäßig gewährleistetes Grundrecht angesehen werden.
See about this case also Markesinis and Unberath (2002), 412–415.
[30] The Constitutional Court (*Bundesverfassungsgericht*) also played an important role in this development; see for instance BVerfG 15 January 1958, BVerfGE 7, 198 = NJW 1958, 257, about which Van Gerven (2000), 142–143; Markesinis and Unberath (2002), 392–397.
[31] BGH 14 February 1958, BGHZ 26, 349 = NJW 1958, 827 (*Herrenreiter*), about which Markesinis and Unberath (2002), 415–420; BGH 19 September 1961, BGHZ 35, 363 = NJW 1961, 2059 (*ginseng*), about which Markesinis and Unberath (2002), 420–423.

705-3 *France*

In France the right to privacy obtained a statutory basis in 1970 with the introduction of article 9 CC ('droit au respect de la vie privée'). This was rather
symbolic since the previous case law already provided far-reaching protection on
the basis of the general provision of article 1382 CC.[32] Pursuant to article 9 CC
the mere infringement of the right to privacy entitles the victim to compensation:
it is not necessary to establish a *faute* or non-pecuniary loss.[33] It could be argued
that this implies a strict liability for infringing another person's right to privacy but
one can also state that the *faute* test is incorporated in the infringement test. An
illustration is the case in which a newspaper published highly personal details of a
singer's life. The singer had published these details himself in another newspaper
but had not given his consent for the second publication, and this publication was
therefore considered to be an infringement of his right to privacy.[34]

705-4 *England*

English law still does not recognise a general liability for invasion of privacy and
infringement of other personality rights.[35] Protection has to be found in specific
torts such as deceit, malicious falsehood, libel (defamation in a permanent form
such as a written text), slander (defamation by spoken words or gestures),
nuisance, breach of confidence, assault, battery, and passing off. Statutory protection can be derived from the Defamation Act 1952 and, more recently, the
Protection from Harassment Act 1997. Most importantly, the Human Rights
Act 1998 obliges the courts to take account of the rights under the European
Convention on Human Rights when interpreting the common law. As a consequence of the direct binding effect of Article 8 of the Convention, the right to
privacy in common law is now protected on a more general basis.[36] This can be
illustrated by a number of celebrity cases.

   A case dating from before the Human Rights Act was about Gordon Kaye, a
well-known television personality, who was interviewed when in hospital after a
serious car accident. He had consented to the interview and its publication but
later it appeared that he had been in no condition to give his informed consent.
Kaye lodged a claim for an injunction but Glidewell LJ stated that ' . . . it is well-
known that in English law there is no right to privacy, and accordingly there is

---

[32] Viney-Jourdain (1998), nr 32–35; Civ. 1re 6 January 1971, D. 1971. 263, comm. Edelman,
JCP 1971. II. 16723, comm. R.L.; Civ. 1re 28 May 1991, D. 1992. 213, comm. Kayser, JCP 1992.
II. 21845, comm. Ringel. See about both decisions Van Gerven (2000), 154–157.

[33] Civ. 1re 5 November 1996, JCP 1997. II. 22805, comm. Ravanas. This decision was more or
less prepared by Civ. 1re 13 February 1985, JCP 1985. II. 20467, comm. Lindon. See Van Gerven
(2000), 156.   [34] Paris 26 March 1987, Sem. Jur. 1987. II. 20904.

[35] See about the need for legislation on this point and about its implications Markesinis and
Deakin (2003), 481 ff.

[36] See also Jane Wright, *Tort Law and Human Rights* (Oxford: Hart, 2001), 163–182.

no right of action for breach of a person's privacy.'[37] However, the Court of Appeal found a solution and granted Kaye an injunction on the basis of malicious falsehood.[38]

In 2004 the House of Lords handed down a milestone decision. The Daily Mirror had published details about a treatment that model Naomi Campbell underwent for her drug addiction. Ms Campbell accepted that the Mirror was entitled to publish the fact that she was addicted, and that she was having therapy, but she argued that details of the treatment were private. In its decision on appeal the House of Lords first of all acknowledged that English law protects privacy. Their Lordships recognized that the relevant national law must be interpreted to ensure that the State complies with its positive obligations under the Convention on Human Rights which require the protection of individual privacy. However, the House of Lords did not create a distinct tort of infringement of privacy but based the protection on the action in equity for breach of confidence.[39] Before the Human Rights Act, breach of confidence had already been pressed into service as a means of protecting privacy but the Act emboldened the courts to hold definitely that this liability could arise even in the absence of prior dealings between the parties. Hence, breach of confidence was expanded not only to cover cases of misuse of private information but also to take account of both Articles 8 (the right to respect for private and family life) and 10 (the right to freedom of expression) ECHR. In the *Campbell* case, the Lords decided with a 3:2 majority that the Mirror's publication of details of Ms Campbell's treatment and a photograph of her leaving the clinic infringed her privacy and was not necessary or justified by the public interest (the right to freedom of expression).[40]

A long-lasting battle with several court decisions concerned the wedding of Michael Douglas and Catherine Zeta-Jones, which was to be covered exclusively by the magazine *OK!*. Two days after the wedding it appeared that another magazine—*Hello!*—was about to publish unauthorized photographs of the wedding. The Douglases sued *Hello!* for breach of privacy. In the first trial the claim for an injunction was awarded but this decision was not upheld by the Court of Appeal.[41] In a second trial the Douglases were awarded £14,750 for distress and inconvenience. Appeal against this decision was dismissed. Lord Phillips MR said: *'Hello!* deliberately obtained photographs that they knew were

[37] *Kaye v Robertson* [1991] FSR 62, at 66.

[38] *Kaye v Robertson* [1991] FSR 62, about which Van Gerven (2000), 160–163. The requirements of malicious falsehood are that the defendant has published about the claimant words which are false, that they were published maliciously, and that special damage has followed as the direct and natural result of their publication. See nr 705-4.

[39] See particularly Gavin Phillipson, 'Transforming Breach of Confidence? Towards a Common Law Right of Privacy under the Human Rights Act', *Mod LR* 66 (2003), 726–758.

[40] *Campbell v MGN Ltd* [2004] UKHL 22.

[41] *Douglas and Others v Hello! Ltd* [2001] 2 All ER 289. The injunction against *Hello!* was dismissed since it was considered to be far more difficult for *Hello!* to prove their loss if the injunction were granted and *Hello!* would win the damages trial, than it would be for *OK!* if the injunction were rejected and they succeeded in the damages trial.

unauthorised and published them to the detriment of the Douglases. This renders them liable for breach of confidence under English law.'[42] Quite remarkably the Court of Appeal also considered that its previous decision about the injunction was wrongly decided, because damages would not have been an adequate remedy to protect private life in the sense of Article 8 ECHR, whereas an injunction would have been. This consideration reflects the major impact of the case law of the ECtHR, particularly the *Caroline von Hannover* case, which will be dealt with in the next section.

705-5 *Article 8 ECHR*

A pivotal instrument for the protection of private life is Article 8 ECHR.[43] See about the European Convention on Human Rights nr 202 and about the remedies for violation of a human right nr 1202-6.

Article 8 ECHR provides for the right to private life and family life. Though this provision has generated a raft of case law it is still unclear what the terms 'private life' and 'family life' mean exactly. The Court has '... avoided laying down general understandings of what each of the items covers and, in some cases, they have utilised the co-terminacy of them to avoid spelling out precisely which is or are implicated'.[44] It should be noted that the Court has extended the protection of private life to activities of a professional or business nature ' ... since it is, after all, in the course of their working lives that the majority of people have a significant, if not the greatest, opportunity of developing relationships with the outside world.'[45]

Although it is essentially the objective of Article 8 to protect the individual against arbitrary interference by the public authorities, it does not merely compel the State to abstain from such interference. The State also has positive obligations inherent in an effective respect for private or family life. These obligations may involve the adoption of measures designed to secure respect for private life even in the sphere of the relationships of individuals between themselves.[46] This is where the horizontal effect of Article 8 comes in.

---

[42] Lord Phillips in *Douglas and Others v Hello! Ltd* [2005] EWCA Civ. 595, nr 53. He openly criticized the House of Lords in *Campbell v MGN Ltd* by saying: 'We cannot pretend that we find it satisfactory to be required to shoe-horn within the cause of action of breach of confidence claims for publication of unauthorised photographs of a private occasion.'

[43] 1. Everyone has the right to respect for his private and family life, his home and his correspondence. 2. There shall be no interference by a public authority with the exercise of this right except such as is in accordance with the law and is necessary in a democratic society in the interests of national security, public safety or the economic well-being of the country, for the prevention of disorder or crime, for the protection of health or morals, or for the protection of the rights and freedoms of others.

[44] Cour d'appel de Paris 13 March 1996, JCP 1996. II. 22632, comm. Derieux, about which Van Gerven (2000), 157–158.

[45] ECtHR 16 December 1992, Case 13710/88 (*Niemetz v Germany*).

[46] ECtHR 24 June 2004, Case 59320/00 (*Caroline von Hannover v Germany*), § 57. See, ECtHR 26 March 1985, Case 8978/80 (*X and Y v Netherlands*), § 23; ECtHR 25 November 1994, Case 18131/91 (*Stjerna v Finland*), § 38.

The protection of personality rights may be restricted by rights or freedoms which the ECHR grants to the other party. In many cases the protection of private life has to be balanced with the freedom of expression (Article 10). Of great importance for the question of how to balance the freedom of expression and the right to private life is the ECtHR's decision in the case of Princess Caroline of Monaco.

Since the early 1990s the Princess had tried to prevent the publication of photos about her private life in the tabloid press. The case that came before the ECtHR was about photos published in various German magazines which were all taken in the public domain. Some of the pictures showed her with actor Vincent Lindon at the far end of a restaurant courtyard in Saint-Rémy-de-Provence, and bore the caption 'These photos are evidence of the most tender romance of our time'.

The German Federal Constitutional Court (*Bundesverfassungsgericht*) considered that Caroline, as a figure of contemporary society '*par excellence*', enjoyed the protection of her private life even outside her home, but only if she was in a secluded place out of the public eye '. . . to which the person concerned retires with the objectively recognisable aim of being alone and where, confident of being alone, behaves in a manner in which he or she would not behave in public'.[47] The Constitutional Court attached decisive weight to the freedom of the press, even the entertainment press, and to the public interest in knowing how the applicant behaved outside her representative functions.

The ECtHR, however, reached a different conclusion. Firstly, it repeated that there is a zone of interaction of a person with others, even in a public context, which may fall within the scope of 'private life'.[48] The Court had no doubt that the publication of photos fell within the scope of her private life (§ 53). Secondly, it considered that the decisive factor in balancing the protection of private life against freedom of expression should lie in the contribution that the published photos and articles make to a debate of general interest.[49] The public's right to be informed is an essential right in a democratic society that, in certain special circumstances, can even extend to aspects of the private life of public figures,[50] particularly where politicians are concerned.[51] To the Court it was clear that, in

[47] BVerfG 15 December 1999, NJW 2001, 2187, § 54. See also BGH 14 May 2002, VersR 2002, 903, ETL 2002, 219 (Fedtke) (*Marlene Dietrich*) and BGH 19 December 1995, BGHZ 128, 1.
[48] ECtHR 24 June 2004, Case 59320/00 (*Caroline von Hannover v Germany*), § 50 ff. See also ECtHR 25 September 2001, Case 44787/98 (*PG and JH v United Kingdom*), § 56; ECtHR 28 January 2003, Case 44647/98 (*Peck v United Kingdom*), § 57.
[49] ECtHR 11 January 2000, Case 31457/96 (*News Verlags GmbH & Co KG v Austria*), § 52 et seq.; ECtHR 26 February 2002, Case 34315/96 (*Krone Verlag GmbH & Co KG v Austria*), § 33 et seq.; ECtHR 18 May 2004, Case 58148/00 (*Plon (Société) v France*), § 60.
[50] Public figures can be described as persons holding public office and/or using public resources and, more broadly speaking, all those who play a role in public life, whether in politics, the economy, the arts, the social sphere, sport or in any other domain: see paragraph 7 of Resolution 1165 (1998) of the Parliamentary Assembly of the Council of Europe on the right to privacy.
[51] ECtHR 18 May 2004, Case 58148/00 (*Plon (Société) v France*).

the instant case, the photos and articles made no such contribution since the applicant exercised no official function and the photos and articles related exclusively to details of her private life (§ 63–66).[52] The Court concluded that in these conditions freedom of expression calls for a narrower interpretation. Furthermore, it considered that the public does not have a legitimate interest in knowing where the applicant is and how she behaves generally in her private life, even if she appears in places that cannot always be described as secluded, and despite the fact that she is well known to the public (§ 76–77). The Court concluded that the German courts had not struck a fair balance between the competing interests and that therefore Article 8 had been breached. The Court reserved its decision on damages.

The Court's decision may have considerable implications for the tabloid press in Europe. As regards public figures the decision is strikingly similar to the Naomi Campbell case in the House of Lords, a decision handed down less than two months before the ECtHR case. It has, however, to be kept in mind that the Court's decision also implies that it could be appropriate for politicians exercising official functions to have a very limited protection of private life or the right to control the use of their image.

706 Wrongful conception (wrongful birth)

706-1 *Protection of the right to self-determination*

Wrongful conception is the term for the birth of an unwanted or unplanned child caused by someone else's wrongful conduct.[53] In fact, the terminology is wrong: what is wrongful in these cases is not the birth of the child but the conduct of a doctor or another third party. The main examples are an ineffective vasectomy or sterilization and a failed abortion. An unwanted pregnancy can also occur after a rape or after a contraceptive appeared to be defective, eg when a condom tears during sexual intercourse. The latter kind of claims will generally be addressed to the manufacturer but they will be difficult to prove (nr 1408-2).

Becoming or staying pregnant because of a contraceptive failure or an ineffective medical treatment can be viewed from a physical point of view. From this perspective, causing a wrongful conception can be considered to be an infringement of the woman's bodily integrity. However, such an approach only deals with one, albeit important, aspect. What is also, and perhaps more

---

[52] ECtHR 26 November 1991, Case 13585/88 (*Observer and Guardian v United Kingdom*), § 59; the Court also referred to the similar scope of Resolution 1165 (1998) of the Parliamentary Assembly of the Council of Europe on the right to privacy.

[53] See for instance Michael Faure and Helmut Koziol (eds.), *Cases on Medical Malpractice in a Comparative Perspective*, (Vienna: Springer, 2001); von Bar (1998), N 581-583; see also the comparative case comments on HR 21 February 1997 (wrongful conception), NJ 1999, 145, comm. CJHB, VR 1998, 182, in *ERPL*, 7/2 (1999), 241–256.

importantly, at stake here is the woman's right to self-determination and the parents' right to choose their way of family life. An unplanned child affects not only the woman but also the child itself, the father and, if applicable, the other children. In other words, it affects private and family life. For this reason an unwanted pregnancy can be considered to be a loss, whereas a not unwanted pregnancy cannot.

This is not only but also a matter of costs. The parents ' . . . have another mouth to feed'[54] and they are statutorily obliged to do so. The Dutch *Hoge Raad* put it this way: 'The damage for which compensation is asked here consists of expenses which, by their very amount, must be deemed to influence in principle the financial situation of the family until the child comes of age.'[55]

The question of whether the interests of the mother and the family ought to be protected is often affected by moral and religious concerns. These concerns are, for instance, expressed in the argument that a wrongful conception claim would imply that the child itself is the damage and that such a claim should therefore be dismissed. An even more reluctant view was expressed by the second *Senat* ('chamber') of the German *Bundesverfassungsgericht* (Constitutional Court). It considered compensation for costs of maintenance to be contrary to the dignity of the child and thus a violation of Article 1 I *Grundgesetz* (Basic Law).[56] Though the German BGH explicitly disagreed with this point of view and principally acknowledged the right to compensation for costs of mainten-ance (nr 706-2), the position of the second *Senat* indicates that the dispute is a serious and a thorough one. It also needs to be emphasized that the discussion in Germany is particularly sensitive because of the experience of gross neglect of respect for human dignity during the Nazi regime. Members of the post-war generation are extremely cautious not to make what they consider to be similar mistakes.[57]

It goes without saying that considering the child itself as damage would be contrary to the dignity of the child. This is explicitly expressed in court decisions acknowledging the right to compensation, for instance by the French *Cour de cassation*: ' . . . the existence of the child (. . .) cannot in itself constitute for the mother a legally reparable loss.'[58]

---

[54] *McFarlane v Tayside Health Board* [1999] 4 All ER 963, 996 (HL).

[55] HR 21 February 1997 (wrongful conception), NJ 1999, 145, comm. CJHB, about which Van Gerven (2000), 133–135, from which the translation is derived.

[56] BVerfG (Zweiter Senat) 22 October 1997, NJW 1998, 523 = JZ 1998, 356. The first *Senat* disagreed with this position: see BVerfG (Erster Senat) 12 November 1997, BVerfGE 96, 375 = NJW 1998, 519 = JZ 1998, 352. See about these cases Markesinis and Unberath (2002), 171–178; Van Gerven (2000), 82–83.

[57] See for instance a similar view as the second *Senat* of the BVerfG, von Bar (1998), N 583.

[58] Civ. 1re 25 June 1991, D. 1991. 566, comm. Le Tourneau (' . . . l'existence de l'enfant qu'elle a conçu ne peut, à elle seule, constituer pour sa mère un préjudice juridiquement réparable.') In the same sense in Germany BGH 18 March 1980, BGHZ 76, 259; BverfG (Zweiter Senat) 22 October 1997, NJW 1998, 523 = JZ 1998, 356 and HR 21 February 1997 (wrongful conception), NJ 1999, 145.

The key issue in wrongful conception cases is that the damage is constituted by the pecuniary and non-pecuniary loss following from the unplanned birth and the interference with family life. Hence, the child does not need to be offended by the fact that damages have been awarded to its parents. So for instance Lord Slynn of Hadley in *McFarlane v Tayside Health Board*: 'An unplanned conception is hardly a rare event and it does not follow that if the conception is unwanted the baby when it is born, or the baby as it integrates into the family, will not be wanted.'[59] Furthermore, it can also be argued that, if a wrongful conception claim is awarded, the parents and the other children can live up to the planned financial standard and the unplanned child does not need to feel embarrassed for taking its part of the family budget. Financial considerations as regards family planning are widely accepted as being legitimate even though a number of people may consider this not to be the highest achievable moral standard for human beings.

An argument against awarding a wrongful conception claim is that the damage can be set off with the benefits of the joy of having a child. The latter is based on the assumption that children are a joy and a blessing but it can be argued that parents do not agree with this assumption on a daily basis. The main objection to a set off is, however, that the costs are material whereas the joy is immaterial. This is an argument to only setting off the non-pecuniary loss with the benefits.[60] And indeed, as will be shown, the courts tend to award damages for non-pecuniary loss for the inconveniences of pregnancy and birth but not for raising the child (nr 706-2).

A final moral point in the discussion is related to the general duty of a victim to restrict his damage: if he does not do so, he has to bear a part of his damage on the basis of contributory negligence (nr 1212). In wrongful conception cases the defendant, for instance the doctor, sometimes takes the view that the claimant could have restricted her damage by terminating the pregnancy. The courts always dismiss this defence, not only in countries in which abortion is a crime, but also in countries with more liberal legislation that could allow the abortion. More generally, it can be argued that one cannot be obliged to restrict the amount of damage by diminishing or destroying his or another's person position as a person.

706-2 *Heads of damage*

Wrongful conception causes specific kinds of damage. Apart from the costs of a second surgery in case of a failed sterilization (for which compensation is

---

[59] *McFarlane v Tayside Health Board* [1999] 4 All ER 963, 971 (HL), about which Van Gerven (2000), 92–96. In the same sense HR 21 February 1997 (wrongful conception), *NJ* 1999, 145, comm. CJHB: the parents ' . . . may contradict such an impression by raising the child with loving care.' See about this case Van Gerven (2000), 133–135, from which the translation is derived.

[60] See in this respect also HR 21 February 1997 (wrongful conception), *NJ* 1999, 145, comm. CJHB, about which Van Gerven (2000), 133–135, from which the translation is derived.

generally provided), three heads of damage can be thought of: the cost of maintaining the child, the loss of income for the mother, and the non-pecuniary loss. The general picture is that if compensation is awarded, this happens in a rather reluctant way.

Compensation for *non-pecuniary loss* is only granted to the mother. German law provides compensation for such a loss on the ground that she suffered physical injury (*Körperverletzung*),[61] whereas English law provides compensation for pain and suffering and for the inconveniences of pregnancy and birth.[62] French law is stricter in that the mother only has a right to compensation for non-pecuniary loss if she has given birth to a handicapped child.[63]

Although loss of income of the mother (if she is not able to continue working or training in the same way as she did before the birth of the child) is generally not compensable,[64] the cost of maintaining a healthy child under certain circumstances is. Here, German law generally compensates the costs of maintenance. However, English law does not but it grants a nominal sum of £15,000. French law does not award compensation at all. If the child is handicapped, all systems provide compensation for the (extra) costs of bringing up the child.

The German BGH grants both parents the right to compensation for the cost of maintaining the child, provided the physician in charge of sterilization or abortion performs the operation incorrectly.[65] However, if the abortion was carried out on medical rather than on social grounds, there is no right to compensation.[66] As has been pointed out (nr 706-1), the second *Senat* of the *Bundesverfassungsgericht* (the Constitutional Court) considered compensation for maintenance costs contrary to the dignity of the child[67] but in a fascinating high-level discussion the BGH did not give in and retained its case law albeit under certain strict conditions.[68]

French law does not award damages at all if the child is born healthy. A right to compensation only exists if the birth gives rise to a special loss (*préjudice particulier*) that exceeds the normal burdens of motherhood. This is particularly the case if the child is handicapped, if the mother is in a bad financial position, or if she suffers from mental problems as a consequence of the birth.[69]

[61] BGH 27 June 1995, NJW 1995, 2407 (wrongful birth).

[62] *McFarlane v Tayside Health Board* [1999] 4 All ER 963 (HL).

[63] CE 2 July 1982, D. 1984. 425, comm. d'Onorio, Gaz. Pal. 1983. 193, comm. Moderne; cp. Civ. 25 June 1991, D. 1991. 566, comm. Le Tourneau, about which Van Gerven (2000), 115.

[64] An exception is HR 21 February 1997 (wrongful conception), NJ 1999, 145, comm. CJHB.

[65] BGH 18 March 1980, BGHZ 76, 249; BGH 30 June 1992, VersR 1992, 1229; BGH 27 June 1995, NJW 1995, 2407; BGH 16 November 1993, BGHZ 124, 128 = JZ 1994, 305, about which Markesinis and Unberath (2002), 164–171.

[66] BGH 25 June 1985, NJW 1985, 2749.

[67] BVerfG (Zweiter Senat) 22 October 1997, NJW 1998, 523 = JZ 1998, 356; BVerfG (Erster Senat) 12 November 1997, BVerfGE 96, 375 = NJW 1998, 519 = JZ 1998, 352. See about these cases Markesinis and Unberath (2002), 171–178; Van Gerven (2000), 82–83.

[68] See for instance Deutsch-Ahrens (2002), N 456.

[69] CE 2 July 1982, D. 1984. 425, comm. d'Onorio, Gaz. Pal. 1983. 193, comm. Moderne; CE 27 September 1989, D. 1991. 80, comm. Verpeaux, about which Van Gerven (2000),

Until 1999 the English courts had awarded damages for the costs of bringing up the child.[70] But in *McFarlane v Tayside Health Board* the House of Lords took a different view. It held unanimously that the parents of a healthy child are not entitled to recover damages for the cost of caring for and bringing up the child.[71] The reasons for this decision were diverse: the majority thought that there was no duty of care and the minority argued it was a matter of irrecoverability of the loss. At the heart of the decision was the consideration that the costs of bringing up a child were pure economic loss and this head of damage is only compensable if the *Caparo* requirements are met (nr 714-1).[72] It was argued that, though the damage caused by the doctor was foreseeable, awarding damages would not be just, fair, and reasonable.[73]

In *Rees*, Lord Bingham of Cornhill summed up what had been, in his view, the policy considerations:

> ... an unwillingness to regard a child (...) as a financial liability and nothing else, a recognition that the rewards which parenthood (...) may or may not bring cannot be quantified and a sense that to award potentially very large sums of damages to the parents of a normal and healthy child against a National Health Service always in need of funds to meet pressing demands would rightly offend the community's sense of how public resources should be allocated.[74]

If the House of Lords uses arguments of public policy, it is to dismiss claims rather than to support them.

Rees v Darlington Memorial Hospital was about a severely visually handicapped woman who did not want to have a baby because she felt unable to discharge the ordinary duties of a mother. The sterilization operation was not carried out properly and the woman had a healthy son. The House of Lords affirmed *McFarlane* and dismissed the mother's claim for the cost of bringing up the child. However, a small majority awarded the mother a nominal sum of £15,000, a sum that would also be available for healthy parents of a healthy child, ' ... in order to recognise that in respect of birth of the child the parent has suffered a legal wrong'.[75] The sum was conventional and not compensatory but

---

115–116; Civ. 1re 25 June 1991, D. 1991. 566, comm. Le Tourneau, about which Van Gerven (2000), 114–115.

[70] *Emeh v Kensington and Chelsea and Westminster Area Health Authority* [1984] 3 All ER 1004 (CA); *Thake v Maurice* [1986] 1 All ER 497 (CA); *Allen v Bloomsbury Health Authority and Another* [1993] 1 All ER 651 (Brooke J).

[71] *McFarlane v Tayside Health Board* [1999] 4 All ER 963 (HL). In *Parkinson v St James and Seacroft University Hospital NHS Trust* [2002] QB 266, the Court of Appeal held that the mother of a handicapped child could recover the additional costs she would incur so far as they would be attributable to the child's disabilities.

[72] *Caparo Industries plc v Dickman* [1990] 2 AC 605, about which Van Gerven (2000), 215–219; see nr 700.   [73] *McFarlane v Tayside HB* [2000] SLT 154.

[74] *Rees v Darlington Memorial Hospital*, [2003] UKHL 52, § 6, per Lord Bingham of Cornhill.

[75] *Rees v Darlington Memorial Hospital*, [2003] UKHL 52, § 17, per Lord Nicholls of Birkenhead.

it made the wrong actionable in negligence (which requires damage). See also nr 1202-3 about general, nominal, and specific damages in English law.

This award of a nominal sum, following Lord Millet in *McFarlane*, indicates that the outcome of *McFarlane* has not been completely satisfactory. Although hardly explicit, the case illustrates the emergence of the idea that also in English law wrongful conception cases are mainly about woman's (human) right to self-determination and the parents' right to family planning. Indeed, Lord Millet indicated that the conventional sum was awarded for the denial of an important aspect of their personal autonomy, namely ' ... the right to limit the size of their family.'[76]

It remains to be seen which position the House of Lords will take in a case of healthy parents having a disabled child with a higher amount of costs of care. In such a case the Court of Appeal allowed recovery of the 'additional' caring costs.[77]

707 Prenatal harm (wrongful life)

707-1 *Actively caused prenatal harm*

The traditional expression of wrongful life refers to a claim for the infringement of the child's health or bodily integrity caused during pregnancy or even before conception. This terminology is not only awkward but also confusing, since it is not the life that is wrongful but the conduct of a third party that has caused or has not prevented harm to an unborn child and the child is born handicapped. A more preferable terminology would be *prenatal harm*.

Such harm may be the consequence of an accident suffered by a pregnant woman (actively caused prenatal harm). Traditionally, however, wrongful life refers to cases in which a child suffers damage because of an illness of the mother during pregnancy, or because the mother has not received proper advice on health risks for her baby, for instance as regards the possibility of a hereditary illness or a genetic defect (not prevented prenatal harm, see nr 707-2).

In these cases a claim for the child can only arise if it is born alive. If it is stillborn the person who would have been entitled to damages did not become a legal subject. Its claim is therefore not inherited by the mother. However, the mother will generally have a claim in her own right for the impairment of her body and health.[78]

If the damage is actively caused by a third party and the child is born alive, all legal systems protect the child's right to bodily integrity and health. This applies, for instance, in the situation in which a pregnant woman and her foetus are injured in a car accident and as a consequence thereof the child appears to be disabled.[79]

---

[76] Lord Millet in *Rees v Darlington Memorial Hospital*, UKHL [2003] 52, § 122. In the same sense Tony Weir, *A Casebook on Tort*, 10th edn., 2004, 17.

[77] *Parkinson v St James and Seacroft University Hospital NHS Trust* [2001] EWCA Civ. 530, [2002] QB 266. [78] Von Bar (2000), N 48.

[79] BGH 11 January 1972, BGHZ 58, 48 = NJW 1972, 1126 = JZ 1972, 363, about which Markesinis and Unberath (2002), 144–147.

Another example is the case in which a doctor carried out an abortion but did not examine the woman to verify the result of the operation. The child was born disabled as a consequence of the abortion attempt, and was awarded FRF 600,000 (approximately €100,000) compensation for non-pecuniary loss.[80]

In England the Congenital Disabilities (Civil Liability) Act 1976 clarified the, by then, unclear situation. Section 1 states that a duty can be owed to a person who is not yet born or even conceived. It holds that the child has an action for damages provided he is born alive and disabled, and that the defendant is liable to either parent of the child for the conduct that caused the disability, for instance on the basis of the tort of negligence. Section 2 provides that the child, once it is born, does not have a claim against its mother except in a case in which she drove a car and negligently caused an accident.[81]

An infringement of the foetus' health can also be caused before conception. A German case was about a woman who received a blood transfusion with contaminated blood. Some months later she got pregnant and when she gave birth to her child it suffered from congenital syphilis. The BGH decided that the child had an action against the hospital based on § 823 I BGB.[82] The BGH dismissed the defendant's argument that he had not infringed the child's health since in fact it had never been in a healthy condition. Thus the court acknowledged that the right to health protects not only against a deterioration of health but also the development of a healthy condition. This case law once again shows how thoroughly tort law protects physical integrity (nr 703).

707-2 *Not prevented prenatal harm*

The most disputed wrongful life cases are those in which a child appears to suffer from a hereditary illness, a genetic defect, or from its mother's illness during pregnancy, for instance rubella. In these cases, claims are addressed to the doctor, not because he caused the disease but because he acted wrongfully in another way. For instance, because he did not advise the mother properly about the risks of a hereditary illness or a possible genetic defect, or because he did not properly prevent the mother's illness that affected the child's health. In these cases all three systems dismiss the child's claim for wrongful life but all allow the mother's claim to a certain extent.

A German wrongful life case was about a child that was born handicapped as the consequence of her mother having suffered from rubella (*Röteln*) during pregnancy. The physician failed to diagnose the condition which would have led the mother to terminate the pregnancy. The BGH decided that the *mother* could

---

[80] CE 27 September 1989, D. 1991. 80, comm. Verpeaux, about which Van Gerven (2000), 115–116.

[81] See for the text of the Act, Markesinis and Unberath (2002), 154–156 and Van Gerven (2000), 91–92.

[82] BGH 20 December 1952, BGHZ 8, 243 = NJW 1953, 416 = JZ 1953, 307, about which Van Gerven (2000), 80–81; Markesinis and Unberath (2002), 147–149.

claim compensation for pain and suffering provided that there was a connection between the injury of the unborn child and the character of the delivery, particularly if it necessarily led to a Caesarean section. The parents had a right to compensation for the extra costs of maintaining the handicapped child, also for costs occurring after the child's majority.[83] In a later case the defendant doctor argued that, at the late stage of the pregnancy, an abortion would not have been legal anyway. However, the BGH held that an abortion at that stage could have been justified in the sense of § 218a II *Strafgesetzbuch* (Criminal Code) because of the potential psychological burdens for the mother.[84]

The BGH decided differently as regards the *child's* claim, for which it could not find a legal basis. It decided that the doctor did not owe a duty towards the child to prevent its birth because of its foreseeable handicap. Such a duty would be inconsistent with the right to bodily integrity, and it would imply a judgement as regards the value of a disabled life:

Human life (...) is a legally protected interest of the highest order deserving absolute protection. No third party may determine its value. For this reason it is recognised that the duty to save the life of a sick person or one who is seriously injured must not be made to depend upon a judgment as to the value of the life to be saved.[85]

In these considerations the horrors of the Hitler era, in which disabled persons were seen as degenerated, echoed even stronger than in the discussions regarding the wrongful conception claims (nr 706-1).

In its decision the BGH referred to the English case of *McKay and Another v Essex Area Health Authority* which had been decided a year earlier.[86] This case was about a pregnant mother who contracted rubella in the early months of her pregnancy. Despite having conducted blood tests, the doctor failed to diagnose the infection and the child was born severely disabled. The Court of Appeal held that the doctor owed the *mother* a duty of care to advise her about the infection and the desirability of an abortion. The doctor was, however, under no

---

[83] BGH 18 January 1983, BGHZ 86, 240, about which Markesinis and Unberath (2002), 156–163. See also Deutsch-Ahrens (2002), N 456 with further references.

[84] BGH 18 June 2002, *Medizinrecht* 2002, 640, *ETL* 2002, 212 (Fedtke). See also the discussion in nr 706-1 in the framework of wrongful conception between the BGH and the BVerfG on the question whether the importance of human dignity allows the existence of a living human being to be legally qualified as a source of harm.

[85] BGH 18 January 1983, BGHZ 86, 241:

Das menschliche Leben (...) ist ein höchstrangiges Rechtsgut und absolut erhaltungswürdig. Das Urteil über seinen Wert steht keinem Dritten zu. Daher ist auch anerkannt, daß die Pflicht, das Leben eines Erkrankten oder schwer Verletzten zu erhalten, nicht von dem Urteil über den Wert des erhaltbaren Lebenszustandes abhängig gemacht werden darf.

See Markesinis and Unberath (2002), 156–163 from which the translation is derived (161).

[86] *McKay and Another v Essex Area Health Authority* [1982] 2 All ER 771 (CA), about which Van Gerven (2000), 97. In this case the Congenital Disabilities (Civil Liability) Act 1976 was not yet applicable but the Court of Appeal considered this Act which excludes wrongful life cases in any event.

obligation to the unborn child to terminate its life. Therefore the court dismissed the *child's* claim because it was contrary to public policy as a violation of the sanctity of human life. Furthermore, the court considered it to be impossible to assess damages because it would require a comparison between the value of existence of a disabled child and the value of non-existence.[87]

In France both the parents and the child are not allowed to claim damage for wrongful life though this was different prior to 2002. For a long time, the *parents'* claim was generally awarded because the doctor's omission to inform or examine the mother as regards health risks for the unborn child prevented the parents from making a well-considered choice as to whether or not to carry out an abortion.[88] In 2000 the *Cour de cassation* also awarded the *child's* claim for wrongful life in the *Perruche* decision. Nicolas Perruche's mother contracted rubella during pregnancy though the doctor had told her she was immunized against it. Subsequently, the child exhibited neurological and sensorial troubles evocative of congenital rubella. The *Cour de cassation* awarded the child's claim for the loss resulting from the handicap, such as psychological, aesthetic, physical, and financial damage.[89]

This decision invoked strong criticism since it was considered to be contrary to the constitutional principle of the dignity of the human person. It was also argued that it suggested that the handicapped have no place in society. Furthermore, doctors felt under increasing pressure to advise abortions since the techniques to diagnose handicaps were not 100 per cent accurate. In early 2002 this resulted in an Act overturning the *Cour de cassation* by outlawing wrongful life claims holding that nobody can be indemnified for his birth, even if handicapped.[90] This provision in its turn was criticized for being the result of a kind of conspiracy between doctors and the legislator in order to remove the burden of liability to national solidarity.[91] The Act can also be considered to be a bridge too far since the *Cour de cassation* did not hold that life should be compensated but only the handicap. Another serious consequence of the Act is that not only the child's claim but also the parents' claim for wrongful life is now blocked, apart from their claim for compensation for

---

[87] *McKay and Another v Essex Area Health Authority and Another* [1982] 2 All ER 771 (CA), about which Van Gerven (2000), 97.
[88] Civ. 1re 26 March 1996, Bull. civ. I, no 56, about which Van Gerven (2000), 116; in the same sense CE 27 September 1989, D. 1991. 80, comm. Verpeaux, about which Van Gerven (2000), 115–116; Crim. 4 February 1998, JCP 1999. II. 10178.
[89] Ass. plén. 17 November 2000 (Perruche), D. 2001. 332, comm. Mozeaud and Jourdain. In Ass. plén. 13 July 2001, Bull. Ass. plén, 2001, no 10, 21, the *Cour de cassation* confirmed its *Perruche* decision though limiting it to cases in which the conditions allowed for a lawful abortion; see also the comparative case comments in *ERPL* 11/2 (2003), 201–234. The *Conseil d'État*, dealing with cases against public hospitals, always dismissed the child's claim for wrongful life but granted the award for the child's damage to the parents, at the same time forbidding the sum to be shared among all the children: CE 14 February 1997, D. 1997. Somm. 322, obs. Penneau, JCP 1997. I. 4025, no 19, obs. Viney (*CHR de Nice c. Époux Quarez*).
[90] Loi no 2002-303 relative aux droits des malades et à la qualité de système de santé. See, inter alia, Philippe Brun, 'France', *ETL* 2002, 179–194 and Simon Taylor, 'Clinical Negligence Reform: Lessons from France?', *ICLQ* 52 (2003), 737–748.
[91] Patrice Jourdain, 'Loi Anti-Perruche: une loi démagogique', D. 2002, C. 891.

psychological damage. Finally, although the Act includes a mechanism of indemnification through national solidarity, there is yet no special fund created to compensate parents for the high costs of raising their handicapped child.[92A]

In all three legal systems, claims of children for not prevented prenatal harm are dismissed and this can be considered to be rather unfortunate.[92] It is often argued that it is not possible to compare the value of an existing disabled life and a non-existing life. However, such a comparison is not necessary if one follows the French *Cour de cassation* in its reasoning that it is the costs of the handicap that need to be compensated and not the handicapped life. The child's life is as valuable as any other human life. This is underpinned rather than denied by awarding compensation for the high costs of raising the handicapped child. Financial support is crucial to prevent the life of the child and its parents from being more troublesome than necessary. The possibility of compensation may also prevent the parents' decision as to whether or not to terminate the pregnancy from being influenced by their financial position.

C PROTECTION OF PROPERTY

708 Introduction

Not only personal interests (nr 702–707) but also interests in objects, either movable or immovable, are generally protected in the different jurisdictions. The same goes for intangible property rights like financial security rights, including mortgages. In common law a distinction is made between the protection of proprietary interests in land (real property) and in movable things (personal property). Forms of (non-physical) interference with a proprietary interest in land will be often qualified as a kind of nuisance and will be discussed in Chapter 15 (Liability for immovable objects).

This section is directly linked to the following section D on the protection of 'pure' economic interests. 'Pure economic loss' is loss not related to or consequential upon harm to personal injury or property loss. If a proprietary interest is infringed, for instance a lorry is damaged, the legal systems acknowledge that the owner is entitled to compensation for the costs of repairing the damage or for the difference between the value of the lorry before and after the accident. However, the owner is also entitled to compensation for the economic loss caused by the infringement of his property, such as the costs of hiring a replacement lorry or the income he loses while not being able to use the lorry.

[92A] The ECtHR considered this to be a violation of Article 1 of the First Protocol ECHR: ECtHR 6 October 2005, Case 1513/03 (*Draon v France*).

[92] The Dutch *Hoge Raad* awarded a wrongful life claim, both from the parents and the child in HR 18 March 2005, *RvdW* 2005, 42, VR 2005, 47.

The latter—consequential—damage is particularly important. As long as the economic loss is consequential upon the property loss, it is not 'pure' and it will be compensated in all jurisdictions. Hence, the more reluctant a legal system is about compensation for pure economic loss, the more important it will be how a property right is interpreted and what damage is considered to be consequential. The wider the interpretation of a property right, the less the loss is 'pure economic' and the more consequential economic loss is compensated.

This section will look at the different interpretations given to property or proprietary interests in order to see which cases remain to be dealt with in the framework of 'pure economic loss'. The emphasis will be on German and English tort law, because French tort law does not hold statutory or systematic obstacles for the recovery of damage to movable or immovable objects. The only requirement as regards damage in French law is that it is direct and certain and that it has affected a legitimate interest (nr 1202-1). Unlike the English and German systems, there is no need in the French system to draw a line between damage to property and pure economic loss.

In this respect it is interesting to refer to Article 1 First Protocol to the European Convention on Human Rights, generally known as the provision that protects the right to property. However, this provision does not use the words 'ownership' or 'property' but the more general concept of 'possession'.[93] This is due to the fact that the former concepts have different meanings in the Contracting States and that it would be confusing to use them in the Convention. This means that the word 'possession' has an autonomous meaning. What needs to be examined is whether the circumstances of the case, considered as a whole, may be regarded as having conferred on the applicant title to a substantive interest protected by that provision.[94] Therefore, the protection provided by Article 1 includes claims with regard to, for instance, patents, shares, goodwill, a building licence, fishing rights, and a planning permission, though it does not include a driving licence.[95] Furthermore, the concept of 'possessions' is not limited to 'existing possessions' but may also cover assets, including claims, in respect of which the applicant can argue that he has at least a reasonable and legitimate expectation of obtaining effective enjoyment of a property right.[96]

---

[93] Article 1 First Protocol ECHR:

1. Every natural or legal person is entitled to the peaceful enjoyment of his possessions. No one shall be deprived of his possessions except in the public interest and subject to the conditions provided for by law and by the general principles of international law. 2. The preceding provisions shall not, however, in any way impair the right of a State to enforce such laws as it deems necessary to control the use of property in accordance with the general interest or to secure the payment of taxes or other contributions or penalties.

The French text of the provision uses the word *'biens'* for 'possession'.

[94] ECtHR 19 June 2001, Case 34049/96 (*Zwierzyński v Poland*), § 63.
[95] Robin White and Clare Ovey, *Jacobs and White, the European Convention on Human Rights*, 3rd edn., (Oxford: Oxford University Press, 2002), 303.
[96] ECtHR 12 July 2001, Case 42527/98 (*Prince Hans-Adam II of Liechtenstein v Germany*), § 83.

709 Germany

§ 823 I BGB does not only mention life, body, and health as protected rights but also property rights. Infringing such a right in an unlawful (*rechtswidrig*) and negligent (*fahrlässig*) way gives rise to liability. The courts have taken a broad view of the concept of infringement of property (*Eigentumsverletzung*). Such an infringement cannot only be established if an object is damaged but also if it is stolen, or even if it remains undamaged but cannot be used properly any more, either partially or completely and either for a certain time or for good.[97]

An example is the case of motor ship that could not sail out for eight months because a quay wall collapsed as a consequence of bad maintenance. It was decided that the latter had infringed the right of the owner of the motor ship even though the ship had remained undamaged. Other ships that were prevented from entering the same canal to carry out contracted business at that place were considered not to suffer damage to their property.[98]

Another case was about a fishery that had been supplied with toxic fish feed as a consequence of which fish were poisoned and died. There was no doubt that the supplier had thus infringed the fishery's property rights. However, the BGH also established an infringement of its property rights as regards the fishes that did not die. Even though they were in good health they could not be sold anymore because their condition had changed.[99] Other examples of infringement of a property right are the wrongful confiscation of a driving licence, the reprogramming of a computer, and the ransacking of an archive.[100]

These examples show that the protection of property includes not only physical damage to an object but also the loss of use of it even though the object itself has remained undamaged. This broad interpretation of the concept of property implies that in German law an important number of cases can be regarded as a matter of infringement of property (*Eigentumsverletzung*) and not as a matter of pure economic loss. The courts have extended the concept of the infringement of a property right because the BGB *Tatbestand* system contains restrictions as regards the compensation of pure economic loss.

However, the BGH has made clear that these extending operations have their limits. An example is the damage to drivers who got stuck in a traffic jam but

---

[97] Münchener Kommentar-Wagner (2004), § 823 N 111–119.
[98] BGH 21 December 1970, BGHZ 55, 153 = NJW 1971, 886 = VersR 1971, 418 (*Motorschiff Christel*), about which Markesinis and Unberath (2002), 219–222. See for a comparable case in England *Rose v Miles* (1815) 105 English Reports 773: the owner of a lighter was prevented from sailing along a stretch of a canal which was blocked by the defendant's barge; the owner of the lighter had to transport his cargo overland; on the basis of public nuisance (nr 506-1), it was held that the owner was entitled to recover his loss which to English standards was considered to be pure economic.
[99] BGH 25 October 1988, BGHZ 105, 346 = NJW 1989, 707 = JZ 1989, 638 (*Fischfutter*).
[100] BGH 31 October 1974, BGHZ 63, 203; BGH 26 February 1980, BGHZ 76, 216.

were not entitled to compensation from the person who negligently caused the accident which in its turn caused the traffic jam. One of the reasons was that the market value of the cars immobilized in the traffic jam was not affected, and thus the property rights were not infringed. The BGH also blocked the alternative route via § 823 II (breach of statutory duty) stating that it is not the scope of traffic regulations to provide that type of protection.[101]

710 England

In England the tort of negligence is the main basis for getting compensation for damage to personal property. The existence of a duty of care is generally no problem, because it is assumed that the tortfeasor owes a duty of care towards persons who may foreseeably suffer property damage because of his negligent conduct (nr 503-3).

Whereas in German law the loss of use of property is considered to be loss of property (thus focusing on the economic function of property), the English tort of negligence in principle considers loss of use as pure economic loss (thus limiting property loss to infringement of the physical integrity of the property). This does not mean that English law does not provide an action for the loss of use. Useful torts in this respect are private nuisance (particularly as regards real property) and public nuisance (nr 506-1) as well as torts like trespass to goods and conversion (nr 505-2). However, the requirements for these latter torts are not crystal clear and the same goes for their mutual relationship.[102] According to Rogers, 'English law governing remedies for interference with goods is exceedingly technical, partly because of the long survival and overlap of a number of different heads of liability and partly because the law, though tortious in form, is largely proprietary in function.'[103]

Another important point of discussion in this respect concerns the question when economic loss is consequential to property loss and when it has to be considered as pure economic loss. In *Spartan Steel* a steel plant suffered damage when a power main was cut during excavation. The Court of Appeal decided that the contractor was liable for the damage to the plant's property (the reduction in value of solidified 'melt') and the profit it would have made from its sale. However, the plant could not recover lost profits caused by the suspension of production because this was not a consequence of damage to their property.[104] If the cable had been damaged on the plant's premises, the plant could have recovered damages for loss of production during the time necessary to repair the cable, just as is the case in German law (nr 709).[105]

---

[101] BGH 21 June 1977, NJW 1977, 2264 = VersR 1977, 965, about which Markesinis and Unberath (2002), 222–226.   [102] Van Gerven (2000), 169 ff.
[103] Winfield and Jolowicz (2002), para. 17.1.
[104] *Spartan Steel and Alloys Ltd. v Martin & Co (Contractors) Ltd* (1973) 1 QB 27, about which Van Gerven (2000), 177–180 and Markesinis and Unberath (2002), 216–219. See also Winfield and Jolowicz (2002), para. 5.32.   [105] Winfield and Jolowicz (2002), para. 5.32.

In 1983, during the summer of the duty of care (nr 503-2) *Junior Books Ltd v Veitchi Co Ltd*[106] cast doubt on the validity of *Spartan Steel*. Subcontractor Veitchi constructed a floor in a Junior Books' production hall but the floor appeared to be defective and had to be replaced. Junior Books claimed damages in tort *inter alia* for the interruption of business during the replacement. Contrary to what could have been expected on the basis of *Spartan Steel*, the House of Lords held that Junior Books' allegation disclosed a cause of action for negligence. When a couple of years later the House of Lords had taken a more conservative approach as regards compensation of pure economic loss, it was 'clarified' that *Junior Books* was a case of property damage and consequential (and thus not pure) economic loss.[107]

Junior Books was distinguished by the Court of Appeal in *Muirhead v Industrial Tank Specialities Ltd*. A fishmonger suffered damage because a tank in which he kept his lobsters did not function properly and the lobsters died (prematurely). Because the seller of the tank was insolvent the fishmonger filed a claim against the French manufacturer. He recovered damages for the dead lobsters and the consequential loss but not for the profit he lost during the time the tank did not function properly.[108]

Eventually, *Spartan Steel* was reconfirmed in two cases: *The Mineral Transporter* (a Privy Council case) and *The Aliakmon* (a House of Lords case).[109] The former case was about a vessel that was damaged and the time charterers of the vessel (not being the vessel's owners or possessors) suffered damage. They filed a claim against the tortfeasor but failed to recover the hire they had to pay during the time the vessel was out of action. Both the Privy Council and the House of Lords decided that the wrongdoer did not owe a duty of care towards the third party who did not himself suffer any property damage. Such damage is considered to be of a pure economic character. The rules for recovering such damage will be pointed out in nr 714.

D PROTECTION OF ECONOMIC INTERESTS

711 Introduction

'Pure economic loss' is the financial loss someone suffers and which is not the consequence of death, personal injury, or damage to movable or immovable

---

[106] *Junior Books Ltd v Veitchi Co Ltd* [1983] AC 520.

[107] *Tate & Lyle Industries v Greater London Council* [1983] 2 AC 509, 530, per Lord Templeman. In *Murphy v Brentwood District Council* [1991] AC 398 (HL) Lord Keith suggested that *Junior Books* fell within the extended *Hedley Byrne* principle; see nr 714-2.

[108] *Muirhead v Industrial Tank Specialties Ltd* [1986] QB 507.

[109] *Candlewood Navigation Corporation Ltd v Mitsui OSK Lines Ltd (The Mineral Transporter)* [1985] 3 WLR 381; *Leigh and Sillivan Ltd v The Aliakmon Shipping Co Ltd (The Aliakman)* [1986] AC 785. In the same sense *Tai Hing Cotton Mill Ltd v Lim Chong Hing Bank* [1985] 3 WLR 317; *Yuen Kun Yeu v Attorney-General of Hong Kong* [1988] AC 175.

objects.[110] This issue is comparable to the protection of mental health which is particularly disputed if the mental harm is not related to physical harm (nr 704).

Most European systems are reluctant in awarding compensation for pure economic loss. This can be illustrated with Article 2:202(4) PETL:

> Protection of pure economic interests or contractual relationships may be more limited in scope. In such cases, due regard must be had especially to the proximity between the actor and the endangered person, or to the fact that the actor is aware of the fact that he will cause damage even though his interests are necessarily valued lower than those of the victim.

Compensation of pure economic loss is complicated both from a technical and a policy point of view. The policy issue regards the fact that it is thought that compensating pure economic loss on a general basis would open the floodgates of claims. For instance, if someone causes an accident on a motorway, other travellers can be affected because of the delays caused. If an auditor wrongfully approves a company's financial statements, investors who relied on this approval can suffer pure economic loss. It has been argued that awarding such claims on a general basis would put such a heavy burden on the tortfeasor and the courts that it would be preferable to leave the loss where it falls.[111]

It is hard to say whether this scenario is nightmare or reality. The best to be said about is that it is the fruit of a political view. There is no evidence whatsoever that compensating pure economic loss on a more general basis would lead to apocalyptic events. Moreover, in personal injury cases the financial consequences can be extensive too. One may for instance think of the *DES* case (see nr 1108-2).[112] Whatever scenario is preferred, choices need to be made to decide when pure economic loss is to be compensated and when not.

The ways in which the legal systems have translated these policy considerations into technical rules differ considerably. French law has the most open approach, seemingly awarding compensation for pure economic loss on a general basis. However, the control mechanisms can be found in the way the requirements for liability (*faute*, causation, and damage) are being applied. English and German tort law both contain high hurdles for compensation of pure economic loss but the policy differences between the two systems are considerable. Whereas

---

[110] See about pure economic loss: Willem H. van Boom, Helmut Koziol and Christian A. Witting, *Pure Economic Loss, Torts and Insurance Law*, 9th vol., (Vienna, New York: Springer 2004); Mauro Bussani and Vernon Valentine Palmer (eds.), *Pure Economic Loss in Europe*, (Cambridge: Cambridge University Press, 2003); Mauro Bussani, Vernon Valentine Palmer and Francesco Parisi, 'Liability for Pure Financial Loss in Europe', *AJCL* 51 (2003), 113–162; Efstathios K. Banakas (ed.), *Civil Liability for Pure Economic Loss*, (Boston: Kluwer International, 1997).

[111] Jaap Spier (ed.), *The Limits of Expanding Liability*, (The Hague: Kluwer International, 1998).

[112] Mauro Bussani and Vernon Valentine Palmer, 'The Notion of Pure Economic Loss and its Setting', in Mauro Bussani and Vernon Valentine Palmer (eds.), *Pure Economic Loss in Europe*, (Cambridge: Cambridge University Press, 2003), 16–21. See also H. Bernstein, 'Civil Liability for Economic Loss', *AJCL* 46 (1998), 111, 126–128; William Prosser, 'Intentional Infliction of Mental Suffering: a New Tort', *Michigan LR*, 37 (1939), 877: '. . . it is a pitiful confession of incompetence on the part of any court of justice to deny relief upon the ground that it will give the courts too much work to do.'

in Germany the judiciary has appeared to be a strong advocate for improving the position of the person or company suffering pure economic loss, the English judiciary broadly supports the principle behind the hurdles and keeps them high. In this respect the real differences seem to exist between France and Germany on the one hand and England on the other. This is because the limits provided by causation in France should not be underestimated, and because the German courts in many ways have overcome the limitations of the BGB. These differences will be further analysed later in this section.[113]

The common feature is that none of the legal systems has succeeded in finding proper general criteria for the compensation of pure economic loss. The three systems use various control mechanisms, both on the part of the defendant (standard of care, scope of the duty) and of the claimant (damage, causation). In other words, this is an area very much governed by *ius in causa positum*: court decisions depend on the specific circumstances of the case. Only in-depth factual analysis can bring more clarity in this misty environment.[114]

712 France

French tort lawyers will raise their eyebrows when reading about pure economic loss. As such this topic does not exist in French tort law. It compensates pure economic loss on a general basis just like all other kinds of damage. At a conceptual level there are no limits.[115]

Behind the screens there are, however, various control mechanisms with which the French courts keep liability for pure economic loss within limits. First of all, the concept of *faute* is different in cases of pure economic loss compared to cases of personal injury and property loss. In the latter category of cases the standard of reference is *le bon père de famille* (nr 302-1) but conduct in economic affairs is judged by the standard of whether one has complied with the principles of *loyauté, honnêteté, et bonne foi* (loyalty, honesty, and good faith).[116]

Two other important control mechanisms are that the damage needs to be 'personal, certain, and legal' (nr 1202-1) and that it is directly caused (nr 1105). An example of causation as a control mechanism is the case of a singer who had an accident and had to cancel a concert. The concert organizer suffered damage and filed a claim against the person who caused the accident. His claim was dismissed because the *Cour de cassation* held that his damage was indirect.[117] Another case was about a creditor who was not able to collect a debt from someone who was killed in a road traffic accident. His heirs rejected the inheritance and the creditor

---

[113] Von Bar (2000), N 44.
[114] See Bussani, and Palmer, op. cit.; Van Boom, Koziol and Witting, op. cit.
[115] See on this topic also Gerhard Wagner, in Zimmermann (ed.), *Grundstrukturen des europäischen Haftungsrecht* (2002), 224 ff. [116] Viney-Jourdain (1998), nr 474.
[117] Civ. 2e 14 November 1958, Gaz. Pal. 1959. 1. 31.

claimed damages from the person who was liable for the accident. The *Cour de cassation* deemed the creditor's damage to be indirect.[118]

Despite these control mechanisms, French law is the most generous of the three systems in awarding claims for pure economic loss since in many cases a direct cause is established. For example, a bus company could recover loss of passenger fares when, due to a traffic accident, buses of the claimant company were delayed.[119] And a factory could recover damage when someone ruptured a gas main which compelled the factory to suspend its production. It was decided that the damage to the factory was the direct consequence of the cutting of the gas main.[120] In these cases it was sufficient that the damage was the direct consequence of the tortious conduct and not merely a hypothetical or indirect consequence.

713 Germany

The BGB only provides for limited grounds for getting compensation for pure economic loss.

From a statutory point of view § 823 II (nr 903) and 826 (nr 402-4) were, *inter alia*, intended to provide compensation for pure economic loss, since § 823 I only deals with personal injury and property loss. § 826 provides for the possibility to lodge a claim for intentional infliction of conduct *contra bonos mores*. This provision is considered to mainly cover loss caused in economic affairs.[121] Its impact is, however, limited due to the requirement that the loss has to be caused intentionally, even though the courts have accepted *dolus eventualis* as sufficient for liability.

Very soon after the entering into force of the BGB it appeared that § 823 II and § 826 were insufficient to do justice to claims for pure economic loss. Hence, in 1904 the *Reichsgericht* called into being the right to business—*das Recht am Gewerbebetrieb* or *das Recht am Unternehmen*—which constituted a *sonstiges Recht* (another right) in the sense of § 823 I BGB (nr 404-1). This right protects operating enterprises against unlawful interference with their business. Its scope is, however, restricted: it does not include professions and the infringement of the right has to be 'direct' (*unmittelbarer* or *betriebsbezogener Eingriff*).

This latter requirement can be illustrated with a case about a company that could not operate for some time because someone had damaged an electricity cable in the neighbourhood of the company's premises. The company claimed damages but the BGH dismissed the claim for infringement of the right to business because

---

[118] Civ. 2e 21 February 1979, D. 1979. IR 344, JCP 1979. IV. 145.

[119] Civ. 2e 28 April 1965, D. 1965. 777, comm. Esmein, about which Van Gerven (2000), 197–198.

[120] Civ. 2e 8 May 1970, Bull. civ. II, no 122, about which Van Gerven (2000), 198. See in the same sense as regards the rupture of a high tension cable: CE 2 June 1972, AJDA 1972. 356, about which Van Gerven (2000), 198–199.

[121] Compare the French standard of *loyauté, honnêteté, et bonne foi* (loyalty, honesty, and good faith), about which nr 712.

it held that the company's right had not been directly infringed.[122] The company would have been entitled to claim damages on the basis of the infringement of property (*Eigentumsverletzung*) if the cable had been on the company's premises, or if the company as a result of the lack of power supply had suffered damage to its goods, eg the failure of eggs to develop in the incubator of a poultry farm.[123] This would have entitled the company to claim compensation on the basis of § 823 I for property damage and the consequential economic loss.

The courts provided a third road to compensation for pure economic loss in addition to the statutory provisions and the right to business, by the so-called contract with protective effects for third parties (*Vertrag mit Schutzwirkung für Dritte*). This contractual liability towards third parties is not easy to fit into the legal system and, of course, this is fuel for a strong debate in the doctrine. It is, however, generally accepted that the defendant is allowed to use all contractual defences towards the third party.[124]

One of the areas in which this *Vertrag mit Schutzwirkung für Dritte* device is applied is the liability of auditors towards third parties. An investor bought shares in a business while relying on a compulsory 'statutory' audit. The approved account showed a surplus of DM 2.5 million (€1.27 million) but it later appeared to have a deficit of DM 11 million. The investor filed a claim against the auditor. The BGH agreed that in this case the principle of the contract with protective effect for third parties could be applied. Subsequently, it stated that

... there are no difficulties about also applying these principles in cases in which an auditor of accounts is entrusted with the compulsory audit of a company provided that it appears sufficiently clear to him that on this audit a particular work product is wanted from him which is to be used as against a third party who trusts in his expert knowledge.[125]

The foregoing shows that the courts, with unflagging zeal, have tried to find ways to compensate pure economic loss. 'One cannot help but think that (...) judges do everything in their power to close any gaps left by the BGB in protecting pure economic loss, by using the provisions on the protection of ownership.'[126] A downside of the judiciary's benevolence is that this is a patchy area of tort law and difficult to get to grips with.

[122] BGH 9 December 1958, BGHZ 29, 65 = NJW 1959, 479, about which Van Gerven (2000), 187–189; Markesinis and Unberath (2002), 203–208.

[123] BGH 4 February 1964, BGHZ 41, 123 = NJW 1964, 720.

[124] Larenz (1987), § 17 II, 224–231; Van Gerven (2000), 601–602 and in depth Hannes Unberath, *Transferred Loss: Claiming Third Party Loss in Contract Law* (Oxford: Hart, 2003).

[125] BGH 2 April 1998, BGHZ 138. 257 = NJW 1998, 1948 = JZ 1998, 1013, about which Markesinis and Unberath (2002), 283–288 from which the translation is derived. A claim against an auditor can also be based on § 826 BGB. See for instance BGH 26 November 1986, NJW 1987, 1758, about which Van Gerven (2000), 234–235: a bank had allowed a company a credit of DM 500,000 (€255,000) on the basis of its financial statements which were approved by an auditor but which later appeared to be incorrect. It was decided that the auditor had acted wilfully (which is sufficient to establish intention) and *contra bonos mores vis-à-vis* the bank.

[126] Von Bar (2000), N 38. According to John Fleming, 'Property Damage–Economic Loss: A Comparative View', *LQR*, 105 (1989), 508, this underscores the German ' ... willingness, indeed eagerness, to extend tort protection' despite the BGB's ' ... categorical exclusion of tort damages for

714 England

714-1 *The* Caparo *rule*

On the basis of the tort of negligence compensation for pure economic loss is only awarded if there is a good reason to do so. As will be set out in more detail below, the tort of negligence requires that the economic loss was foreseeable, that there was sufficient proximity between claimant and defendant, and that it is fair, just, and reasonable to impose a duty of care upon the defendant.

The claimant may also rely on other torts to get compensation for pure economic loss. On the one hand one may think of breach of statutory duty (nr 902) and private and public nuisance (nr 506-1) which do not always require negligence.[127] There are also other torts available but these usually require that the wrongdoer caused the harm intentionally or in bad faith (nr 714-3).[128]

The tort of negligence provides modest means to get compensation for pure economic loss, especially after the House of Lords turned to a more conservative approach in the mid 1980s (nr 500). Compensation for pure economic loss on the basis of this tort is now mainly to be determined on the basis of *Caparo*. A second important basis for liability is the extended *Hedley Byrne* rule which assumes that there can be a duty of care in order to prevent third parties suffering economic loss from improper statements or any assumption of responsibility for the provision of services (nr 714-2).

Caparo claimed to have suffered damage when purchasing Fidelity, a stock exchange listed company. In doing so, it relied on the statutory audit in which Dickman approved Fidelity's annual account. However, this account wrongly showed a profit of £1.3 million before tax; in fact the loss was more than £400,000. Caparo filed a claim against Dickman, the auditor. The key question was whether Dickman owed Caparo a duty of care.

Lord Bridge said:

What emerges is that, in addition to the foreseeability of damage, necessary ingredients in any situation giving rise to a duty of care are that there should exist between the party owing the duty and the party to whom it is owed a relationship characterized by the law as one of 'proximity' or 'neighbourhood' and that the situation should be one in which the court considers it fair, just and reasonable that the law should impose a duty of a given scope on the one party for the benefit of the other.[129]

---

pure economic loss and the great weight reputedly given by German law to theoretical orthodoxy over pragmatism.'

[127] It may be doubted whether breach of statutory duty should be included here, since there seems to be no 'economic' case law: Markesinis and Deakin (2003), 517–518.

[128] See, for example, Tony Weir, *Economic Torts* (Oxford: Clarendon Press, 1997).

[129] Lord Bridge in *Caparo Industries plc v Dickman* [1990] 2 AC 605 at 617, about which Van Gerven (2000), 215–219.

This implies that in cases of pure economic loss a duty of care requires (a) foreseeability, (b) proximity, and (c) fair-just-reasonableness.

In *Caparo* the House of Lords decided that a special relationship (foreseeability and proximity) between Caparo and the auditor could only be established if the auditor knew or ought to have known that the annual account

... would be communicated to the plaintiff either as an individual or as a member of an identifiable class, specifically in connection with a particular transaction of a particular kind and that the plaintiff would be very likely to rely on it for the purposes of deciding whether or not to enter upon that transaction or upon transactions of that kind.[130]

714-2 *The extended* Hedley Byrne *principle*

In cases of pure economic loss a duty of care can also be based on the extended *Hedley Byrne* principle. It started in 1964 with *Hedley Byrne*. Advertising agency Hedley Byrne & Co asked the Heller bank for information about the solvency of one of its clients. The bank gave positive information based on inadequate research. A little later the client went bankrupt and Hedley suffered damage. The House of Lords decided unanimously, referring to the Atkinian principle in *Donoghue v Stevenson* (nr 503-1) that there can be a duty of care in order to prevent third parties suffering economic loss from improper statements, provided that there is a special relationship between the one who owes the duty and the one who suffers the damage.[131]

In *Henderson v Merrett Syndicates Ltd*, the *Hedley Byrne* principle was reformulated into the extended *Hedley Byrne* principle. The principle was no longer confined to statements but it can be applied to any assumption of responsibility for the provision of services, and one of the crucial requirements is that the defendant relied upon the assumption of responsibility by the other party. If the requirements are met, a duty of care cannot be denied for reasons of fairness, justice, and reasonableness.[132]

The *Henderson* case was about individual insurers at Lloyds (the so-called *Names*) who had incurred heavy personal liabilities caused by negligent underwriting by the managing agents of syndicates of which they were members. Lord Goff held that there was plainly an assumption of responsibility by the managing agents towards the Names. They also represented themselves as possessing a

---

[130] *Caparo Industries plc v Dickman* [1990] 2 AC 605, [1990] 1 All ER 568, about which Van Gerven (2000), 215–219 and Markesinis and Unberath (2002), 306–309. See for comparison *JMPG v Nicks Anderson* [1991] All ER 134 and *Morgan Crucible v Hill Samuel Bank and Others* [1991] All ER 148. In France no specific hurdles have to be taken by the claimant: *faute, dommage* and *lien de causalité* are sufficient; see for instance Com. 17 October 1984, JCP 1985. II. 20458, comm. Viandier, about which Van Gerven (2000), 241.

[131] *Hedley Byrne & Co Ltd v Heller and Partners Ltd* [1964] AC 465. See also *Ministry of Housing and Local Government v Sharp* [1970] 2 QB 223; *Howard Marine Ltd v Ogden & Sons Ltd* [1978] QB 574; *Tai Hing Cotton Mill Ltd v Liu Chong Hing Bank Ltd* [1985] 3 WLR 317, 330.

[132] Lord Steyn in *Williams v Natural Life Health Foods Ltd* [1998] 2 All ER 577, [1998] 1 WLR 830, explaining *Henderson v Merrett Syndicates Ltd* [1995] 2 AC 145.

special expertise to advise the Names on the suitability of risks to be underwritten. Furthermore, the managing agents well knew that the Names placed implicit reliance on that expertise. He concluded that a duty of care was owed in tort by the agents to the Names and '... since the duty rests on the principle in *Hedley Byrne*, no problem arises from the fact that the loss suffered by the names is pure economic loss.'[133]

It was, for instance, decided on the basis of the extended *Hedley Byrne* principle that an economic adviser who was responsible for information given in a brochure owed a duty of care towards those initially buying shares in a business and also towards everybody purchasing shares from the initial buyers.[134] The principle was also used to impose a duty of care on an educational psychologist (employed by a local authority), holding him liable for failing to diagnose a child's dyslexia. For this reason the child did not receive necessary educational provision for her dyslexia and did not learn to read and write as well as she could have done.[135]

The most well known application of the extended principle was *White v Jones* in which the House of Lords acknowledged that a solicitor can owe a duty of care towards a third party. Solicitor Jones failed to make a new will Mr Barratt, in which he would bequeath money to his daughters and his five grandchildren. Eventually Jones did make an appointment with Barratt but Barratt died three days earlier. The disappointed legatees claimed damages from Jones. With the smallest possible majority the House of Lords decided that Jones owed a duty of care towards the legatees. Lord Goff said:

> ... under the *Hedley Byrne* principle by holding that the assumption of responsibility by the solicitor towards his client should be held in law to extend to the intended beneficiary who (as the solicitor can reasonably foresee) may, as a result of the solicitor's negligence, be deprived of his intended legacy in circumstances in which neither the testator nor his estate will have a remedy against the solicitor.[136]

Neither the *Caparo* rule nor the extended *Hedley Byrne* principle provide for easy decisions. It would be '... reaching for the moon... to expect to accommodate every circumstance which may arise within a single short abstract formulation.'[137] Whereas *Caparo* focuses on proximity and fair-just-and-reasonableness, *Hedley Byrne* requires assumption of responsibility and reliance. It very much depends on

---

[133] *Henderson v Merrett Syndicates Ltd* [1995] 2 AC 145 at 182. See for a critical analysis of the Hedley Byrne case law: Christian Witting, *Liability for Negligent Misstatements* (Oxford: Oxford University Press: 2004).

[134] *Possfund Custodian Trustee Ltd and Another v Diamond and Others* [1996] 2 All ER 774 (Lightman J).   [135] *Phelps v Hillingdon London Borough Council* [2001] 2 AC 619.

[136] *White v Jones* [1995] 1 All ER 691, 710, per Lord Goff, about which Van Gerven (2000), 219–224 and Markesinis and Unberath (2002), 338–348. The case is also interesting because of Lord Goff's references to German, French, and Dutch cases. France: Civ. 1re 23 November 1977, JCP 1979. II. 19243; Civ. 1re 14 January 1981, JCP 1982. II. 19728; Civ. 1re 21 February 1995, Bull. civ. I, no 95, about which Van Gerven (2000), 242–243; Germany: BGH 6 July 1965, NJW 1965, 1955 (Testamentfall); the Netherlands: Hof Amsterdam 31 January 1985, NJ 1985, 740.

[137] *Merrett v Babb* [2001] 3 WLR 1 at 41, per May LJ.

the circumstances of the case as to whether a duty of care is established on the basis of one of these rules. However, it has been argued that the two should not be seen as rivals but as complementary rules yielding to the same result.[138]

714-3 *Intentional interference with economic interests*

Pure economic loss can also be recovered on the basis of a number of torts dealing with intentional interference with economic interests. One may think of (a) inducing breach of contract and interference with contract, (b) interference with trade or business by unlawful means, (c) economic duress, and (d) conspiracy to injure or to use unlawful means.

(a) Broadly speaking, a person who deliberately procures the breach of a contract to the detriment of another will be liable in tort under certain circumstances. It is a prerequisite that in all such cases the claimant first shows that he had a pre-existing legal right to performance under a valid and non-rescindable contract.[139]

The tort of directly inducing breach of contract requires that the defendant intended to interfere with the claimant's contractual right or that he was at least reckless in creating the risk of a breach of this contract.[140] The actionable conduct itself may take two forms: firstly, the defendant may directly induce a third party to breach his contract with the claimant. For example, there will be liability where the defendant enticed an opera singer into performing for his theatre rather than for the claimant with whom she had already concluded a contract.[141] Courts have applied this principle to exclusive dealing contracts and commercial supply contracts.[142] Secondly (although this scenario is less clear-cut in case law), there will be liability where the defendant himself is bound by a contract to the claimant, and breaches this contract so as to leave the claimant unable to fulfil his obligations under a *separate* contract to a third party. An example is a breach of contract by Shirley Bassey with record production company Dreampeace by refusing to perform, thus leaving Dreampeace unable to honour its contracts with the musicians which it had hired for the recording. The Court of Appeal allowed Dreampeace's action in tort against Bassey. In such cases, the claimant's action in tort remains distinct and independent of his action in contract (where the difference in rules of liability may mean that he is ultimately left undercompensated).[143]

Further extending the two categories mentioned above, case law has held that *indirect* inducement to a breach is also actionable in principle. For example, a trade union may be liable if it puts pressure on a company to stop supplying

[138] *Bank of Credit and Commerce International (Overseas) Ltd v Price Waterhouse (No 2)* [1998] PNLR 564 at 582, per Neill LJ. [139] *Grieg v Insole* [1978] 1 WLR 302.
[140] *Torquay Hotel Co Ltd v Cousins* [1969] 2 Ch 106, 138, per Lord Denning.
[141] *Lumley v Gye* (1853) 2 E & B 216.
[142] *Jasperson v Dominion Tobacco Co* [1923] AC 709; *Temperton v Russell* [1893] 1 QB 715.
[143] *Millar v Bassey* [1994] EMLR 44.

material to another company under a valid contract.[144] Similarly, a parent
company which withdraws funds from its subsidiary may be held liable if the
latter is as a consequence unable to honour its contractual obligations towards
another company.[145] The required mental element for liability is tempered: it is
sufficient for the defendant to have intended to obtain the breach of contract and
it is irrelevant that the ultimate victim of this breach was in fact someone who
had not been 'targeted' by him.[146]

There is no liability where the defendant's conduct neither induces a breach of
the contract nor interferes with performance under it. A person who illegally
records concerts cannot be liable to the record company with whom the per-
former had signed an exclusive contract simply on the basis that he has in some
way 'decreased the value of' the contract.[147]

(b) The key requirement for liability for *interference with trade or business by
unlawful means* is that the defendant used unlawful means to interfere with the
claimant's trade or business.[148] Adopting a rather free market *laissez-faire*
approach, English courts have considered that this formal, objective criterion is
essential to establishing liability:[149] a person cannot be liable for simply acting in
his own economic self-interest and the claimant must realise that his 'right . . . to
pursue his trade or calling is qualified by an equal right of others to do the same
and compete with him'.[150]

In order to temper this deferential standard of review, judges have been active
in construction of the notion of 'unlawful means'. It is not necessary that these
means are actionable *per se*.[151] They include making threats of physical violence
to the claimant,[152] as well as cases of fraud. One high-profile example of the
latter is provided by the case of *Lonrho plc v Fayed*, in which the House of Lords
reinstated an action by the claimant alleging that fraud perpetrated by the
defendant (businessman Mr Al-Fayed) upon a government minister had meant
that the defendant had been given an unfair opportunity to bid for the Harrods
department store.[153] Other unlawful means include threatening to breach a
contract or to induce such a breach.[154]

The requisite intention in these torts is more stringent than in the economic
torts relating to contractual obligations (above) and serves as a control mechanism to limit the scope of liability. The defendant must have intended to inflict
economic damage on an identified person whom he had in some way targeted;
incidental victims of 'collateral damage' will have no claim.[155]

---

[144] *DC Thomsons & Co Ltd v Deakin* [1952] Ch 646.
[145] *Stocznia Gdanska SA v Latvian Shipping Co* [2002] 2 Lloyd's Rep 436.   [146] Ibid.
[147] *RCA Corp v Pollard* [1983] 1 Ch 135.   [148] *Rookes v Barnard* [1964] AC 1129.
[149] *Mogul Steamship Co Ltd v McGregor, Gow & Co* (1889) LR 23 QBD 598; [1892] AC 25.
[150] *Allen v Flood* (1898) AC 1, 173.   [151] [1992] 1 AC 448.
[152] *Messenger Group Newspapers v NGA* [1984] ICR 397.   [153] [1992] 1 AC 448.
[154] *Rookes v Barnard* [1964] AC 1129; see also *Stratford v Lindley* [1965] AC 269 and *Hadmor
Productions Ltd v Hamilton* [1983] 1 AC 191.
[155] *Lonrho Ltd v Shell Petroleum Co Ltd (No 2)* [1982] AC 173 (per Lord Diplock).

(c) A defendant will be liable for *economic duress* if he brings illegitimate pressure to bear upon the claimant, thereby vitiating his consent. An example is a union extracting money from the claimant in order to free its ship from being blacklisted.[156] It has been held that economic duress is an autonomous tort which is actionable in its own right[157] and this has led some commentators to fear that the requirement of 'unlawful means' will be undermined.[158]

(d) For the tort of *conspiracy to use unlawful means*, it is sufficient to establish that the defendants simply intended to use such means. No justification is available (cf conspiracy to injure *infra*): indeed, the issue of whether a defendant was personally capable of committing the illegality in question appears to be irrelevant. For example, in *Rookes v Barnard*[159] one of the defendants was held liable for conspiracy even though he personally was not bound to the employer by a contract of employment.

The tort of conspiracy to injure does not require proof of use of unlawful means. However, the claimant must overcome the difficult hurdle of showing that the defendants had predominantly intended to inflict 'deliberate damage without any (...) just cause'.[160] This is a deferential, subjective test, which in practice demands that the defendants exhibited personal malice.[161] It is a sufficient defence for them to show that they acted in their economic self-interest in some way: significantly, there is no control of proportionality by the courts between the alleged economic motive and the means taken achieve it.[162] For example, the courts have accepted this justification defence where the defendants had concluded a closed shop agreement with the aim of boycotting the claimant's supplies.[163]

E CONCLUDING REMARKS

715 Balancing freedom and protection

The analysis of this chapter shows that there is no such thing as a limitative list of protected interests: '... tort law can be employed to protect whatever interests are deemed worthy of protection in any particular society; the list of protected interests is not set in stone.'[164] In each legal system life, bodily integrity, physical

[156] *Universe Tankships Inc of Monrovia v International Transport Workers' Federation* [1983] 1 AC 366.
[157] *Universe Tankships Inc of Monrovia v International Transport Workers' Federation* [1983] 1 AC 366 at 400, per Diplock LJ.   [158] Markesinis and Deakin (2003), 524.
[159] *Rookes v Barnard* [1964] AC 1129.
[160] *Crofter Hand Woven Harris Tweed Co v Veitch* [1942] AC 435; see also *Quinn v Leathem* [1901] AC 495.   [161] See for example, *Huntley v Thornton* [1957] 1 WLR 321.
[162] Markesinis and Deakin (2003), 526.
[163] *Crofter Hand Woven Harris Tweed Co v Veitch* [1942] AC 435.
[164] Ken Oliphant, 'The Nature of Tortious Liability', in Andrew Grubb (ed.), *The Law of Tort* (London: Butterworths, 2002), 9.

and mental health, personality rights, property rights, and also pure economic interests are protected, albeit to a different extent and in different ways.

As regards personality rights this protection includes the right to self-determination and family planning. These rights are at stake for parents, at least for the mother, in the cases on wrongful conception and prenatal harm (wrongful life) (nr 706–707). These cases are illustrative for the development of personality rights in general which have gained great weight in the second half of the 20th century. In particular, the influence of human rights has led to a less casuistic and more conceptual approach of the protection of personality rights in tort law. In England this development has only just begun since the enactment of the Human Rights Act which made human rights directly applicable in English law.

The only interest not protected in the three legal systems is that of the child for not prevented prenatal harm (wrongful life). Legal as well as moral objections are at the basis of dismissing such claims. A legal reason is that there is no causation: if the doctor had advised the mother properly the child would probably not have been born; or, similarly, it is held that causation cannot be established since it requires a comparison of an existing disabled life and a non-existing life. The moral objection is that it would be denigrating towards handicapped persons to consider a handicapped life as damage. If, however, as has been pointed out, one would not take the handicapped life but the costs of the handicap as the damage to be compensated this moral issue could be 'neutralized'. Such a claim would not differ from a claim for damages for loss of mental and physical health in general.

Apart from the disputed prenatal harm claim of the child, all sorts of interests are, in principle, protected by tort law. Hence, a catalogue of protected interests does not add much to understanding tort law. The pivotal issue is that interests are *more or less* protected. The higher the value, the better the protection is. Life and bodily integrity are strongly protected: on the part of the defendant not much is needed to trigger liability: in many cases he is (almost) strictly liable. However, these interests are not absolutely protected: protection of life and bodily integrity are not guaranteed under each and every circumstance. In the end there is always a balance to be struck with the interests of the potential tortfeasor.

Pure economic interests, on the other hand, are less strongly protected. On the part of the defendant more is needed to trigger liability: in a number of cases liability for pure economic loss requires intentional conduct (England and Germany) or at least a 'direct' causal connection (France). In many cases even intentionally caused pure economic loss is not compensable, particularly if this happens in fair competition. This also shows that the level of protection depends on the interests of the potential tortfeasor.

This idea of a relative protection of interests is also adopted in Article 2:102 PETL:

(1) The scope of protection of an interest depends on its nature; the higher its value, the precision of its definition and its obviousness, the more extensive is its protection. (...)
(5) The scope of protection may also be affected by the nature of liability, so that an interest may receive more extensive protection against intentional harm than in other cases.

This provision is drafted as a principle rather than a rule and in this function it makes sense.[165]

In Tony Weir's unbeatable description:

In fact a tort claim is really more of a boxing match than a hurdle race; (...) success depends on the number of points you make overall. The plaintiff gets extra points if the harm he has suffered is of serious nature—especially personal injury—or if he is particularly deserving or especially reliant on the defendant; so too if the defendant's conduct was very reprehensible, or if the contribution his conduct made to the harm was very obvious and direct, or if he was very close to the plaintiff so that he should have been especially concerned for his well-being and interest.[166]

The lesson of this chapter is that unlawfulness or wrongfulness cannot be based one-sidedly on the infringement of a right (as is the primary approach in § 823 I BGB) or one-sidedly on a certain kind of conduct (as is the primary approach in the English tort of negligence).[167] Unlawfulness or wrongfulness is rather determined by *balancing* the interests of both the claimant (the protection of his life, goods, and financial assets) and the defendant (the protection of his freedom to act).[168] This makes tort law a special branch of the fine art of balancing. In the end the balancing act results in an answer to the question of what kind of conduct may be required from someone with respect to the interests of others. Or, turning the question around, it provides an answer to the question of what kind of conduct people may expect from each other.

The protection of life and property on one hand, and the protection of the freedom to act on the other, cannot be fully warranted at the same time. Full freedom to act would make society extremely dangerous, whereas full protection of rights and interests would paralyse society. Tort law is about balancing the freedom of conduct against the protection of rights and interests:

As has often been pointed out, if all the trains in this country were restricted to a speed of 5 miles an hour, there would be fewer accidents, but our national life would be intolerably slowed down. The purpose to be served, if sufficiently important, justifies the assumption of abnormal risk.[169]

It is exactly this balancing act that will be the topic for analysis in Chapter 8. It will be shown that the requirement of negligence, in particular, provides the

---

[165] The ECC puts strong emphasis (eleven Articles) on the idea that damage needs to be legally relevant. In a number of these provisions the legal relevance of damage is, however, also determined by the defendant's conduct. The most striking example is Article 1:101(2), holding: 'Particular rules may provide that damage is legally relevant only if caused intentionally.'

[166] Tony Weir, *A Casebook on Tort*, 10th edn. (London: Sweet & Maxwell, 2004), 5.

[167] This only concerns the matter of principle as regards unlawfulness. As a practical matter there are important benefits for the claimant in the German approach in which the infringement of a right also provides for advantages as regards the burden of proof. In fact, this brings fault liability a step closer to liability for rebuttable negligence: see nr 903 and 1004-2.

[168] Larenz-Canaris (1994), 350: 'Das Grundproblem jeder Deliktsordnung besteht in dem Spannungsverhältnis zwischen Güterschutz und Handlungsfreiheit.'

[169] Asquith LJ in *Daborn v Bath Tramways Motor Co Ltd* [1946] 2 All ER 333, at 336. See also Kötz-Wagner (2004), N 39.

tools to balancing the freedom to act on one hand and the protection of interests on the other.

716 The role of insurance

Balancing freedom and protection is not just a matter of technique. The court's decision is also driven by opinions about justice, fairness, and reasonableness. It is biased by the importance attached to freedom and protection and this in its turn is determined by political, social, cultural, and policy preferences (nr 608–610).

Of course, a very important role in this balancing act is played by the availability of insurance. Unlike scarcely a century ago, the defendant will now often be backed by a liability insurer, the claimant can usually rely on other sources of payment, such as sick pay from his employer or payments from his health care or disability insurer, and the claimant's insurer or employer may have a right of recourse against the defendant. Hence, the mentioning of the names of the main actors on the credit titles of many cases is generally misleading. In fact, the parties are often not much more than the puppets on a string held by their insurers who also pronounce the text of the play from backstage. In this way, tort law determines less whether the tortfeasor or the victim has to bear the loss, but more whose insurance company, and therefore which group of insured people, has to.[170]

The availability of insurance liability has boosted the function of tort law as a compensation system, virtually at the same time as national legislators started setting up social security systems. In tort law the scope of strict liability was gradually extended and the courts developed high standards of care, including objective rather than subjective tests (nr 811), affirmative duties (nr 808), and duties to prevent victims against their own negligence (nr 807).[171] Thus, the standard of care moved away from normal life standards and required more from the defendant than could reasonably be expected from a normal human being (nr 1004), in order to provide compensation to the claimant. For example, in *Daly v Liverpool Corporation*, Stable J stated that the standard of care and skill which the law requires from a driver is in fact a standard 'which it is impossible to reconcile with the discharge of the duties of drivers'.[172] It has been argued more than once that the influence of insurance has thus perverted the tort law requirements.[173]

---

[170] André Tunc, 'Les causes d'exonérations de la responsabilité de plein droit de l'article 1384 alinéa 1er, du code civil', D. 1975. 86: 'Les problèmes de responsabilité civile ne doivent pourtant plus être envisagés comme s'ils se posaient entre deux individus. La plupart du temps, aujourd'hui, l'assurance en transforme les données.' See also, for example, Geneviève Viney, *Le déclin de la responsabilité individuelle* (Paris: Librairie Générale de Droit et de Jurisprudence, 1965); Hein Kötz, *Sozialer Wandel im Unfallrecht* (Karlsruhe: Müller, 1976); P.S. Atiyah, *The Damages Lottery* (Oxford: Hart, 1997).
[171] By the end of the 20th century the courts also developed rules to ease the victim's burden of proof for causation (nr 1107).　　　[172] *Daly v Liverpool Corporation* [1939] 2 All ER 142.
[173] B.S. Markesinis, 'La perversion des notions de la responsabilité délictuelle par la pratique de l'assurance', *RIDC*, 1983, 301–317; Le Tourneau (2004), nr 51: 'L'indemnisation de la victime en

'Liability for personal fault had undoubtedly appealed to the strongly individualistic strain in Victorian moralising; but as a basis for a workable system of accident compensation it had required significant compromise.'[174]

For this reason liability insurance has become of the utmost importance to understand contemporary tort law. Initially, such insurance aimed to protect the tortfeasor's solvency and, indeed, liability insurance still is a person's or company's crushable financial zone. In the course of time it has also been the basis for raising the required level of care in fault liability and to develop rules of strict liability. More generally, it has also been instrumental in striking a balance between allowing dangerous activities because of their social benefits on the one hand, and the protection against the consequences of these risks on the other. Without liability insurance a high level of care or strict liability would substantially limit the freedom to act. With such insurance, however, the main limitation on the freedom to act is the necessity of paying the premium for the liability insurance policy. These premiums are generally rather modest, especially in relation to the total costs of a risky activity.

With this insurance background in mind, the following chapters will further analyse the balancing of the interests of the claimant and the defendant, first of all the judge's balancing act in the framework of intention and negligence (Chapter 8), subsequently the balancing act of the legislator in the framework of liability for violation of a statutory rule (Chapter 9) and rules of strict liability (Chapter 10), and finally the balancing of the mutual interests in the framework of causation (Chapter 11) and damage and damages (Chapter 12).

---

est grandement facilitée. Mais cela au prix d'une perversion de la responsabilité qui n'est plus commutative (comme elle devrait l'être) mais distributive.' See also Lord Denning, *The Discipline of Law* (London: Butterworths, 1979), 280: 'In theory the Courts do not look behind the masks. But in practice they do. That is the reason, why the law of negligence has been extended so as to embrace nearly all activities in which people engage.' Christian von Bar, 'Das "Trennungsprinzip" und die Geschichte des Wandels der Haftpflichtversicherung', *AcP*, 181 (1981), 326: the judge ' . . . macht ein Haftungsrecht schließlich unglaubwürdig, wenn er nicht den tragenden Grund der Verurteilung angibt: die Versicherung' (the judge makes tort law in the end incredible, if he does not indicate the basis for his decision: insurance).

[174] W. Cornish and G. Clarke, *Law and Society in England* (1750–1950) (London: Sweet & Maxwell, 1989), 538.

8

Intention and Negligence

A INTRODUCTION

801 Fault liability: intention and negligence

After having analysed the protected interests in the previous chapter, this chapter will deal with the requirements of intention and negligence. Liability can exist for both intentional and negligent conduct. These are the two bases for fault liability which is usually opposed to strict liability. In this book the term 'negligence liability' will also sometimes be used to indicate liability rules which are neither strict nor based on the intentional infliction of harm. It has to be kept in mind that these three categories are not strictly separated (nr 803 and 1005).

On the continent, fault is sometimes identified with blameworthiness and considered to imply a subjective test: someone is at fault if he can be personally and morally blamed for his conduct.[1] However, in practice, such a disqualification of the defendant is not required for liability, neither on the continent nor in common law, because the courts generally apply the objective test of the reasonable man or the good family father (*le bon père de famille*) (nr 805). Even in liability for intentional conduct, subjective elements do not always play a decisive role. In this book fault liability will be used in this more neutral sense and will include liability for intentional and negligent conduct as opposed to strict liability.

A defendant's intentional or negligent conduct cannot be analysed in isolation but has to be considered in connection with the interests of the claimant. In areas of highly valued interests, such as life and bodily integrity, generally a high level of care is required (if a rule of strict liability applies, the level of care is, in principle, not relevant at all; see Chapter 10). In areas of less highly valued interests, such as pure economic interests, generally a less high level of care is required; sometimes liability only exists in case of the defendant's intentional conduct (nr 715).

---

[1] Von Bar (2000), N 314 uses the term 'misconduct': 'The term "fault" relates to the mental and behavioural possibilities of the individual. "Misconduct" refers to the average achievable performance for the group to which the individual in the particular circumstances is attributed.'

In the following section of this chapter (B) attention will be paid to the concept of intention. The role which liability for intentionally inflicted harm plays in each of the three systems will be described, and this will be put in a comparative perspective.

Sections C and E will analyse the key role which negligence plays in the various jurisdictions in establishing liability. There are, indeed, other major grounds for liability in tort: the violation of a statutory rule (Chapter 9) and strict liability (Chapter 10). However, if liability for violation of a statutory rule and strict liability are tort law's chorus line, liability for negligence is its *prima donna*.[2] The main part of this chapter will provide an analysis of her anatomy and of the way she moves.[3] How do courts establish that a defendant's conduct was negligent? What does it mean to compare the defendant's conduct with that of a standard of reference such as the *reasonable man*? The focus in these sections will be both on the negligent conduct (balancing the risk and the precautionary measures, section C) as well as on the negligent person (assessing the required knowledge and ability, section D). Section E will deal with the grounds of justification, in some jurisdictions also known as defences.

B INTENTION

802 Intention in the legal systems

802-1 *France*

French law scarcely acknowledges rules which require intentional conduct for liability in damages. In many cases negligence will suffice and in many other cases the basis for liability is strict. One of the few examples of liability for intentional conduct is based on the theory of *abus de droit* (abuse of a right) (nr 302-2). The idea is that someone cannot escape liability by hiding behind a subjective right of which he is the legal holder. In principle, the exercise of a right can only give rise to liability if the owner of the right acted intentionally or in bad faith. There is, however, no consensus—either among French legal writers, or in case law—as to the precise criteria for defining 'abuse'. Broadly speaking, there are two diverging trends among academics.

The *objective* theory of abuse of rights is premised on a societal (as opposed to an individualistic) conception of subjective rights. They serve a socially useful

---

[2] Apart from France (nr 303-306), rules of strict liability are generally an exception to the main rule. Reminiscences of negligent conduct can be recognized in many strict rules; see nr 1005.

[3] See for a comparative view: Helmut Koziol (ed.), *Unification of Tort Law: Wrongfulness*, (The Hague, London, Boston: Kluwer, 1998); Van Gerven (2000), 280–394.

function and must be exercised in a manner consistent with this end. If one fails
to do so, any purported exercise of the right will be disqualified as an abuse.
In contrast, the *subjective* theory focuses on the defendant's motive for exercising
his right: it sets the threshold for required fault much higher than simple
negligent conduct. Specifically, the defendant will only abuse his right in a case
of malicious intention to harm the victim (*intention de nuire*). In practice,
evidence of this *mens rea* may be deduced from the lack of personal benefit which
a defendant draws from choosing to exercise his right in a particular manner
(*absence d'intérêt personnel d'agir*).[4]

The *Cour de cassation* has in general refused to take sides in this debate: the
ensuing casuistic reasoning may be explained by its primary concern to deliver
practical justice on the merits of each case. However, a judicial tendency for a
subjective approach may be discerned. In examining the defendant's mental
state, the *Cour* often makes reference made to his intention to harm (*intention de
nuire*)[5] or fraudulent fault (*faute dolosive*);[6] or sometimes to more attenuated
forms of moral guilt, such as the defendant's bad faith (*mauvaise foi*)[7] or culpable
levity of conduct (*légèreté blamable*).[8]

802-2 *Germany*

In German law liability on the basis of fault requires *Verschulden*. According to
§ 276 I BGB this is either intention (*Vorsatz*) or negligence (*Fahrlässigkeit*).[9]
Intention (*Vorsatz*) is not defined in the BGB, unlike negligence (*Fahrlässigkeit*)
of which a definition is provided in § 276 II (nr 804-2). The legislator has left it
to the courts and the doctrine to explore the meaning of *Vorsatz*.

The concept is used, for example, in all three general rules. In both § 823 I
(infringement of a right) and § 823 II (violation of a statutory rule) intention
features in addition to negligence. *Vorsatz* in this respect generally includes *dolus
eventualis*, ie the acting person is aware that occurrence of harm is possible and
consents to the harm if it should occur.[10] The translation as mere 'intention' is
therefore slightly imprecise. A person acting with *dolus eventualis* does not
actually intend to do harm but may well hope that it does not occur. In this
chapter, 'intention' will be used in the broad sense, including *dolus eventualis*.

As a general rule, it can be said that there must be a knowledge requirement,
consisting at least in the awareness that the occurrence of harm is possible, and a

---

[4] Civ. 1re, 19 November 1996, Bull. civ. I, no 404, RTD civ. 1997.156, obs. Gautier.
[5] Civ. 3e, 12 October 1971, Bull. civ. III, no 480.
[6] Civ. 2e, 11 January 1973, Gaz. Pal. 1973. 2. 710.
[7] Civ. 2e, 11 January 1973, Gaz. Pal. 1973. 2. 710.
[8] Com. 22 February 1994, Bull. civ. IV, no 79.
[9] § 276 I: 'Der Schuldner hat Vorsatz und Fahrlässigkeit zu vertreten'.
[10] Deutsch-Ahrens (2002), N 116: 'Vorsätzlich handelt, wer im Bewußtsein des Handlungser-
folges und in Kenntnis der Rechtswidrigkeit des Verhaltens den Erfolg in seinen Willen aufge-
nommen hat.' See also Kötz-Wagner (2001), N 105.

voluntary requirement, consisting at least in consenting to the harm in case it occurs. Both requirements must be present with regard to the violation of the protected interest or the statutory rule, and the unlawfulness of this violation or conduct.

Mistakes of fact generally exclude *Vorsatz*, ie there is no *Vorsatz* if a stone aimed at a bush injures a person hiding in that bush. Mistakes of law, notably about the unlawfulness of the act, are somewhat controversial. The BGH seems to treat them in a similar way to mistakes of fact.[11] This does not of course affect the possible appreciation of a conduct as negligent.

Yet, in § 823 the distinction between *Vorsatz* and *Fahrlässigkeit* does not play a significant role because the latter is easier to establish and sufficient for *Verschulden*. However, the distinction is important in § 826 (intentional infliction of damage *contra bonos mores*; nr 402-4), where only intentional infliction of damage is sufficient to establish liability. This is the main instance where higher courts and doctrine deal more extensively with intentional infliction of harm. On one hand the courts have taken a broad view by also accepting forms of recklessness as being sufficient for liability. On the other hand, however, the BGH limits the tortfeasor's liability: he is not liable for all the consequences of his conduct (as is usually the case with intentional conduct, see nr 1101) but only for the consequences he intended to cause or recklessly accepted might happen (*dolus eventualis*).[12]

802-3 *England*

Liability for intentional conduct plays an important role in English law, much more important than in German and French law. English law still holds numerous intentional torts (nr 504–505). It is interesting to note the variation in the defendant's requisite mental state for establishing liability in the so-called 'intentional torts'. It is possible to observe a continuous spectrum.

Arguably the highest threshold is set with regards to torts requiring malice (malicious falsehood, malicious prosecution). They go beyond the detection of conduct which is simply voluntary and imply an inquiry into the defendant's *motive*. To make out the tort of malicious prosecution, the claimant must establish that the defendant harboured a personal animus: this is a distinct requirement for liability going over and above the need to prove that the prosecution was without reasonable cause. Similarly, for the economic tort of conspiracy to injure, malice is given a restricted meaning and courts are deferential to any economic self-interest motive advanced by the defendant by way of justification. In relation to economic torts, it has been said that malice

... in its pure form means more than an intention to inflict some temporal injury. All competition, and most economic activity, will do that. Instead it refers to actions done

---

[11] Deutsch-Ahrens (2002), N 118–119.
[12] BGH 8 March 1951, NJW 1951, 596; BGH 5 November 1962, NJW 1963, 148; BGH 20 November 1990, NJW 1991, 634.

out of spite or ill will, whereby someone is prepared to impose costs upon himself solely to make someone else worse off.[13]

At a slightly less stringent level, the tort of deceit requires that the defendant knew of the falsity of his statement or had been reckless as to its veracity. This must be coupled with a deliberate intention to induce the claimant to rely upon it.

Further down the spectrum, the mental requirement in the tort of battery requires that the defendant had intended the consequences of his actions or that he was at least reckless as to them—a test of subjective indifference.[14] This subjective test is watered down under the Protection from Harassment Act 1997, which sets the requisite standard for liability according to an objective test of 'reasonable forseeability'.

Meanwhile, regarding the torts of false imprisonment, trespass to chattels, conversion, and trespass to land, the 'intentional' element is diluted further still. These are strict liability torts which are actionable as soon as the requisite objective conditions are met. It is sufficient to establish that an unwitting defendant had the intention simply to perform the immediate voluntary material act which ultimately amounted to harming the claimant. His ignorance as to the consequences of his actions is irrelevant—proof of absence of fault is ineffective in exonerating him.

Finally, the intentional element for defamation is attenuated almost to vanishing point: 'liability . . . does not depend on the intention of the defamer; but on the fact of defamation'.[15] Indeed, it has been held that a defendant may be liable towards a victim whom he never even knew existed.[16]

803 Comparative observations

The legal systems differ considerably as regards the scope of application of liability for intentional conduct. Whereas in France it applies to the exercise of rights only and in Germany to liability for damage caused *contra bonos mores*, ie mainly for pure economic loss, in English law it plays a role across the board: in cases of economic loss, of property loss, and of personal injury. This is consonant with the general approaches of the various jurisdictions, with English law generally holding the highest hurdles to establishing liability (nr 604–605). Particularly in the area of personal injury, however, the importance of intentional torts has diminished

---

[13] R.A. Epstein, 'A Common Law for Labor Relations: A Critique of the New Deal Labor Legislation', *Yale LJ* 92 (1983), 1357, 1368.

[14] *Fowler v Lanning* [1959] 1 QB 426; and *Letang v Cooper* [1965] 1 QB 232.

[15] *Cassidy v Daily Mirror Newspapers Ltd* [1929] 2 KB 331, 354.

[16] See *Newstead v London Express Newspaper Ltd* [1940] 1 KB 377.

over the past decades where, to a certain extent, they have been absorbed by the generalization of the tort of negligence (nr 503).

There are some parallels to draw in the way the legal systems deal with the requirement of intention. In all countries there is a tendency to relax the requirement of intention and to include forms of recklessness or acting in bad faith. This effect of 'watering down' the requirement of intention shows the need for more flexibility than the core requirement of intention can provide. A similar adaptation is visible in the framework of negligence where the requirement has moved into a more (and more) objective direction (nr 811).

Requiring intentional or reckless conduct for liability implies a protection of the freedom to act. This is generally accepted if there are no highly protectable values at stake or the activity is highly valued as such. One may think of conduct in economic competition. A similar reasoning leading to a protection of the freedom to act can be recognized in the area of liability of public authorities. Traditionally, courts have generally been reluctant to impose liability on these bodies because they are supposed to work in the general interest, and policy issues are involved in the issues they are dealing with. This reluctance is some-times reflected in the fact that governmental liability requires a qualified fault, such as a *faute lourde* in French law or acting in bad faith in the English tort of misfeasance in public office. These issues will be dealt with in more detail in Chapter 18.

If someone has caused damage intentionally, the question of causation is usually easy to answer. In such cases, also, remote consequences are generally put on the defendant's account (nr 1101). This is, however, different in the framework of § 826 BGB where the liability of the tortfeasor is limited to the damage he intended to cause or which he was aware could occur, and consents to the harm if it should occur.

C NEGLIGENT CONDUCT

804 Negligence in the legal systems

804-1 *England*

In the English tort of negligence the key requirement for negligent conduct is not the duty of care (which only restricts the tort's scope of application, nr 503) but the breach of duty. The breach test focuses on the question of whether the defendant exercised sufficient care towards the claimant. A breach of duty is generally established by comparing the conduct of the defendant with that of a *reasonable man*.[17] The classical description of this mythical person is by Alderson B. in *Blyth v Birmingham Waterworks*, decided in 1856: 'Negligence is the omission to do something which a reasonable man, guided upon those considerations which ordinarily regulate the conduct of human affairs, would do, or doing something which a prudent and reasonable man would not do.'[18]

This objective test implies that it is not relevant whether the defendant personally knew the risk or personally could have avoided it. It will not even do that the defendant has acted to the best of his judgment:

> Instead (...) of saying that the liability for negligence should be co-extensive with the judgment of each individual, which would be as variable as the length of the foot of each individual, we ought rather to adhere to the rule which requires in all cases a regard to caution such as a man of ordinary prudence would observe.[19]

Lack of experience is no obstacle to concluding that someone has breached his duty. In *Nettleship v Weston* the Court of Appeal compared someone who was having a driving lesson with someone with a driving licence. Lord Denning said: 'The learner driver may be doing his best but his incompetent best is not good enough. He must drive in as good a manner as a driver of skill, experience and care, who is sound in mind and limb, who makes no errors of judgment, has good eyesight and hearing, and is free from infirmity.'[20]

Specific circumstances can lead to an adaptation of the objective standard. Firstly, the courts judge children's conduct on the basis of the *standard of a reasonable child* (nr 813-4).[21] Secondly, a more subjective test is applied to a defendant acting in an emergency situation. If he cannot be blamed for getting into this situation, neither will he generally be blamed for personal incapacities (nr 812-1).[22]

804-2 *Germany*

§ 276 I BGB describes *Verschulden* as either intention (*Vorsatz*) or negligence (*Fahrlässigkeit*). Hence, the generic term encompasses both intention and negligence. However, it is more common to use the term *Verschulden* than *Fahrlässigkeit*, even though in practice the defendant's conduct will usually be *fahrlässig* and not *vorsätzlich*. § 276 II defines *Fahrlässigkeit* as conduct contrary to the care required in society.[23]

---

[17] Salmond and Heuston (1996), 222.

[18] *Blyth v Company of Proprietors of the Birmingham Waterworks* (1856) 156 ER 1047, 1049. Winfield and Jolowicz (2002), para. 5.52; Salmond and Heuston (1996), 222–223; Markesinis and Deakin (2003), 167.

[19] *Vaughan v Menlove* (1837) 132 ER 490. Markesinis and Deakin (2003), 167–168; Winfield and Jolowicz (2002), paras 3.4 and 5.52; Dobbs I (2001), § 120, 284–285; Warren A. Seavey, 'Negligence—Subjective or Objective?', *Harvard LR*, 41 (1927), 1–27.

[20] Lord Denning in *Nettleship v Weston* [1971] 2 QB 691, 699: a majority of the court held the learner driver liable.

[21] *McHale v Watson* (1966) 115 CLR 199; see also *Finlow v Domino* (1957) 11 DLR 2d 493. Markesinis and Deakin (2003), 172–173. [22] Markesinis and Deakin (2003), 170–172.

[23] § 276 II: 'Fahrlässig handelt, wer die im Verkehr erforderliche Sorgfalt außer Acht läßt'.

It has to be emphasized that the question of *Verschulden* only comes up if the defendant's conduct violated a normative rule (*Tatbestand*) and that he acted unlawfully (*rechtswidrig*).[24] However, the test for negligent conduct is not only dealt with under *Verschulden* but also under *Rechtswidrigkeit*.[25] Two situations need to be distinguished. If someone directly infringes a protected right in the sense of § 823 I, the negligence test takes place under the heading of *Fahrlässigkeit* in the framework of *Verschulden*. For example, if someone has infringed another person's bodily integrity he has acted unlawfully, unless he can invoke a ground of justification (§ 823 I). The question of whether his conduct was negligent (or intentional) is dealt with under *Verschulden*.

In other situations, however, for example in cases of indirect infringements and infringements of the right to business and the general personality right, the negligence test partly finds a home in the *Rechtswidrigkeit* requirement. This implies an impersonalized qualification of the conduct. For instance, if a rotten tree falls and causes injury to a passer-by, the owner breaches his *Verkehrspflicht* (safety duty) if he omitted securing or removing the tree. The breach of this safety duty implies unlawfulness and deals in fact with the outer aspects of negligence: *äußere Sorgfalt* (outer care).[26]

In both situations the *Fahrlässigkeits* test in the framework of *Verschulden* is a test as regards the person of the tortfeasor, particularly his knowledge of the risk and his abilities to prevent it. This is also sometimes described by the term *innere Sorgfalt* (inner care).[27]

Fahrlässigkeit cannot be established if, even for a careful person, it would not have been possible to recognize and to prevent the risk. The courts apply an objective standard (*objektivierter* or *typisierter Fahrlässigkeitsmaßstab*) which means that the tortfeasor's personal knowledge and abilities are not decisive, but the typical knowledge and abilities of the professional group or the social or age group of the tortfeasor are. The judge compares the conduct of a doctor with that of a typical doctor and the conduct of a driver with that of a typical driver. The person who does not meet this standard acts with *Verschulden*, even if he

[24] *Verschulden* also plays an important role in other tort law provisions, such as § 831 (liability of the employer) and § 832 (liability of supervisors of children). See nr 1602 and 1606.

[25] BGH 20 October 1987, NJW 1988, 909; BGH 9 June 1967, VersR 1967, 808 = JZ 1968, 103 (*Kraftfahrer*); see about the latter case Markesinis and Unberath (2002), 507–508; Larenz (1987), § 20 III, 286; § 20 IV, 289–290.

[26] In fact the German discussion is even more complicated because of the dispute between the tenets of *Erfolgsunrecht* (generally the approach described in the main text) and *Handlungsunrecht*. The advocates of the latter tenet do not consider the direct infringement of a protected right as *rechtswidrig* but only if, at the same time, the defendant's conduct did not meet the general standard of care. See Kötz-Wagner (2001), N 94–103.

[27] See about this distinction Deutsch-Ahrens (2002), N 121; Christian von Bar, *Verkehrspflichten* (Cologne: Heymann, 1980), 172; Larenz (1987), § 20 IV, 291. Its value is disputed by Kötz-Wagner (2001), N 118. The BGH holds that violation of outer care is an indication for the violation of inner care ('*indiziert innere Sorgfalt*'): BGH 11 March 1986, NJW 1986, 2757, 2758; BGH 31 May 1994, NJW 1994, 2232. However, there is no case in which there was a violation of the outer care, but not of the inner care.

personally cannot be blamed for his conduct. Shortcomings in knowledge or abilities, tiredness, nervousness, excitement, or dejection are no defence against liability.[28] The objective test does not apply to disabled persons and children. This follows from § 827–829 BGB (nr 813-3).

The burden of proof as regards negligence is on the claimant, but if unlawfulness follows from the breach of a safety duty (*Verkehrspflicht*) (nr 403-2) or the violation of a statutory rule (nr 903), provided they prescribe the required conduct in a sufficiently specific way, the burden of proof is shifted to the defendant.[29] He has to prove with effective certainty (compare nr 1103-1) that it was not possible to recognize the risk or to prevent it. This is advantageous for the claimant, though this was never intended by the drafters of the BGB. The rules were developed by the BGH thus bringing the negligence rule in effect closer to the rules of strict liability (nr 1004-2).

804-3 *France*

Apart from causation and damage, French tort law only requires a *faute* in order to establish liability (articles 1382 and 1383 CC). The French legislator has left the interpretation of *faute* to the courts and the doctrine, thus giving rise to lots of discussions and theories (nr 302-1).

The main part of the French doctrine distinguishes two elements of *faute*: an objective element focusing on the conduct of the wrongdoer, and a subjective element relating to his personal capacities. An alternative way of expressing this is that the objective element covers the external circumstances and the subjective element the internal circumstances of the wrongdoer (*circonstances externes* and *circonstances internes*). However, in practice the subjective element does not play a role any more (nr 302-1).

If a *faute* cannot be based on the violation of a statutory rule (nr 904), the doctrine has developed two ways to establish a *faute*. Either a *faute* is considered to be the breach of a pre-existing obligation (*l'obligation préexistante*), or it is conduct that does not meet the standard of the good family father (*le bon père de famille*). These two ways are generally considered to be complementary.

The theory of the pre-existing obligation has the oldest history. The idea behind it is that liability does not arise from nowhere at the moment the harm occurs but that it is based on the breach of an existing obligation. Sources of such obligations are, for instance, regulations applying to certain professions or sports, morality, custom, and technical standards. Authors advocating this theory talk about a duty (*un devoir*), an obligation (*une obligation*) or, more generally, about conduct contrary to the law (*contrairement au droit*).[30] Conduct that breaches a

---

[28] RG 14 January 1928, RGZ 119, 397 = JW 1928, 1049 (*Segelschiff*), about which Markesinis and Unberath (2002), 505–506; BGH 16 March 1976, VersR 1976, 775; Kötz-Wagner (2001), N 112; Larenz (1987), § 20 III, 285; Deutsch-Ahrens (2002), N 123.
[29] Kötz-Wagner (2001), N 253–259.   [30] Carbonnier (2000), § 231, 418.

pre-existing obligation is often indicated as a *fait illicite* (unlawful act). If a pre-existing obligation cannot be derived from the aforementioned sources, the defendant's conduct is compared with that of a standard, especially *le bon père de famille*.

A minority in the doctrine consider the idea of a pre-existing obligation to be artificial. They argue that it is not the pre-existing obligation that constitutes the faulty character of the conduct, but that it is the faulty character of the conduct (imprudence, unreasonableness) that constitutes the *faute*.[31] They consider a *faute* as erroneous conduct that would not have been committed by a careful person (*une personne avisé*), placed in the same external circumstances as the wrongdoer.[32]

Although the doctrine shows a fierce discussion between the adherents of these two theories, there is hardly any difference in outcome.[33] There are, however, differences in policy approach. These differences run parallel with the delicate French distinction between right and left (*droite et gauche*). An author using the concept of *fait illicite* will probably think in a more conservative direction, whereas his opponent may be more progressive. The latter will generally refuse to use the concept of *faute morale* and will prefer to apply the notion of *faute social*. If he lives in Paris it will probably be on the Left Bank of the Seine.

805 The reasonable person balancing risk and care

805-1 *The elements of negligence*

It follows from the foregoing that the general negligence test in the legal systems involves a comparison of the conduct of the tortfeasor with that of the reasonable man or the *bonus pater familias*. In other words: the factual 'is' conduct of the actual defendant is compared with the normative 'should' conduct of an average careful person in the same situation and, where there is a difference because the defendant's conduct did not meet this standard of care, negligence can be established.[34]

This idea is also is reflected in Article 3:102(b) ECC providing that a person causes damage negligently if his conduct ' . . . does not amount to such care as could be expected from a reasonably careful person in the circumstances of the case.'

---

[31] Aubry et Rau-Dejean de la Bathie (1989), nr 22 note 9; Mazeaud-Tunc (1965), nr 431 en 439.
[32] Mazeaud-Tunc (1965), nr 439: ' . . . une erreur de conduite telle qu'elle n'aurait pas été commise par une personne avisée placée dans les mêmes circonstances "externes" que l'auteur du dommage.' [33] Viney-Jourdain (1998), nr 443; Carbonnier (2000), § 231, 418–420.
[34] Kötz-Wagner (2001), N 106:

Es wird also das 'Ist-Verhalten' des konkreten Schädigers am 'Soll-Verhalten' eines durchschnittlich besonnenen Mensch in gleicher Lage gemessen, und ergibt sich hier eine Differenz, weil der Beklagte mit seinem Verhalten underhalb jenes Sorgfaltsstandards geblieben ist, so liegt Fahrlässigkeit vor.

In assessing this standard of care, all circumstances of the case need to be taken into account. A reflection of this European common core can be found in Article 4:102(1) PETL:

The required standard of conduct is that of the reasonable person in the circumstances, and depends, in particular, on the nature and value of the protected interest involved, the dangerousness of the activity, the expertise to be expected of a person carrying it on, the foreseeability of the damage, the relationship of proximity or special reliance between those involved, as well as the availability and the costs of precautionary or alternative methods.

The list is neither exhaustive nor binding. Not all circumstances will play a role or will get the same emphasis in all the cases that come before the courts. The weight attributed to the various circumstances may also differ, not only by case but also by legal system. For example, the expected level of expertise of a doctor may differ by country and so may the balance between the value of the protected interest and the costs of precautionary matters. Hence, the courts can gear the reasonable person up and down at their discretion.

The negligence test of the reasonable person focuses both on his conduct and his personal capacities. It has an outer (visible) aspect and an inner (invisible) one. Both aspects play a role in order to establish negligence. The questions to be answered thus are: (1) whether the defendant behaved as a reasonable person would have done in the same circumstances (careful conduct, outer care) (section B), and (2) whether the defendant possessed the reasonable person's knowledge and skills (careful person, inner care) (section C).

It should be emphasized that the two aspects (conduct and person) are very much intertwined[35] if only because a person's conduct is supposed to be based on available knowledge and skills—however unlikely this may be in daily life when a person's behaviour sometimes seems to be disengaged from the operation of his mind.

In all three legal systems the establishment of negligence is very much a matter of *ius in causa positum*: the law is found in the facts of the case. In assessing whether someone has acted with due care, many factors and elements play a role and they all vary in weight. Hence, the structure of this chapter deviates somewhat from that of the other chapters. In order to get to grips with the elusive negligence standard, the two aspects of negligence (conduct and person) will be analysed and divided into factors and elements. These factors and elements will then be *illustrated* with the help of case law from the various legal systems. Although the courts do not as such use the analysis provided in this chapter, it is submitted that the analysis is compatible with the way the courts usually assess negligence.

805-2 *The four factors of negligent conduct*

As regards careful conduct, it is generally accepted that the required level of careful conduct has to be established by balancing due care and the expected

---

[35] Von Bar (2000), N 229.

risks: 'As the danger increases, so must the precautions increase.'[36] This balancing of care and risk reflects the general task of tort law to balance freedom and protection (nr 715). A closer look at the content of both these concepts reveals that the level of risk can be determined by: (1) the seriousness of the expected damage, and (2) the probability that an accident will happen. And the level of care can be broken down into: (3) the character and the benefit of the conduct, and (4) the burden of precautionary measures.

Historically, this approach goes back to the considerations of the famous American judge Learned Hand in *United States v Carroll Towing Co.* The case was about vessels that were not fastened to their moorings thus causing damage. Learned Hand said:

Since there are occasions when every vessel will break away from her moorings, and since, if she does, she becomes a menace to those about her; the owner's duty, as in other similar situations, to provide against resulting injuries is a function of three variables: (1) the probability that she will break away; (2) the gravity of the resulting injuries, if she does; (3) the burden of adequate precautions.[37]

At a later stage a fourth factor—the character and benefit of the conduct—was added.

Working with these factors has a stronger basis in common law than in civil law, but in France and Germany the factors are also mentioned in the legal literature.[38] This four-factor approach does not differ much from the above-cited Article 4:102(1) PETL which sums up relevant factors to be taken into account in assessing the required standard of conduct.[39] This latter 'listing', however, illustrates less clearly that setting the standard of care implies balancing the interests of defendant and claimant.

The economic analysis of tort law is based on this four-factor approach.[40] This analysis provides an extremely interesting way of looking at (tort) law issues but it is also disputed, *inter alia*, because of the simple free market approach taken by

[36] Denning LJ in *Lloyds Bank Ltd v Railway Executive* [1952] 1 All ER 1248, 1253. See also BGH 21 April 1977, VersR 1977, 817, 818.
[37] *United States v Carroll Towing Co* (1947) 159 F. (2d) 169, 173.
[38] Von Bar (2000), N 225; Lord Reid in *Morris v West Hartlepool Co Ltd* [1956] AC 552, 574; Kötz-Wagner (2001), N 36–41 and 109; Münchener Kommentar-Grundmann (2003), § 276 N 61; Viney-Jourdain (1998), nr 477. See also Dobbs I (2001), § 143, 334–337.
[39] The nature and value of the protected interest involved (PETL) is similar to the first factor: seriousness of the expected damage. The dangerousness of the activity (PETL) is similar to the second factor: the probability that an accident will happen. The expertise to be expected of a person performing it and the foreseeability of the damage (PETL) are dealt with in section C about the negligent person. Aspects of the relationship of proximity or special reliance between those involved (PETL) can be subsumed under the third factor: character and benefit of the conduct. Finally, the availability and the costs of precautionary or alternative methods (PETL) is similar to the fourth factor: the burden of precautionary measures.
[40] Classic books in this respect are Guido Calabresi, *The Costs of Accidents* (New Haven: Yale University Press, 1970); Richard A. Posner, *Tort Law* (Boston: Little, Brown & Co., 1982); Steven Shavell, *Economic Analysis of Accident Law* (Cambridge, Mass.: Harvard University Press, 1987).

some of its advocates.[41] The debate shows that economic analysis (as with legal analysis) does not provide for value-free outcomes. However, this does not mean that such an analysis cannot be useful.

The four-factor approach can be illustrated by the English case of *Bolton v Stone*. During a cricket match the ball was hit over an intervening house and into a street where it injured the claimant. In the previous thirty years the ball had been hit into the street only six times. The House of Lords dismissed the woman's claim, holding that the risk was foreseeable but taking such a small risk did not amount to negligence. Lord Reid said: 'I do not think that a reasonable man considering the matter from the point of view of safety would or should disregard any risk unless it is extremely small.'[42]

This case can also be approached with the help of the four factors. On the risk side: (1) the seriousness of the expected damage concerned personal injury, and (2) the probability that an accident would happen was very low. On the conduct side: (3) the burden of precautionary measures involved the costs of erecting a high fence. Their Lordships apparently considered that the risk (probability and seriousness) did not outweigh the costs of precautionary measures such as erecting a high fence. It may also have crossed their Lordships' minds: (4) that cricket is a useful activity—at least by English standards. But then they may have contemplated that the character and benefit of the conduct can be a ground of justification in exceptional circumstances only (nr 809).[43]

The four factors for establishing negligent conduct can be used as a formula but, as the case above suggests, this is not a matter of simply carrying out a calculation and reaching a conclusion. One should keep in mind the words of Cooke P:

Ultimately the exercise can only be a balancing one and the important object is that all relevant factors be weighed. There is no escape from the truth that, whatever formula be used, the outcome in a grey area case has to be determined by judicial judgment. Formulae can help to organise thinking but they cannot provide answers.[44]

The formulae can give the judge the tools to determine the outcome of the case; this is the finding function of the formulae. If the judge has made his initial judicial judgment he can explain the reasons for it with the help of the formulae; this is the justification function of the formulae.[45]

[41] See also Richard J. Wright, 'Standards of Care in Negligence Law', in David G. Owen (ed.), *Philosophical Foundations of Tort Law*, (Oxford: Clarendon Press, 1995), 249–275, who criticizes the utilitarian efficiency theory in the framework of an economic approach of tort law. In Europe, however, this utilitarian theory has not gained strong support.

[42] Lord Reid in *Bolton v Stone* [1951] AC 850, 867–868.

[43] Custom, habits, traditions, or practices are no defence against liability. Negligence is a matter, not of ordinary care but of required care. Von Bar (2000), N 225, note 307.

[44] Cooke P in *South Pacific Manufacturing Co Ltd v New Zealand Security Consultants & Investigations Ltd* [1992] 2 NZLR 282, 294. See also Stapleton, Jane, 'Duty of Care Factors: a Selection from the Judicial Menus', in Peter Cane and Jane Stapleton (eds.), *The Law of Obligations: Essays in Celebration of John Fleming*, (Oxford: Clarendon Press; New York: Oxford University Press, 1995), 59–95.

[45] T. Koopmans, 'Comparative Law and the Courts', *ICLQ*, 45 (1996), 550.

As has been said, the characteristics of the reasonable person are related not only to his conduct but also to his personal capacities, in particular his knowledge and abilities. What did the defendant know about the risk and what ought he have to know about it? And what could the defendant have done to avoid the risk and what ought he to have done to avoid it? In principle, people have to match the knowledge and skills of the reasonable person. If they are not able to do so, they are liable for their shortcomings. However, the application of an objective test is disputed as regards children and mentally disabled people (nr 813) and in emergency situations (nr 812-1). The two personal elements (knowledge and abilities) differ from the above-mentioned four elements of conduct. The latter ones are *factors* that have to be balanced, whereas the former ones are *conditions* for liability.

805-3 *Background and plan of the chapter*

There are many reasons why we require a certain level of care from other people. One of the reasons is the necessary trust in society that a certain level of safety will be provided.

Communities depend on mutual trust (. . .). Trust is the expectation that arises within a community of regular, honest and co-operative behaviour, based on commonly shared norms, on the part of members of the community. Those norms can be about deep 'value' questions like the nature of God or justice, but they also encompass secular norms like professional standards and codes of behaviour. That is, we trust a doctor not to do us deliberate injury because we expect him to live by the Hippocratic Oath and the standards of medical profession.[46]

Trust, legitimate expectations, and due care are three important aspects of establishing negligent conduct. This can also be illustrated by Article 6 of the European Directive on Liability for Defective Products, providing that a product is defective ' . . . when it does not provide the safety which a person is entitled to expect, taking all circumstances into account.' It is generally accepted that, apart from manufacturing defects, this defectiveness test is similar to the negligence test (nr 1003-2). There is, however, a difference in perspective. Article 6 does not require that the producer has acted as a reasonable producer but it approaches defectiveness from the claimant's perspective and his legitimate expectations. Also, in negligence cases, courts are often inclined to approach cases from the claimant's perspective and to take into account his legitimate expectations. This implies a shift in perspective from the defendant's duty to act carefully to the claimant's right to safety. Though these are two sides of the same coin, the shift illustrates a different starting point.

In the following sections the elements of negligent conduct will be further analysed. Assessment of the magnitude of the risk requires an analysis of the

---

[46] Francis Fukuyama, *Trust: the Social Virtues and the Creation of Prosperity*, (New York: Free Press, 1995), 27.

seriousness of the expected loss and the *probability* that a loss will be caused (nr 806). When the risk has been established it has to be balanced with the burden of precautionary measures. This burden involves costs, effort, and time (nr 807).

When assessing the required level of care, a number of other considerations have to be taken into account. Firstly, one has to take into account that other people will not always act with due care as regards their own interests, and that they have to be protected against their own mistakes (nr 807). Secondly, due care can imply that someone has to remove or reduce risks in an active way. This potential liability for omissions means that one can owe an affirmative duty to potential victims (nr 808). Finally, the character of the conduct is a strong indication for the required level of care, whereas in some cases the benefit of the conduct can be a justification for causing damage (nr 809).

806 Magnitude of the risk

806-1 *Seriousness of the harm*

The magnitude of a risk is determined by: (1) the amount and seriousness of the expected loss, and (2) the probability that the loss will be caused. The more serious the expected loss and the more likely it is that it will be caused, the bigger the risk. The faster someone drives through a residential area, the more likely it is that an accident will happen, and the more serious the consequences will be.

In certain cases legal systems do not compensate a certain kind of loss, for example pure economic loss. In the analysis provided here the amount of the loss in such a case amounts to zero. Regardless of the probability of the risk, the magnitude of the risk will be zero too. Even though someone actually suffers pure economic loss, there is no legally relevant risk. And where there is no risk, no care is required. Within the framework of the English tort of negligence, these are cases in which the author of the damage did not owe the victim a duty of care. And in German tort law the argument is that there has not been an infringement of a protected right. One could argue that in such a case the author of the damage was free to cause the damage.

In this respect a major difference exists with cases in which death or personal injury is caused. In many cases, causing personal injury simply outweighs the other elements. Negligence is established even if the probability of the harm was very low (nr 806-2) or if the burden of precautionary measures was very high (nr 807-2). This amounts to the fact that causing death or personal injury in many cases leads to the conclusion that the damage was caused negligently.

When assessing the amount or seriousness of the damage it is sometimes important to take into account the specific circumstances of the case. An English example is *Paris v Stepney Borough Council*. At work, an employee got a splinter in his sole healthy eye. The activity as such did not require the employees to wear protective glasses since the probability of such an accident was very low. However, the employer was held liable because he had to make an exception for his one-eyed employee: the damage to his sole healthy eye would cause him greater damage than it would to other persons. Lord Morton said: '... that the more serious the damage which will happen if an accident occurs, the more thorough are the precautions which an employer must take.'[47]

806-2 *Probability of the harm*

The magnitude of the risk is not only determined by the amount and seriousness of the expected loss (nr 806-1) but also by the probability of the harm. The degree of probability has to be established from the perspective of the moment directly before the harmful event. However, once a case is brought before the court and the judge has heard the facts, it is tempting for him to look at a case with hindsight.

This probability factor in negligence requires a double specification. Firstly, the probability that someone will cause harm is not decisive, but the increase in the probability over the accepted risk level is. Many social and economic activities (such as driving and producing dangerous goods) are risky but they have been socially accepted. As such, it is not negligent to carry out such activities. This means that probability is relevant only so far as it exceeds the socially accepted level, ie if such an activity is carried out in a negligent way.

Secondly, it is the probability of the harmful event (the accident) which is decisive, not the probability of the ultimate damage. It is, for example, not necessary to assess the probability that a victim of a road traffic accident will experience serious complications during his recovery process, or the probability that the victim is a pregnant woman.[48] It is sufficient to assess the probability that they would suffer personal injury of some kind. Probability has to be established in a generalized way.

Since the degree of probability can be underestimated in daily life, the use of available empirical data can be useful. In *Haley v London Electricity Board* these data were available. The case was about a blind man who fell into a hole in the pavement. As a consequence of this fall he lost his sense of hearing. The workmen had only marked the hole with the handle of a hammer. The House of Lords decided that an accident to a blind person could have been expected with a reasonable degree of probability, referring to statistics showing that a number of unaccompanied blind people use the pavement.[49]

[47] Lord Morton in *Paris v Stepney Borough Council* [1951] AC 367, 385.
[48] See as regards the latter for instance BGH 11 January 1972, BGHZ 58, 48 = NJW 1972, 1126, about which Markesinis and Unberath (2002), 144–147.
[49] *Haley v London Electricity Board* [1965] AC 778. See also BGH 30 October 1990, VersR 1991, 358: the operator of a hotel has to reckon on people being lame and has to protect them against the risks of a slippery parquet floor.

When assessing probability it has to be taken into account that other people will not always act attentively and carefully as regards their own interests. This means that ' . . . a person is required to realize that there will be a certain amount of negligence in the world'.[50] This aspect will be analysed below with respect to the burden of precautionary measures towards potentially negligent victims (nr 807-4).

A low probability is as such no obstacle for liability. If someone crosses a road on which only a few cars a day travel, it is very unlikely that an accident will occur. However, negligence can be established because of the seriousness of the possible damage (personal injury and property damage), and the low burden of precautionary measures (slow down or pay attention). The same goes when a tree falls exactly at the moment that a pedestrian passes by. This is also very unlikely but the owner is still obliged to take precautionary measures by inspecting and maintaining the tree on a regular basis.[51] Lord Dunedin said: 'People must guard against reasonable probabilities, but they are not bound to guard against fantastic possibilities.'[52] However, the courts are sometimes inclined, particularly in cases of personal injury, to regard fantastic possibilities as reasonable probabilities.

807 Precautionary measures

807-1 *Costs, efforts, and time*

As has been said (nr 805), negligence is established by balancing risk and care: the bigger the risk, the more precautionary measures are required.[53]

Precautionary measures are not free: they cost time, effort, and money. One may think of the cost of materials for physical safety measures or labour costs for maintenance and supervisory tasks. It is clear that there is a limit to what can be afforded as regards precautionary measures, and therefore precautionary measures are not required if the risk is not worth taking them. One may think of *Bolton v Stone*, in which it was decided that the costs of a high fence were too high in relation to the low risk, particularly the very small probability that someone outside the field would be hit by a ball (nr 805-2).

The risk that someone will suffer personal injury generally induces the courts to require considerable precautionary measures. This makes sense since the value of a human being and his bodily integrity is considered to be very high. In some cases the courts put the amount of precautionary measures at such a level that the tortfeasor's duty is in fact a duty to guarantee a result (ie not causing damage) rather than a duty of care. An example is the way in which, in England,

---

[50] Prosser and Keeton (1984), 198.
[51] *Schiller v Council of the Shire of Mulgrave* (1972) 129 CLR 116.
[52] Lord Dunedin in *Fardon v Harcourt Rivington* [1932] 146 LT 391, 392. See also BGH 11 January 1972, BHGZ 58, 48 = NJW 1972, 1126 = JZ 1972, 363, about which Markesinis and Unberath (2002), 144–147.   [53] See also von Bar (2000), N 225.

negligence liability is applied to drivers of motor vehicles. The courts require a very high standard of care from drivers, which is hard to reconcile with a 'human' negligence standard.[54] In such cases it can be argued that precautionary measures are in fact hardly relevant and that strict liability has disguised itself in the clothing of negligence liability (nr 1004). In these cases the standard is intended not to enable corrective justice but to enable distributive justice by granting damages to victims.

Precautionary measures can be divided into permanent measures and one-off measures. In cases of one-off measures the costs will generally be outweighed by the magnitude of the risk. A spectator at an ice hockey game, sitting at the long side of the rink, was hit in the face by a puck. She claimed damages for her injuries from the organizer of the game. The German BGH decided that the organizer had to protect not only the spectators who were sitting at the short sides of the rink but also the spectators at the long side, by erecting a transparent wall. The cost of around DM 130,000 (€67,000) for such was considered to be not too burdensome for the organizer. The BGH dismissed the impudent organizer's defence that the woman had been contributory negligent by not ducking in time to avoid the puck.[55]

In many cases precautionary measures have a permanent character. One may think of research, maintenance, and supervising activities. Compared with one-off measures, the costs, time, and effort of taking permanent measures are generally much higher and will more easily outweigh the magnitude of the risk. A highway authority has to check the road for risks such as debris, oil, or tree branches. The risk for drivers would be much lower if the highway authority checked the road twice an hour rather than twice a week. However, the costs of more maintenance need to be balanced against the lower risk in order to find the appropriate level of care (nr 1510).

An example is a decision of the Court of Brussels dismissing a claim against a shop owner for damage to cars caused by shopping trolleys in the shop's car park. It was established that the shop owner had taken adequate measures such as a sign with do's and don'ts, frequent collection of the trolleys, and had indicated places where customers could leave their trolleys. Requiring more precautionary measures would be too expensive in relation to the character and extent of the risk.[56]

The law and economic approach of this balancing act focuses on the costs of taking precautionary measures on one hand, and the costs related to accidents on the other. Preventing all accidents at all costs is deemed to be inefficient. The idea is that it is only efficient to take precautionary measures as long as the costs of these measures are lower than the losses due to accidents (to be precise: lower than the magnitude of the risk, ie the chance that an accident will occur multiplied by the expected damage which it will cause).[57]

[54] *Daly v Liverpool Corporation* [1939] 2 All ER 142.
[55] BGH 29 November 1983, NJW 1984, 801.
[56] Rb. Brussel 23 October 1986, TBBR 1987, 187.
[57] See for example Kötz-Wagner (2001), N 39–41.

This can be nicely illustrated by a German case about a driver who collided with an animal crossing the road. The driver claimed damages from the highway authority alleging it should have erected a fence along the road. The BGH considered the existing warning signs to be sufficient and dismissed the claim.[58] Kötz and Schäfer criticized this decision, arguing that prevention of 50 to 60 accidents a year largely outweighed the annual depreciation and costs of maintenance for a fence of DM 60,000 (€30,500).[59]

807-2 *Reducing the risk*

In many cases it is too costly or even impossible to eliminate a risk. This is generally the case if eliminating the risk would make the activity impossible to carry out. In such cases it is sufficient to reduce the risk.

Firstly, one may think of sports like football or rugby. A duty to eliminate the risk of injuries during such activities would imply that these sports cannot be practised in a normal way. Hence, the character and benefit of the conduct implies that players do not have to be more careful than is required within the rules of the game, even though this low duty of care will not eliminate, but only slightly reduce, the risk of injuries.[60]

The same goes for other useful but risky activities, such as driving. Eliminating the risk would be possible by reducing the maximum speed to five miles an hour but that would deprive the activity of its core benefit: speed. However, in this area, this has not led to the conclusion that the risk could be reduced: on the contrary. Most legislators have provided for rules of strict liability. The driver (or the keeper of the motor vehicle) also has to be liable for the risk that cannot be eliminated (nr 1404–1405).

A second category of cases in which a risk is hard to eliminate relates to drugs. Many drugs have side-effects, even if they are properly used, ie in the correct dosage, at the right times, etc. Eliminating these risks can be accomplished by not allowing these drugs onto the market. This is, of course, undesirable. Hence, the manufacturer is allowed to bring these drugs onto the market provided the benefit of the drug outweighs the remaining side-effects, and the manufacturer adequately advises the consumer about these effects in the information leaflet.

Thirdly, eliminating the risk is almost always difficult if the precautionary measures consist of supervision and maintenance. For instance, a secure mental hospital will generally owe third parties a duty to supervise its patients in order to prevent them from causing harm. However, hospitals cannot be forced to eliminate this risk. The latter would only be possible by locking up the patient, and this would be a violation of his fundamental rights and contrary to the goals of psychiatric and medical treatment. Hence, a mental hospital can generally

---

[58] BGH 13 July 1989, NJW 1989, 2808.
[59] Kötz and Schäfer, 'Judex, calcula!', *JZ* 1992, 355.   [60] Von Bar (2000), N 253.

confine itself to supervising the patient in a proper way (nr 1605). This will reduce the risk but certainly not eliminate it.[61]

Though this solution may be reasonable from a defendant's perspective and a corrective justice point of view, it is less satisfactory for the claimant and from a distributive justice point of view. The French *Cour de cassation* took the claimant's side in its *Blieck* decision by imposing strict liability on, *inter alia*, the mental hospital (nr 305). Such a strict liability rule avoids the discussion on the feasibility and acceptability of precautionary measures and, in fact, imposes on the hospital a duty to guarantee that no damage will be caused to third parties (nr 1004-1). Such a strict liability rule is only acceptable if appropriate liability insurance is available.

807-3 *Duty to warn or to inform*

Closely connected to the previous section is the issue of the duties to warn and to inform. Generally, a duty to warn refers to risks for death or personal harm, whereas a duty to inform refers to other areas but this is no matter of principle.

No duty to warn or to inform exists when someone is justified in believing that the potential victim knows about the risk, is aware of it, and is able to behave accordingly. This goes for generally known facts, for example that it is possible to fall off a staircase or, for the past few decades, that smoking threatens a person's health.

A duty to inform can be only at stake if the risk cannot be eliminated in another way, such as by physical means. In such cases, providing proper information can reduce the risk. For instance, supervisors owe a duty to inform their visitors about the inevitable risks regarding premises, grounds, and roads (nr 1506), and manufacturers owe a duty to inform their consumers about the inevitable risks of their products (nr 1408-1). Generally, a duty to inform is owed in cases in which an information gap exists, ie if someone (the supervisor, the manufacturer) knows about a risk that the other person (the visitor, the consumer) does not know about or is insufficiently aware of.

Although a warning will make a potential victim a better informed person, it is not definite that it will also make him wiser in the sense that he will use the information provided properly. For instance, in places with many potential victims, such as stadiums or underground stations, elimination of the risk should be preferred over warnings. In such places, people will be less attentive and therefore less aware of information provided (nr 1506-4). Also, as regards children, consumers, and employees, warnings are considered to be less effective because these persons often are inclined to underestimate the risk. More far-reaching

---

[61] As regards prisoners these counter-arguments cannot be invoked and the duty of the prison or, more generally, the supervisors is less problematic. See, for example, *Home Office v Dorset Yacht Co Ltd* [1970] AC 1004, 1027; Winfield and Jolowicz (2002), para. 5.6.

measures are to be preferred unless they are too expensive or would considerably reduce the benefit of the activity (nr 809).

Information has to be provided in such a way that it informs the potential victim in time. Furthermore, the information has to be understandable and clear about the nature and content of the risk, and particularly about the consequences of not following the instructions. Warnings aimed at children have to be comprehensible and have to properly inform the child about the way to act safely. Very young children should be warned by pictures rather than by written text (nr 1506-4).

Often even potentially negligent victims need to be warned against risks, for example, to prevent a patient from using a drug in a wrong way. An example is a German case in which the BGH decided that if a drug has to be taken by the patient himself in emergency situations (in this case acute asthma attacks), the manufacturer also has to warn of the risks in case of excessive use.[62]

However, a duty to warn does not exist in cases of obvious abuse. Here, one may think of another German case about someone who used a coolant as a narcotic. The BGH decided that the manufacturer did not owe the abuser a duty to warn that the product was poisonous if it was used in this way.[63]

If there is doubt about the existence of a certain risk, or if the risk is known but not (yet) avoidable, someone may nonetheless owe a duty to inform other people. This has been decided as regards the duty of physicians to advise their patients about HIV and the Hepatitis C virus at a stage when these viruses were only just known of (see nr 810-4). Such information can state that there might be a risk but that this is not yet certain, or that it is known that there is a risk but that it is not yet known how this risk may be avoided.

807-4 *Negligent victims*

In many cases it is not just the defendant but also the claimant who can influence the risk. In such cases the question arises as to whether the defendant has to take into account the victim's potential negligent conduct. The *leitmotiv* in negligence liability is that '... people should not assume that others always act carefully and that, therefore, failure to guard against folly is sometimes folly in itself.'[64] In many cases potential victims have to be protected against their own mistakes. The potential victim's negligent conduct influences the level of care that is required from the defendant.

The key issue is who possesses information about the risk (knowledge) and who has the best possibility of restricting or eliminating it (ability) (nr 810). Hence, the negligent conduct of a potential victim has particularly to be taken into account if the victim does not have enough knowledge of the risk, if he is

---

[62] BGH 24 January 1989, NJW 1989, 1542.   [63] BGH 7 July 1981, VersR 1981, 957.
[64] *Lang v London Transport Executive* [1959] 1 WLR 1168, 1174-8. See also Viney-Jourdain (1998), nr 456-1.

inclined to underestimate it, or if he is insufficiently able to avoid the risk effectively, for instance because of impulsiveness, carelessness, habit, lack of time, and lack of alternatives. The latter is especially the case with children. In this respect Hamilton LJ stated, '. . . that in the case of an infant, there are moral as well as physical traps. There may accordingly be a duty towards infants not merely not to dig pitfalls for them, but not to lead them into temptation.'[65]

A manufacturer also has to protect consumers against their own negligent conduct. It is well-known that consumers will not always take all precautionary measures, for example because they underestimate the risk or because of carelessness. This can imply that the manufacturer has to adapt the design of his product or to inform the customer of the residual inevitable risk. In certain circumstances, manufacturers also have to warn consumers against a particular abuse of the product, for instance in the case of a drug against acute asthma attacks (nr 807-3). The issue does not only rise in cases of negligence liability but also within the strict liability framework of the EC Directive on defective products; see nr 1408-1.

808 Omissions

808-1 *General remarks*

Precautionary measures may imply not only that someone has to *refrain* from certain conduct, for instance not driving too fast, but also that he has to *do* something, for instance clearing the street of snow or informing other people of a risk. The distinction between acts and omissions is often also indicated by the words *misfeasance* and *nonfeasance*. Problems as regards liability for omissions have risen in all jurisdictions.

It is hard to draw a clear line between acts and omissions.[66] For example, one could argue that in *Donoghue v Stevenson* (nr 503) the manufacturer was *acting* by putting a defective product into circulation, but it could also be considered that he *omitted* to check the content of the bottle. The main approach in the jurisdictions is that there is misfeasance if the omission is part of an activity (as was the case in *Donoghue v Stevenson*). The French call this *l'omission dans l'action*. Genuine omissions (nonfeasance) are considered to be the ones without an action, in French: *l'omission sans action*.[67] Such omissions are related to risks which are not created by the defendant but by the victim (by entering a construction site without permission), by a third person (a teacher's pupil throwing a

---

[65] *Latham v R Johnson & Nephew Ltd* [1913] 1 KB 398, 416, per Hamilton LJ. See also Markesinis and Deakin (2003), 172.

[66] See also Jeroen Kortmann, *Altruism in Private Law. Liability for Nonfeasance and Negotiorum Gestio* (Oxford: Oxford University Press, 2005), 5 ff.

[67] See for instance Le Tourneau (2004), nr 7203–7209.

stone through a window), by nature (a tree falling in heavy winds), or by the condition of an object (the floor of a shop being slippery).

Imposing an affirmative duty on someone implies a bigger restriction to the freedom to act than a duty to refrain from something whilst carrying out a certain activity (nr 808-1). In the former case someone has to enter into an activity rather than adapt his behaviour during an activity in which he is already involved. It is less burdensome to take precautionary measures when carrying out an activity than having to act in order to take such measures.

However, many cases of so-called omissions are about failures to act in activities the defendant has already entered into. One may think of opening a highway, a house, or a stadium to the general public, of hiring an employee, of raising a child, of keeping an animal, or of using dangerous substances. In all these cases affirmative duties can easily arise and the burden of imposing such duties is not as dramatic as is suggested in the above-mentioned juxtaposition of acts and omissions.

Responsibility for premises, for moving goods, or for other persons implies that someone has knowledge of certain risks, that he is able to prevent, remove or limit them, and that the potential victim lacks this knowledge and ability or is not sufficiently aware of the risks. Many omission cases are characterized by this difference in knowledge and ability by the person who owes an affirmative duty, and this difference is also an important justification for imposing such a duty.

A good illustration of the reluctance in English law as regards liability for omissions is *Stovin v Wise*. A highway authority had planned to improve a junction but then let the matter rest. An accident took place which probably could have been prevented if the authority had not omitted to improve the junction. By the smallest majority, their Lordships decided that the highway authority did not owe road users a duty of care. In his speech Lord Hoffman took a clear conservative view as regards liability for omissions:

There are sound reasons why omissions require different treatment from positive conduct. It is one thing for the law to say that a person who undertakes some activity shall take reasonable care not to cause damage to others. It is another thing for the law to require that a person who is doing nothing in particular shall take steps to prevent another from suffering harm from the acts of third parties (. . .) or natural causes. (. . .). Except in special cases (such as marine salvage) English law does not reward someone who voluntarily confers a benefit on another. So there must be some special reason why he should have to put his hand in his pocket.[68]

In his speech Lord Hoffmann played down the responsibility people have for their premises, their property, or for other persons, in order to prevent them

---

[68] Lord Hoffman in *Stovin v Wise* [1996] 3 All ER 801, 819. Von Bar (2000), N 194, note 106, commented that this argument was ' . . . strongly reminiscent of the views so typical of the 19th C.' See also nr 1507 and 1804-2.

from causing damage to third parties. His focus was strongly on the protection of personal freedom and not on the protection of life and property. His speech is an illustration of the gap in policy between English law and the continental systems: the French hardly see the point of discussing the difference between acts and omissions and the Germans have developed a huge range of affirmative duties in the framework of the *Verkehrspflichten* (safety duties) (nr 808-3).

Liability for omissions is a crucial issue for the development of tort law since it is at the heart of the division between the defendant's and the claimant's responsibility. How far does the defendant's responsibility for the claimant's interests go? There might be a common ground to protect the claimant from his own mistakes, but the question is whether he should also be protected against his more foolish behaviour.

As regards establishing affirmative duties, a number of salient features can be described, depending on the relationship someone has with the place of the accident, with the movable thing that caused the damage, with the tortfeasor, and with the victim. They are set out in nr 808-2.

808-2 *Indications for affirmative duties*

It goes without saying that not ' . . . every individual has a duty to save everybody else from all possible dangers.'[69] Therefore, the key issue for the courts is to whom to attribute the duty to prevent the harm.

It is clear that someone who is involved in an activity is also responsible for taking precautionary measures. But if someone else has created the risk (the victim, a third party) or it is created by nature or by the condition of an object, it is not self-evident who is the person in charge, responsible for taking measures. However, the jurisdictions show important similarities as regards the question of who can owe an affirmative duty. The main indications are: (a) a relationship with the place of the accident, (b) a relationship with the movable thing that caused the damage, (c) a relationship with the tortfeasor and (d) a relationship with the victim.[70] Cases in which none of these relationships exist will fall into the category of cases of pure omission. They mainly concern rescue cases and will be analysed in Chapter 17.

(a) *Relationship with the place of the accident.* The first clue for the creation of affirmative duties is the place where the accident occurred, for example, the premises, the road, or the land. The owner or tenant often has a duty to supervise the safety of a locality. In England the supervisor is usually the

---

[69] Von Bar (2000), N 194.
[70] Compare Article 4:103 PETL:

A duty to act positively to protect others from damage may exist if law so provides, or if the actor creates or controls a dangerous situation, or when there is a special relationship between parties or when the seriousness of the harm on the one side and the ease of avoiding the damage on the other side point towards such a duty.

occupier who owes duties towards the visitor. These duties are enumerated in the two Occupier's Liability Acts. In France the owner of land or a building owes a duty of care towards the visitor, towards his neighbour, and towards passers-by, for instance to prevent snow falling from the roof onto the high-way.[71] The first German *Verkehrspflichten* related to roads, land, and buildings and imply that someone allowing another person to enter his road, land, or building is obliged to make or keep it sufficiently safe. He has, for example, to fill holes in the road, scatter sand or salt on an icy road, and equip stairs with banisters.[72]

In this category, rules of stricter liability also apply in French law (article 1384 s. 1 and article 1386) and German law (§ 836–838 BGB). See in more detail about liability for premises, grounds, and roads Chapter 15.

(b) *Relationship with the movable object that caused the damage.* The second clue for the creation of an affirmative duty is the fact that someone owns or uses the movable object that directly or indirectly caused the damage. If this is the case, the owner or user often does not only have the opportunity, but also the duty of supervising the object in order to prevent damage. In Germany the *Verkehrspflichten* provide for many affirmative duties that are intended to prevent damage caused by a movable object, such as machines and dangerous substances. English duties to prevent damage caused by a movable object are not dealt with separately by the courts or the doctrine; they are mainly based on the tort of negligence.

In this area rules of stricter liability also apply, in all systems for defective products (based on the European Directive, see nr 1406) and animals, and in Germany and France for motor vehicles also. In France, liability for omissions as regards things is almost completely absorbed by the general strict liability rule for damage caused by a *chose* (article 1384 s. 1 CC). See in more detail about liability for movable objects, Chapter 14.

(c) *Relationship with the tortfeasor.* The third category of affirmative duties applies to persons who owe a duty to prevent another person from causing damage to third parties. In this area, rules of vicarious and strict liability apply in most legal systems, particularly for parents (for damage caused by their children) and employers (for damage caused by their employees). French tort law even holds a judge-made general strict liability rule for damage caused by other persons. If no strict rule applies, it has to be established that the supervisor breached his duty of care. One may think of the duty of a school as regards its pupils, a hospital as regards its patients, and a prison as regards its prisoners. See in more detail about the duty to supervise other persons, Chapter 16.

---

[71] Civ. 2e 23 December 1969, JCP 1970. IV. 242; Civ. 2e 26 November 1980, D. 1981. IR. 276; Civ. 2e 4 May 1983, Gaz. Pal. 1983. 2. 261, obs. Chabas; Civ. 2e 18 January 1963, JCP 1963. II. 13316, comm. Blaevoët; Civ. 2e 9 July 1975, D. 1975. IR. 215, JCP 1977. II. 18544, comm. Mourgeon (1re esp.).   [72] Kötz-Wagner (2001), N 235–244.

(d) *Relationship with the victim.* The fourth category of affirmative duties refers to cases in which someone has to supervise and take care of another person, particularly if this person is not able to protect himself in a normal way. One may think of the duty of a physician towards his patient, of a host towards his guest, a prison towards its prisoner, a driver towards his passenger, a parent towards his child, and a school towards its pupil. Apart from some aspects dealt with in Chapter 14 about the liability for premises, grounds, and roads, for practical reasons this topic will not be further elaborated in this edition of the book.

Generally, the courts show more reluctance in establishing liability in cases of nonfeasance than in cases of misfeasance.[73] In the former category, the reasonable man can be less perfect than in the latter category (nr 812). This means that in certain circumstances it can be required that the defendant knew or could have easily known about the risk for the claimant.

Affirmative duties are usually not owed by children, if only for the fact that they will generally not possess the means and the authority to supervise movable objects, premises, or other persons. This does not necessarily apply in relation to rules of strict liability. For example in France a child can also be the *gardien de la chose* (nr 303-3).

808-3 *Fitting affirmative duties into the legal systems*

Affirmative duties have been mainly discussed in English and German law, since the tort of negligence and the BGB did not provide sufficient possibilities for affirmative duties of care. From this starting point, the courts in both jurisdictions have developed these duties, though the German courts with clearly more enthusiasm and perseverance than the English (nr 808-1). In France the general *faute* liability did not raise obstacles for establishing affirmative duties and this caused omissions to play a rather modest role in doctrinal discussions.

In English law the issue is dealt with within the framework of the duty of care in the tort of negligence (nr 503). In principle, a duty to act has to be based on precedent. When there is no precedent, a duty can only be established if there was foreseeable harm and a sufficient proximity between defendant and claimant; furthermore, it has to be fair, just, and reasonable to impose a duty of care on the defendant.[74] As regards affirmative duties, the key element is proximity: 'The use of "proximity" is only the beginning of the analysis, however, since the precise scope and extent of the duty will differ from one situation to another; but without some pre-tort relationship of this kind, it is unlikely that an affirmative

---

[73] Terré-Simler-Lequette (2002), nr 721; Carbonnier (2000), § 221, 402–403. See also Zimmerman, *The Law of Obligations* (Oxford: Clarendon Press, 1996), 1045.

[74] *Caparo Industries plc v Dickman* [1990] 1 All ER 568, about which Van Gerven (2000), 215–219; see nr 714-1.

duty of any degree can be imposed.'[75] Sufficient proximity and thus affirmative duties are generally accepted with regard to the protection and supervision of other persons. In the doctrine these categories are often both treated under the heading of the 'duty to control others.'[76]

In Germany affirmative duties revealed a hole in the legislative framework soon after the entering into force of the German BGB. The *Reichsgericht* had to decide a case about someone who was injured by a tree which had fallen onto the highway. §823 I primarily refers to damage caused by positive conduct by focusing on the infringement of a right (nr 402-3). However, the *Reichsgericht* decided that §823 I also applied in cases in which the infringement of the right of another person was the consequence of an omission.[77] Of course, the sole infringement could not be sufficient for a *Tatbestand* and *Rechtswidrigkeit* in the sense of §823 I. This would lead to undesirable consequences because producers of knives or fireworks could be liable even if they had put a perfect product onto the market, simply because it had caused harm. Hence, the *Reichsgericht* developed safety duties (*Verkehrspflichten*) to determine whether an omission was unlawful or not. These duties to act are generally based on the relationship which someone has with a building or land, with a movable thing, or with the potential victim. They apply, *inter alia*, to contractors, pharmacists, chemists, architects, doctors, car wash companies, swimming pools, railways, organizers of demonstrations, hotels, pubs, guest houses, hunters, shops, operators of sports and playing grounds, sports centres and ski-runs, skiers, and road constructors towards all foreseeable victims.[78]

Article 1383 of the French *Code civil* explicitly holds that liability for damage may follow not only from someone's act but also from someone's negligence or carelessness. On this basis the courts have competence to establish affirmative duties. As in all *faute* cases, it is decisive whether and how a reasonable person in the same circumstances would have acted. Liability for omissions therefore does not raise specific questions in French tort law.[79] Moreover, in French law strict liability rules apply to cases that in other jurisdictions would be treated as omission cases. It is, therefore, illustrative—both from a legal-systematic and a literary-cultural point of view—that the most famous French omission case is not about an affirmative safety duty but about the affirmative duty of an author. In an article in a socialist almanac, written by Professor Turpain, entitled 'Historique de la T.S.F.' (History of Wireless Telegraphy) the Catholic Édouard

---

[75] Markesinis and Deakin (2003), 150.
[76] Markesinis and Deakin (2003), 149–150; Fleming (1998), 168. See also Lord Bridge of Harwich in *Curran v Northern Ireland Co-Ownership Housing Association Ltd* [1987] 2 WLR 1043.
[77] RG 30 October 1902, RGZ 52, 373.
[78] Deutsch-Ahrens (2002), N 86: 'Die Unterlassung spielt im Zivilrecht eine erhebliche Rolle. Das Gebiet der Verkehrssicherungspflichten wird sogar von ihr beherrscht. Unterlassungen sind nach allgemeiner Ansicht nur dann widerrechtlich, wenn sie einer Pflicht zum Tun widersprechen.'
[79] Mazeaud-Tunc (1965), nr 540; Viney-Jourdain (1998), nr 453; Aubry and Rau-Dejean de la Bathie (1989), nr 37.

Branly was consistently not mentioned though it was generally known that Branly had been at the T.S.F.'s birth. The *Cour de cassation* considered this omission to be a *faute* because the omitted fact had to be demonstrated on the basis of a legal, statutory, contractual, or customary obligation or, in a professional setting, according to the requirements of objective information.[80] Although the general decision on the liability for omissions was favoured by the doctrine, the specific decision on this duty to provide objective information was strongly criticized. How could objective historiography be possible?[81] In 1994 the *Cour de cassation* overruled this disputed aspect of its decision, stating that liability for an omission in a publication only occurs if the presentation of the thesis causes, by denaturization, falsification, or gross negligence, a flagrant denial of the truth.[82]

809 Character and benefit of the conduct

809-1 *General remarks*

As has been pointed out, the magnitude of the risk determines the required level of care: the greater the risk, the higher the level of care (nr 805-1). In establishing the level of care, the character and benefit of the defendant's conduct also has to be taken into consideration.

Firstly, the character and benefit of the defendant's conduct can play a role on a specific level in the framework of the grounds of justification. For example, a doctor's infringement of someone's bodily integrity can be justified by the patient's consent. In such a case the benefit of the doctor's conduct is deemed to outweigh the infringement of the patient's right (nr 815).

On a general level one may think of cases in which it is not possible or desirable to require the defendant to take certain precautionary measures, even though his conduct harms other people's interests or fails to protect it. Various examples can illustrate this.

Firstly, the character and benefit of the defendant's conduct plays a role in cases of opposing fundamental rights and freedoms, for example the right to privacy and the right to freedom of expression. One may think of the *Caroline*

---

[80] Civ. 27 February 1951, D. 1951. 329, comm. Desbois, S. 1951. 1. 158; JCP 1951. II. 6193, comm. Mihura, Gaz. Pal. 1951. 1. 230:

... que l'abstention, même non dictée par l'intention de nuire, engage la responsabilité de son auteur lorsque le fait omis devait être accompli soit en vertu d'une obligation légale, réglementaire ou conventionnelle, soit aussi, dans l'ordre professionnel, s'il s'agit notamment d'un historien, en vertu des exigences d'une information objective.

See for more details about this case Van Gerven (2000), 282–283.

[81] J. Carbonnier, 'Le silence et la gloire', D. 1951. 119.

[82] Civ. 2e 15 June 1994, Bull. civ. II, no 218.

von Hannover case before the European Court of Human Rights in which it was decided that freedom of expression did not outweigh Caroline's right to privacy (nr 705-5). In other cases, for instance as regards the privacy of politicians, it can be the other way round. In such cases it is not desirable from a human rights point of view to require the press to refrain from publishing facts even if these are harmful for the politician involved.

Secondly, the character and benefit of the defendant's conduct plays a major role in the liability of public bodies. Though public benefit as such cannot be regarded as an absolute defence,[83] liability for public bodies differs from liability of private individuals, particularly because under certain circumstances a public body is allowed to be subject to a marginal test only. It is believed that this is justified by the special task of public bodies to work in the public interest, and having to balance various interests on a daily basis. See in detail nr 1810.

Thirdly, the character and benefit of the defendant's conduct plays a role in economic competition between businesses. Competition is considered to be one of the cornerstones of western economic policy, which implies that the defendant's freedom to compete is of such a high value that it usually outweighs the competitor's interest to be protected. The defendant is only liable if he caused the damage in an unfair way, for instance by unfair practices (*concurrence déloyale, unlauterer Wettbewerb*),[84] by forbidden agreements or concerted practices with other businesses (cartels), or by abusing a dominant market position (Articles 81 and 82 EC).

Finally, the character and benefit of the defendant's conduct plays a role in sports with an inherent risk of causing physical harm to opponents. One may think of football, rugby, hockey, or squash. Such sports cannot be practised without allowing the players to create risks which would not be acceptable outside the playing grounds. However, players can be liable if they cause damage to another player in a (most) unfair way, for instance by grossly negligently violating the rules of the game. In this category of cases, it is impossible from a sporting point of view to require players to refrain from conduct that can harm other players.

A parallel can be drawn between sports competition and economic competition. Both areas accept competition as a useful and beneficial incentive for action and therefore emphasize the value of the freedom to act. Protection of a competitor's or an opponent's interests only comes into play in cases of unfair conduct according to the characteristics of the competition.

---

[83] See for example for England *Bamford v Turnley* (1862) 122 ER 27.

[84] See also Directive 2005/29/EC on Unfair Commercial Practices which only applies to business-to-consumer relations but a number of the forbidden practices are also relevant in business-to-business relations. See about this Directive, Hugh Collins (ed.), *The Forthcoming EC Directive on Unfair Commercial Practices* (The Hague, London, Munich: Kluwer Law International, 2004).

809-2 *Assumption of risk*

In most legal systems the so-called 'assumption of risk' (*Handeln auf eigene Gefahr, acceptation du risque*) plays an important role in the above-mentioned sports cases (nr 807-1).[85] Though generally accepted throughout the legal systems, this defence raises more questions than answers.

Systematically the concept is hybrid, since it is related to contributory negligence (nr 1200), grounds of justification (nr 800), and negligence.[86] In practice the concept has chameleon-like features, since its application very much depends on the circumstances of the case. For practical reasons this topic will be dealt with in this chapter because the focus will be on the question of how the standard of care is assessed in activities such as sports with an inherent risk in which someone is voluntary engaged.

In sports cases, assumption of risk is generally considered to be a defence against liability but not if the tortfeasor has grossly violated a rule of the game. This implies that participants only accept the 'normal' risks of the game—risks which are inherent in the game's character—provided that the risks are sufficiently clear beforehand. Participants do not accept abnormal risks (*risque anormal*), such as an intentional or manifest breach of a rule of the game.[87] For example, the French *Cour de cassation* decided that participants in an ocean regatta did not accept the abnormal risk of a fatal accident.[88] Interestingly, the BGH has linked the defence of *Handeln auf eigene Gefahr* to the general principle of good faith (*Treu und Glauben*, § 242 BGB). If the defendant has acted intentionally or grossly negligently, he cannot in good faith invoke the defence of assumption of risk.[89]

It makes sense to look at this issue from the opposite angle. Someone who participates in a football match not only assumes that he may break his leg but he will first and foremost assume that his opponents will play fairly. Hence, the key issue can also be identified as whether the person who caused the damage played fairly. In principle, the sole fact that a player caused harm to an opponent by

[85] Von Bar (2000), N 512–513. See also Art. 5:101(2) ECC providing that a person has a defence as against the injured person if the latter, '. . . knowing the risk of damage of the type caused, voluntarily exposes himself to that risk and is to be regarded as accepting it.' A classic is Hans Stoll, *Das Handeln auf eigene Gefahr: Eine rechtsvergleichende Untersuchung*, (Berlin: De Gruyter, 1961). Another important category of cases relates to people accepting a lift from a drunken driver. It is generally accepted that this does not imply the acceptance of the risk that an accident will occur. The courts usually decide to attribute contributory negligence to the victim. See nr 1200.
[86] Von Bar (2000), N 512.
[87] Van Gerven (2000), 734–736. Civ. 2e 28 January 1987, Bull. civ. 1987. II. 32 (squash); Viney-Jourdain (1998), nr 573-1; Carbonnier (2000), § 232, 421; *Woolridge v Sumner* [1963] 2 QB 43 (liability towards a spectator at races).
[88] Civ. 2e 8 March 1995 (cons. Bizouard), Bull. civ. II, no 83, D. 1995. IR. 99, JCP 1995. II. 22499, note J. Gardach, RTC 1995, 905, note P. Jourdain.
[89] BGH 5 November 1974, BGHZ 63, 140, 144 = NJW 1975, 109, 110. See also BGH 14 March 1961, BGHZ 34, 355 = NJW 1961, 655 = JZ 1961, 602, about which Markesinis and Unberath (2002), 678–683; BGH 1 April 2003, VersR 2003, 775, ETL 2003, 190 (Fedtke).

breaching a rule of the game is not sufficient for liability. This will generally only be the case if the referee shows a player the red card or should have shown him one.

English law explicitly requires that the violation was intentional or grossly negligent. Basi (Khalsa Football Club) tried to tackle Condon (Whittle Wanderers) to get the ball. He missed the ball and hit Condon who broke his leg. The referee sent Basi off the field with a red card because he considered the sliding tackle to be performed in a dangerous and reckless manner.[90] Condon's damages claim was awarded because Basi had grossly negligently violated the rule of the game.[91] In Germany, the earlier case law of the BGH seems to suggest that the sole breach of a rule of the game can give rise to liability but it is unclear whether this is really the case.[92] Wagner clarified that a violation only gives rise to liability if a player does not act reasonably, mainly if he intends to injure the other player, or if he acts unreasonably dangerously, there is room for a damages claim.[93] More recent case law indicates that a substantial infringement of the relevant rules is required.[94] Interpreted in this way, there would not be a difference in outcome between English and German law.

D NEGLIGENT PERSON

810 Knowledge and ability

810-1 *Introduction*

It has been pointed out that negligence refers to two aspects: conduct and person. If it is established that the defendant's *conduct* was negligent, the question has to be answered whether his *personal capacities* met the required standard. Personal capacities comprise two elements: knowledge and ability. Someone acts below the required standard if he knew the risk or ought to have known it, and when he could avoid the risk or ought to have avoided it. Conduct and person are two sides of the same coin since they cannot be separated from each other (nr 805-1).

[90] *Condon v Basi* [1985] 1 WLR 866.
[91] See also *Blake v Galloway* [2004] 3 All ER 315 about teenagers engaged in 'high-spirited and good natured horseplay' which involved throwing twigs and pieces of bark at each other. One of the teenagers was hit in the eye by a piece of bark. The Court of Appeal held that the boy who threw the bark did not do this recklessly or with a very high degree of carelessness and dismissed the negligence claim. It also dismissed the battery claim (nr 504-1) because the claimant, by participating in the game, had impliedly consented to the risk of a blow to any part of his body.
[92] BGH 5 November 1974, BGHZ 63, 140; see also BGH 10 February 1976, BGHZ 63, 866 = NJW 1976, 957.   [93] Münchener Kommentar-Wagner (2004), § 823 N 523.
[94] BGH 1 April 2003, VersR 2003, 775, ETL 2003, 190 (Fedtke).

Someone will generally be negligent if he causes damage although he personally knew the risk and had the capacity to avoid it. However, someone will not be negligent if no one on earth knew the risk or could have avoided it, not even on the basis of the most recent and available scientific data. The key question in negligence mostly lies between these extremes: what ought the defendant to have known about the risk and which abilities should he have had to avoid the risk? This question is not a factual one (what did the defendant know or what were his abilities) but a normative one. It implies that someone can be liable on the basis of negligence even though he *personally* did not know the risk and personally could not have avoided it. As regards personal negligence the 'ought' question is the *leitmotiv* (nr 811).

In order to establish the required knowledge and ability, the court has to look at the situation immediately before the time of the event that gave rise to the claim. However, in daily life it is often tempting to judge the defendant's conduct with hindsight. 'Nothing is so easy as to be wise after the event.'[95] The fact that the damage has occurred is usually the best indication that a reasonable person should have foreseen it. And if one knows which sequence of events has led to the damage, it is rather easy to conclude which safety measure or measures would have prevented the damage.[96] This mechanism adds to a higher standard of care and sometimes brings it close to rules of strict liability (nr 1004).

The following sections will discuss the meaning of knowledge and ability (nr 810), the objective and subjective standards (nr 811), the standards of reference (nr 812), and the position of children and mentally disabled persons (nr 813).

810-2 *Knowledge*

The required knowledge is related to the risk. Therefore, what the tortfeasor knew or ought to have known about the risk is decisive, ie the seriousness and probability of the harm. See about the elements of the risk nr 806.

The requirement of knowledge is to be applied in a generalized way. Usually, knowledge is related to the fact that a particular conduct can cause harm of a general kind, such as damage to health or to property. The required knowledge does not have to be related to the sequence of events that resulted in the damage;

[95] Branwell B in *Cornmann v Eastern Counties R Co* (1859) 157 ER 1050.
[96] Kötz-Wagner (2001), N 261:

Daß der Schaden überhaupt eingetreten ist, ist unter diesen Umständen der beste "Beweis" dafür, daß ihn ein sorgfältiger Mensch auch hätte vorhersehen müssen, und wenn man weiß, welch Ursachenkette zu dem Schaden geführt hat, läßt sich nachträglich auch besonders leicht eine Sicherungsmaßnahme ermitteln, die—wäre sie ergriffen worden—den Schaden verhindert hätte.

See also Winfield and Jolowicz (2002), para. 5.57.

this sequence does not have to be foreseeable.[97] This generalization technique has boosted the number of claims awarded: 'The history of negligence is the story of the unexpected. The books are full of odd occurrences, strange conjunctions, and unpredictable contingencies.'[98]

An example can be found in a decision of the German BGH. A pregnant woman was injured in a car accident. When she delivered the baby three months later, it was found that the child suffered from brain damage. The BGH decided that it was not required that the driver knew or could have known that he would injure a pregnant woman or her child. 'It suffices to render the person liable who inflicted the injury if he should have realised the possibility of a damaging result in general; it need not be foreseeable what form the damage would take in detail and what damage might occur.'[99] This issue is also considered as a matter of causation and the BGH decision is a clear application of the adequacy theory (nr 1103-1).

Knowledge refers not only to the risk itself but sometimes also to the existence of a safety rule. The maxim is that every person is supposed to know the law, not only the written but also the unwritten law. This makes sense: safety rules generally aim to prevent or restrict risks that unreasonably endanger the interests of others, and knowledge of the rules implies knowledge of these risks.

An interesting example is a decision of the German BGH. The case was about a 15-year-old boy, who was skiing on the Bavarian *Zugspitzplatt* when he lost control over his skis, collided with the square iron pillar of a ski tow, and was severely injured. According to the BGH, the ski tow operator owed the users a duty to cover the sharp-edged pillars with pallets or similar material. Though the operator had breached its safety duty (*Verkehrspflicht*) and had thus acted unlawfully (*rechtswidrig*), the BGH considered that there was no *Verschulden*. The operator could not have known this new safety duty at the time of the accident; neither did the rule logically follow from earlier decisions.[100]

Sometimes the risk is unclear or it is unclear whether there is a risk at all. Doubt generally requires research and investigations. The impossibility of investigating is no general defence against negligence. If an investigation is not possible one has to be cautious. For example, in the case of an unclear priority situation (was it an exit or a side road?) the BGH decided that if the situation is not clearly in someone's favour, he has to take more care.[101] In the same vein it

---

[97] See also nr 806-2 about the same role the probability of the sequence of events plays in establishing negligent conduct and nr 1112 about the role probability of the sequence of events plays in establishing causation.

[98] Lord Justice-Clerk Aitchison in *Bourhill v Young* [1941] SLT 364, 387, about which also nr 704.

[99] BGH 11 January 1972, BGHZ 58, 48, 56 = NJW 1972, 1126 = JZ 1972, 363, about which Markesinis and Unberath (2002), 144–147 from which the translation is derived (147). See about this case also nr 707; Münchener Kommentar-Grundmann (2003), § 276 N 70; BGH 5 November 1976, NJW 1977, 763.

[100] BGH 23 October 1984, NJW 1985, 620, 621 = VersR 1985, 64, 66. See also BGH 14 March 1995, NJW 1995, 2631 (see nr 1503-2).

[101] BGH 5 October 1976, VersR 1977, 58. See also Münchener Kommentar-Grundmann (2003), § 276 N 74.

can be argued that if there is doubt about the risk of a certain conduct and less risky conduct is possible, one has to choose the latter option.[102]

810-3 *Ability*

The personal aspect of negligence does not only refer to knowledge (nr 810-2) but also to ability. It is not only about 'I did not know' (knowledge of the risk) but also about 'I could not help' (ability to avoid the risk).

The element of ability refers to the personal ability to avoid the risk, and it is closely related to the element of the burden of precautionary measures (nr 807). The difference is that personal ability refers to the precautionary measures that can only be taken by someone as an individual (eg the ability of a driver to react and to steer to avoid a sudden dangerous situation), whereas the precautionary measures discussed in nr 807 are those which do not depend on someone's personal abilities.

In order to answer the question of whether the tortfeasor possessed the required ability or skill to avoid the risk, a generalized approach is to be preferred, just as in matters of required knowledge (nr 810-2). Hence, the ability to avoid the risk should not relate to the possibility of avoiding the consequential damage but, in principle, only to the possibility of avoiding the accident.

It goes without saying that someone cannot act negligently if the risk could not have been avoided by anybody. One simply cannot require conduct that is impossible for a human being to exercise. However, even if the risk was unavoidable for everybody, the defendant can still be negligent if the situation in which the unavoidable risk occurred could have been avoided by earlier safety measures. One may think of a driver who is blinded by the sun; at that moment he might be unable to avoid a particular risk such as not giving way to another driver. But he could have avoided this situation by wearing proper sunglasses. The less you can see, the more you have to foresee.[103]

810-4 *State of the art*

Universities and companies' research departments are working to expand the borders of human knowledge and technique. This scientific state of the art is the bottom line for knowledge and ability in the framework of negligence. If harm could only have been prevented on the basis of knowledge and technique which nobody possessed at the time of the accident, the state of the art defence can successfully be invoked. This is the case not only in negligence liability but also in some strict liability rules such as in the EU Directive on defective products (nr 1410-2).

---

[102] BGH 9 February 1951, NJW 1951, 398; BGH 28 September 1992, VersR 1993, 112. Münchener Kommentar-Grundmann (2003), § 276 N 74.
[103] BGH 23 May 1967, VersR 1967, 862; BGH 17 December 1968, VersR 1969, 373. See also Dobbs I (2001), § 129, 304–305.

An example is the English case of *Roe v Minister of Health* decided in 1954. In preparation for an operation a patient had a spinal injection. The glass ampoule containing the anaesthetics had been disinfected in a phenol solution but this phenol had contaminated the anaesthetics via invisible hairline cracks in the glass of the ampoule. As a consequence the patient was permanently paralysed. However, the anaesthetist did not have to prevent this unknown risk: 'He did not know that there could be undetectable cracks, but it was not negligent for him not to know it at that time. We must not look at the 1947 accident with 1954 spectacles.'[104]

The state of the art question usually arises with respect to medical diagnoses and therapies, professionally used substances, such as asbestos and chemicals, and products (especially drugs).

When is a risk considered to be known according to the state of the art? Usually, risks are not discovered from one day to the next. At a certain point there might be an assumption of the existence of a risk, then the assumption of a cause may come into play, and in the end, such causation is scientifically proved. In other cases, causation cannot be proved except with statistical evidence and often researchers will not even reach that stage.

Subsequently, if the risk is discovered it will take time before articles are published in specialist journals, and more time will go by before the knowledge of the risk has reached the practitioners who need to know about it. Though new media might enable a quicker dissemination of the news around the world, it is obvious that the borderline between a known and an unknown risk is not always crystal clear. It can be argued that, in order to establish the time as from which a certain risk is supposed to be known, the judge should take into account the content of the article, the authority of the journal in which it was published, and the extent to which the content and scope of the article are endorsed within the relevant discipline. As regards the speed and scale of dissemination of the outcome of legal research there exist quite major differences

... between a study of a researcher in a university in the United States published in an international English-language international journal and (...) similar research carried out by an academic in Manchuria published in a local scientific journal in Chinese, which does not go outside the boundaries of the region.[105]

Requirements for big companies and professionals do not need to be the same as for small businesses, though the latter should at least know what is published in newspapers, by their branch organizations, or on general news sites on the internet. See about problems as regards different opinions within a discipline nr 812-2.

Even if information is available about the risk it is not always clear which measures can be taken to avoid the risk since there may be no technique yet available. One may think of HIV. The existence of this virus and its

---

[104] *Roe v Minister of Health* [1954] 2 QB 66, 84.
[105] AG General Tesauro before ECJ 29 May 1997, C-300/95, ECR 1997, I-2649 (*Commission v United Kingdom*).

consequences started to become clear in 1983 and 1984. However, the test for checking donor blood for HIV, which was essential to avoid infection by way of blood transfusion, was only available in early 1985.[106] Comparable problems occurred with the Hepatitis C virus.[107] In such cases, a duty to inform about the risk and about the impossibility of preventing it can exist. The same goes if there are serious doubts about safety but the risk as such is not sufficiently clear.

811 Subjective and objective tests

811-1 *Subjective test*

If the court applies an *objective test* it takes a normative approach and decides what the defendant ought to have known about the risk and what he ought to have done to avoid it (nr 811–2). A *subjective test* implies that the court takes the tortfeasor as it finds him: it establishes whether the defendant personally knew the risk and whether he was personally able to avoid it.[108]

The latter is the classical approach in which the fault proper is decisive and in which liability can only exist if the wrongdoer can be personally blamed for his conduct.[109] Though the frequently used terminology of fault liability suggests that the subjective approach is the general rule in tort law, this is certainly not the case. On the contrary, the general rule is that knowledge and ability are judged in an objective way and that a subjective test is applied in exceptional cases only. The reasons to prefer an objective test over a subjective one are threefold.[110]

Firstly, the subjective test causes practical problems because the judge needs to examine what facts the defendant knew and what his abilities were at the moment of his harmful conduct. To get an answer to his questions the judge will either have to turn the defendant inside out or ask an expert to do so. Even with the current possibilities of psychology this is impossible.[111]

Secondly, the subjective test confuses liability and crime. In criminal law the wrongdoer is the centre of interest; this is demonstrated, for instance, in the fact that a prosecution ends with the death of the wrongdoer.[112] In tort law an action for damages can also be filed against the defendant's successors. Moreover, the discussion is not about penalty but about damages. This does not exclude the fact that tort law and the obligation to pay damages may have a corrective function.

[106] See about the HIV blood scandal in France nr 304.
[107] See about the Hepatitis C virus in the context of product liability *A v The National Blood Authority* [2001] 3 All ER 289, nr 63, about which nr 1410-2.
[108] Von Bar (2000), N 227.
[109] Xavier Blanc-Jouvan, 'La responsabilité de l'infans', *RTD civ.* 1957, 36; Larenz (1987), § 20 III, 284, stresses that the German law does not apply such a subjective test; see nr 804-2.
[110] See also Gerhard Wagner in Zimmermann (ed.), *Grundstrukturen des Europäischen Deliktsrechts*, (Baden-Baden: Nomos, 2003), 189 ff. [111] Larenz (1987), § 20 III, 286.
[112] Mazeaud-Tunc (1965), nr 421; Terré-Simler-Lequette (2002), nr 678; Larenz (1987), § 20 III, 286.

Finally, liability generally does not imply a moral judgment about the defendant's conduct. The judge is not a confessor, and someone who is liable for damage does not have to put on a hair shirt. Liability is not based on moral but on social responsibility.[113] Yet, morality can play a role in tort law but the moral opinions of one social group are not decisive.[114]

The objections against the subjective test all boil down to the fact that a subjective test puts too much emphasis on the defendant and his freedom to act, and that it is hard to properly take into account the victim's interests.[115] In the end, it would support the footballer who injured an opponent and argued '... that he was such a bad player he owed no duty not to break his opponents' legs with awful tackles.'[116]

Hence, a subjective test will only be applied if the defendant's interests *a priori* substantially outweigh those of the victim. One may think of emergency and rescue cases (Chapter 17).

811-2 *Objective test*

If a judge applies an objective test he has to establish what the defendant ought to have known about the risk, and what he ought to have done to avoid it. In this respect the courts make use of standards of reference, usually the *reasonable man* and the *bonus pater familias*. These are not very exciting and rather odious goody-goodies, who have proper knowledge of all situations, are sufficiently skilled to avoid risks, and never make a mistake.

If the defendant did not act according to the knowledge and ability of the reasonable person this does not mean that he is personally to blame for his conduct. Holmes' famous words are more than a century old:

The standards of the law are standards of general application. The law takes no account of the infinite varieties of temperament, intellect, and education which make the internal character of a given act so different in different men. (...). If, for instance, a man is born hasty and is always having accidents and hurting himself or his neighbours, no doubt his congenital defects will be allowed for in the courts of Heaven, but his slips are no less troublesome to his neighbours than if they sprang from guilty neglect. His neighbours accordingly require him, at his proper peril, to come up to their standard, and the courts which they establish decline to take his personal equation into account.[117]

---

[113] See also Aubry et Rau-Dejean de la Bathie (1989), nr 325; Terré-Simler-Lequette (2002), nr 724.

[114] Percy H. Winfield, 'Ethics in English Law', *Harvard LR*, 45 (1931), 112–135; Terré-Simler-Lequette (2002), nr 678.

[115] Viney-Jourdain (1998), nr 444; Mazeaud-Tunc (1965), nr 421; Larenz (1987), § 20 III, 286.

[116] C. Gearty, 'Liability for Injuries Incurred During Sports and Pastimes', *Cam LJ* [1985] 371.

[117] Oliver Wendell Holmes, *The Common Law*, edited by Mark DeWolfe Howe (London, Melbourne: Macmillan, 1960), 86–87.

The objective test is the basic rule in all legal systems (see in more detail nr 802). The French *faute* of article 1382 CC is established by using an abstract (objective) and not a concrete (subjective) test. The best known standards of reference are *l'homme droite et avisé* and *le bon père de famille*. Germany assesses negligence (*Fahrlässigkeit*) in the sense of § 276 BGB by applying an objective test (*objektivierter Fahrlässigkeitsmaßstab*). The usual standard of reference has been described as a careful person of average circumspection and capability (*ein sorgfältiger Mensch von durchschnittlicher Umsicht und Tüchtigkeit*).[118] In the English tort of negligence an objective test is also applied by comparing the defendant's conduct with that of the *reasonable man*. Sir Alan Herbert concluded that '. . . in all mass of authorities which bears upon this branch of the law there is no single mention of a reasonable woman.'[119] Neither, it can be said, is there any reference to *la bonne mère de famille*. In this book the neutral *reasonable person* is used as the general standard of reference.[120]

In Community tort law the ECJ has refrained from making liability dependent on the concept of fault. Elements of fault are only accepted as far as they are implied in the concept of a sufficiently serious breach. Indeed, the element of knowledge can play a role in this respect but this element is subject to an objective test (nr 1805-1).

The objective test implies the application of the *faute sociale*. Social life requires that people meet proper standards of conduct, knowledge, and skills. If someone is not able to do so, he has to pay for the consequences of his temporary or permanent shortcomings. This rule can be harsh but generally anyone can have a momentary lapse. The objective test makes clear that tort law is not about punishing someone for his wrongful behaviour or blaming him for it. Tort law is rather about protecting the public's reasonable safety expectations: as regards their pecuniary and non-pecuniary interests. People may expect other people to behave in an objectively careful way. If this standard is not met, there is good reason to compensate the harm caused. Of course, the use of an objective test would not have been conceivable without the fuel of modern tort law: the availability of liability insurance (nr 716).

In some areas of accident law and also outside this area, lower standards of knowledge and ability are applied. One may think of some kinds of affirmative duties (nr 808). However, this does not make the test subjective. It only means that the reasonable person is less odiously perfect. An example is the occupier's liability towards trespassers in English law (nr 1504-1).

Subjective tests have not been completely extinguished. Firstly, a more subjective test is sometimes applied to children and mentally disabled persons (nr 813). A genuine subjective test is applied in so-called rescue cases in which someone has a duty to rescue a person who is in peril. However, such a duty is unknown in common law and is quite exceptional in other European legal systems (nr 1702).

[118] Kötz-Wagner (2001), N 108.
[119] Sir Alan Herbert, *Uncommon Law. Being 66 Misleading Cases*, (London: Methuen 1969), 5.
[120] This is also the case in Arts. 3:201 and 4:102 of the PETL.

A quite recent development is the establishment of a subjective test for the protection of service providers of websites in the framework of the E-commerce Directive. This is performed by applying a subjective test as regards the knowledge of the illegal information or activity on the websites. Service providers are not liable for the information on websites to which they provide access on condition that:

(a) the provider does not have actual knowledge of illegal activity or information and, as regards claims for damages, is not aware of facts or circumstances from which the illegal activity or information is apparent; or (b) the provider, upon obtaining such knowledge or awareness, acts expeditiously to remove or to disable access to the information.[121]

812 Standards of reference

812-1 *General remarks*

The reasonable person appears in many different ways, depending on the character of the defendant's activity (nr 809). In daily life people play different roles. Sometimes we are drivers, sometimes we are experts or professionals, then again amateurs and finally also laymen or laywomen.[122] The standard of reference varies with the social role.[123] This explains why in one situation more knowledge and abilities are required than in the other.[124] A functional standard of reference enables the judge to differentiate according to the social role of the defendant and the circumstances of the case. From the perspective of reasonable expectations, this means that people may trust that nobody undertakes activities for which he does not have the proper knowledge and abilities.

This goes not only for professionals but also for amateurs. A person was injured when a door handle, which the resident had fixed with a do-it-yourself kit, broke off. Jenkins LJ said:

...the degree and skill required of him must be measured not by reference to the degree of competence in such matters which he personally happened to possess, but by reference to the degree of care and skill which a reasonably competent carpenter might be expected to apply to the work in question.[125]

The judge decided that the resident had acted according to that standard.[126]

---

[121] Article 13(1) Directive 2000/31/EC of 8 June 2000 (Directive on electronic commerce); see nr 1302.
[122] Deutsch, Erwin, *Allgemeines Haftungsrecht*, 2nd edn., (Cologne: Heymann, 1996), N 403: '...der Mensch schlüpft im Laufe eines Tages in manche Gewänder, einmal nimmt er am allgemeinen Verkehr teil, ein andermal ist er Fachmann oder Professional, dann wieder Amateur, schließlich auch Laie.'
[123] Viney-Jourdain (1998), nr 464 '...le standard de "l'homme raisonnable" n'est pas unique, mais qu'il varie en fonction de la difficulté et des caractères propres à l'activité exercée.'
[124] Larenz (1987), § 20 III, 287; Noël Dejean de la Bathie, *Appréciation in abstracto et appréciation in concreto en droit civil français* (Paris: Pichon & Durand-Auzias, 1965), nr 18 ff.
[125] *Wells v Cooper* [1958] 2 QB 265. See also Dobbs I (2001), § 122, 290.
[126] Markesinis and Deakin (2003), 170.

The possibility of adapting the standard of reference to the social role and to the circumstances of the case is of particular importance in an emergency situation (nr 811-1). In such a situation there is no time to ponder and weigh out alternatives; impulses are mostly decisive for behaviour, and a wrong decision will not automatically establish liability: 'Errors of judgment committed in an emergency will not normally be classified as negligence.'[127] Hence, the standard of reference in emergency situations will generally not differ much from the person of the defendant. However, an objective standard will be applied if someone has caused the emergency situation himself or if he can prepare for such a situation on a professional basis (nr 1703-2). One may think of doctors and paramedics. In an emergency situation their standard of reference will be the reasonably competent and skilled first aid doctor and paramedic.

812-2 *Professionals*

Nobody expects the passenger on the Clapham omnibus to have any skill as a surgeon, a lawyer, a docker, or a chimney-sweep unless he is one; but if he professes to be one, then the law requires him to show such skill as any ordinary member of the profession or calling to which he belongs, or claims to belong, would display.[128]

This professional standard of reference can be differentiated according to the differences in subdisciplines, between general practitioners and specialists, and between doctors in a local hospital and a university hospital.[129]

What should be the level of the professional standard? Does it need to be excellent, good, fair, reasonable, average, or ordinary? In England, McNair J in *Bolam v Friern Hospital Management Committee* preferred the ordinary professional:

The test is the standard of the ordinary skilled man exercising and professing to have that special skill. A man need not possess the highest expert skill at the risk of being found negligent. It is well-established law that it is sufficient if he exercises the ordinary skill of an ordinary competent man exercising that particular art.[130]

This standard can be confusing because many mistakes and inaccuracies are inevitable in human (and hence also professional) conduct and thus 'ordinary' or 'average'. Prosser and Keeton are more to the point when they argue that a

---

[127] Markesinis and Deakin (2003), 170. In the same sense Deutsch-Ahrens (2002), N 123; Larenz, *Lehrbuch des Schuldrechts I* (1987), § 20 III, 283; Dobbs I (2001), § 129, 304; see also BGH 25 October 1951, NJW 1952, 217.

[128] Winfield and Jolowicz (2002), para. 3.6; see also *Wells v Cooper* [1958] 2 QB 265, 271; *Ashcroft v Mersey Regional Health Authority* [1983] 2 All ER 245, 247; *Duchess of Argyll v Beuselinck* [1972] 2 Lloyd's Rep. 172 (solicitor). See furthermore Viney-Jourdain (1998), nr 471; Noël Dejean de la Bathie, *Appréciation in abstracto et appréciation in concreto en droit civil français* (Paris: Pichon & Durand-Auzias, 1965), nr 44–53; Dobbs I (2001), § 122, 290.

[129] BGH 10 February 1987, NJW 1987, 1479 (specialized lawyer).

[130] McNair J in *Bolam v Friern Hospital Management Committee* [1957] 2 All ER 118, 121.

professional has to be good: 'Sometimes this is called the skill of the "average member" of the profession; but this is clearly misleading, since only those in good professional standing are to be considered.'[131] The difference between ordinary or average and good is for instance that the ordinary or average professional will not always read the professional literature, whereas the good professional will do that in time.[132]

Professionals in apprenticeship or during pupillage have to consult a more experienced colleague if there is a reason to do so; they are being judged according to the knowledge and ability of the experienced colleague.[133] A German case was about an inexperienced doctor who made a mistake during surgery. The doctor was deemed to have acted negligently, not for making the mistake, but for not realizing that he was not skilled enough to do the surgery and not consulting a colleague.[134] This is an instance of *Übernahmeverschulden* (fault to undertake an activity), a concept allowing someone to be found negligent, not because he was negligent in the specific situation which he could not handle because of his lack of abilities, but because he undertook to enter that situation in the first place.[135]

Assessing the professional standard may cause problems if, within a certain discipline, differences of opinion exist about the correctness of an analysis, a diagnosis, a treatment, or a therapy. In many disciplines 'schools' dispute each others' positions. This issue played a role in *Maynard v West Midlands Regional Health Authority*. Doctors in a hospital were in doubt whether Blondell Maynard's illness was tuberculosis or Hodgkin's disease. Without waiting for the tuberculosis test the doctors decided to perform surgery in order to make the Hodgkin's diagnosis. This surgery damaged the patient's vocal cords; a risk inherent in this kind of surgery. In the end it appeared that Ms Maynard suffered from tuberculosis and she stated that the surgery had been unnecessary. The professional opinions with regard to the doctors' conduct were divided. Lord Scarman said, and all their Lordships agreed with him:

It is not enough to show that there is a body of competent professional opinion which considers that theirs was a wrong decision, if there also exists a body of professional opinion, equally competent, which supports the decision as reasonable in the circumstances. It is not enough to show that subsequent events show that the operation need never have been performed, if at the time the decision to operate was taken it was reasonable in the sense that a responsible body of medical opinion would have accepted it as proper.[136]

---

[131] Prosser and Keeton (1984), 187.   [132] *Hunter v Hanley* [1955] SLT 213.
[133] *Wilsher v Essex Area Health Authority* [1986] 3 All ER 801; compare *Nettleship v Weston* [1971] 3 All ER 581 in which the standard of reference for a learner driver was someone with a driver's licence (nr 804-1).
[134] BGH 27 September 1983, NJW 1984, 655; BGH 26 April 1988, NJW 1988, 2298.
[135] Kötz-Wagner (2001), N 115.
[136] Lord Scarman in *Maynard v West Midlands Regional Health Authority* [1985] 1 All ER 635, 638. See also *Bolam v Friern Barnet Management Committee* [1957] 2 All ER 118; *Whitehouse v Jordan* [1981] 1 All ER 246; *Sidaway v Bethlem Royal Hospital Governors* [1985] 1 All ER 643.

The next question is what a *responsible body of medical opinion* implies:

Where there are different schools of medical thought (...), the doctor is entitled to be judged according to the tenets of the school the doctor professes to follow. This does not mean, however, that any quack, charlatan or crackpot can set himself up as a 'school', and so apply his individual ideas without liability. A 'school' must be a recognized one within definite principles, and it must be the line of thought of a respectable minority of the profession.[137]

813 Children and mentally disabled persons

813-1 *Introduction*

Though the objective test is the rule in tort law (nr 811-2), a special position is taken by children and mentally disabled persons. Children under the age of 6 are generally not capable of answering for their behaviour. When they have learned how to behave they are not always able to apply that knowledge because of their impulsiveness. Neither can people who are seriously mentally disabled in the sense that they cannot control their behaviour answer for their acts. The disability can be permanent or temporary, the latter for instance as the consequence of a stroke.

Applying an objective test is not in the interest of these persons because they are not able to meet the standard of 'the reasonable person'. It would seem more appropriate to apply a subjective test and to take their shortcomings into account but such a test would give priority to the interests of the child and the mentally disabled person to the detriment of the claimant, for whom it will make no difference by whose conduct he suffered damage. The dilemma is between emotional objections against liability of children and mentally disabled persons on the one hand, and the social desirability of liability to protect victims on the other. The question is how to merge common sense and justice into a legal rule.[138]

A possible solution of this dilemma can be found in the Dutch Civil Code. It provides that a child under the age of 14 cannot be liable for its own personal conduct (article 6:164). In its place the parent is strictly liable, provided the child's act would have been negligent if it would have been carried out by an adult person, in other words if it was objectively negligent (article 6:169 s. 1). A mentally disabled person cannot invoke a mental shortcoming as a defence against liability (article 6:165 s. 1) but he has a right of recourse against his supervisor if the latter also acted negligently towards the victim (article 6:165 s. 2).[139]

In French, German, and English law the solutions to the dilemma differ. As regards *children*, French law compares the child's conduct and knowledge with

[137] Prosser and Keeton (1984), 187.
[138] Xavier Blanc-Jouvan, 'La responsabilité de l'infans', *RTD civ.* 1957, 28–60, nr 1: '...à déterminer dans quelle mesure les exigences élémentaires du bon sens et de la justice peuvent ici se traduire en règle de droit.' [139] See also von Bar (1998), N 91–92 and 132–133.

that of an adult person. German and English law opt for a comparison with 'a child of the same age', provided the child has reached the age of discretion (England) or 7 years of age (Germany, in traffic accidents, 10 years of age). German law additionally provides the possibility of an equity liability if the child did not meet the standard of its age group; this liability depends on the financial means of the child and the needs of the victim (§ 829 BGB).

From the claimant's perspective the parents' liability is of the utmost importance, particularly in German and English law. However, only French law holds a strict liability for parents and other supervisors, whereas German law contains a liability for rebuttable negligence. England, as usual, relies on negligence liability (nr 1602). The two rules are therefore not communicating: in England the small chance of liability of the child is not compensated by a bigger chance of liability of its parent. In France the big chance of liability of the child is combined with a likewise big chance of its parents' liability.

As regards the child's personal liability, the draft for a European Civil Code adopts the German and English solution by comparing the child's conduct with that of a child of the same age (Article 3:103). Unlike these countries, however, this is combined with a rule of strict liability for parents of minors under the age of 14 (Article 3:201).[140]

The drafters of the Principles of European Tort Law show more reluctance. Article 4:102(2) provides that the general negligence standard '... may be adjusted when due to age, mental or physical disability [...] the person cannot be expected to conform to it.' At the same time the PETL only provides a liability for rebuttable negligence for parents (Article 6:101). This combination of provisions does not produce an attractive result for victims. See about liability of parents, nr 1602–1604.

As regards *mentally disabled persons* French law applies an objective test. English law applies a subjective test but restricts it to cases in which the person has lost all control over his conduct. German law generally also applies a subjective test but this is combined with an equity liability depending on the financial means of the disabled person and the needs of the victim.

The Draft ECC opts for an equity liability in case of mental incompetence, very much similar to the German situation (Article 5:301).[141] The PETL states

---

[140] Art. 3:103 ECC provides:

(1) A person under 18 years of age is only accountable for legally relevant damage (...) in so far as that person does not exercise such care as could be expected from a reasonably careful person of the same age in the circumstances of the case. (2) A person under seven years of age is not accountable for causing damage intentionally or negligently.

[141] Art. 5:301 ECC:

(1) A person who is mentally incompetent at the time of causing legally relevant damage is liable only if this is equitable, having regard to the mentally incompetent person's financial means and all the circumstances of the case. Liability is limited to reasonable compensation. (2) A person is

that the general negligence standard may be adjusted when someone cannot conform to it due to mental or physical disability. This would set a lower level of care than in current legal practice in the legal systems, as will be shown below.

The objective or more objective approach seems to be highly influenced by the availability of liability insurance, particularly in cases of a heart attack or a stroke of the driver of a motor vehicle for which compulsory liability insurance exists. According to Fleming this is ' ... a welcome recognition of the fact that considerations of moral fault are out of place, especially in relation to traffic accidents where personal liability has been displaced by insurance.'[142]

813-2 *France*

The requirement of *faute* in article 1382 CC contains an objective and a subjective element (nr 302-1). In practice, the subjective element scarcely plays a role any more.

As regards *mentally disabled persons* article 489-2 CC holds that a mental disorder is no defence against liability. This provision came into force in 1968 and the Minister of Justice (*Le Garde des Sceaux*) introduced it with *aplomb*: 'What we are witnessing here is a small legal revolution.'[143]

Article 489-2 is neither a special rule nor a rule based on equity. A pedestrian, obviously tired of life, had thrown himself in front of a bus. The driver tried to avoid him but the manoeuvre caused injury to one of the passengers, who claimed damages from the pedestrian. His liability insurer argued that it only covered liability on the basis of articles 1382 and 1383 and that article 489-2 applied to a special kind of liability. The *Cour de cassation* did not accept this argument and decided that article 489-2 is a part of the framework of article 1382 ff CC.[144]

Article 489-2 also applies to minor persons. In a criminal case a 17-year-old murderer was discharged because it was held he was mentally ill at the time of the crime. The victim's mother claimed damages from the murderer. The *Cour de cassation* awarded the claim, deciding that article 489-2 applies to adults and minors who have injured another person under the influence of a mental disorder.[145]

---

mentally incompetent if that person lacks sufficient insight into the nature of his or her conduct, unless the lack of sufficient insight is the temporary result of his or her own misconduct.

[142] Fleming (1998), 126–127.

[143] 'Nous sommes ici en présence d'une petite révolution juridique.' Cited by Geneviève Viney, 'Réflexions sur l'article 489-2 du Code civil', *RTD civ*, 1970, 263.

[144] Civ. 2e 4 May 1977, D. 1978. 393, comm. Legeais, RTD civ. 1977, 772, obs. Durry: ' ... que l'art. 489-2 c. civ. ne prévoit aucune responsabilité particulière et s'applique à toutes les responsabilité prévues aux art. 1382 et s. dudit code.' See also Civ. 2e 24 June 1987, Bull. civ. II, no 137.

[145] Civ. 1re 20 July 1976, D. 1977. IR. 114, RTD civ. 1976, 783, obs. Durry: ' ... que l'obligation à réparation prévue à l'art. 489-2 c. civ. concerne tous ceux–majeurs ou mineurs–qui, sous l'empire

Article 489-2 applies irrespective of the cause or duration of the disorder and irrespective of any regime of legal protection.[146] However, a short period of unconsciousness because of a heart attack is considered not to be a mental disorder in the sense of this provision.[147]

Before 1968 *children* could only be liable if they had reached the age of discretion (*l'âge de raison*). This caused uncertainties since this age had to be established in each individual case.[148] The entering into force of article 489-2 CC did not affect the liability of children, but the new provision seemed to be the expression of a more general idea that subjective shortcomings should not be an obstacle for liability.[149] In this spirit the courts started to knock down the barricades for liability of children.

In 1984 this development resulted in five judgments of the *Cour de cassation's Assemblée plénière*. One of the decisions implied that objective wrongful conduct (*comportement fautive*) of a 5-year-old child justified its contributory negligence and therefore a reduction of the amount of compensation. The case was about a 5-year-old girl who, without looking, ran onto the road where she was fatally hit by a vehicle. The *Cour de cassation* agreed that the parents' claim for damages needed to be reduced by 50 per cent because of the child's objective contributory negligence. The court did not consider it relevant whether the child was able to understand the consequences of her conduct.[150] A number of authors consider this as undesirable and argue that the objective rule should not apply to the child's contributory negligence.[151]

Soon after these decisions the *Cour de cassation* took the same view as regards liability of the child for damage caused. In a school playground a 7-year-old boy deliberately bumped into another boy, as a consequence of which the latter hit a bench and was seriously injured. The 7-year-old was held liable: his conduct could be qualified as a *faute* regardless of whether he had reached the age of

d'un trouble mental, ont causé du dommage à autrui.' Cf Viney-Jourdain (1998), nr 591; Aubry and Rau-Dejean de la Bathie (1989), nr 346.

[146] Terré-Simler-Lequette (2002), nr 733.

[147] Civ. 2e 4 February 1981, JCP 1981 IV. 136.

[148] Xavier Blanc-Jouvan, 'La responsabilité de l'infans', *RTD civ.* 1957, nr 13: 'Cela montre que l'on se trouve, en fait, en plein arbitraire.'   [149] Viney-Jourdain (1998), nr 578.

[150] Ass. plén. 9 May 1984, JCP 1984. II. 20255, comm. Dejean de la Bathie, D. 1984. 525, comm. Chabas, RTD civ. 1984, 509, obs. Huet:

... la cour d'appel, qui n'était pas tenue de verifier si la mineure était capable de discerner les consequences de tells actes, a pu, sans se contredire, retenir, sur le fondement de l'article 1382 c.civ., que la victime avait commis une faute qui avait concouru avec celle de M. Tidu, à la realisation du dommage dans une proportion souverainement appréciée.

This case would now be decided differently under the regime of the *loi Badinter* (see nr 1404-1). See also Civ. 2e 28 February 1996, D. 1996. 602, JCP 1996. IV. 942.

[151] Geneviève Viney, 'La réparation des dommages causés sous l'empire d'un état d'inconscience: un transfert nécessaire de la responsabilité vers l'assurance', *JCP* 1985. I. 3189; Terré-Simler-Lequette (2002), nr 732; Carbonnier (2000), § 229, 414–416.

discretion.[152] The standard of reference is not the child of the same age but an adult, more specifically *le bon père de famille.*[153]

The consequences of this case law seem to be harsh for the child since it has to meet an adult standard of care. In practice, the consequences are limited, since in addition to the child the parents are strictly liable and they are statutorily obliged to insure their liability (nr 1602-1). In practice the insurance policy will also cover the child's liability.

813-3 *Germany*

Whereas unlawfulness (*Rechtswidrigkeit*) represents the test of the outer conduct, *Verschulden* (intention or negligence) is the heading under which the test of the defendant's inner capacities takes place (nr 804-2). Generally, negligence implies an objective test, but special statutory rules apply to children and mentally disabled persons.[154] These persons are deemed to be not capable of acting with *Verschulden* (intention or negligence), ie they are not *verschuldensfähig.*

Only if someone is *verschuldensfähig* can it be established whether the child or the disabled person acted with *Verschulden* (intentionally or negligently).

According to § 827 BGB a *mentally disabled or unconscious person* is not *verschuldensfähig* if he does not have the discretion to understand the unlawfulness of his conduct or if he is not able to act according to that knowledge. The burden of proof for absence of *Verschuldensfähigkeit* is on the defendant.[155] Mentally disabled persons are persons with a mental or psychological disorder which affects the mental capacity to an important extent; this includes cases of poisoning and high fever.[156] Examples of unconsciousness are hypnosis, sleep, and a cerebral haemorrhage.[157]

§ 827 also holds that, if someone acts unlawfully and causes damage to another person in a temporary state of mental disorder which he has caused by using alcohol or drugs, the unlawful act is deemed to imply negligence. However, if the person did not know or ought to have known that the substances consumed could seriously decrease the level of consciousness, there is no negligence. One may think of someone who took a medicine with an unknown side-effect.[158]

§ 828 I BGB holds that *children* under the age of 7 are never liable for damage caused by their own conduct, neither can they be contributorily negligent

---

[152] Civ. 2e 12 December 1984, Gaz. Pal. 1985, 235 (Sabatier).
[153] Terré-Simler-Lequette (2002), nr 631; Le Tourneau (2004), nr 1331.
[154] The privileged position of deaf mute persons was repealed in the legislative reform of the law of damages in 2002 (nr 1202-2).
[155] BGH 25 April 1966, VersR 1966, 579. Deutsch-Ahrens (2002), N 136–137.
[156] BGH 25 January 1977, VersR 1977, 430. Deutsch-Ahrens (2002), N 136.
[157] BGH 15 January 1957, BGHZ 23, 90. Deutsch-Ahrens (2002), N 137; Münchener Kommentar-Wagner (2004), § 827 N 5–7.
[158] Deutsch-Ahrens (2002), N 138; Münchener Kommentar-Wagner (2004), § 827 N 9.

(§ 254 BGB).[159] The reason is that they are deemed to be not *verschuldensfähig*, ie not capable of acting negligently. For children under the age of 10, the same reasoning applies in cases of accidents involving motor vehicles, railroads, or funiculars (§ 828 II). This rule aims to prevent an *existenzvernichtende Haftung* (a life ruining liability), especially in cases in which the child's liability is not covered by liability insurance.[160] § 828 II was inserted after the *Bundesverfassungsgericht* (Constitutional Court) had concluded that an unlimited liability of a minor is contrary to human dignity and therefore unconstitutional.[161] § 828 II intends to provide a privilege for children only when they are confronted with traffic situations they are not able to handle in light of their age. Hence, the BGH has decided that this provision does not apply if a child negligently damages a parked vehicle.[162]

Apart from what is provided in § 828 I and II, someone under the age of 18 is not liable if he is *verschuldensunfähig* (not able to act intentionally or negligently: § 828 III). This is the case if the child, taking into account its mental development, is not able to understand the unlawfulness of its conduct and to answer for the consequences of its acts.[163] This is a subjective test: the development of this child is decisive. It is advocated that courts need to be reluctant in establishing a child's *Verschuldensfähigkeit*, particularly as regards children under the age of 10 with regard to accidents other than traffic accidents.[164] If the child is not *verschuldensfähig*, it is not liable for the damage caused. If the child is *verschuldensfähig* (capable of acting negligently), *Verschulden*, (intention or negligence) needs to be established.

Establishing negligence (*Fahrlässigkeit*) depends on a comparison of the child's conduct with that of a normally developed child of the same age group. This test is particularly about the child's ability to refrain from its conduct (*Steuerungsfähigkeit*), which relates to the child's impulsiveness and childish unconcern.[165] A bus passenger was injured when the driver suddenly had to brake for a 7-year-old boy who crossed the street to catch a ball. The BGH decided that the boy knew the risk but that it could not be required of a boy of his age and development to act according to his knowledge because of the attraction of the ball.[166] Another case was about a 12-year-old boy who hit another boy with a

---

[159] § 254 does not mention children but in the context of this provision § 827 is applied analogically. Deutsch-Ahrens (2002), N 134; Münchener Kommentar-Wagner (2004), § 828 N 3–5. See about contributory negligence nr 1212–1216.

[160] LG Dessau 25 September 1996, VersR 1997, 242; Hans-Jürgen Ahrens, 'Existenzvernichtung Jugendlicher durch Deliktshaftung?', VersR 1997, 1064–1065 and Klaus Goecke, *Die unbegrenzte Haftung Minderjähriger im Deliktsrecht*, (Berlin: Duncker & Humblot, 1997).

[161] BVerfG 13 August 1998, NJW 1998, 3557.

[162] BGH 30 November 2004, NJW 2005, 354, ETL 2004, 311 (Fedtke).

[163] BGH 22 November 1966, VersR 1967, 158; see also BGH 21 May 1963, BGHZ 39, 281 en BGH 14 November 1978, NJW 1979, 864; Deutsch-Ahrens (2002), N 135. Kötz-Wagner (2001), N 317; Larenz (1987), § 20 VI, 294.

[164] Münchener Kommentar-Wagner (2004), § 828 N 8–10; Deutsch-Ahrens (2002), N 135.

[165] Münchener Kommentar-Wagner (2004), § 828 N 7; Larenz (1987), § 20 VI, 295.

[166] BGH 27 January 1970, VersR 1970, 374: '... trotz dem starken Aufforderungscharakter des wegfliegenden Balles möglich und zumutbar wäre, sich der Einsicht gemäß zu verhalten (...). Nach der Lebenserfahrung muß das bezweifelt werden.'

piece of wood during a game. It was established that the boy was old enough to answer for his conduct (he was *verschuldensfähig*), but that he did not act negligently, taking the character and attractiveness of the game for a boy his age.[167]

If liability cannot be established because of the provisions of § 827 or § 828, the defendant can be obliged to pay damages on the basis of equity according to § 829. This is only possible if no damages can be obtained from a supervisor, either on factual (insolvency) or on legal grounds.[168]

Whether someone is obliged to pay damages on the basis of § 829 depends on the circumstances of the case, such as the nature and extent of the damage, the contributory negligence of the victim, the mental development of the tortfeasor, and particularly the parties' financial positions.[169] This latter aspect explains why this provision is also known as the *Millionärsparagraph*.

According to the BGH, compulsory liability insurance (such as for motor vehicles) can be a basis for equity liability, whereas voluntary liability insurance cannot trigger liability but only influence the amount of damages.[170] Most authors disagree with this distinction, arguing that voluntary insurance is also aimed to protect the interests of the victim.[171]

§ 829 requires *Verschulden* unless this cannot be established because of the defendant's age or mental condition.[172] In fact, the provision applies if the defendant's conduct did not meet the objective standard of a non-disabled adult person. For example, during a game a boy hit another boy in the eye with a wooden knife. He was supposed to know the risk (*verschuldensfähig*), but negligence (*Fahrlässigkeit*) was denied only because of his age. § 829 could thus be applied.[173] Another example concerned a driver who lost control over the wheel because of a cerebral haemorrhage and hit two pedestrians on the pavement. *Fahrlässigkeit* was only denied because of the driver's unconsciousness, therefore § 829 applied.[174]

813-4 *England*

There is not much authority in English law on the liability of *mentally disabled persons* and the few indications in the case law are not

[167] BGH 21 May 1963, BGHZ 39, 281; See also BGH 14 November 1978, NJW 1979, 864 and BGH 28 February 1984, NJW 1984, 1958.
[168] BGH 11 October 1994, BGHZ 127, 186 = NJW 1995, 452, about which Markesinis and Unberath (2002), 1000–1004; BGH 26 June 1973, NJW 1973, 1795; BGH 24 January 1969, NJW 1969, 1762.
[169] BGH 24 April 1979, NJW 1979, 2096; BGH 26 June 1973, NJW 1973, 1795; Münchener Kommentar-Wagner (2004), § 829 N 14–17.
[170] BGH 18 December 1979, BGHZ 76, 279, 285, 286; BGH 11 October 1994, BGHZ 127, 186 = NJW 1995, 452; see about the latter case Markesinis and Unberath (2002), 1000–1004.
[171] Kötz-Wagner (2001), N 328; Münchener Kommentar-Wagner (2004), § 829 N 19–20; Christian von Bar, 'Das "Trennungsprinzip" und die Geschichte des Wandels der Haftpflichtversicherung', *AcP*, 181 (1981), 326.
[172] Münchener Kommentar-Wagner (2004), § 829 N 7–8.
[173] BGH 21 May 1963, BGHZ 39, 281. Münchener Kommentar-Wagner (2004), § 829 N 7–8.
[174] BGH 15 January 1957, BGHZ 23, 90, 98; see also BGH 21 May 1963, BGHZ 39, 281.

unequivocal.[175] The principle seems to be that a mental disorder as such is no obstacle for liability, but this does not apply for each tort in the same way.[176] In the framework of the tort of negligence, liability can be excluded in the case of a mental disorder because '... even the reasonable man can have a heart attack'.[177] 'If a sleepwalker, without intention or without carelessness, broke a valuable vase, that would not be actionable.'[178]

In *Waugh v James K Allan* the House of Lords dismissed the claim against a lorry driver who collided with a pedestrian on the pavement after he had lost control of his vehicle as the consequence of a heart attack.[179] In this case it was established that he did not have any control of himself any more. This is an exception rather than the rule since the courts are generally reluctant to dismiss claims in case of an attack or a stroke. In another case a driver had a stroke, was able to drive a short distance, but then collided with two cars. Neill J concluded that the driver was liable because he had some control of the car and had not been fully unconscious.[180] In another case, a driver caused an accident because of his diabetes and did not succeed in proving that his driving was not a conscious act; therefore, the court dismissed the defence of an inevitable accident.[181] Along these lines, a driver's conviction that his vehicle is driven by an extra-terrestrial power is no real defence.[182]

There are only few clear decisions about the liability of *children*.[183] It is assumed that an early age as such is no obstacle for liability. 'In the law of tort there is no defence of infancy as such and a minor is as much liable to be sued for his torts as is an adult.'[184] This is uncontested for children around the age of 12. When they perform adult activities, such as driving or operating particular machines, the courts judge their conduct by using an adult standard and treat the minor in the same way as an inexperienced adult.[185] For example, when a 12-year-old boy tried to throw a dart at a post he missed the post but hit a bystander.

---

[175] Winfield and Jolowicz (2002), para. 24.26; Fleming (1998), 126–127; Salmond and Heuston (1996), 415.
[176] For instance battery and assault only require a voluntary act: see *Morriss v Marsden* [1952] 1 All ER 925.   [177] Winfield and Jolowicz (2002), para. 24.26.
[178] Stable J. in *Morriss v Marsden* [1952] 1 All ER 925. Winfield and Jolowicz (2002), para. 24.26, concluded that his Lordship '... thus evidently contemplated negligent and non-negligent sleepwalkers as legal possibilities.'
[179] *Waugh v James K Allan Ltd* [1964] 2 Lloyd's Rep. 1; see also *Kay v Mills* (1961) 28 DLR (2d) 554 (driver fell asleep) and *Hill v Baxter* [1958] 1 QB 277 (epilepsy-stroke).
[180] *Roberts v Ramsbottom* [1980] 1 WLR 823.
[181] *Boomer v Penn* (1965) 52 DLR (2d) 673. See also *Gordon v Wallace* (1973) 2 DLR (3d) 342.
[182] *Buckley v Smith Transport Ltd* (1946) 4 DLR 721; Winfield and Jolowicz (2002), para. 24.26.
[183] Fleming (1998), 321–322 and Winfield and Jolowicz (2002), para. 24.16.
[184] Winfield and Jolowicz (2002), para. 24.16; Salmond and Heuston (1996), 411.
[185] *Buckpitt v Oates* [1968] 1 All ER 1145 (17-year-old driver); *Gorely v Codd* [1967] 1 WLR 19 (liability of a 16-year-old boy, shooting with a gun without reason). Dobbs I (2001), § 124, 293. Compare *Nettleship v Weston* [1971] 2 QB 691 (nr 804-1).

Kitto J. said:

... it does not follow that he cannot rely in his defence upon a limitation upon the capacity for foresight or prudence, not as being personal to himself but as being characteristic of humanity at his stage of development and in that sense normal. By doing so he appeals to a standard of ordinariness to an objective and not a subjective standard.[186]

If the child is younger, the standard is an objective one: a child of the same age. The comparison is related to '... the child's capacity to perceive the risk as well as his sense of judgment and behaviour.'[187] It has for instance been decided that a 5-year-old boy did not act negligently by shooting arrows and that an 8-year-old boy did not act negligently by lighting matches in a barn.[188] Edmund Davies LJ said: 'At some stages of life, one year's difference in age matters nothing; but in youth and early manhood when knowledge is rapidly blossoming, a 12-month is a very long time.'[189]

E DEFENCES AND GROUNDS OF JUSTIFICATION

814 Overview

If someone intentionally (see section A above) or negligently (see sections B and C above) has caused legally relevant damage (see Chapter 7) this will not always imply that he is liable for the damage caused. Apart from the fact that causation cannot be established, the defendant has a number of arguments at his disposal to contest his liability. In common law these are usually known as *defences*, whereas in civil law *grounds of justification (fait justificatif, Rechtfertigungsgründe)* is the common language. The former concept is broader than the latter since it includes not only grounds of justification like an Act of God, but also contributory negligence (nr 1212) and limitation of actions, which is generally dealt with separately on the continent.[190]

Within the area of justification the conceptual diversity between the legal systems is also considerable. For example, in Germany the *Rechtfertigungsgrund*

---

[186] Kitto J in *McHale v Watson* (1966) 115 CLR 199, 213.   [187] Fleming (1998), 126.
[188] *Walmsley v Humenick* (1954) 2 DLR 232 and *Yorkton Agriculture and Industrial Exhibition Society v Morley* (1967) 66 DLR (2d) 37. Fleming (1998), 126; Salmond and Heuston (1996), 411–412.   [189] Edmund Davies LJ in *Kerry v Carter* [1969] 1 WLR 1372, 1377.
[190] See for example Markesinis and Deakin (2003), 740 ff. Winfield and Jolowicz (2002), nr 25.1 ff. take a more continental view.

(ground of justification) neutralizes the *Rechtswidrigkeit* (unlawfulness), whereas in France the concept of *faute* itself implies the absence of a *fait justificatif* (ground of justification).[191] Furthermore, the grounds of justification are related to the defences which are available in strict liability. However, in common law an Act of God is only a defence under the *Rule in Rylands v Fletcher* (nr 1414-2) but on the continent it is a defence of a much more general character (*höhere Gewalt, cause étrangère* (nr 303-1 and 1404-2).

Hence, it is not surprising that von Bar, usually rather optimistic about the feasibility of common European concepts, sighed: 'Such diversity can pose a considerable obstacle for a common European law of delict.'[192]

An effort to provide an overview of the European common core as regards the grounds of justification can be found in article 7:101 PETL which runs as follows:

(1) Liability can be excluded if and to the extent that the actor acted legitimately
   a) in defence of his own protected interest against an unlawful attack (self-defence),
   b) under necessity,
   c) because the help of the authorities could not be obtained in time (self-help),
   d) with the consent of the victim, or where the latter has assumed the risk of being harmed, or
   e) by virtue of lawful authority, such as a licence.
(2) Whether liability is excluded depends upon the weight of these justifications on the one hand and the conditions of liability on the other.[193]

815 Consent

Somewhat related to the tenet of the *assumption of risk* (nr 809-2) is the defence of *informed consent*.[194] The latter plays a prominent role in the framework of medical treatment, such as a surgery. In principle, a physician does not act negligently if he treats a patient with the latter's informed consent (*volenti non fit iniuria*). It is assumed that this consent should be given freely and on the basis of correct and sufficient information.

[191] Carbonnier (2000), § 232, 420: 'L'absence de fait justificatif est rationnellement impliqué dans le concept légal de la faute.'
[192] Von Bar (2000), N 488 and more generally about defences in a comparative perspective N 485–490.
[193] See for more detailed provisions Art. 5:201–202 ECC. See about the defence of *ex turpi causa non oritur actio* Art. 5:103 ECC:

Legally relevant damage caused unintentionally in the course of committing a criminal offence to another person participating or otherwise collaborating in the offence does not give rise to a right to reparation if this would be contrary to public policy.

See about this action also von Bar (2000), N 514–516.
[194] Compare Art. 5:101(1) ECC: 'A person has a defence as against the injured person (. . .) if the injured person validly consents to the legally relevant damage and is aware or ought to be aware of the consequences of that consent.'

Generally, someone gives his consent to allow certain specific intentional (medical) treatment, whereas risk acceptance is a much vaguer concept related to more general consequences which will not necessarily take place.[195]

In practice, the key issue is whether the patient has been adequately informed by the physician. This is not always easy to assess. For example, it might be necessary that, during an operation, a surgeon takes measures which have not been discussed with the patient and he therefore could not have given his consent. The question then is, whether the patient's original consent covered these extra measures or whether the surgeon can prove that there was a necessity to take these extra measures.

Here also, the benefit and character of the physician's conduct influence the level of precautionary measures. The aim of medical treatment is to cure, not to cause harm. However, this worthy cause, which is related to the physician's Hippocratic Oath, is at odds with the patient's right to self-determination. It is broadly accepted nowadays that, in principle,[196] the latter prevails over the former. This implies that it is not the physician but the patient who decides about medical treatment. Therefore, he needs to be properly and adequately informed.

F CONCLUDING REMARKS

816 Comparative observations

In this chapter a kaleidoscopic picture of the elements of intention and negligence has been presented. The analysis provided is not aimed at developing a formula for intention or negligence. This would have been a mission impossible: '. . . to search for any single formula which will serve as a general test of liability is to pursue a will-o'-the wisp.'[197] Rather, the function of this chapter is to demonstrate how manifold are the elements that a court needs to take into consideration when establishing intention and negligence. It also shows that harmonizing European approaches in this respect will not be easy. Although it might be possible to find common ground as to the main factors to be taken into account, the balancing of these factors is ultimately a matter of policy and for this reason less tangible. Additionally, the variety of cases is so enormous that it can

---

[195] Von Bar (2000), N 505 and 512; Kötz-Wagner (2001), N 96; Münchener Kommentar-Wagner (2004), § 823 N 309–310; Viney-Jourdain (1998), nr 575-576; Terré-Simler-Lequette (2002), nr 738; Carbonnier (2000), § 232, 420–421; Winfield and Jolowicz (2002), paras 5.56 and 25.4.

[196] This can be different if the patient is not able to give his consent, for example if he is too young, mentally ill, unconscious, or in a bad way after an accident.

[197] *Caparo Industries plc v Dickman* [1990] 2 AC 605, 628 per Lord Oliver.

be said that the courts actually find intention and negligence in the facts of each case: *ius causa positum.*

As has been indicated in the concluding remarks of Chapter 7, tort law is very much influenced by, and cannot be understood without, the development of insurance possibilities, both on the part of the defendant and the claimant (nr 716). Liability insurance has enabled people to carry out more dangerous activities (manufacturing processes, driving) without the prospect of going bankrupt when substantial damage is caused, for which one is held liable. It has made activities available for everyone who can pay for the activity and for a liability insurance coverage.

Without the availability of liability insurance, a subjective fault principle would make sense as a basis for liability, by requiring a level of care which is feasible in daily life and feasible for the defendant as an individual. Liability insurance, however, has changed the qualities and properties of the reasonable man balancing risk and care (nr 805). Nowadays, he often has to observe a much higher level of care than is feasible in daily life or for the average tortfeasor personally. In fact, assessing the level of care is not so much a way to answer the question of whether the tortfeasor's conduct was negligent, but whether the loss needs to be at his expense or needs to remain a cost to the claimant.

This change caused by the availability of liability insurance has also enabled a change of perspective. Whereas fault traditionally focuses on the tortfeasor's duty, the focus is now more on the claimant's legitimate expectations. The question has become: what is the level of safety the claimant was entitled to expect from the tortfeasor? Most importantly, this change in perspective illustrates a shift in focus from the tortfeasor's duty to the claimant's right. This development is articulated more strongly in French and German law than in English tort law, where the focus is traditionally on the defendant's duty (of care) rather than on the claimant's right (to compensation) (nr 610).

Exceptions to the intertwinement of fault and liability insurance are cases in which intentional conduct is a prerequisite for liability, since liability insurance generally does not cover intentionally inflicted harm. This can be different if it is not the insured who is acting intentionally but the person for whom he is liable. For example, if a child causes damage intentionally and the parents are liable for this damage on the basis of fault or strict liability. In cases of intentionally inflicted harm, tort law plays a less important role as an instrument for compensation and distributive justice. Here, the emphasis will generally be on its function of corrective justice.

9

Violation of a Statutory Rule

901 Introduction

Legislators in all legal systems have produced and continue producing an abundant amount of statutory regulations, for example, in the area of health and safety such as road traffic safety, product safety, safety at work, and protection of the environment. For a couple of decades the national legislators have been joined by the European legislator, which is now responsible for a substantial part of the legislation in the Member States.

Violation of a statutory rule may first of all have an administrative law or a criminal law impact, by imposing a penalty such as a fine or imprisonment. However, such a violation also has consequences in tort law. If things go wrong because a statutory safety rule is not adhered to, a claim for damages can, in principal, be based on the violation of such a rule. Whereas statutory safety rules are the warning signs and barriers at the top of the cliff, tort law can be considered to be the ambulance waiting at the bottom of the cliff.

In all tort law systems, statutory rules play an important role in establishing liability in damages but, as will be pointed out, the conditions differ from system to system. With a statutory rule as a basis for a damages claim, we move away from the fault basis as discussed in the previous chapter, to the stricter forms of liability which will be discussed in the following chapter. This move towards strict liability is most apparent in French and English law because a claim based on the violation of a statutory rule does not necessarily require that the defendant has acted intentionally or negligently. In such a case, the statutory rule imposes an obligation to provide or guarantee a result (nr 906-2).[1]

A claimant can invoke the violation of a statutory rule to prove the French *faute*, the German *Rechtswidrigkeit*, or the English tort of breach of statutory duty. Statutory rules include every written rule, including administrative orders, enacted by a governmental body, be it the European Union, a Member State, or a local authority.[2] Generally, the violation of such a statutory rule can give rise to liability, but each legal system contains some restrictions to this rule and these differ from system to system.

---

[1] Von Bar (1998), N 27–35; 302–307.   [2] Von Bar (2000), N 223.

Between common law and civil law an important difference exists in legislative technique. In civil law countries such as France and Germany, the legislature usually confines itself to adopting the main outlines of a rule and leaves it to the executive to work out the details by means of secondary legislation. In the common law tradition, however, a certain rivalry exists between the legislature and the judiciary. The legislature drafts laws in a detailed manner, which leaves little to be regulated by the executive and as little scope as possible for interpretation by the courts. Though differences between common law and civil law have decreased, also because of the influence of EC law, they are still relevant to understand the different ways of interpreting statutory rules.[3]

In statutory provisions both the victim's protected interests (Chapter 7) and the defendant's conduct (Chapter 8) are at stake. Statutory provisions are the fruit of the balancing process by the legislature between the freedom to act and the protection of interests (nr 715). This process is comparable to that of the courts in the framework of unwritten law in order to establish the level of care, as has been pointed out in Chapter 8. The difference is that a court decision will carry out this process on an individual basis, whereas the legislature will rather focus on the rights and interests of one group and the restrictions to the freedom of the other.

This chapter will describe the rules in the legal systems as regards liability for damage caused by the violation of a statutory rule. The following sections will focus on the national rules in England (nr 902), Germany (nr 903), and France (nr 904). Subsequently, the first requirement of liability for breach of Community law—the conferment of rights on individuals—will be described and will be illustrated with the *Peter Paul* case (nr 905). Subsequently, an overview will be provided, comparing the Community requirement of conferment of rights and the English requirement of a private right of action. The relationship between the requirement of the scope of the statutory rule and the general requirement of causation will also be examined. Finally, the question will be answered as to whether breach of statutory duty is strict or negligence liability (nr 906).

902 England

902-1 *Private right of action: introduction*

Whereas in other legal systems the violation of a statutory rule and the general negligence claim are more or less intertwined, in English law breach of statutory duty and the tort of negligence are two separate and independent causes of action: 'A claim for damages for breach of a statutory duty intended to protect a person in the position of the particular plaintiff is a specific common law right

---

[3] Walter Cairns and Robert McKeon, *Introduction to French Law* (London: Cavendish, 1995), 5–6.

which is not to be confused in essence with a claim for negligence.'[4] Hence, as will be shown below, someone can be liable for breach of statutory duty and not under the tort of negligence and vice versa.

A claim for a breach of statutory duty requires that there is a statutory duty, that this duty has been breached, and that this breach has caused damage. The peculiarities of this tort are that it is required that the legislator intended to create a private right of action (can a damages claim be based on the statute at all?, nr 902-1/2) and that the provision aims to protect the victim against the damage he suffered (can this victim base his claim on the statute?, nr 902-3).

A private right of action can be explicitly awarded by the legislator. One may think of the Consumer Protection Act (nr 1406), the Highways Act and the Occupier's Liability Acts (nr 1507 and 1504-1, respectively). However, in many other cases the court has to find out whether the legislator intended to confer a private right of action for damages for breach of a statutory duty.

The question of conferral of private law rights is essentially an exercise in statutory construction by the courts, whose role it is to discern the intention of Parliament by adopting a purposive approach. The test is whether Parliament intended to provide a private right of action for breach of statutory duty and this depends '... on a consideration of the whole Act and the circumstances, including the pre-existing law, in which it was enacted.'[5] In a legal system where the judiciary is considered to be the inferior body in a hierarchical relationship with a sovereign Parliament (nr 501-4), it is not surprising that the courts have traditionally been reluctant to find implicit private law duties hidden in a statute. The basic proposition is that there is no tort of careless performance of a statutory duty *per se*.[6] However, it will be interesting to see whether this inertia can be overcome as English courts are increasingly put under pressure by the European Court of Human Rights to infer a private law action in certain areas. For example, in the area of child protection, the UK was found to be in violation of Article 13 ECHR (lack of an effective domestic remedy).[7]

The general reluctance of the courts to allow concurrent private law actions has resulted in them adopting various control mechanisms. Admittedly, the rules regards reading an implied private law action into a statute are few, arbitrary, and applied inconsistently by the courts. Indeed, in one of his well-known provocative one-liners Lord Denning said: 'The dividing line between the pro-cases and the contra-cases is so blurred and so ill-defined that you might as well toss a

---

[4] Lord Wright in *London Passenger Transport Board v Upson* [1949] AC 155 at 168–169. Markesinis and Deaking (2003), 358; Winfield and Jolowicz (2002), para. 7.1, point out that other common law countries and a majority of jurisdictions in the United States generally consider the statute to 'concretize' the common law duty under the tort of negligence. To a certain extent this resembles the German and French approach; see nr 903 and 904.
[5] Lord Simonds in *Cutler v Wandsworth Stadium Ltd* [1949] AC 398 at 407.
[6] *X (Minors) v Bedfordshire County Council* [1995] 2 AC 633, per Lord Browne-Wilkinson.
[7] ECtHR 10 May 2001, Case 29392/95 (*Z v United Kingdom*).

coin to decide it.'[8] However, it can be said with some certainty that courts tend to take account of a number of factors when deciding upon the actionability of a breach of statutory duty at common law.

902-2 *Private right of action: relevant factors*

Firstly, an important indication for a private or civil right of action is related to the remedy provided by the statute. If the statute only provides for criminal sanctions, there is no private action. It has occasionally been decided that, if the statute makes the defendant liable to pay a fine to a public body, then there will in general be no claim by the private law victim.[9] From the position of the defendant this rule could be seen as an application of the maxim *non bis in idem* and it contrasts with the position in, for example, French law (nr 904).

Secondly, if a statute does not provide for any remedy it is assumed that an action in tort is possible, particularly if the statute protects a limited class of people.[10] Hence, an important prerequisite for a private right of action seems to be that the statute imposes a duty for the benefit of a certain class of individuals.[11] An important example is the area of industrial activities, in which safety legislation generally protects the employees, providing them with a private right of action. The safety rules in this area require a high standard of care from the employer and are often strict. This contributes substantially to the strong legal protection of employees if they have suffered personal injury (or their relatives, in cases of fatal accidents).[12]

In the area of social welfare, such as education and housing, it is generally unlikely that statutory legislation creates private rights of action. In *X v Bedfordshire CC*, a case about the failure of local authorities to deal properly with a case of serious child abuse, the House of Lords dismissed the damages claim based on the violation of child protection legislation.[13] In *R v Deputy Governor of Parkhurst Prison* it was held: 'The fact that a particular provision was intended to

---

[8] Lord Denning in *Ex parte Island Records* [1978] 3 All ER 824 (CA), Ch. 122 at 135.

[9] *Keating v Elvan Reinforced Concrete Ltd* [1968] 1 WLR 722: no common law claim in tort under the Public Utilities Street Works Act 1950.

[10] *X (Minors) v Bedfordshire County Council* 1995] 2 AC 633. In *Lonhro Ltd v Shell Petroleum Co Ltd (No 2)* [1982] AC 173 per Lord Diplock, citing Brett J in *Benjamin v Storr* (1874) LR 9 CP 400 at 407, however, this 'identifiable class' requirement is waived. An individual claimant will have an action in tort if he is able to establish that he suffered 'particular, direct and substantial' damage 'other and different from that which was common to all the rest of the public'. This is notwithstanding the fact that the statute created a mere public right as opposed to an individual or 'class' right.

[11] *X (Minors) v Bedfordshire County Council* [1995] 2 AC 633 at 731; *O'Rourke v Camden LBC* [1998] AC 188 at 194; Lord Diplock in *Lonrho Ltd v Shell Petroleum Co Ltd (No 2)* [1982] AC 173 at 182. Markesinis and Deakin (2003), 364–365.

[12] Winfield and Jolowicz (2002), para. 7.3; *Lonrho Ltd v Shell Petroleum Co Ltd* [1981] 2 All ER 456; *Lonrho plc v Fayed and Others* [1989] 2 All ER 65.

[13] *X (Minors) v Bedfordshire County Council* [1995] 2 AC 633 at 731. The House of Lords also rejected the common law claim based on negligence because of the delicate nature of the local

protect certain individuals is not of itself sufficient to confer private law rights of action upon them, something more is required to show that the legislature intended such conferment.'[14] As regards this 'something more' one may think of a statement in Hansard or of a regulatory or historic context which makes it likely that the legislator intended to confer a private right of action.

Thirdly, the adequacy of pre-existing or parallel remedies provided for at common law gives another indication. For example, the victim of a road accident cannot dispense with having to make out a common law claim in negligence simply by invoking a violation of the Highway Code (statutory liability).[15] To allow otherwise would be ' . . . to introduce isolated pockets of strict liability into an area generally governed by negligence'.[16] This point is a corollary of factor a) above: they both demonstrate how the courts often ensure that the boundary demarcating the material domains of common law tortuous liability and statutory liability is respected.

Fourthly, the formulation of the statutory provision is also relevant. An amorphous, nebulous duty to act in the general interest is unlikely to crystallize into something concrete which would be enforceable by a private law claim. For example, neither the duty to house homeless persons under the Housing Act 1985, nor the duty to provide sufficient education under the Education Acts are actionable by a private litigant in tort.[17]

Finally, if the loss likely to be suffered as a result of the breach of a statutory duty is not recoverable under common law or only on a limited basis, this seems to be an indication that there is no private right of action.[18] One may particularly think of cases of pure economic loss, which is difficult to recover under common law (nr 714). Circumventing the tort of negligence via the tort of breach of statutory duty is considered to be undesirable.

902-3 *Scope of the statutory duty*

Breach of statutory duty not only requires that the legislator intended to create a private right of action (nr 902-2) but also that the rule aims to protect the victim against the kind of damage he suffered. This scope requirement comprises two elements.

---

authority's function in investigating allegations of child abuse. However, the European Court of Human Rights considered the failure to intervene to be a breach of Article 3 ECHR (inhuman or degrading treatment). See in more detail nr 1808-1.

[14] *R v Deputy Governor of Parkhurst Prison, ex parte Hague* [1992] AC 152 at 177. Winfield and Jolowicz (2002), paras 7.2 and 7.3; Markesinis and Deakin (2003), 363–368.

[15] For example, see *Phillips v Britannia Hygienic Laundry Co* [1923] 2 KB 832; *Coote v Stone* [1971] 1 WLR 279.   [16] See Winfield and Jolowicz (2002), para. 7.8.

[17] *O'Rourke v Camden LBC* [1998] AC 188 and *Phelps v Hillingdon LBC* [2001] 2 AC 619. See generally, Winfield and Jolowicz (2002), para. 7.4.

[18] Winfield and Jolowicz (2002), para. 7.8, with reference to *Pickering v Liverpool Daily Post and Echo Newspapers plc* [1991] 2 AC 370.

Firstly, the victim must belong to the *group of persons* which the legislator aimed to protect. In *Hartley v Mayoh & Co* a fire fighter was electrocuted when he was extinguishing a fire in a factory. His widow claimed damages from the owner of the factory, arguing he had violated certain statutory safety rules. The Court of Appeal held that these rules were intended only to protect the employees' safety and not the fire fighters' safety. For this reason the widow's claim based on breach of statutory was dismissed but, on different grounds, the claim based on the tort of negligence was allowed.[19]

Secondly, the statutory provision must aim to protect the victim against the *kind of damage* he suffered. *Gorris v Scott* was about a statutory duty owed by the owner of a ship, to tether cattle to rings during sea transport in order to restrict the risk of cattle plague. During a storm at sea, sheep were swept overboard because they were not tethered to rings. The ship owner was deemed not to be liable for the loss of the sheep on the basis of breach of statutory duty, because the statute was intended to protect against the spreading of diseases and not the animals' safety.[20] Such an interpretation seems to be too restricted nowadays. For example, in *Grant v National Coal Board* a mining company was liable when a miner was hurt because a stone fell from a tunnel roof onto the rail which caused a truck to derail. The company was liable to the miner because it had not met its statutory duty to maintain the roofs of mine tunnels.[21]

Generally, it is sufficient for an action for breach of statutory duty that the claimant suffered harm of the kind which the statute aimed to prevent, even if it did not occur exactly in way foreseen by the statute. This explains why the scope issue is generally considered to be related to the question of causation (nr 1104) rather than to the question of breach.[22] This is also the case in other jurisdictions (nr 903–904).

There is only a thin line between the requirement of a private right of action and that of the scope of the statutory duty. For example, in *Capital and Counties plc v Hampshire CC* the Court of Appeal held that a fire authority's statutory duty to take reasonable measures to ensure an adequate supply of water for fire-fighting did not give rise to a private right of action.[23] In such a case it can also be argued that the fire authority's statutory duty did not aim to protect householders against (extra) fire damage caused by the lack of water supply.

---

[19] *Hartley v Mayoh & Co* [1954] 1 QB 383; *Knapp v Railway Executive* [1949] 2 All ER 508, 515. Winfield and Jolowicz (2002), para. 7.11; Markesinis and Deakin (2003), 370–371.
[20] *Gorris v Scott* (1874) LR 9 Ex 125.   [21] *Grant v National Coal Board* [1956] AC 649.
[22] *Donaghey v Boulton & Paul Ltd* [1968] AC 1, about which Van Gerven (2000), 415–416; Markesinis and Deakin (2003), 370–371; Winfield and Jolowicz (2002), para. 7.12; Dobbs I (2001), § 138, 326–328. See about generalization techniques also nr 806-2 (probability) and nr 810-2 (knowledge).
[23] *Capital and Counties plc v Hampshire CC* [1997] QB 1004.

902-4 *Negligence and strict liability*

If a statutory rule contains a private right of action and the duty aims to protect the victim against the harm, liability depends on the wording of the statutory duty. This can imply that someone has to act carefully or that he has to take precautionary measures. If this is the case, breach of statutory duty and the tort of negligence, though different torts, are quite similar in outcome.

Statutory provisions can, however, also hold a duty to guarantee a certain result. This means that someone can be liable for breaching a statutory duty even if he had acted carefully.[24] This is why the English consider the tort of breach of statutory duty to be a type of strict liability, and it implies that, though English law only holds few general strict liability rules, statutory provisions provide specific strict liability rules. 'If strict liability is rare at common law, it is relatively common by statute.'[25] This is consonant with the English allergy to general rules (nr 604–605).

One of the many examples of the application of a strict statutory duty can be found in *John Summers & Sons Ltd v Frost*. A grinding wheel injured an employee's thumb. According to s. 14(1) of the Factories Act 1961 each dangerous part of a machine had to be covered. In this case, the employer could not comply with this provision because a small part of the wheel had to be kept uncovered to enable proper use of the machine. This was, however, no obstacle to awarding the employee's claim for damages.[26]

903 Germany

§ 823 II BGB is one of the three general rules in German tort law, in addition to § 823 I (infringement of a right, nr 402-3) and § 826 (intentional infliction of damage *contra bonos mores*, nr 402-4). § 823 II implies that someone acts unlawfully (*rechtswidrig*) and is liable for the ensuing damage if he violates a statutory rule that is aimed to protect the claimant against the damage he has suffered (*Schutzgesetzverstoß*).[27]

---

[24] Winfield and Jolowicz (2002), para. 7.1; Markesinis and Deakin (2003), 369. *Brown v National Coal Board* (1962) AC 574; *Scott v Green & Sons* [1969] 1 WLR 301; *Denyer v Charles Skipper and East Ltd* [1970] 1 WLR 1087; *Bux v Slough Metals Ltd* [1973] 1 WLR 1358; *Quintas v National Smelting Co* [1961] 1 WLR 401.

[25] Tony Weir, *Tort law*, (Oxford: Oxford University Press, 2002), 86.

[26] *John Summers & Sons Ltd v Frost* [1955] AC 740. See also Dobbs I (2001), § 141, 331–333. Another example is *London Passenger Transport Board v Upson* [1949] AC 155, about which nr 1404-3.

[27] § 823 II: 'Die gleiche Verpflichtung trifft denjenigen, welcher gegen ein den Schutz eines anderen bezweckendes Gesetz verstößt. Ist nach dem Inhalte des Gesetzes ein Verstoß gegen dieses auch ohne Verschulden möglich, so tritt die Ersatzpflicht nur im Falle des Verschuldens ein.' Münchener Kommentar-Wagner (2004), § 823 N 317 ff. See BGH 27 November 1963, BGHZ 40, 306; BGH 8 June 1976, BGHZ 66, 388 = NJ 1976, 1740 = VersR 1976, 1043, about which Markesinis and Unberath (2002), 209–211;

The significance of § 823 II lies particularly in the area of liability for pure economic loss, since § 823 I does not protect against pure economic loss and § 826 requires intentional behaviour of the tortfeasor. An example is the manager of a GmbH (a limited liability company) who fails to file a bankruptcy petition where the GmbH is unable to pay its debts. In such a case the manager cannot be liable on the basis of § 823 I because he did not encroach on one of the rights mentioned in this provision. Also, a claim based on § 826 can fail if intention cannot be proved. However, a claim can be based on the breach of the manager's statutory duty following from § 64 I GmbHG (Limited Liability Company Act).[28]

The main requirement is that the statutory rule (also) protects individual interests. If only general or public interests are protected, the rule is considered not to be a protective one (*Schutzgesetz*) in the sense of § 823 II.[29] For example, the statutory rule in the Criminal Code regarding the duty to help someone who is in peril does not intend to protect the victim in the sense of § 823 II BGB (nr 1702-2). Another example is the statutory duty of the financial supervisor to supervise banks in a proper way. This statutory duty only protects the general interest and not individuals who suffer damage from inadequate supervision. See nr 905-2.

If the statutory rule (also) protects individual interests, § 823 II contains two more requirements.[30] Firstly, the victim must belong to the group of people who are intended to be protected by this rule. One may think of § 248b StGB (Criminal Code), which prohibits the unauthorized use of a motor vehicle but if someone uses a motor vehicle without being authorized the statutory provision only protects the owner, not the other road users.[31] Secondly, the infringed interest must be within the scope of protection of the rule, and finally, certain rights are only protected against infringements by certain conduct.[32] In this respect one may think of the Act for the protection of plants (*Pflanzenschutzgesetz*). This Act protects against the dangerous effects of pesticides but not against the harm caused by a product for the protection of plants which appears to be defective.[33]

Violation of a statutory rule establishes *Rechtswidrigkeit*. In addition to this requirement, *Verschulden* has to be established as is the case in other German tort law provisions (nr 402-2). The second sentence of § 823 II provides that, if the statutory duty itself does not require *Verschulden* (intention or negligence), this

---

[28] BGH 6 June 1994, BGHZ 126, 181, about which Van Gerven (2000), 228–229. See for more examples Markesinis and Unberath (2002), 943–953.

[29] See for instance BGH 27 January, BGHZ 12, 146 = NJW 1954, 675; BGH 13 December, BGHZ 106, 204 = NJW 1989, 974. Münchener Kommentar-Wagner (2004), § 823 N 340 ff.

[30] See Kötz-Wagner (2001), N 176–185.   [31] BGH 4 December 1956, BGHZ 22, 293.

[32] BGH 25 September 1990, NJW 1991, 292; Deutsch-Ahrens (2002), N 213–215; Münchener Kommentar-Wagner (2004), § 823 N 344.   [33] BGH 17 March 1981, VersR 1981, 636.

has still to be established. However, the BGH has improved the claimant's position by ruling that, if the defendant violated a statutory rule and this rule prescribes a specific standard of conduct, it is presumed that the defendant acted negligently (*fahrlässig*). The defendant can rebut this presumption by proving that he did not act negligently.[34] This means that in these cases § 823 II implies liability for rebuttable negligence. If, however, the statute only prohibits a result, for example putting unhealthy food onto the market, negligence is not presumed and needs to be proved by the claimant.[35]

904 France

In French tort law, violation of a written legal rule (*un devoir légal*) constitutes a *faute* in the sense of article 1382 CC, unless the defendant can prove a ground of justification. The principle applies to all rules with an imperative character.[36] Courts take an expansive approach when it comes to deciding if there has been a *violation de la loi*. *Loi* (law) is interpreted *lato sensu* and includes, for example: statutes, secondary legislation, administrative sanctions, the Highway Code (*Code de la Route*)[37], deontological rules,[38] rules of urbanism,[39] and even spouses' marital and statutory duty to live together.[40]

Two aspects will be mentioned: (i) the statutory rule does not have to intend to protect the victim or the harm he suffered, and (ii) the violation of the written rule is decisive: an additional negligence test is not required.

(i) Scope of the statutory duty. Liability for violation of a statutory rule does not require that the rule aims to protect the victim against the harm he suffered. This means that French law generally rejects the relevance of the scope of the rule (*théorie de la relativité aquilienne*). The idea is that statutory provisions are issued in the general interest, that they apply to everyone and protect everyone. Statutory duties thus have an absolute and not a relative character.[41]

---

[34] BGH 12 March 1968, NJW 1968, 1279; BGH 13 December 1984, NJW 1985, 1774; BGH 19 November 1991, BGHZ 116, 104 = NJW 1992, 1039 = JZ 1993, 671; see about the latter case Markesinis and Unberath (2002), 579–584; see furthermore Kötz-Wagner (2001), N 174–174a; Münchener Kommentar-Wagner (2004), § 823 N 354–355. The same rule of evidence applies to the violation of a *Verkehrspflicht* (nr 804-2).

[35] BGH 19 November 1991, BGHZ 116, 104, 115 = NJW 1992, 1039, 1042.

[36] Viney-Jourdain (1998), nr 448; Le Tourneau (2004), nr 6717.

[37] Civ. 2e 22 January 1969, JCP 1969, II, 15917.

[38] Civ. 1re 4 November 1992, D.1992. IR 270.

[39] Civ. 3e 29 November 1983, Bull. civ. III, no 247.

[40] Article 215 CC: Civ. 9 November 1965, JCP 1965. II. 14462. Le Tourneau (2004), no 6735.

[41] Viney-Jourdain (1998), nr 441, states that it is simply not possible to define the scope of application of a general principle: '... il est illusoire de chercher à definir par avance le domaine d'application du principe général qu'il formule aussi bien quant aux personnes protégées que quant aux dommages couverts.' Terré-Simler-Lequette (2002), nr 718; Aubry and Rau-Dejean de la Bathie (1989), nr 28; Carbonnier (2000), § 231, 418.

This rather forceful way of absolute thinking (the French like *les grands principes*, nr 608-3) is moderated by the requirement of causation: it goes without saying that a causal connection between the loss and the violation of the statutory rule has to be established. Just as in other jurisdictions, the scope of the duty and causation are closely connected. If the loss was not caused by the violation of the statutory rule, it can also often be said that the statutory provision did not protect the victim or his interests.[42]

This occurs, for instance, if the claim is based on the violation of a general statutory provision. In such a case the courts are inclined to dismiss the claim and require the violation of a more specific rule. This is, for example, the case if a claim for damages is filed in a criminal law suit and the claim is dismissed because the violated statutory rule is written in the general rather than in the claimant's interest.[43] This shows that, despite the French devotion to absolute and general rules, the courts are not without sin as they sometimes cannot resist the temptations of the concept of a relative statutory duty.

If a statutory provision only prohibits an attitude, such as carelessness and negligence, which is the case in many criminal law provisions, the court has to establish the *faute* in another way, particularly by establishing the violation of a pre-existing obligation or comparing the defendant's conduct with that of *le bon père de famille* (nr 302-1).[44]

(ii) Negligence and strict liability. The required level of care depends on the wording of the statutory rule. This level can vary from a duty to take safety measures to a duty to guarantee safety. If someone breaches such a duty and causes damage, it is no defence that he acted carefully, unless negligence is a statutory requirement.[45]

For instance, the driver who collides with another car in front of him breaches article R 10 Highway Act (*Code de la Route*) because he has failed to adapt his speed in order to be able to react properly to foreseeable obstacles and thus commits a *faute*. It is no defence that under the specific circumstances he drove carefully.[46]

---

[42] Jean Deliyannis, *La notion d'acte illicite. Considéré en sa qualité d'élément de la faute délictuelle* (Paris: Libr. Gén. de Droit & Jurispr., 1952), nr 78: '. . . si la disposition violée n'avait pas pour but de protéger le lésé le rapport de causalité entre l'acte illicite et le dommage n'est pas adéquat.'

[43] Civ. 3e 3 December 1980, JCP 1980. IV. 70; Civ. 1re 24 March 1981, JCP 1981. IV. 212; Viney-Jourdain (1998), nr 441.

[44] Carbonnier (2000), § 231, 418; Viney-Jourdain (1998), 448.

[45] Viney-Jourdain (1998), nr 448; Le Tourneau (2004), nr 6717 ff. with further examples and references.

[46] Civ. 2e 4 February 1976, D. 1976. IR. 140. Art. R 10 Code de la Route reads as follows: 'Tout conducteur doit constamment rester maître de sa vitesse et mener avec prudence son véhicule (. . .) il doit régler sa vitesse en fonction des obstacle prévisibles.' Viney-Jourdain (1998), nr 448; Terré-Simler-Lequette (1996), nr 687; Le Tourneau (2004), nr 6718–6722.

905 Liability for breach of Community law

905-1 *Violated rule must confer rights on individuals*

Violation of a statutory rule is connected to European Community law in two ways. Firstly, violation of a European rule can give rise to liability according to national law. In principle, such a violation implies a breach of statutory duty (England), a *Schutzgesetzverstoß* (Germany), or a *faute* (France). Besides the different national requirements for liability (nr 902–904), it is required that the rule has direct effect which means that the provision has to be clear, precise and unconditional (nr 204-2).

Secondly, the *Francovich* case law of the ECJ provides a framework for liability for breach of Community law which can be considered as the violation of a statutory rule by a Community institution, a Member State, or an individual (nr 205).[47] In addition to the requirements of sufficiently serious breach (nr 1805), causation (nr 1106), and damage (nr 1202-4), it is required that the violated Community rule aims to confer rights on individuals. This last requirement will be dealt with in this section.

It needs to be kept in mind that the requirement of the conferment of rights on individuals differs from the requirement of direct effect. If a rule has direct effect it may be directly invoked by the claimant. A rule has direct effect if the provision is clear, precise and unconditional—is 'self-executing': it must not leave the implementing Member State any margin of discretion. Direct effect relates to the status of the rule. The question of whether a rule confers rights on individuals relates to the content of the rule. Compensation for damage caused by breach of Community law cannot be claimed by invoking a (statutory) rule that merely aims to protect general interests: the scope of the violated rule has to be the protection of individuals.

Contrary to the conferment of rights on individuals, direct effect is not a condition for liability. For example, in *Francovich* the provisions of the Directive did not have direct effect but they did confer rights on individuals. If a rule has no direct effect, liability for damages and purposive or consistent interpretation (nr 204-4) are the ways to redress and to support compliance with Community rules and principles.

If a claimant can invoke the direct effect of a rule, this will not always help him since he may have suffered damage which cannot be repaired by the direct effect. This was one of the important reasons for the ECJ to create Member State liability in *Francovich* and *Brasserie du Pêcheur and Factortame* (nr 205-1). Thus, regardless of whether a rule has direct effect, liability for damages requires that the rule confers rights on individuals.

---

[47] In English law the nature of Member State's liability for breach of Community law is explicitly considered to be in the nature of a breach of statutory duty: *R v Secretary of State, ex parte Factortame Ltd (No 7)* [2001] 1 WLR 942.

Examples of the latter are Article 43 EC, securing the freedom of establishment of nationals of a Member State in the territory of another Member State, and Article 28 EC, guaranteeing the freedom to export goods to other Member States. In *Brasserie du Pêcheur and Factortame III*, the ECJ decided that these provisions confer rights on individuals. This indicates that generally formulated provisions can also confer rights on individuals. Hence, it is not the character of the rule (general or specific) that is decisive but the character of the interests which it aims to protect. If this is only a general interest, the rule cannot be invoked by claimants as the basis for a claim for damages.[48]

Also, a provision in a Directive can confer rights on individuals. This is the case if the result prescribed by the Directive so implies. The question of whether this is the case particularly plays a role if a Member State has not, or has not correctly, transposed a Directive into national law. In *Francovich* it was, for instance, decided that Directive 80/987 conferred rights on individuals, particularly on employees in case of insolvency of their employer (nr 205-1).

To establish whether the scope of the rule has an individual or a more general character, the preamble of the Regulation or Directive in which the rule is embodied may provide important information. Community rules that aim to protect life, health, or property usually confer rights on individuals. Examples are provisions regarding the permitted level of harmful substances in air and water, for instance rules regarding a limit for lead content in the air[49] and rules regarding the protection of groundwater against pollution by certain dangerous substances.[50] One may also think of safety rules as regards dangerous substances at work, such as asbestos.[51]

However, many other rules merely aim to protect parts of the environment, such as areas, biotopes, habitats, animals, or plants. One may think of the Birds Protection Directive of which it has been argued that, by this Directive, the administration of the common inheritance of mankind in Europe has been entrusted. This implies that individuals cannot invoke the violation of provisions in this Directive.[52]

---

[48] ECJ 5 March 1996, Joined cases C-46/93 and C-48/93, ECR 1996, I-1029 (*Brasserie du Pêcheur and Factortame III*), paras 50–51; ECJ 8 October 1996, Joined cases C-178/94, C-179/94, C-188/94, C-189/94 and C-190/94, ECR 1996, I-4845 (*Dillenkofer and Others v Germany*), paras 23, 26, 41 and 42.

[49] Directive 80/779/EEC of 15 July 1980 on air quality limit values and guide values for sulphur dioxide and suspended particulates, OJ L 229, 30.08.1980, 30–48.

[50] Directive 80/68/EEC of 17 December 1979 on the protection of groundwater against pollution caused by certain dangerous substances, OJ L 20, 26.01.1980, 43–48. Immission levels (eg the maximum pollution of air or water) will generally protect the individual, whereas emission levels (eg the maximum output of substances from a certain source) will generally not.

[51] Directive 83/477/EEC of 19 September 1983 on the protection of workers from the risks related to exposure to asbestos at work, OJ L 263, 24.09.1983, 25–32.

[52] This issue is also discussed under the question of whether an individual or an interest group has a right of standing; see for instance Edward Brans, *Liability for Damage to Public Natural Resources: Standing, Damage and Damage Assessment*, (The Hague: Aspen Publishers, 2001).

905-2 *Illustration: liability for inadequate banking supervision*

The previous paragraph and the link between national and Community law can be illustrated with two important cases about financial supervision. The English *Three Rivers* case was about clients of the collapsed Bank of Credit and Commerce International (BCCI).[53] They claimed damages from the Bank of England for improper supervision of the BCCI, alleging that the Bank had wrongfully granted a banking licence (or had failed to timely revoke the existing licence), which caused loss to over 6,000 depositors. The claimants based their claim, *inter alia*, on a violation of the (transposed) provisions of the 1977 Banking Directive.[54] However, the House of Lords held that this Directive was only intended as a measure to harmonize the regulation of banking, and did not confer a right to damages for depositors who suffered loss by reason of the failure by the supervisory bodies. In other words, the Directive protected the public interest rather than the individual interests of the bank's clients. The House of Lords' decision was criticized for the fact that it did not ask preliminary questions to the ECJ about the scope of the Directive.[55]

A couple of years later, however, the ECJ was requested to answer a similar question in *Peter Paul*. In the 1990s Paul and others had lost money when the German BVH bank with which they had opened term deposit accounts went bankrupt. The bank was not a member of any deposit guarantee system. Article 3(1)(ii) of Directive 94/19 on deposit guarantee schemes holds that a credit institution can only take deposits if it is covered by a deposit guarantee system for losses up to ECU 20,000 per deposit (Article 7(1)).[56] In Germany this Directive was implemented three years late. On the basis of breach of Community law (nr 205-1) the German court of first instance awarded damages corresponding with the minimum coverage of ECU 20,000.[57]

As regards their remaining damage, the claimants argued that this was caused by negligent supervision of the BVH Bank by the German banking supervisor (*Bundesaufsichtsamt für das Kreditwesen*). § 6(4) Law on Credit Institutions (*Gesetz über das Kreditwesen*) limited the liability for breach of official duties of the financial supervisor by imposing on it official obligations only in the public interest. Hence, the scope of the rule was not to protect individual victims.[58]

---

[53] *Three Rivers District Council v Bank of England (Three Rivers I)* [2000] 2 WLR 1220; see about the other aspect of this case—liability for misfeasance in public office—nr 1804-5.

[54] Directive on the co-ordination of laws, regulations and administrative provisions relating to the taking up and pursuit of the business of credit institutions; EEC 77/80 (First Banking Directive).

[55] Mads Andenas and Duncan Fairgrieve, 'Misfeasance in Public Office: Governmental Liability and European Influences', in Duncan Fairgrieve, Mads Andenas and John Bell (eds.), *Tort Liability of Public Authorities in Comparative Perspective* (London: BIICL, 2002), 193–194.

[56] OJ 1994 L 135/5.   [57] LG Bonn 16 April 1999, NJW 2000, 815.

[58] This is now held in § 4(4) Gesetz über die Bundesanstalt für Finanzdienstleistungsaufsicht (FinDAG) (Law on the Supervision of Financial Services). The current federal body for supervision of financial services is the *Bundesanstalt für Finanzdienstleistungsaufsicht (BAFin)*. The BGH confirmed its case law in BGH 20 January 2005, NJW 2005, 742.

This is the so-called requirement of the *Drittbezogenheit der Amtspflicht*: the official duty has to be owed to a third person (nr 1803-2). The BGH asked the ECJ preliminary questions whether this rule was compatible with Community law, in particular the Deposit Guarantee Schemes Directive 94/19/EC and the Bank Directive 2000/12/EC.[59]

The ECJ considered that the First Banking Directive and other Directives as regards financial supervision do not confer rights on depositors in the event that their deposits are unavailable as a result of defective supervision on the part of the competent national authorities. The fact that the interests of the banking clients were mentioned in the Directive's recitals as one of the balancing factors does not imply the conferment of rights on individuals. Furthermore, the provisions in the Directives do not preclude a national rule to the effect that the functions of the national authority responsible for supervising credit institutions are to be fulfilled in the public interest only, which under national law precludes individuals from claiming compensation for damage resulting from defective supervision on the part of that authority.[60]

After the ECJ decision, the BGH decided the case on the basis that the German statutory rules as regards banking supervision were compatible with Community law. It also decided, without referring the case to the *Bundesverfassungsgericht*, that the rules were not infringing the constitution.[61] This is somewhat surprising for two reasons. Firstly, prior to the introduction of the concealed statutory immunity in 1984, the BGH had taken the view that the banking supervisor also acted in the individual interest of the clients.[62] The BGH was, however, overruled by the German legislator acting in the interest of the State. Secondly, this is still a very controversial issue in the German literature and the majority of the authors consider the provisions to be unconstitutional.[63]

The German situation differs from England and France. In England the supervisor also has a statutory immunity (s. 102(1) of the Financial Services and Markets Act) but it can be held liable if its conduct amounts to a violation of a provision in the ECHR, or if it acted in bad faith. In common law, an action can be based on the tort of misfeasance in a public office (nr 1804-5). In France the supervisor does not have immunity at all and can be liable under administrative tort law, albeit that the claimant needs to prove a *faute lourde* (nr 1802-2). These differences are at odds with the fact that banking supervisors increasingly coordinate their work in order to supervise and regulate the European banking market.[64] In some countries the supervisor can be held liable whereas in others it

---

[59] BGH 16 May 2002, NJW 2002, 2464.
[60] ECJ 12 October 2004, C-222/02 (*Peter Paul v Federal Republic of Germany*), paras 40–47.
[61] BGH 20 January 2005, NJW 2005, 742.
[62] BGH 15 February 1979, BGHZ 74, 144 = NJW 1979, 1354; BGH 12 July 1979, BGHZ 75, 120 = NJW 1979, 1879; BGH 15 March 1984, BGHZ 90, 310.
[63] See Matthias Gratias, *Staatshaftung für fehlerhafte Banken- und Versicherungsaufsicht im Europäischen Binnenmarkt* (Baden-Baden: Nomos, 1999), with further references.
[64] Particularly in the CEBS, the Committee of European Bank Supervisors.

benefits from immunity. Sooner or later the European legislator needs to address this lack of a level playing field.

At first sight *Peter Paul* contrasts with *Brasserie du Pêcheur* (nr 205-2). In the latter case, the question was whether Germany was liable for the violation of the prohibition to impede the free movements of goods in the Community (Article 28 EC) by imposing the *Reinheitsgebot* (purity regulation) on imported beers. Just as in *Peter Paul*, German law barred liability of the State because the purity regulation was issued in the interest of the public at large and was not directed towards any particular person or class of persons (requirement of *Drittbezogenheit*). Hence, according to German law there was no duty towards *Brasserie*. The ECJ considered this requirement to be incompatible with Community law:

> Total exclusion of loss of profit as a head of damage for which reparation may be awarded in the case of a breach of Community law cannot be accepted. Especially in the context of economic or commercial litigation, such a total exclusion of loss of profit would be such as to make reparation of damage practically impossible.[65]

The difference with *Peter Paul* is that, in *Brasserie*, Germany had violated a Community rule that conferred rights on individuals, and in *Peter Paul* this could not be established. Hence, if the ECJ had found in *Peter Paul* that the Banking Directives confer rights on individuals and there had been a sufficiently serious breach, the bank supervisor's immunity would have been incompatible with Community law.

906 Comparative observations

906-1 *Conferment of rights and private right of action; scope and causation*

As is clear from the foregoing, the rules for liability based on the violation of a statutory rule differ substantially throughout the legal systems. This will be further analysed in this section.

Another difference can be found in the various relationships between the violation of a statutory rule and the general liability rules. In France violation of a statutory duty is just another way of establishing a *faute*, in addition to the violation of unwritten law. In Germany and England the two rules are considered to provide two separate bases for liability. However, the relationship between these bases for liability differs. In Germany § 823 II BGB (violation of a statutory rule) is intended to supplement the possibilities under § 823 I BGB (infringement of a right), particularly in the area of compensation for pure

---

[65] ECJ 5 March 1996, Joined cases C-46/93 and C-48/93, ECR 1996, I-1029 (*Brasserie du Pêcheur and Factortame III*), para. 87.

economic loss (nr 903). In England breach of statutory duty runs parallel to the tort of negligence and does not supplement it. A good illustration of the difference between the systems is road traffic accidents: whereas in France, the breach of a provision of the *Code de la Route* amounts *ipso facto* and systematically to a tortious *faute*, in England it will not be conclusive of the defendant's liability since this is exclusively regulated by the tort of negligence.

The requirement of conferring rights on individuals in Community law (nr 905-1) is akin to the English requirement of the private right of action (nr 902-1/2). The latter refers to the question of whether the legislator, when issuing the statutory rule, intended to provide claimants with an action for damages in tort. It has been shown that this question is far from easy to answer (nr 900).

German and French law do not require establishing that the legislator intended to provide potential victims with a private right of action in tort. Such a requirement is neither mentioned in the Draft European Civil Code nor in the Principles of European Tort Law. Both require, just like German and English law that the statutory rule aims to protect the victim against the damage he has suffered.[66]

However, these differences should not be exaggerated. It can be argued that the requirement of conferment of rights is an aspect of the scope of the statutory rule. If a statutory rule does not confer rights on individuals, not one individual is protected; in such a case the statutory duty is to be fulfilled in the public interest only. However, if a rule does confer rights on individuals, the scope issue refers to the question whether the claimant belongs to the class of protected individuals.

If the ECJ is to decide on scope of the rule issues it is not unlikely that the Court will follow the French path, by finding the answer within the framework of causation. As has been pointed out, in French law the scope of a statutory rule is not relevant for establishing a *faute* (nr 904). However, it requires a direct and certain causal connection between the harm suffered and the breach of the statutory duty (nr 1105). Hence, in a number of cases one could argue that, if the statutory provision in fact does not aim to protect the victim against the damage suffered, it will not be unlikely that the requirement of causation is not fulfilled.

The strong link between the scope of the statutory duty and causation can also be illustrated with the English case of *Donaghey v Boulton & Paul*. The case was about a workman who fell through a hole in the roof sheeting of an aircraft hangar. The applicable statutory regulations required the use of crawling boards on 'roofs ... covered with fragile materials through which a person is liable to fall a distance of more than 10 feet.' The accident occurred in a different way than was foreseen in the regulation: the worker did not fall through the fragile material but through a hole in the roof.[67] The House of Lords held that the workman's damage

---

[66] Article 3:102 ECC and Article 4:102(3) PETL.
[67] *Donaghey v Boulton & Paul Ltd* [1968] AC 1; about which Van Gerven (2000), 415–416. Lord Reid took a purposive view of the provision and in fact applied the *Mischief rule*; see nr 501-4.

was within the scope of protection of the statutory rule. Lord Reid deemed it decisive that the workman suffered the kind of damage against which the statutory rule aimed to protect, even though it happened in a way not contemplated by the maker of the regulation. He referred to two important causation cases in which it was decided that it is decisive whether the accident which occurred is of a type which should have been foreseeable by a reasonable careful person; the precise concatenation of circumstances need not be envisaged.[68]

It is also interesting to note that, whereas English judges see provisions for criminal sanctions as hinting at the absence of a private law action in tort— which is seen as an unnecessary 'additional extra'—in France, the presence of the former only serves to reinforce the existence of the latter.[69] This once again illustrates the different policy approaches between France and England (nr 609). The English generally consider corrective justice to be the main function of tort law. They are not inclined to accumulate a criminal sanction with the tort law sanction. In France the main function of tort law is distributive justice. The purpose of liability is not so much to sanction the defendant's behaviour as to compensate the claimant's damage. Hence, a criminal sanction can easily accumulate with liability for damages because they serve different purposes and, in fact, this happens by the principle that a *faute criminelle* automatically implies a *faute civile* (nr 302-1).

906-2 *Negligence and strict liability*

A statutory rule is strict if it holds an obligation to provide or guarantee a result. In France and England violation of such a statutory duty establishes liability unless there is a ground of justification. Negligence is only required if it is required by the statutory provision, for example if the rule prescribes to take due care. If the court applies such a rule, it has to establish negligence by its own authority in the same way it does in establishing and applying unwritten duties of care (nr 804).[70]

In German law § 823 II BGB requires *Verschulden* (intention or negligence) besides the violation of a statutory rule, even if the rule only holds a (strict) obligation to guarantee a result. However, the BGH has reversed the burden of proof of negligence if the statutory rule prescribes a specific standard of conduct. In such a case negligence is assumed and the defendant must prove that his conduct was not negligent.

This implies that the practical differences between the German system, on the one hand (negligence liability, in case of specific statutory duties a liability for

---

[68] See particularly *Overseas Tankship (UK) Ltd v Morts Dock & Engineering Co Ltd* (*The Wagon Mound No 1*) [1961] AC 388; *Hughes v Lord Advocate* [1963] AC 837, about which Van Gerven (2000), 411–412 and nr 1104.

[69] Carbonnier (2000), no 231: 'Le droit pénal (...) agit (...) comme un révélateur de l'illicite dans la responsabilité civile'.   [70] Von Bar (2000), N 221.

rebuttable negligence), and the French and the English system on the other (only negligence liability if negligence is an element of the specific statutory provision, in other cases strict liability), are limited.

What is the position taken by the ECJ? Just as in French and English law and yet again unlike German law, a breach of a (statutory) Community duty can imply strict liability. For example, a failure to take any measure to transpose a Directive in order to achieve the result it prescribes within the period laid down for that purpose constitutes *per se* a sufficiently serious breach of Community law, ie a violation of the transposition provision in the Directive.[71]

In other cases, however, for instance as regards the question of whether a Directive is correctly implemented, the Member State has a margin of discretion. In *Brasserie du Pêcheur* the ECJ has indicated that, in such a case, the following factors have to be taken into account when establishing a sufficiently serious breach:

... the clarity and precision of the rule breached, the measure of discretion left by that rule to the national or Community authorities, whether the infringement and the damage caused was intentional or involuntary, whether any error of law was excusable or inexcusable, the fact that the position taken by a Community institution may have contributed towards the omission, and the adoption or retention of national measures or practices contrary to Community law.[72]

In these cases negligence is required for liability. This, however, has perhaps more to do with the fact that liability for breach of Community law is mainly about liability of public bodies. It remains to be seen how the ECJ will decide in cases against individuals or companies for breach of Community law (nr 205-3).

The Draft ECC and the PETL solely connect breach of statutory duty with negligence liability. Article 3:102 ECC (negligence) holds:

A person causes legally relevant damage negligently when that person causes the damage by conduct which ... does not meet the particular standard of care provided by a statutory provision whose purpose is the protection of the injured party from the damage suffered.

Article 4:102(3) PETL (required standard of conduct) provides: 'Rules which prescribe or forbid certain conduct have to be considered when establishing the required standard of conduct.' Whereas the ECJ in this respect focuses on English and French elements, both drafts seem to advocate a more German approach in which breach of statutory duty is always a negligence liability.

---

[71] ECJ 8 October 1996, Joined cases C-178/94, C-179/94, C-188/94, C-189/94 and C-190/94, ECR 1996, I-4845 (*Dillenkofer and Others v Germany*).

[72] ECJ 5 March 1996, Joined cases C-46/93 and C-48/93, ECR 1996, I-1029 (*Brasserie du Pêcheur and Factortame III*), para. 56. See also nr 1805-1.

10

Strict Liability

1001 Introduction

Strict liability is usually described as liability without fault (*responsabilité sans faute, verschuldensunabhängige Haftung*). Fault is generally considered to be a synonym for intentional or negligent conduct, and this implies that strict liability is liability without intentional or negligent conduct. In this sense strict liability is also referred to as objective liability (*responsabilité objective*) or risk liability (*Gefährdungshaftung*), which means that liability is to be established independent from the tortfeasor's conduct.[1]

However, in practice strict liability is far from a clear concept. Indeed, strict liability can be considered as liability without negligence, but elements of negligence often play a role in rules of strict liability. For example, strict liability of the employer for damage caused by his employee requires the employee's negligent conduct. Strict liability for a defective product holds elements in the requirement of defect that are akin to the elements of negligent conduct. Even 'pure' strict liability rules for damage caused usually hold defences which bear traces of negligence. For example, one of the defences in liability for things in French law is the external cause (*cause étrangère*) which was unforeseeable and insurmountable (*imprévisible et insurmontable*). The various national rules of stricter liability will be pointed out and categorized in nr 1003. See for an overview by legal system nr 300–306, 405 and 506.

The concept of strict liability is even more blurred because not only does strict liability hold elements of negligence, but negligence liability also holds elements of strict liability. The courts use various techniques to make negligence liability stricter, such as applying an objective standard of care,[2] increasing the required knowledge and ability to a high level (nr 812), and substantially raising the required level of precautionary measures (nr 807). Within the framework of negligence liability, the courts also make use of various subtle evidence rules in

---

[1] See about strict liability from a comparative law perspective: Bernhard A. Koch and Helmut Koziol (eds.), *Unification of Tort Law: Strict Liability* (The Hague, London, Boston: Kluwer, 2002); Van Gerven (2000), 539–687; von Bar (2000), N 306–410.

[2] Von Bar (2000), N 307: '...even liability for misconduct is no-fault liability: it is only exceptionally linked with personal blameworthiness.' He uses the term 'misconduct': Von Bar (2000), N 314.

order to shift the burden of proof as regards negligence or elements of negligence to the defendant. Particularly in Germany the legislator has enacted rules of negligence liability with a reversed burden of proof, such as for the employer and for the parent. Such liability is stricter than liability for proven negligence, since the risk of not being able to prove facts is no longer with the claimant but with the defendant. See nr 1004-2.

This all illustrates that a clear distinction between negligence and strict liability is not possible. In nr 1005 it will be further argued that in practice such a distinction does not exist, and that legislators and courts apply a mixture of elements in order to find the right balance between fault and strict liability. Hence, this chapter deals with rules of *stricter* liability rather than *strict* liability. This will be extensively illustrated in the third part of this book in which the most important categories of liability will be analysed and discussed.

1002 Background of strict liability

All legal systems provide strict liability rules in addition to the basic negligence liability rule. The latter rule implies that the victim has to prove facts that justify the conclusion that the defendant acted negligently. In France this concerns liability based on articles 1382 and 1383 CC (*faute*), in Germany § 823 and § 826 BGB (*Tatbestand, Rechtswidrigkeit,* and *Verschulden*), and in England the tort of negligence (duty of care and breach of duty).

If fault liability does not lead to satisfactory results strict liability is often provided as a solution. There are various reasons for imposing rules of strict liability.[3]

Strict liability rules often apply to damage caused by movable objects representing a higher than average risk, such as motor vehicles, animals, or defective products such as drugs. These objects are considered to be inherently or inevitably dangerous: accidents may happen with a considerable level of probability and if they happen they are likely to cause severe damage, namely death and serious personal injury. See about the elements of risk nr 806. The bigger the potential risk, the more there will be food for thought of a rule of strict liability.

Such a rule serves the goal of strict liability to improve the claimant's position by no longer requiring that the right to compensation depends on the claimant's proof of negligent conduct. For example, if the claimant faces a complex organization as a defendant he may have considerable difficulties in proving his case, such as in product liability cases. This problem cannot only be solved by a rule of strict liability but also by a liability for rebuttable negligence.

Another reason to impose strict liability rules is that it may lead to more efficiency since extensive discussions on the required level of care and the level of

---

[3] See also Koch and Koziol (2002), 407–413.

care which was effectively maintained are no longer necessary. As has been pointed out in the framework of liability for negligence, high risks generally require a high level of precautionary measures to avoid accidents (nr 806–807). The higher the level of care applied in negligence cases, the smaller the difference between these grounds for liability is. Rules of strict liability do not take the required level of care as a starting point but link liability, in principle, to the realization of a risk.

Strict liability rules can also be considered as a matter of setting off: on one hand the law allows the activity, but on the other claimants can more easily prove their claim and get compensation. This relates to the idea that the costs of socially valuable but dangerous activities (driving, mass production) should not be borne by the unlucky and arbitrary individual who suffers damage from them. These costs should be borne by society or by the specific group involved in the activity. This is, in fact, a matter of equality before the public burdens, not so much the burdens imposed by governmental misfeasance or nonfeasance (nr 1811) but the burdens imposed by risky and at the same time valuable and beneficial social activities.

Also, loss spreading within a certain group can be a goal of strict liability. An illustration is strict liability for defective products: mass production makes it impossible or at least very costly to guarantee that each and every product is manufactured in a safe way. Hence, a slightly lower safety standard is allowed, provided the manufacturer is strictly liable to the people who have the bad luck to be harmed by a defective product. Subsequently, the manufacturer can re-distribute the costs of his liability to all consumers by raising the product's price.

Liability insurance further enables and supports rules of strict liability. The driver, the manufacturer, or the owner of the animal can continue his activities without having to worry that liability for damages will ruin his financial position (nr 716). The fact that the compensation is generally paid for by the insurer means that the burden is in fact carried by the group of insured and they can often re-distribute these costs to the customers. In this sense, big companies and insurers are not only 'deep pockets' but also loss spreaders.[4]

Another argument for strict liability is that someone who has the (commercial) benefits of a certain activity also has to answer for the damage he causes (*cuius commodum, eius damnum*), or, *ubi emolumentum, ibi onus* (where the advantage is, there should be the burden). This is a fairness argument that has long standing and is supported throughout the legal systems.

In Germany rules of strict liability often hold a maximum for the amount for damages to be paid. If the damage is higher, compensation can only be obtained on the basis of fault liability. Such a maximum amount of compensation is also one of the options for the Member States provided in the European Directive on

---

[4] Channelling strict liability to one person happens by excluding liability of all other potentially liable persons. This does not happen in European strict liability rules, apart from liability for damage caused by nuclear plants. See Koch and Koziol (2002), 419–420.

liability for defective products (nr 1406), and it can also be found in international treaties such as the Paris Convention on Third Party Liability in the Field of Nuclear Energy (1960 nr 1415-2). Such a limitation makes stricter rules more feasible since the insurer can better assess the limits of the financial risks to be covered. However, this argument is much stronger for nuclear risks than for the capped liability sums in Germany where they seem rather to be an instrument to make strict liability more acceptable. The compensation cap is strongly criticized in Germany and, indeed, does not seem to be a necessary measure to keep the burden of liability within limits.[5]

1003 Three variations on strict liability

1003-1 *Liability with an extra debtor*

The content and structure of stricter rules show a wide variation. In this section the four major variations will be briefly set out: negligence liability with an extra debtor; strict liability for a defective object; and strict liability with a limited defence. All these forms of strict(er) liability contain elements of negligence, either direct or indirect.

The first category comprises rules according to which someone is jointly liable with the person who actually caused the damage by his negligent conduct. This is also called negligence liability with an extra (strictly liable) debtor.

The main example of this category is the employer's liability for damage caused by his employee. In England and France it is sufficient to establish that the employee acted negligently and that his conduct was related to the employer's business. If these requirements are met, the employer is strictly liable; he does not have any defence but contributory negligence. In Germany the situation is different: the employer may prove that he was not negligent in selecting, instructing, and supervising his employee. However, the courts have considerably restricted this liability for rebuttable negligence (nr 1606-1/2). French law has a number of other rules providing negligence liability with an extra debtor, particularly the general rule of strict liability for persons (nr 305) and the liability of parents according to article 1384 al. 4 (nr 1602-1).

The aim of rules like this is to provide the victim with a more solvent debtor than the person who in fact caused the damage, in order to improve his chances of getting damages.[6] From the debtor's perspective this is a strict liability. From the victim's perspective, however, this is a negligence liability since he has to prove negligent conduct from the employee. If he succeeds he will automatically (England and France) or in principle (Germany) have a second debtor.

---

[5] Koch and Koziol (2002), 428–429 with further references.
[6] See for instance Terré-Simler-Lequette (2002), nr 804: '...une responsabilité destinée à améliorer, au profit de la victime, les chances de réparation.'

1003-2 *Liability for a defective object*

Strict liability for a defect refers to liability for things. In such a rule, liability is based on the condition and safety of a thing rather on the negligence of its owner, user, or producer.

An important and well known example of strict liability for a defect can be found in the EC Directive on liability for defective products. According to Article 1 of the Directive, the manufacturer is liable for damage caused by a defect in its product. Article 6 provides that a product is defective ' . . . when it does not provide the safety which a person is entitled to expect, taking all circumstances into account.' This is the mirror of the negligence test which, though focusing on the defendant's negligent conduct, in many cases actually refers to the safety the claimant was entitled to expect. The close relationship between defect and negligence is also illustrated by Article 2 providing that, as regards the defectiveness of a product, the court has to take into account the presentation and the reasonable expected use of the product. These factors are also relevant in order to establish negligence (para. 8.1).[7] However, the defectiveness test differs principally from the negligence test because it takes the product and not the producer as a reference. Though this may lead to similar results in cases of design defects, it makes a difference in cases of manufacturing defects (nr 1408-1).

The idea behind this rule is that it is no longer required that the claimant proves the defendant's negligent conduct (which often involves facts as regards the defendant's internal organization) and to limit the burden of proof to facts regarding the visible elements of a thing (product). In fact, the defendant owes an obligation to guarantee a result, ie a certain standard of safety in the product, no matter how this is done. It illustrates the development of depersonalization in tort law.

1003-3 *Liability with a limited defence*

Strict liability with a limited defence is perhaps the most classic and genuine form of strict liability. In principle, this liability is independent of the defendant's religious conduct; more specifically it is not dependent on whether the defendant took sufficient precautionary measures. The materialization of the risk establishes liability.

The defences vary: for example in English law *Act of God* is (regardless of the defendant's religious conviction) a defence under the *Rule in Rylands v Fletcher* and relates to natural events only. A slightly broader defence is available under French and German strict liability rules, namely *force majeure* or *höhere Gewalt*. Under this defence, acts of third parties or the claimant can also be invoked provided they were objectively unforeseeable and unavoidable, in other words, they were completely beyond his control.

[7] See for instance Fleming (1998), 540–541.

As a consequence of the reform of the law of damages in German law (nr 1202-2) the defence of *höhere Gewalt* as described above replaced the defence of *ein unabwendbares Ereignis*. Though the difference with the former defence is subtle, the latter defence allowed the defendant to argue that he could not have avoided the harm even if he had taken the utmost care. This is in fact a negligence test with the most perfect man as standard of reference (nr 812) and a reversal of the burden of proof (nr 1004-2). It shows how reminiscences of fault liability are still traceable in strict liability.

Examples of this category of strict liability can be found in most legal systems: one may think of liability for animals (nr 1402–1403), liability for things and persons in France (nr 303–306), liability for motor vehicles and for installations in Germany (nr 405). One may also think of rules in land law such as trespass to land and nuisance (nr 1413). The German legislator, in particular, scrupulously follows newly emerging risks and quickly provides for strict liability rules, ranging from strict liability for motor vehicles to strict liability for genetic engineering (nr 405).

Liability for damage caused by motor vehicles in France goes even a step further: in these cases *force majeure* is no defence against liability (nr 1404-1). This kind of strict liability is in fact an absolute liability also, because it excludes the defence of contributory negligence apart from an inexcusable fault. Another example in this respect is the liability of the operator of a nuclear plant, which is absolute and only accepts intentional self-infliction of harm as a defence. Combined with a mandatory liability insurance system, as is the case for the keeper of a motor vehicle and the operator of a nuclear plant, such systems provide maximum protection to victims of accidents and are, in fact, insurance systems for the benefit of third parties paid for by the collective of insured.

Finally, such a rule of strict liability could initially also be found in the area of Community law, particularly in the Member State's obligation to timely implement a Directive. According to the ECJ's *Francovich* case law, the sole transgression of the time for implementation amounts to a sufficiently serious breach. This could be considered to be a form of strict liability. Currently, this liability for not timely implemented Directives depends on balancing a number of factors and this comes close to the balancing act in negligence (nr 1805), but in practice it remains close to strict liability.

1004 Strict elements in negligence

1004-1 *Raising the standard of care*

Rules of stricter liability not only play an explicit role as described in nr 1003 but they also enjoy a more implicit and hidden existence behind the scenes of negligence liability. With the help of the fluid concept of negligence, the courts have often in fact applied forms of stricter liability, particularly in the area of liability for personal injury.[8] The waters of negligence liability run into the waters of strict liability, and it is impossible to indicate the exact borderline between the two.

The courts use several 'techniques' to stretch the standard of care. One is to increase the level of required precautionary measures; another one is to increase the required level of knowledge and ability. A third way is to make use of the rules of evidence (1004-2).

Firstly, to establish negligent *conduct* it is required that the defendant did not take sufficient precautionary measures. The extent of the required precautionary measures depends on the extent of the risk: the higher the risk, the more measures will be required (nr 806–807). Particularly in personal injury cases, the courts require a high level of care. In this area the courts often decide that the defendant did not take sufficient precautionary measures, even if the probability of the accident was very low. Due to the fact that the balancing process to establish negligence cannot always be quantified and, in practice, is hardly quantified at all, the elements of negligence provide several ways along which the courts can stretch the standard of care in the direction of a stricter one.

A court can require burdensome precautions even if the risk is not big enough to justify them. If, for example, a patient fainted when he stood up after blood was taken at a hospital, the court has to balance the risk (what is the chance that a patient faints? what is the expected damage if this happens?) and the precautionary measures.[9] The court could, for instance, decide that the hospital owes each patient a duty to assist and supervise when the patient stands up after blood has been taken, even if the risk does not outweigh the burden of precautionary measures. The temptation for the court to do so is quite substantial, since this duty will make the difference for the claimant and in personal injury cases courts are seldom oblivious to the fate of a seriously injured victim. Ultimately, such a decision could imply that in certain situations the costs or burdens of precautionary measures are in fact not relevant, which would mean that the defendant's duty is stricter than negligence.

Secondly, as regards the negligent *person*, it is required that the defendant knew or ought to have known the risk, and that he was able or ought to have been able to avoid its realization. The courts usually apply an objective test, typically referring to a standard of reference such as the *reasonable man* or the *bonus pater familias*. The required level of knowledge and ability mainly depends on the nature and risk of the defendant's activity (nr 810).

[8] In the same sense for instance Christian von Bar, *Verkehrspflichten* (Cologne: Heymann, 1980), 128, who has pointed out that it is possible *Verkehrspflichten* '... in der Mitte der Bandbreite möglicher Zurechnungskriterien anzusiedeln, d.h. mit Hilfe der Verkehrspflichten ein Hin- und Herwandern des Blicks zwischen Verschulden und unbedingter Einstandspflicht zu ermöglichen.'
[9] Compare HR 6 November 1981, NJ 1982, 567, comm. CJHB (blood sample).

The objective test can be considered to be a kind of strict liability, even though in most areas of tort law it is the regular form of negligence liability (nr 811). An objective test implies that the defendant is liable if, with reference to an objective standard such as the reasonable man, he ought to have known the risk and he ought to have been able to prevent the risk. This implies that, if the reasonable person has better qualities than the actual defendant, the latter has to bear the risk for his shortcomings.[10] A court does not take the tortfeasor as it finds him. This can be illustrated by the rule that a doctor has to answer for the knowledge and ability of a good doctor. The personal knowledge and abilities of the doctor are not relevant. He bears the risks for not having the qualities which can be required from a reasonably competent doctor (nr 812-2).

A court can go a step further. It can equip the reasonable person with excellent knowledge and abilities and shape it like the perfect person. If the courts do so, an average defendant will be faced with high challenges and a great many strict elements. As far as negligence liability applies, such as in England, this happens for example as regards drivers of motor vehicles, who have to behave like perfect drivers, seeing everything, swiftly anticipating unexpected events, and steering like the best Formula 1 driver (nr 1404-3). Stretching knowledge and ability to such a high level can imply that these requirements are, in fact, not relevant for establishing liability. The ultimate step would be to completely skip the requirements of knowledge and ability.

1004-2 *Shifting the burden of proof*

Finally, without altering or stretching the negligence rule itself, the position of the victim can also be improved by shifting the burden of proof. This can happen in various ways.

Firstly, the courts can apply *prima facie* rules or rules of *res ipsa loquitur* evidence. This means that at first sight the facts of the case speak for the claimant. For example, if a driver collides with the back of the car in front of him, the court will generally presume that he acted negligently and will allow the defendant to rebut this presumption. The same can go for product liability cases, particularly cases of manufacturing defects (one may think of an exploding bottle): it is hardly possible for a victim to prove that the manufacturer knew or should have the known that this product was defective and or that he should have taken more care in preventing it from happening. The German *Chicken Pest* case illustrates this very well. A farmer had his chickens vaccinated but the vaccine turned out to be contaminated and the birds died. However, it could not be determined what had caused the contamination. The German BGH decided that

---

[10] Larenz (1987), § 20 III, 287.

... if the correct use of an industrial product violates the objects of legal protection pursuant to § 823 I BGB because the product was defective, it is incumbent upon the manufacturer to find out what caused the defect and to prove that he was not at fault.[11]

According to the EC Directive the claimant has to prove that the product was defective. If he succeeds in doing so, the manufacturer cannot escape liability by proving that he was not negligent. He has, however, a limited number of other defences (nr 1410).

Not only courts, but also legislators, can enact rules of negligence liability with a reversed burden of proof. This means that the tortfeasor is liable for the damage caused unless he can prove that his conduct was sufficiently careful. 'Where the defendant is burdened with proving that he acted with the care of the paterfamilias, breach of that duty is no longer a prerequisite for liability: the defendant will be liable even where he acted correctly if he cannot discharge that burden.'[12] Such rules can mainly be found in Germany. For example, the German liability of persons having to supervise minors is a negligence liability with a reversed burden of proof (nr 1602-2). In this area a similar rule was applied in France but in the 1990s the *Cour de cassation* transformed this rule into a strict liability with a limited defence (*force majeure*) (nr 1602-1). The German employer's liability for damage caused by his employee is also a negligence liability with a reversed burden of proof, whereas in England and France strict liability rules apply (nr 1606). Finally, the German liability of the possessor of a collapsing building is a liability for rebuttable negligence whereas the French rule contains a strict liability with a limited defence (nr 1502–1503).

By shifting the burden of proof as regards negligence, the claimant's risk is shifted to the defendant, in that the latter bears the risk that he is not able to prove that he acted carefully. If the defendant cannot prove that he was not at fault, his liability is not based on proved fault but solely on the presumption of fault. This is, in fact, a form of strict liability.[13] Rules of liability for rebuttable negligence are often applied in cases in which the defendant possesses more information about the cause of the damage than the claimant. In Germany the BGH refers to these rules to (partly) shift the burden of proof as regards product liability (see nr 1407-1) and accidents in hospitals, for example because of a slippery floor, an injection with contaminated fluid, or a defective machine. In such cases the claimant can confine himself to proving the defective product or situation, and it is then up to the defendant to prove that he did not act negligently.[14] In English law the *Rule in Rylands v Fletcher* which was long thought

---

[11] BGH 26 November 1968, BGHZ 51, 91 (*Hühnerpest*), about which von Bar (2000), N 277, with further references.   [12] Von Bar (2000), N 308.

[13] In the same sense Koch and Koziol (2002), 434.

[14] Münchener Kommentar-Wagner (2004), § 836 N 4, with reference to BGH 26 November 1968, BGHZ 51, 91; BGH 10 January 1984, BGHZ 89, 263 = NJW 1984, 1400; BGH 24 June 1975, VersR 1975, 952; BGH 18 December 1990, NJW 1991, 1540; BGH 9 May 1978, NJW 1978, 1683; BGH 11 October 1978, NJW 1978, 584; BGH 3 November 1981, NJW 1982, 699.

to be a form of strict liability, has been reshaped by the courts to a rule which comes close to a liability rule for rebuttable negligence.

Finally, to put things in a further confusing perspective, liability for rebuttable negligence can come close to the 'pure' strict liability as set out in nr 1003-3. The more difficult it is for the defendant to rebut the presumption of negligence, the more akin this will be to a strict liability with a *force majeure* defence.

The development of strict liability and of raising the standard of care in negligence is due to the widespread availability of liability insurance. Markesinis and Deakin argue that

> ... there is no denying the fact that, as a result of modern insurance practices, the notions of 'duty' (and causation) are at times used to conceal insurance dictates and the term 'negligence' is employed in contexts where the defendant could not humanly have avoided the accident in question.[15]

Indeed, without liability insurance high level standards of care and strict liability would considerably limit the freedom to act to the rich and the lucky. With liability insurance, however, everybody can be rich in this respect and need not be too afraid of being unlucky.

1005 The blurred border between strict and fault liability

It can be concluded that elements of stricter liability can be found inside the framework of fault liability, and that elements of fault can be found inside the framework of strict liability. This means that there is no exact borderline to be drawn between negligence and strict liability.

Liability rules are to be found on the continuum between pure subjective negligence liability and absolute liability. Subjective negligence liability requires that the defendant is personally to blame for his conduct, because he personally knew better and was personally able to act differently (nr 811-1). This subjective negligence liability scarcely plays a role in current tort law. As an exception one may think of liability for not providing emergency aid (nr 1703). Absolute liability requires no more than a causal connection between a certain event and the damage; even the defence of *force majeure* is not accepted. Here also, examples are rather scarce but one may think of the liability of the operator of a nuclear installation and the French liability of drivers for damage caused in road traffic accidents (nr 1404-1).

The dichotomy between negligence and strict liability is outdated. Legislators and courts look for the right balance by mixing negligence and strict elements, sometimes fine-tuning this mix by (partially) shifting the burden of proof from the claimant to the defendant.[16] Hence, there are not just two tracks: negligence

---

[15] Markesinis and Deakin (2003), 3.

[16] See for instance the burden of proof as regards the German requirement of *Verschulden* in the framework of the *Verkehrspflichten* (nr 804-2) and the violation of a statutory rule (nr 903).

and strict liability, but a broad road with several lanes, containing different mixes of elements of both.[17] The theoretical distinction between negligence and strict liability cannot be maintained and a clear distinction between the two concepts is neither useful nor feasible.[18] The old steeled frameworks of 19th and 20th century tort law (*fault and risk, faute et risque, Verschulden und Gefährdung*) are no longer opponents but need to cooperate in order to achieve the appropriate results for the 21st century.

---

[17] See for an interesting proposal for a mixed general liability rule: Hans Stoll, *Richterliche Fortbildung und gesetzliche Überarbeitung des Deliktsrechts*, (Heidelberg: CF Müller, 1984), 17–18.

[18] Kötz-Wagner (2001), N 264; Zweigert-Kötz, *Introduction to Comparative Law* (1998), 647 ff; Ernst von Caemmerer, *Das Verschuldensprinzip in rechtsvergleichender Sicht*, RabelsZ 1978, 5–27, particularly 12 ff.; Koch and Koziol (2002), 432–435.

11

Causation

A INTRODUCTION

1101 General remarks

If someone has acted negligently (Chapters 7–8), violated a statutory rule (Chapter 9), or a strict cause has materialized (Chapter 10), the question arises as to whether there is a causal connection with the consequential damage (Chapter 12). This chapter will provide an overview of the main problems as regards causation in tort law.[1]

Despite the fact that causation plays a crucial role in tort law, none of the jurisdictions holds a specific statutory provision on this subject.[2] They provide rules in almost all areas of liability, but there is no provision giving guidance for the application of the requirement of causation. Hence, causation rules have all been developed by the courts.

It is not easy to get to grips with the notion of causation and it is hard to fruitfully design a generally applicable causation test:

. . . causation is no more than the connection deemed necessary in tort law between, on one hand, a defendant's misconduct, that of a person for whom the defendant is responsible, or the existence of a source of danger, and on the other, compensable damage. There is no generalized answer as to the qualities of that link.[3]

In the legal systems various tests are applied, but in practice the courts' approaches are also driven by policy considerations. This explains why the application of the same test can lead to various outcomes, whereas the application of

---

[1] See in depth about causation H.L.A. Hart and A.M. Honoré, *Causation in the Law* (Oxford: Clarendon, 1985); A.M. Honoré, 'Causation and Remoteness of Damage', in A. Tunc (ed.), *International Encyclopedia of Comparative Law*, Vol. XI, Chapter 7 (Tübingen: Mohr, 1971); Jaap Spier (ed.), *Unification of Tort Law: Causation* (The Hague, London, New York: Kluwer Law International, 2000); von Bar (2000), N 411–484; Van Gerven (2000), 395–466.

[2] Art. 6:98 Dutch BW is one of the few statutory provisions as regards causation and it codified the case law of the Dutch Supreme Court: 'Reparation of damage can only be claimed for damage which is related to the event giving rise to the liability of the obligor, which, also having regard to the nature of the liability and of the damage, can be attributed to him as a result of such event.'

[3] Von Bar (2000), N 440.

different tests can lead to similar outcomes. Hence, it is necessary to look at causation in a more practical way. 'Once one moves away from general theories towards (. . .) typical cases, the large extent of commonality between the various legal systems (. . .) becomes more apparent.'[4]

An important reason for the difficulties of designing a general concept of causation and also of comparing the various legal systems is that causation is determined and influenced by the other requirements for liability. This is what makes causation an elusive phenomenon.

Firstly, the requirements of negligence and causation are closely related to each other. In both, probability and foreseeability play an important role. In the negligence test, the question is how likely it is that harm *would be* caused by the negligent conduct (nr 806-2), whereas in causation the question is how likely it is that the damage *was* caused by the negligent conduct or by the cause for which the defendant is liable.

Secondly, foreseeability (knowledge) plays a role in negligence as well as in causation. In the framework of negligence, the knowledge requirement is related to the fact that a particular conduct can cause harm of a general kind, such as damage to health or to property. Knowledge is not related to the sequence of events that resulted in the damage. Particularly in personal injury cases, this sequence does not have to be foreseeable (nr 810-2).

Thirdly, the more negligently someone acts, the easier it is to attribute remote or unforeseeable consequences. Someone who intentionally injures someone else has to answer for all direct consequences, whether they are likely or not: 'intention to injure the plaintiff disposes of any question of remoteness'.[5] This means that the damage does not need to be foreseeable, but rather that all damage directly flowing from the intentional act is recoverable. For example, the idea in the English tort of deceit is that ' . . . as between fraudster and the innocent party, moral considerations militate in favour of requiring the fraudster to bear the risk of misfortunes directly caused by his fraud'.[6] And in the framework of § 826 BGB (intentional infliction of harm *contra bonos mores*) the German courts tend to accept rather remote consequences as damage once the other requirements have been proven.[7] The only limitation is that the scope of the rule test is applied in this instance.[8]

Fourthly, negligence elements such as the scope of the duty or the scope of the rule absorb a number of causation issues. For example, if a rule does not protect against pure economic loss, the causation issue will never rise (nr 714 and 906-1).

---

[4] Van Gerven (2000), 466.
[5] *Quinn v Leathem* [1901] AC 495, 537. In the same sense BGH 27 January 1981, BGHZ 79, 259, 262: ' . . . vorsätzlich herbeigeführte Tatfolgen sind immer adäquat'. Von Bar (2000), N 457–459.
[6] *Smith New Court Securities Ltd v Scrimgeour Vickers (Asset Management) Ltd* [1997] AC 254, 279–280, per Steyn LJ.   [7] Münchener Kommentar-Wagner (2004), § 826 N 5f.
[8] Kötz-Wagner (2001), N 199; Münchener Kommentar-Wagner (2004), § 826 N 27.

Fifthly, causation is influenced by the kind of loss, more specifically by the character of the infringed right or interest. Causation is more easily established in cases of death and personal injury than in cases of property damage or pure economic loss. One may think of the maxim 'the tortfeasor takes the victim as he finds him' one the on hand (nr 1112), and the *English Wagon Mound* case on the other (nr 1104).

Finally, the causation requirement is also closely connected to contributory negligence. Lord Atkin said: 'I find it impossible to divorce any theory of contributory negligence from the concept of causation.'[9] If the claimant has contributed to the damage this will lead to a reduction in the amount of compensation to which he is entitled. This reduction is often related to the claimant's causal contribution to the damage (nr 1212–1215).

The problem of defining causation also leads to complications when comparing the causation requirement in the different jurisdictions. What is being regarded as a causation question in France might be a duty question in England and a scope question in Germany. One may particularly think of the so-called *Cable* cases about loss caused to people and businesses depending on the delivery of gas or electricity. In England the issue will be dealt with under the question of whether the person who damaged the cable owed the victim a duty of care. In Germany the question will be whether the author of the damage has infringed one of the rights protected by § 823 I. In France, however, the filters of duty of care and protected interests do not exist and thus the limits of liability have to be found in the requirement of causation (nr 1105).

It can be concluded that the territory for causation depends on the way the liability battle is played as regards negligence and stricter cause on the one hand, and damage on the other. This explains why causation does not have a shape of its own. It is an elastic feature which can be stretched and shrunk according to the magnitude of the other requirements. The fact that the burden of proof as regards causation can be (partially) shifted from the claimant to the defendant (nr 1107) adds further to the flexible concept of causation.

1102 Establishing and limiting causation; factual and legal causation

Generally, a distinction is made between establishing causation and limiting causation. The first issue refers to the question of whether a causal connection can be *established* between the negligent conduct or the strict cause on the one hand, and the loss on the other. In order to establish causation all jurisdictions apply the *conditio sine qua non* test. This test literally means: condition without which the damage would not have occurred. In the Anglo-American systems this

---

[9] Lord Atkin in *Caswell v Powell Duffryn Associated Collieries Ltd* [1940] AC 152, 165.

test is usually known as the *but for* test. The key question in this test is: would the damage also have occurred if the tortfeasor had not acted in the way he did?[10] If the answer is negative, the requirement of causation is met. If the answer is yes, the causal connection is not established. In many cases the test is rather easy to apply. For example, if a driver collides with a pedestrian at a crossing it will be clear that the driver has caused physical damage to the pedestrian: the latter would not have suffered damage if the driver had stopped in time.

Though at first sight the test is rather simple, a closer look reveals a number of problems. As regards establishing causation these problems are twofold. Firstly, the claimant can be in a difficult and sometimes impossible position to prove causation if there are two or more possible causes for his damage. Secondly, the *conditio sine qua non* test only provides for an all-or-nothing solution: it does not provide a solution for cases in which the defendant has caused the claimant to lose a chance, for example to win a tournament or to be cured from a disease. In these cases, policy considerations have invoked the courts to look for ways to deviate from the *conditio sine qua non* test. These will be discussed in more detail in nr 1107–1110.

Once causation has been established, the work is not yet finished. In many cases it has only just begun. This refers to the second issue of limiting causation. The problem is that the test to establish liability accepts all events and circumstances as possible *causes* regardless whether they are a legally relevant or irrelevant cause.[11] For example, an important 'cause' for an accident is that the tortfeasor is at that place at that time. If his neighbour had not asked him something when he had left the house ten minutes before, he would not have been at the place of the accident at that very moment. However, the neighbour's conduct is not considered to be a relevant legal cause. In the end, this all goes back to Adam and Eve's sin in paradise. As Vaisey J once said: 'The argument in the old fable in which the loss of a kingdom is traced back to an originating and ultimate cause in the loss of a single nail from a horse's shoe does not commend itself to me as adaptable to this case.'[12]

Another problem is that the *conditio sine qua non* test considers all *consequences* as equal regardless whether they are likely or unlikely, foreseeable or unforeseeable, direct or remote. One may think of an electricity mains cable that is negligently cut, causing damage not only to the owner of the cable but also to a neighbouring tile factory which cannot operate for some time. As a consequence the factory cannot deliver to the constructors and thus the constructor is not able to finish the house within the time limit agreed with his customer. Finally, the customer has to put up at a hotel where he gets seriously injured in a fire. For all these consequences the broken main is *conditio sine qua non* but the legal systems limit the consequences for which the tortfeasor has to answer.

---

[10] Article 3:101 PETL: 'An activity or conduct (hereafter: activity) is a cause of the victim's damage if, in the absence of the activity, the damage would not have occurred.'
[11] Von Bar (2000), N 437.
[12] Vaisey J in *Norris v William Moss & Sons Ltd* [1954] 1 WLR 346, 351.

The instruments used to limit the consequences are manifold: reasonable foreseeability, probability, scope of the rule, and the directness of the consequential damage (nr 1103–1106). These are the mythical formulae applied by the national priests of tort law to avert the dangers of consequences going too far for the tortfeasor. Behind the masks of these tests policy reasons play a significant role.[13] For example, an important policy consideration acknowledged throughout the legal systems is that protection of personal injury victims is considered to be of a higher importance than the protection of someone who only suffered property loss or a pure economic loss (nr 1111).

The *conditio sine qua non* test is generally considered to focus on *factual* causation, whereas the problem about limiting causation is also indicated as *legal* causation.[14] This distinction is, however, not clear cut. Though the *conditio sine qua non* test is in many ways factual, the deviation from the test in multi-causation cases, in particular, is driven by legal and policy considerations (nr 1107–1110). Also the selection of relevant and not relevant causes in the framework of the *conditio sine qua non* test can be considered to be of a legal character: not all causes of the damage are considered as relevant, only the ones related to negligent conduct or the cause for which the defendant is liable.[15]

Section B will provide an overview of the various legal systems (nr 1103–1106). Subsequently, a couple of issues regarding the *conditio sine qua non* test will be further analysed in section C: the burden of proof of causation (nr 1107), multiple causes (nr 1108–1109) and loss of a chance (nr 1110). Finally, section D is about the question how legal systems deal with unlikely and unexpected consequences: on the one hand how they limit the consequences for which the tortfeasor has to answer (nr 1111) and on the other how they extend these consequences following the maxim *the tortfeasor takes the victim as he finds him* (nr 1112).

B CAUSATION IN THE LEGAL SYSTEMS

1103 Germany

1103-1 *Adequacy theory*

German tort law distinguishes between two aspects of causation: the liability-founding causation (*haftungsbegründende Kausalität*) and the liability-specifying causation (*haftungsausfüllende Kausalität*).

---

[13] See, *inter alia*, Kötz-Wagner (2001), N 156, with regard to the scope-of-the-rule tenet: 'Vielfach fungiert diese Lehre nur als verbale Umrahmung für normative Überlegungen, die in Wahrheit für die Schadenszurechnung in jeder Gruppe typischer Fälle maßgeblich sind.' (Often this tenet only serves as the verbal framing for normative considerations which in fact are decisive for the attribution of damage in each group of typical cases.)
[14] Von Bar (2000), N 413.   [15] In this sense also von Bar (2000), N 414.

The liability-founding causation refers to the relation between the conduct and the infringement of a right (*Rechtsgutsverletzung*) and requires full proof and effective certainty that the defendant's conduct caused some kind of harm (§ 286 ZPO).

The liability-specifying causation (or the causation determining the extent of liability) refers to the relation between the infringement of a right (*Rechtsguts-verletzung*) and the ultimate damage. Unlike in § 286 ZPO, effective certainty that the accident caused the damage is not required; it is sufficient if the court has a sensible and reasonable level of conviction about causation between the loss and the damage (§ 287 ZPO).[16] The doctrine has thoroughly elaborated the distinction between these two aspects of causation even though in practice it is not always easy to make.[17]

The question as to how to limit the attribution of the consequences for which the accident is a *conditio sine qua non* is known under the heading of legal causation (*Kausalität im rechtlichen Sinne*). German authors firstly developed the adequacy theory (*Adäquanztheorie*). This theory was born around the turn of the last but one century and, as might be expected from the German doctrine, many variants of this theory have been developed. Some authors put the focus on reasonable foreseeability of the damage, some on the question of whether the cause was adequate to create the damage and others on the increase of the chance that damage will occur. In each variant the probability element plays a pre-dominant role.[18] The different approaches boil down to the principle that the defendant is only obliged to compensate harmful consequences that were rea-sonably expected or foreseeable or not very likely for an objective and optimal observer.[19]

The BGH considers the adequacy theory to be a 'filter' in order to establish which consequences should be the burden of the defendant.[20] An event is an adequate condition for a consequence

... if it has in a general and appreciable way enhanced the objective possibility of a consequence of the kind that occurred. In making the necessary assessment account is to be taken only of (a) all the circumstances recognisable by an 'optimal' observer at the time the event occurred, (b) the additional circumstances known to the originator of the condition.[21]

---

[16] See for example BGH 11 November 1997, VersR 1998, 201, 202 and BGH 28 January 2003, ZfS 2003, 287, ETL 2003, 183 (Fedtke).   [17] Von Bar (2000), N 449.

[18] In this sense also Honoré, in *International Encyclopedia of International and Comparative Law* (1971), 49, para. 80.

[19] Münchener Kommentar-Oetker (2001), § 249 N 103–113; Larenz (1987), § 27 III b, 436; Kötz-Wagner (2001), N 151.

[20] BGH 4 July 1994, NJW 1995, 126, 127. In the same sense BGH 27 January 1981, BGHZ 79, 259, 261.

[21] BGH 23 October 1951, BGHZ 3, 261 = VersR 1952, 128. See about this case Markesinis and Unberath (2002), 633–638, from which the translation is derived, and Van Gerven (2000), 399–403. See also RG 22 June 1931, RGZ 133, 126, about which Markesinis and Unberath (2002), 629–630; RG 4 July 1938, RGZ 158, 34; BGH 11 January 1972, BGHZ 58, 48,

An example is a case that is reminiscent of the better Laurel and Hardy slapsticks though its reality makes it rather sad. After separating from her husband, a wife enters into a relationship with another man. A couple of days later the furious husband demands access to the flat of this man's brother, and breaks through the main entrance and living room doors of the apartment. The brother, fearing for his life, jumps out of the window and falls 8–10 metres. He claims damages from the husband. The court of first instance did not regard the husband's act as an adequate cause for the claimant's decision to jump out of the window: it was not something the husband could have reasonably expected the brother to do (the court apparently assumed that the husband was able to have reasonable expectations at that time at all). The BGH quashed the decision, arguing that the claimant's decision to jump in order to avoid physical confrontation was indeed within the scope of reasonable reactions to the husband's extremely aggressive activity.[22]

In the longer run, the adequacy theory appeared to be insufficiently satisfactory to deal with legal causation issues. The various variants of the adequacy theory (objective or subjective knowledge, objective or subjective probability, the degree of probability, the probability of the general consequence, or the probability of the specific consequence) have made it intangible in practice, and it appeared to be unsuitable to solve all causation problems in a clear and reasonable way. Hence, the German doctrine and courts have developed the scope of the duty theory (*Schutzzweck der Norm*). See nr 1103-2.

1103-2 *Scope of the rule*

In the course of the 20th century, German lawyers developed the scope of the duty theory which focuses on the question of whether it was the purpose of the violated rule to protect the victim against the damage he has suffered (*Schutzzweck der Norm*). This theory is applied in the framework of § 823 II BGB (breach of statutory duty), § 839 (governmental liability), and § 823 I as regards safety duties (*Verkehrspflichten*), the right to business (*das Recht am Gewerbebetrieb*), and the general personality right (*allgemeine Persönlichkeitsrecht*).[23] The theory fits well into § 823 I in which the emphasis is on protected interests and in which it makes sense to restrict causation to damage to interests which are protected by the law. Honoré has called it a 'legal policy theory'.[24]

An example of the application of this protective scope theory is an accident on the highway, as a consequence of which the driver of a motor vehicle who was

---

56 = NJW 1972, 1126 = JZ 1972, 363, about which Markesinis and Unberath (2002), 144–147 and BGH 23 September 1998, VersR 1998, 1410, 1411.

[22] BGH 2 May 2002, ZfS 2002, 329, ETL 2002, 217 (Fedtke).

[23] BGH 22 April 1958, BGHZ 27, 137 = NJW 1958, 1041 = JZ 1958, 742, about which Markesinis and Unberath (2002), 652–653; BGH 2 July 1991, BGHZ 115, 84; Von Caemmerer (1956), 395–410; Kötz-Wagner (2001), N 157.

[24] Honoré, *International Encyclopedia of Comparative Law* (1971), 60, para. 97.

not involved in the accident suffered economic loss because he was delayed by the accident. A highway authority owes a duty of care towards road users as regards their safety, but, according to the BGH, if the highway authority breaches this duty and an accident occurs it is not liable for the economic loss a person suffers because of a delay: the scope of the duty to take care of road safety does not include protection against pure economic loss.[25] The BGH expressed the same opinion when impatient drivers caused damage by driving on the pavement to avoid the scene of an accident. This damage could not be imputed to the person who was responsible for the accident since it was outside the scope of the violated traffic rule.[26] Another example is the case in which an accident occurred after someone had omitted to give way, and the persons involved had an argument, as a consequence of which the victim suffered a stroke. It was held that the person who did not give way was not liable for this damage because the scope of the right-of-way rule is not to protect someone against this kind of damage.[27]

The scope of the rule theory is of particular use and interest in cases of strict liability.[28] It is less appropriate to limit the consequences of strict liability with the help of the foreseeability requirement, since this very much belongs to the framework of liability in negligence. Requiring foreseeability for causation in cases of strict liability would let in a negligence element via the backdoor of causation. Hence, the scope of the rule theory indeed seems to be a better way of limiting the consequences of strict liability.

An example is the case of the pig farmer who claimed damages after his pigs panicked because of the noise of a traffic accident close to the farm. The BGH considered that the noise was one of the risks of motorized traffic, and that the keeper of a motor vehicle in principle had to answer for the consequences on the basis of § 7 StVG (see nr 1404-2). In other words, it was the scope of § 7 StVG to also protect against the damage caused by noise. However, in the end the BGH concluded that the farmer had only himself to blame on the basis of contributory negligence because of his factory farming which made the pigs more likely to panic.[29] Kötz criticized this latter part of the decision, arguing that it was unconvincing that the court directed its criticism at the modern way of pig-breeding while letting the modern motorized traffic have its way. In his opinion

[25] BGH 18 December 1972, NJW 1973, 463; see also BGH 27 May 1963, BGHZ 39, 358 = NJW 1963, 1821 = JZ 1963, 707, about which Markesinis and Unberath (2002), 615–617. BGH 6 June 1989, BGHZ 107, 359 = NJW 1989, 2616 = JZ 1989, 1069, about which Markesinis and Unberath (2002), 835–839; BGH 22 April 1958, BGHZ 27, 137 = NJW 1958, 1041 = JZ 1958, 742 about which Markesinis and Unberath (2002), 652–653; Kötz-Wagner (2001), N 160–163.
[26] BGH 16 February 1972, BGHZ 58, 162 = NJW 1972, 904 = JZ 1972, 559, about which Van Gerven (2000), 403–405 and Markesinis and Unberath (2002), 654–657.
[27] BGH 6 June 1989, BGHZ 107, 359 = NJW 1989, 2616 = JZ 1989, 1069, about which Markesinis and Unberath (2002), 835–839. Kötz-Wagner (2001), N 160 with many other examples in N 161–163.   [28] Kötz-Wagner (2001), N 359.
[29] BGH 2 July 1991, BGHZ 115, 84, about which Van Gerven (2000), 405–406.

it should have been decisive whether pig farms or motor vehicles were customary at that place.[30]

Another case was about a helicopter of the German army that flew over a building; as a consequence of the air pressure a part of the roof fell in. The BGH granted the claim of the owner of the building on the basis of § 33 LuftVG (Air Traffic Act),[31] considering that the key issue was '... whether the injury represented a specific manifestation of the danger against which the general public was meant to be indemnified, according to the liability regime.'[32]

On the basis of the scope of the rule theory, quite unlikely consequences can also be attributed to the defendant. Generally, the author of the damage cannot invoke particular vulnerabilities of the victim: he has to take the victim as he finds him.[33] In other words, remote consequences are attributed to the defendant, unless they are the materialization of the general risks of life (*das allgemeine Lebensrisiko*), also referred to as 'sphere of the risk' theory.[34] Examples of more remote consequences are cases in which a person is injured in an accident and more seriously injured in a second one that happens on his way to hospital, or he is more seriously harmed by an infection during his stay at the hospital. The consequences of the more serious harm will generally be attributed to the first defendant.[35] Another example is the florist who is injured in an accident, as a consequence of which his flowers did not get attention during his stay in hospital. The defendant will have to answer for this extra damage.[36]

Exceptional cases in which no causation was established were the overly nervous

[30] Kötz-Wagner (2001), N 360b:

Wenig einleuchtend ist (...), daß der BGH die ganze Schale seines Zorns über die moderne Massentierhaltung ausgegossen hat, den modernen Kraftverkehr hingegen ganz ungeschoren davonkommen ließ. Es sollte für die Haftung darauf ankommen, ob in der Gegend, in der es zu dem Unfall kam, der Betrieb von Kraftfahrzeugen oder die Schweinezucht 'ortsüblich' war.

[31] § 33 LuftVG: 'Wird beim Betrieb eines Luftfahrzeuges durch Unfall jemand getötet, sein Körper oder seine Gesundheit verletzt oder eine Sache beschädigt, so ist der Halter des Luftfahrzeuges verpflichtet, den Schaden zu ersetzen.'

[32] BGH 27 January 1981, BGHZ 79, 259, about which Van Gerven (2000), 549–550, from which the translation is derived.

[33] BGH 29 February 1956, BGHZ 20, 137, 139 = VersR 1956, 305, about which Markesinis and Unberath (2002), 665–668; BGH 6 June 1989, BGHZ 107, 359, 363 = NJW 1989, 2616 = JZ 1989, 1069, about which Markesinis and Unberath (2002), 835–839; BGH 30 April 1996, BGHZ 132, 341, 345 = NJW 1996, 2425 = VersR 1996, 990 = JZ 1996, 1080; BGH 11 November 1997, BGHZ 137, 142 = NJW 1998, 810 = JZ 1998, 680 = VersR 1998, 200 = JZ 1998, 680, about which Markesinis and Unberath (2002), 668–673.

[34] Matthias Mädrich, *Das allgemeine Lebensrisiko* (Berlin: Duncker & Humblot: 1980); Larenz (1987), § 27 III b, 439; Kötz-Wagner (2001), N 167; BGH 1 June 1959, BGHZ 30, 154; BGH 22 April 1958, BGHZ 27, 137 = NJW 1958, 1041 = JZ 1958, 742 about which Markesinis and Unberath (2002), 652–653; BGH 9 July 1985, BGHZ 95, 199.

[35] RG 13 October 1922, RGZ, 105, 264, about which Markesinis and Unberath (2002), 628–629; see also BGH 15 April 1966, VersR 1966, 658.

[36] BGH 15 April 1966, VersR 1966, 658.

woman who collapsed because of a barking non-dangerous dog and the man who had a stroke following a minor verbal altercation.[37]

It was at an early stage that the BGH emphasized that the adequacy theory and the scope of the rule theory are in fact not real causation theories but tools to establish the consequences for which the defendant has to answer. In the end, policy choices play a decisive role, particularly in borderline cases.[38]

The German doctrine has produced many interesting ideas about causation. However, the legal writers are far from unanimous as regards the question of which causation theory or concept is to be preferred.[39] The courts do not take a position in this domestic conflict. They just select the concept that provides the most convincing tool to deal with the causation issue in order to decide the individual case. The diverging commentaries on the case law also make clear that the application of a certain causation theory does not necessarily lead to the same results. This casts some doubt on the value of developing causation theories and concepts in this area (nr 1100). The main benefit of it seems to be to feed the judiciary with arguments and possible convincing solutions to the problem, of which it then may choose the one it deems to fit the present case.

1104 England

The factual causal connection between the negligent conduct and the damage is established on the basis of the *more likely than not* test. This test, which is also described as the *balance of probabilities* test, implies that liability is established when the probability is over 50 per cent and that no liability exists when the probability is 50 per cent or lower.[40] Complete certainty about causation is not required, and generally the victim will benefit from this rule.

The issue of limiting causation is described as *legal causation* or *remoteness of damage*, and in the US as *proximate cause*. English law first took the view that, if a reasonable man had foreseen any damage as likely to result from his act, he is liable for the direct consequences suffered by the claimant. The *Re Polemis* case was about stevedores who negligently allowed a plank to fall into the hold of a ship. This caused a spark resulting in a fire that destroyed the ship. In this case, the Court of Appeal held that foreseeability of some damage resulting from allowing the plank to fall was sufficient for causation.[41]

[37] RG 9 December 1907, JW 1908, 41 (barking dog); BGH 3 February 1976, NJW 1976, 1143, 1144.
[38] BGH 23 October 1951, BGHZ 3, 261, 267 = VersR 1952, 128, about which Markesinis and Unberath (2002), 633–638; BGH 1 June 1959, BGHZ 30, 154, 157; BGH 4 July 1994, NJW 1995, 126, 127; BGH 11 November 1997, BGHZ 137, 142 = NJW 1998, 810 = VersR 1998, 200 = JZ 1998, 680, about which Markesinis and Unberath (2002), 668–673.
[39] Larenz (1987), 455–457.
[40] Markesinis and Deakin (2003), 189. See *Barnett v Chelsea and Kensington Hospital* [1969] 1 QB 428 and *Bolitho v City and Hackney Health Authority* [1998] AC 232.
[41] *Re Polemis and Furness, Withy & Co* [1921] 3 KB 560.

In 1961 the Privy Council slightly tightened the ties in *The Wagon Mound (No. 1)*. In Sydney harbour, oil was discharged from a ship in a negligent way. After some time the oil became mixed in the harbour basin with cotton oddments. Welding activities in the neighbourhood caused the mixture to catch fire. The fire caused severe damage to a wharf and ships. Viscount Simonds said: 'It is a principle of liability (. . .) that a man must be considered to be responsible for the probable consequences of his act. To demand more of him is too harsh a rule.'[42] It was held that harmful consequences are *too remote* if they were unforeseeable for a reasonable person. The case is explained by the fact that damage by pollution was foreseeable, but damage by fire was not because it was established to be not foreseeable that fuel oil spread on water would catch fire.[43] Hence, since *The Wagon Mound (No. 1)*, it is no longer required that the reasonable man could have foreseen any damage as likely to result from his act. It is decisive whether he could have foreseen that damage of some type or kind of damage would ultimately be suffered, in this case damage through pollution. It is not necessary that the extent of the damage was foreseeable.

Despite this seemingly reluctant approach, foreseeability of consequences is often accepted even if they occur in an unusual way, particularly in personal injury cases. In fact, it can be argued that the *Re Polemis* rule governs this area: as long as some kind of personal injury or harm was foreseeable, the extent of the damage is no longer relevant.[44]

In *Hughes v Lord Advocate*, workmen had opened a manhole to maintain underground telephone equipment. After work, they left the manhole uncovered, with a tent and red warning paraffin lamps beside it. An 8-year-old boy went into the tent with one of the lamps. After dropping or accidentally knocking over one of the lamps an explosion occurred, which threw the boy into the hole and injured him severely. The claim against the employer's workers was dismissed by the court of first instance and the Court of Appeal but the House of Lords allowed the claim. In his leading speech Lord Guest said:

... it is sufficient if the accident which occurred is of a type which should have been foreseeable by a reasonable careful person (. . .); the precise concatenation of circumstances need not be envisaged. Concentration has been placed in the courts below on the explosion which, it was said, could not have been foreseen because it was caused in a unique fashion by the paraffin forming into vapour and being ignited by the naked flame of the wick. But this, in my opinion, is to concentrate on what is really a non-essential element in the dangerous situation created by the allurement.[45]

---

[42] Viscount Simonds in *Overseas Tankship (UK) Ltd v Morts Dock & Engineering Co (The Wagon Mound No. 1)* [1961] AC 388, 422–423 (PC).

[43] Winfield and Jolowicz (2002), paras 6.15 and 6.18; Markesinis and Deakin (2003), 207.

[44] Markesinis and Deakin (2003), 207. This also exemplifies the egg-shell skull principle, implying that the tortfeasor has to take the victim as he finds him (nr 1112). In cases of property damage and pure economic loss, causation is approached in a more reluctant way: see Markesinis and Deakin (2003), 210–213.

[45] *Hughes v Lord Advocate* [1963] AC 837, about which Van Gerven (2000), 411–412. See also *Smith v Leech Brain & Co Ltd* [1962] QB 405; *Jolley v Sutton London Borough Council* [2000] 1

The foreseeability test is even applied in cases of strict liability, for example in the *Rule in Rylands v Fletcher* and in cases of nuisance.[46] This is peculiar because foreseeability is strongly intertwined with the negligence requirement (nr 810). For this reason other jurisdictions consider foreseeability and strict liability not to sit very well together (nr 1103-2 and 1105).

Though the foreseeability test has a dominant position in English causation law it does not have a monopoly. Other techniques are also applied to restrict causation, including the scope of the rule theory. The House of Lords has emphasized ' ... that in deciding the scope of the defendant's liability for the consequences of his wrong it is necessary to consider the nature of the loss against which the legal rule in question is designed to keep the claimant harmless.'[47] Furthermore, it should be borne in mind that causation issues are prevented from arising by the requirements set for the existence of a duty of care. Specifically, a duty of care is conditional upon there being sufficient 'proximity' between the parties prior to the commission of the tort, and whether it would be 'fair, just, and reasonable' to impose a duty of care (nr 714-1). Moreover, pure policy considerations can also explicitly play a role in denying causation.[48]

A good example is *Meah v McCreamer*. A young man sustained brain damage in a road accident, which caused him to brutally attack women. For these crimes he was sentenced to life imprisonment. The man tried to recover the damages he had to pay to the women from the person liable for the road accident. Indeed, the defendant was held liable for the fact that the claimant was sentenced to life imprisonment. However, his claim for compensation for the damages he had to pay to the women was rejected. In this respect it was considered that no one should profit from his own crime.[49]

WLR 1082. See also Lord Denning MR in *Stewart v West African Terminals Ltd* [1964] 2 Lloyd's Rep. 371, 375:

It is not necessary that the precise concatenation of circumstances should be envisaged. If the consequence was one which was within the general range which any reasonable person might foresee (and was not of an entirely different kind which no one would anticipate) then it is within the rule that a person who has been guilty of negligence is liable for the consequences.

See furthermore Hart and Honoré, op. cit., 6.

[46] See as regards the *Rule in Rylands v Fletcher*: *Cambridge Water Co Ltd v Eastern Counties Leather plc* [1994] 2 AC 264, about which nr 1414-2. See as regards nuisance: *Overseas Tankship (UK) Ltd v Miller Steamship Co Pty Ltd. (The Wagon Mound No. 2)* [1967] AC 617 (PC).

[47] Winfield and Jolowicz (2002), para. 6.23, referring to *Nykredit Mortgage Bank Plc v Edward Erdman Group Ltd (No. 2)* [1997] 1 WLR 1627, 1638 at which Lord Hoffmann denied that this is a matter of causation. The scope issue also plays a role within the framework of the breach of statutory duty which requires the courts to examine whether the harm suffered by the claimant falls within the scope of protection of the statute (nr 902-3).

[48] See for an overview Winfield and Jolowicz (2002), para. 6.23 ff.

[49] *Meah v McCreamer (No. 2)* [1986] 1 All ER 943. See also *W v Meah* [1986] 1 All ER 935, in which case aggravated damages were awarded (nr 1200). Comparable from a causation point of view is BGH 8 May 1979, NJW 1979, 1654: a 14-year-old boy sustained brain damage as the consequence of an accident which *inter alia* resulted in a significant change of personality, sexual disorders, and ending up keeping 'bad company'; the Oberlandesgericht (Court of Appeal) established the causal connection with the accident and this decision was upheld by the BGH.

Overall, when deciding upon questions of causation, as is the case in other issues of liability, English judges claim they are applying common sense standards. 'Causation is to be understood as the man in the street, and not as either the scientist or the metaphysician would understand it.'[50]

1105   France

French law simply requires that a causal connection needs to be certain and direct (*certain et directe*).[51] This rule stems from article 1151 CC, a provision in the section on the law of contract. In practice it has appeared difficult to draw a line between direct and indirect causes and between certain and uncertain causes.[52] Generally, the requirement rarely leads to inherent restrictions of the scope of liability and very often the generous conclusion is that a causal link is established.[53] An example is the case of a tram company that lost income when the tramlines were blocked because of a traffic accident. The *Cour de cassation* held that this loss was an immediate and direct consequence of the traffic accident.[54] An example of a case in which the loss was not considered to be a direct consequence was when someone's debtor was killed in a car accident and the heirs of the debtor refused to accept the inheritance. The creditor claimed damages from the person responsible for the death of the debtor but the *Cour de cassation* held that the causal connection was not sufficiently direct.[55]

French legal writers have not expressed a strong inclination to develop profound theories and thoughts about causation.[56] They have only developed some small scale theories, none of which has gained a firm foothold in the doctrine, and their voices are not being heard in the case law.[57] This goes, for instance, with the adequacy theory to which legal writers sometimes refer but to which the French *Cour de cassation* has never converted itself explicitly.[58] However, in many cases the probability of damage seems to have played a decisive role in establishing causation. This is not only the case in negligence liability[59] but also

---

[50] *Yorkshire Dale Steamship Co Ltd v Minister of War Transport* [1942] AC 691, 706 per Lord Wright.
[51] Le Tourneau (2004), nr 1719. See for instance Civ. 2e 3 October 1990, Bull. civ. II, no 184, about which Van Gerven (2000), 422; civ. 2e 20 June 1985, Bull. civ. II no 125, about which Van Gerven (2000), 424.   [52] Viney-Jourdain (1998), nr 348.
[53] Viney-Jourdain (1998), nr 353–355.
[54] Civ. 28 April 1965, D 1965. 777, comm. Esmein.
[55] Civ. 2e 21 February 1979, JCP 1979. IV. 145. See also Civ. 2e 12 June 1987, JCP 1987. IV. 286.
[56] Viney-Jourdain (1998), nr 335 speaks about '. . . le refus de toute effort systématique de définition.'
[57] See for instance the explanatory theory which seems to be related to the adequacy theory: Aubry and Rau-Dejean de la Bathie (1989), § 444ter; Viney-Jourdain (1998), nr 346-1; Van Gerven (2000), 419–420.   [58] Le Tourneau (2004), nr 1716; Viney-Jourdain (1998), nr 338-340.
[59] See for instance Civ. 2e 20 December 1972, JCP 1973. II. 17541, comm. Dejean de la Bathie, about which Van Gerven (2000), 425.

in the framework of strict liability (article 1384 s. 1). If, for instance, a thing has caused damage but has only played a passive role, causation can be denied for the reason that the thing was not the legal cause of the damage and the damage was a *conséquence normale*.[60]

In the framework of strict liability, elements of the adequacy theory and the foreseeability requirement play a role, albeit a modest one.[61] This is particularly the case as regards the defence of an external cause (*cause étrangère*). Such a cause can be established if the event was external, unforeseeable, and unavoidable (*externe, imprévisible, insurmontable*). The causal link can also be broken by proof of a *faute* of the victim or a *faute* of a third party, provided that the *faute* was an external cause for the defendant.

The scope theory is rarely applied in the framework of causation though there are some decisions in which the theory seems to have been applied implicitly. For instance, when a firework was sold to persons under the legal age and the firework caused a fire, the *Cour de cassation* denied causation. However, if personal injury had been caused, causation would have been established.[62]

Causation is an important control mechanism for keeping liability in French law within limits (nr 604-3). This happens, for example, if third parties suffer damage because of someone's personal injury. An example is the case of the concert organizer who tried to claim money from the person who was liable for the accident which caused a singer to cancel a concert. The *Cour de cassation* deemed his damage to be indirect and dismissed the claim.[63] See also nr 712. In other legal systems a similar solution could be reached by applying the purposive scope of the rule theory: the purpose of the rule not to injure another person is to protect that person and not the economic loss of third parties. This reasoning, however, can hardly be said to be more transparent than the French requirement that the damage has to be directly caused. Both requirements cover the policy reasons behind the decision, which is to keep the tortfeasor's burden within limits.

1106 European Union

A clear communitarian concept of causation does not yet exist. In its case law the ECJ has developed a framework concerning liability for breach of Community law (nr 205–206), of which causation is one of the obvious requirements next to a sufficiently serious breach and damage.[64]

---

[60] Viney-Jourdain (1998), nr 332 ff.; Van Gerven (2000), 454.
[61] Viney-Jourdain (1998), nr 403.
[62] Civ. 8 April 1986, D. 1986. IR. 312. See also Civ. 3e 2 July 1974, D. 1975. 61, about which Van Gerven (2000), 426–427. See also von Bar (2000), N 475.
[63] Civ. 2e 14 November 1958, Gaz. Pal. 1959. 1. 31.
[64] A.G. Toth, 'The Concepts of Damage and Causality as Elements of Non-Contractual Liability', in T. Heukels and A. McDonnell, *The Action for Damages in Community Law* (1997),

As in all national jurisdictions, the basic requirement for causation is that the *conditio sine qua non* test or *but for* test is met. Causation is not established if the same damage would have occurred in the same way in the absence of the wrongful Community act or omission in question.[65] In cases of omissions, causation is established if the consequences would not have occurred provided the affirmative action had been carried out.[66]

Passing the *conditio sine qua non* test is not sufficient to draw conclusions as regards causation. In many cases the consequences for which the defendant has to answer have to be restricted. In their Opinions, some Advocates-General have pointed out that Community law requires adequate causation, but these thoughts have not been further elaborated.[67] Though there are also decisions in which the ECJ requires a sufficient level of foreseeability or probability, in most cases the ECJ requires a direct link between the breach and the damage. In *Bergaderm*, in which the ECJ set out the three requirements for Community liability, it held not only that the breached rule must confer rights on individuals and that the breach must be sufficiently serious, but also that there must be a direct causal link between the breach of the obligation and the damage sustained by the injured party.[68]

In this respect the court seems to be inspired by the way the French *Cour de cassation* deals with causation issues (nr 1105). In its application, however, the Court has proved to be more reluctant than its French counterpart. An explanation for this reluctance is that the case law of the ECJ is mainly related to cases of pure economic loss and liability of public authorities. In these kinds of cases, national courts are usually reluctant to award damages. Particularly in the framework of liability for legislative acts, the ECJ generally takes a restrictive view:

In the field of non-contractual liability of public authorities for legislative measures, the principles common to the laws of the Member States to which the second paragraph of Article [288] of the EEC Treaty refers cannot be relied on to deduce an obligation to make good every harmful consequence, even a remote one, of unlawful legislation.[69]

179–198; Wolfgang Wurmnest, *Grundzüge eines europäischen Haftungsrecht*, (Tübingen: Mohr, 2003), 159–191.

[65] ECJ 7 April 1992, Case C-358/90, ECR 1992, I-2457, 2505 (*Compagnia Italiana Alcool v Commission*).

[66] CFI 6 July 1995, Cases T-572/93, ECR 1995, II-2025, 2050 (*Odigitria v Council and Commission*); CFI 18 September 1995, Case T-167/94, ECR 1995, II-2589, 2624 (*Nölle v Council and Commission*); CFI 25 June 1997, Case T-7/96, ECR 1997, II-1061, 1076 (*Perillo v Commission*).

[67] See for instance AG Gand, ECJ 14 July 1967, Cases 5, 7, 13–24/66, ECR 1967, 245, 284 (*Kampffmeyer v Commission*).

[68] ECJ 4 July 2000, Case 352/98, ECR 2000, I-5291 (*Laboratoires Pharmaceutique Bergaderm SA and Gouplin v Commission*), paras 42–44. See also ECJ 28 April 1971, Case 4/69, ECR 1971. 325, 337 (*Lütticke v Commission*); ECJ 2 July 1974, Case 153/73, ECR 1974, 675, 693 (*Holtz & Willemsen v Council*); ECJ 17 December 1981, Case 247/80, ECR 1981, 3211, 3246 (*Ludwigshafener Walzmühle v Council and Commission*); CFI 24 February 2000, Case T-178/98. ECR 2000, II-3331 (*Fresh Marine Company v Commission*).

[69] ECJ 4 October 1979, Joined Cases 64 and 113/76, 167 and 239/78, 27, 28 and 45/79, ECR 1979, 3091, 3117 (*Dumortier Frères v Council*).

As regards the burden of proof, the ECJ requires the claimant to be precise and specific in stating and proving the facts as regards causation. In a case against the Commission, Roquette alleged it had to pay compensatory amounts on the importation into France of certain products, that its foreign competitors enjoyed more favourable marketing conditions, and that this had distorted the conditions of competition to its disadvantage. This statement appeared to be too broad and too unspecific since the ECJ concluded that Roquette had failed to prove the necessary causal connection between the alleged damage and the fixing of compensatory amounts by the Commission.[70]

In *Mulder* the ECJ considered that, ' . . . in order for the Community to incur non-contractual liability, the damage alleged must go beyond the bounds of the normal economic risks inherent on the activities in the sector concerned.'[71] In other words, he must bear the damage himself if it is within his sphere and he thus would have suffered anyway in the normal course of his activities. This approach can be related to the German 'sphere of risk' theory (nr 1103-2).[72] However, it is also possible to consider it as a matter of recoverable damage in the sense that damage someone suffers in the normal course of his activities is legally not relevant and thus not recoverable. Although *Mulder* was about an unlawful act, this issue is closely related to compensation for legal acts in which the costs imposed on individuals by governmental conduct do not always have to be borne by these individuals. However, they have to bear the burden when the damage was within the bounds of normal economic risks. See nr 1806.

In Community law, the requirement of actual damage does not exclude the recoverability of a lost chance: see nr 1110-4.

C ESTABLISHING CAUSATION

1107 Shifting the burden of proof

1107-1 *Germany*

The basic rule in all jurisdictions is that the burden of proof as regards causation is on the claimant. However, they take different starting points as to *what* the claimant has to prove.

German law requires that the claimant proves the relationship between the conduct and the infringement of a right (*Rechtsverletzung* or *Rechtsgutsverletzung*) with effective certainty. Effective certainty is not required as regards the relationship between the infringement of a right and the ultimate damage

---

[70] ECJ 21 May 1976, Case 26/74, ECR 1976, 677, 687 (*Roquette v Commission*).
[71] ECJ 19 May 1992, Joined Cases C-104/89 and C-37/90, ECR 1992, I-3061 (*Mulder v Council*).   [72] Van Gerven (2000), 456.

(nr 1103-1). English law, on the other hand, in both cases applies the *more likely than not* test: causation can be established if the probability is just over 50 per cent (nr 1104).

Though German law seems to be tougher for the claimant than English law, the courts apply procedural legal techniques to relieve the claimant's burden of proof. The most well known are the notion of *res ipsa loquitur* and *prima facie* evidence, which refers to the idea that if the facts speak for themselves the court may decide that causation is so likely that it is assumed unless the defendant can rebut it or prove the opposite.[73]

Closely related to the notion of *res ipsa loquitur* and *prima facie* evidence is the so-called reversal rule. If the claimant has proved that the defendant has acted negligently by increasing the likeliness of an accident and this risk has materialized, a causal connection between the defendant's conduct and the accident is assumed and it is up to the defendant to rebut this assumption or to prove that the accident would also have occurred if he had not acted negligently.

One may think of omission cases, for example if someone hits his head on a low ceiling and the occupier of the building has failed to comply with his duty to warn of the possibility. In such cases the assumption is that the claimant would have read the warning and would have acted accordingly, and that it is up to the defendant to prove that the claimant would have ignored the warning.[74]

In Germany a reversal rule can be found in the framework of the violation of a statutory rule (*Schutzgesetzverstoß*) and the breach of a safety duty (*Verkehrs-pflicht*). If the damage is within the scope (*Schutzbereich*) of the statutory or safety duty, a causal connection between the breach and the accident is assumed (*Anscheinsbeweis*); it is then up to the defendant to prove that there is no causal connection.[75]

Perhaps the most well-known reversal rule was introduced by the BGH in the area of product liability. A vaccine for chickens turned out to be contaminated and the birds died. The cause of the contamination remained unclear and the BGH reversed the burden of proof of this causation question, as well as the question as regards *Verschulden* and *Rechtswidrigkeit*. The risk of not being able to prove the cause of the damage was no longer for the claimant but for the defendant. However, this reversal rule can only be applied if the claimant has proved that the cause of damage was of an organizational nature within the

---

[73] Von Bar (2000), N 449. These techniques are also applied in other areas such as establishing negligence (nr 804-2) and stretching negligence (nr 1004-2).

[74] Von Bar (2000), N 476:

The result of such duties to warn, to grant hearings, to provide information and to advise is that he who breaches them must demonstrate that the person concerned would have ignored the warning, opportunity, information, or advice and taken the risk in any event. (. . .). It is common European law that a doctor must prove that the victim of an unsuccessful operation would have taken the risk even with adequate information and advice.

[75] Münchener Kommentar-Wagner (2004), § 823 N 356; Deutsch-Ahrens (2002), N 275.

manufacturer's area of responsibility and if the damage occurred due to an actual defect in the product.[76]

1107-2 *France*

Under French law, there are a number of instances where there is an attenuation of the rule which places the burden of proof upon the claimant.[77]

Firstly, French courts adopt a flexible approach in allowing the claimant to establish causation by a method of proof by exclusion (*la prevue par exclusion*).[78] The argument is essentially based upon the *a contrario* logic of negative deduction: for example, where the claimant has suffered viral contamination in the aftermath of a blood transfusion, and has succeeded in showing that there were no possible causes other than the operation itself, it will be for the defendant clinic to prove that the blood product supplied was not contaminated.[79]

Secondly, whereas the general technique of 'proof by exclusion' gives rise in practice to a *rebuttable* presumption of *fact*, in certain specific cases the French courts have also decided upon a number of *legal* 'policy' presumptions which are *irrebuttable*. Several examples are available from case law. (i) Where one of the protagonists is culpable of a criminal fault (*faute pénale*), it is considered counter to public policy to allow him to escape tortious liability altogether. *De facto*, he is legally reputed to be liable for at least part of the resulting damage. It is interesting to note that this presumption is comparable to that found in the English case of *Meah v McCreamer*,[80] and that it shows a face of French tort law which often remains hidden: tort law as a punitive, conduct-regulating system. Indeed, the material domain of the presumption is arguably greater than the corresponding one in English law, due to the wide meaning of *faute penale*. For example, the presumption has been held to operate in relation to car passengers who had omitted to fasten their seatbelts.[81] (ii) As regards accidents at work, all injuries which manifest themselves at the workplace and during working hours are, by operation of law, deemed imputable to the employer.[82] (iii) Other cases where the claimant is effectively excused from having to prove causation include cases of liability in respect of buildings, where the unusual (*anormal*) role played by a building (often its explosion) is *per se* deemed conclusive of liability.[83]

---

[76] BGH 26 November 1968, BGHZ 51, 91 *Hühnerpest*; BGH 17 March 1981, BGHZ 80, 186; BGH 11 June 1996, VersR 1996, 1116. Von Bar (1998), N 277. Under the German law governing genetically modified organisms a rebuttable presumption applies that the harm was caused by the altered properties of such organisms: see § 34(1) Gentechnikgesetz. A similar rule applies to certain harm caused to the environment; see Koch and Koziol (2002), 425.

[77] See Viney-Jourdain (1998), nr 369 and 373; see also the cases mentioned in Van Gerven (2000), 428 under 4.2.3.

[78] Le Tourneau (2004), nr 1710.   [79] Civ. 1re, 9 May 2001, D. 2001. 2149, rapp Sargos.

[80] *Meah v McCreamer (No. 2)* [1986] 1 All ER 943, about which nr 1104.

[81] Civ. 2e 27 April 1979 and Civ. 2e 3 March 1979, Gaz. Pal. 1979. 2. Somm. 422; Civ. 2e 15 May 1992, Bull. civ. II, no 140.

[82] Soc. 15 November 1979, Bull. civ. V, nos 862 and 863; Soc. 3 March 1982, Bull. civ. V, nos 140 and 141.   [83] Civ. 2e 14 November 2002, Bull. civ. II, no 258.

Thirdly, the *loi Badinter* on liability for road traffic accidents goes one step further than either of the two previously mentioned techniques and it is arguably the most extreme application of the reversal rule (nr 1404-1). It is sufficient for the claimant to show that the defendant's vehicle was *implicated* in the accident; or, more (im)precisely, that it had '... intervened, in any fashion, in the production of the accident'.[84] *Implication* in the *accident* is a much lower threshold than the standard requirement of 'causation' of the *damage* itself. Indeed, it has been argued that the text of the *loi Badinter* symbolizes an outright rejection of the notion of causation since article 2 of the Act excludes *force majeure* from all considerations of liability.[85]

1107-3 *England*

English law does not accept the reversal of the burden of proof as a rule but the matter is extensively discussed, and in a number of cases the courts nevertheless have reversed the burden of proof. The first example, *McGhee v National Coal Board*, was about an employee alleging he had contracted dermatitis during his work at brick kilns. His employers admitted they had been negligent in taking precautionary measures but they argued that providing showers probably would not have prevented the illness. The House of Lords held that the breach of safety regulations by the employer had significantly increased the risk of dermatitis and allowed the claim in the absence of proof by the defendants that their breach of duty was not causative.[86] Lord Wilberforce formulated a general principle: 'It is a sound principle that where a person has, by breach of duty of care, created a risk, and injury occurs within the area of that risk, the loss should be borne by him unless he shows that it had some other cause.'[87] His view was advocated by legal authors[88] but no such rule has been acknowledged by the courts. The rule remains that the claimant has to prove causation and, if he is not able to do this satisfactorily, he has to rely on the possibility that the court accepts the proven facts as a *prima facie* evidence. This means that, on the basis of the facts presented to the court, it may decide that causation is so likely that it is assumed unless the defendant can rebut it or prove the opposite.[89]

Secondly, in *Fairchild* the House of Lords refused to adopt Lord Wilberforce's reversal rule as a general rule but the rule was accepted for cases of indivisible

[84] Civ. 2e 21 June 2000, Bull. civ. II no 122 ('... intervene, à quelque titre que ce soit, dans la survenance de l'accident').   [85] Le Tourneau (2004), nr 1718.
[86] *McGhee v National Coal Board* [1973] 1 WLR 1, [1972] 3 All ER 1008 (HL). Winfield and Jolowicz (2002), para. 6.11.
[87] Lord Wilberforce in *McGhee v National Coal Board* [1973] 1 WLR 1, [1972] 3 All ER 1008 (HL).
[88] Markesinis and Deakin (2003), 192, with reference to the American case *Summers v Tice* (1948) 119 P.2d. 1 and the Canadian hunting case *Cook v Lewis* [1951] SCR 830, (1952) 1 DLR 1, SCC. See also Winfield and Jolowicz (2002), para. 6.12.   [89] Von Bar (2000), N 449.

diseases.[90] The case was about employees who had worked for several employers, all of whom had exposed them to asbestos. As a consequence of these exposures they contracted mesothelioma but they were not able to prove by whose wrongful conduct they had contracted the disease.[91] Adhering to the traditional approach by laying the burden of proof on the claimant would be 'deeply offensive to instinctive notions of what justice requires and fairness demands.'[92] In line with *McGhee* their Lordships held that the employers' tortious acts had increased the risk of contracting a disease and that each such act can be said to have made a material contribution to the contracting of that disease. On this ground it was decided that the employees could claim damages from each employer who had wrongfully exposed them to asbestos while all employers were jointly and severally liable.[93]

Thirdly, *Chester v Afshar* was about a woman who had back surgery with a small (1–2 per cent) but unavoidable risk of even more harm when the surgery was duly carried out. The doctor did not inform her about this small risk which indeed materialized during the surgery. The trial judge found that the woman had established a causal link between the breach of the duty to inform and the injury she had sustained, where she could prove that if she had been properly informed she would not have undergone the surgery *at that moment*. This decision was upheld by the Court of Appeal and the House of Lords. The majority of the House of Lords did not consider it material that the risk could have anyway materialized in surgery at a later stage. Though the case is not entirely clear, the probable main reason was pointed out by Lord Hope:

> The function of the law is to enable rights to be vindicated and to provide remedies when duties have been breached. Unless this is done the duty is a hollow one, stripped of all practical force and devoid of all content. It will have lost its ability to protect the patient and thus to fulfil the only purpose which brought it into existence.[94]

Despite the fact that the courts have made exceptions to the rule that the burden of proof of causation is on the claimant (*prima facie* evidence, indivisible diseases), the reluctance to accept a general reversal rule in English law is well described by Markesinis and Deakin:

> The mere fact that [someone] was at fault in the sense of breaching a duty of care is not a good reason for imposing liability. To do so may be to impose a powerful incentive for careful behaviour on the part of defendants. But this runs up against the objection that it

---

[90] *Fairchild v Glenhaven Funeral Services Ltd. & Others* [2002] 3 All ER 305, ETL 2003, 144 (Oliphant) and the comparative case comments in *ERPL* 12 (2004) 2, 215–258.

[91] Mesothelioma is a severe form of lung cancer generally causing the death of the patient within six months of the diagnosis. The disease can only be caused by the inhalation of asbestos fibres; the incubation period is between 20 and 40 years.

[92] *Fairchild v Glenhaven Funeral Services Ltd & Others* [2002] 3 All ER 305, § 36, per Lord Nicholls.

[93] *Chester v Afshar* [2004] UKHL, 41, AC 2005 134, All ER 2004/4, 587, ETL 2004, 230 (Oliphant). [94] *Chester v Afshar* [2004] UKHL 41, § 87, per Lord Hope of Craighead.

is not the role of the tort of negligence to penalise careless behaviour *as such*. If this is seen as desirable, there may be an argument for leaving it to Parliament to achieve through statutory regulation of the kind which is widespread in relation to employer's liability.[95]

However, one can also look at this problem from a different angle. The idea behind the reversal rule is that, the more likely a causal connection between the defendant's conduct and the claimant's loss, the more justified it will be to shift the burden of proof. The justification for the rule is that, if the law imposes a duty on someone in order to prevent a certain risk, the duty would be ineffective if the person breaching the duty can escape liability if the victim cannot prove causation even though a causal connection is (very) likely.[96]

It may be concluded that differences between the legal systems should not be overestimated. English law does not hold a general reversal rule but it is more victim-friendly by establishing causation using the 'more likely than not' test. German and French law, on the other hand, have a stricter rule for establishing causation but its drawbacks are compensated by the use of the reversal rule.[97]

1108 More than one possible cause

1108-1 *Comparative overview*

Damage always has more than one factual cause and usually the question is: what is the legal cause for the damage? (nr 1102). However, there are also cases in which there is more than one legal cause for the damage, for example if the damage can be caused by more than one tortfeasor.[98] These tortfeasors can have acted with a common design, for instance vandals throwing stones at passers-by and one of the stones hits a person's head. They can also have acted severally without a common design. One may think of hunters firing, one of the bullets hitting another person, or a defective drug put into circulation by a number of manufacturers. In all these cases, the victim's problem is to prove causation by identifying the person who caused the damage.

Closely related are cases in which it is certain that more than one person has caused the same damage, for example when someone is hit by two bullets fired by

---

[95] Markesinis and Deakin (2003), 190.

[96] In this sense also Lord Hope of Craighead in *Chester v Afshar* [2004] UKHL 41, § 87, as regards the more limited question whether the causation test was satisfied when a doctor had failed to inform a patient about a small but inevitable surgery risk:

The function of the law is to enable rights to be vindicated and to provide remedies when duties have been breached. Unless this is done the duty is a hollow one, stripped of all practical force and devoid of all content. It will have lost its ability to protect the patient and thus to fulfil the only purpose which brought it into existence.

[97] Von Bar (2000), N 449.

[98] See for a more extensive comparative view on this issue W.V. Horton Rogers (ed.), *Unification of Tort Law: Multiple Tortfeasors* (The Hague, London, New York: Kluwer, 2004).

two people, where either bullet could have been fatal (alternative causes). In such a situation both can argue that the *conditio sine qua non* test is not met, since the damage would have occurred anyway because of the other tortfeasor's conduct.[99]

The position is different if two independent events did not cause the same damage. One may think of someone who is hit by two bullets, one in each leg. If it can be identified who caused which damage—for example because they used different guns—each of the tortfeasors is liable for the damage he caused. In all jurisdictions each tortfeasor is liable for the damage he actually caused.[100]

German law possesses two provisions to tackle multiple causation problems. § 830 I 1 BGB holds that, when two or more persons have caused injury through an unlawful act which they committed jointly, they are jointly and severally liable for the damage. The BGH has strongly limited the scope of application by requiring that the participants knowingly and intentionally co-operated to cause the damage. If this is the case, the sole psychological support (*psychisch vermittelte Kausalität*) is sufficient for establishing causation.[101] In cases of large scale demonstrations § 830 I 1 only applies to protesters who have exercised violence in an active way. The mere fact that they participated in a demonstration is not sufficient for establishing liability, an approach inspired by the need to protect the constitutional freedom of assembly (Article 8 *Grundgesetz*).[102]

§ 830 I 2 BGB holds tortfeasors severally liable if, independently from each other, they could have caused the same damage and it cannot be established which of them has caused the injury or to what degree. Unlike § 830 I 1, intentional cooperation is not required. This provision was, for example, applied when two people independently from one another beat a third person and it could not be established which of them caused the injuries.[103] If each potential tortfeasor could have caused the full damage, the victim does not have to prove the causal contribution of each person to the damage and the provision reverses the burden of proof as regards the *conditio sine qua non* test.[104] As a result of this

[99] Art. 3:102 PETL provides: 'In case of multiple activities, where each of them alone would have caused the damage at the same time, each activity is regarded as a cause of the victim's damage.'
[100] Van Gerven (2000), 432; Le Tourneau (2004), nr 1739; Larenz-Canaris (1994), 580–581; Winfield and Jolowicz (2002), para. 21.1.
[101] BGH 14 January 1953, BGHZ 8, 288 = NJW 1953, 499; BGH 25 May 1955, BGHZ 17, 327 = NJW 1955, 1274; BGH 4 March 1960, VersR 1960, 540; BGH 31 January 1978, BGHZ 70, 277 (labour union jointly liable with air controllers for the consequences of an unlawful strike). § 830 II equates instigators and accomplices with participants. Both for instigators and accomplices it is required that they acted (induced or helped) intentionally.
[102] BGH 24 January 1984, BGHZ 89, 383 = NJW 1984, 1226 = JZ 1984, 521, comm. Stürner; BGH 4 November 1997, BGHZ 137, 89 = NJW 1998, 377, about which Markesinis and Unberath (2002), 230–235. The author, co-authors, instigators and accomplices are jointly and severally liable on the basis of § 840 BGB (*Gesamtschuldner*), unless they can prove that their conduct did not cause the damage. They have a right of recourse towards the other tortfeasor(s).
[103] BGH 15 June 1982, NJW 1982, 2307. Münchener Kommentar-Wagner (2004), § 830, N 52.
[104] BGH 1 October 1957, BGHZ 25, 271, about which Van Gerven (2000), 444–445.

provision, persons who are connected in some way to the damage can be liable if they cannot prove that they did not have anything to do with the damage. § 830 I 2 does not apply if one of the possible causes is a natural one or lies within the sphere of the victim. The same applies if one of the possible tortfeasors is not liable, either on the basis of negligence or on the basis of strict liability.[105]

In French law damage caused by more than one possible tortfeasor is discussed under the heading of *faute collective*, a *faute* in the sense of article 1382 CC committed by more than one person. An example is a case in which hunters marked the end of their hunt with a salvo. One of the hunters, who had left the group just before the salvo, was hit by a bullet and suffered an eye injury. The collective *faute* of the hunters was considered to be the *cause réelle* of the accident.[106] The position of the claimant is strongly enhanced by the fact that he does not have to identify all possible tortfeasors, which is particularly helpful for him when there are more than just a few. He can confine himself to suing just one (insured or solvent) tortfeasor and recover the whole damage from him. He does not have to prove that there are no other tortfeasors involved.

If a collective *faute* is established, the defendants may prove that the conduct of a third party (including the victim) yields an external cause (*cause étrangère*) which was unforeseeable and unavoidable (*imprévisible et irrésistible*). If they cannot prove this they are bound *in solidum*, which means that they are each fully liable towards the victim. Each has a right of recourse towards the other tortfeasor(s).[107] A parallel to the *faute collective* is the *garde collective* in the framework of the strict liability for things (article 1384 al. 1 CC).[108]

English law does not possess a general rule to reverse the burden of proof as regards *conditio sine qua non* where the damage can be caused by more than one tortfeasor. An exception can be found in the *Fairchild* case (nr 1107-3) in which the House of Lords decided that in cases of *indivisible diseases* the burden of proof as regards causation can be shifted to the defendants, provided that their tortious acts have increased the risk of contracting a disease and that each such act can be said to have made a material contribution to the contracting of that disease.[109] In other cases of indivisible damage the traditional rule stands that the victim has to prove that the defendant caused his damage.[110] However, as has been pointed out (nr 1104), causation does not have to be certain; according to

---

[105] BGH 17 December 1952, VersR 1953, 146; BGH 30 January 1973, BGHZ 60, 177 = NJW 1973, 993. Münchener Kommentar-Wagner (2004), § 830 N 35.

[106] Civ. 2e 5 June 1957, D. 1957. 439, comm. Savatier, JCP 1957. II. 10205, comm. Esmein, about which Van Gerven (2000), 442; see furthermore Viney-Jourdain (1998), nr 378.

[107] Civ. 2e 4 March 1970, Bull. civ. 1970. II. 76, JCP 1971. II. 16585, about which Van Gerven (2000), 433; Civ. 2e 17 March 1971, D. 1971. 494, about which Van Gerven (2000), 433–434; Le Tourneau (2004), nr 1752ff; Viney-Jourdain (1998), nr 402 and 414.

[108] Civ. 2e 15 December 1980, D. 1981. 455, comm. Poisson-Drocourt; see furthermore Viney-Jourdain (1998).

[109] *Fairchild v Glenhaven Funeral Services Ltd & Others* [2002] 3 All ER 305. See also *McGhee v National Coal Board* [1973] 1 WLR 1, [1972] 3 All ER 1008 (HL) and *Wilsher v Essex Area Health Authority* [1988] 2 WLR 557 (HL).   [110] Van Gerven (2000), 431–432.

the *more likely than not* test it is sufficient if the probability was higher than 50 per cent.[111]

1108-2 *Conclusion*

If damage can be caused by two or more events for which different persons are liable, and it is certain that the damage can only have been caused by one of them, the question is how to help claimants out of the evidentiary quagmire. German and French law provide specific rules to reverse the burden of proof, whereas under English law the victim, apart from cases of invisible diseases, has to rely on the *more likely than not* test. French law further simplifies the claimant's position by not requiring that he identify and summon all possible tortfeasors.[112]

A justification for relieving the burden of proof is that it is not reasonable to dismiss a claim just because the victim cannot prove causation while it is certain that all tortfeasors have acted wrongfully and at least one of them has caused the damage. An interesting example in this respect is the Dutch *DES* case, which gained international attention and was also mentioned in the English *Fairchild* case.[113] The case is illustrative for the way in which courts have to balance the interests of claimant and defendants and for the policy choices that can be made.

DES was a defective drug which was put onto the market by a large number of manufacturers (pharmacists were also allowed to produce DES) and which caused damage to a large number of plaintiffs. The drug was intended to protect against premature birth and was used by pregnant women in the 1940s, 1950s and 1960s. Their daughters and sons suffered from fertility problems and their daughters had a high risk of cervical cancer. The claimants could not prove from which manufacturer they had obtained DES.

The decision of the Dutch Supreme Court (*Hoge Raad*) was inspired by article 6:99 Dutch Civil Code (BW),[114] holding that it is required that: (a) the

---

[111] Markesinis and Deakin (2003), 189; *Barnett v Chelsea and Kensington Hospital* [1969] 1 QB 428; *Bolitho v City and Hackney Health Authority* [1998] AC 232. If the tortfeasors caused the same damage they are *several concurrent tortfeasors* if they acted independently from each other. They are *joint tortfeasors* if they acted with a common design. See *Brooke v Bool* [1928] 2 KB 578; *CBS Songs Ltd v Amstrad Consumer Electronics plc*. [1988] AC 1013. Markesinis and Deakin (2003), 850.

[112] In Article 3:103(1) PETL an intermediate solution was chosen: 'In case of multiple activities, where each of them alone would have been sufficient to cause the damage, but it remains uncertain which one in fact caused it, each activity is regarded as a cause to the extent corresponding to the likelihood that it may have caused the victim's damage.'

[113] HR 9 October 1992, NJ 1994, 535, comm. CJHB (DES), about which Van Gerven (2000), 447–452. Compare von Bar (1998), N 319 ff.

[114] Article 6:99 BW:

Where the damage may have resulted from two or more events for each of which a different person is liable, and where it has been determined that the damage has arisen from at least one of these events, the obligation to repair the damage rests upon each of these persons, unless he proves that the damage is not the result of the event for which he himself is liable.

This provision entered into force on 1 January 1992 and did not apply to this case but the *Hoge Raad* considered that the provision reflected the law as it stood as from the 1940s.

summoned manufacturers[115] had put DES into circulation in the relevant period and that they had acted unlawfully for doing this; (b) that other producers also had put DES into circulation in the relevant period and that they were also liable for doing that; and (c) that the claimant has suffered damage as a consequence of using DES but that it cannot be established from which manufacturer the used DES was obtained. If these requirements are met, the summoned parties are jointly and severally liable, unless this was unacceptable from a reasonableness point of view in the given circumstances. A relevant factor in this respect is the probability that the damage to the victim is caused by an event for which no liable person can be determined.

The decision was clearly in favour of the claimants who were in an impossible position to prove causation and, inevitably, it has caused mixed reactions. The decision was, for instance, criticized for the fact that the manufacturer could be liable for a larger amount of damage than he could have caused.[116] This could have been prevented by choosing a kind of market share liability which means that an identified producer is only liable for the percentage of the damage that corresponds with its market share.[117] However, this would have compelled victims to claim damages from all manufacturers in order to get fully compensated, and in practice they would probably have confined themselves to the companies with the largest market share to recover the biggest chunk of their damage. This could be unfair in the sense that only the big companies have to pay and the smaller ones do not. A solution for this would be to require all manufacturers to pay into a fund according to their market share. This problem is typical for what are called mass torts: torts that cause damage to a high number of people, often because of a defective product.

1109   Successive causes

1109-1   *Second event would have caused same damage as first event*

In the above-mentioned cases the causes were indivisible since it was not possible to establish who caused the damage and to what extent. There are also cases in which the events occur successively or in which at least a sequence of events can be distinguished. Examples are the pedestrian who is hit by a car and, before he

---

[115] Just as in French law the *Hoge Raad* held that it was not required that the claimant identify and summon all possible liable persons.

[116] See for an overview Van Gerven, 449 comm. 227.

[117] As the Californian Supreme Court decided in *Sindell v Abbott Laboratories* (1980), 607 P.2d 924. This was also a case about the liability of the manufacturers of DES. This solution is also advocated in Article 3:103(2) PETL:

If, in case of multiple victims, it remains uncertain whether a particular victim's damage has been caused by an activity, while it is likely that it did not cause the damage of all victims, the activity is regarded as a cause of the damage suffered by all victims in proportion to the likelihood that it may have caused the damage of a particular victim.

can be rescued, is hit by a second car; the victim of an accident who suffers further damage in hospital because of medical negligence by a doctor; or someone who is not able to leave a house on fire in time because of an injury caused by a previous accident.[118]

Two situations can be distinguished. Firstly, the situation in which a second event would have caused the same damage as the first event has caused. And secondly, the situation in which the second event has worsened the claimant's situation caused by the first event (nr 1109-2).

The three legal systems take similar views in that the first tortfeasor remains liable for the claimant's damage even if the second tortfeasor would have caused the same damage. In such cases the first tortfeasor will generally have a right of recourse against the second tortfeasor.[119] In Germany the problem is dealt with under the heading of overtaking causation (*überholende Kausalität*). The English case of *Baker v Willoughby* is a good example. Baker permanently injured his leg as the consequence of an accident. After a certain time his business was raided and he received bullet wounds in the same leg and it had to be amputated. The first tortfeasor argued that he only had to compensate the damage until the day of the raid because Baker had suffered the same damage because of the amputation. However, the House of Lords decided that this would yield 'a manifest injustice'. It held that the damage caused to Baker by the first defendant was not so much the leg injury as such but his loss of earning capacity, and this loss had hardly increased because of the amputation. If the House of Lords had focused on the injury as such, the aggravated damage because of the amputation would have hardly yielded a claim for the victim and the latter would have been crushed between the two tortfeasors.[120]

Differences between the legal systems occur if no one is liable for the second event. One may think of a person who suffers loss of earning capacity as the consequence of an accident, and where he subsequently and independently from the accident would have suffered the same damage because of an illness or another physical infirmity, for instance a heart attack. In such a case, German law and English law only hold the first tortfeasor liable until the second event, because the latter cause is in the claimant's own sphere and has to be attributed to him.[121]

Jobling v Associated Dairies Ltd was about a man who was permanently and completely incapacitated because of a back injury caused by an accident for

[118] See Case 6 in Spier (ed.), *The Limits of Expanding liability. Eight Fundamental Cases in a Comparative Perspective*, 1998, 20.
[119] Van Gerven (2000), 462–463. Compare Article 3:104(3) PETL: 'If the first activity has caused continuing damage and the subsequent activity later on also would have caused it, both activities are regarded as a cause of that continuing damage from that time on.'
[120] *Baker v Willoughby* [1970] AC 467. Markesinis and Deakin (2003), 194–195.
[121] Article 3:106 PETL: 'The victim has to bear his loss to the extent corresponding to the likelihood that it may have been caused by an activity, occurrence or other circumstance within his own sphere.'

which Associated Dairies was liable. A few years later he developed back complaints (myelopathy) which were unrelated to the accident and originated only after the accident. The House of Lords rejected the application of *Baker v Willoughby*, because myelopathy had to be considered as a *vicissitude of life*.[122] Associated Dairies only had to pay until the moment at which myelopathy would have led to complete incapacity. Lord Bridge explained this as follows:

When the supervening illness or injury, which is the independent cause of the loss of earning capacity, has manifested itself before trial, the event has demonstrated that, even if the plaintiff had never sustained the tortious injury, his earnings would now be reduced or extinguished. To hold the tortfeasor, in this situation, liable to pay damages for a notional continuing loss of earnings attributable to the tortious injury is to put the plaintiff in a better position than he would be in if he had never suffered the tortious injury.[123]

French law takes a different view, holding the first tortfeasor liable towards the claimant regardless of the character of the second event. In practice, a second cause in the victim's sphere will have no consequences if the first tortfeasor has completely and unconditionally paid the damages as a once and for all capital. This will be different if future damages are awarded as periodical payments and the payment can be adapted to new developments. This is for instance the case in Germany. See about future damage nr 1205.

1109-2 *Second event increases damage caused by first event*

If the second event would not have caused the same damage but has aggravated the claimant's personal injury, the first tortfeasor will be jointly liable with the second tortfeasor if the second event can be attributed to the first event. An example of such an attributable second event is a French case about someone who got injured in a road accident and was more severely injured in a fire in hospital: his burns were considered to be a result of the initial accident.[124] Also attributable to the first tortfeasor was the contamination with HIV from blood transfusions given to the victim of a road traffic accident. The French blood transfusion authority paid damages to the claimant and was granted a right of recourse against the driver who was liable for the first event.[125]

If the second event is too remote from the first one, the second tortfeasor can be solely liable for the aggravated damage. The second accident can be too remote if too much time has passed between the first and second event. In 1937

[122] *Jobling v Associated Dairies Ltd* [1982] AC 794. According to Winfield and Jolowicz (2002), para. 6.8, *Jobling* has cast doubts on the authority of *Baker* in the field of causation.
[123] Lord Bridge in *Jobling v Associated Dairies Ltd* [1982] AC 794, 820. Markesinis and Deakin (2003), 196, refer to the parallel with the American case of *Dillon v Twin State Gas and Electric Co* (1932) 163 A.2d 111.
[124] Civ. 2e 8 February 1989, Bull. civ. II, no 32, JCP 1990. II. 21544.
[125] Civ. 2e 6 March 2003, RTD civ. 2003, 310, obs. Jourdain, ETL 2003, 163 (Lafay, Moréteau and Pellerin-Rugliano).

a German was injured in a car accident, as a consequence of which his right leg
was amputated. Eight years later, during the last days of the war, he could not
reach a bunker in time to take shelter against artillery fire because of his handicap. The BGH denied causation between the first and the second event and
thus the first tortfeasor was not liable for the claimant's aggravated damage.[126]

In principle, both these rules (as regards the second event which is attributable
to the first event and the second event which is not) apply in all three systems.[127]

Whereas personal injury is generally considered in terms of loss of earning
capacity and thus a kind of continuous loss, property loss is considered to be a
one-off loss and is therefore treated differently. One may think of cases in which
someone collides with a car that was already damaged by a previous accident. It
seems to make sense that, as far as the damage is the same, the first tortfeasor
would stay liable, that he has a right of recourse against the second tortfeasor,
and that the second tortfeasor has to compensate the extra damage he caused.
However, there does not seem to be consensus on this point from a comparative
point of view.[128]

1110 The loss of a chance

1110-1 *France*

If a doctor wrongfully fails to diagnose a patient with a certain illness, for
example cancer, this failure implies that treatment can only start later and that
the patient's chances to recover or to live longer have been worsened. If the tenet
of the loss of a chance is applied the doctor will be only liable for a percentage of
the patient's damage, ie the percentage of the patient's lost chance to recover.

French tort law has the longest history as regards the application of the tenet
of the loss of a chance (*la perte d'une chance*). It is applied to a lost chance of a
profit, for instance passing an exam or winning a prize, and to the loss of a
chance of preventing a loss, for instance recovering from a disease. The latter
may be the case either because of a failure to provide medical treatment or a
failure to provide proper information about the risks of a medical treatment.[129]

[126] BGH 24 April 1952, NJW 1952, 1010 = VersR 1952, 352, about which Markesinis and
Unberath (2002), 643–645 (eight years between first and second accident, causation denied).
[127] *France*: Crim. 11 January 1961, Bull. crim. 1961. 18; Crim. 12 January 1970, Bull. crim.
1970. 23; Civ. 1re 17 February 1993, Bull. civ. I, no 80, JCP 1994. II. 22226. *Germany*: RG 13
October 1922, RGZ 105, 264, about which Markesinis and Unberath (2002), 628–629; RG 5
December 1927, RGZ 119, 204; BGH 15 December 1970, VersR 1971, 442. *England*: *Overseas
Tankship (UK) Ltd v Morts Dock & Engineering Co* (*The Wagon Mound (No. 1)*), [1961] AC 388;
Wieland v Cyril Lord Carpets Ltd [1969] 3 All ER 1066; *McKew v Holland & Hannen & Cubitts
(Scotland) Ltd* [1969] 3 All ER 1621; *Pigney v Pointers Transport Services Ltd* [1957] 2 All ER 807.
See in more detail J. Spier (ed.), *Unification of Tort Law: Causation*, 2000, 141–146.
[128] J. Spier (ed.), *Unification of Tort Law: Causation* (2000), 141–146.
[129] Civ. 1re 12 November 1985, Bull, civ, I, no 298, about which Van Gerven (2000), 428; Civ.
1re 7 February 1990, Bull, civ, I, no 39, about which Van Gerven (2000), 428; Civ. 1re 3 November

It is required that the loss of the chance was real and that the causal connection between the defendant's conduct and the loss of the chance was clear. In such a case the lost chance is estimated as a percentage, and the defendant has to compensate this percentage of the claimant's damage.[130]

The loss of a chance rule is applied in personal injury cases as well as in cases of property damage or pure economic loss. An example of the latter is the case of a horse breeder who, as the consequence of an accident for which the defendant was liable, was incapable of training his mares for two races. The *Cour de cassation* considered the damage constituted by the lost chance to be direct and certain, the latter even though the realization of a chance can never be certain. The breeder could recover the damage for the loss of his chance to win races with his mares, and to establish this chance the case was referred to a lower court.[131]

Another example concerned a skier who collided with another skier who subsequently left the place of the accident and remained untraceable. The injured skier claimed damages from her instructor who had failed to identify the other skier while she lay on the ground. If the instructor had identified the other skier this might have given her the chance to get compensation from him. The *Cour de cassation* awarded her claim for this lost chance.[132]

1110-2 *England*

In English law the notion of the loss of a chance has long since been applied in contractual relationships as regards financial loss.[133] *Chaplin v Hicks* was about a lady who, as a consequence of a breach of contract, lost the chance to win an acting competition.[134] In *Kitchen v Royal Air Forces Assocation* a solicitor was held liable for the loss of a chance of his client to get damages on the basis of the Fatal Accidents Act. The latter was granted compensation of 66 per cent of the damage for the loss of a chance of 66 per cent.[135] And in *Allied Maples Group Ltd v Simmons & Simmons* the claimants received damages from their solicitors for the loss of the chance to negotiate on the conditions of a lease contract.[136]

1983, Bull, civ. I, no 253, about which Van Gerven (2000), 427. In the doctrine application of the loss of a chance in medical negligence cases is disputed: see Viney-Jourdain (1998), nr 370–373.

[130] Req. 17 July 1889, S. 1891. I. 399; Civ. 1re 14 December 1965, JCP 1966. II. 14753, comm. Savatier; Civ. 1re 17 November 1982, JCP 1983. II. 20056, D. 1984. 305, about which Van Gerven (2000), 428; Civ. 1re 8 January 1985, D. 1986. 390, comm. Penneau; Civ. 10 June 1986, Bull. civ. 1986. I. 163; Viney-Jourdain (1998), nr 370; Le Tourneau (2004), nr 1417 ff.

[131] Crim. 6 June 1990, Bull. crim. 1990. 224, about which Van Gerven (2000), 200–201.

[132] Civ. 1re, 10 June 1986, Bull. civ. I, no 163.

[133] Winfield and Jolowicz (2002), para. 6.9-10; Markesinis and Deakin (2003), 198–200; Helen Reece, 'Losses of Chances in the Law', *Mod LR*, 59 (1996), 188; Jane Stapleton, 'Cause-in-Fact and the Scope of Liability for Consequences', *LQR* (2003) 119, 388–425.

[134] *Chaplin v Hicks* [1911] 2 KB 786 (CA).

[135] *Kitchen v Royal Air Forces Association* [1958] 2 All ER 241.

[136] *Allied Maples Group Ltd v Simmons & Simmons* [1995] 1 WLR 1602, about which Van Gerven (2000), 224–226.

It is striking that the tenet of the loss of a chance is not applicable in medical negligence cases in which the patient lost a chance to be cured or to survive. *Hotson v East Berkshire Area Health Authority* was about a 13-year-old boy who fell out of a tree. The hospital where the boy was admitted discovered only five days later that he had broken his hip. Ultimately, the boy became disabled. It was established that, at the moment the boy was hospitalized, he already had a chance of 75 per cent of suffering from such a complication. The House of Lords dismissed the claim: on the basis of the 'more likely than not test' (50 per cent) the disability would have occurred anyway.[137]

This implies that a lost chance of 50 per cent or less will result in 0 per cent compensation, and the lost chance of more than 50 per cent in 100 per cent compensation. In the Court of Appeal the Master of the Rolls, Sir John Donaldson, took a clearly different position:

> As a matter of common sense, it is unjust that there should be no liability for failure to treat a patient, simply because the chances of a successful cure by that treatment were less than 50%. Nor, by the same token, can it be just that, if the chances of a successful cure only marginally exceed 50 per cent, the doctor or his employer should be liable to the same extent as if the treatment could be guaranteed to cure. If this is the law, it is high time that it was changed.[138]

However, his position did not get support in the House of Lords.

More recently in *Gregg v Scott*, the House of Lords sought to justify this solution in two ways: firstly, it is the only logical solution which follows strictly from the procedural fiction that only a contention which has a 51 per cent likelihood of being true is legally deemed to be fact in the eyes of the court. Secondly, the House invoked a policy explanation: if courts were to allow damages proportional to the corresponding decrease in chance of survival, this would reduce the *efficiency* of tort law as a system of compensation. Specifically, it would involve considerable extra expense (in time and money) in determining the precise 'before' and 'after' percentages, while at the same time resulting in only partial awards of damages. Apparently, in cases of financial loss the House seems to consider this to be less of a problem. *Gregg v Scott* was about a general practitioner who did not refer a person with a benign tumour to a specialist; after it was revealed that the patient had non-Hodgkin's lymphoma it was established that his chance of long-term survival was reduced from 42 per cent to 25 per cent; on the basis of a balance of probabilities the House of Lords dismissed his claim.[139]

---

[137] *Hotson v East Berkshire Area Health Authority* [1987] 2 All ER 909 (HL). In the same sense *Wilsher v Essex Area Health Authority* [1988] 2 WLR 557 (HL): a child was born blind after getting an overdose of oxygen during birth; a causal connection was denied because there could have been five other causes for the blindness which were all about equally likely.

[138] *Hotson v East Berkshire Area Health Authority* [1987] 2 WLR 287, 294 (CA); Tony Weir, *Tort Law* (Oxford: Oxford University Press, 2002), 75 qualified this speech as an 'outburst from a normally sensible judge'.   [139] *Gregg v Scott* [2005] UKHL 2.

1110-3 *Germany*

The German BGH has always refused to apply the tenet of the loss of a chance.[140] The alternatives in German law are, firstly, that according to the general rules the claimant's burden of proof can be relieved on the basis of *prima facie* evidence (*Anscheinsbeweis*), and secondly, that the reversal rule may apply (nr 1107-1).

In its third way to meet the claimant's problems with the burden of proof, German law is probably unique. In cases of gross medical negligence (*grober Behandlungsfehler*) which was the adequate cause of the damage, the burden of proof is reversed if the treatment provided a chance of recovery of more than 50 per cent. It is then up to the doctor to prove that his negligence was not, the cause of the damage.[141] If he succeeds, the patient will get no compensation at all, but, if he does not succeed, the doctor will be fully liable.[142] For example, if a doctor grossly negligently makes a wrong diagnosis and the patient dies, the doctor is liable for the death of the patient unless he proves that the patient could not have been saved anyway.[143]

Examples of gross negligence are when a doctor does not carry out simple research for diagnosis or therapy (blood and urine tests) or where he did not document data properly.[144] The reversal rule also applies to other persons owing a safety duty, such as nursing staff and swimming pool attendants.[145]

1110-4 *Comparative overview*

Applying the tenet of the loss of a chance brings the causation issue close to the area of damages since the causation question is in fact wrapped up in the assessment of damages, more particularly the assessment of future damage. Future damage is usually established on the basis of an estimation of the victim's future chances as regards his (financial) prospects. For example, if a student misses his exams because of an accident, the question may be what chance he had to pass his exams (loss of a chance), but it can also be established that he will certainly enter a profession, but a year later than if the accident had not happened (lost profits in the framework of the assessment of damages).[146] See about future damage nr 1205.

It can be concluded that only French tort law generally acknowledges the possibility of awarding the claim for the loss of a chance to win or the loss of a chance not to lose. This means that the tortfeasor is liable for the amount of

---

[140] Kötz-Wagner (2001), N 149; Deutsch-Ahrens (2002), N 428 is one of the few German authors who advocates application of the tenet of the loss of a chance.

[141] BGH 1 February 1994, VersR 1994, 562; Kötz-Wagner (2001), N 258.

[142] BGH 11 June 1968, NJW 1968, 2291.   [143] Kötz-Wagner (2001), N 258.

[144] BGH 13 February 1996, BGHZ 132, 47; see also BGH 21 September 1982, BGHZ 85, 212 and BGH 27 June 1978, BGHZ 72, 132.

[145] BGH 10 November 1970, NJW 1971, 241; BGH 11 April 1967, NJW 1967, 1508.

[146] See also von Bar (2000), N 444.

damage that corresponds with the loss of the chance he has caused. English law applies the rule in cases of financial loss but not in cases of physical harm. German law only applies an all-or-nothing rule.

In medical malpractice cases, English law will be generally more generous to the victim than will German law. In English law the claimant will get full compensation on the basis of the *more likely than not* test if the claimant's loss of a chance was over 50 per cent. In Germany the claimant can only benefit from a reversal of the burden of proof if the chance of a successful treatment was over 50 per cent where the doctor was grossly negligent. If the loss of a chance is over 50 per cent, English and German law can sometimes be more beneficial for the claimant than French law, because the consequence in England and Germany is that the claimant gets full compensation whereas in France he will only get damages to the amount of his lost percentage.

Community law does not exclude the recoverability of a lost chance. This can be concluded from the *Farrugia* case. Farrugia, specializing in surgery, applied for a Community grant to do a research training fellowship in the United Kingdom. The Commission rejected his application on the ground that the applicant was a British citizen but, in fact, he was a Maltese national with British *overseas* citizenship. The CFI held:

In the present case, concerning non-material damage flowing from the applicant's loss of his chance to pursue his studies and research in the United Kingdom, the requirement that such damage be actual presupposes that the applicant must establish at least that his application satisfied the substantive conditions for being accepted, so that it was only the Commission's unlawful refusal (. . .) which deprived him of the chance of having his application taken into consideration for award of the fellowship requested.

On the basis of facts, the CFI held that the applicant had not satisfied this substantive condition: Farrugia's application would also have failed if the Commission had assessed his citizenship correctly.[147] Hence, the loss of a chance is recoverable in Community law but the chance must have been realistic, at least to a certain extent.

D UNEXPECTED AND UNLIKELY CONSEQUENCES

1111 Confusion and principles

Legal systems apply different techniques to limit the causal consequences for which the defendant has to answer. In a way, these techniques are an expression

---

[147] CFI 21 March 1996, Case T-230/94, ECR 1996, II-195, 212 (*Farrugia v Commission*). See also cases of Community staff claims, for example CFI 16 December 1993, Case T-20/89, ECR 1993, II-1423, 1440.

of the different legal cultures. The most general approach is adopted in French law (direct cause), the most traditional approach in English law (foreseeability), and the most sophisticated one in German law (adequacy, scope of the rule, and sphere of risk). These different techniques, though they are of some practical use, do not provide a real distinguishing standard for finding clear answers to causation questions in individual cases. What has been said about the use of formulae in establishing negligence (nr 805-2) also goes for establishing causation. 'Formulae can help to organise thinking but they cannot provide answers.'[148]

Hence, it is not surprising that in this respect the drafts for European rules are rather vague and do not provide much guidance. Article 4:101(1) ECC holds: 'A person causes legally relevant damage to another if the damage is to be regarded as a consequence of that person's conduct or the source of danger for which that person is responsible.'[149]

In practice, policy considerations play a very important, if not a decisive role. In many cases the court decides the outcome it wishes to reach on the basis of policy considerations as to what would be fair, just, and reasonable in the given case. Subsequently, it gives its decision in the language the national law provides. For example, the court says that the consequences were foreseeable or not, that they were very unlikely or not so unlikely, that they were direct or indirect, or that they were within or outside the protective scope of the rule. In this respect, it is interesting to see that in England the maxim *the tortfeasor takes the victim as he finds him* (nr 1112) is considered to be an exception to the reasonable foreseeability test whereas in Germany it is seen as a consequence of the adequacy theory.[150] Particularly in England and Germany, the courts are also inclined to discuss causation matters explicitly on a policy level.

Causation is not just about vagueness and elusiveness. Some general principles are apparent from the comparative overview and they are inspired by policy considerations to improve victim protection. Firstly, personal injury consequences for the claimant will be more easily attributed to the defendant's conduct than consequences in the sphere of property damage and pure economic loss: '... it appears that the test of remoteness for property damage (and, by extension, for pure economic loss) is stricter than for interferences with physical safety and health'.[151] This is reflected in English and German law, in which economic loss is rather easily compensable if it is caused by personal injury or property damage but not if the economic loss is 'pure' (nr 713–714). And

---

[148] Cooke P in *South Pacific Manufacturing Co Ltd v New Zealand Security Consultants & Investigations Ltd* [1992] 2 NZLR 282, 294. See also Jane Stapleton, 'Duty of Care Factors: a Selection from the Judicial Menus', in Peter Cane and Jane Stapleton (eds.), *The Law of Obligations: Essays in Celebration of John Fleming* (Oxford: Clarendon Press; New York: Oxford University Press, 1998).

[149] The other provision in the ECC is about the claimant's predisposition. The PETL contains a provision on the conditio sine qua non rule (Article 3:101, nr 1102) and a number of provisions focusing on rules regarding concurrent, alternative, and potential causes. See nr 1108–1109.

[150] Van Gerven (2000), 454.

[151] Markesinis and Deakin (2003), 208; von Bar (2000), N 470.

although French law does not restrict the compensation of pure economic loss as such (nr 700), the causation requirement plays an important role to keep the amount of compensable damage within limits.[152]

Secondly, if someone's conduct can cause personal injury of some kind, it is not relevant how the harm eventually occurred. In such cases causation can also be established if the damage was caused after an unlikely sequence of events.[153] An American case was about a cleaner using benzene in a room where a gas heater was burning with a naked flame. The cleaner opened a machine to clean it when a rat jumped over his hand. The rat was splashed with benzene, ran away with benzene-coated fur and crawled under the heater where the rat's fur ignited. Then the rat panicked and ran back to the machine causing the benzene bottle to explode. It was very unlikely that such a bizarre sequence of events would occur, but the judge considered the explosion to be foreseeable; the way the explosion had occurred was considered not to be relevant.[154]

Thirdly, and related to the second principle, the eggshell skull rule implies that the tortfeasor has to take the victim as he finds him. He also has to compensate the consequences of the claimant's specific vulnerabilities (nr 1112).

1112 Tortfeasor takes victim as he finds him

In all jurisdictions an important maxim as regards causation in cases of personal injury is described in Lord Parker's historic words: 'It has always been the law of this country that a tortfeasor takes his victim as he finds him.'[155] This implies that the defendant also has to answer for the consequences of the claimant's vulnerabilities and predispositions, even if he is extremely vulnerable. This is for example the case if he has an eggshell skull, suffers from an alcohol addiction, or if he has a weak heart.[156] However, this principle is not without exceptions or corrections.

In Germany the victim can be contributorily negligent if he has not taken reasonable measures to protect himself against his vulnerability.[157] One may

---

[152] Von Bar (2000), N 44 and 470.   [153] Von Bar (2000), N 454.

[154] *United Novelty Co v Daniels (Miss)* (1949) 42 So 2d 395.

[155] Lord Parker in *Smith v Leech Brain Co* [1962] 2 QB 405, 414, about which Van Gerven (2000), 462.

[156] Civ. 13 January 1982, JCP 1983. II. 20025 (delirium tremens of alcoholic victim); Civ. 17 February 1993, JCP 1994. II. 22226 (HIV-contamination by a haemophiliac victim); BGH 29 February 1956, BGHZ 20, 137 = VersR 1956, 305, about which Markesinis and Unberath (2002), 665–668; BGH 6 June 1989, BGHZ 107, 359 = NJW 1989, 2616 = JZ 1989, 1069, about which Markesinis and Unberath (2002), 835–839; BGH 30 April 1996, BGHZ 132, 341 = NJW 1996, 2425 = VersR 1996, 990 = JZ 1996, 1080, comm. Schlosser and the comparative case comments in *ERPL*, 6/2 (1998), 249–255. See furthermore Article 4:101(2) ECC: 'In cases of personal injury or death the injured person's predisposition with respect to the type or extent of the injury sustained is to be disregarded.' Von Bar (2000), N 466–469.

[157] BGH 22 September 1981, NJW 1982, 168. See also BGH 5 July 1963, VersR 1963, 1161.

think of someone with an eggshell skull who does not wear a helmet when cycling even if he is not statutorily obliged to wear one. In France this principle does not apply if the victim is in a stable and consolidated pathological condition. Damage in connection with this condition will not be attributed to the defendant. However, the tortfeasor has to answer for predispositions that do not have any external injurious manifestation.[158]

Reluctance as regards the application of the maxim exists in cases of psychological vulnerability. This is, of course, related to the more general reluctance as regards compensation for psychological damage. In English law it has to be foreseeable that a person of reasonable fortitude would suffer some psychological harm. Once this is proved, the claimant's oversensitivity is no defence (nr 704).[159] The German approach is different but will probably lead to similar results: psychological consequences are not attributed to the defendant if the psychological harm is disproportionate compared with the physical harm suffered (*Bagatellfälle*). This is the case when the harmful event had '. . . quite insignificant consequential injuries and the psychological reaction of the plaintiff to this was in gross disproportion to the cause and not comprehensible.'[160]

It is disputed whether the tortfeasor has to answer for a compensation neurosis. According to German law:

> . . . the attribution of harmful psychological consequences is ruled out if the plaintiff has a compensation neurosis or wish neurosis. The claimant would thus be using the accident merely as a pretext in his neurotic striving for assistance and security in order to evade the difficulties and burdens of the working life. The denial of compensation for harm in the case of such neuroses is based on the idea that the psychological disorder obtains its character from a conscious or unconscious 'wish' idea to safeguard one's life or exploitation of an assumed legal position. It is so prominent that the necessary attributable connection with the accident cannot be affirmed. This is so despite the fact that a direct causal connection between such neuroses and the preceding accident exists.[161]

The idea is that compensation is aimed to support the victim and to relieve his recovery but in the case of a neurosis compensation would lead to the contrary by strengthening the victim in his neurosis, which hinders his return to social life.[162]

---

[158] Civ. 2e 19 July 1966, D. 1966. 598, about which Van Gerven (2000), 462.

[159] *Page v Smith* [1996] AC 155; Winfield and Jolowicz (2002), para. 6.28.

[160] BGH 11 November 1997, BGHZ 137, 142 = NJW 1998, 810 = VersR 1998, 200 = JZ 1998, 680, about which Markesinis and Unberath (2002), 668–673 from which the translation is derived. See also BGH 30 April 1996, BGHZ 132, 341 = NJW 1996, 2425 = VersR 1996, 990 = JZ 1996, 1080; BGH 14 January 1992, NJW 1992, 1043 = VersR 1992, 504; BGH 12 November 1985, VersR 1986, 240.

[161] BGH 11 November 1997, BGHZ 137, 142 = NJW 1998, 810 = VersR 1998, 200 = JZ 1998, 680, about which Markesinis and Unberath (2002), 668–673, from which the translation has been derived. See also BGH 30 April 1996, BGHZ 132, 341 = NJW 1996, 2425 = VersR 1996, 990 = JZ 1996, 1080; BGH 29 February 1956, BGHZ 20, 137 = VersR 1956, 305.

[162] BGH 29 February 1956, BGHZ 20, 137, 142. See also BGH 12 November 1985, NJW 1986, 779: a greater need for treatment is nevertheless compensable, even if this need is partly caused by psychological instability.

12

Damage and Damages

A INTRODUCTION

1201 Purposes

1201-1 *Reparation and compensation*

Damage (*dommage, Schaden*) is, just like causation, a general requirement for liability in damages, not only for contractual liability but also for non-contractual liability, be it based on negligence or on strict rules.[1] In France these requirements of damage and causation are very aptly called *les constantes de la responsabilité.*[2]

Liability rules can only be effective if the law provides a remedy.[3] Besides the remedy of damages, the legal systems provide the possibility of an injunction, which is particularly effective in order to prevent or stop ongoing infringement of the claimant's rights, for example nuisance by causing noise or smell. Such a situation can be stopped by way of a prohibitive injunction (England), an *Unterlassungsklage* or *Beseitungsklage* (§ 1004 German BGB), and a procedure to *supprimer la situation illicite* (France). The courts under certain circumstances also have the power to impose a mandatory injunction by virtue of which the defendant is ordered to take positive action to rectify the consequences of what already has been done. This order is in fact a form of reparation in kind. The difference is that an injunction generally does not require proof of fault: causing the infringement of a protected interest will do.[4]

---

[1] See about the law of remedies and damages from a comparative perspective: H. Stoll, 'Consequences of Liability', in A. Tunc (ed.), *International Encyclopaedia of Comparative Law, Vol. XI/8, Torts*, (Tübingen: Mohr, 1986); Harvey McGregor, 'Personal Injury and Death', in A. Tunc (ed.), *International Encyclopedia of Comparative Law, Vol. XI/9: Torts*, (Tübingen: Morh, 1986); Van Gerven (2000), 740–887; von Bar (2000), N 119–178; Ulrich Magnus (ed.), *Unification of Tort Law: Damages* (The Hague, London, Boston: Kluwer, 2001).

[2] See for example Carbonnier (2000), § 205, 351; Le Tourneau (2004), nr 1300.

[3] See also Article 13 ECHR (Right to an effective remedy): 'Everyone whose rights and freedoms as set forth in this Convention are violated shall have an effective remedy before a national authority notwithstanding that the violation has been committed by persons acting in an official capacity.'

[4] Winfield and Jolowicz (2002), paras 22.46–22.49; Deutsch-Ahrens (2002), N 499–505; Le Tourneau (2004), nr 2440–2446; von Bar (2000), N 122–125. See also Article 1:102 ECC.

In this chapter the emphasis will be on the damages remedy: the defendant's obligation to pay the claimant a certain amount of money in order to repair the harm done. Reparation can happen in two ways: either reparation in kind— which aims to restore the *status quo ante*—or reparation through monetary compensation—which provides for an equivalent. If someone's car is damaged in a road traffic accident, the tortfeasor generally has to pay the costs of reparation and the difference between the value of the car before and after the accident. If someone suffers personal injury, the tortfeasor has to pay the victim's costs of medical treatment and his loss of income and/or loss of earning capacity. Generally, compensation relates to losses (*damnum emergens*) as well as lost profits (*lucrum cessans*).

Compensation of harm not only takes place via the tort law system. Indeed, tort law and the law of damages generally do not properly provide first aid in getting compensation. A victim will often also and mostly primarily rely on other sources for the compensation of his damage, particularly social security, labour law, and private insurance. For example, in most countries people are compulsory or voluntarily insured against costs of medical health care. If they are ill they are also entitled, at least for some months, to the continuation of the payment of their salary by their employer. Finally, many car owners have insurance coverage for damage caused to their car, regardless of who is responsible for it.[5]

1201-2 *Recognition and satisfaction*

Reparation and compensation are not the only functions of damages. Sometimes other goals are also intended to be achieved, for instance recognition. This can be the case if someone has not suffered appreciable harm. In such cases the French courts may award a *franc symbolic* (nr 1202-1) and the English courts *nominal damages*, particularly as regards torts that are actionable per se like trespass and libel (nr 1202-3). One may also think of Article 41 ECHR which requires the Court to afford just satisfaction to the injured party of a violation of human rights. Such satisfaction may consist of the declaration that there has been a violation of the rights protected by the Convention or in the award of a nominal sum (nr 1202-6).

The function of such a symbolic award is to vindicate the claimant's legally protected interests rather than to compensate his harm. Lord Halsbury described nominal damages as

...a technical phrase which means that you have negatived anything like real damage, but that you are affirming by your nominal damages that there is an infraction of a legal

---

See in a broader perspective the EC Directive 98/27 on Injunctions for the Protection of Consumers' Interests.

[5] The intertwinement between these different sources of compensation has been extensively analysed and discussed. See for example Ulrich Magnus (ed.), *The Impact of Social Security on Tort Law* (Vienna, New York: Springer, 2003).

right which, though it gives you no right to any real damages at all, yet gives you a right to the verdict or judgment because your legal right has been infringed.[6]

In Germany a similar effect can be reached by a so-called *Feststellungsurteil*, a decision in which the court declares, for example, that someone's right is infringed (§ 256 ZPO). However, this action does not give rise to damages, not even symbolic damages.

Also compensation for non-pecuniary loss, for example damages for pain and suffering, can be considered to contain elements of recognition. Awards for this kind of loss are symbolic insofar as money cannot really make good (compensate) the damage. Indeed, the notion of *solatium* is referred to explicitly in some English judgments.[7] Particularly in cases of compensation of non-pecuniary loss of an unconscious claimant, the recognition function plays a predominant role (nr 1207).

German law expressly considers damages for non-pecuniary loss (*Schmerzensgeld*) to have a double function: compensation (*Ausgleich*) and satisfaction (*Genugtuung*).[8] Firstly, the money compensates for the loss suffered and enables the claimant to buy himself new amenities instead of the ones he is no longer able to enjoy. Secondly, the money aims to provide the claimant satisfaction for the infringement of his right. It aims not only to sooth the negative feelings caused by the infringement but also to punish intentional and grossly negligent conduct as well as serious infringements of personality rights such as privacy (nr 705).[9] In these latter cases awards can be even higher than for persons who have suffered personal injury.[10] In this sense damages can also have a deterrent effect; see nr 1201-3.

1201-3 *Punishment and prevention*

Not only are awards meant to compensate the loss suffered by the claimant but they can also function to punish the defendant, to give him an incentive to prevent him from further wrongdoing in the future, or to skim the profits he has made by his unlawful conduct.[11] In such cases the focus is on the defendant's behaviour rather than on the claimant's interest.

In the United States tort law has become (in)famous for its punitive damages: extraordinary high awards of millions of dollars awarded by juries who want to punish the tortfeasor for his wrongful conduct. Although the amounts in Europe are much lower, here also elements of punitive damages can be recognized in

---

[6] *The Mediana* [1900] AC 113, 116 (HL).

[7] For example in *Uren v John Fairfax & Sons Pty Ltd*, 117 CLR 118, 150, per Windeyer J.

[8] BGH 6 July 1955, BGHZ 18, 149, about which Markesinis and Unberath (2002), 981–991.

[9] Deutsch-Ahrens (2002), N 475–476.

[10] Many German legal writers consider this function to be a kind of penalty since it disembarks from the position of the claimant but the BGH adheres to the view that satisfaction is entirely of a private law nature. See Larenz (1987), 423.

[11] See for instance the classic article of H. Stoll, 'Penal Purposes in the Law of Tort', *AJCL*, 18 (1970), 3.

different shades of explicitness, especially in cases of infringement of a person's personality rights, such as reputation and privacy. Generally, these awards are high compared to awards for personal injury and they are intended to both compensate the claimant's loss and deter the defendant from further wrongdoing.

A good English example in which the various functions of compensation, recognition, punishment, and deterrence come together is defamation. In these cases a jury decides on the damages award.[12] In the early 1990s there was a tendency to grant very high awards of up to £600,000 (€870,000).[13] This led to legislation empowering the Court of Appeal to set limits (section 8 of the Courts and Legal Services Act 1990). In *Rantzen v Mirror Group Newspapers* the Court of Appeal referred to Article 10 ECHR (freedom of speech) and considered: 'The question becomes: could a reasonable jury have thought that their award was necessary to compensate the claimant and to re-establish his reputation.' By way of guidance juries are now advised about the general range of damages for non-pecuniary loss in personal injury cases, with a maximum award of around £200,000 (€290,000).[14] This top level is, however, not considered to be a binding maximum for a defamation case. In an earlier case Lord Hailsham of St Marylebone LC stressed the interest of the claimant by pointing out that ' . . . he must be able to point to a sum awarded by a jury sufficient to convince a by-stander of the baselessness of the charge . . . This is why it is not necessarily fair to compare awards of damages in this field with damages for personal injuries.'[15]

Over and above these compensatory damages, English law acknowledges the possibility to award so-called exemplary damages. These damages are awarded on the basis of the defendant's conduct rather than the claimant's damage. They give expression to the fact that the defendant deserves to be civilly punished for his outrageous conduct. An example is where a newspaper decides to proceed to publish material which it knows to be defamatory, taking a risk that an eventual out-of-court settlement will be offset against a greater profit from increased sales.[16] Regarding the quantum of exemplary damages, the award should be the minimum necessary to achieve punishment and deterrence. Concretely, the Court of Appeal has suggested a range of £5,000–£50,000 in the first category (punishment), whereas in the second category (deterrence) it is thought that the upper limit is potentially much higher.[17]

---

[12] The appellate court is, however, bound to quash a jury's verdict on the question of defamation or no defamation if this verdict is perverse: see *Grobbelaar v News Group Newspapers Ltd* [2002] 1 WLR 3024, ETL 2002, 161 (Oliphant).   [13] *Sutcliffe v Pressdram Ltd* [1991] 1 QB 153.

[14] *John v Mirror Group Newspapers Ltd* [1997] QB 586 (damages awarded to singer Elton John for an allegation that he had been bulimic were lowered from £350,000 (€500,000) to £50,000 (€70,000)); Winfield and Jolowicz (2002), para. 12.67; Markesinis and Deakin (2003), 687–688.

[15] *Broome v Cassell & Co Ltd* [1972] AC 1027, at 1072, [1972] 2 WLR 645, [1972] 1 All ER 801, about which Van Gerven (2000), 745.

[16] *Broome v Cassell & Co Ltd* [1972] AC 1027, [1972] 2 WLR 645, [1972] 1 All ER 801, about which Van Gerven (2000), 745.

[17] *Thompson v MPC* [1998] QB 517; Winfield and Jolowicz (2002), nr 22.10.

The German position can be illustrated with the Caroline of Monaco case. A German appeal court had awarded the Princess DM 30,000 (€15,300) for non-material harm caused by the infringement of her personality rights through publication of a made-up interview, photographs, and incorrect allegations concerning her personal life. The BGH quashed the decision, considering that the award should be higher to have a genuinely deterrent effect in order to protect the claimant against the deliberate infringement of her personality right by the defendant in the pursuit of its own commercial interests.[18] The court to which the case was referred awarded DM 180,000 (€92,000).[19]

These amounts for the infringement of private life contrast with the generally lower awards for personal injury and this difference has been challenged before the German Constitutional court (*Bundesverfassungsgericht*) by parents who had suffered severe mental and physical harm from the death of their three children in a traffic accident. Though they had claimed more than twice as much, the mother received DM 70,000 (€35,800) and the father DM 40,000 (€20,500). They argued that the decision was a violation of the principle of equal treatment (Article 3 *Grundgesetz*). The Constitutional court dismissed the claim, considering the different treatment to be justified by special reasons, thus fully focusing on the preventive effects. A high award of damages could prevent the commercial exploitation of another person's personality whereas this effect could not be achieved in traffic accidents since the award was not to be paid by the tortfeasor but by his insurance company.[20]

In French law reparation of harm is the main function of the law of damages and not the punishment of the tortfeasor.[21] However, in the legal literature the concept of a private law penalty (*peine privée*) has been acknowledged, particularly in the area of *dommage moral* (non-pecuniary).[22] *Dommage moral* includes injury to a person's honour, his modesty or his religious convictions.[23] The sums awarded under these heads of damages are rather generous and there is the suspicion amongst French legal writers that the quantum is often deliberately exaggerated in order to show the court's disapproval of the defendant's conduct.[24]

---

[18] BGH 15 November 1994, BGHZ 128, 1 = NJW 1995, 861:

Where interference in the rights of privacy of the affected person is intended to increase circulation and hence profits, then the notion of prevention commands that the profit realized be included as a factor when calculating the quantum of damages.

Von Bar (1998), N 521. See also the comparative case comments in *ERPL*, 5/2 (1997), 237–260.
[19] OLG Hamburg 25 July 1996, NJW 1996, 2870. See about the case of Caroline von Hannover before the European Court of Human Rights, nr 705-5.
[20] BVerfG 8 March 2000, NJW 2000, 2187, about which Markesinis and Unberath (2002), 1008–1011.
[21] Civ. 2e 8 May 1964, JCP 1965. II. 14140, comm. Esmein, about which Van Gerven (2000), 765: the court is not allowed to take into account the previous liability of the defendant in establishing the damages.
[22] Viney-Jourdain (1998), nr 254. See for instance Suzanne Carval, *La responsabilité civile dans sa function de peine privée* (Paris: LGDJ, 1995).
[23] Civ. 2e 13 October 1955, D. 1956, Somm. 32; Lille 6 June 1907, D. 1907. 2. 191; Civ. 17 June 1914, DP 1919. 1. 36.   [24] Terré-Simler-Lequette (2002), nr 712.

Specifically, French courts have used a number of techniques. Firstly, the concept of *prejudice moral* is very elastic. Next, large sums are also awarded for *préjudice moral* to companies: for example, the court in Nanterre awarded for a breach of trademark an amount of FRF 6,360,000 (€970,000).[25] It is also significant that trial judges—who retain sovereign discretion in fixing the quantum of an award—expressly take into account the behaviour of the defendant: for example, the fact that a competitor who markets a product almost identical to the claimant indirectly takes unfair benefit from the latter's investment in market research, and also (more directly) steals his existing clients.[26] Finally, the *Cour de cassation* has on occasion gone one step further and dispensed the claimant from having to bring proof of specific *prejudice moral* which is deemed to exist 'by necessary inference' in cases of unfair competition.[27]

The fact that a damages award may have a punishing and preventive function is a typical example of the application of the principle of corrective justice (nr 609). It also shows that there is only a thin line to be drawn between tort law and criminal law. Although there is much more to say about the differences and commonalities between these areas of the law, two remarks will be made here. Firstly, aspects of punishment and prevention in tort law particularly play a role in cases (protection of privacy, honour, and reputation) in which criminal rules are usually of modest importance. Rules of privacy, honour, and reputation are effectively enforced by tort law and a collision or an accumulation of punishing sanctions (civil and criminal) will generally not occur. Secondly, damages awards in these areas are often paid from the defendant's own purse rather than by his liability insurer. The latter is the usual situation in personal injury cases and, hence, in this area the punishing function of the damages award does not play a significant role.

1202 Features of the legal systems

1202-1 *France*

The founding fathers of the *Code civil* left the word *dommage* (damage) for interpretation by the courts, just as they did with the word *faute* (nr 302). *Dommage* in itself does not contain any restriction as to the scope of the protected rights and interests. The only requirements the case law has developed are that someone has suffered damage, that this damage was suffered in a legitimate

---

[25] Nanterre 12 March 1993, (*CPC France c. Kruger GmbH et NACO*).
[26] Cour d'Appel Paris 23 June 1993 (*BN c. Atlantic Snacks*).
[27] Com. 22 October 1985, Bull. civ., IV, no 245 (*Sté générale Mécanographie c. Sté Saint Etienne Bureau*): '...le prejudice s'inférait nécessairement des actes déloyaux constatés l'existence d'un préjudice, fût-il seulement moral'; see also com. 9 February 1993, Bull. civ. IV, no 53 (*Mercédès Benz France c. Tchumac*). See also M.A. Frison Roche, 'Les principes originels du droit de la concurrence déloyale et du parasitisme', *RJDA*, 1994, 483.

interest, and that it was *certain and personal* to the claimant.[28] In doing so, the courts relied on provisions in the *Code civil* as regards damages for contractual liability. In particular articles 1146–1155 CC are considered to be the expression of general principles and are therefore also applied in cases of non-contractual liability. Since damage is a substantive prerequisite condition to liability, French law does not recognize the concept of a tort which is actionable *per se*. Liability in French tort law is thus seen primarily as a means of compensating loss, as opposed to sanctioning wrongful conduct.

The damage needs to be certain but this requirement has always been taken modestly because '... certainty does not belong to this world'.[29] Hence, damage needs to be very likely, at least likely enough to be taken into consideration. In this vein the tenet of the loss of a chance (*la perte d'une chance*, nr 1101-1) is accepted by the courts as a situation in which damage is considered to be certain, albeit only to the percentage of the probability that an advantageous event will not happen (has been lost).[30]

Damage also needs to be personal but this does not amount to considerable limitations. On the contrary, if someone dies or gets injured as the consequence of an accident, third parties also may have a right to compensation, for example as regards non-pecuniary loss for grief and sorrow. Such a third party is called *un victime par ricochet*: a victim by reflection.[31] The requirement of personal damage is one of the instruments (next to causation) to limit the number of third parties which are entitled to compensation. For example, a grandmother who became custodian of her grandchild after his parents died in an accident was not considered to be a *victime par ricochet*. She could not obtain damages from the tortfeasor: her damage was supposed to be compensated via the child under her care.[32]

This broad approach corresponds with the interpretation of *faute* which does not focus on a duty of the tortfeasor towards the victim, as is the case in English law (nr 503), nor on the question of whether the victim suffered damage as the consequence of the infringement of a protected right, as is the case in Germany (nr 402). For the same reason the notion of 'pure economic loss' is unknown in French tort law, whereas in the casuistic systems of Germany and England the distinction between physical loss and loss of property on the one hand, and pure economic loss on the other, is of paramount importance (nr 604).

The *Cour de cassation* considers the establishment of the amount of damages as a factual matter which cannot be challenged in cassation. The *Cour* does not consider it to be its task to develop or unify the law of damages and leaves this to

[28] See for instance Civ. 2e 3 October 1990, Bull. civ. II, no 184; Civ. 2e 20 June 1985, Bull. civ. 1985. II, no 125, about which Van Gerven (2000), 422 and 424. Le Tourneau (2004), nr 1410ff.
[29] Le Tourneau (2004), nr 1411: '... la certitude n'est pas de ce monde.'
[30] Crim. 6 June 1990, Bull. crim., no 224, RTD Civ. 1991, 121, obs. Jourdain.
[31] Le Tourneau (2004), nr 1453–1457.
[32] Crim. 9 October 1996, Bull. crim., no 352, RTD civ. 1997, 398, obs. Hauser, RTD civ. 1997, 946, obs. Jourdain.

the lower courts. These are free to choose the most appropriate form of redress.[33] This can also imply the payment of a *franc symbolique*, currently an *euro symbolique*, provided the decision confirms that this makes good the suffered harm, for instance in the case of a violation of an intangible property right.[34] The freedom for the courts to assess damages has caused a lack of transparency and consistency in the compensation process.[35]

No head of damage is *a priori* excluded from compensation. The main distinction is considered to be between pecuniary loss (*dommage patrimonial*) and non-pecuniary loss (*dommage moral*). Compensation for non-pecuniary loss is granted for personal injury,[36] for the loss or serious injuries of a loved one (nr 1206), and even for the death of a beloved animal.[37] It also covers harm to human feelings, especially in cases concerning the protection of personality and privacy (nr 705-3).

Finally, a loss cannot be compensated if it is suffered in an illegitimate or illicit interest, but the opinions as to what is illegal have changed in the course of time. For example, until the 1970s an unmarried partner did not have a right to compensation for the loss of maintenance because of the death of her companion. Her infringed interest was considered to be illegitimate (*intérêt illégitime*) (nr 1209).[38] The *Cour de cassation* considers to be an illegal interest the loss of income from a non-declared activity: this is not a kind of damage that is eligible for compensation.[39] However, things were different in the case of a passenger who was injured in an accident whilst he had not paid his fare. The *Cour de cassation* held that the passenger had suffered damage in a legally protected, interest, ie his bodily integrity. This legal interest did not become illegitimate by travelling illegally,[40] whereas in the other case the loss of income in the non-declared activity was damage suffered in an illegitimate interest.

---

[33] See for instance Civ. 2e 9 July 1981, Gaz. Pal. 1982, Jur. 109, comm. Chabas, about which Van Gerven (2000), 806; Civ. 2e 20 January 1993, Gaz. Pal. 1993. 2. 491, comm. Evadé.

[34] Crim. 16 May 1974, D. 1974. 513; Civ. 26 September 1984, JCP 1984. IV. 327. Le Tourneau (2004), nr 5861.

[35] In this respect it is worth mentioning a working group under chairmanship of Yvonne Lambert-Faivre which has made recommendations to the Minister of Justice in the *Rapport sur l'indemnisation du dommage corporel*, June 2003. See Lafay, Moréteau and Pellerin-Rugliano, *ETL*, 2003, 177–178.   [36] Civ. 22 October 1946, JCP 1946. II. 3365.

[37] Civ. 1re 16 January 1962, D. 1962. 199; JCP 1962. II. 12557, comm. Esmein: FFR 1,500 for a mare; Caen 30 October 1962, D. 1962. 92, JCP 1962. II. 12954, RTD civ. 1963, 93, obs. A. Tunc: FFR 900 for a dachshund. Mazeaud-Tunc (1965), nr 320 ff. and Viney-Jourdain (1998), nr 266.

[38] Civ. 27 July 1937, DP 1938. I. 5, comm. Savatier; Ch. mixte 27 February 1970, D. 1970, 201, comm. Combaldieu, Gaz. Pal. 1970. 1. 163. See also the English case of *Burns v Edmann* [1970] 2 QB 541 (burglar) and the German case of BGH 6 July 1976, BGHZ 67, 119: a prostitute who was injured in an accident did not have the right to compensation of her loss of real income but only of the income she would have earned with unskilled work. Since prostitution in Germany is no longer illegal it is questionable whether this decision still reflects the law.

[39] Civ. 2e 24 January 2002, Bull. civ. II, no 47, D. 2002. 259, comm. Mazeaud; ETL 2002, 195 (Brun) and the comparative case comments in *ERPL*, 12/4 (2004), 509–542.

[40] Civ. 2e 17 November 1993, RTD civ. 1994, 115, obs. Jourdain.

1202-2 *Germany*

The German law of damages is laid down in a number of provisions of the BGB which have been modestly reformed in 2002. The so-called *Zweites Gesetz zur Änderung schadensersatzrechtlicher Vorschriften* (Second Act Amending the Provisions on Damages) took effect on 1 August 2002.[41] One of the most important changes for tort law was the introduction of the right to damages for non-pecuniary loss in cases of strict liability. Before 2002 a claimant also had to base his claim on provisions regarding liability for negligence (§ 823 and 826) in order to get damages for non-pecuniary loss.[42]

§ 249–254 BGB hold general rules which apply to all obligations to pay compensation, regardless of their legal foundation (tort, breach of contract, or unjust enrichment). § 842–845 BGB contain provisions specifically dealing with the right to damages in case of tortious liability.

§ 249 I holds: 'A person who is obliged to make reparation for harm must restore the situation which would have existed if the circumstances giving rise to the obligation to make reparation had not occurred.'[43] This provision implies that, as a rule, reparation is to be implemented by way of *Naturalrestitution* (reparation in kind). This means that the tortfeasor himself must buy a new thing to replace the one he has destroyed, repair the car he damaged, take it to a garage to have it repaired, or that he himself must cure the victim, or call and pay a doctor to treat the victim.

If the obligation concerns reparation for personal injury or damage to property, the victim may claim the amount of money necessary to restore the *status quo ante* (§ 249 II).[44] In theory this is an exception to the rule of *Naturalrestitution* (§ 249 I) but in practice it will rather be the rule. The amount of money necessary to restore the *status quo ante* is not necessarily the same as the actual costs of repair. For example, if the claimant himself repairs the damaged car there will be no labour costs but he will nevertheless be able to recover the costs of professional repair. The possibility to claim the money necessary to restore the *status quo ante* does not exist in cases of harm to other protected rights.

---

[41] See for an overview Jörg Fedtke, *ETL*, 2002, 206–212 and extensively Gerhard Wagner, *Das neue Schadensersatzrecht* (Baden-Baden: Nomos, 2002); Hans-Georg Bollweg and Matthias Hellmann, *Das neue Schadensersatzrecht* (Cologne: Bundesanzeiger, 2002) and Andreas Cahn, *Einführung in das neue Schadensersatzrecht* (Munich: C.H. Beck, 2003).

[42] An exception is liability on the basis of the only strict liability rule in the BGB: § 833 regarding liability for damage caused by a luxury animal (nr 404-1).

[43] Translation Van Gerven (2000), 753. § 249 BGB: '(1) Wer zum Schadensersatz verpflichtet ist, hat den Zustand herzustellen, der bestehen würde, wenn der zum Ersatz verpflichtende Umstand nicht eingetreten wäre.'

[44] § 249 BGB: '(2) Ist wegen Verletzung einer Person oder wegen Beschädigung einer Sache Schadensersatz zu leisten, so kann der Gläubiger statt der Herstellung den dazu erforderlichen Geldbetrag verlangen.'

Besides § 249 II the second exception to the rule of *Naturalrestitution* (§ 249 I) is § 251.[45] § 251 I provides that, in as much as reparation is not possible or not sufficient to restore the *status quo ante*, the defendant has to compensate the claimant through a monetary award. One may think of a car that is repaired but whose value is nevertheless lower than it was before the accident. According to § 251 II the defendant can compensate the claimant through a monetary award if reparation would be possible but disproportionately expensive.[46]

According to § 253 I BGB a victim is only entitled to compensation for non-pecuniary loss if a statutory provision so provides. The most important exception to the non-compensability of non-pecuniary loss can be found in § 253 II. This provision grants damages for non-pecuniary loss in cases of the infringement of the claimant's body, freedom, health, or sexual self-determination and it applies irrespective of the basis of the claim, ie in tort cases as well as in cases of breach of contract. Before 2002 this provision could be found in § 847 BGB and was therefore only applicable in tort cases. One of the consequences of the new system is that damage for non-pecuniary loss can also be claimed in contractual medical negligence cases. Similar provisions to § 253 II can be found in the Acts containing rules of strict liability, for instance § 8 ProdHG (Product Liability Act) and § 11 StVG (Road Traffic Act).

These BGB provisions are a nice example of German legislative technique using a rule-exception model. But the limits of this technique are similarly clear. For example, the BGB did not provide a right to compensation of non-pecuniary loss in the case of the infringement of the general personality right. After it had called into being such a right in 1954 (nr 404-2), the BGH considered that the protection of human dignity would not be effective without a proper remedy.[47] The *Herrenreiter* case was about a tonic designed to increase sexual performance. For advertising purposes the manufacturer used a picture of a well-known industrialist, who was also an amateur equestrian, but he had not given his consent to do so. He was granted damages for non-pecuniary loss of DM 10,000 (€5,100). The BGH justified its deviation from the BGB by referring to Articles 1 and 2 *Grundgesetz* (Basic Law).[48] These constitutional provisions are superior in the hierarchy of norms and could therefore fill the gap in the BGB provision

---

[45] § 251 BGB:

(1) Soweit die Herstellung nicht möglich oder zur Entschädigung des Gläubigers nicht genügend ist, hat der Ersatzpflichtige den Gläubiger in Geld zu entschädigen. (2) Der Ersatzpflichtige kann den Gläubiger in Geld entschädigen, wenn die Herstellung nur mit unverhältnismäßigen Aufwendungen möglich ist.

[46] See for example BGH 29 April 2003, VersR 2003, 920, ETL 2003, 193 (Fedtke) and BGH 29 April 2003, NJW 2003, 2085, ETL 2003, 194 (Fedtke). Kötz-Wagner (2001), N 480.

[47] BGH 14 February 1958, BGHZ 26, 349 = NJW 58, 827 (*Herrenreiter*), about which Markesinis and Unberath (2002), 415–420.

[48] BGH 5 December 1995, NJW 1996, 984. For this reason the new § 253 II did not need to mention the infringement of the general personality right as a basis for compensation of non-pecuniary loss.

by way of *verfassungskonforme Auslegung* (interpretation in conformity with the constitution). This judge-made right to compensation has neither been changed by the 2002 reform of the law of damages, nor has it been codified. The legislator feared that codification would cause more confusion than clarity.

1202-3 *England*

Just like the English law of torts, the English law of damages is patchy and hard to get to grips with. The different kinds of remedies, such as damages, have been developed throughout the centuries and are closely connected to the old English writ system. This system determined not only the available rights but also the available remedies, of which damages are now the most important ones (nr 502). English law (and common law more generally) provides a broad spectrum of damages: pecuniary and non-pecuniary, general and special, nominal and substantial, compensatory and punitive. These various heads of damages are not always easy to distinguish and they are also subject to differing opinions in the legal literature.

The common ground is that damages are given as a sum of money. They are considered to be '... obtainable by success in an action, for a wrong which is either a tort or a breach of contract'.[49]

Many torts, such as the tort of negligence, require that the claimant has suffered a loss. If he can prove the amount of the damage he suffered he can obtain special damages. Other torts do not require proof of a loss: these torts are actionable *per se*, for instance trespass to land and libel (nr 504). Damages for these torts are symbolic, nominal, or general (though if the claimant can prove he has suffered damage special damages can be awarded). Nominal or general damages are also awarded in cases in which the fact of a loss is shown but the necessary evidence as to its amount is not given.[50] Nominal damages can be said to further the purpose of tort law as a means of vindicating the infringement of individual rights. However, English law does not show unequivocal commitment to this aim of recognition, since courts may on the contrary decide to award the claimant *contemptuous* damages where it disapproves of his behaviour. For example, it is not exceptional for a court to award the winner in a libel action the sum of £0.01,[51] and to even deny him recovery of his costs.[52]

Exemplary damages are available where the claimant has suffered loss at the hands of an unscrupulous and cynical tortfeasor who had, by his deliberate calculation, aimed to make a 'net profit' from committing the tort.[53] These

---

[49] Harvey McGregor, *On Damages*, 17th edn. (London: Sweet & Maxwell, 2003), para. 1-001.
[50] McGregor on Damages (2003), para. 10-001.
[51] *Reynolds v Times Newspapers* [2001] 2 AC 127.
[52] Markesinis and Deakin (2003), 784.
[53] *Rookes v Barnard* [1964] AC 1129, about which Van Gerven (2000), 743. Exemplary damages are also available in the particular case of 'oppressive, arbitrary or unconstitutional' conduct by Government servants, such as detention without a legal warrant: see *Huckle v Money* (1763) 2 Wils 205.

damages serve to civilly punish the defendant for his outrageous conduct but they are applied in moderation. They are not awarded for personal injury, not even in case of severe injury or gross negligent conduct.[54]

The reluctance of English judges compared with the approach in the US may be explained by the ambivalence of the very nature of punitive damages: there is considered to be a risk of confusion between the functions of civil and criminal law, whereas the latter alone provides adequate safeguards for the defendant. Indeed it is interesting to note that it has been decided that, where the defendant has been convicted of (and served the appropriate sanction for) a crime, exemplary damages are no longer available in a private law action in tort (*non bis in idem*).[55] However, the punitive role of exemplary damages remains ambiguous: while it is true that they are 'means-tested' (the defendant's financial status is taken into account when fixing the quantum of the award), they may also be awarded against a person vicariously liable for the direct tortfeasor's actions.[56]

Exemplary damages need to be distinguished from aggravated damages.[57] Whereas exemplary damages focus on the defendant's conduct, aggravated damages refer to a compensatory amount that takes into account the aggravated injury caused to the claimant's feelings of dignity and pride. Aggravated damages can be awarded in personal injury cases but this is unusual.[58]

Unlike many US jurisdictions, juries only play a modest role in the English law of damages though they still assess damages in, for example, defamation cases (nr 1201-3). In personal injury cases the role of the jury has in fact been abolished in 1966 by the Court of Appeal's decision in *Ward v James*. It considered that the necessary accessibility, uniformity, and predictability of damages awards cannot be warranted by a jury since a jury is not allowed to know what a conventional award of money is. The Court held that, in a personal injury, case, judges should order a trial by jury in exceptional circumstances only, for example for the award of exemplary damages.[59]

---

[54] *Rookes v Barnard* [1964] AC 1129, [1964] 2 WLR 269, [1964] 1 All ER 367, about which Van Gerven (2000), 743; *Cassell & Co Ltd v Broome* [1972] AC 1027, [1972] 2 WLR 645, [1972] 1 All ER 801, about which Van Gerven (2000), 745.   [55] *Archer v Brown* [1985] QB 401.

[56] *Thompson v MPC* [1998] QB 517.

[57] See *Thompson v Comr. of Police of the Metropolis* and *Hsu v Comr. of the Metropolis* [1997] 2 All ER 762, [1997] 3 WLR 403; *Kuddus v Chief Constable of Leicestershire Constabulary* [2001] UKHL 29. The Law Commission has recommended the abolition of aggravated damages and their absorbtion into a strict compensatory model: see Consultation Paper No. 132 on Aggravated, Exemplary and Restitutionary Damages, 1993, para. 8.18.

[58] See for instance *W v Meah* [1986] 1 All ER 935, a case of rape and vicious sexual assault (nr 1104).

[59] *Ward v James* [1966] 1 QB 273, 300, per Lord Denning MR, about which Van Gerven (2000), 776. This was confirmed in *H v Ministry of Defence* [1991] 2 QB 103; *Thompson v Comr. of the Police of the Metropolis* and *Hsu v Comr. of the Police of the Metropolis* [1997] 2 All ER 762, [1997] 3 WLR 403.

1202-4 *Community law: liability of Member States*

As regards remedies in Community law a distinction needs to be made between liability of Community institutions on the one hand and liability of Member States on the other.

The Member State liability developed in the so called *Francovich* case law (nr 205) requires the conferment of rights on individuals, a sufficiently serious breach of Community law and a direct causal link between the breach and the damage sustained. Remedies are not provided by Community law but by national law:

> ... it is for the domestic legal system of each Member State to designate the courts having jurisdiction and to determine the procedural conditions governing actions at law intended to ensure the protection of the rights which citizens have [under] (...) Community law, it being understood that such conditions cannot be less favourable than those relating to similar actions of a domestic nature.[60]

Hence, national remedies need to be in line with the principles of effectiveness and non-discrimination.

The principle of effectiveness also requires that reparation ' ... for loss or damage caused to individuals as a result of breaches of Community law must be commensurate with the loss or damage sustained so as to ensure the effective protection for their rights.'[61]

The consequences of these principles have been fleshed out in *Brasserie* and *Factortame III*. The Court held: 'National legislation which generally limits the damage for which reparation may be granted to damage done to certain, specifically protected individual interests not including loss of profit by individuals is not compatible with Community law.'[62] For example, the principle of non-discrimination implies that in English law it must be possible to award exemplary damages (nr 1202-3) pursuant to claims or actions for breach of Community law if such damages may be awarded pursuant to similar claims or actions founded on domestic law. At the same time the Court held that the German requirement of *Drittbezogenheit* is not compatible with *Francovich* liability (nr 1803-2) as is the English tort of misfeasance in a public office (nr 1804-5).

---

[60] ECJ 16 December 1976, Case 33/76, ECR 1976, 1989, at 1997–1998 (*Rewe-Zentralfinanz eG and Rewe Zentral AG v Landwirtshaftskammer für das Saarland*); see also ECJ 7 July 1981, Case 158/80, ECR 1981, 1805 (*Rewe v Hauptzollamt Kiel*).
[61] ECJ 5 March 1996, Joined cases C-46/93 and C-48/93, ECR 1996, I-1029 (*Brasserie du Pêcheur and Factortame III*), para. 82.
[62] ECJ 5 March 1996, Joined cases C-46/93 and C-48/93, ECR 1996, I-1029 (*Brasserie du Pêcheur and Factortame III*), para. 90.

1202-5 *Community law: liability of Community institutions*

In the area of the liability of a Community institution, the ECJ has provided Community law rules as regards the requirements of damage and damages, following Article 288(2) EC 'in accordance with the general principles common to the laws of the Member States.'[63] Initially, the Court used various definitions for recoverable damage varying from 'actual, significant and definite', 'direct', 'real' and 'actual and certain'. This did not exactly provide a clear path through the jungle. Leaving aside the requirement of directness (which is in fact a causation matter, see nr 1106), the most relevant requirements now seem to be that the damage is *actual* and *certain*. However, the formulations in the case law in this respect are not stable and conclusions can only be provisional.

That the damage has to be actual and certain does not mean that it must already have occurred. In *Kampffmeyer* the ECJ has acknowledged the possibility to file a claim for future damage, ie ' ... for imminent damage foreseeable with sufficient certainty even if the damage cannot yet be precisely assessed. To prevent even greater damage it may prove necessary to bring the matter before the Court as soon as the cause of damage is certain.' The ECJ referred to the Advocate-General's Opinion, pointing out that this approach matches the ones taken in the national legal systems where claims for future loss are generally allowed provided that the cause of the loss is sufficiently certain (nr 1205).[64]

The requirement that the damage is certain is a matter of proof rather than a matter of substance. The applicant has to provide factual evidence to enable the Court to assess the damage in question.[65]

Since the standard of proof required by the Court is very high and the furnishing of adequate evidence may be difficult or even impossible, the failure or inability of the applicant to satisfy this requirement has led to the dismissal of the application in a number of cases.[66]

---

[63] See for example A.G. Toth, 'The Concepts of Damage and Causality as Elements of Non-Contractual Liability', in Ton Heukels and Alison McDonnell, *The Action for Damages in Community Law* (The Hague, Boston: Kluwer Law International, 1997), 179–198; Wolfgang Wurmnest, *Grundzüge eines europäischen Haftungsrechts* (Tübingen: Mohr, 2003), 193–322.

[64] ECJ 2 June 1976, Joined Cases 56-60/74, ECR 1976, 711, at 741 (*Kampffmeyer v Commission and Council*). See also ECR 14 January 1987, Case 281/84, ECR 1987, 49 (*Zuckerfabrik Bedburg v Council and Commission*); ECJ 6 December 1984, Case 59/83, ECR 1984, 4057 (*Biovilac NV v EEC*). In ECJ 2 June 1965, Joined Cases 9 and 25/64, ECR 1965, 311 (*FERAM v High Authority*) it was held that future damage was not certain and actual yet and could therefore not be compensated.

[65] ECJ 9 June 1964, Joined Cases 55-59/63 and 61-63/63, ECR 1964, 211, at 229 (*Modena v High Authority*); CFI 14 September 1995, Case T-571/93, ECR 1995, II-2379, 2410 (*Lefebvre v Commission*).

[66] A.G. Toth, 'The Concepts of Damage and Causality as Elements of Non-Contractual Liability', in Ton Heukels and Alison McDonnell, *The Action for Damages in Community Law* (The Hague, Boston: Kluwer Law International, 1997), 184–185, with further references.

Cases are mainly about pure economic loss and it is often hard to prove which damage a company has actually sustained in the course of its business as a consequence of the Community institution's unlawful conduct. Particularly, the Court generally does not accept statistical evidence about disadvantageous trends in trade.[67]

Nominal damages are not awarded by the ECJ: the applicant has at least to make clear that damage has been suffered. In the *Roquette* case the applicant alleged it had suffered damage because its competitors were allowed certain benefits which were wrongly denied to the applicant. He claimed that he was entitled to nominal damages. The Court held: 'The fact that the applicant has reduced its claim to nominal damages does not relieve it of providing conclusive proof of the damage suffered.'[68]

See for the requirement of specific, and unusual damage in the framework of liability for lawful acts, nr 1806.

1202-6 *European Convention on Human Rights*

If a human right which is protected by the European Convention on Human Rights is infringed, such as the right to life or to privacy, a remedy is needed to make good the harm.[69] Article 41 (formerly Article 50) ECHR provides: 'If the Court finds that there has been a violation of the Convention or the protocols thereto, and if the internal law of the High Contracting Party concerned allows only partial reparation to be made, the Court shall, if necessary, afford just satisfaction to the injured party.' The principle of just satisfaction should not be understood in the specific way as was pointed out in nr 1201-2. On the contrary, the starting point for the Court is that the applicant should be brought to the position in which he or she would have been had there not been a breach of the Convention: *restitutio in integrum*.

This follows from a landmark decision of the Court in 1995, in which it set out the consequences if a State has violated the Convention. It considered that a judgment

... in which the Court finds a breach imposes on the respondent State a legal obligation to put an end to the breach and make reparation for its consequences in such a way as to restore as far as possible the situation existing before the breach. The Contracting States that are parties to a case are in principle free to choose the means whereby they will

[67] ECJ 21 May 1975, Case 26/74, ECR 1976, 677, 687 (*Roquette v Commission*); ECJ 17 December 1981, Joined Cases 197–200, 243, 245 and 247/80, ECR 1981, 3211, 3254 (*Ludwigshafener Walzmühle v Council and Commission*).

[68] ECJ 21 May 1975, Case 26/74, ECR 1976, 677, 688 (*Roquette v Commission*).

[69] See about this topic Tim Eicke and David Scorey, *Human Rights Damages: Principles and Practice* (London: Sweet & Maxwell, 2001); Gerhard Danneman, *Schadensersatz bei Verletzung der Europäischen Menschenrechtskonvention: eine rechtsvergleichende Untersuchung zur Haftung nach Art. 50 EMRK* (Cologne: Heymann, 1994) and from a more general perspective Dinah Shelton, *Remedies in International Human Rights Law*, 2nd edn. (Oxford: Oxford University Press, 2005).

comply with a judgment in which the Court has found a breach. This discretion as to the manner of execution of a judgment reflects the freedom of choice attaching to the primary obligation of the Contracting States under the Convention to secure the rights and freedoms guaranteed (Article 1). If the nature of the breach allows of restitutio in integrum, it is for the respondent State to effect it, the Court having neither the power nor the practical possibility of doing so itself. If, on the other hand, national law does not allow—or allows only partial—reparation to be made for the consequences of the breach, Article [41] empowers the Court to afford the injured party such satisfaction as appears to it to be appropriate.

Hence, it is primarily up to the Contracting State to make good the damage suffered by the applicant as a consequence of the violation of the Convention. The Court only steps in when national law does not allow (or only partially allows) reparation for the consequences of the breach.

If *restitutio in integrum* is not possible, which will often be the case, the Court awards just satisfaction under various heads: financial satisfaction can be awarded for pecuniary loss, non-pecuniary loss, and costs and expenses. Immaterial satisfaction can be provided by the mere declaration that there has been a violation of the rights protected by the Convention. This is a rather regular though perhaps unsatisfactory way of providing just satisfaction. There are also instances in which the applicant by way of just satisfaction was afforded nominal damages, for example ' . . . a token indemnity of one hundred Dutch guilders'.[70]

1203 Collateral benefits

Tort systems try to avoid overcompensating the victim, since the object of tort law is not only to achieve *restitutio in integrum* (nr 1201-1) but is also *limited* to that (*compensatio lucri at damni*). Specifically, courts aim to deduct collateral benefits from an award of damages where this is appropriate. In Germany this is called *Vorteilsausgleichung* and the French deal with this issue under the heading of *réglementation du cumul d'indemnité*. German, English, and French courts take a similar purposive approach to the question of setting off collateral benefits received by the claimant against damages awards.[71]

The general rule is that payments made to the victim which are intended to be a substitute for damages, and which are awarded in respect of an identical loss, are deductible, for example, payments under certain insurance schemes. One can also see it this way: that these payments reduce the claimant's damage and that, insofar as the damage is reduced, he does not have a claim. In respect of monies paid out under private *medical* insurance schemes, English law considers that: 'The insurances under these schemes (. . .) are regarded as indemnity insurances

---

[70] ECtHR 23 November 1976, Case 5100/71 (*Engel and Others v The Netherlands*).

[71] See generally Markesinis and Deakin (2003), 796 ff; Le Tourneau (2004), no 2590 ff; Münchener Kommentar-Oetker (2003), § 249 N 222 ff.

which entitle the insurers themselves to recover their outlays directly from the tortfeasor through the medium of subrogation'. The individual victim '. . . has no standing to claim the medical expenses; he has been made whole by the insurers who in their turn step into his shoes and make the claim for the moneys expended by them'.[72] The principle is the same in French law: there is subrogation where the purpose of the payment by the third party is to indemnify the victim.[73] Similarly, in German law, social and private insurers have a right of recourse against the tortfeasor: social insurers as far as they were obliged to provide the victim sick pay or a disability pension (§ 116 *Sozialgesetzbuch X*, Social Code) and private insurers as far as they compensate the victim (§ 67 *Versicherungsvertragsgesetz* (Insurance Contract Act)).[74]

Generally, payments of social and private insurers lower the claimant's damage but, because of the insurer's right of recourse, the tortfeasor does not benefit from the claimant's insurance coverage. Thus, from the defendant's perspective, there is no net reduction in the extent of his liability: he simply pays the same quantum but to a different claimant (the victim's private or social insurer).

In England, courts have also accepted the deduction of *ex gratia* payments made directly by the tortfeasor, and also any wages paid by the employer under the name of sick pay or otherwise.[75] In principle, the latter are deductible from any award for loss of earnings because they are a partial substitute for these wages: 'The purpose of the payment is directly to reduce the loss and not to allow the injured party a bonus in addition to compensation received from the tortfeasor for that loss.'[76] This may be likened to the French and German position, where benefits paid out to the victim (for example, representing income replacement) under a social security scheme or by the employer are also deducted from the damages award.[77] If the employer and the social insurer have a right of recourse, as is the case in France and Germany, the tortfeasor does not benefit from the employer's and social insurer's payments.[78]

In contrast, a number of collateral benefits are deemed non-deductible. Firstly, charitable donations are deemed non-deductible. English courts consider that to allow the tortfeasor to be unjustly enriched by a benevolent gift intended for the claimant would be 'revolting to the ordinary man's sense of justice, and therefore contrary to public policy'.[79] In Germany the ratio is that these donations are aimed to be for the benefit of the victim, not that of the tortfeasor.[80]

---

[72] McGregor on Damages (2003), para. 35-182. [73] Le Tourneau (2004), nr 2590.
[74] Kötz-Wagner (2001), N 508–509.
[75] *Williams v BOC Gases* [2000] PIQR Q253 (ex gratia payments); *Hussain v New Taplow Paper Mills Ltd* [1988] AC 514 (wages); see also *Parsons v BNM Leyland (UK) Ltd* [1964] 1 QB 95.
[76] Clerk and Lindsell on Torts (2000) nr 29-43.
[77] Civ. 2e 9 November 1976, Bull. civ. II, no 302; Civ. 2e 17 April 1975, Bull. civ. II, no 110; Civ. 2e 28 January 1998, Resp. civ. et ass. 1998, no 117, comm. Groutel. Le Tourneau (2004), nr 2621. [78] Kötz-Wagner (2001), N 508-509; Le Tourneau (2004), nr 2619.
[79] *Parry v Cleaver* [1970] AC 1, at 14.
[80] Münchener Kommentar-Oetker (2003), § 249 N 242.

Next, monies paid under private *accident* insurance schemes subscribed to by the victim are considered non-deductible from awards for loss of earning capacity. In France, the justification for this is that these payments are not considered to be compensatory, since they simply represent the *quid pro quo* of the premiums which had been previously paid under the insurance scheme and so are a legitimate contractual 'bonus'.[81] German law takes a similar stand by holding that the insurance is intended to be for the benefit of the insured, not the tortfeasor.[82] English courts reach the same result but here the ground is related to causation and remoteness. The insurance payout is a 'completely collateral matter [which is] predominately caused by some extraneous and independent cause'.[83] It may be suggested that the result in the three systems is essentially one of policy: to avoid discouraging individuals from taking out first-party insurance.[84]

Finally, the deductibility of disablement pensions poses a particular problem. In France, the *Cour de cassation* has deemed that the aim of such payments is to provide assistance (*assistance*) to the claimant and not to compensate (*indemniser*) him.[85] Again, the same position is taken by German law.[86] The English House of Lords has also decided, by a bare 3–2 majority, upon the non-deductibility of an occupational disability pension: this applies (logically) if the payment is made under a contribution-based scheme since it is seen as a form of 'deferred remuneration', which has been rightly earned by the claimant in his distinct capacity as employee. But the House of Lords held that this solution should also cover non-contribution based disability pensions.[87] These concurring approaches in the legal systems run counter to that of the English Law Commission which has asked for the disability pension to be deductible.[88]

B PERSONAL INJURY

1204 Introduction

If someone suffers personal injury for which another person is liable, he may suffer various kinds of damage.[89] As regards pecuniary (financial) loss one may think of costs for health care, loss of income, and other costs incurred by the accident. In many cases the practical application of the rules can be complicated,

[81] Le Tourneau (2004), nr 2590.
[82] Münchener Kommentar-Oetker (2003), § 249 N 249; BGH 19 November 1955, BGHZ 19, 94 = NJW 1956, 222; BGH 17 October 1957, BGHZ 25, 322 = NJW 1957, 1876.
[83] *Parry v Cleaver* [1970] AC 1.   [84] Markesinis and Deakin (2003), 798.
[85] Le Tourneau (2004), nr 2590.   [86] Münchener Kommentar-Oetker (2003), § 249 N 249.
[87] *Parry v Cleaver* [1970] AC 1, per Lord Pearce at 36 and per Lord Wilberforce at 42.
[88] Law Commission Consultation Paper No 147 (1997) at para 4.67.
[89] See for an overview S. Lindenbergh (ed.), *Personal Injury Compensation in Europe* (Deventer: Kluwer, 2003).

for example as regards the proof of the existence of an illness or the causal connection with the accident (nr 1107–1108). Also, it may take a long time, often many years, to establish the victim's final medical position and to settle the case. At this final stage, the claimant's future damage needs to be established. This generally raises difficult questions to which there are no easy answers, and perhaps not even correct answers (nr 1205).

Personal injury does not only cause pecuniary (material) loss but also non-pecuniary (immaterial) loss, such as pain and suffering and loss of amenities. Though all systems acknowledge this head of damage, there are considerable differences in the way they are being structured (nr 1206). In this respect the jurisdictions also provide various answers to the question of whether an unconscious person has a right to compensation of immaterial loss. The answer to this question reveals aspects of the function of compensation of non-pecuniary loss (nr 1207).

If someone dies as the consequence of an accident this sole fact will not give rise to compensation, apart from the funeral costs. The loss of life as such is not compensable (nr 702). Generally, only the relatives will have a claim for damages: for pecuniary loss if they are financially dependant on the deceased, sometimes for non-pecuniary loss (grief and sorrow), and sometimes for mental harm (nr 1211).

Not only physical harm but also mental harm can cause pecuniary loss (costs for health care, loss of income) and non-pecuniary loss (pain and suffering, loss of amenities). The right to compensation for mental harm is generally acknowledged throughout the legal systems, provided it is related to the physical injury. More reluctance exists as regards 'pure mental harm', ie mental harm not connected to physical harm, for example if someone witness a serious accident and suffers a severe shock. See about the relation between physical and mental harm and between pecuniary and non-pecuniary loss, nr 704.

In this section three issues will be dealt with. Firstly, the question of future damage and the various ways in which damages for this head of damage are awarded: in a lump sum or in periodical payments (nr 1205). Secondly, the question of compensation of non-pecuniary loss and what the various levels of compensation for personal injury in the legal systems are (nr 1206). Finally, the question of whether an unconscious person has a right to compensation for non-pecuniary loss; in this respect the legal systems come to similar solutions in answering this question in the affirmative (nr 1207).

1205 Future damage

If a car is damaged in an accident, this can be considered to be a once-and-for-all loss. It goes without saying that such a loss can be compensated by an amount equal to the costs of repair and the loss of value.

This is different if someone suffers a personal injury which has consequences for the rest of his life. This is continuing damage which will mainly consist of lost earnings following from the fact that the victim is not able to work anymore or to do work at the same income level. The injured person will also have increased needs, such as for medical care and for aids like a wheelchair or a special car.

It is a complicated matter to establish the amount of compensation as regards the claimant's future damage. This amount will depend on various factors that are hard to assess: the nature of the injury, the age the victim will reach, his mental and physical strength, and the expected future development of the victim's position: is his condition expected to deteriorate or to improve? Moreover, exogenous factors like inflation, the rise in wages and prises, as well as changes in tax law, also and social security law have to be taken into account.

Particularly as regards social security, it is important to note that in more recent years many governments have cut back their social security expenses. It is beyond doubt that in the past many court decisions or out-of-court settlements have relied on future compensation for the claimant by the social security system. The subsequent changes in legislation may have caused gaps in many claimants' financial positions.

Future damage can be compensated by a lump sum (*capital* in France, *Kapitalabfindung* in Germany) or by a periodical payment (*rente* in France, *Rente* in Germany). Whereas a lump sum is a non-revisable, once-and-for-all award, a periodical payment will often be revisable and thus adaptable to changed circumstances.[90] In this respect the traditions of the legal systems differ.[91]

In England the non-revisable once-and-for-all award is still the rule.[92] In establishing future damages the courts generally apply simple calculation methods. They seem to be disinclined to trust scientific methods:

As a method of providing a reliable guide to individual behaviour patterns or to future economical and political events, the predictions of an actuary can be only a little more likely to be accurate (and will almost certainly be less interesting) than those of an astrologer.[93]

[90] Periodical payments subject to adaptation are well known in family law, for example alimony payments between divorced persons.
[91] Art. 10:102 PETL does not make a choice: Damages are awarded in a lump sum or as periodical payments as appropriate with particular regard to the interests of the victim.' Article 6:203 ECC prefers the lump sum: 'Compensation is to be awarded once and for all unless a good reason requires periodical payment.
[92] See for example *Brunsden v Humphrey* (1884) 14 QBD 141, about which Van Gerven (2000), 818–819 and *Lim Poh Choo v Camden and Islington Area Health Authority* [1980] AC 174 (HL), about which Van Gerven (2000), 819–820. See also *Fournier v Canadian National Railway* [1927] AC 167.
[93] Oliver LJ in *Auty v National Coal Board* [1985] 1 All ER 930, 939. See also nr 501-5 about the relation between the English judiciary and the academic world.

For a few years, periodical payments have been allowed on the basis of the Damages Act 1996. Section 2, as revised by the Courts Act 2003, provides that a court may award damages for future pecuniary loss in respect of personal injury in the form of periodical payments. For the award of other damages in respect of personal injury such payments need the parties' consent. A court may not award periodical payments unless it is satisfied that the continuity of payment is reasonably secure. There is no provision for adapting the payment following changes in the claimant's personal circumstances although the Lord Chancellor may by order enable a court which has made an order for periodical payments to vary the order in specified circumstances.[94]

As regards loss of earnings and costs caused by an impairment of body and health, German law adheres to the revisable periodical payments. This follows from § 843 I BGB. The same rule applies to the compensation of loss of income of dependants of a deceased victim (§ 843 II). § 843 III provides the court with the possibility to grant a lump sum award if there is a serious reason to do so.

The French requirement that the damage must be certain (nr 1202-1) is no obstacle to assessing future damage.[95] The lower courts are free to choose between a lump sum and a periodical payment though the former is clearly preferred to the latter. In both cases a revision is possible but only if this is advantageous for the claimant.[96]

The main advantage of the once-and-for-all award is that parties can put an end to their dispute. This can help the claimant to concentrate on the future rather than to stick to the past. The advantage for liability insurance companies is that they can close the file. However, an inevitable risk of a once-and-for-all award is the over- or undercompensation of the claimant, since it is very difficult for the court to establish future damage with sufficient certainty.

Knowledge of the future being denied to mankind, so much of the award as is to be attributed to future loss and suffering—in many cases the major part of the award—will almost surely be wrong. There is really only one certainty: the future will prove the award to be either too high or too low.[97]

In this respect revisable payments are to be preferred but this leads to higher social costs, for it will be mainly up to the courts to establish the new periodical payment.

---

[94] Section 2B(1) of the Damages Act 1996 as amended by the Courts Act 2003. See Oliphant, *ETL*, 2002, 143–144 and *ETL*, 2003, 113.   [95] Req. 1 June 1932, D. 1932. I. 102.
[96] Civ. 2e 29 April 1994, Resp. civ. et ass. 1994, 243, about which Van Gerven (2000), 838–840; Req. 30 December 1946, D. 1947. 178, about which Van Gerven (2000), 842–843; Civ. 2e 12 October 1972, D. 1974. 536, comm. Malaurie, JCP 1974. II. 17609, comm. Brousseau, about which Van Gerven (2000), 843.
[97] Lord Scarman in *Lim Poh Choo v Camden and Islington Area Health Authority* [1980] AC 174, 183; see also about this case Van Gerven (2000), 819–820. See in the same sense Lord Steyn in *Wells v Wells* [1998] 3 WLR 329, 351. It is considered to be the task of the legislator to change the law.

1206 Non-pecuniary loss for personal injury

Physical or psychological injury usually causes not only pecuniary but also non-pecuniary loss. One may think of pain and suffering, loss of amenity, loss of expectation of life, or disfigurement. In Germany this head of damage is generally known as *immaterieller Schaden* (immaterial damage) and in France as *dommage moral* (moral damage). In the latter country pecuniary loss is considered to be loss of *avoirs* (having) and non-pecuniary loss to be loss of *être* (being).[98]

The aspects of non-pecuniary loss for personal injury vary throughout the systems. French law distinguishes between *souffrances morales ou physiques* (mental or physical suffering or *pretium doloris*), *préjudice esthétique* (aesthetic damage), and *préjudice d'agrément* (loss of leisure). For each of these heads of damage separate sums are awarded.[99] English law distinguishes between pain and suffering and loss of amenity, the latter being the damaging effect upon the claimant's ability to enjoy life.[100] German law does not distinguish between the heads of non-pecuniary loss but it does as regards the functions of the award (*Schmerzensgeld*): compensation and satisfaction (nr 1201-2). Neither English nor German law award separate sums of money for the various aspects of non-pecuniary loss. More generally, the division of people's sufferings as the consequence of physical damage may be of some use for analytical reasons, but it is to be criticized because they are all intertwined aspects of one affected personality and these aspects cannot be treated separately.[101]

The amounts of damages for non-pecuniary loss differ considerably from system to system. There are also differences in emphasis as to which aspects of non-pecuniary loss are relevant. Though each case is different and so is each victim, an important guideline for the courts is to look at the amounts awarded in similar cases. Awards deviating in this respect from the median will need a more thorough justification by the court. In Germany so-called *Schmerzensgeldtabellen* are regularly published.[102] These are lists of what ranges of *Schmerzensgeld* have been awarded for what injury. This instrument plays an

---

[98] Le Tourneau (2004), nr 1309:

Une chose est la lésion, l'atteinte, celle des corps (dommage corporel), des choses (dommage materiel), des sentiments (dommage moral); autre choses sont les repercussions de la lesion, de l'atteinte, répercussions sur le patrimoine, répercussions sur la personne de la victime, sur ses avoirs (préjudice patrimoniale) et sur son être (préjudice extra-patrimoniale).

[99] Le Tourneau (2004), nr 1583–1587. He also mentions *le préjudice sexuel*: the partial or complete impossibility to maintain regular intimate contacts or to procreate.
[100] Winfield and Jolowicz (2002), para. 22.19; Markesinis and Deakin (2003), 827–829. A third ground—loss of expectation of life—was abolished by the Administration of Justice Act 1982. This was an indirect way for damages for bereavement in certain cases but this is now dealt with directly by statute (nr 1210). [101] Le Tourneau (2004), nr 1588–1592.
[102] Susanne Hacks, Ameli Ring and Peter Böhm, *Schmerzensgeld*, 23th edn. (Bonn: Dt. Anwalt-verl., 2005); Andreas Slizyk, *Schmerzensgeld-Tabelle*, 4th edn. (Munich: Beck, 2001).

increasing rule in the harmonization of the law, in addition to the role of the BGH.[103] In England the Court of Appeal sets the level of awards and issues guidelines.[104]

Compensation of non-pecuniary loss is generally paid as a lump sum. However, in cases of severe physical impairment the German courts are also entitled to award a periodical payment for the duration of the claimant's life.[105]

One of the possibilities to compare legal systems is to look at the amounts paid for the most severe kinds of physical injury such as quadriplegia or very severe brain damage.[106] In this respect the highest sum of compensation for non-pecuniary loss awarded by an English judge is £205,000 (€300,000).[107] The highest German award for *Schmerzensgeld* in such cases is currently €500,000 as a lump sum. This can be combined with a periodical payment of €1,000 or more per month.[108] Somewhat surprisingly, the highest French awards for *dommage moral* are not much higher than €100,000.[109]

These amounts show that, though English law is generally considered to be less generous towards claimants than French law, the sums awarded in the English system are more generous. The chance of getting compensation is lower but if one is successful the compensation is higher. In other words, the top of the compensation pyramid is higher but the base, ie the number of people who are compensated, is smaller. If this is correct, it may be thought that the French pyramid of damages has the classical Egyptian shape whereas the English pyramid will look more like the *Tour d'Eiffel*. Continuing this metaphor the German picture would look like an Egyptian pyramid with twice the height of the Eiffel tower.

1207 Unconsciousness

The legal systems are unanimous that consciousness is not required to award a claim for non-pecuniary loss but a difficult issue in this respect is the question as to what extent someone can obtain damages for non-pecuniary loss if he suffered physical harm that caused loss of consciousness.

[103] BGH 8 June 1976, VersR 1976, 967.   [104] *Heil v Rankin* [2000] 2 WLR 1173.

[105] See for instance BGH 13 October 1992, BGHZ 120, 1 = NJW 1993, 781 in which a lump sum of DM 50,000 (€25,500) was awarded and a monthly payment of DM 500 (€255), about which Markesinis and Unberath (2002), 997–999.

[106] See for a Europe wide comparative overview of personal injury awards: David McIntosh and Marjorie Holmes (eds.), *Personal Injury Awards in EU and EFTA Countries* (The Hague, London: Kluwer Law International, 2003).   [107] *Heil v Rankin* [2000] 2 WLR 1173.

[108] See for example OLG Hamm 16 January 2002, VersR 2002, 1163, ETL 2002, 214 (Fedtke). In this respect is interesting to note that German law does not award compensation for *Bagatellschaden*, ie damages for non-pecuniary loss caused by minor personal harm.

[109] This amount included damages for pain and suffering, aesthetical injury and loss of leisure. See David McIntosh and Marjorie Holmes (eds.), *Personal Injury Awards in EU and EFTA Countries* (The Hague, London: Kluwer Law International, 2003), 319.

French tort law awards damages for non-pecuniary loss, ie pain and suffering, as well as loss of amenity (*préjudice d'agrément*), to victims who are fully unconscious or in a coma. The victim's position is assessed in an objective way. In 1995 the *Cour de cassation* considered that ' . . . the vegetative state of a human being does not exclude any head of damages and the claimant's loss must be made good in its entirety.'[110]

In the same way the German BGH has awarded damages for non-pecuniary loss to an unconscious victim. After having been more reluctant in previous cases, it decided in 1992: ' . . . damage to the personality and the loss of personal quality as a consequence of severe brain damage represent in themselves non-material harm which is to be compensated for independently of whether the person affected feels the impairment.' Accordingly, the BGH held that the damages should be more than just symbolic, because they reflect a loss of personality and human dignity.[111]

In the case of unconsciousness, English law provides compensation for loss of amenity (to which an objective test applies) but not for pain and suffering (to which a subjective test applies; it is presumed that the victim is not in any pain). This was decided by a small majority of the House of Lords in *West & Son v Shephard*.[112] In this case Lord Morris said:

The fact of unconsciousness is therefore relevant in respect of and will eliminate those heads or elements of damage which can only exist by being felt or thought or experienced. The fact of unconsciousness does not, however, eliminate the actuality of the deprivations of the ordinary experiences and amenities of life which may be the inevitable result of some physical injury.

Compensation of non-pecuniary loss provides the claimant with the possibility to buy amenities he can enjoy instead of amenities he is no longer able to enjoy. It can also satisfy the claimant's disturbed feelings. However, these functions are not of much use for an unconscious person. Hence, the legal systems assess non-pecuniary loss in an objective way, thus moving away from the compensation and satisfaction functions towards recognizing the victim's infringed interest: his loss of personality and dignity (nr 1201).

---

[110] Civ. 2e 22 February 1995, D. 1995. Somm 233, obs. Mazeaud, JCP 1995. I. 3853, obs. Viney; Civ. 2e 28 June 1995, D. 1995. IR. 215. Terré-Simler-Lequette (2002), nr 708; see also Van Gerven (2000), 118–120.

[111] BGH 13 October 1992, BGHZ 120, 1 = NJW 1993, 781, comm. Deutsch, about which Markesinis and Unberath (2002), 997–999, from which the translation is cited (998) and comparative case comments in *ERPL*, 4/2 (1996), 221–261. See also BGH 16 February 1993, NJW 1993, 1531. OLG Hamm 16 January 2002, Vers 2002 1163, ETL 2002, 214 (Fedtke) awarded the maximum amount of €500,000 in a case in which the person's personality was practically destroyed due to medical malpractice.

[112] *West & Son v Shephard* [1964] AC 326, [1963] 2 WLR 1359, [1963] 2 All ER 625, about which Van Gerven (2000), 99–100; in the same sense *Lim Poh Choo v Camden Area Health Authority* [1980] AC 174, about which Van Gerven (2000), 819–820. See also *Wise v Kaye* [1962] 1 QB 638.

C FAMILY TIES

1208 Introduction

If someone dies as the consequence of an accident for which another person is liable, third parties may also suffer damage, particularly the parents, the partner, or the child of the victim. These are what the French call *victimes par ricochet*. Here, they will also be referred to as secondary victims. The loss they suffer can be fourfold: costs of the funeral, loss of maintenance (nr 1209), non-pecuniary loss (grief and sorrow) (nr 1210), and mental harm as a consequence of witnessing a fatal accident or a very serious non-fatal accident (nr 1211).

The question of whether a right to compensation for third parties exists is often linked to questions of causation and the scope of the duty: was the damage to the relatives 'caused' by the tortfeasor and did the infringed rule aim to protect the rights of the relatives? In many jurisdictions, however, these questions are governed by specific statutory provisions.

In all three countries the tortfeasor of a fatal accident is obliged to pay for the costs of the funeral or cremation. Compensation is owed to the person who has paid the costs, mostly the relatives but sometimes the employer or the municipality.[113] It could be argued that there is no causal connection between the tortfeasor's conduct and the damage, because at some point the victim would have died anyway and funeral or cremation costs would have to be made anyway. This argument is, however, dismissed in all three systems.

As regards compensation for relatives, be it for pecuniary or non-pecuniary loss, the question is who qualifies as 'relative'.[114] This is particularly disputed as regards unmarried partners, be they heterosexual or homosexual. This dispute reflects the changes that have taken place in the past decades in the way people organize their private life and their relationships. For example, until recently German law only acknowledged a right to compensation for loss of maintenance by married partners. French and English law acknowledged the right of unmarried partners but only if they were heterosexual; the right of same-sex partners was dismissed.

In recent years all three countries have created possibilities to conclude some kind of registered partnership. In England this is the *Civil Partnership* and in Germany the *eingetragene Partnerschaft*. Both apply to same-sex partners only. In France the *Pacte civil de solidarité* (*PACS*) can also be concluded by heterosexual partners.

---

[113] *France*: Crim. 1 July 1986, Sem. Jur. 1986. IV. 267; *Germany*: § 844 Abs. 1 jo. § 1968 BGB; *England*: Section 3(5) Fatal Accidents Act 1976. Von Bar (2000), N 47. In the same sense Article 2:202(2)(b) ECC.

[114] The 'illegitimate' child (a child born outside marriage and not recognized by the father) has the same rights as other children since ECtHR 13 June 1979, Case 6833/74 (*Marckx v Belgium*).

Since the enactments of the respective Acts these registered partners are included in the group of persons who have a right to compensation for loss of maintenance.

As regards other European countries it can be argued that denying same sex partners the same rights as heterosexual partners could be in variance with the ECHR. Although same sex relationships do not amount to 'family life' in the sense of Article 8 ECHR, the Court provides some protection to these relationships. An Austrian case was about the right to succeed to a tenancy to which the applicable law entitled the spouse and the life companion. The Austrian Supreme Court (*Oberster Gerichtshof*) held that the latter did not include homosexual companions as this was not the legislature's intention in 1974. Before the ECtHR the Austrian government argued that the aim of the provision at issue was the protection of the traditional family unit. However, the Court held that Austria had failed to show that it was necessary to exclude persons living in a homosexual relationship from the scope of application of the statutory rule in order to protect the 'traditional family'.[115] Hence, it can be argued, in the framework of the law of damages, that if a right to compensation is provided to an unmarried partner this includes the same-sex partner, unless it can be shown that a different treatment is necessary to protect the 'traditional family'—and this is very unlikely.

1209 Loss of maintenance

In Germany § 844 II BGB provides that only persons whom the deceased had a statutory duty to maintain have a right to compensation from the tortfeasor. These are the spouse (§ 1360), the registered partner (§ 5 *Lebenspartnerschaftsgesetz*), the children (§ 1601 ff.), and the adopted children (§ 1766).[116] Registered partnerships are only possible between persons of the same sex.

It follows from this list that an unmarried or unregistered partner and a stepchild are not entitled to claim. A right to compensation for loss of maintenance only exists if the deceased was legally obliged to maintain the claimant (§ 844–845). The fact that he actually maintained the deceased is not relevant. This means that a stepson does not have a right to compensation even though his stepfather maintained him for many years as his own child. Also if someone dies shortly before his marriage, his future wife will not have a right to compensation for loss of maintenance since the obligation to maintain starts only from the day of marriage.[117] Given this restricted approach it is not surprising that employers,

---

[115] ECtHR 24 July 2003, Case 40016/98 (*Karner v Austria*), paras 40–41.

[116] These rules also apply in cases of strict liability: see §§ 10 StVG, 5 HPflG, 35 LuftVG, 28 AtomG.

[117] Kötz-Wagner (2001), N 544–545; Deutsch-Ahrens (2002), N 439; Christian Schubel, 'Ansprüche Unterhaltsberechtigter bei Tötung des Verpflichteten zwischen Delikts-, Familien- und Erbrecht', *AcP*, 198 (1998), 1–34.

employees, creditors, or clients of the deceased do not have a right to compensation either.[118]

The amount of compensation is mostly paid as a periodical payment and not as a lump sum (§ 843 II BGB, nr 1205) and is determined by the amount the deceased was obliged to pay, considering his income.[119] In the case of the death of someone who took care of the household (in most cases this is still the woman), the costs of household assistance are the starting point for assessing damages.[120]

English law provides a right to compensation of the costs of maintenance for the spouse and the former spouse, the parents, children, step- and foster children as well as the partner, provided he or she has lived with the deceased for at least two years. Only these dependants enumerated in section 1(3) of the Fatal Accidents Act 1976 are entitled to damages for the costs of maintenance (pecuniary loss).[121] Until the Civil Partnership Act 2004, same sex partners were not included since section 1(3)(iii) required that the claimant had been living *as the husband or wife* of the deceased. Section 83 of the Civil Partnership Act 2004, however, has included the civil partner. According to s. 1(1) of this Act a civil partnership is an officially registered relationship between two people of the same sex.

Section 5 of the Fatal Accidents Act 1976 provides that contributory negligence of the deceased may reduce the amount of compensation. The statutory enumeration of persons entitled to compensation for loss of maintenance is exhaustive which means that, just like in German law, English law does not grant employers or other third parties a right to compensation.

Contrary to German law, in English law it is not necessary that the deceased was obliged to maintain the relative. The relative also has a right to compensation if the deceased paid for maintenance on a voluntary basis.[122] The amount of compensation depends on the reasonable expectation as to how long the deceased would have maintained the dependant. Hence, a right to compensation was denied in the case of a woman who had left her husband five weeks before he died.[123] Also, if the relative ran a business together with the deceased, he can only claim damages for the loss caused by the death of his spouse but not for the loss he suffers because the business had to be terminated. So, when a dancer died, her partner received compensation for the loss of his lady as a spouse but not for his lady as a dance partner.[124]

---

[118] Kötz-Wagner (2001), N 544.　　　[119] Kötz-Wagner (2001), N 546.

[120] BGH 26 November 1968, BGHZ 51, 109; BGH 8 February 1983, BGHZ 86, 372 = NJW 1983, 1425.

[121] As amended by the Administration of Justice Act 1982 (c. 53). See for the main provisions Van Gerven (2000), 107–109. Winfield and Jolowicz (2002), paras 23.9–23.17; Markesinis and Deakin (2003), 833–842.　　　[122] Winfield and Jolowicz (2002), paras 23.12–23.13.

[123] *Davies v Taylor* [1972] 3 All ER 836 (HL).

[124] *Burgess v Florence Nightingale Hospital for Gentlewomen* [1955] QB 349 (Devlin J). See also *Malyon v Plummer* [1964] 1 QB 330 (CA): the woman worked in the business of her deceased husband but did not get compensation for loss of salary.

On the basis of the word *dommage* in article 1382 CC the French courts have assessed which third parties have a right to compensation. The case law requires that the infringed interest was legitimate and that the damage was certain and directly caused. This implies that French law does not require that the deceased had an obligation to maintain the claimant but that it is sufficient if he in fact maintained him.[125] Also, the employer and the business partner can claim damages for the loss caused by the death of their employee or business partner, provided that a causal connection between the loss and the accident can be established.[126]

French family ties do not need to be of a formal kind. The partner of an unwed couple can claim damages if the other partner died as a consequence of an accident for which a third party is liable. The *Cour de cassation* thus decided in 1970 in a case in which M. Dangereux (*nomen est omen*) was liable for a car accident causing the death of M. Paillette. The court allowed his partner, Mlle Gaudras, an action for damages, acknowledging that the surviving partner has a legitimate interest (*intérêt légitime*) to bring an action in tort, but it has to be established that the relationship of the couple was sufficiently stable and continuous (the *dommage* has to be *certain*).[127] In a later decision it was added that this implied a relationship '. . . between a man and a woman.'[128] This position, however, has been condemned by the legislator. It created a registered partnership for heterosexual and same sex couples, the so-called PACS (*pacte civil de solidarité*) in articles 515–518 CC (nr 1208).

The draft ECC and the PETL both provide a right to compensation to the natural person whom the deceased maintained or would have maintained if death had not occurred, thus excluding other third parties like employers or business partners from claiming damages. Both proposals provide a right to compensation to the person to whom the deceased actually provided care and financial support, regardless of whether he was statutorily obliged to do so, thus preferring the French and English approach over the German.[129] This latter difference is particularly relevant for unmarried couples. Indeed, considering the way people currently organize their private lives and their relationships, it is doubtful that it should make a difference whether the deceased had formally or actually taken responsibility for someone else.

[125] Ch. mixte 27 February 1970, D. 1970. 201, comm. Combaldieu.

[126] Civ. 2e 12 June 1987, Bull. civ. II, no 128; Civ. 12 December 1979, Gaz. Pal. 1980. 1. 247.

[127] Ch. mixte 27 February 1970, D. 1970. 201, comm. Combaldieu, JCP 1970. II. 16305, comm. Parlange. See about this case also Van Gerven (2000), 125.

[128] Civ. 3e 17 December 1997, D. 1998. 111, comm. Aubert: '. . . le concubinage ne peut résulter que d'une relation stable et continue ayant l'apparence du mariage, donc entre un homme et une femme'.

[129] Art. 2:202(2)(c) ECC: '. . . loss of maintenance is legally relevant damage to a natural person whom the deceased maintained or, had death not occurred, would have maintained under statutory provisions or to whom the deceased provided care and financial support.' Article 10:202(2) PETL: 'In the case of death, persons such as family members whom the deceased maintained or would have maintained if death had not occurred are treated as having suffered recoverable damage to the extent of loss of that support.'

The tortfeasor can invoke the deceased's contributory negligence against the persons claiming compensation for the costs of maintenance.[130] This is considered to be justified because the cause of the damage is the same even though it is someone else's damage.[131] In England contributory negligence is based on section 5 of the Fatal Accidents Act 1976; in Germany § 846 provides that the tortfeasor can invoke the deceased's contributory negligence (§ 254) against the dependants,[132] and in France the rule has been developed by the courts.[133] In the same sense Article 8:101(2) PETL.

1210 Non-pecuniary loss for loss of a loved one

The loss of a close relative or another loved one can give rise not only to loss of maintenance but also to immaterial loss, such as sorrow, grief, and the loss of companionship. If relatives do not have a claim for loss of maintenance, for example if a child dies as the consequence of an accident, compensation of non-pecuniary loss will be particularly important from a recognition point of view (nr 1201-2). It needs to be emphasized that claims for non-pecuniary loss are strongly related to claims for nervous shock. The latter cases also concern people who suffer damage as a secondary victim, for example because they witness the accident (nr 1211).

In Germany no damages are awarded for non-pecuniary loss following from the death or severe injury of a relative. The relevant provisions in the BGB (§ 844 ff.) do not provide for compensation of this head of damage. The BGH has argued that these provisions and the legal system may not be undermined by granting such compensation.[134] This lack of a right to compensation for relatives has been strongly criticized[135] but in the latest reform of the law of damages this rule has remained unchanged.[136] The 'alternative' is to file a claim on the basis of an infringement of the right to health, provided the relative suffered from a mental illness because of the death of his or her loved one (nr 704).

In England the closest relatives of a person who died as the result of an accident for which another person was liable are entitled to so-called damages for bereavement. Section 1A(2) of the Fatal Accidents Act 1976 provides that a claim for damages for bereavement shall only be for the benefit of the spouse, the registered partner, and the parents of a minor person who was never

[130] As regards the child's claim this is considered to be an exception to the rule that the parent's or supervisor's conduct cannot be attributed to the child as contributory negligence. See about this rule for example Crim. 10 October 1963, D. 1964. 20, comm. Esmein; BGH 8 March 1951, BGHZ 1, 248; Münchener Kommentar-Oetker (2003), § 254 N 135.

[131] Viney-Jourdain (1998), nr 435.

[132] BGH 6 April 1976, NJW 1976, 1501; Kötz-Wagner (2001), N 550.

[133] Ass. plén. 19 June 1981, D. 1982. 85, comm. Chabas, JCP 1982. II. 19712, Gaz. Pal. 1981. 529, comm. Boré, RTD civ. 1981, 857, obs. Durry.

[134] BGH 19 December 1978, VersR 1979, 323.

[135] Kötz-Wagner (2001), N 541; Walter Odersky, *Schmerzensgeld bei Tötung naher Angehöriger* (Munich: Beck, 1989), 10 ff.   [136] Münchener Kommentar-Wagner (2004) § 844 N 4.

married.[137] In the latter case the mother will be the only beneficiary if the child was illegitimate. The list of persons entitled to bereavement damages does not include the fiancé(e), the unmarried and unregistered partner, and the children of the deceased. According to s. 1A(3) the award is a fixed amount of £10,000 (€14,000).[138] This amount will be equally divided if both parents have a right to damages (s. 1A(4)).

The French law of damages takes a more liberal view than Germany and England. Damages for a so-called *perte d'affection* are not only granted to the deceased's relatives by blood or marriage,[139] but also to his fiancé(e),[140] his unmarried partner, and his registered partner.[141] All persons having a relationship with the deceased by blood or by marriage (parents, children, brothers, sisters, sons- and daughters-in-law, nephews, and nieces) are entitled to claim compensation for non-pecuniary loss (*préjudice d'affection*). In these cases there is a rebuttable presumption that there is an affectionate relationship with the victim. Other persons, such as an illegitimate child, a fiancé(e), and an unmarried partner have the same right provided they can prove they were very close to the deceased and seriously affected by his death.[142]

French law also acknowledges a claim for non-pecuniary loss for the relative of someone who is injured.[143] If someone, as the consequence of an accident, is in a state of unconsciousness or in a coma the parents, brothers, and sisters have a right to compensation for their non-pecuniary loss.[144] The injury of the relative does not need to be exceptionally serious; it is enough that it is established with sufficient certainty.[145]

Until now, Community law has not acknowledged the relative's right to compensation for non-pecuniary loss where the primary victim was injured. Mr Leussink, a Commission official, suffered serious harm when the Commission car in which he drove went out of control. This was due to the rear tyre coming off. The Commission was held liable for bad maintenance of the car and Mr Leussink's claim for damages was awarded. His wife and four children claimed compensation for the immaterial effects on their family life on the basis of Article 235 and 288(2) EC. The ECJ dismissed this claim, considering:

Although there can be no doubt about the reality of those effects or about the existence of a link with the accident, they are nevertheless the indirect result of the injury suffered

---

[137] The civil partner was added by the Civil Partnership Act 2004. According to s. 1(1) of this Act a civil partnership is an officially registered relationship between two people of the same sex.
[138] Until 2002 this amount was £7,500 (€10,700). The reform partially followed the proposal of the Law Commission in its report on Damages for Wrongful Death, Report No. 269 (1999). See Oliphant, ETL 2002, 142.   [139] Req. 2 February 1931, S. 1931. 1. 123.
[140] Crim. 5 January 1956, D. 1956. 216.
[141] Ch. mixte 27 February 1970, D. 1970. 201; Crim. 19 June 1975, D. 1975. 679, comm. Tunc.
[142] Viney-Jourdain (1998), nr 310 ff. Van Gerven (2000), 125–129.
[143] Crim. 9 February 1989, D. 1989. 614, comm. Bruneau.
[144] See for instance Cour d'appel de Paris 10 November 1983, D. 1984. 214, about which Van Gerven (2000), 118–119.   [145] Civ. 2e 23 May 1977, JCP 1977. IV. 187.

by Mr Leussink and do not constitute part of the harm for which the Commission may be held liable in its capacity as employer. This is borne out by the fact that the legal systems of most Member States make no provision for compensating such effects.[146]

It is most remarkable that the ECJ used French causation terminology (the damage was 'indirect', nr 1105) to dismiss a claim which would have been awarded under French law using this very terminology.

It is doubtful whether the legal systems of most Member States still do not compensate non-pecuniary loss of relatives as the ECJ considered in the above-mentioned case. Both the ECC and the PETL hold provisions regarding the right to compensation of non-pecuniary loss for persons close to the primary victim, not only in cases of death but also in cases of (serious) personal injury. For such a right, the ECC and the PETL consider 'a particularly close personal relationship' (ECC) or a 'close relationship' (PETL) with the injured person to be sufficient.[147] Connecting the right to compensation to persons having a close personal relationship with the primary victim makes sense, since compensation for non-pecuniary loss is for suffered grief, sorrow, and loss of companionship. This means that formal family ties should not be a prerequisite for compensation. For the seriousness of the loss suffered it does not make a difference whether a married or an unmarried (heterosexual or homosexual) person loses his or her partner for life.

1211 Nervous shock

Finally, the death of a loved one can also cause more serious harm than grief or sorrow. A relative may suffer mental harm as the consequence of the death of a beloved, particularly, though not solely, if he was a witness to the fatal accident.[148] See about the right to compensation for mental harm in general, nr 704.

French law takes a liberal position by not requiring that the claimant suffered a medically acknowledged psychological disorder or that he was a witness to the accident. All kinds of mental harm caused by the death or severe injury of another person, including natural grief, are eligible for compensation provided the harm is a certain and direct consequence of the tortfeasor's conduct.[149] Hence, in French law the difference between mental harm and grief is fluid.

---

[146] ECJ 8 October 1986, Joined Cases 169/83 and 136/84, ECR 1986, 2801 (*Leussink and Others v Commission*), para. 22.

[147] Art. 2:202(1) ECC provides: 'Non-economic loss caused to a natural person as a result of another's personal injury or death is legally relevant damage if at the time of injury that person is in a particularly close personal relationship to the injured person.' Article 10:301(1) PETL: 'Non-pecuniary damage can also be the subject of compensation for persons having a close relationship with a victim suffering a fatal or very serious non-fatal injury.'

[148] Von Bar (2000), N 62 ff.

[149] Civ. 2e 22 February 1995, D. 1996. 69, note Chartier and Cour d'appel Paris 10 November 1983, D. 1984. 214, about which Van Gerven (2000), 118–119. Terré-Simler-Lequette (2002), nr 700–703.

According to German law only close relatives such as the fiancé(e) and the partner of an amatory relationship are entitled to claim, but their impairment of health needs to exceed the 'normal' degree of grievance and sorrow expected in such a case. This means that a claim is generally only awarded in case of a traumatic disorder with consequences lasting for a certain time.[150] The BGH, for instance, awarded the claim of a woman who received a shock after she heard that her husband had been killed in a car accident for which a driver was liable.[151] However, the BGH dismissed the claim for loss of income of a woman who became addicted to alcohol after her husband was killed in a car accident.[152] The relative does not need to have witnessed the accident although this might be of relevance in cases of less severe injuries.[153]

The claim for nervous shock needs to be seen in connection to the fact that it is not possible in German law to get compensation for grief and sorrow following from the death of a loved one (nr 1210). Particularly where the loved one, for example a child or an elderly person, did not maintain other persons, there is no other legally relevant damage than what follows from the infringement of the right to (mental) health. This means that in such cases there is an incentive to challenge the limits of protection of this right.[154]

English law erects the highest hurdles for compensation: it requires that it was foreseeable that the claimant (the 'secondary victim') would suffer mental harm as a consequence of the death of the primary victim, and that he has witnessed the accident or its immediate aftermath.

The closer the claimant and the primary victim are related, the more foreseeable it is that someone may suffer a nervous shock. In one of the *Hillsborough* cases, relatives and friends claimed compensation for psychological damage after witnessing spectators being crushed to death in a surging crowd during an FA Cup match. The House of Lords dismissed the claims of brothers, brothers-in-law, uncles, grandparents, and friends of the victims, considering their relationship not to be close enough, and therefore mental harm was not foreseeable.[155] This does not mean that damages are never granted to a brother or a grandparent but this will depend on the question of whether the

---

[150] BGH 4 April 1989, NJW 1989, 2317, about which Markesinis and Unberath (2002), 119–122.

[151] BGH 11 May 1971, BGHZ 56, 163 = NJW 1971, 1883 = VersR 1971, 905: '... bei der Klägerin über noch im Bereich normaler Reaktion liegende Erscheinungen von Schmerz, Trauer und Niedergeschlagenheit hinaus unmittelbar zu einer "traumatischen" Schädigung der physischen oder psychischen Gesundheit geführt hat.' See Markesinis and Unberath (2002), 115–119. See also BGH 5 February 1985, BGHZ 93, 351 = NJW 1985, 1390.

[152] BGH 31 January 1984, NJW 1984, 1405.

[153] BGH 5 February 1985, BGHZ 93, 351 = NJW 1985, 1390.

[154] In these cases § 254 is not directly applicable because the relative has a separate claim on the basis of § 823 I (infringement of health). Hence, in these cases courts apply § 254 analogously (nr 1212). BGH 11 May 1971, BGHZ 56, 163 = NJW 1971, 1883 = VersR 1971, 905, 1140, about which Markesinis and Unberath (2002), 115–119.

[155] *Alcock v Chief Constable of South Yorkshire* [1992] 1 AC 310, about which Van Gerven (2000), 101–103.

relationship is close and loving enough to establish foreseeability of the psychological damage.[156]

Generally, the claimant needs to have been within sight or hearing of the event or its immediate aftermath. In *McLoughlin v O'Brian* a woman got a message that members of her family were brought into hospital after a serious car accident. When she arrived there, she found one of her children dead and two other children and her husband seriously injured. The House of Lords awarded her claim for psychological damage because she was faced with the direct consequences of the accident ('the immediate aftermath').[157]

Communication of the accident by a third party will not do, not even if the scene was on television, because the Broadcasting Code excludes depiction of the suffering of recognizable individuals.[158] Apart from the fact that English courts seem to have confidence in broadcasters complying with this rule, this does not rule out that someone is shocked by viewing the scenes of the disaster even though he is not able to identify individuals. However, in one of the *Hillsborough* cases the House of Lords considered:

> The viewing of these scenes cannot be equiparated with the viewer being within ' . . . sight or hearing of the event in question' to use the words of Lord Wilberforce (in *McLoughlin v O'Brien*), nor can the scenes reasonably be regarded as giving rise to shock, in the sense of a sudden assault on the nervous system.[159]

The English toolkit to control the flood of claims in this area is quite sophisticated. However, the witness requirement seems to be rather arbitrary since it is coincidental whether someone has witnessed the accident or not, whereas the mental impact of the accident and its consequences can be similar. This puts pressure on the courts to interpret the *immediate aftermath* in a rather flexible way.[160]

---

[156] Markesinis and Deakin (2003), 105–107. After the Hillsborough tragedy police officers claimed compensation from their employer for damage they suffered as a result of a post traumatic stress disorder. These claims were partly awarded since policemen can be considered as rescuers to whom the employer owes a duty of care: *Frost v Chief Constable of the South Yorkshire Police* [1997] 1 All ER 540. But the House of Lords considerably limited the possibilities for such a claim in *White v Chief Constable of South Yorkshire* [1998] 3 WLR 1510; see Markesinis and Deakin (2003), 110–111.   [157] *McLoughlin v O'Brian* [1983] AC 410.

[158] *Alcock v Chief Constable of South Yorkshire* [1992] 1 AC 310.

[159] Lord Keith in *Alcock v Chief Constable of South Yorkshire* [1992] 1 AC 310, 398, about which Van Gerven (2000), 101–103. See also *Hicks and Others v Chief Constable of South Yorkshire Police* [1992] 2 All ER 65. See furthermore K.J. Nasir, 'Nervous Shock and Alcock: The Judicial Buck Stops Here', *Mod LR* 55 (1992), 705–713; B. Lynch, 'A Victory for Pragmatism? Nervous Shock Reconsidered', *LQR* 108 (1992), 367–371.

[160] In *Atkinson v Seghal*, The Times, March 2003, the Court of Appeal extended the immediate aftermath to the moment a mother had left the mortuary an hour and a half after the accident where she had witnessed the disfigured body of her daughter. *Walters v North Glamorgan NHS Trust* [2002] EWCA Civ. 1792, ETL 2002, 157 (Oliphant), was about a woman witnessing her baby son suffering for 36 hours from severe brain damage caused by a major epileptic seizure, which the hospital had wrongfully failed to prevent. The Court of Appeal considered the full 36 hours being the immediate aftermath causing the mother's 'shock'.

The differences can be well illustrated by referring to Article 2:201(2b) ECC and Article 10:202(1) PETL. Both proposals pretend to have found a European compromise by virtually copying the German rule and requiring that mental harm needs to amount to a medical condition or a recognized illness, but that it is not required to have been a witness to the accident or its immediate aftermath. This compromise would imply that English law needs to remove the witness requirement and that French law needs to introduce the requirement of a medical condition. This is a nice compromise indeed, but not one which will be easily acceptable for both England and France if only for the question of what Germany is prepared to offer in this respect.

D CONTRIBUTORY NEGLIGENCE

1212 Introduction

The previous chapters focused on the tortfeasor's wrongful or negligent behaviour respectively, the risks of which he had to answer. However, the claimant may also have contributed to the damage.[161] In practice, questions of contributory negligence or risk are of major importance. This importance is not fully reflected in the legal literature since the questions raised very much depend on the circumstances of the case and are insofar less eligible for more abstract considerations.[162]

Until the 20th century, the claimant's negligence implied dismissal of his claim. This went back to Roman law though in this respect opinions differ. According to some authors a claim was dismissed unless the tortfeasor had acted intentionally; according to others this was only the case if the victim's fault was more serious than the tortfeasor's.[163]

Currently, the consequence of the victim's negligence is that he cannot claim compensation for the full loss he suffered: the court will reduce the amount of

[161] See about contributory negligence from a comparative point of view: A.M. Honoré, 'Causation and Remoteness of Damage', in A. Tunc (ed.), *International Encyclopedia of Comparative Law* (Tübingen: Mohr, 1983); Ulrich Magnus and Miquel Martín-Casals (eds.), *Unification of Tort Law: Contributory Negligence* (The Hague, London, New York, Kluwer, 2004); Van Gerven (2000), 689–728; von Bar (2000), N 517–539.

[162] See for an exception for instance Christian Grüneberg, *Haftungsquoten bei Verkehrsunfällen*, 7th edn. (Munich: C.H. Beck, 2002).

[163] Reinhard Zimmermann, *The Law of Obligations: Roman Foundations of the Civilian Tradition* (Cape Town: Juta, 1996), 1010 ff. In the US *contributory negligence* indicates that the tortfeasor is not liable at all if the victim has done something wrong, whereas *comparative negligence* indicates that the victim's negligence leads to a division of the damage. Until 1934, in France the custodian of a thing (nr 303-1) was not strictly liable in the sense of art. 1384 al. 1 CC if the victim had acted negligently: Req. 13 April 1934, DP 1934. I. 41.

damages. In France this is known as *faute de la victime* and it has been developed by the courts, whereas in other countries statutory provisions apply: in England the Law Reform (Contributory Negligence) Act 1945, and in Germany § 254 BGB (*Mitverschulden*).[164]

The key question is whether the claimant ' . . . did not in his own interest take reasonable care of himself and contributed, by want of his care, to his own injury'.[165] It is considered to be decisive whether the claimant has behaved as could be expected from a reasonable person in the given circumstances.

In England the test of the reasonable person applies not only to the conduct of the defendant but also to that of the claimant. Section 4 of the Law Reform (Contributory Negligence) Act 1945 defines the claimant's fault as 'negligence, breach of statutory duty or other act or omission that gives rise to liability in tort or would, apart from this Act, give rise to the defence of contributory negligence.' The latter part of this definition refers to the claimant's lack of care. This implies that ' . . . the standard applied to the claimant in contributory negligence is the same as that of the "reasonable person" in negligence liability generally.'[166]

In Germany contributory negligence (*Mitverschulden*) can be established if the claimant has acted negligently as regards his own interests (§ 254 BGB). The negligence test of § 276 (*Fahrlässigkeit*) applies accordingly. In principle, this implies an objective test of the victim's conduct: the conduct of a careful person of average circumspection and capability is decisive (*ein sorgfältiger Mensch von durchschnittlicher Umsicht und Tüchtigkeit*) (nr 804-2).[167]

In French law also contributory negligence (*la faute de la victime*) can give rise to a lower amount of compensation. It can even leave the victim with empty hands if the defendant can prove that the victim's conduct was the only cause of the damage, which means that it must have been unforeseeable and unavoidable (*inprévisible et irrésistible*).[168] Generally, an objective test applies (*l'appréciation in abstracto*) to the victim's conduct and it is striking that this even goes for young children (nr 813-2 and 1215).[169] The defence of *faute de la victime* is also allowed in cases of strict liability and requires a comparison of the mutual *fautes* of defendant and claimant.[170] In road traffic accidents the defence of contributory negligence has been completely abolished (nr 1404-1).

---

[164] See also Art. 5:102(1) ECC and Art. 8:101 PETL.

[165] Viscount Simon in *Nance v British Columbia Electric Railways Co Ltd* [1951] AC 601, 611. In the same sense Civ. 2e 8 March 1995, Bull. civ. II, no 82: ' . . . avait commis une faute en négligeant de veiller à sa propre sécurité'.   [166] Markesinis and Deakin (2003), 745.

[167] Münchener Kommentar-Oetker (2003), § 254 N 35; Kötz-Wagner (2001), N 108

[168] Le Tourneau (2004), nr 1863 and 1889.

[169] Terré-Simler-Lequette (2002), nr 802; Le Tourneau (2004), nr 1882.

[170] Le Tourneau (2004), nr 1890 justifies this by stating that comparing the defendant's strict liability and the claimant's fault would amount to 'd'additionner des tomates et des pommes'.

1213 Contributory risk

Not only can the claimant's *negligent conduct* lead to a decrease of the damages to be paid by the tortfeasor, but also other *causes* for which the claimant has to answer can reduce the amount of the awarded damages.[171] Rules of strict liability for persons (Chapter 16) and for movable objects (Chapter 14) are of relevance here.

In determining the proportion by which the plaintiff's damages are to be reduced, attention must be paid to the respective blameworthiness of the parties as well as to the causative potency of their acts or omissions... after all, if attention were not paid to causative potency, a careless plaintiff would recover nothing from a defendant who was free from fault but strictly liable.[172]

As regards liability for persons, one may for example think of the employers' liability for the conduct of their employees (*vicarious liability*) (nr 1606).[173] The conduct of these persons is only imputed to the victim in cases of damage to property loss and pure economic loss and not in cases of death and personal injury. In the former cases there may often be an internal agreement between the victim and the person for whom he has to answer.[174] In Germany the BGH analogously applies § 278 BGB (contractual liability for persons) to contributory negligence. This means that the conduct of someone with whom the victim has a contract can be attributed to the victim as contributory negligence. The requirement of a contract is broadly interpreted because organs of legal bodies are also considered to fall within the ambit of this rule.[175]

Also rules of strict liability for things (animals, motor vehicles) may be relevant in the framework of contributory negligence but this is a much more disputed area.[176] In Germany and England, rules of strict liability for animals are taken into account. If, for instance, damage is caused by the tortfeasor and

---

[171] Art. 8:101(1) PETL:

Liability can be excluded or reduced to such extent as is considered just having regard to the victim's contributory fault and to any other matters which would be relevant to establish or reduce liability of the victim if he were the tortfeasor.

Arts. 5:102(3) and 5:102(4) ECC:

Paragraphs (1) and (2) apply correspondingly where a person for whom the injured person is responsible within the scope of Article 3:202 contributes by their fault to the occurrence or extent of the damage. (4) Compensation is to be reduced likewise if and in so far as any other source of danger for which the injured person is responsible under Chapter 3 contributes to the occurrence or extent of the damage.

Art. 8:101(3) PETL:

The contributory conduct or activity of an auxiliary of the victim excludes or reduces the damages recoverable by the latter according to para. 1.

[172] Weir, *A Casebook on Tort* (2000), 244.
[173] *Carberry v Davies* [1968] 1 WLR 1103 (CA). Winfield and Jolowicz (2002), para. 6.47; compare Salmond and Heuston (1996), 497.   [174] Von Bar (2000), N 533–535.
[175] Münchener Kommentar-Oetker (2003), § 254 N 140.   [176] Von Bar (2000), N 532.

the claimant's horse, the latter will be a ground for lowering the amount of damages to be paid by the tortfeasor regardless of the claimant's negligence.[177]

In France the victim's contributory negligence is not influenced by the strict liability for things (article 1384 al. 1 CC). Here, only the victim's fault (*faute de la victime*) can amount to contributory negligence.[178] This means that, if the defendant's things are involved in the accident, this does not amount to contributory negligence. This is not surprising because French law has a general rule and a number of specific rules of strict liability for things, which are particularly applicable in cases of accidents. Attributing all strict liability rules to the victim's conduct would put most claimants at least in an uncomfortable position.

Another example in this respect is the German strict liability of the owner or keeper of a motor vehicle (§ 7 StVG, see nr 1404-2). This strict liability can be attributed to him as contributory negligence if he himself has suffered damage in a traffic accident. Generally this is the attribution of the *Betriebsgefahr* (operational risk) of the vehicle.[179] In many cases the attribution of the operational risk varies from 20 per cent to 33 per cent.[180]

1214 Systematic observations

Contributory negligence does not imply that the claimant owes the tortfeasor a duty nor that he is under an enforceable duty to take care for his own interests. The claimant's duty is in fact what the Germans like to call an *Obliegenheit*. This is a legal position, not being a right or a duty, which someone can improve or lose by his own behaviour. Hence, in the case of the victim's lack of care as regards his own interests, he cannot call on the other party to compensate him in full.[181]

It goes without saying that in order to qualify for contributory negligence a causal connection has to be established between the claimant's negligence or risk on the one hand, and the damage on the other (Chapter 11). A driver who is under the influence of alcohol and is hit by another vehicle is not, for this sole

---

[177] *Germany*: BGH 6 July 1976, BGHZ 67, 129 = NJW 1976, 2130 (strict liability for animals: § 833). *England*: Section 10(1) jo. 2–4 Animals Act 1971; see about this Act nr 1402.

[178] Civ. 2e 21 July 1982, D. 1982. 449, comm. Larroumet, JCP 1982. II. 19861, comm. Chabas, RTD civ. 1982, 807, obs. Durry (*Desmares*); compare Le Tourneau (2004), nr 1869–1872.

[179] BGH 23 June 1952, BGHZ 6, 319 = NJW 1952, 1015; BGH 13 April 1956, BGHZ 20, 259, about which Markesinis and Unberath (2002), 839–841. See also Kötz-Wagner (2001), N 560 ff.   [180] Münchener Kommentar-Oetker (2003), § 254 N 114.

[181] Von Bar (2000), N 518; Kötz-Wagner (2001), N 553. Larenz (1987), § 31 I a, 540; BGH 18 April 1997, BGHZ 135, 235, 240; *Davies v Swan Motor Co* [1949] 2 KB 291, [1949] 1 All ER 620; *Dawrant v Nutt* [1961] 1 WLR 253; Civ. 2e, 8 March 1995, Bull. civ. II, no 82, D. 1995. Somm. 232, obs. Delebecque. See also the critical remarks by Le Tourneau (2004), nr 1872, arguing that, considering that most tortfeasors are insured against liability, the claimant is the only person who personally bears the consequences of his negligent conduct: 'Paradoxalement, seule la victime va subir personnellement les conséquences de ses fautes qui ont contribué à la realisation du dommage.'

reason, contributorily negligent. Lord Atkin said: 'If the claimant was negligent but his negligence was not a cause operating to produce the damage there would be no defence. I find it impossible to divorce any theory of contributory negligence from the concept of causation.'[182]

The amount of compensation can be reduced not only if the claimant contributed to the accident but also if he contributed to the extent of his damage. If a passenger did not wear a seat belt, he did not contribute to the accident but he did contribute to the damage. In such a case the amount of compensation to which he is entitled may be reduced.[183] For the same reason contributory negligence can be invoked against a motorcyclist who has contributed to his damage by not wearing a helmet.[184]

Generally, the claimant has a duty to restrict the damage as far as this can be reasonably expected from him.[185] If he negligently does not take reasonable measures to get medical aid, to follow medical instructions, to look for work, or to follow courses to increase his opportunities, he will lose his right to claim full compensation for his damage. It depends on the circumstances of the case as to what can be reasonably expected from the victim. For example, a woman who is pregnant as the consequence of a negligent vasectomy can restrict her damage by way of an abortion but it is generally admitted that there is no obligation for her to do so, not even if such an abortion can be carried out within the legal period of time (nr 706-1). In a similar vein, a person is not obliged to undergo a serious operation, particularly if the outcome is uncertain. French law, in particular, goes a step further by accepting that even the refusal to undergo a minor operation does not lead to contributory negligence.[186] More recently, the *Cour de cassation* has held that a victim is not required to limit the damage or injury in the interest of the liable party. This is another sweeping general principle (*grand principe*) for which the *Cour de cassation* is quite (in)famous (nr 301-3 and 608-3). It remains to be seen whether it will always lead to reasonable results in the circumstances of the particular case. However, this latter aspect does not seem to be of the greatest concern to the *Cour de cassation* in its case law as regards liability.

If a passenger knows that the driver is drunk and an accident occurs, the driver cannot claim that the passenger assumed the risk (nr 809-2). The driver cannot say '... that the fact of his passenger travelling in a vehicle in circumstances in which for one reason or another it could be said that he had willingly accepted a

---

[182] Lord Atkin in *Caswell v Powell Duffryn Associated Collieries Ltd* [1940] AC 152, 165. See also Lord Denning in *Davies v Swan Motor Co (Swansea) Ltd* [1949] 2 KB 291, [1949] 1 All ER 620.
[183] See for England *Froom v Butcher* [1976] QB 286 and for Germany BGH 9 February 1965, NJW 1965, 1075; BGH 30 January 1979, NJW 1979, 980; BGH 20 March 1979, BGHZ 74, 25; BGH 2 February 1982, BGHZ 83, 71; BGH 29 September 1992, BGHZ 119, 268.
[184] *O'Connell v Jackson* [1972] 1 QB 270; *Capps v Miller* [1989] 1 WLR 839, [1989] 2 All ER 333.
[185] Von Bar (2000), N 530.
[186] Von Bar (2000), N 531, with further references. This case law seems to be particularly triggered by article 16-3 CC, enacted in 1994 and protecting the integrity of the body (*l'intégrité corporale*).

risk of negligence on the driver's part relieves him of liability for such negligence.'[187] However, he may invoke contributory negligence, which will generally be estimated around 20 per cent.[188] The ECJ has held that reduction of the compensation in such cases must not be disproportionate (see 1405-2).[189] In France the percentage will generally be zero, since according to article 3 *loi Badinter* the passenger's right to damages is only affected if he committed an inexcusable fault (*faute inexcusable*) and this fault was the sole cause of the accident (nr 1404-1).

If the tortfeasor has acted intentionally, he will generally not have a contributory negligence defence.[190] For England this follows from the fact that the Law Reform (Contributory Negligence) Act 1945 does not apply to bribery,[191] deceit,[192] conversion, and intentional trespass to goods.[193] French case law shows the same picture.[194] This means that a thief cannot invoke the contributory negligence of the robbed person, for instance because the latter did not lock his belongings in a safe place. The opportunity makes the theft possible but it does not provide him a contributory negligence it defence. More generally, contributory negligence of the claimant is not taken into account if, compared to this, the tortfeasor's negligence was overwhelming.[195] An exception to this rule is accepted if the claimant provoked the defendant's intentional conduct. In such a case the amount of damages can be reduced on the basis of contributory negligence of the provoker.[196]

Whereas until the 20th century, the claimant's negligence led to dismissal of his claim (1212), by the end of the same century the opposite situation occurs: in certain circumstances the claimant's negligent conduct does not even lead to a reduction of his right to compensation. Particularly in Germany and France, victims of road traffic accidents are thus strongly protected against the consequences of their own mistakes (1215 and 1404). This reflects the compensation function which tort law has increasingly gained in the course of the past decades (nr 716).

---

[187] Beldam LJ in *Pitts v Hunt* [1991] 1 QB 24; see s. 149 of the Road Traffic Act 1988.

[188] Winfield and Jolowicz (2002), para. 25.10. *Owens v Brimmell* [1977] QB 859, [1976] All ER 765 (contributory negligence of the passenger of a drunken driver); *Nettleship v Weston* [1971] 2 QB 691, (CA) (contributory negligence of someone who gives a friend driving lessons). See however also *Morris v Murray* [1991] 2 QB 6, [1990] 3 All ER 801 (drunken pilot), an exceptional case, in which the court dismissed the claim of a passenger of a crashed aeroplane on the basis of *volenti non fit injuria* (nr 815). See for Germany Kötz-Wagner (2001), N 557.

[189] ECJ 30 June 2005, Case C-537/03, nyp, (*Candolin and Others v Pohjola and Others*).

[190] Compare nr 1101 about the consequences of intention for establishing the causal chain.

[191] *Corporación Nacional del Cobre de Chile v Sogemin Metals Ltd and Others* [1997] 2 All ER 917.

[192] *Alliance v Leicester v Hamptons* [1993] NPC 19.   [193] Von Bar (2000), N 521.

[194] Crim. 4 October 1990, D. 1990. IR. 284; Crim. 16 May 1991, D. 1991. IR. 220; Civ. 26 February 1991, Bull. civ. I, no 73; Civ. 16 June 1992, D. 1993. Somm. 212; Viney-Jourdain (1998), nr 430.   [195] In the same sense Art. 5:102(2)(a) ECC.

[196] M. Martín-Casals, in *Principles of European Tort Law, Text and Commentary* (Vienna, New York: Springer, 2005), 134–135.

1215 Children

A delicate issue is the question of whether a young victim can be contributorily negligent, just like the question of whether children can be liable for damage they have caused by their own conduct (nr 813). In some jurisdictions the possibility to invoke contributory negligence against a young victim is limited.

In Germany children under the age of 7 cannot be contributorily negligent. For children under the age of 11 the same goes for accidents with motor vehicles, railways, or ski lifts. Children under the age of 18 cannot be contributorily negligent if they do not know what they are doing (lack of *Einsichtsfähigkeit*) (§ 828 III jo § 254). If they are *einsichtsfähig* their conduct will be compared to that of someone of the same age. Unconscious and mentally disabled persons cannot be contributorily negligent on the basis of § 827 jo. § 254 BGB, provided they were not able to understand the negligence of their conduct or to act accordingly. However, § 829 applies accordingly: this means that, despite lack of accountability, a child or a handicapped person can be contributorily negligent if equity so demands (nr 813-3).[197]

English law also uses the child of the same age as type of comparison in order to establish contributory negligence[198] but there is no fixed age under which a child cannot be contributorily negligent.[199] The starting point is whether the child ' . . . is of such an age as reasonably to be expected to take precaution for his or her own safety.'[200] The test is not entirely objective since the courts also take into account the child's individual circumstances and handicaps.[201]

French case law follows a remarkable track by comparing the conduct of the child-victim to that of the *bon père de famille* just as is the case if the child causes the damage himself (nr 813-2).[202] Legal authors have criticized this because it too easily establishes the child's contributory negligence, which means that the child only gets compensation for part of his damage. They argue that the test for the conduct of the tortfeasor should not be the same one as for the conduct

---

[197] BGH NJW 1969, 1762; BGH NJW 1973, 1795; Münchener Kommentar-Oetker (2003), § 254 N 34.

[198] See for instance *Gough v Thorne* [1966] 3 All ER 398, [1966] 1 WLR 1387 (no contributory negligence of a 13-year-old girl). See, however, also *Morales v Ecclestone* [1991] RTR 151 (75 per cent contributory negligence of an 11-year-old boy dashing onto the road). See furthermore Occupier's Liability Act 1957, s. 2(3)(a): ' . . . an occupier must be prepared for children to be less careful than adults.'

[199] The Pearson Commission advised a minimum age of 12: The Royal Commission on Civil Liability and Compensation for Personal Injury, Vol. 1, Cmnd 7054 (1978), nr 1077.

[200] Compare Lord Denning in *Gough v Thorne* [1966] 3 All ER 398, [1966] 1 WLR 1387.

[201] *Daly v Liverpool Corporation* [1939] 2 All ER 142.

[202] Ass. plén. 9 May 1984, JCP 1984. II. 20255, comm. N. Dejean de la Bathie, D. 1984. 525, comm. F. Chabas, RTD civ. 1984, 509, obs. J. Huet; in the same sense Civ. 2e 28 February 1996, D. 1996. 602, JCP 1996. IV. 942.

of the victim.[203] However, the *Cour de cassation* does not seem to be inclined to change its view.[204]

Things are different under the *loi Badinter* as regards traffic accidents, on the basis of which contributory negligence of children in cases of road traffic accidents is almost completely excluded (nr 1404-1). Also contributory negligence of young (under 16), of old (over 70) and of handicapped (more than 80 per cent) persons is no longer a defence in traffic accidents, provided that these persons are not themselves drivers of a motor vehicle. As has been pointed out, the same rule goes for Germany for children until the age of 10. England does not have a hard and fast rule in this respect but: 'Damages of traffic victims may not always be reduced for contributory negligence if the victims are very young children or old persons.'[205]

This brief overview shows different opinions as regards the age until which children should be immune to contributory negligence. In Germany this applies to children until the age of 7 and in many cases until the age of 10. In France a special rule applies to road traffic accidents in which persons up to the age of 16 are fully protected. In England, however, children are not protected though the subjective approach to the child's conduct is much more favourable to its position than the French objective approach in cases other than traffic accidents.

Guido Calabresi, one of the fathers of law and economics in accident law, wrote in 1970:

In deciding who should be liable, the fault system pays little attention to which of the possible categories of costbearers is most likely to be aware of the risk involved. As a result, although it may seem to choose a party that can avoid the accident cheaply, it actually often picks one that will bring about very little cost avoidance.[206]

This is particularly the case if they are not able to avoid the accident. Although children seem to be the *cheapest cost avoiders* (look out, stay away), they are generally not aware of the potential risks or they are not able to act accordingly. Hence, liability in these cases ought to be with the adult persons who possess of the required knowledge and ability. Moreover, all potential victims benefit from their precautionary measures.

---

[203] Viney, 'La réparation des dommages causés sous l'empire d'un état d'inconscience: un transfert nécessaire de la responsabilité vers l'assurance', *JCP* 1985. I. 3189; Terré-Simler-Lequette (2002), nr 732; Carbonnier (2000), § 229, 414–416.

[204] Civ. 2e 19 February 1997, Bull. civ. II, no 53 (contributory negligence of a child that approached a moving swing). However, there are also decisions pointing in another direction: see for example Civ. 6 March 1996, D. 1997. 93, comm. Lebreton (no contributory negligence of a 15-year-old boy who, despite strong warnings, started a descent in the mountains and got injured).

[205] *Gough v Thorne* [1966] 3 All ER 398, [1966] 1 WLR 1387; Salmond and Heuston (1996), 510.

[206] Guido Calabresi, *The Costs of Accidents* (New Haven: Yale University Press, 1970), 244–245.

E CONCLUDING REMARKS

1216 Comparative observations

Throughout the legal systems the heads of damage to be compensated are fairly similar. After all, people throughout Europe suffer similar kinds of damage: loss of income, loss of maintenance, costs of health care, damage to property, loss of profit, immaterial damage like pain and suffering or grief, etc.

There are, however, some differences as to the heads of damage compensated, for example as regards the loss of maintenance (nr 1209) and the compensation for grief for the loss of a loved one (nr 1210). As regards loss of maintenance, German law requires that the deceased was obliged to maintain the relative, whereas English and French law also allow for a claim if the deceased had maintained the relative on a voluntary basis. Also, as regards compensation for grief, German law is the exception by not allowing such a claim at all.

The right to compensation for relatives is strongly influenced by family policy as to who is supposed to be a close relative of the deceased. The position of unmarried partners in particular has been valued differently over the years. More recently, the position of same-sex partners has been improved. All three systems now provide the opportunity of a registered partnership which gives same-sex partners in this respect the same rights as married partners (nr 1208).

Even where all three legal systems compensate a certain head of damage, this does not always happen in the same way. One may think of the different ways in which future damage is being paid out: as a lump sum, as a pension, or as a combination (nr 1205) and of the two the different levels of compensation for pain and suffering (nr 1206).

Low amounts for non-pecuniary loss in France and high amounts in England are an illustration of the French preference for the equality principle. It makes compensation available for many by keeping the threshold for liability low. This almost inevitably means that there is less money available per individual. On the other hand, the high liability threshold in England implies that the level of available money per individual is also higher. However this may be, Germany takes a different view by allowing compensation for many more than in England and not much less than in France, at the same time keeping the amounts for compensation at a high level.

As regards the available opportunities for remedies, English law shows its roots with its many different forms of available damages. As has been pointed out (nr 502), English tort law was developed on the basis of the writ system which provided for specific and distinctive remedies, which has led to a diverse palette of available damages (nr 1202-3). In this way, the English law of damages seems to be more sophisticated than the French and German equivalents which only hold one form of damages. However, under this one umbrella different aspects (compensation, satisfaction, recognition, deterrence) are dealt with in a way that does not differ much from the way this happens in English law.

1217 Community law and effective national remedies

Community law has hardly touched upon this area of the law. In Directives such as the Product Liability Directive and in the *Francovich* case law (nr 205) it is left to the national law of the Member States to apply the concept and provide for an effective remedy. The form and content of this remedy is at the discretion of the Member States provided that the remedy is non-discriminatory and effective.[207]
The Product Liability Directive provides for a strict liability regime for damage caused by a defective product. Article 9 of the Directive covers damage caused by death, personal injury, and loss of private property. Non-pecuniary loss is entirely left to the laws of the Member States. As regards compensation for *pecuniary loss* the ECJ considered in the *Veedfalds* case that it is up to the Member States to determine the precise content of death, personal injury, and damage to private property. Nevertheless, full and proper compensation for persons injured by a defective product must be available. Application of national rules may not impair the effectiveness of the Directive and the national court must interpret its national law in the light of the wording and the purpose of the Directive.[208]
Within these broad margins, compensation for pecuniary and non-pecuniary loss will still differ considerably depending on the applicable law of damages. It is characteristic for the fragmentation of Community law that the ECJ has held that the interpretation of a concept like damage in one Directive does not have authority in another Directive using the same concept.[209] This implies that Community law provides for different meanings of the same word.
The Common Frame of Reference initiated by the Commission could bring more harmony in these matters (nr 611). When drafting these references advantage should be taken '. . . of existing national legal orders in order to find possible common denominators, to develop common principles and, where appropriate, to identify best solutions.'[210] This will certainly not be an easy task regarding the analysis provided in this chapter.

---

[207] ECJ 16 December 1976, Case 33/76, ECR 1976, I-1989 (*Rewe-Zentralfinanz eG et Rewe-Zentral AG v Landwirtschaftskammer für das Saarland*) and ECJ 16 December 1976, Case 45/76, ECR 1976, I-2043 (*Comet BV v Produktschap voor Siergewassen*). See also R.H.G. Hesper, 'Op weg naar Europeesrechtelijke aansprakelijkheid voor schade bij schending van Europees kartelrecht', *RM Themis* 1999, 143–162, at 154.

[208] ECJ 10 May 2001, Case C-203/99 (*Veedfalds v Århus Amtskommune*), para. 27. ECJ 15 May 1990, Case C-365/88 [1990] ECR I-1845 (*Hagen GmbH v Zeehoge*); ECJ 10 April 1984, Case 14/83, ECR 1984, 1981 *Von Colson and Kamann v Nordrhein-Westfalen*.

[209] ECJ 12 March 2002, C-168/00 [2002] ECR I-2631 (*Simone Leitner v TUI Germany*); see the comparative case comments in *ERPL*, 11/1 (2003), 91–102.

[210] Communication of the Commission to the European Parliament and the Council. A more coherent European contract law. An Action plan, COM(2003) 68 final (OJ C 63, 15.3.2003), no. 63.

The Commission's project for a Common Frame of References runs parallel with the Commission's search for the development of remedies in order to enhance the possibilities for private enforcement of Community law, in particular competition law. The reform of the European competition policy by Regulation 1/2003 has decentralized enforcement powers from the Commission to the national competition authorities and the national courts. At the same time the Commission has emphasized the importance of private enforcement of competition law by individuals and companies who suffer damage from unfair competition, for example by abuse of market power.[211]

In 2004 the Commission published a study which found that levels of private enforcement through damages claims in Europe are currently very low. The study also found that not only is there 'total underdevelopment' of actions for damages for breach of EC competition law, but also that there is 'astonishing diversity' in the approaches taken by the Member States. Among the obstacles to a wider use of private enforcement actions were limitations on forms of compensation available; the need to prove negligence or intention, and high standards of proof.[212]

Based on the results of the study the Commission published a Green Paper in order to identify potential ways forward for the encouragement of private enforcement of EU competition law. The main argument for this is that the threat of such litigation can have a strong deterrent effect and result in a higher level of compliance with the competition rules.[213]

The idea of private enforcement of competition law has been bolstered by the ECJ's decision in *Courage v Crehan* in which a private party sought redress for infringement of competition law rules (nr 205-3). Of importance for the private enforcement of Community law in general is the ECJ's decision in *Muñoz*. The case was about a trader who, in civil proceedings, sought enforcement of Community food quality standards against a competitor. The ECJ held that compliance with these food quality standards '...must be capable of enforcement by means of civil proceedings instituted by a trader against a competitor.' The Court considered that tort law claims strengthen the *effet utile* of quality standards, and that they supplement enforcement by public

---

[211] See for different views on the value and effectiveness of private enforcement of competition law: Wouter P.J. Wils, 'Should Private Antitrust Enforcement Be Encouraged in Europe?', *World Competition*, 26 (2003), 473–488 (public enforcement is superior to private enforcement) and Clifford A. Jones, 'Private Antitrust Enforcement in Europe: A Policy Analysis and Reality Check, *World Competition*, 27 (2004), 13–24 (private enforcement has great value as a supplement to public enforcement and as the primary means of compensating victims of infringements whose interests are to be protected by national courts).

[212] Denis Waelbroeck, Donald Slater and Gil Even-Shoshan, *Study on the conditions of claims for damages in case of infringement of EC competition rules*, Brussels, 31 August 2004 http://europa.eu.int/comm/competition/antitrust/others/private_enforcement/index_en.html.

[213] Green Paper, *Damages Action for Breach of the EC Antitrust Rules*, 19.12.2005, COM (2005) 627 final.

authorities and discourage practices, '...often difficult to detect, which distort competition'.[214]

The *Muñoz* decision further opens the gate to private enforcement of Community law, not only in food standard cases but most likely in all other situations in which Community law confers rights on individuals. This implies that the national laws have to provide remedies (in particular actions for damages and injunctions) for the private enforcement of Community law and these remedies need to be effective and non-discriminatory. This may impel reinterpretation of parts of the national laws and other parts of them may even be disapplied.[215]

An important issue for the near future is how to balance the Commission's ideas in the Green Paper as regards private enforcement of competition law on the one hand and private enforcement of other Community rules—as emphasized in *Muñoz*—on the other. It is hard to see that there would be a justification for a fundamental change of national tort laws and laws of damages in order to bolster private enforcement of competition law and not to strengthen the private enforcement of rules in other areas of Community law, including, for example, the product liability Directive (nr 1406–1411) and Member State liability (nr 205). In other words, is the Green Paper a first step in a broader approach to private enforcement of Community law, leading to more consistency in the area of European tort law? Or is it a development on its own with no consequences for other areas of Community law, leading to more inconsistency in the area of European tort law?

---

[214] ECJ 17 December 2002, Case C-253/00, ECR I-7289 (*Antonio Muñoz y Cia SA and Superior Fruiticola SA v Frumar Ltd and Redbridge Produce Marketing Ltd*), paras 30–31.

[215] See Gerrit Betlem, 'Torts, A European *Ius Commune* and the Private Enforcement of Community Law', *Cam LJ*, 64 (2005), 126–148.

PART III

CATEGORIES OF LIABILITY

13

Introduction

1301 Supervising persons, immovable and movable objects

This third part of the book will deal with various categories of liability which are mainly related to someone's quality as a supervisor over persons or things. One may think of supervisors of movable objects (Chapter 14), of premises, grounds, and roads (Chapter 15), and of other persons (Chapter 16). From a comparative point of view, negligence and strict liability rules are at stake in each of these categories. Hence, the chapters will provide a comparison of the various rules and cases in the different legal systems in comparable situations. In some areas, rules of strict liability can be compared, in other areas rules of negligence liability, and finally there are areas where strict liability is the rule in one jurisdiction and negligence liability in the other.

One of the important issues in all these areas is who qualifies as supervisor. As regards strict liability rules, the liable person is generally indicated by the rule itself. For instance in France the custodian (*gardien*) is strictly liable for damage caused by a thing (*chose*) in the sense of article 1384 al. 1 CC (nr 303) and in Germany the keeper (*Halter*) of a motor vehicle is strictly liable for the damage caused by its operation (*Betriebsgefahr*) in the sense of § 7 StVG (nr 1404-2). Generally, the person who is able to influence the magnitude of the risk or who is able to get a proper insurance coverage for his liability is strictly liable.

Also within the framework of negligence liability the question arises who the supervisor is, for example if someone suffers damage because of a missing railing of a staircase. In principle, the responsible person will be the one who has a special relationship with the building, for instance because he is the owner, the tenant, or the operator, and for that reason is able and authorized to influence the magnitude of the risk by taking precautionary measures. Persons who do not have a special relationship with the building, for instance visitors, generally do not owe a duty of care to potential victims, not even if they can factually influence the magnitude of the risk. The same goes, for instance, for children, even if they live on the premises where the dangerous situation occurs. These persons are not authorized to interfere. Hence, even if they could interfere, they are not obliged to do so.

The question as to who is the supervisor particularly occurs in cases of omissions. As has been pointed out (nr 808), liability for omissions is related to someone's special relationship with the place of the accident, with the movable object that played a role in the occurrence of the damage, with the potential victim, and with the potential tortfeasor. Indeed, if something or someone needs to be actively supervised, it is crucial to know by whom such an affirmative duty is owed. The following chapters are, however, not restricted to liability for omissions. Also active negligent conduct, for instance of the driver of a motor vehicle, will be dealt with, but in such cases it is much easier to identify the supervisor.

It is important to note that responsibility in itself does not imply liability. Someone is *responsible* if he owes a duty to supervise objects or persons or if a rule of strict liability applies to him. Someone can only be *liable* if he has breached this duty or if the requirements for strict liability are met. Human responsibility may relate to our own conduct, to the responsibility that we choose to take on for other people, things, and events, and to the responsibility that society thrusts upon us.[1]

In some instances there is no responsibility for someone or something but society may nonetheless thrust a duty of solidarity upon us. These are the so-called rescue or emergency cases which will be analysed in Chapter 17. These so-called 'pure omissions' occur in situations in which no special relationship exists with premises, a movable thing, or another person. In these situations the question arises whether someone can be obliged to act, particularly to come to another person's rescue.

Finally, Chapter 18 is devoted to liability of public authorities which is a category of liability of growing importance throughout Europe, particularly because of the intertwinement of the development of national law with the case law of the European Court of Justice and the European Court of Human Rights.

1302 Liability for lack of information and for defective information

Another important category, besides the ones mentioned above, is responsibility for information. Information is one of the most important features in our information society. In order to make decisions we need information about our physical safety, our health, risks for our property, and our financial means and opportunities.

Lack of information impairs one's ability to make decisions of the fully rational kind postulated in economic discourse (. . .). In many instances uncertainty will cause people to take decisions different from what they would have been under circumstances of abundant information. As information becomes subsequently available, such decisions may appear in retrospect to have been erroneous. They entail a loss or a failure to obtain a

---

[1] Honoré, *Responsibility and Fault* (1999), 125–129.

gain which it would have been possible to avoid with better information. Uncertainty is generally a source of disutility and information is the antidote to it. In most cases efficiency will be enhanced by moves which improve the flow of information in society.[2]

Hence, lack of information and defective information are the risks of the information society, just like defective products and environmental damage are the risks of the industrialized society, motor vehicles of the motorized society, and animals of the agricultural society.

The need for timely, adequate, and reliable information plays a role in many areas. A duty to warn can be of pivotal importance (nr 807-3), for instance in the framework of product liability (nr 1408-1), or liability for damage caused by immovable objects (nr 1506). In many of these cases the duty to warn has to be balanced with the victim's duty to be attentive and careful (nr 805). Other important areas in this respect are medical services (the duty of a doctor to inform a patient about the impact of a treatment) and financial services (the duty of a bank to inform a client about the risks of an investment and the duty of an auditor to provide correct information about a company's accounts).

An important issue in this respect is whether the person providing the information ought to have known that the recipient would rely on it and that the receiver of the information was entitled to do so (see also nr 1302).[3] See also Article 2:207 ECC, holding

> Loss caused to a person as a result of making a decision in reasonable reliance on incorrect advice or information is legally relevant damage if: (a) the advice or information is provided by a person in pursuit of a profession or in the course of trade; and (b) the provider knew or ought to have known that the recipient would rely on the advice or information in making a decision of the kind made.

An important illustration on a Community level of liability for timely, adequate, and reliable information is the Prospectus Directive, holding that the public offer of securities requires the prior publication of a prospectus. According to Article 5(1),

> ... the prospectus shall contain all information which, according to the particular nature of the issuer and of the securities offered to the public or admitted to trading on a regulated market, is necessary to enable investors to make an informed assessment of the assets and liabilities, financial position, profit and losses, and prospects of the issuer and of any guarantor, and of the rights attaching to such securities. This information shall be presented in an easily analysable and comprehensible form.[4]

---

[2] Ejan Mackaay, *Economics of Information and Law* (Montreal: Groupe de recherche en consommation, 1980), 115.

[3] See for example S. Banakas, 'Liability for Incorrect Financial Information: Theory and Practice in a General Clause System and in a Protected Interests System', *ERPL*, 7 (1999), 261–286 and more generally Christian Witting, *Liability for Negligent Misstatements* (Oxford: Oxford University Press, 2004).

[4] Directive 2003/71/EC of 4 November 2003 on the prospectus to be published when securities are offered to the public or admitted to trading and amending Directive 2001/34/EC. See

Incorrect information published in the media can also infringe the honour, reputation, or privacy of a person. See for example the *Coroline von Hannover* case in nr 705-5, and the *Branly* case in nr 808-3. One may also think of the case of someone who was sentenced for a certain crime and the commentator of the published sentence omitted to mention that the sentence was provisional.[5] Also organizations and companies may suffer damage from published defective information, for example in the case of negligently conducted consumer tests or where a tourist information office omits to put a hotel on a list of recommended hotels.[6]

A topical issue in this respect is the liability of an internet service provider for defamatory or otherwise wrongful information put on a website which it has made accessible. Does the internet service provider have a duty to take pre-cautionary measures in order to limit, terminate, or prevent damage caused by this wrongful information? The answer to this question is negative and here also, Community law has left its traces. Article 13(1) of the E-commerce Directive holds that service providers are not liable for the information on websites to which they provide access on condition that:

(a) the provider does not have actual knowledge of illegal activity or information and, as regards claims for damages, is not aware of facts or circumstances from which the illegal activity or information is apparent; or (b) the provider, upon obtaining such knowledge or awareness, acts expeditiously to remove or to disable access to the information.

According to Article 15, a service provider does not have an obligation to monitor the information it transmits or stores but it may be required to ter-minate or prevent an infringement as soon as it receives information about it.[7]

Particularly in Germany, rules of strict liability have followed the emergence of new technological risks albeit with a certain delay (nr 405-1). The risks of the information society, however, have led to a development in an opposite direc-tion, holding the internet provider only liable for a subjective fault: only if he factually knows about illegal content (not just if he ought to know about it) has he a duty to act. This is a rare instance of liability being restricted rather than expanded, as the general tendency has been over the last century. See also nr 811 about the subjective test of knowledge and ability.

Commission Regulation (EC) No 809/2004 of 29 April 2004 implementing Directive 2003/71/EC of the European Parliament and of the Council as regards information contained in pros-pectuses as well as the format, incorporation by reference and publication of such prospectuses and dissemination of advertisements.

[5] Seine 19 April 1967, D. 1968. 253, comm. P. Voirin.
[6] Civ. 2e 7 February 1963, Bull. civ. II, no 132.
[7] Directive 2000/31/EC of 8 June 2000 (Directive on electronic commerce); see nr 1302. See BGH 23 September 2003, MDR 2003, 92, ETL 2003, 192 (Fedtke): the provider has a duty towards the person affected if it has positive knowledge concerning the illegal content and the technical ability to remove the content with a reasonable amount of effort.

14

Liability for Movable Objects

A INTRODUCTION

1401 Overview

In the vast majority of cases in which someone suffers personal injury or property loss, a movable object has played a role by actively causing the damage (for example, an exploding gas cylinder) or by being otherwise instrumental in causing the damage (for example, someone stumbles over a piece of wood on the street). More particularly, this chapter will focus on liability for damage caused by animals, motor vehicles, products, and dangerous substances. It will deal with both rules of strict and fault liability for damage caused by movable objects in order to enable a better comparison between the legal systems.

The legal systems hold various strict rules as regards liability for movable objects. If no such specific rule exists, liability for damage caused by a movable object has to be based on the defendant's fault, his intentional or negligent conduct. All legal systems provide for strict liability regimes for damage caused by animals and defective products, and France and Germany also for a general strict liability for damage caused by motor vehicles.[1]

The statutory strict liability regimes for damage caused by *animals* mainly date from the 19th century but they are mostly based on older rules. Animals have for long been considered as a special risk for which a special liability regime was needed. The current liability regimes in the different legal systems show different shades of strictness (nr 1402–1403). Liability generally rests on the person who keeps the animal for his own use and benefit.[2]

Since the beginning of the 20th century, in most countries strict liability regimes for damage caused by *motor vehicles* have been developed. In France the system is now virtually absolute and in Germany the regime is strict (nr 1404).[3] In 2002 the European Commission proposed to oblige liability insurers to cover personal injuries

---

[1] In addition to these movable objects one may also think of strict liability rules for damage caused by trains and planes: see Koch and Koziol (2002), 398–401.   [2] Von Bar (1998), N 208–222.
[3] In 1970 the Law Commission dismissed proposals to introduce strict liability of car owners: Law Commission, *Civil Liability for Dangerous Activities and Things*, Report No. 32 (1970), para. 14–16.

suffered by pedestrians and cyclists as a consequence of an accident in which a motor vehicle was involved, irrespective of whether the driver of the vehicle was at fault. This was in fact a copy of the absolute French system. The European Parliament and the Council, however, were not convinced of the virtues of such a system and rejected it. Strict liability for motor vehicles rests not only on the long-term keeper or the owner but also on the third party liability insurer (nr 1400).

The most European liability regime applies to defective *products*. This European Directive of 1985 (85/374/EEC) provides for strict liability for manufacturing defects and for an objective negligence liability for design defects. This is a maximum harmonization Directive and it has achieved a higher level of harmonization in the area of tort law in the European Community. However, many important differences remain and the European Commission is investigating the possibilities of a further harmonization of the national liability regimes. Liability rests on the manufacturer and not on the keeper of the product. Though he has brought the product out of his control by putting it onto the market, it is necessary and justified that the product remains within his scope of responsibility. The manufacturer is the most eligible actor in the distribution chain that is able to control and prevent defectiveness, whereas the wholesale dealer and the seller often lack the means to check every single item they sell.

Since the end of the 20th century, strict liability regimes for damage caused to the *environment* have been imposed in Germany and even in England. In France the traditional general strict liability rules apply to this contemporary problem (nr 1400). At an international level a number of treaties are in force (nr 1414–1415). Finally, the European Union has put its stamp on this field, albeit a rather vague one, by adopting a Directive with regard to the prevention and remedying of environmental damage. In these various rules liability rests primarily on the polluter, and not on the owner or keeper of the polluted water, similarly to the manufacturer's liability. Someone who discharges waste aims to bring it out of his control but the consequences need to remain within his scope of responsibility. Indeed, there does not seem to be a good reason to treat responsibility for products differently from the responsibility for waste produced in the manufacturing process.

Liability for animals and motor vehicles generally does not rest on the owner of the movable object but on *le gardien* (France), *der Halter* (Germany), or *the keeper* (England). These are persons who have factual control over the movable object. In Germany and France children and mentally handicapped persons can also be *gardien* or *Halter*. As regards motor vehicles the driver is considered to be the potentially liable person (nr 1405).[4] This approach contrasts with liability for immovable objects where it is more usual that liability rests on the owner of the premises or building or on the operator of the plant (nr 1506-1). Both rules, however, serve the same purpose, ie to impose liability on someone who can be easily traced and identified.[5]

---

[4] Koch and Koziol (2002), 413–420.
[5] The *seller* can be liable towards the buyer on the basis of breach of contract. As regards his liability to third parties the Directive aims to channel all claims to the manufacturer thus exempting

In this chapter the various special liability regimes for damage caused by animals (B), motor vehicles (C), products (D), and for damage caused to the environment (E) will be analysed.

Regarding liability for movable objects, the most important and most general French provision is, of course, article 1384 al. 1 holding a strict liability regime for things (*responsabilité du fait des choses*). This rule has been analysed in nr 303. In addition to this provision, special strict liability regimes apply to specific things, particularly for animals, motor vehicles, and products. The special rule for damage caused by animals is, however, virtually absorbed by the general rule of article 1384 al. 1. No special rule applies to liability for damage caused to the environment and in these cases the general rule is of great importance.

In Germany, the *Verkehrspflichten*, the judicial safety duties (nr 403) are of great importance regarding liability for damage caused by movable objects. However, in German law the categories of cases dealt with in this chapter (animals, products, motor vehicles, and environmental liability) are all covered by special strict liability regimes. For this reason the *Verkehrspflichten* will not play a role in this chapter.

The English *tort of negligence* is the rule that will often be applied in cases of liability for damage caused by movable objects; see nr 503. This will also be the case in this chapter, since English law does not have a strict liability regime for damage caused by motor vehicles and only a very limited strict rule for damage caused to the environment. Only damage caused by animals and products is covered by a strict liability regime.

As regards environmental damage all legal systems provide rules in the framework of the law of neighbours. In all regimes these rules have a mainly strict character (nr 1413).

B ANIMALS

1402 National rules

The English Animals Act 1971 contains, with some changes, the common law rules with regard to liability for damage caused by animals.[6] Liability regimes in

the seller from the strict liability regime of the Directive (unless the manufacturer cannot be identified). This does not exclude the seller's liability on the basis of tort (fault), but for the claimant this may be difficult to prove. In French law the seller has been strictly liable on the basis of the breach of a judge-made *obligation de sécurité*. However, it is uncertain whether this rule can be maintained next to the regime of the Directive (nr 1407-2).

[6] Winfield and Jolowicz (2002), para. 16.1 ff; Markesinis and Deakin (2003), 548–559. Liability for animals can also be based on the strict torts of trespass (*Manton v Brocklebank* [1923] 2 KB 212; *League Against Cruel Sports v Scott* [1985] 2 All ER 489) and nuisance (*Pitcher v Martin* [1937] 3 All ER 918; *Gilleck v O'Reilly* [1984] ILRM 402 (HC)).

the Animals Act differ according to the kind of animal causing damage. Because of the limited scope of the strict liability rules in the Animals Act, many cases remain to be decided on the basis of the tort of negligence.[7]

Strict liability applies to damage caused by livestock straying onto another person's land, to damage caused by dangerous animals which are usually not domesticated in the British Isles, and to damage caused by dogs that kill or injure cattle. The consequence of this latter rule is that cattle are better protected against dogs than human beings are. A less strict rule applies to damage caused by non-dangerous animals under section 2(2): a keeper is strictly liable if the animal has posed a risk of severe damage, a risk that is attributable to the animal's abnormal characteristics 'which are not normally so found except at particular times or in particular circumstances' and those characteristics were known to the keeper.[8]

The lack of clarity and precision in this and other provisions in the Act is causing ongoing confusion. For example, in a case about a horse that had been frightened, escaped from the field where it was kept, and ran across a main road causing an accident, the House of Lords decided by the smallest majority that the keeper of the horse was strictly liable because the horse's abnormal characteristics in the present case could be found in particular circumstances. The minority held that in the present case the horse's characteristics were considered to be normal.[9] Indeed, this opaque statutory text provides the judge with a bran-tub rather than a rule.

Generally, liability is on the keeper of the animal: this is the owner or the person who has the actual power over the animal. The keeper can avoid or restrict liability by proving risk acceptance or contributory negligence.[10]

In German law the liability regime also varies according to the kind of animal causing damage. Strict liability applies to damage caused by a luxury animal (*Luxustier*) and negligence liability with a reversed burden of proof applies to damage caused by a *Nutztier*. A *Nutztier* is a domestic animal serving the business, earnings, or prosperity of the keeper, whereas a *Luxustier* is every other animal that does not serve these economic purposes (§ 833 BGB). The distinction between these kinds of animals was incorporated in the BGB in 1908 under pressure of an agricultural lobby opposing strict liability for damage caused by their animals. In practice, it is often difficult to distinguish between the two kinds of animals and even the BGH would prefer the distinction to be abolished but it considers this to be a task of the legislator rather than the judiciary.[11]

---

[7] Markesinis and Deakin (2003), 548–549.

[8] In *Glanville v Sutton* [1928] 1 QB 571 this rule did not apply: the keeper of the animal knew that his horse had a propensity to bite other horses but not to bite men. Winfield and Jolowicz (2002), paras 16.3–16.14; Markesinis and Deakin (2003), 550–559.

[9] *Mirvahedy v Henley* [2003] UKHL 2003, 16, ETL 2003, 127 (Oliphant).

[10] See for example *Cummings v Grainger* [1977] 1 QB 397; [1977] 1 All ER 104. Markesinis and Deakin (2003), 556–558; Winfield and Jolowicz (2002), para. 16.8.

[11] BGH 27 May 1986, NJW 1986, 2501, 2502: it can '... nicht Aufgabe richterlicher Rechtsfortbildung sein, diese Korrektur vorzunehmen, die der Gesetzgeber trotz Kenntnis der Reformvorschläge bislang nicht vorgenommen hat.' See also Kötz-Wagner (2001), N 355.

However, in a country where agricultural interests are of major political importance this is not very likely to happen.

In both rules the keeper of the animal is the liable person. The keeper is the person who has, for his own interest and for certain duration, the supervision of the animal. For example, someone who for some days hires a horse from a riding school does not become the animal's keeper.[12] The aim of the statutory rules is to protect against specific animal risks (*die spezifische Tiergefahr*), ie death, personal injury, and property damage caused by the specific danger inherent in the keeping of an animal. This implies that the rules do not apply if a drain is clogged by cow dung and after rain this blockage causes the flooding of the basement of a neighbouring house: the blockage could also have been caused in another way. The person who suffers damage could not invoke § 833 but had to rely on § 823.[13] It is yet unclear whether a horse rider has a claim against the keeper of the animal or that he has accepted the risk of damage.[14] § 29 ff. *Bundesjagdgesetz* (Federal Game Act) impose strict liability on hunting associations for property damage in its hunting district caused by game.

In France, article 1385 CC holds the owner or the person who uses the animal strictly liable for damage caused by the animal, also if it is lost or has escaped, provided there is a sufficient causal connection with the damage.[15] In fact, strict liability based on article 1385 rests on the animal's custodian (*gardien*). In the course of time, this provision has been almost completely absorbed by the general strict liability for things of article 1384 al. 1 (nr 303). This means that the custodian (*gardien*) is liable for the damage caused by the animal, unless he can prove *force majeure*. Article 1385 still has the advantage for a claimant to file a claim against the owner who then has to prove that he was not the custodian.[16] No distinction is made as regards the nature of the animal.[17]

1403 Comparative observations

In all legal systems strict regimes apply to liability for damage caused by animals but the content of these rules differs in many respects.[18] It has been suggested that a common ground across the legal systems for strict liability is the inadequate control by humans.[19]

---

[12] Münchener Kommentar-Wagner (2004), § 833 N 20–26; Kötz-Wagner (2001), N 358.

[13] Kötz-Wagner (2001), N 360.

[14] BGH 9 June 1992, NJW 1992, 2474; BGH 22 December 1992, NJW 1993, 2611.

[15] Civ. 12 November 1986, JCP 1987. II. 20731.

[16] Civ. 2 and 8 July 1970, D. 1970. 704.

[17] Carbonnier (2000), § 250, 451–452; Viney-Jourdain (1998), nr 632; Terré-Simler-Lequette (2002), nr 760.

[18] Compare Art. 3:203 ECC: 'A person who independently exercises control over an animal and has it for their own use is accountable for the causation by the animal of personal injury and consequential loss, loss within Art. 2:202, and for loss resulting from property damage.'

[19] Koch and Koziol (2002), 397.

The English and German systems relate liability rules to the nature of the animal. In English law this is the potential risk the animal causes, whereas German law distinguishes between 'luxury' and 'utility' animals. From a liability point of view the German distinction does not make much sense since it is at least doubtful whether a 'utility' dog causes a smaller risk than a 'luxury' dog. How would one appreciate such a distinction if it had been made as regards motor vehicles?

In most systems strict liability rests on the keeper. This can be the owner but it may also be another person who, for a certain duration, is the supervisor of the animal, which means he has actual control over it and uses it for his own purposes. Thieves are always keepers but children generally are not. For the latter see for example s. 6(3)(b) of the Animals Act 1971: '... a person is a keeper of an animal if... he is the head of a household of which a member under the age of 16 owns the animal or has it in his possession.'[20] The fact that someone does not qualify as keeper does not rule out that his liability can be based on the general rules of negligence liability.

Damage caused by 'wild' animals is covered neither by strict nor by negligence liability rules for the simple reason that they do not belong to anyone: there is neither an owner nor a keeper. In practice this may play a role in traffic accidents caused by wild animals suddenly crossing the road. This, however, does not rule out that the owner of the premises where the wild animals live (for example a public authority) owes a duty of care to third persons, for example a duty to warn and inform.[21]

The strict liability rules apply to damage 'caused' by the animal. In German law the risks covered are limited to damage caused by the specific animal risk. This includes the risks caused by the animal's unpredictable behaviour and avoids the English confusion about the question of whether the animal risk is attributable to the animal's abnormal characteristics.

The defences of the animal keeper differ from system to system. All jurisdictions allow the defendant to invoke the victim's contributory negligence. The same goes for risk acceptance, which generally also leads to a reduction of the amount of damages (nr 809-2).

A recent discussion concerns the applicability of strict liability for animals to micro-organisms like bacteria and viruses.[22] The risks caused by animals generally concern personal injury, whereas bacteria and viruses generally cause damage to health (nr 703). As far as it is possible to 'keep' these micro-organisms, no doubt they will be kept for reasons of utility rather than luxury. One may think of laboratories keeping bacteria and viruses for research reasons and manufacturers using bacteria for their products, for example certain kinds of yoghurt. The issue is also related to discussions on liability for damage caused by

---

[20] See also nr 1506-1 about a similar position for children as regards the premises on which they live.   [21] Von Bar (1998), N 208. See also the fence example mentioned in nr 807-1.
[22] Von Bar (1998), N 209.

genetically modified organisms (GMOs). Though this has been advocated in the doctrine, no case law is yet known in which a strict liability rules for damage caused by animals is applied to micro-organisms. However, it is clear that risks caused by micro-organisms are sufficiently large and unpredictable to justify a rule of strict liability. If the courts are not prepared to analogically apply the strict rule for animals, the legislators have to enact a special strict liability rule as regards damage caused by micro-organisms as, for example, has been done by the German legislator in § 32 *Gentechnikgesetz* (Genetic Engineering Act).

C MOTOR VEHICLES

1404 National rules

1404-1 *France:* loi Badinter

Since 1986 very strict rules have been in force in France, providing an almost absolute liability for road traffic accidents: pedestrians, cyclists, and passengers have a right to compensation for damage caused by an accident in which a motor vehicle was involved. The custodian (*gardien*) or driver of the motor vehicle can only avoid liability by proving intentional conduct or an inexcusable fault (*faute inexcusable*) of the victim.[23]

The French Act regarding liability for damage caused by traffic accidents is known as the *loi Badinter* and is named after Robert Badinter, the Minister of Justice (*Garde des Sceaux*) who was politically responsible for the Act.[24] The preparations took more than two decades and to a great extent the Act is based on the ideas of André Tunc, the godfather of French tort law, although the legislator made simplifications and political compromises.[25] The *loi Badinter* was evaluated at its tenth anniversary in 1996 and the outcome of this evaluation was an unqualified positive: the premiums for liability insurance had not increased considerably and the number of court proceedings had been substantially lower than before the Act's coming into force.[26]

---

[23] See for a translation of the main provisions of the *loi Badinter*: Van Gerven (2000), 587–588.

[24] Loi no. 85-677 of 5 July 1985, S. 7584; JCP 1985. III. 57405. See Chabas, *Le droit des accidents de la circulation* (1988); Viney, *L'indemnisation des victimes d'accidents de la circulation*, (Paris, 1992).

[25] André Tunc, *La sécurité routière. Esquisse d'une loi sur les accidents de la circulation* (1966); André Tunc, *Pour une loi sur les accidents de la circulation* (1981) and from a comparative perspective André Tunc, *Traffic Accident Compensation* (1998).

[26] Dixième anniversaire de la loi Badinter sur la protection des victimes d'accidents de la circulation: Bilan et perspectives, Resp. civ. et assur. 1996, nr 4bis; Tunc, *Traffic Accident Compensation* (1998), 461–471. The Rapport Catala of 2005 (nr 301-2) only proposes some minor changes to the current system, *inter alia*, to bring the position of the driver onto the same footing as

The main rule of the *loi Badinter* is that the victim of a road traffic accident in which a motor vehicle is involved has a right to compensation against the driver and the custodian (*gardien*). The victim is entitled to compensation on the sole ground that the motor vehicle was *involved* in the accident (*implication du véhicule*). It is not necessary to establish that this implication was also the cause of the damage.[27] The courts very easily accept that this is the case, for example even if a car is parked without hindering other traffic.[28] The criterion used is comparable to the one developed in the case law as regards *fait de la chose* (act of a thing) in the framework of article 1384 al. 1 (nr 303-2). If there has been no contact between the car and the victim it is generally required that the car played an active role, for example by being in the proximity at the time of the accident. Examples are the case of a driver who is dazzled by the headlights of another vehicle and the case of a cyclist who loses his balance when he is suddenly confronted with the arrival of a truck.[29] A motor vehicle can even be implicated in an accident if some time has lapsed between the cause and the accident. In a case in which a road-sweeping machine had ejected gravel onto the pavement and some time later a person slipped on it, the *Cour de cassation* held that the machine had been implicated in the accident.[30]

Article 2 excludes *force majeure* and the act of a third party as defences against liability for personal injury.[31] According to Article 3(1), the driver or custodian of the motor vehicle can only escape liability if he proves that the victim intentionally sought the damage he suffered (*le victime a volontairement recherché le dommage qu'elle a subi*) or that the victim's inexcusable fault (*faute inexcusable*) was the sole cause of the accident.

According to the *Cour de cassation* an inexcusable fault is the intentional fault of an exceptional gravity which, with no valid reason, has exposed the victim to a danger which he should have realized.[32] In this respect the courts are looking for a clear and unambiguous intention to commit suicide or for extremely reckless

---

that of other victims (see below). See *Avant projet de réforme du droit des obligations (Articles 1101 à 1386 du Code civil) et du droit de la prescription (Articles 2234 à 2281 du Code civil)* (Rapport Catala) at www.justice.gouv.fr.

[27] Le Tourneau (2004), nr 8102.

[28] At least this is the position of the second civil chamber: Civ 2e 23 March 1994, D. 1994, 229, comm. Groutel, JCP 1994. II. 22292, comm. Conte, RTD civ. 1994, 627, obs. Jourdain; Civ. 2e 25 January 1995, Bull. civ. II, no. 27, RTC 1995, 382, obs. Jourdain; Civ. 2e 12 June 1996, D. 1996. IR. 175; Le Tourneau (2004), nr 8108.

[29] Civ. 2e 8 June 1994, Bull. civ. II, no. 147, D. 1994. IR. 181; Civ. 2e 13 January 1997, JCP 1997. II. 22883. See also Civ. 2e 14 November 2002, Bull. civ. II, no. 252.

[30] Civ. 2e 24 April 2003, D. 2003, IR. 266, RTD civ. 2003, 515, ETL 2003, 162 (Lafay, Moréteau and Pellerin-Rugliano).

[31] Article 5 II provides that if damage to goods is claimed the defendant can invoke the regular contributory negligence defence (nr 1212).

[32] Ass. plén. 10 November 1995, D. 1995. 633, JCP 1996. II. 22564, comm. Viney, RTD civ. 1996, 183, obs. Jourdain: '...seule est inexcusable au sens de ce texte la faute volontaire d'une exceptionnelle gravité exposant sans raison valable son auteur à un danger dont il aurait dû avoir conscience.' In the same sense already Civ. 2e 20 July 1987, Bull. civ. II, no 160.

behaviour. For example, the fault of a drunken pedestrian who crossed the road at a blind and dark bend was not inexcusable and neither was the fault of a drunken pedestrian who was lying down in the middle of the street in the middle of the night.[33] An example of an inexcusable fault can be found in the case of young men seating themselves on the roof of a stationary bus; when the bus drove off, one of them fell off and died. The relatives' claim was nevertheless awarded because the inexcusable fault was not the sole cause of the accident: the bus driver was also negligent because he knew about the persons on the roof of his bus.[34]

According to Article 3(2) and 3(3) the defence of inexcusable fault does not apply to persons under the age of 16, persons older than 70, and persons who were already disabled for more than 80 per cent.[35] These are the so-called super-privileged victims (*les victimes superprivilégiées*). Against these victims a custodian or driver is only allowed to invoke the defence of intentional conduct.

If the *driver* of a motor vehicle suffers damage from a road traffic accident, his position is less favourable than that of passengers, cyclists, and pedestrians. He is entitled to compensation against the other driver or custodian of a motor vehicle, but the amount of compensation is reduced if he has committed a *faute* (article 4). However, the *Cour de cassation* has decided that, even if the *faute* of the victim-driver was the only cause of the accident, this does not necessarily mean that he is not entitled to compensation at all.[36]

A peculiarity is, furthermore, that the Act only applies to accidents and not to intentionally caused damage. For example, when a driver frightens a hitch-hiker and the latter gets injured as a consequence of this intentional conduct, the victim cannot file a claim on the basis of the *loi Badinter* but he has to base his claim on criminal procedure provisions with regard to damages for victims of crimes in article 706-3 ff. *Code de procédure penal* (Criminal Procedure Code).[37]

Belgium followed the French example in 1995 (article 29bis WAM, Act on Liability Insurance of Motor Vehicles). The Belgian legislator was inspired by the wish to improve the position of social security funds rather than to protect victims of road accidents. The idea was that a strict liability for owners and keepers of motor vehicles, combined with a right of recourse for public health

---

[33] Ass. plén. 10 November 1995, D. 1995. 633, JCP 1996. II. 22564, comm. Viney, RTC 1996, 183, obs. Jourdain; Civ. 2e 23 January 2003, ETL 2003, 174 (Lafay, Moréteau and Pellerin-Rugliano). [34] Civ. 2e 8 November 1993, Bull. civ. II, no 316, JCP 1994. IV. 84.
[35] Terré-Simler-Lequette (2002), nr 971 ff.
[36] Ch. mixte 28 March 1997, D. 1997. 294, comm. Groutel; Civ. 2e 6 May 1997, D. 1997. 503, comm. Groutel; Civ. 2e 2 July 1997, D. 1997. 183. The Rapport Catala of 2005 (nr 301-2) proposes to include the driver in the protected persons. This would imply that only the driver's inexcusable fault will be an defence against liability. See *Avant projet de réforme du droit des obligations (Articles 1101 à 1386 du Code civil) et du droit de la prescription (Articles 2234 à 2281 du Code civil)* (Rapport Catala) at www.justice.gouv.fr.
[37] Crim. 6 February 1992, RTC 1992, 571, obs. Jourdain. Less clear are Civ. 2e 2 March 1994, Bull. civ. II, no 79, RTC 1995, 132, obs. Jourdain; Civ. 2e 30 november 1994, Bull. civ. II, no 243, RTC 1995, 132, obs. Jourdain.

care and disability insurers, implies that a bigger part of social security expenses can be shifted to liability insurers.[38] Unlike the French system, the Belgian obligation to compensate does not rest on the custodian or driver of the motor vehicle but solely on the liability insurer of the motor vehicle that is involved in an accident.[39] Whereas the French approach implies an almost absolute *liability system*, the Belgian law provides for an *insurance system* in which the liability insurer has an obligation to pay compensation for the damage suffered. This difference is, however, not a matter of principle. In scarcely any other area are liability insurance and tort law so closely connected as in the law regarding compensation for road accidents (nr 706 and 1405).

1404-2 *Germany:* Straßenverkehrsgesetz

The German strict liability regime for damage caused by motor vehicles is embodied in § 7 *Straßenverkehrsgesetz* (StVG, Road Traffic Accident), which entered into force in 1909. The provision holds the keeper of a motor vehicle strictly liable for damage caused by the risk of its operation (*Betriebsgefahr*), unless he can prove *höhere Gewalt* (an external cause). § 7 StVG applies to all personal and property damage of pedestrians, cyclists, passengers, and drivers caused by a motor vehicle.[40]

The keeper is the person who has the supervision of the motor vehicle; usually the owner is also the keeper.[41] Someone who for a couple of days borrows the vehicle from the owner does not become a keeper, but if he uses the vehicle on the basis of a lease contract, he will be considered to be the keeper.[42]

The strict liability rule does not apply to the driver who is not also the keeper of the vehicle, for example the spouse of the keeper or someone who borrows the car for a short time. According to § 18 StVG the driver is liable, unless he proves that he did not cause the damage intentionally or negligently (*Verschulden*). This is a negligence liability with a reversed burden of proof. The driver is jointly liable with the keeper of the motor vehicle.

If the driver, who is not also the keeper, suffers damage, for example because of a defect of the vehicle's brakes, § 8 StVG does not allow him to base his claim against the keeper on § 7 StVG. He has to rely on the general negligence rules of § 823 I and II BGB.

---

[38] H. Bocken and I. Geers, 'De vergoeding van letselschade en schade door overlijden bij verkeersongevallen', *TPR*, 1996, 1199–1263; B. Tuerlinckx, 'Artikel 29bis W.A.M.-Wet: Toepassing in de praktijk na de wetswijziging van 13 april 1995', *TPR*, 1996, 11–27.

[39] Another difference is that in Belgium pedestrians, cyclists, and passengers have a right to compensation, unless the liability insurer can prove intentional conduct of the victim. The initial defence of inexcusable fault was scratched in 2000. See about (the former version of) Belgian law von Bar (2000), N 369.   [40] Deutsch-Ahrens (2002), N 380–385a.

[41] RG 27 January 1930, RGZ 127, 175; BGH 29 May 1954, BGHZ 13, 351, 354.

[42] BGH 22 March 1983, BGHZ 87, 133 = VersR 1983, 656.

§ 7 StVG applies to damage caused by the risk of the operation (*Betriebsgefahr*) of the motor vehicle, particularly the risks caused by the speed and the mass of the vehicle. This can also be the case if the vehicle has not touched the victim, for example when a motorcyclist falls during overtaking by an articulated lorry.[43] However, liability on the basis of this provision does not require that the vehicle is in motion; § 7 StVG can also apply to the keeper of a motor vehicle standing still on a motorway.[44] The operational risk of the motor vehicle (*Betriebsgefahr*) has to be related to traffic. Hence, § 7 StVG does not apply where a motor vehicle is used to pump fodder into a silo but it does apply if debris is thrown out of a sander.[45] The provision also applies if traffic noise causes personal injury or property damage, for example if a collision of cars near a farm causes pigs to be panic-stricken (nr 1103-2).

The keeper of a motor vehicle can avoid liability by proving *höhere Gewalt*. This requires an external cause (such as the powers of nature or the act of a third party) which is unforeseeable and unavoidable. This defence makes liability of § 7 II StVG independent of negligence considerations.[46] Until 2002 this was different when the keeper disposed of the defence of an *unabwendbares Ereignis* (unavoidable event). An event was unavoidable if it was caused by the victim, a third party, or an animal, and the keeper as well as the driver had observed all due care. The courts compared the conduct of the driver with that of the ideal driver who takes into account the considerable chance that other people make mistakes.[47] In practice the difference between the old and the new defence will be small since the courts applied a very high standard of care before accepting the defence of unavoidable event.

The keeper of the motor vehicle can reduce the amount of compensation to be paid by invoking contributory negligence of the victim. This defence is, however, not allowed against victims of less than 10 years of age (nr 1215).

The amount of damages for death and personal injury is limited to a maximum capital of €600,000 or €36,000 as an annual pension (§ 12 I StVG). In case of more victims the limits are €3,000,000 and €180,000 respectively (§ 12 II StVG). As far as the damage exceeds these limits, the victim has to base his claim on the negligence rules of § 823 I and II BGB.

Since 2002 it is possible to claim compensation for non-pecuniary loss under a strict liability rule. Until then many traffic accident cases were decided on the basis of § 823 I and II in order to be able to get compensation for non-pecuniary loss (nr 1202-2).

1404-3 *England: tort of negligence*

While most continental legal systems provide for strict liability rules for damage caused by motor vehicles, English law mainly sticks to traditional negligence

---

[43] BGH 11 July 1972, NJW 1972, 1808.   [44] BGH 18 March 1969, VersR 1969, 668.
[45] BGH 5 July 1988, BGHZ 105, 65.   [46] Deutsch-Ahrens (2002), N 385a.
[47] BGH 17 March 1992, BGHZ 117, 337; BGH 28 May 1985, NJW 1986, 183.

liability.[48] In this respect the courts require a high standard of care from drivers of motor vehicles, especially towards pedestrians and cyclists: '. . . negligence in fact works much more strictly here than in other areas, so much so that in many instances it has become artificial to continue calling it by that name.'[49] This strict interpretation of negligence (nr 1004) somewhat limits the differences with the strict liability regimes in France and Germany.[50] However, two important gaps remain: firstly, the difference in the burden of proof which, in the practice of road accidents, is often decisive for liability, and secondly, the driver's contributory negligence defence which is not excluded like in France or limited like in Germany. In England it is fully applicable, also towards young children.

A number of cases illustrate that in traffic accidents the required level of care is high. In *Nettleship v Weston* the conduct and capacities of a driving pupil were compared to those of an experienced driver;[51] in *Roberts v Ramsbottom* it was established that a driver acted negligently when he lost consciousness for which he could not be blamed;[52] and in *Henderson v HE; Jenkins & Sons and Evans* the owner of a lorry was held liable for the unforeseeable failure of the hydraulic braking system (see also nr 1004-1).[53] However, *Worsley v Hollins* was about a minibus whose brakes failed to function causing it to run into the back of a car waiting at traffic lights. The defendant was able to prove that the minibus had recently passed the MOT test and had been fully serviced, and this was enough to dismiss the victim's claim for negligence.[54A]

The latter case is an example of the application of the maxim of *res ipsa loquitur*. Though this application can be beneficial for the claimant, it does not provide the same level of protection for claimants as strict liability does. *Ng Chun Pui v Lee Chuen Tat*, a Privy Council case, was about a coach suddenly crossing the central reservation and colliding with a public light bus on the other carriage way. At the trial the claimant did not call oral evidence and relied upon the fact of the accident as evidence of negligence or the doctrine of *res ipsa loquitur*. In other words, he relied upon the mere fact that the accident occurred and argued that this very fact could only have come about if negligence was involved. According to Lord Griffiths, there

. . . can be no doubt that the plaintiffs were justified in taking this course. In ordinary circumstances if a well maintained coach is being properly driven it will not cross the central reservation of a dual carriageway and collide with on-coming traffic in the other carriageway.[54]

---

[48] In the 1970s the Pearson Commission pleaded for a strict liability regime but this proposal was rejected: *Report of the Commission on Civil Liability and Compensation for Personal Injury*, Cmnd. 7054.   [49] Markesinis and Deakin (1998), 268.

[50] The tort of trespass to the person and trespass to goods could have been developed into a strict liability regime but it was already at an early stage in history negligence became a requirement for trespass to the person in traffic accidents: see *Holmes v Mather* (1875) LR 10 Ex. 261 and nr 500.

[51] *Nettleship v Weston* [1971] 2 QB 691(CA).

[52] *Roberts v Ramsbottom* [1980] 1 WLR 823.

[53] *Henderson v HE Jenkins & Sons and Evans* [1970] AC 282.

[54A] *Worsley v Hollins* [1991] RTR 252 (CA).

[54] *Ng Chun Pui v Lee Chuen Tat* [1988] RTR 298.

This approach differs from a reversal of the burden of proof in that it shifts the risk of providing evidence as regards (lack of) negligence to the defendant. *Res ipsa loquitur* only implies that if the defendant does not adduce evidence, the claimant has proved his case. But if the defendant does adduce evidence, this evidence must be evaluated to see if it is still reasonable to draw the inference of negligence from the mere fact of the accident. In this case the defendant adduced the evidence by showing that the coach had to swerve to the right because of a car suddenly cutting into his lane. The victims' claims were dismissed.

Breach of statutory duty could provide for complementing the predominant negligence rules, but the English courts have consistently refused traffic legislation as a source of liability in order to prevent isolated pockets of strict liability coming into an area generally covered by negligence (nr 902-2).[55]

An exception is *London Passenger Transport Board v Upson*, about a pedestrian who crossed the street at a pedestrian crossing while the traffic lights showed red for pedestrians. When she 'emerged' at the crossing from behind a waiting taxi she was knocked down by a bus driving at a speed of approximately 15 mph. The Court of Appeal found that the driver had not been *negligent* because reasonably he could not have seen the pedestrian and he had not driven too fast, but it established that the driver was liable for breach of his statutory duty. The House of Lords upheld this decision.[56] The relevant statutory duty reads as follows: 'The driver of every vehicle approaching a crossing shall, unless he can see that there is no passenger thereon, proceed at such a speed as to be able if necessary to stop before reaching such crossing.'[57] This provision implies that a driver has to guarantee to stop in time before the crossing regardless of any unexpected event at the crossing. It is no defence that he approached the crossing at a very moderate speed, or that he could only see the pedestrian at the last moment. Though the negligence of his conduct is in principle not relevant he may invoke *force majeure*, for instance a defect in the braking system of his vehicle for which he was not to blame.[58]

The contributory negligence is fully applicable; there are no exclusionary rules such as in Germany and France. Generally, it is hard to establish contributory negligence of young children under the age of 7.[59] Above this age the applicable objective standard is that of the child of the same age (nr 1215). An example of a case in which the contributory negligence defence was dismissed is *Gough v Thorne*. A 13-year-old girl wanted to cross a busy road in London. A lorry driver stopped alongside her, with one hand indicating the other traffic to stop and with the other that she should cross. When she crossed she was hit by a car

---

[55] Winfield and Jolowicz (2002), para. 7.8.

[56] *London Passenger Transport Board v Upson* [1949] AC 155, about which Van Gerven (2000), 574 ff. The driver's employer was vicariously liable for this breach of statutory duty; see nr 1606-4.

[57] Reg. 3 of the Pedestrian Crossing Places (Traffic) Regulations 1941, replaced by the 'Zebra' Pedestrian Crossing Regulations 1971, SI 1971, No. 1524.

[58] See for instance *Burns v Bidder* [1967] 2 QB 227.

[59] See for instance the Scottish case of *Barns v Flucker* [1985] SLT 142.

passing the lorry at high speed. The trial judge decided that her contributory negligence was one-third. The Court of Appeal allowed the appeal. Lord Denning MR said:

A judge should only find a child guilty of contributory negligence if he or she is of such an age as reasonably to be expected to take precautions for his or her own safety (. . .). A child has not the road sense or the experience of his or her elders. He or she is not to be found guilty unless he or she is blameworthy.

In this case Lord Denning concluded that the girl was not to blame for crossing the road as she did without leaning forward and looking to see whether anything was coming.[60] In this case it will also have played a role that the child could reasonably rely on the adult's advice she was given.

1405 International perspective

1405-1 *Comparative observations*

Travelling, both for business and private purposes, has got a strong border-crossing character over the last decades. However, at each border within the European Union the traveller is still inadvertently subject to a change of the applicable liability rules for road traffic accidents.[61] Though harmonizing Directives have been issued in this area (nr 1405-2), this only concerned the compulsory insurance for liability for damage caused by motor vehicles and not the heart of the matter: the content of the applicable liability rules.

As regards compensation for damage caused by motor vehicles, the national regimes differ considerably. France holds a no fault liability, Germany a strict liability, and England a traditional negligence liability. Though in many road accidents the tortfeasor has acted negligently, a negligence regime causes a problem for the victim in that the burden of proof of negligence is on him. This means that he has to prove what has actually happened, and how the accident occurred, and to prove this he will very much depend on witnesses and technical evidence. In this respect, the English road traffic victim is much worse off than his French and German counterpart. Compared to this, the practical differences between the French and German system are rather small.

Another aspect which makes the position of the English victim less favourable than French and German victims is the tortfeasor's defence of contributory negligence. In England the defence of contributory negligence is, in principle, possible towards all

---

[60] *Gough v Thorne* [1966] 3 All ER 398, [1966] 1 WLR 1387.

[61] The rules of international private law determine the applicable law in international traffic accident. See the Hague Convention of 4 May 1971 on the Law Applicable to Traffic Accidents: www.hcch.net and the Rome Convention (Rome II) on the applicable law concerning non-contractual obligations. The European Commission has proposed to adopt and broaden this Convention in an EU Regulation: COM (2003) 427 final.

persons regardless their age. In Germany this defence is generally available but not against children until the age of 10 and against mentally disabled persons. Finally, in France the victim's contributory negligence can only be invoked in cases of intent or inexcusable *faute* (for certain vulnerable categories only in case of intent). These different rules make a substantial difference in the victim's legal position, since in many road traffic accidents the victim's conduct is not perfect, for example because of a (split) second of absent-mindedness.

The key issue for strict liability in France is the involvement of the motor vehicle in the accident (implication), whereas in Germany this is the operation of the vehicle. In practice the difference is not big since none of the systems requires contact between the motor vehicle and the victim. Furthermore, in both systems the strict liability rule applies to vehicles standing still. Despite these commonalities, the French concept of *implication* is definitely broader than the German *Betriebsgefahr*. There is, again, a sharp contrast with the English approach which focuses on the correctness of the driver's conduct.

The differences illustrate the various approaches of tort law in the three jurisdictions. Whereas English law primarily focuses on the conduct of the driver and the victim, the German and the French approach are based on the materialization of the risks of the motor vehicle. In short, this is an illustration of the difference between putting the emphasis on the freedom to act on the one hand, and putting the emphasis on solidarity in the burdens of the costs of road traffic accidents on the other.

The development of liability for damage caused by motor vehicles cannot be understood without taking into account the fact that there is compulsory liability insurance for damage caused by motor vehicles throughout Europe (nr 1405-2). The focus of tort law in this area is very much on distributive rather than corrective justice and the goal is to provide compensation to victims of traffic accidents. The rules are instrumental for that goal. From a comparative view, this seems to be less apparent in English law than in French and German law but from a domestic English point of view, the liability rules for road traffic accidents are indeed more instrumental than in other areas of liability.[62] Compulsory insurance of liability for damage caused by motor vehicles in fact attributes damage to the risk community of the insured rather than to the tortfeasor personally. Though it is also apparent in other areas of accident law (nr 100), road traffic accidents are the example par excellence of this development. We are still inclined to apply liability rules as a matter of compensation between individuals, but for the area of road traffic accidents this is wrong as far as liability is covered by insurance.[63] See also nr 716.

---

[62] Traffic accidents are virtually the only area in English law in which distributive justice prevails over corrective justice (nr 609-2).

[63] Kötz-Wagner (2001), N 377:

Wir sind es zwar immer noch gewöhnt, uns bei der Anwendung haftungsrechtlicher Normen von der Vorstellung leiten zu lassen, daß es dabei um eine Frage des Schadensausgleichs zwischen

1405-2 *European law*

A Europe without borders does not exist, not even in the area of traffic accidents. Despite the goals of free movement of people and of goods, this is not an important issue for European harmonization since these differences are not a real obstacle for cross-border traffic.[64] Indeed, the influence of the European Union as regards liability for road traffic accidents has been rather modest and up until now it has confined itself to five Directives concerning liability insurance. These Directives provide for compulsory liability insurance for liability to which a motor vehicle can give rise to and for a direct right to compensation for the claimant against the liability insurer of the vehicle (*action directe*).

The First Directive introduced compulsory third party liability insurance for personal injury and brought to an end the checks by Member States as to whether the motor vehicle carried a so-called green card (which showed that the liability to which the vehicle could give rise was insured).[65] The Second Directive extended the compulsory third party liability insurance to property damage, at the same time providing for a minimum level of insurance cover. Moreover, it obliged Member States to set up funds to compensate for personal injury or property damage caused by an unidentified or uninsured vehicle.[66] The Third Directive obliged Member States to ensure that all passengers of vehicles, other than a driver or passenger who has knowingly and willingly entered a stolen vehicle, is covered by compulsory civil liability insurance.[67] The Fourth Directive assists someone who suffers damage because of a road accident outside his country of residence to identify the insurer of the liable vehicle. It provides for an efficient mechanism for quick settlement of claims for these so-called 'visiting victims'.[68] Finally, the Fifth Directive makes it easier to get temporary liability insurance when staying abroad for study or work. It also substantially increases

Individuen geht. Für das Gebiet des Schadensausgleichs bei Straßenverkehrsunfällen ist die Vorstellung jedoch, soweit der Versicherungsschutz reicht, ausnahmslos falsch.

[64] An early attempt to harmonize rules was the European Convention of 14 May 1973 on Civil Liability for Damages caused by Motor Vehicles. This Council of Europe Convention was never enforced because it did not get the minimum of three ratifications. Von Bar (2000), N 378, footnote 70. Another attempt by the Council of Europe in the area of product liability was followed by action from the European Community; see nr 1406.

[65] Directive 72/166/EEC of 24 April 1972 on the approximation of the laws of member states relating to insurance against civil liability in respect of the use of motor vehicles and to the enforcement of the obligation to insure against such liability, OJ L103/1 2.5.1972, amended by Directive 72/430/EEC of 19 December 1972 (First Motor Insurance Directive), OJ L291/162 of 28.12.1972.

[66] Directive 84/5/EEC of 30 December 1983 on the approximation of the laws of the member states relating to insurance against civil liability in respect of the use of motor vehicles (Second Motor Insurance Directive), OJ L8, 11.1.1984.

[67] Directive 90/232/EEC of 14 May 1990 on the approximation of the laws of the member states relating to insurance against civil liability in respect of the use of motor vehicles (Third Motor Insurance Directive), OJ L129, 19.5.1990.

[68] Directive 2000/26/EC of 16 May 2000 on the approximation of the laws of the member states relating to insurance against civil liability in respect of the use of motor vehicles and amending

the levels of minimum insurance cover for personal injury to €1 million per victim and €5 million per accident, and for property damage to €1 million per accident.[69]

The first four Directives have already been implemented into the French *Code des Assurances* (article L 124 ff. Insurance Code), the German *Pflichtversicherungsgesetz* (Compulsory Insurance Act), and in England *inter alia*, in the European Communities (Rights Against Insurers) Regulations 2002. This system of compulsory liability insurance has provided a solid basis for legislators to develop rules of strict and absolute liability. It has also stimulated the courts—in cases in which negligence rules are applicable—to raise the level of required care (nr 1404).

In 2002 the European Commission attempted to harmonize the rules regarding liability for damage caused by motor vehicles to pedestrians and cyclists. This proposal was embodied in the above-mentioned proposal for the Fifth Directive. It held that compulsory liability insurance for motor vehicles 'shall cover personal injuries suffered by pedestrians and cyclists as a consequence of an accident in which a motor vehicle is involved, irrespective whether the driver is at fault' (Article 4 s. 2).[70] This implied a no fault insurance system for damage to pedestrians and cyclists caused by a motor vehicle.

The Commission explained the background of this proposal by stating that, while pedestrians and cyclists may be the cause of some accidents, motor vehicles cause most accidents, and that pedestrians and cyclists usually suffer more in accidents involving motor vehicles. Therefore, a

new provision is inserted in Directive 84/5/EEC in order to include in the cover provided by the vehicle insurance personal injuries suffered by pedestrians and cyclists in accidents involving a motor vehicle. This cover under the compulsory insurance of the vehicle should apply, irrespective of whether the driver is at fault.[71]

As far as the Commission is aware, 'such inclusion of pedestrians and cyclists in some Member States' legislation does not seem to have had a significant impact on the cost of the insurance.'[72]

The Commission's proposal seemed to a great extent to be inspired by the Belgian system (the country of the Commission's headquarters) and it was also consonant with the Swedish and Finnish system. In these systems the liability

Council Directives 73/239/EEC and 88/357/EEC (Fourth Motor Insurance Directive), OJ L181/65, 20.7.2000.

[69] Directive 2005/14/EC of 11 May 2005 amending Council Directives 72/166/EEC, 84/5/EEC, 88/357/EEC, 90/232/EEC and Directive 2000/26/EC relating to insurance against civil liability in respect of the use of motor vehicles (Fifth Motor Insurance Directive), OJ L149/14, 11.06.2005.

[70] Proposal for a Directive of the European Parliament and of the Council amending Council Directives 72/166/EEC, 84/5/EEC, 88/357/EEC, 90/232/EEC and Directive 2000/26/EC on insurance against civil liability in respect of the use of motor vehicles, 07.06.2002, COM(2002) 244 final, 2002/0124 (COD), 24.

[71] COM (2002) 244 final (7 June 2002), 14. Liability of the pedestrian or cyclist as well as the level of damages should be governed by the applicable national legislation and the national courts.

[72] COM (2002) 244 final (7 June 2002), 8.

insurer is the 'liable' party. A difference was that the Commission's proposal was confined to pedestrians and cyclists and did not include passengers. Nonetheless, the proposal was considered to be a step too far and the European Council as well as the European Parliament rejected it, preferring this sensitive matter to be dealt with by separate legislation. Even though the proposal could have been tempting for governments wanting to cut the costs of social security by passing them on to private liability insurers (see the Belgian example, nr 1404–1), strong ideas about the foundations of liability and the arguments put forward by a lobby of liability insurers and drivers prevailed.

Soon after the adoption of the Fifth Directive the ECJ handed down an important decision in which it drew conclusions from the Second and Third Directives for the substantive laws of the Member States as regards liability for damage caused by traffic accidents. The case was about an accident with a car where the driver and all passengers were drunk. As a consequence of the accident one of the passengers died and the others were seriously injured. On the basis of the Finnish Law on motor vehicle insurance, two of the passengers were denied compensation because they should have noticed the driver's drunken state. The ECJ held that Article 2(1) of the Second Directive and Article 1 of the Third Directive

preclude a national rule which allows the compensation borne by the compulsory motor vehicle insurance to be refused or limited in a disproportionate manner on the basis of the passenger's contribution to the injury or loss he has suffered. The fact that the passenger concerned is the owner of the vehicle the driver of which caused the accident is irrelevant.

Although this decision does not mean that national law has to follow that of other countries, a benchmark for a proportional reduction or limitation in such cases could be derived from the fact that in many countries the reduction is about 25 per cent (nr 1214).[73]

D PRODUCTS

1406 History, future, and context of the EC Product Liability Directive

The EC Directive of 25 July 1985 concerning liability for defective products is the oldest and still most powerful example of European harmonization in the field of tort law.[74] The Directive is applicable not only in the Member States of

---

[73] ECJ 30 June 2005, Case C-537/03, nyp, (*Candolin and Others v Pohjola and Others*).
[74] Directive 85/374/EEC, OJ L 210/29, 7.8.1985; see, *inter alia*, about product liability in Europe: Christopher J.S. Hodges (ed.), *Product Liability: European Law and Practice* (London: Sweet & Maxwell, 1993); Jane Stapleton, *Product Liability* (London, Boston: Butterworths, 1994); Patrick

the European Union but also in the European Economic Area.[75] Moreover, the Directive has been an important example for other jurisdictions to reform their product liability regime.[76]

The aims of the Directive are manifold: it is not just about consumer protection or just about providing a level playing field for competition between businesses throughout the European Union. According to the ECJ, the limits of the scope of the Directive

... are the result of a complex balancing of different interests. As is apparent from the first and ninth recitals in the preamble to the Directive, those interests include guaranteeing that competition will not be distorted, facilitating trade within the common market, consumer protection and ensuring the sound administration of justice.[77]

The Member States were obliged to transpose the EC Directive by 30 July 1988 but most Member States took more time. In this respect it can be argued that the Directive has direct effect and that it must be applied to products which are put into circulation after 29 July 1988, irrespective of the date of implementation. However, in France it is argued that the Act implementing the Directive is only applicable to products which were put onto the market after its enactment on 19 May 1998.[78] This highly disputable position could be challenged before the European Court. See about direct effect, nr 204-2.

The first country to implement the Directive was the United Kingdom. This happened in the Consumer Protection Act 1987.[79] In 1989 Germany transposed the Directive in the *Produkthaftungsgesetz* (Product Liability Act).[80] France was the last Member State to implement the Directive and this only happened in 1998 in article 1386-1 ff CC.[81] France was not very fond of implementing the Directive because it provided for a lower level of protection than French law did (nr 1407-2). It was only after a convicting decision of the ECJ that the French legislator implemented the Directive in the *Code civil*.[82]

Kelly and Rebecca Attree (eds.), *European Product Liabilities*, 2nd edn., (London, Edinburgh, Dublin: Butterworths, 1997); Geraint Howells, 'Product Liability—A History of Harmonisation', in *Towards a European Civil Code* (2004), 645–656; Duncan Fairgrieve (ed.), *Product Liability in Comparative perspective*, (Cambridge: Cambridge University Press, 2005).

[75] The European Economic Area (EEA) consists of the EU and the EFTA countries: Iceland, Liechtenstein, Norway, and Switzerland.

[76] Mathias Reimann, 'Product Liability in a Global Context: the Hollow Victory of the European Model', *ERPL*, 11/2 (2004), 128–154. He argues that the global dissemination of system of the Product Liability Directive has influenced the law in the books rather than the law in action. In most countries the European model has not significantly affected the nature and the number of claims. This illustrates, so he argues, how deceptive and ineffective mere blackletter law harmonization can be.   [77] ECJ 25 April 2002, Case C-52/00 (*Commission v French Republic*), para. 29.

[78] Philippe Brun, 'France', *ETL*, 2002, 194.

[79] Consumer Protection Act 1987, c. 43. See for the main provisions Van Gerven (2000), 667–668.

[80] Produkthaftungsgesetz 15 December 1989, BGB l. I. 2198. See for an English translation of the main provisions Van Gerven (2000), 650–651.

[81] Act of 19 May 1998 (Loi 98-389), about which *inter alia* Ghestin, JCP 1998. I. 148. See for an English translation of the main provisions Van Gerven (2000), 661–662.

[82] See *inter alia* Jacques Ghestin, JCP 1998. I. 148.

In January 2001 the European Commission published a Report on the Application of the Directive.[83] Its main conclusion was that there was still limited experience with regard to the application of the Directive. This was considered to be mainly due to two factors: firstly, in some Member States the Directive was transposed too late, and secondly, parallel to the regime of the Directive, national contractual or extra-contractual law and specific liability regimes are still applied. The scarce information available has not permitted the identification of any major problems with the application of the Directive. Hence, the Commission considers it premature to envisage any changes to the current liability system under the Directive. It nonetheless launched several studies, especially to investigate the practical, economical, and financial consequences of the Directive and the possibilities for greater harmonization of the current product liability system.[84]

In addition to the Directive on product liability, product safety regulations, particularly the General Product Safety Directive, play an important role in this respect.[85] Article 3(1) of this Directive provides that producers '... shall be obliged to place only safe products on the market.' Paragraphs 3(2) and 3(3) indicate under which circumstances a product is safe in the sense of this Directive. To a great extent the concept of a safe product (Product Safety Directive) runs parallel to the concept of a not defective product (Product Liability Directive). Although an unsafe product will generally imply that it is also defective, it remains to be seen whether a defective product will always have to be considered as unsafe. The Product Liability Directive has a repressive character, aiming at reaching a fair apportionment of the risks between the interests of the individual manufacturer and the individual victim, whereas the emphasis of the Product Safety Directive is very much on the prevention of damage, thus balancing the risks between the individual manufacturer and the public at large.

The Product Safety Directive also provides for a duty of the producer to monitor the products he has put on the market. Article 5(1) provides that producers shall adopt measures enabling them to '... (a) be informed of risks which these products might pose; (b) choose to take appropriate action including, if necessary to avoid these risks, withdrawal from the market, adequately and effectively warning consumers or recall from consumers.' Well before the adoption of this Directive product recalls were already a well-known and regularly applied measure taken by producers to prevent (further) damage. To a certain extent the Product Liability Directive was an incentive for product recalls in order to prevent or limit liability risks. However, it is very likely that other incentives play a much bigger role, particularly the interest of a company to protect its reputation, brand, and market value.

---

[83] COM (2001) 893 final (31 January 2001).

[84] COM (2001) 893 final (31 January 2001), 28 ff.

[85] Directive 2001/95/EC of 3 December 2001 on general product safety, OJ L 11/4, 15.01.2002. See about this area for example Christopher Hodges, *European Regulation of Consumer Product Safety*, (Oxford: Oxford University Press, 2005).

1407 Level of harmonization

1407-1 *Options in the Directive; differences in the laws of damages*

The Directive on product liability aims to harmonize European regimes but it only does so to a certain extent.[86] Substantial differences remain because of the options in the Directive, the remaining differences in the national laws of damages (this section) and the application of pre-existing liability regimes next to the Directive (nr 1407-2).

The Directive provided for three options for the Member States when implementing the Directive (Articles 15–16). Firstly, they could rule that manufacturers of raw agricultural products and game would not fall under the scope of the Directive and thus, in practice, only under the general national tort law provisions.[87] However, this option was abolished in 2000 as a result of measures taken by the EU in order to fight the BSE crisis.[88] BSE, also called 'Mad Cow Disease', is presumed to be a cause of the human Creutzfeld-Jakob disease which caused a high number of casualties in the course of the 1990s, particularly in the United Kingdom. This measure was aimed at political rather than legal effect, since it is hard to imagine how it would be possible to track down the farmer who put the meat onto the market which caused the patient's disease.

Secondly, Member States could also exclude the development risk defence by derogating from Article 7(e), and provide that the producer shall be liable even if he proves that the state of scientific and technical knowledge at the time when he put the product into circulation was not such as to enable the existence of a defect to be discovered. This was unconditionally done by Finland and Luxembourg. France, Germany, and Spain do not allow the defence in the medical area. See about this defence in more detail nr 1410-2.[89]

Finally, Member States could provide that a producer's total liability for damage resulting from death or personal injury and caused by identical items with the same defect shall be limited to an amount not less than ECU 70 million. Limitations have been adopted by Germany, Greece, Spain, and Portugal.

---

[86] This implies that the rules of international private law stay of great importance to assess the applicable law in international product liability accidents. See the Hague Convention of 2 October 1973 on the Law Applicable to Products Liability: www.hcch.net and the Rome Convention (Rome II) on the applicable law concerning non-contractual obligations; the European Commission has proposed to adopt and broaden this Convention in an EU Regulation: COM(2003) 427 final.

[87] This was done by all Member States except for Finland, Luxembourg, and Sweden.

[88] Directive 1999/34/EC of 10 May 1999, amending Council Directive 85/374/EEC on the approximation of the laws, regulations and administrative provisions of the Member States concerning liability for defective products, OJ L 141/20.

[89] Initially, France required that the producer had taken appropriate steps to avert the consequences of a defective product in order to be able to invoke the development risk defence.

A second reason for remaining differences between the Member States is that important issues such as regards damages are mainly decided on the basis of national law. It is true that Article 9 of the Directive provides for compensation for damage caused by death or personal injury, and for damage to property intended for private use, but the amount of compensation has to be established according to national law. It has been pointed out earlier that these laws differ from country to country, particularly as regards compensation for non-pecuniary loss and the rights to compensation for third parties (nr 1209–1210). In theory the ECJ could push for more harmonization in this area but this is not very likely to happen, be it only for the reason that the ECJ is reluctant to develop case law in fields that are not related to fundamental issues of Community law.[90] Up until now the ECJ has confined itself to obliging the Member States to ensure that the national law of damages provides an effective remedy.[91]

A harmonizing development can be found in Germany. The Directive was implemented in the *Produkthaftungsgesetz* (Product Liability Act) but this was not an attractive basis for liability since German law did not award damages for non-pecuniary loss on the basis of a strict liability rule. Hence, most product liability claims were based on negligence liability (§ 823 I BGB), a rule the BGH has developed into a victim-friendly basis with a reversed burden of proof. However, since 2002 damages for pain and suffering can be granted on the basis of strict liability (nr 1202-2). This means that the chances for the Directive (*Produkthaftungsgesetz*) to be the main German basis for product liability claims have increased.

1407-2 *Previously existing liability systems*

A final element of divergence is related to the Directive's harmonization character. Minimum harmonization, on the one hand, would imply that Member States are allowed to issue stricter rules for the manufacturer. Maximum harmonization, on the other, would mean that deviation from the Directive is not allowed at all. In an infringement procedure against France for not correctly implementing the Directive, the ECJ pointed out that, apart from those matters for which the Directive provides an option or refers to national law, it seeks to achieve complete (or maximum) harmonization of the laws.[92]

A crucial provision in this respect is Article 13, holding that the Directive shall not affect any rights which an injured person may have according to the rules of

---

However, in ECJ 25 April 2002, Case C-52/00 (*Commission v French Republic*) decided that Article 15 entitled Member States to remove the exemption from liability for development risks but not to alter the conditions under which that exemption is applied.

[90] Walter van Gerven, 'The ECJ-Case law as a Means of Unification of Private Law?' in *Towards a European Civil Code* (2004), 103.

[91] ECJ 10 May 2001, Case C-203/99 (*Veedfalds v Arhus Amtskommune*), about which nr 1409.

[92] ECJ 25 April 2002, Case C-52/00 (*Commission v French Republic*), paras 19 and 24. In the same wording ECJ 25 April 2002, Case C-154/00, ECR I-3879 (*Commission v Hellenic Republic*); ECJ 25 April 2002, Case C-183/00, ECR 2002, I-3901 (*Maria Victoria González Sánchez v Medicina Asturiana SA*).

the law of contractual or non-contractual liability or a special liability system existing at the moment when this Directive is notified. In the same case against France the Court held, *inter alia*, that Article 13 of the Directive does not allow a Member State to maintain a general system of product liability different from that provided for in the Directive. However, it does not preclude the application of other systems of contractual or non-contractual liability based on other grounds, such as fault or a warranty in respect of latent defects.[93]

It is beyond doubt that general fault liability regimes can be maintained besides the Directive regime, but the question is whether this also goes for the existing French general strict liability regime. In French law, product liability can be based on article 1384 al. 1 (strict liability for the *garde de la structure de la chose*, nr 303-3) but in the early 1990s the *Cour de cassation* constructed a more straightforward route.[94] It imposed security obligations (*obligations de sécurité*) on the manufacturer as well as on the reseller of the *chose*.[95] This obligation exists independent of any contractual obligation and is not only owed to the buyer (contractual) but to all third parties who suffer damage because of a defect (*vice*) or a default (*défaut*) of the chose.[96] The liable person can escape liability by proving an external cause: *force majeure* or an act of a third party or the victim (*fait du tiers* or *fait de la victime*). It is interesting to note that the *Cour de cassation* developed this case law precisely to compensate the fact that the French legislator had not transposed the Product Liability Directive into French law.[97]

Now this case law is in jeopardy by the ECJ decision and it will probably have to be abolished. The French tort law world is in turmoil because the ECJ decision does not only affect the applicability of a strict liability rule but it also cuts deep into the essential values of French tort law: its high level of victim protection and its principle of solidarity (nr 609-3). It is illustrative that the ECJ decision has been described in no less terms than a 'European threat'[98] and that it has been summarized as that, in the eyes of Luxembourg, it is ' . . . la directive, rien que la directive, toute la directive . . . l'exégèse: le retour!'[99] Traditionally, the

---

[93] ECJ 25 April 2002, Case C-52/00 (*Commission v French Republic*), paras 21–23.

[94] Civ. 1re 11 June 1991, Bull. civ. I, no 20; Civ. 3e 3 March 1998, D. 1999. 36, comm. Pignarre and Brun. See already Civ. 1re 16 May 1984, RTD civ. 1985, 179, obs. Rémy. Le Tourneau (2004), nr 6073.

[95] Civ. 1re 27 January 1993, Bull. civ. I, no 44; Civ. 1re 17 January 1995, D. 1995. 351, comm. Jourdain: the supplier of defective playground equipment is obliged to deliver products without a defect that can cause danger to persons or goods; this obligation is owed to the buyer as well as third parties; Le Tourneau (2004), nr 6073.   [96] Le Tourneau (2004), nr 6073.

[97] Le Tourneau (2004), nr 6075. See about other examples of 'inter-power-play' between the French legislator and the *Cour de cassation*: nr 303-1 (liability for accidents at the workplace) and nr 1404-1 (liability for road traffic accidents).

[98] J. Calais-Auloy, 'Menace européenne sur la jurisprudence française concernant l'obligation de sécurité du vendeur professionel [CJCE, 25 avril 2002]', D. 2002. 2458.

[99] ' . . . the Directive, nothing but the Directive, the whole Directive . . . meaning: the way back!': ECJ 25 April 2002, RTD civ. 2002, 868, obs. Marguenaud and Raynard. See also Geneviève Viney, 'L'interprétation par la CJCE de la directive du 25 juillet 1985 sur la responsabilité du fait des produits défectueux', JCP 2002. I. 177.

positive French approach towards Europe reaches its boundaries where French and European interests start to diverge.[100]

In line with the *Cour de cassation's* case law, article 1386-7 held that the supplier of a defective product is liable in all cases and on the same basis as the manufacturer. It is not surprising that the ECJ decided that with the enactment of this provision France had not fulfilled its obligations under Article 3(3) of the Directive. This provision holds the supplier of the product liable only if he does not inform the claimant, within a reasonable time, of the identity of the producer or the person who supplied him with the product.[101] The question about the interpretation of Article 13 went a step further, namely whether the case law of the *Cour de cassation* on security obligations could be maintained as an existing general liability regime.

Article 13 also holds that the Directive does not affect rights of an injured person according to an existing *special liability system*. The 13th recital of the Directive refers implicitly to the German *Arzneimittelgesetz* (Drugs Act), holding a rule of strict liability for pharmaceutical products which also blocks the development risk defence (§ 84). This means the drug manufacturer is liable, even if, according to the state of medical knowledge, it was impossible to discover the harmful consequences.[102] The transposition of the European Directive into the German *Produkthaftungsgesetz* (Product Liability Act) has not affected the applicability of this rule: in case of a defective medicine the Drugs Act applies and not the implemented Directive, due to the principle of *lex specialis derogat legi generali*.[103]

The question is which other existing strict liability regimes can be sustained next to the Directive. In *Sánchez v Medicina Asturiana*, the ECJ considered that the Spanish Act regarding the protection of consumers and users of health care of 1984 (Act 26/84) was not a special Act in the sense of Article 13 because it was not restricted to a specific production sector.[104]

1408 Defective product

1408-1 *Relevant provisions*

The producer shall be liable for damage caused by a defect in his product (Article 1). This rule raises questions as regards the notions of producer, damage,

---

[100] See for the possible consequences of the ECJ decision for the sustainability of the BGH's product liability case law based on § 823 I: Renate Schaub, 'Abschied von nationalen Produkthaftungsrecht? Anspruch und Wirklichkeit der EG-Produkthaftung', *ZEuP*, 2003, 562–589.
[101] ECJ 25 April 2002, C-52/00 (*Commission v French Republic*). The decision also obliged France to implement the €500 threshold (nr 1409) and to relax the manufacturer's possibility to exonerate on the basis of a development risk (nr 1410-2). [102] Kötz-Wagner (2001), N 478.
[103] Deutsch-Ahrens (2002), N 404.
[104] ECJ 25 April 2002, C-183/00, ECR 2002, I-3901 (*Maria Victoria González Sánchez v Medicina Asturiana SA*); ECJ 25 April 2002, C-52/00, (*Commission v French Republic*), para. 23.

causation, defect, and product. The Directive contains definitions of all these notions, except for causation. Since the definitions do not always give sufficient clarification, the case law of the ECJ and the national courts is important. In this and the following sections the main issues of the Directive will be pointed out.

For the purpose of the Directive, 'product' means all movables even if incorporated into another movable or into an immovable, including electricity (Article 2). In several cases throughout the Member States it was held that blood supplied by a blood bank can be considered to be a product in the sense of this provision.[105]

Article 6 provides that a product is defective ' . . . when it does not provide the safety which a person is entitled to expect, taking all circumstances into account.' The Directive does not make a distinction between different types of defects. In practice, however, a distinction is usually made between manufacturing defects on the one hand, and design and instruction defects on the other. Design and instruction defects are shortcomings that are inherent in the product, for example side-effects of drugs or an insufficient warning in the directions for use. These shortcomings occur in all products of a specific type. Manufacturing defects are shortcomings that are not inherent in the product. This is the case if the individual product does not meet the standard of the general quality of its specific type. The classic example is the exploding bottle. These shortcomings are mainly, but not solely, caused during the manufacturing or distribution process.[106]

As regards manufacturing defects the Directive provides for a strict liability regime. Consumers do not need to expect that products are defective because of failures in the manufacturing process. As regards design and instruction defects, things are different. These defects particularly, though not solely, play a role as regards drugs, for instance if a drug has side-effects or if there has been an insufficient warning in the directions for use. In such a case the consumer is not entitled to expect a drug to be 100 per cent safe if he has been properly informed about its side effects.

Article 6 mentions three circumstances to be taken into account when establishing the defect. It is generally agreed that this enumeration does not have a limitative character.

Firstly (sub a), the Article mentions the presentation of the product. In this respect one may think of information about the product which is provided by advertising and publicity, and of information in an insert or in directions for use. It can be argued that warnings are generally insufficient if it is possible to

---

[105] *A. v National Blood Authority* [2001] 3 All ER 289, nr 63; Rb. Amsterdam 3 February 1999, NJ 1999, 621 (*Scholten v Sanquin Bloedvoorziening*); see also Civ. 1re 4 March 2003, D. 2003. IR 866 (*X v Ètablissement français du sang*). See also the French Act 91-1406 of 31 December 1991 *pour l'indemnisation des victimes contaminées par le virus de l'immuniodéficience humaine*, creating a special fund for persons who were infected with HIV as a result of blood transfusions; see Van Gerven (2000), 629–630; Le Tourneau (2004), nr 8502–8577.
[106] See about this distinction, for example, Kötz-Wagner (2001), N 435–437.

produce a safer product without extra financial burden and this higher safety level does not affect the benefit of the product (nr 809). This aspect is particularly relevant in assessing the defectiveness of a medicine. One of the dilemmas in this respect is that, if a manufacturer needs to mention all known side effects, how unlikely or minor they may be, the consumer might be confused and miss the relevant and essential information he needs. For this reason, the French *Cour de cassation* requires only communication of the reasonably foreseeable risks.[107]

Secondly (sub b), the court must also take into account the use to which it could reasonably be expected that the product would be put. In other words: what kinds of negligent use might the producer expect from the consumer? The general answer is that the producer must take into consideration that consumers make mistakes and do not always use the product in a safe or even in a proper way. He has to anticipate such user's conduct, either by designing the product in a safer way or, if this is not reasonably feasible, by effectively warning the consumer. For example, a manufacturer of toys has to take into account that younger children may not just play with the toys but may also try to put them into their mouth or even try to swallow them. A similar consideration principle applies in the field of negligence (nr 807-4). Thus product liability for a large part is about justified and defeated expectations: those of the general public as regards the safety of the product, and those of the producer as regards the way the product was used by the consumer.

Finally (sub c), the court has to take into account the time when the product was put into circulation. The defectiveness of the product must be determined on the basis of safety rules that were in force when the product was put into circulation. Hence, a product shall not be considered to be defective for the sole reason that a better product was subsequently put into circulation (Article 6 s. 2). This system differs from negligence, in which the test as regards conduct and knowledge is related to the moment immediately before the realization of the risk (nr 810-2). A product can be defective if it wears out too quickly and causes damage. In such a case the product was already inherently defective when it was put into circulation. This issue is connected to the producer's defence under Article 7(b): he is not liable if he can prove that it is probable that the defect did not exist at the time when the product was put into circulation by him or that this defect came into being afterwards (nr 1410-1).

1408-2 *Case law*

Cases from the national courts can illustrate the foregoing rules as regards the defective product. An English case was about claims of people who had been infected with the Hepatitis C virus as a result of receiving blood transfusions.

---

[107] Civ. 1re 8 April 1999, JCP 1999. II. 20721. A different view is taken by Cour d'Appel Paris 23 September 2004, D. 2005. 1012, about which nr 1410-2.

The donor blood contained the Hepatitis C virus and the claimants contracted the disease. All claimants were infected at a time when the existence of the virus was already known but no test was yet available to screen the blood. They claimed damages from the National Blood Authority (NBA). The NBA argued that the blood was not defective, because all the public was entitled to expect was that the blood would not be affected by any reasonable *detectable* contaminants. This was in fact an 'avoidability' argument (nr 810-3) and Burton J rightly rejected it as being incompatible with the strict liability system of the Directive.[108] He also considered that the general public was entitled to expect that the blood was safe.

The District Court of Amsterdam came to a similar conclusion. The case was about a claimant who received HIV-infected blood during heart surgery. It was assumed that the blood had been given by a donor who had only just contracted HIV, such that his infection could not be detected by a test during what has been called 'the window period'. The Court agreed with the claimant that,

... taking into account the vital importance of blood products and that in principle there is no alternative, the general public expects and is entitled to expect that blood products in the Netherlands have been 100% HIV-free for some time. The fact that there is a small chance that HIV could be transmitted via a blood transfusion, which the Foundation (defendant) estimates at one in a million, is in the opinion of the Court not general knowledge. It cannot therefore be said that the public does not or cannot be expected to have this expectation.[109]

A comparable decision can be found in a case decided by the German BGH. The claimant had suffered damage when a mineral water bottle exploded. It was established that this explosion resulted from a very fine hairline crack which was not discovered, although the technical and supervisory procedure in the producer's factory was in accordance with the very latest state of technology, including seven different inspections. The BGH concluded:

As the court below rightly held, a product is defective (...) if it does not afford the safety which in all circumstances can justifiably be expected, and consumers expect soda water bottles to be free from faults such as hairline splits and micro fissures which could make them explode. The consumer's expectation that the bottle be free from faults would not be diminished even if it were technically impossible to identify and remove such faults.[110]

One may conclude from the foregoing that the expectation of the general public as regards the safety of the product is not a factual but a normative one.

[108] *A v The National Blood Authority* [2001] 3 All ER 289, nr 63. This decision discusses in depth the interpretation of Articles 6 and 7(e) of the Directive in an exemplary comparative way.
[109] Rb. Amsterdam 3 February 1999, NJ 1999, 621 (*Scholten v Sanquin Bloedvoorziening*) (translation from *A v The National Blood Authority* [2001] 3 All ER 289, nr 44 iii). The Court considered the blood to be defective but it allowed the defendant's 'development risks' defence (Article 7 sub e).
[110] BGH 9 May 1995, BGHZ 129, 353 = NJW 1995, 2162 = JZ 1995, 1060, about which Markesinis and Unberath (2002), 584–589 from which the translation is derived.

The general public is not entitled to expect the safety the product actually has, which can be 99.9 per cent, but it is entitled to expect the safety the product ought to have. This means that the general public is entitled to expect that products are 100 per cent free of manufacturing defects. This is even the case if the public is aware of the risk of, for example, invisible hairline cracks in a bottle which can make it explode. A different interpretation would lead to a form of Russian roulette[111] and to an unfair apportionment of the risks inherent in the modern technological manufacturing process.[112]

The general public is not entitled to expect that products are 100 per cent free of design or instruction defects. In these cases there is often a balance to be struck between the benefits of the product and the harm it causes, for example by having harmful side-effects. The manufacturer can prevent the product from being defective by properly advising the consumer about the side-effects.

As regards blood products, the question is whether contamination is a manufacturing defect or a design defect: whether the defect is inherent or not inherent in the product. The severe health consequences of receiving contaminated blood (HIV, Hepatitis C), and the fact that patient does not have a choice or an alternative, induce courts to consider blood defects as not inherent in the product and to consider a blood product to be a product of which people may expect that it is 100 per cent safe even if, in fact, it is not. A warning that the product is not 100 per cent safe should not be enough to prevent the product from being defective. Hence, there should be no Russian roulette for people who are treated with blood products.

If the product is considered to be defective, the fact that the producer was not technically or financially able to avoid the defect is not relevant. See nr 1410-2 about the 'development risks' defence of Article 7(e) of the Directive.

1409 Damage

Article 9 considerably restricts the Directive's field of application by only providing compensation for damage caused by death or personal injury, and for damage to private property. The Directive does not provide for compensation of

---

[111] Winfield and Jolowicz (2002), para. 10.17 with reference to *Richardson v LRC* [2000] *PIQR*, 164 (broken condom): a couple used condoms as a means of contraception. After sexual intercourse it appeared that the teat had parted from the body of a condom. The claimant filed claims against LRC alleging that the split of the condom was caused by a weakening of the latex occurring before the condom left the factory, and that the fact of the split itself evidenced the existence of a defect. The court rejected both claims.

[112] See the second recital in the Preamble of the Directive:

Whereas liability without fault on the part of the producer is the sole means of adequately solving the problem, peculiar to our age of increasing technicality, of a fair apportionment of the risks inherent in modern technological production.

pure economic loss and of damage to commercial property.[113] If a defective product has caused such damage a claim has to be filed on the basis of the national tort law provisions. Neither does the Directive apply to damage to the product itself; compensation for such damage will usually be claimed from the supplier on the basis of contract law. The right to compensation for non-pecuniary loss depends on the applicable national law.

The Member State can provide that a producer's total liability for damage resulting from death or personal injury, and caused by identical items with the same defect, shall be limited to an amount which may not be less than €70 million (Article 16). Such limitations have been adopted by Germany, Greece, Spain, and Portugal, countries which are familiar with limitations in national tort law.

As regards damage to property, it is required that the item of property (i) is of a type ordinarily intended for private use or consumption, and (ii) was used by the injured person mainly for his own private use or consumption. A lower threshold of €500 applies to damage to property. This means that the Directive is not applicable to damage below that amount; hence, small claims have to be based on national law. If the damage exceeds this amount the total amount can be compensated under the Directive, provided the other requirements for liability are met. When France and Greece did not implement this threshold in their legislation, the ECJ decided that they thus failed to fulfil their obligations under the Directive. According to the Court, this provision was adopted in order to avoid an excessive number of disputes. Hence, in the event of minor material damage the victim of a defective product cannot rely on the Directive's liability regime but must bring an action based on ordinary contractual or non-contractual liability.[114]

In the Danish *Kidney* case the ECJ gave some clarification as regards the proper meaning of Article 9.[115] The case was about Mr Veedfalds who was due to undergo a kidney transplant operation at the Danish Skejby hospital. After a kidney had been removed from the donor, Mr Veedfald's brother, it was prepared for transplantation through flushing with a perfusion fluid designed for that purpose. This fluid proved to be defective and a kidney artery became blocked during the flushing process, making the kidney unusable for any transplant. The fluid had been manufactured in the laboratories of the dispensary of the Århus District Hospital, and prepared with a view to its use at the Skejby hospital. Both hospitals were owned and managed by the Amtskommune. Mr Veedfalds claimed damages from the Amtskommune. In the national procedure the Danish court asked the ECJ preliminary questions.

---

[113] There is a parallel in this respect with the Unfair Commercial Practices Directive (nr 204-1) which also applies to business-to-consumer relations (B2C) and not to business-to-business relations (B2B).

[114] ECJ 25 April 2002, Case C-52/00 (*Commission v French Republic*); ECJ 25 April 2002, C-154/00 (*Commission v Hellenic Republic*).

[115] ECJ 10 May 2001, Case C-203/99 (*Veedfalds v Århus Amtskommune*).

As regards non-pecuniary loss the ECJ confirmed that compensation is solely governed by national law. Save for this head of damage and the exclusions in Article 9 as regards property damage, a Member State may not restrict the types of material damage, resulting from death, from personal injury, or from property damage:

> Although it is left to national legislatures to determine the precise content of those two heads of damage [death and personal injury on the one hand and damage to private property], nevertheless, save for non-material damage whose reparation is governed solely by national law, full and proper compensation for persons injured by a defective product must be available in the case of those two heads of damage. Application of national rules may not impair the effectiveness of the Directive (see, to this effect, the judgment in Case C-365/88 *Hagen* [1990] ECR I-1845, paragraph 20) and the national court must interpret its national law in the light of the wording and the purpose of the Directive (see, in particular, the judgment in Case 14/83 *Von Colson and Kamann* [1984] ECR 891, paragraph 26).[116]

The national provisions as regards the law of damages differ from country to country and generally it will be hard to argue that the application of these national provisions will impair the effectiveness of the Directive (nr 1217). However, impairment of effectiveness could be at stake in cases in which the legal systems hardly provide any compensation at all, for example where a child dies as the consequence of a defective product. In such a case there is hardly pecuniary loss (apart from the costs of the funeral or the cremation) and the compensation of non-pecuniary loss differs from country to country but if amounts are awarded these are generally rather modest (nr 1210). It is questionable whether the national laws in such cases impair the effectiveness of the Directive but it is clear that they do not really support its effectiveness either.

1410 Defences

1410-1 *General observations*

Article 7 provides the producer with six ways to escape liability, including the development risk defence. In addition to these defences he may also invoke contributory negligence of the victim (Article 8(2)) but not the act or omission of a third party (Article 8(1)). The latter provision means that the producer is still liable towards the victim even if a third party has intentionally sabotaged his product. This restriction of the producer's defences is without prejudice to the provisions of national law concerning his right of recourse against the saboteur.

According to Article 7(a), the producer is not liable if he proves that he did not put the product into circulation. He can, for instance, do so by proving that

---

[116] ECJ 10 May 2001, Case C-203/99 (*Veedfalds v Århus Amtskommune*), para. 27.

the product was stolen from his premises. In the *Veedfalds* case (nr 1409), the Amtskommune stated that it had not put the product—the perfusion fluid used to prepare the kidney for transplantation—into circulation. The ECJ, however, decided that Article 7(a) implies that a product is put into circulation when it is used during the provision of a specific medical service, consisting in preparing a human organ for transplantation, and the damage caused to the organ results from that preparatory treatment. This means that the requirements of Article 7 are met if the producer has put the product at the disposal of a third party; this can be the consumer but also the conveyor. It is not relevant where this happens. It can be argued that a product is also put into circulation if the product is used by a test subject or if it is given to visitors of a factory during a guided tour.

Article 7(b) provides that the producer is not liable if he proves that, having regard to the circumstances, it is probable that the defect which caused the damage did not exist at the time when the product was put into circulation by him, or that this defect came into being afterwards. In this respect one may think of defects which are a consequence of normal wear and tear. However, if the product wears and tears too quickly, the product will be considered to be defective when it was put into circulation.

It follows from Article 7(c) that the producer is not liable if the product was neither manufactured by him for sale or any form of distribution for economic purpose, nor manufactured or distributed by him in the course of his business. This defence is intended to apply to privately manufactured products (for example, a cake) outside any commercial purpose. In *Veedfalds* the hospital invoked this defence but the ECJ held that a defective product which has been manufactured and used in the course of a specific medical service does not fall within the scope of Article 7(c), even if it is financed entirely from public funds and provided to the patient without his having to pay for the product as such. This means that medical products manufactured by hospitals and blood banks for this reason cannot be excluded from the application of the Directive. Though the Directive seems to make a distinction between commercial and non-commercial manufacturing, the relevant distinction appears to be between private and non-private manufacturing. This corresponds with the broad interpretation by the ECJ of 'commercial activities' in EU law, for instance in the framework of Article 81 EC.

According to Article 7(d), the producer is not liable if the defect was due to compliance of the product with mandatory regulations issued by the public authorities. It is thought that it is no defence for a manufacturer that he has complied with all legally required safety standards, but it could be a defence if he was obliged to manufacture the product in a specific way. This defence relates to the situation that the imposed legal norm was wrong and the manufacturer has to choose between two evils: violating the imposed standard or putting a defective product onto the market. According to Clarke such a situation ' . . . is a very unlikely eventuality and accordingly the defence is of minimal value to many potential defendants.'[117]

Finally, the manufacturer of a component is not liable if the defect is attributable to the design of the product in which the component has been fitted, or to the instructions given by the manufacturer of the product into which the component was fitted (Article 7(f)). This defence is superfluous and has been inserted on political grounds since it is clear from the other Directive provisions that the manufacturer of the component is only liable if his product is defective.[118]

1410-2 *Development risk defence*

The defence giving rise to most interesting discussions as regards the Directive is the so-called development risk defence of Article 7(e). The Directive describes the defence as follows: '. . . that the state of scientific and technical knowledge at the time when he put the product into circulation was not such as to enable the existence of the defect to be discovered'. This is a substantial difference from the negligence rule where, in principle, the claimant has to prove that the defendant knew or ought to have known about the risk (nr 810-2).

This defence has been interpreted in the sense that, taking into account all the available scientific and technical knowledge, it was *impossible* for the producer to discover the risk.[119] However, in a case about the way this defence was transposed into UK law, the ECJ seemed to leave a little more space for the producer. On the one hand, the Court stated that it is up to the producer to prove that it was impossible to discover the defect on the basis of the objective state of the available scientific and technical knowledge including the most advanced level and not restricted to the relevant industrial sector. But on the other hand, this knowledge must have been accessible at the moment the product was put into circulation.[120] It can be argued that information that can be found on the internet with the help of search machines is accessible for producers. This is also the case for knowledge published in international scientific journals. Accessibility may, however, be doubtful if the knowledge has only been published in a journal which is disseminated in one country and which is not written in a main language.

The development risk defence only applies to the fact of whether the risk could be known, not whether it could be avoided. This item was discussed in the English *NBA* case (nr 1408-2) in which the existence of the Hepatitis C virus was

[117] Alistair M. Clark, *Product Liability* (London: Sweet & Maxwell, 1989), 188. In the same sense H.C. Taschner, *Produkthaftung* (Munich: Beck, 1986), 110.

[118] H.C. Taschner, *Produkthaftung* (Munich: Beck, 1986), 125.

[119] See for instance BGH 9 May 1995, BGHZ 129, 353, 359 = NJW 1995, 2162 = JZ 1995, 1060, about which Markesinis and Unberath (2002), 584–589.

[120] ECJ 29 May 1997, Case C-300/95 ECR 1997, I-2649 (*Commission v United Kingdom*). See also Howells, *Product Liability*, (1998), 453–454.

acknowledged but a screen test to discover the virus was not yet available. Burton J held that the development risk only applies to knowledge issues and not to avoidability issues. Hence, the defence could only be accepted if the claimant was infected before the existence of the Hepatitis C virus was acknowledged in the scientific and technical literature.[121]

The defence also played a role in the German case of the exploding mineral water bottle. The case was about a 9-year-old girl carrying a mineral water bottle when it exploded, as a consequence of which she suffered an eye injury. The explosion was caused by hairline cracks in the bottle's glass. The BGH held that the bottle was defective because of a manufacturing defect. Such defects (*Ausreißer*) are not defects for the purpose of Article 7(e): 'Liability should only be excluded when the potential danger of the product could not be detected because the possibility to detect it did not (yet) exist at the time of marketing.'[122] In other words, if the defect is known—and risks caused by hairline cracks were known for a long time—unavoidability of the defect in the particular product is no answer.[123]

There are only very few cases in which the development risk defence has been accepted. In the above-mentioned case of the District Court of Amsterdam (nr 1408-2), about a claimant who received HIV-infected blood during heart surgery by a donor who had only just contracted the virus, the court accepted the defence with regard to the scientific impossibility to detect HIV contamination during the window phase. This, however, can be considered to be an incorrect decision because the defence did not relate the knowledge to the risk but to its avoidability.[124] In France the *Cour d'Appel de Paris* accepted the defence in a case about a man who suffered from an intestinal haemorrhage and underwent a therapy consisting of taking a medicine called Pantasar. Subsequently, he suffered a serious kidney disease. The court agreed with the claimant that the medicine was defective because the leaflet did not warn the user about the potential, though very unusual, side-effect. However, the court held that the manufacturer was not liable because the state of scientific and technical knowledge at the time when the medicine was put into circulation was not such as to enable the existence of the defect to be discovered.[125]

Article 15 provided the possibility for Member States to strike out the 'development risk' defence and to hold the producer liable even if he proves that,

---

[121] Burton J in *A v The National Blood Authority* [2001] 3 All ER 289, nr 74.

[122] BGH 9 May 1995, BGHZ 129, 353 = NJW 1995, 2162 = JZ 1995, 1060 (translation derived from *A v The National Blood Authority* [2001] 3 All ER 289, nr 53 iii), about which Markesinis and Unberath (2002), 584–589.

[123] In the same sense Burton J in *A v The National Blood Authority* [2001] 3 All ER 289, nr 53 iii.

[124] Rb. Amsterdam 3 February 1999, NJ 1999, 621 (*Scholten v Sanquin Bloedvoorziening*).

[125] Cour d'Appel Paris 23 September 2004, D. 2005. 1012. The duty to inform as formulated by the *Cour d'Appel* suggests that the manufacturer needs to mention all kinds of known side-effects, whether big or small, likely or unlikely (see nr 1408-1).

at the time when he put the product into circulation, the state of scientific and technical knowledge was not such as to enable the existence of a defect to be discovered. This was done by Luxembourg and Finland, by Spain with respect to medicines and food, and by France as regards human products such as blood and blood products. Germany allows the manufacturer the development risk defence of Article 7(e). However, in this country the development risk cannot be invoked by the drug manufacturer. This follows from the German § 64 *Arzneimittelgesetz* (Drugs Act) (nr 1407-2).

France allows the development risk defence but initially made it subject to the requirement for the manufacturer to monitor its products. If a manufacturer had not complied with his monitoring duty, he could not invoke the development risk defence. In an infringement procedure the ECJ held that France had thus failed to fulfil its obligations under Article 7 of the Directive. It considered that this provision does not authorize Member States to alter the conditions under which that exemption is applied.[126]

1411 Other requirements

Burden of proof. It goes without saying that the manufacturer has to prove the facts as regards the defences of Articles 7 and 8 s. 2 (nr 1410). The burden of proof with regard to damage, defect and causation between defect and damage is on the victim (Article 4). It is plausible that national courts will apply general procedural rules with regard to the burden of proof, such as *prima facie* evidence or the *res ipsa loquitur* principle. For example, if a television catches fire because of short-circuiting, the court may conclude that there is *prima facie* evidence that the television was defective. It is then up to the manufacturer to show that this provisional conclusion was unjustified. In medical cases, however, this technique may be less easy to apply. *Prima facie* evidence was, for example, not accepted by the *Cour de cassation* in a case in which a woman received a vaccination against Hepatitis B and shortly thereafter developed multiple sclerosis. She had to prove that the vaccine (product) was somehow likely to cause such a disease but she did not succeed and her claim against the manufacturer was dismissed.[127]

Producer. According to Article 3 'producer' means the manufacturer of a finished product, the producer of any raw material, or the manufacturer of a component part and any person who, by putting his name, trademark, or other

---

[126] ECJ 25 April 2002, Case C-52/00 (*Commission v French Republic*), para. 47.

[127] Civ. 1re 23 September 2003, D. 2004. 898, comm. Serinet and Mislawski, ETL 2003, 164 (Lafay, Moréteau and Pellerin-Rugliano). See also BGH 14 June 2005, NJW 2005, 2614 (liability for HIV-contaminated blood products). See for a similar problem the controversial MMR immunization (against measles, mumps, and rubella) and its alleged consequences for the immunized children.

distinguishing feature on the product presents himself as its producer (Article 3(1)). It can be concluded from the *Veedfalds* case that a hospital can also be regarded as a producer in the sense of the Directive.[128]

The person who imports into the EEA a product for sale, hire, leasing or any form of distribution in the course of his business shall be deemed to be a producer within the meaning of this Directive (Article 3(2)). This means that if the product is manufactured outside the EEA, for example in China or Brazil, the victim can file a claim against the company that imported the product into the EEA. This rule considerably simplifies the position of the victim of a defective product from outside the EEA.

If the producer of the product cannot be identified, each supplier of the product shall be treated as its producer unless he informs the injured person, within a reasonable time, of the identity of the producer or of the person who supplied him with the product (s. 3).

Jointly and severally liable. Where, as a result of the provisions of the Directive, two or more persons are liable for the same damage, they shall be liable jointly and severally, without prejudice to the provisions of national law concerning the rights of contribution or recourse (Article 5).

Limitation and extinction periods. Two limitation periods are applicable, the first counts three years, the second ten years. The short term starts to run from the day on which the plaintiff became aware, or should reasonably have become aware, of the damage, the defect, and the identity of the producer (Article 10). Suspension and interruption of the limitation period is determined by the applicable national law. The long term ends ten years after the date on which the producer put into circulation the actual product which caused the damage, unless the injured person has in the meantime instituted proceedings against the producer (Article 11). These limitation periods in fact exclude liability for defects that only cause damage on the longer term. One may think of the dangerous substances which have an incubation period of more than ten years and of side-effects of drugs that only occur in the long term or even in a following generation. See as regards the latter the Dutch *DES* case (nr 1108-2).

Limitation and exclusion of liability. Liability of the producer arising from this Directive may not, in relation to the injured person, be limited or excluded by a provision limiting his liability or exempting him from liability (Article 12). This relates to the Directive on Unfair Terms in Consumer Contracts, according to which may be regarded as unfair terms which exclude or limit the legal liability of a seller or supplier in the event of the death of a consumer or personal injury to the latter resulting from an act or omission of that seller or supplier.[129]

---

[128] ECJ 10 May 2001, Case C-203/99 (*Veedfalds v Århus Amtskommune*).
[129] Directive 93/13/EEC of 5 April 1993: Article 3(3) in connection with the Annex sub a.

E DANGEROUS SUBSTANCES AND THE ENVIRONMENT

1412 Introduction

This section will deal with liability for dangerous substances, though in France, Germany, and England this, as such, is not subject to special liability regimes.[130] In a more indirect way, however, liability for dangerous substances can be recognized in rules regarding environmental liability and in so-called neighbourhood rules. As will be pointed out, these categories of liability are strongly intertwined.[131] Dangerous substances such as gas, oil, or explosives are usually movable things and they often play a role in causing damage. Even though this is not always the case (one may think of producing noise or vibrations), this topic is for practical reasons best dealt with in this chapter since the types of cases are so closely connected. At the same time it has to be kept in mind that the issue is rather hybrid. It is also closely linked to liability for immovable things and to property law since the law of neighbours usually requires some kind of proprietary interest in land (nr 1413).

For lack of special rules liability for damage caused by dangerous substances requires the application of the traditional tort law provisions. One may not only think of the general negligence rules but also of stricter rules like the English *Rule in Rylands v Fletcher*, the French general rule of strict liability for things, and generally the violation of a statutory rule concerning the protection of the environment (nr 1413).

The legal systems hold some strict liability rules for damage caused to the environment but these vary considerably in their field of application. The broadest examples can be found in the German *Umwelthaftungsgesetz* (Environmental Liability Act) and the *Wasserhaushaltsgesetz* (Water Resources Act). English law holds a strict liability rule in the Environmental Protection Act 1990 but its scope is rather narrow (nr 1414).

---

[130] Some other countries, however, hold such liability for damage caused by dangerous substances, for example art. 6:175 Dutch Civil Code. In France, the general strict liability for things applies to both dangerous and non dangerous things: nr 1400. Art. 3:206 ECC:

A person who independently exercises control over a substance or an installation and has it for their own use is accountable for the causation by that substance or by emissions from that installation of personal injury and consequential loss, loss within Article 2:202, loss resulting from property damage or burdens within Article 2:209, if, (a) having regard to their quantity and attributes, it is very likely that the substance or emissions will cause such damage unless adequately controlled, and (b) the damage results from the realisation of that danger.

[131] See also Elspeth Reid, 'Liability for Dangerous Activities: A Comparative Analysis', *ICLQ*, 48 (1999), 731–756, at 752.

Finally, sanctions for impairment of the environment can also be found in the 'neighbourhood' rules: the English tort of private nuisance, the French rules on *trouble de voisinage*, and the German rules of § 906 ff. BGB. These rules have old historic roots. They regulate the inconveniences of living together, particularly in populous areas, and aim to reconcile the various social and economic interests of people and businesses living and operating in each other's vicinity. Compared with the above-mentioned rules, neighbourhood rules generally deal with continuing nuisance rather than one-off damage. Also, they focus on remedies to stop nuisance (prohibitive injunction) or to restore the situation (mandatory injunction) rather than to compensate it by providing damages. This is because the neighbourhood rules are strongly linked to property law which shows that the borders between tort law and property law are permeable (nr 1415-1).

1413 Law of neighbours

1413-1 *Germany: § 906 and 1004 BGB*

The German law of neighbours is mainly regulated in the section of the BGB that deals with property law. According to § 1004 I BGB, the owner can file a claim to terminate the infringement of his property. If further infringements are expected, he can ask the court for a prohibitive injunction. § 1004 II provides that such claims are excluded if the owner has a duty to tolerate the infringement (*Duldungspflicht*).[132]

§ 1004 I BGB is the most basic and most important norm used to defend property from interferences. It lays down the rule that, in principle, all others can be prevented from interfering with someone's property, such as prohibiting the post office from putting adverts in a mailbox or demanding from a garage owner that he remove petrol that has dripped into the soil.

Another important provision in the German law of neighbours is § 906 I BGB, holding that a landowner has to endure gases, steam, smells, smoke, soot, heat, noise, vibrations, and the like originating from another property, as long as this interference does not represent a substantial impairment of the use or enjoyment of the land or property. The latter is usually the case if the rules as regards emissions are adhered to.[133]

---

[132] § 1004 BGB:

(1) Wird das Eigentum in anderer Weise als durch Entziehung oder Vorenthaltung des Besitzes beeinträchtigt, so kann der Eigentümer von dem Störer die Beseitigung der Beeinträchtigung verlangen. Sind weitere Beeinträchtigungen zu besorgen, so kann der Eigentümer auf Unterlassung klagen. (2) Der Anspruch ist ausgeschlossen, wenn der Eigentümer zur Duldung verpflichtet ist.

[133] § 906 (1):

Der Eigentümer eines Grundstücks kann die Zuführung von Gasen, Dämpfen, Gerüchen, Rauch, Ruß, Wärme, Geräusch, Erschütterungen und ähnliche von einem anderen Grundstück ausgehende

An exception to § 906 I is § 906 II, holding that also a substantial interference needs to be tolerated provided this is caused by a use of the neighbouring land which is typical for that area (*ortsüblich*), provided it cannot be prevented against reasonable costs for the user (*Benutzer*) of the neighbouring land from which the impairment emanates. If someone has a duty to tolerate a substantial interference, he has a right to compensation from the user of the land from which the impairment emanates if the interference, to an inacceptable extent compromises the typical local use of the land or the returns gained from that land.[134]

The main goal of this rule is to enable activities which are beneficial for society. For example industrial activities that are a nuisance for the neighbourhood cannot be prevented by an injunction of other landowners. The price to be paid by the industry is to compensate neighbouring landowners according to the rules in § 906 II BGB. It can be argued that the interfering activity is lawful since it cannot be prohibited, but the prevailing opinion is that it is considered to be unlawful because this is the basis for compensation to be paid.[135]

A leading case was about two properties on a slope, one above the other. After heavy rain chemicals were carried from the higher to the lower land which was organically farmed. The farmer suffered damage since his vegetables could no longer be sold as being organic. The BGH held that § 906 was applicable since the interference had a natural cause and allowed the claim for damages. It was not relevant whether the claimant could have asked for an injunction before the damage occurred.[136]

1413-2 *England: private nuisance*

Private nuisance is an act which, without being trespass, interferes with a person's enjoyment of his land or premises or a right which he has over the land of another person.[137] In private nuisance a single act will not do: there must be either a repetition or a continuing state of affairs. However, a single act of nuisance may fall within the scope of the statutory nuisance rule of section 73(6)

Einwirkungen insoweit nicht verbieten, als die Einwirkung die Benutzung seines Grundstücks nicht oder nur unwesentlich beeinträchtigt. Eine unwesentliche Beeinträchtigung liegt in der Regel vor, wenn die in Gesetzen oder Rechtsverordnungen festgelegten Grenz- oder Richtwerte von den nach diesen Vorschriften ermittelten und bewerteten Einwirkungen nicht überschritten werden.

[134] § 906 (2):

Das Gleiche gilt insoweit, als eine wesentliche Beeinträchtigung durch eine ortsübliche Benutzung des anderen Grundstücks herbeigeführt wird und nicht durch Maßnahmen verhindert werden kann, die Benutzern dieser Art wirtschaftlich zumutbar sind. Hat der Eigentümer hiernach eine Einwirkung zu dulden, so kann er von dem Benutzer des anderen Grundstücks einen angemessenen Ausgleich in Geld verlangen, wenn die Einwirkung eine ortsübliche Benutzung seines Grundstücks oder dessen Ertrag über das zumutbare Maß hinaus beeinträchtigt.

[135] See about liability for lawful acts nr 1803-1.
[136] BGH 20 April 1990, BGHZ 111, 158; BGH 18 November 1994, NJW 1995, 714.
[137] Winfield and Jolowicz (2002), para. 14.1 ff.

of the Environmental Protection Act 1990 (nr 1414-2). In *Hunter v Canary Wharf Ltd* Lord Lloyd distinguished three kinds of private nuisance: 'They are (1) nuisance by encroachment on a neighbour's land; (2) nuisance by direct physical injury to a neighbour's land; and (3) nuisance by interference with a neighbour's quiet enjoyment of his land.'[138]

Examples of private nuisance are bringing about smoke, noise, and smells, or causing crowds to assemble and thus preventing other persons from entering their land or premises. Private nuisance also plays an important role as regards liability for damage to the environment. The available remedies are the award of damages and an injunction, though the award of the latter is solely within the discretion of the court.

It has for long been held that private nuisance does not require negligence and thus that taking all reasonable care is no defence against liability.[139] In order to establish private nuisance, the interest of the owner to interfere and that of the other owner not to be disturbed have to be balanced. The outcome of this balancing act very much depends on the circumstances of the case. It was for instance decided that 750 crowing cocks provided nuisance, but crying children in a crèche did not.[140] However, this balancing act is not very different from the balancing act in negligence (nr 805) and therefore it is not surprising that there is some confusion as to the role of negligence in private nuisance.[141]

The tort of private nuisance can only be invoked by persons who have a proprietary interest: This '. . . distinguishes a tenant holding a leasehold estate from a mere licensee. Exclusive possession *de jure* or *de facto*, now or in the future, is the bedrock of English land law.'[142] Here, the tort of private nuisance is preserved as a monument for the protection of property rights.[143] Hence, an adult daughter living in her parents' home will not be entitled to an injunction on the basis of private nuisance against persistent nuisance calls to the home.[144] She needs to rely on the tort of negligence or on s. 1(1)(2) of the Protection from Harassment Act 1997 (nr 503 and 504-1).

In *Hunter v Canary Wharf* residents in the London Docklands argued that their TV reception was adversely affected by the newly built 250 metres high *Canary Wharf Tower*. The House of Lords decided that only someone with a proprietary interest is entitled to file a private nuisance claim: '. . . a mere licensee

---

[138] *Hunter v Canary Wharf Ltd* [1997] AC 677, at 695, per Lord Lloyd.
[139] *Rapier v London Tramways Co* [1893] 2 Ch. 588.
[140] *Leeman v Montagu* [1936] 2 All ER 1677 and *Moy v Stoop* [1909] 25 TLR 262.
[141] See for instance *Smith v Littlewood* [1987] AC 241, about which B.S. Markesinis, 'Negligence, nuisance and affirmative duties of action', *LQR*, 105 (1989), 104.
[142] *Hunter v Canary Wharf Ltd* [1997] AC 677, at 703, per Lord Hoffmann.
[143] See nr 500. See also the minority opinion of Lord Cooke in *Hunter v Canary Wharf* [1997] AC 677.
[144] The Court of Appeal awarded such a claim on the basis of private nuisance in *Khorasandjian v Bush* [1993] QB 727 but this was four years before the private nuisance claim was restricted to persons with a proprietary interest.

on the land has no right to sue.'[145] Thus the landowners had a *locus standi* in private nuisance but the House of Lords dismissed their claim, considering that everyone has the right to build on his land what he likes, even if he interferes with light, air, views, or TV reception of the neighbour. Liability for this kind of nuisance would be, taking into account the extent of it, very troublesome for the builder or owner of the tower.[146] Moreover, as one of the commentators wrote: '... there was always satellite and cable (...). Let them watch BSkyB!'[147] This is exactly what they decided to do...

In the above-mentioned *Cambridge Water* case (nr 1400), about a company which in the 1970s had leaked chemicals on its own land, the claim for damages was *inter alia* based on private nuisance. According to the House of Lords such a claim required that the possibility of nuisance of the occurred type was reasonably foreseeable for someone such as the defendant. The Law Lords concluded that foreseeability of the harm could not be established and that the company was not liable on the basis of private nuisance.[148]

Someone who suffers damage by nuisance caused by a statutory undertaker can be in a rather unfortunate position. At times of heavy rain the sewers of the water company, Thames Water, became overloaded and caused repeated flooding of Mr Marcic's garden, and his house to be affected by damp. The House of Lords, however, dryly dismissed Mr Marcic's claim against Thames Water. It held that an action for nuisance would set at nought the statutory scheme: the intention of the Water Industry Act 1991 was that individuals should not be able to bring court proceedings for the failure to build more sewers but should apply for an enforcement order by the water regulator. Only the failure by the water company to comply with such an order could give rise for an action for damages.[149] According to Oliphant, 'by making the statutory remedy exclusive, the House of Lords has effectively allowed private rights to be overridden in the public interest.'[150] The scope of this decision is supposed to be limited to situations where responsibility for the management and maintenance of property is imposed by statute.

1413-3 *France:* trouble de voisinage

The French nuisance rules—*trouble de voisinage* (vicinity trouble)—are judge-made rules. They are not based on articles 1382, 1383 or 1384 CC but on the maxim

---

[145] *Hunter v Canary Wharf Ltd* [1997] AC 677, at 679.

[146] *Hunter v Canary Wharf Ltd* [1997] AC 677. See also BGH 21 October 1983, BGHZ 88, 344 = NJW 1984, 729.

[147] Allastair Mullis and Donal Nolan, 'Tort', *All ER Annual Review* 1997, 513.

[148] *Cambridge Water Co v Eastern Counties Leather plc* [1994] 2 AC 264, about which Van Gerven (2000), 172–175. See already *The Wagon Mound (No. 2)* [1967] 1 AC 617 (PC); *Home Brewery v Davis* [1987] 2 WLR 117, 128; Winfield and Jolowicz on Tort (1994), 415.

[149] *Marcic v Thames Water Utilities Ltd* [2003] UKHL 2003, 66, ETL 2003, 122 (Oliphant). The House of Lords dismissed a claim under the Human Rights Act, holding that the statutory scheme provided a remedy for the vindication of the claimant's right under Article 8 ECHR; see nr 1808-2.   [150] Ken Oliphant, op. cit., 123. See also nr 1811 in fine.

according to which '. . . nul ne doit causer à autrui un trouble anormal de voisinage' (no one must cause another atypical disturbance of the neighbourhood).[151]

Voisinage does not mean that the land that causes troubles has to be adjacent to the land that suffers from it. It suffices if the lands are in each others vicinity (*voisinage*) in the normal sense of the word.[152] The right to claim is not only with the owner of the land but also with the person who has the right to use the land, such as the beneficiary or the tenant, and even a person who does not live on the premises but suffers damage from the nuisance. Similarly, persons other than the owner of the land or building can also be sued, for example, the operator of a factory or a cafe.[153] All kinds of activities can be subject to an action for *troubles de voisinages*, including noises, vibrations, smoke, smell, water pollution, and blocking out light or sun.[154] Such an action can lead to an injunction or to the obligation to pay damages, either in kind or in money.[155]

The standard to be applied in these cases is whether there is 'un trouble *anormal*', in other words: damage exceeding the inconveniences of the neighbourhood. Hence, the trouble needs to be of certain intensity. The application of this standard very much depends on the circumstances of the case. It is up to the court to assess the reality, the nature, and the seriousness of the troubles suffered.[156]

For example, it has been decided that, in an industrial zone, certain inconveniences are typical. Moving to such an area implies that, in principle, one has to accept such existing risks. To a certain extent the social benefits of the industry justify noise and pollution.[157] It is standing case law that a licence is no justification for causing *troubles de voisinages* because a licence is given on the basis of a balancing of interests by a public body and this does not affect the protected rights and interests of individuals and businesses. However, if a plant has a licence, courts will not award a claim to shut it down.[158]

1413-4 *Comparative observations*

The neighbourhood rules are mainly strict and apply to liability for disturbing the neighbourhood environment, for example by producing gas, steam, vibrations, noises, or radiation. Such conduct can affect not only the flora, fauna,

---

[151] See already Civ. 27 November 1844, DP 1845. 1. 13 and more recently for example Civ. 2e 28 June 1995, Bull. civ. II. 1990, no 222, D. 1995. IR. 182; Civ. 3e 11 February 1998, D. 1998. IR 67.   [152] Le Tourneau (2004), nr 7160.

[153] Civ. 2e 28 June 1995, Bull. civ. II. 1990, no 222, D. 1995. IR. 182; Civ. 3e 25 October 1972, D. 1973. 756; Civ. 3e 8 March 1978, D. 1978. 641, comm. Larroumet. Le Tourneau (2004), nr 7161.   [154] Le Tourneau (2004), nr 7165–7169.

[155] Le Tourneau (2004), nr 7179–7182.

[156] Civ. 2e 16 June 1976, Bull. civ. II, no 202; Civ. 2e 21 March 1997, D. 1998. Som. 61, obs. Robert. Interference by noise is governed by Décret no 88-523, 5 May 1988 *relative aux règles propres à préserver la santé de l'homme contre les bruits de voisinage*, jo. 6 May 1988, 6307.

[157] Civ 1e 27 May 1975, D. 1976. 318, comm. Viney; Civ. 3e 3 November 1977, D. 1978. 434, comm. Caballero.

[158] Civ. 27 August 1861. S. 1861. 1. 840; Civ. 2e 25 October 1978, Bull. civ. II, no 220; Civ. 1 23 January 1996, Bull. civ. I, no 43; Terré-Simler, *Droit civil. Les biens*, 4th edn., no 318.

water, air, soil, and more generally the ecological equilibrium, but also human beings. The key question is which level of nuisance does one not need to accept and, as a consequence, which level of nuisance is one obliged to endure. In this respect, the area where the nuisance takes place is of great importance: in a city other rules apply than in the countryside.

Establishing the acceptable level of nuisance implies a balancing of interests and this is not very different from the one made in negligence. The first question is whether the nuisance can be reduced or stopped at reasonable costs (nr 807-1). If this is not possible, it can be argued that the character and benefit of the activity (nr 809-1) may lead to the conclusion that the activity can be allowed to continue, but if the nuisance exceeds a certain level the claimant has a right to compensation (nr 800). In all these cases the central issue is whether the interference is substantial. This is a matter which very much depends on the circumstances of the case.[159]

As regards these neighbourhood rules a strong relationship exists between tort law and property law though in common law this relationship still differs from that on the continent.[160] However, in all three systems neighbourhood law was initially mainly seen as dealing with an interference with the property of land but it now also applies to users of land such as tenants and beneficiaries. This has loosened the ties between tort law and property law in this respect.

1413-5 *Article 8 ECHR*

Protection against nuisance can also be derived from the positive obligations the ECtHR has developed in the framework of Article 8, protecting the right to respect for private and family life and the home. These positive obligations imply that Contracting States must take reasonable and appropriate measures to secure the citizens' rights under Article 8, also in cases in which the nuisance is not caused by public authorities.[161]

López Ostra v Spain[162] was about a new water treatment plant that was built 12 metres from Mrs López Ostra's home in Lorca, a centre of the Spanish leather industry. The plant was intended to treat waste from the tanneries but it did not have a licence and it had not applied for one either. The plant caused gas fumes, noise, and smells with consequential health problems for the applicant. The ECtHR considered that, in order to establish an infringement of Article 8 '... regard must be had to the fair balance that has to be struck between the competing interests of the individual and of the community as a whole, and in any case the State enjoys a certain margin of appreciation' (para. 51). The Court

---

[159] Von Bar (1998), N 534.   [160] Von Bar (1998), N 526–531 with further references.
[161] See more generally about this Alastair Mowbray, *The Development of Positive Obligations under the European Convention on Human Rights by the European Court of Human Rights*, (Oxford: Hart, 2004).   [162] ECtHR 9 December 1994, Case 16798/90 (*López Ostra v Spain*).

concluded that such a fair balance had not been struck in this case and that Article 8 had been infringed:

... despite the margin of appreciation left to the respondent State, the Court considers that the State did not succeed in striking a fair balance between the interest of the town's economic well-being—that of having a waste-treatment plant—and the applicants effective enjoyment of her right to respect for her home and her private and family life. (para. 58)

The Court awarded Mrs López Ostra ESP 4,000,000 (approx. €24,000) for non-pecuniary loss caused by distress and anxiety she suffered as a consequence of the nuisance (para. 65).

A similar decision was handed down in *Moreno Gómez v Spain*,[163] a case about nuisance caused by noise. The applicant lived in a residential area in Valencia in which a couple of years later the municipality allowed bars and discos to operate. This caused severe noise nuisance, with consequential loss of sleep and health complaints. In a report written for the municipality experts assessed the level of noise as unacceptable: the applicant's residential area was qualified as an 'acoustically saturated zone'. The Court considered: 'In view of its volume—at night and beyond permitted levels—and the fact that it continued over a number of years, the Court finds that there has been a breach of the rights protected by Article 8' (para. 60). The regulations issued by the Valencia City Council should in principle have been adequate to secure respect for the guaranteed rights. However, regulations to protect guaranteed right

... serve little purpose if they are not duly enforced and the Court must reiterate that the Convention is intended to protect effective rights, not illusory ones. The facts show that the applicant suffered a serious infringement of her right to respect for her home as a result of the authorities' failure to take action to deal with the night-time disturbances. In these circumstances, the Court finds that the respondent State has failed to discharge its positive obligation to guarantee the applicant's right to respect for her home and her private life, in breach of Article 8 of the Convention. (para. 61)

Ruling on an equitable basis, as required by Article 41, the Court found that the authorities' failure to take action undeniably caused the applicant non-pecuniary damage and awarded her the €3,005 she had claimed (para. 67).

Another case of noise nuisance was filed by people living in the neighbourhood of one of Heathrow Airport's runways.[164] They alleged that the United Kingdom had violated its positive obligation to protect them against the noise caused by night flights, particularly in the early morning, which caused sleep disturbances and health problems. The Chamber of the Court awarded the claim but the Grand Chamber did not find a violation of Article 8 (with a 12 to 5

---

[163] ECtHR 16 November 2004, Case 4143/02 (*Moreno Gómez v Spain*). See also ECtHR 20 April 2004, Case 48995/99 (*Surugiu v Romania*); ECtHR 10 November 2004, Case 46117/99 (*Taskin and Others v Turkey*).
[164] ECtHR 8 July 2003, Case 36022/97 (*Hatton v United Kingdom*).

majority). It decided that the United Kingdom had struck a fair balance between the economic and public interests on the one hand, and the interests of the individuals on the other.

One of the important differences between this case and *Ostra* and *Gómez* cases is that in *Hatton* the night flight scheme was considered to be legal (the legality of the scheme was idly challenged in national judicial review procedures) and that the airport complied with the rules laid down in the scheme. However, it would be undesirable to draw a formal line exactly there. It is important to also take into account the strictness with which noise level regulations can be challenged in a judicial review procedure before the national court. The less intense the legality of such regulations is assessed in national judicial review procedure, the more space the Court may have to decide that the regulation does not strike a fair balance between public and individual interests. In *Hatton* the Court held that the English scope of judicial review was limited to the classic English public law concepts, such as irrationality, unlawfulness, and patent unreasonableness, and then did not allow consideration of whether the claimed increase in night flights represented a justifiable limitation on the right to respect for the private and family lives of those who live in the vicinity of Heathrow Airport (para. 141). The Court therefore concluded that there had been a violation of Article 13 (for lack of an effective remedy) but considered that the finding of this violation constituted in itself sufficient just satisfaction in respect of any non-pecuniary damage (para. 148).

1414 Environmental liability

1414-1 *Germany:* Umwelthaftungsgesetz and Wasserhaushaltsgesetz

German tort law holds some important general environmental liability rules. They are part of a high amount of strict liability rules enacted by a very active legislator (nr 405-1). Like the other countries Germany has a detailed legislation aiming to protect the environment. Violation of such a rule can give rise to liability on the basis of § 823 II BGB (violation of a statutory rule). However, this will always be a negligence liability since this provision always requires that the person who violated the statutory rule acted intentionally or negligently (nr 903).

Umwelthaftungsgesetz. The *Umwelthaftungsgesetz* (Environmental Liability Act) entered into force in 1991. § 1 protects against damage caused by an infringement of the right to life, body, health, or property. Pure economic loss cannot be recovered on the basis of this provision. These interests are protected only against certain types of infringement, ie pollution through substances, vibrations, noise, pressure, radiation, steam or heat which affects soil, air, or water. The liable person is the operator *(Inhaber)* of an installation *(Anlage)* which is listed in the Annex to the Act. This Annex counts 96 categories of installations, varying from the area of power supply, via the production of food, to waste disposal.

An important support for claimants is § 6 UmweltHG which holds that, if an installation is suitable to have caused the damage, it is assumed that the installation was the cause of the damage. It is then up to the operator to prove that this was not the case. The assumption does not apply if the installation was used according to the applicable rules and there was no failure in its functioning.

§ 4 UmweltHG provides the operator the defence of *höhere Gewalt* (external cause), for example, force of nature or sabotage by a third party.[165] If liability is established the operator of the installation is only liable to a maximum amount of €85 million (§ 15 UmweltHG).

Wasserhaushaltsgesetz. A specific strict liability provision applies to the protection of the quality and the composition of water. § 22 I *Wasserhaushaltsgesetz* (Water Resources Act) holds a strict liability for someone who affects the water so as to alter its physical, chemical, or biological nature by introducing or directing substances into the water (lakes, brooks, rivers, ponds, and groundwater) thus causing damage to someone. This provision does not only protect against personal or property damage; also pure economic loss can be recovered. Unlike most other German strict liability rules (nr 405-1) the amount of compensation is not limited.

The provision is applied in cases of water pollution by industrial plants as well as by private oil tanks, water purification plants, and pollution by lorries or ships. Liability rests on the operator of an installation which is intended to produce, employ, store, transport, or dispose of substances which cause damage if they get into the water (§ 22 II).[166]

§ 22 I presupposes '... an intention to use the water, beyond merely causing the introduction of damaging material.'[167] This conduct-related requirement is a rather strange element in a strict liability rule (nr 1004) but it aims to somewhat limit the scope of the rule. For example, the BGH held that there is no liability under this provision for spreading salt onto roads in winter which is then washed into the ground water.[168]

The defendant has the defence of *höhere Gewalt* (Act of God) (§ 22 II). This defence was, for example, not allowed when high waters flushed a dunghill into a brook which caused trout to die and the farmer had not in any way safeguarded the dung.[169]

1414-2 *England:* Rylands v Fletcher *and breach of statutory duty*

The torts dealt with in this section are closely connected to the tort of private nuisance (nr 1413-2). The statutory duties in the Environmental Protection Act

---

[165] Deutsch-Ahrens (2002), N 402.   [166] Deutsch-Ahrens (2002), N 399.
[167] Von Bar (2000), N 404.   [168] BGH 20 July 1994, BGHZ 124, 394.
[169] BGH 17 October 1985, VersR 1986, 92.

1990 (particularly Part III of this Act) are also known as rules of statutory nuisance. The *Rule in Rylands v Fletcher* dates from the 1860s and initially embodied a rule of strict liability. This Rule was subsequently dressed down with elements of negligence liability (though from an English point of view it might have rather been a matter of dressing up) but, in 2003, in *Transco plc v Stockport Metropolitan Borough Council* the House of Lords decided to consider the Rule to be a sub-species of private nuisance.[170]

Fletcher instructed a contractor to build a water reservoir on his land, under which were unused galleries of a mine. These were connected with a mine that Rylands operated on the adjacent land and the water in Fletcher's reservoir filled Rylands' mine. Fletcher could not be liable on the basis of negligence since he could not have known about the unused galleries and the contractor had not informed him about them. However, Fletcher was held liable for the damage. Blackburn J said:

> We think that the true rule of law is, that the person who for his own purposes brings on his lands and collects and keeps there anything likely to do mischief if it escapes, must keep it in at his peril, and, if he does not do so, is *prima facie* answerable for all the damage which is the natural consequence of its escape.[171]

The Rule applied to escaped cattle eating corn or grass at the neighbour's land and to fumes and noises from a workshop.

Less than a century later, the House of Lords in *Read v Lyons* considerably restricted the scope of the Rule by stating that the *Rule in Rylands v Fletcher* did not apply in cases of a *natural use of land*.[172] According to many authors, the appliance of the Rule by the courts since then tends towards a negligence liability with a reversed burden of proof.[173]

One of the few applications of the *Rule in Rylands v Fletcher* can be found in the *Cambridge Water* case. In the 1970s, Eastern Counties Leather (ECL) had leaked chemicals (PCE) on its own land, and these chemicals reached the claimant's underground water source which was about one mile distant. The water could no longer be used. In its decision the House of Lords qualified the storage of considerable amounts of chemicals as a classical example of a *non natural use of land*.[174] It also stated that the *Rule in Rylands v Fletcher* would only apply if it would have been foreseeable that as a cause of the escape relevant

---

[170] *Transco plc v Stockport Metropolitan Borough Council* [2003] UKHL 61, §9 per Lord Bingham of Cornhill.

[171] *Rylands v Fletcher* (1866) LR 1 Ex 265, 279. See also (1868) LR 3 HL 330.

[172] *Read v Lyons & Co. Ltd.* [1947] AC 156.

[173] Winfield and Jolowicz (2002), para. 15.1 ff; Markesinis and Deakin (2003), 543–547. In Australia the Rule is absorbed by the tort of negligence: *Burnie Port Authority v General Jones Pty Ltd* (1994) 120 ALR 42.

[174] *Cambridge Water Co Ltd v Eastern Counties Leather plc* [1994] 1 All ER 77 [1994] 2 WLR, 83, about which Van Gerven (2000), 172–175. See about the nuisance claim in the *Cambridge Water* case nr 1413-2.

damage would occur. The escape itself does not need to be foreseeable but the consequences of the escape are limited with the help of the foreseeability criterion. Lord Goff said:

> ... when ECL created the conditions which have ultimately led to the present state of affairs (...) it could not possibly have foreseen that damage of the type now complained of might be caused thereby. Indeed, long before the relevant legislation came into force, the PCE had become irretrievably lost in the ground below. In such circumstances, I do not consider that ECL should be under any greater liability than that imposed for negligence.[175]

For this reason the House of Lords dismissed the claim based on the *Rule in Rylands v Fletcher*. Since the nuisance claim was also rejected (nr 1413-2), ECL was not liable for damage suffered by Cambridge Water Co. Though both torts provide for strict liability, the claim was dismissed for lack of causation because the damage was deemed to be not foreseeable. See about the use of this causation criterion in strict liability cases, nr 1104.

It can be concluded from *Cambridge Water* that the *Rule in Rylands v Fletcher* is not dead yet. However, the Rule has lost its relevance for legal practice because, since World War II, no one seems to have succeeded in a claim under the Rule.[176] It has become very unlikely that the House of Lords will redevelop the Rule in the direction of a more general rule of strict liability. It considers this to be not a matter for the judiciary but for the legislator: 'If such liability is imposed by statute, the relevant activities can be identified, and those concerned can know where they stand. Furthermore, statute can where appropriate lay down precise criteria establishing the incidence and scope of such liability.'[177]

Breach of statutory duty. General strict liability in common law is rare but statutory rules may provide for specific rules of strict liability (nr 902). An example of a rather general statutory liability rule in the environmental area is section 73(6) of the Environmental Protection Act 1990:

> Where any damage is caused by waste which has been deposited in or on land, any person who deposited it, or knowingly caused or knowingly permitted it to be deposited, in either case so as to commit an offence ... is liable for the damage except where the damage (a) was due wholly to the fault of the person who suffered it; or (b) was suffered by a person who voluntarily accepted the risk of the damage being caused.

The field of application of this provision is rather narrow since it only applies to the pollution of land by waste.

---

[174] Lord Goff in *Cambridge Water Co Ltd v Eastern Counties Leather plc* [1994] 2 AC 264, 307.
[176] Oliphant, ETL 2003, 136. A *Rylands v Fletcher* claim also failed in *Transco plc v Stockport Metropolitan Borough Council* [2003] UKHL 61, ETL 2003, 135.
[177] *Cambridge Water Co Ltd v Eastern Counties Leather plc* [1994] 2 AC 264, 305. See also Gary T. Schwarz, 'Rylands v Fletcher, Negligence, and Strict Liability' in Peter Cane and Jane Stapleton, *The Law of Obligations: Essays in Celebration of John Fleming*, (Oxford: Clarendon Press; New York: Oxford University Press, 1998), 209–239.

1414-3 *France: art. 1384 al. 1 CC and violation of a statutory rule*

French tort law does not hold general rules on liability for environmental damage. However, liability can be based on the general strict liability rule for things of article 1384 al. 1 or on the violation of a statutory rule via the general *faute* rule in article 1382.[178]

Article 1384 al. 1. In 1993 in a landmark decision the *Cour de cassation* shaped the requirements for article 1384 al. 1 in order to implement the 'polluter pays' principle. After an explosion in a granary of *La Société La Malterie de la Moselle*—a company processing barley into malt, an important ingredient of beer—the *Société* concluded a contract with the *Sociétés Cardem et Somafer* to demolish the granary and to transport the rubble to a dumping-ground. This dumping-ground was within a water procurement zone serving the municipality of Montigny-les-Metz. Some time later the local authorities discovered that the disposed materials included the remains of fermented barley which created a risk of pollution and the authorities decided to stop pumping up water and to buy water elsewhere. The Court of Appeal held *La Malterie* and *Cardem et Somafer* jointly and severally liable, the former on the basis of article 1382 and the latter on the basis of article 1384 al. 1. The *Cour de cassation* quashed this decision, holding that there had not been a transfer of the custodianship (*transfer de la garde*) from *La Malterie* to *Cardem et Somafer* (nr 300). Such a transfer could only have taken place if the latter had been informed about the risk of pollution, in order to have the possibility to prevent the damage itself and this had not happened in this case. In other words, the *Cour de cassation* confirms that liability for industrial pollution rests on the company whose activity is at the origin of the pollution risk. The conveyor or the demolishing company can only be liable on the basis of article 1382 requiring a *faute* and knowledge of the risk. This approach complements the rules for product liability: the manufacturer is liable not only for the harmful consequences of the defective product he has put onto the market, but also for the harmful consequences of what results from the manufacturing process, including waste.[179]

Statutory provisions. Besides the general strict liability rule of article 1384 al. 1, liability for violation of a statutory rule (article 1382) plays an important role as regards environmental liability. Various Acts contain provisions the violation of which implies a *faute* in the sense of article 1382. Since the provisions generally do not require any form of negligence, environmental liability on this basis is

---

[178] See for example Gilles J. Martin, 'La responsabilité civile du fait des déchets en droit français', *RIDC* 1992, 65–82.

[179] Civ. 1 re 9 June 1993, D. 1994. 80, JCP 1994. II. 22202, comm. Viney, who also points out that this decision is an illustration of the distinction between the *garde de la structure* and *garde de la comportement*: if the damage is caused by a defect or a danger in the structure of the *chose*, liability can stay with someone even if the *chose* has been passed onto someone else (nr 303-3). See also Civ. 2e 29 April 1997, JCP 1997. IV. 1273.

strict. See about this topic generally, nr 904. Important Acts in this respect are about water pollution and waste removal.[180]

In this respect it is important to note that the *Cour de cassation's* interpretation of article 1384 al. 1 in the above-mentioned *La Malterie* case also finds a ground in the statutory system of environmental liability. Article 2 of the Act of 15 July 1975 regarding waste removal and recycling of materials (*relative à l'élimination des déchets et à la récupération des matériaux*) holds that the producer of waste is regarded as the person who is in charge of the production, and who has the obligation to prevent the harmful consequences.[181] Both the legislator and the *Cour de cassation* put the emphasis on the producer's liability, the latter by restricting the possibility to transferring the custodianship of waste in the sense of article 1384 al. 1.

1415 International perspective

1415-1 *Comparative observations*

The most targeted legislation as regards liability for damage to the environment can be found in Germany. This is also the country where, compared with England and France, protection of the environment plays the most important role on various political and societal levels. The *Umwelthaftungsgesetz* and the *Wasserhaushaltsgesetz* cover a wide range of cases of environmental damage and they provide for strict liability.

France does not hold general strict liability rules focusing on environmental damage. The need for such rules is limited because the general strict liability rule for things (article 1384 al. 1) applies to waste and other (dangerous) substances negatively affecting the environment. Additionally, the many specific Acts protecting the environment provide for strict liability on the basis of article 1382 (violation of a statutory rule).

In both legal systems the direction is clear: to damage caused by dangerous substances some kind of strict liability applies. The paths to this goal are, however, quite different. Whereas France holds a very general strict liability rule for things, Germany does not focus on the dangerous substance but on the listed institutions (*Anlagen*) in the Annex to the *Umwelthaftungsgesetz*. Hence, on the one hand the German provisions are broader because they apply not only to substances but also to vibrations, noise, and the like. On the other hand they are

---

[180] For example the Act of 16 December 1964 against water pollution (*relative au regime et à la repartition des eaux et à lutte contre leur pollution*) and the Act of 15 July 1975 regarding waste removal and recycling of materials (*relative à l'élimination des déchets et à la récupération des matériaux*), amended by the Act of 13 July 1992.

[181] Art. 2 Act of 15 July 1975 regarding waste removal and recycling of materials (*relative à l'élimination des déchets et à la récupération des matériaux*), amended by the Act of 13 July 1992, holds: 'Le producteur des déchets est désormais regardé comme celui qui est en charge de cette production et qui a l'obligation d'en prévenir les effets dommageables.'.

more limited, because it is required that the physical or property damage is caused by environmental pollution.

On the other side of the Channel the situation deviates substantially from the continental mainstream. English law only holds one general strict liability rule for environmental damage. The only common rule of strict liability in this respect (the *Rule in Rylands v Fletcher*) has been restored to a rule in which negligence plays an important role. Hence, the fact of the matter is that in England polluters and users of dangerous substances can escape liability more easily than in France and Germany.

In the *Cambridge Water* case (nr 1414-2) the House of Lords held that creating strict liability is not a matter for the courts but for the legislator. No doubt this is constitutionally correct. However, in a country reluctant to adopt general strict liability rules and alternatively governed by a Labour party and a Conservative party, it is hard to conceive that legislation as regards strict liability for environmental damage will get high on the political agenda.

1415-2 *International law*

From an international law point of view a number of developments can be mentioned.[182]

Firstly, in the area of nuclear liability and oil pollution of the sea, international treaties are in force providing liability rules.

The *Paris Convention of 29 July 1960 on Third Party Liability in the Field of Nuclear Energy* was extended by Protocols and by the supplementary Brussels Convention of 31 January 1963.[183] This Convention aims to ensure adequate and equitable compensation for persons who suffer damage caused by nuclear incidents, while taking the necessary steps to ensure an unhindered development of the production and uses of nuclear energy for peaceful purposes. The Convention holds the operator of a nuclear plant liable for death, personal injury, and property damage caused by a nuclear event, provided that such damage or loss was caused by a nuclear incident in such installation or involving nuclear substances coming from such installation (Article 3). The operator's liability is almost absolute: he may only invoke an act of armed conflict, hostilities, civil war, insurrection, or a grave natural disaster of an exceptional character (Article 9). Article 10 obliges the operator to maintain third party liability insurance coverage.[184]

---

[182] See extensively R. Wolfrum and C. Langenfeld, *Environmental Protection by Means of International Liability Law* (Berlin: Erich Schmidt, 1999).

[183] Von Bar (1998) N 379 with further references. See also *Nuclear Energy Agency, Liability and Compensation for Nuclear Damage: An International Overview* (Paris: Organisation for Economic Co-operation and Development, 1994). Parties to this Convention are, *inter alia*, France, Germany, and the United Kingdom.

[184] See also the Vienna Convention of 21 May 1963 on Civil Liability for Nuclear Damage, as well as the Protocol of 12 September 1997 to amend this Convention, and the Convention of 12

The *Convention of 29 November 1969 on Civil Liability for Oil Pollution Damage*, subsequently updated by a number of Protocols, provides strict liability rules for the ship owner. A guarantee fund was established by the *International Convention of 18 December 1971 on the Establishment of an International Fund for Compensation for Oil Pollution Damage*.[185]

Secondly, a number of Conventions have been signed and ratified but have not (yet) entered into force. An interesting one in this respect is the *European Convention of 21 June 1993 on Civil Liability for Damage Resulting from Activities Dangerous to the Environment (Lugano Convention)*. Article 6 holds a strict liability for the operator in respect of a dangerous activity for the damage caused by the activity. The regime would have covered personal injury, damage to property, and expenses for measures of reinstatement. The Convention also provides extensive and detailed definitions of dangerous activities, dangerous substances, and the environment.[186] This Convention is clearly the fruit of the heydays of environmental policy, and considering the current economic-political situation it is highly unlikely that it will ever enter into force.

Thirdly, the case law of the European Court of Human Rights on Article 8 (protection of private life and family life) imposes on Contracting States obligations to prevent their citizens from nuisance. See nr 1413-5 and 1808-2.

Fourthly, European Community law provides for an abundance of rules regulating conduct and activities that can affect the environment, varying from limiting emissions of noxious substances to protecting the habitat of various animals. Violation of these statutory rules can give rise to liability depending on the conditions set by the national laws (nr 902–904).

Finally, the European Directive concerning liability for damage caused to the environment. This Directive was adopted in April 2004 and has to be implemented by the Member States before May 2007. See in more detail about this Directive nr 1415-3.

1415-3 *European Union law*

In 1991, in the midst of negotiations on the *Lugano Convention on Civil Liability for Damage Resulting from Activities Dangerous to the Environment* (nr 1415-2), the European Commission issued a proposal for a Directive on Civil Liability for Damage caused by waste.[187] The, by then, draft Convention and the Commission proposal covered similar issues but were partly inconsistent with each other. In the end neither the Directive nor the Convention entered into force.

September 1997 on Supplementary Compensation for Nuclear Damage. The Paris, Brussels, and Vienna Conventions are linked by the so-called Joint Protocol adopted in 1988.

[185] Von Bar (1998) N 380 with further references.
[186] Von Bar (1998) N 383 with further references.
[187] OJ C 251, 4.10.1989, 3.

In 2002 the European Commission presented a new proposal concerning liability for damage caused to the environment. This Environmental Liability Directive was adopted on 21 April 2004 by the European Parliament and the Council.[188] The Directive aims to prevent environmental damage by forcing industrial polluters to pay prevention and remediation costs. The Directive is supposed to be one of the flagships of a vast communitarian legislation to protect the environment. However, the fruit of a long and bitter political fight has rather made it look like a mud boat. Also, its scope of application is considerably reduced by excluding compensation for personal injury and damage to property. In fact, the whole concept of collecting payments in response to harmful activities has been shifted from tort law to administrative law, albeit disguised in tort law terminology.[189] Member States have until 30 April 2007 to transpose the Directive's provisions into national law.

The purpose of the Directive is to establish a framework of environmental liability based on the 'polluter pays' principle, to prevent and remedy environmental damage (Article 1).

Article 3(3) substantially limits the scope of the Directive by holding that it does not give private parties a right of compensation as a consequence of environmental damage or of an imminent threat of such damage. Natural and legal persons are only entitled to submit to the competent authority any observations relating to instances of environmental damage (Article 12). Articles 5(4) and 6(3) entrust the enforcement of the liability rules to the Member States. These are under a duty to ensure that the necessary preventive or restorative measures are actually taken.

Environmental damage is defined in Article 2(1) of the Directive by reference to biodiversity protected at Community and national levels. Water damage is any damage covered by the Water Framework Directive, and land damage is covered if the land contamination creates a significant risk to human health. In order to establish liability the environmental damage caused has to be significant. This is elaborated in Annex I of the Directive.

Liability rests primarily on the operator. Article 2(6) holds that an operator is any natural or legal, private or public person who operates or controls the occupational activity or to whom decisive economic power over the technical functioning of such an activity has been delegated, including the holder of a permit or authorization for such an activity or the person registering or notifying such an activity.

According to Article 3(1), the operator who carries out 'hazardous activities' (listed in another Annex of the Directive) is strictly liable for preventing or restoring any damage caused by those activities to land, water, and protected habitats and species. The operator carrying out other, less harmful, activities will

---

[188] Directive 2004/35/EC of the European Parliament and of the Council of 21 April 2004 on environmental liability with regard to the prevention and remedying of environmental damage, OJ L 143/56, 30.4.2004.

[189] See also Bernhard A. Koch, 'European Union', *ETL*, 2004, 595–596.

be held liable when damage to protected habitats and species has been caused by their fault or negligence.

Article 4(1) exempts operators from liability in case of damage caused: (a) by an act of armed conflict, hostilities, civil war or insurrection, or (b) by a natural phenomenon of exceptional, inevitable, and irresistible character (Act of God). Article 8(3) provides the same as regards damage: (a) caused by a third party and occurred despite the fact that appropriate safety measures were in place, or (b) resulted from compliance with a compulsory order or instruction emanating from a public authority. Finally, Article 8(4) holds that the Member States may allow the operator not to bear the cost of remedial actions where he demonstrates that he was not at fault or negligent, and that the environmental damage was caused by: (a) an emission or event expressly authorized by, and fully in accordance with the conditions of, an authorization conferred by or given under applicable national laws including implemented communitarian rules, and (b) an emission or activity or any manner of using a product in the course of an activity which the operator demonstrates was not considered likely to cause environmental damage, according to the state of scientific and technical knowledge at the time when the emission was released or the activity took place.

Damage from nuclear and maritime accidents falls outside the regime's scope and remains subject to existing treaties (Article 4(2)–(4)(nr 1415-2)).

The German statesman Otto von Bismarck (nr 401-1) is supposed to have said that the less people know about how sausages and Acts are made, the better they sleep.[190] The Environmental Liability Directive is a proper example of this maxim. It suffers from a lot of scars and bruises as a consequence of the political battle preceding its adoption as well as of poor drafting: ' . . . apart from a blatant disregard of the most basic concepts of tort law, its contents show one more time how the lobbying of the industry and other possible polluters can effectively ruin the prospects of an important endeavour.'[191] The proposal not only lacks teeth, it also leaves a lot of space for the Member States to choose the ways in which the proposed goals have to be reached, thus not providing a high level of harmonization.

F CONCLUDING REMARKS

1416 Comparative observations

This chapter on liability for damage caused by movable objects has illustrated the English reluctance as regards rules of strict liability (apart from the European

---

[190] 'Je weniger die Leute davon wissen, wie Würste und Gesetze gemacht werden, desto besser schlafen sie.'   [191] Bernhard A. Koch, 'European Union', *ETL*, 2003, 439.

product liability regime, only liability for damage caused by animals is strict and even this is not without exception), the German love for detailed strict and fault rules (both to be found in the *Verkehrspflichten* and the various specific rules of strict liability), and the French fondness for rules of strict liability (even the strict liability for defective products does not go far enough for the French).

Despite these differences, one can argue that, from a distance, liability for damage caused by animals and by defective products show relatively small differences between the legal systems (see nr 1403 and 1407 for a more detailed analysis). More substantial differences exist in the area of liability for damage caused by motor vehicles and for damage caused by dangerous substances (environmental damage). Indeed, in addition to product liability the latter areas have attracted the European Commission's legislative attention. This is not surprising since these three categories all have a strong transboundary character. However, the Commission's success in its efforts to harmonize these areas was mixed. There has been some success in the area of product liability and hardly any result in the area of environmental damage and road traffic accidents.

Firstly, the Product Liability Directive has been an important contribution to harmonizing the laws of the Member States. The latest case law of the ECJ has further enhanced the harmonizing power of the Directive. However, since the Directive only covers part of the liability issue (it does not harmonize the law of damages), important differences between the Member States will necessarily remain (nr 1407).

Secondly, as regards motor vehicles the European Community has been successful in harmonizing the laws regarding compulsory liability insurance. However, the substance of tort law in this area is still untouched by European legislation, and it is quite likely that in the foreseeable future this will remain the case, particularly after the almost reckless effort to harmonize the position of pedestrians and cyclists was wrecked by the other Community institutions (nr 1405).

Thirdly, 'Europe' has issued an abundance of regulations as regards dangerous substances in order to protect health and safety and the environment. These rules have an indirectly harmonizing effect in as much as they can be invoked under national law in the framework of liability for violation of a statutory rule (nr 902–904). However, the efforts to directly harmonize the *liability* rules for damage caused by dangerous substances have run aground. The strong opposition to the Directive proposal on liability for environmental damage has resulted in an instrument that does not make use of tort law tools and whose effectiveness has been put in doubt (nr 1415-3).

The prospects for European legislation in the areas of road traffic accidents and environmental liability are rather gloomy. An important reason for the (modest) success of the Product Liability Directive was the momentum: when, in the course of the 1970s, the Directive proposal was developed, a number of recent cases of serious consequences of defective drugs had occurred, consumer protection had recently become part of the Community's tasks, most Member States did not have specific tort law provisions for product liability, and the EC counted 'only' ten Member States. All these circumstances endorsed the momentum for the Product Liability Directive. Currently, in the areas of liability for traffic accidents and for environmental damage, not even one of these circumstances occurs.

15

Liability for Immovable Objects

A NATIONAL RULES

1501 Introduction

People can suffer damage when visiting or using houses, grounds, roads, or public buildings. This can happen in many ways. Firstly, it is conceivable that the construction of the premises or road does not meet the required safety standards, because of bad design or bad maintenance. One may think of a collapsing building, roofing-tiles falling down, or holes in a road. Secondly, visitors can get injured because the supervisor did not warn them properly or in time about inevitable risks, such as low ceilings in a building or dangerous bends in a road. Thirdly, visitors can be harmed by other visitors, particularly in crowded public buildings such as stadiums, swimming pools, and the like.[1]

From a comparative point of view the applicable liability rules show a wide variety in structure and form: negligence liability, negligence liability with a reversed burden of proof, liability for defects, strict liability, and liability for breach of a statutory duty.

Some of the liability rules for buildings and premises go back to Roman law, particularly the rule that someone is liable for the (partial) collapse of a building, provided that this collapse is due to bad construction or bad maintenance. In France the great grandchild of this rule is the strict liability rule of article 1386 CC (nr 1502-1), whereas in Germany § 836–838 BGB provide a fault liability with a reversed burden of proof (nr 1503-1). In England the tort of public nuisance applies to collapsing buildings, but this tort has its roots in the common law rather than in Roman law (nr 1504-2).

In addition to these rules French law holds a strict liability for damage caused by things (*choses*) (nr 303). This rule was developed by the *Cour de cassation* as regards movable things, but from the mid 20th century the court has also applied the rule to liability for immovable things (nr 1502-2).[2]

---

[1] One may also think of liability for damage caused by (nuclear) energy plants and by mains or pipelines through which liquid or gas is transported under high pressure. They will not be separately discussed here. See Koch and Koziol (2002), 401–402.

[2] See also von Bar (1998), N 223–236.

German law does not have other rules of strict liability but here an important role is played by safety duties (*Verkehrspflichten*). These were initially designed by the *Reichsgericht* and applied to liability for damage suffered on premises, grounds, and roads (nr 1503-2).

In English law, liability has to be based on the tort of negligence or the breach of a statutory duty. As regards the latter, one may particularly think of the Occupiers' Liability Acts and the Highways Act. All these rules require negligent conduct (nr 1504-1).

In the following sections, the specific national rules applying to liability for immovable objects will be analysed in more detail, both rules of stricter and rules of negligence liability (1502–1504). Nr 1505 will deal with differences and similarities between strict and negligence liability for immovable objects.

Issues arising in both strict and negligence liability will be the subject of nr 1506. One may think of the question of who the liable person is (nr 1506-1), what role the character of the premises plays in establishing liability (nr 1506-2), whether unauthorized visitors (trespassers) are protected (nr 1506-3), to what extent the supervisor has to take into account the visitor's imprudence (nr 1506-4), and to what extent the visitor has to be protected against other visitors' negligent or criminal conduct (nr 1506-5).

Finally, the spotlight will be put on a special immovable object: roads. The duties of the highway authority in the various jurisdictions show a number of commonalities if only because strict liability is not accepted and the liable person is usually a public body (nr 1507–1510).

1502 France

1502-1 *Strict liability for collapsing buildings (art. 1386 CC)*

French law holds the owner (*le propriétaire*) of a building strictly liable for damage caused by the collapse of the building as the consequence of inadequate maintenance or a defect in the construction (*la ruine d'un bâtiment*). This rule has been laid down in article 1386 CC and is a *lex specialis* to article 1384 al. 1. However, as will be pointed out below, its importance has substantially decreased with the development of article 1384 al. 1 into a general rule of liability for things.[3]

A building is defined as a man-made construction intended to be permanently connected with the ground (*une construction immobilière*).[4] This implies that a tree or a rock is not a building in the sense of this provision. Damage caused by falling trees or by a stone falling from a hill has to be dealt with under the regime of art. 1384 al. 1.

---

[3] Viney-Jourdain (1998), nr 719.
[4] Aubry and Rau (1989), nr 118; Terré-Simler-Lequette (2002), nr 781; Viney-Jourdain (1998), nr 721.

The first requirement of article 1386 is that the damage is caused by the collapse of the building. The case law takes 'collapse' very broadly and includes the damage of any part of the construction or of any movable or immovable element that is indissolubly connected to the construction.[5] A partial collapse suffices, for example the collapse of a balcony or the door of a hangar.[6]

Secondly, the collapse has to be caused either by a defect in the maintenance (*défaut d'entretien*) or a defect in the construction (*vice de construction*). It is up to the claimant to prove the facts pertaining the collapse and its origin. If he is not able to do so, he may rely on article 1384 al. 1 which does not require a collapse (or a building).[7] However, the courts are inclined to rather easily establish a defect in maintenance or construction. An often cited case is about an 18th century bridge which collapsed under the weight of a 1.5 tonne 20th century lorry. On the basis of the 19th century article 1386 CC, the Court of Appeal in Angers decided that this provision applied and that the owner of the bridge was liable for the damage because the construction of the bridge was defective. It was not considered to be relevant that the bridge was not used for the purpose for which it was built, rather the court seemed to focus on the legitimate expectations of the user of the building (bridge).[8]

The owner's only defences are *force majeure* and contributory negligence. *Force majeure* requires a fact of an external character (*caractère extérieur*), which is unforeseeable and insurmountable (*imprévisible et insurmontable*). However, in the framework of article 1386, this defence has a limited character. If the collapse and its origin (bad maintenance or a defective building) have been established, it is not easy to think of facts that can amount to *force majeure*. One could perhaps think of a lack of possibilities to maintain the building, for example because of state orders or an armed conflict.[9]

1502-2 *General strict liability for things (art. 1384 al. 1 CC)*

The general strict liability rule for things (*responsabilité du fait des choses*), created by the *Cour de cassation* at the end of the 19th century on the basis of article 1384 al. 1 CC (nr 303), not only applies to damage caused by movable things but also by immovable things. This was decided in 1928 by the *Cour de cassation* in a case in which someone suffered damage as the consequence of an accident with a lift. Later the court also applied the provision to a falling tree, a landslide, the bursting of a dyke, and an accident on an escalator.[10]

---

[5] Terré-Simler-Lequette (2002), nr 782; Aubry and Rau (1989), nr 119; Viney-Jourdain (1998), nr 722.

[6] Civ. 2e 12 July 1966, D. 1966. 632, JCP 1967. II. 15185, comm. Dejean de la Bathie, RTD civ. 1968, 362, obs. Durry (balcony); Civ. 2e 17 October 1990, Bull. civ. II, no 201 (door).

[7] Terré-Simler-Lequette (2002), nr 782.

[8] Cour d'Appel Angers 4 November 1971, D. 1972. 169, comm. J.L., RTD civ. 1972, 787, obs. Durry.   [9] Terré-Simler-Lequette (2002), nr 783.

[10] Req. 6 March 1928, DP 1928. I. 97, comm. Josserand, S. 1928. I. 225, comm. Hugueney (lift); Civ. 30 April 1952, D. 1952. 471, JCP 1952. II. 7111, comm. Blaevoet (tree); Civ. 2e 12 May 1966,

This case law raised the question of whether there was any ground left for the application of article 1386. The *Cour de cassation* had to decide about this in a case involving tiles falling off the roof, a typical article 1386 case. The claimant tried to circumvent the requirement of the latter provision that the collapse was caused by defective maintenance or a defective construction. However, the *Cour de cassation* did not accept this argument and held that in a collapse case only article 1386 is applicable.[11] This case law still stands despite criticism from the doctrine.[12]

Liability on the basis of article 1384 al. 1 requires the 'act of the thing' (*fait de la chose*). This implies that the *chose* must have contributed to the realization of the damage. The *Cour de cassation* distinguishes three categories of cases.[13] Firstly, if a moving *chose* touches the claimant or his property there is a rebuttable assumption that the *chose* has contributed to the realization of the damage. One may think of a rolling stone and a falling tree.

Secondly, if there is contact between the claimant and the non-moving *chose* the claimant has to prove that the thing was the cause of the damage. As regards an immovable thing, this will particularly be the case if it 'behaved abnormally' (*comportement anormal de la chose*). This is the case if the thing was defective or if it was put in a wrong place. For example, when someone fell through an open door in a lift shaft, it was decided that the harm was caused by the fact of a thing (*fait de la chose*).[14]

Another case concerned Mme Cadé, who suffered a fit in the changing room of a swimming pool and fell. When she was lying unconscious on the ground her arm rested on a heating pipe and she suffered injury. The *Cour d'Appel* in Colmar dismissed her claim because the swimming pool had not committed a *faute*. The *Cour de cassation*, however, decided that the appeal court should also have established whether liability could have been based on article 1384 al. 1.[15] However, neither on this basis was Mme Cadé successful because the court held that the heating installation was installed in a normal way.[16] A final illustration is the case about someone who slipped on snowy stairs in a ski resort. Slippery snowy stairs are normal in a ski resort and the *Cour de cassation* concluded that there was no *fait de la chose*. The custodian of the stairs was not liable for the damage.[17]

Thirdly, article 1384 al. 1 can also apply in cases in which there is no contact between the *chose* and the claimant. One may think of someone who is shocked

D. 1966. 700, comm. Azard (tree); Civ. 25 June 1952, D. 1952. 614, JCP. 1952. II. 7338, comm. Esmein (landslide); Civ. 2e 26 April 1990, JCP 1990. IV. 235 (burst dyke); Civ. 2e 2 April 1997, D. 1997. IR. 105 (escalator); see about the latter case also nr 1505).

[11] Civ. 4 August 1942, D.C. 1943. 1, comm. Ripert.
[12] According to Viney-Jourdain (1998), nr 739, art. 1386 is '... un instrument de chicane dont notre système de responsabilité civile délictuelle (...) aurait (...) tout avantage à se passer.' See also Aubry and Rau (1989), nr 120.   [13] Civ. 19 February 1941, D.C. 1941. 85, note Flour.
[14] Civ. 2e 29 May 1996, Bull. civ. II, no 117, D. 1996. IR. 156.
[15] Civ. 19 February 1941, D.C. 1941. 85, comm. Flour.
[16] Civ. 19 February 1941, D.C. 1941. 85, comm. Flour; in the same sense Civ. 19 November 1964, D. 1965. 93.   [17] Civ. 2e 15 March 1978, D. 1978. IR. 406.

by seeing a building collapsing but is not hit himself. In these cases, the claimant has to prove that the *chose* was the cause of his damage but the court will not easily award such a claim.

The custodian (*gardien*) has the same defences as the owner has under the rule of article 1386: *force majeure* and the victim's contributory negligence.[18] See nr 1502-1.

1503 Germany

1503-1 *Liability for collapsing buildings (§ 836–838 BGB)*

§ 836–838 BGB provide a liability for damage caused by the collapse of a building or a work connected with the ground (*Einsturz eines Gebäudes oder eines anderen mit einem Grundstück verbundenen Werkes*) or the breaking off of parts of the building or the work. A work does not need to be permanently connected with the ground and includes booths, scaffoldings, gates, exposition tents, gravestones, and bridges.[19] The provisions are, for instance, applied in cases of planks falling off scaffolding and of a sunshade or a screwed on shower cubicle coming down.[20]

§ 836–838 are for example not applicable when snow slides off a roof, because snow is not a part of the building.[21] In such a case liability has to be established on the basis of the breach of a safety duty (*Verkehrssicherungspflicht*) of § 823 I (nr 1503-2).

These rules as regards liability for collapsing buildings only protect against personal injury and property loss; pure economic loss cannot be recovered on the basis of these provisions.[22]

§ 836 holds liable the possessor (*Besitzer*) of the ground on which the building or the work stands. This will usually be the owner. It implies that, for example, a tenant cannot be liable in the sense of this provision. If someone possesses a building on someone else's ground, then the possessor of the building and not the possessor of the ground is liable, because the former is in a better position to avert risks (§ 837).[23] § 838 imposes the same liability on the person who takes over the maintenance of the building or the work from the possessor, or on the

---

[18] Terré-Simler-Lequette (2002), nr 802.

[19] RG 23 March 1916, JW 1916, 1019 (booth); BGH 27 April 1999, NJW 1999, 2593 = VersR 1999, 1424; BGH 4 March 1997, NJW 1997, 1853 = VersR 1997, 835; BGH 21 April 1959, VersR 1959, 694 (walls, gates, and scaffolding); BGH 29 March 1977, NJW 1977, 1392 = Vers 1977, 668 (gravestone); BGH 9 July 1959, VersR 1959, 948 (bridge).

[20] BGH 4 March 1997, NJW 1997, 1853 = VersR 1997, 835 (scaffolding); RG 13 October 1930, JW 1931, 194 (sunshade); BGH 12 March 1985, NJW 1985, 2588 = VersR 1985, 666 (shower cubicle).   [21] BGH 8 December 1954, NJW 1955, 300.

[22] Münchener Kommentar-Wagner (2004), § 836 N 17.

[23] § 837 BGB: 'Besitz jemand auf einem fremden Grundstück in Ausübung eines Rechts ein Gebäude oder ein anderes Werk, so trifft ihn anstelle des Besitzers des Grundstücks die im § 836 bestimmte Verantwortlichkeit.'

person who has a duty to maintain on the basis of his right to use the building (*Nutzungsrecht*).[24]

§ 836–838 provide for a concretization of the general safety duty (*Verkehrspflicht*) as regards the direct and indirect consequences of gravitation.[25] The relevance of these rules lies in the shift of the burden of proof. If the claimant has proved that the collapse or the breaking off is caused by a defective construction (*fehlerhafte Errichtung*) or an objective defective maintenance (*objektiv mangelhafter Unterhaltung*), the possessor of the ground or the work is, in principle, liable for the damage. He can only escape liability by proving that he did not act negligently (§ 836 I 2), which means that he has taken all measures which can be required from a careful person in order to avert the risk. This burden of proof is considered to be reasonable since the possessor of the building or work will be better informed about these facts than the claimant.[26]

These rules imply that the possessor needs to inspect the building or the work and check whether it meets the safety standards. This is the same standard as applies in the general framework of the *Verkehrspflichten* in § 823. If a defect is discovered the possessor needs to take appropriate and timely measures. The standard of the inspections depends on the nature and the condition of the building or work, particularly its use and the risks which are related to this use. In public buildings which are used by many visitors, the possessor needs at least to have an inspection plan. The case law requires a high standard of care in this respect. However, a possessor may have discharged his duties, even if he could have known of the defect, if the building had been inspected by an expert shortly before the event.[27]

The possessor or the person liable on the basis of § 837–838 can also prove the claimant's contributory negligence, which will lead to a lower amount of damages to be paid (§ 254).

German law also holds a number of specific strict liability rules which partly apply to the liability for premises, grounds, and roads. One may particularly think of the strict liability of operators of gas and electricity mains (§ 2 Haftpflichtgesetz) (nr 405-2).

1503-2 *Verkehrspflichten*

The German safety duties (*Verkehrspflichten*) made their first appearance in a case about the safety of a road: someone suffered damage when a rotten tree fell onto the highway (nr 403-1). In this case the BGB appeared to have a lacuna

---

[24] § 838 BGB: 'Wer die Unterhaltung eines Gebäudes oder eines mit einem Grundstück verbundenen Werkes für den Besitzer übernimmt oder das Gebäude oder das Werk vermöge eines ihm zustehenden Nutzungsrechts zu unterhalten hat, ist für den durch den Einsturz oder die Ablösung von Teilen verursachten Schaden in gleicher Weise verantwortlich wie der Besitzer.'

[25] Deutsch-Ahrens (2002), N 338.   [26] Münchener Kommentar-Wagner (2004), § 836 N 2.

[27] Larenz-Canaris (1994), § 79 VI 1b, 488; Münchener Kommentar-Wagner (2004), § 836 N 19–22; Deutsch-Ahrens (2002), N 339–340.

in dealing with damage caused by omissions. Hence, the *Reichsgericht* created safety duties (*Verkehrspflichten*), affirmative duties imposed on persons who had opened their roads, premises, or grounds to the general public.[28] Though the scope of the *Verkehrspflichten* later also included other areas, it all started with the safety duty of the supervisors of roads, premises, and grounds to ensure the safety of the visitors.

The duty is owed by the person who has opened and keeps open his premises for public use, and who has the legal and factual potential to take measures in order to improve the visitors' safety. He is called the *Verkehrspflichtige* and he is comparable to the French *gardien* and the English *occupier* (nr 1502-2 and 1504-1).

The *Verkehrspflichtige* is liable on the basis of § 823 I for personal injury or property loss caused by the insufficient maintenance of the premises, by the failure not to remove obstacles, or by the failure to keep the premises in a sufficiently safe condition.[29] Safety duties are in principle owed to all visitors. Warning and prohibition signs can make someone a trespasser instead of a visitor. For example, adult people entering the building site of a new estate are sufficiently warned for risks if they have passed a sign with the words 'Unauthorized persons are not allowed to enter' (*Unbefugten ist das Betreten untersagt*). In such a case the supervisor has fulfilled his safety duty (*Verkehrspflicht*)[30] and does not owe the trespassers any other duty. In other cases, the *Verkehrspflichtige* should know that visitors can be sometimes curious[31] and may find themselves, though by mistake, in places where they do not need to be.[32] However, in 1915 the *Reichsgericht* dismissed the claim of a male hotel guest who suffered damage as the consequence of an accident at the unlit corridor to the ladies' room because, according to the (male) members of the court, he had no business to be there.[33]

More care is required as regards children unlawfully entering the premises. An 8-year-old boy visited a quarry that was converted into a recreation lake. Outside the marked swimming area the boy suddenly sank at a place where the bottom invisibly ran down steeply to a depth of 18 metres. He could not swim and drowned. His father claimed damages for the costs of the funeral but the operator of the quarry argued it had provided warning signs saying 'Building site, entering not allowed' (*Baustelle, Betreten verboten*). The BGH considered this to be too undifferentiated to indicate the specific occurring risk. More effective precautionary measures should have been taken and, at least for children, more understandable warning signs should have been used.[34] In contrast, when

---

[28] RG 30 October 1902, RGZ 52, 373.   [29] Kötz-Wagner (2001), N 235.
[30] BGH 11 December 1956, NJW 1957, 499 = VersR 1957, 165, about which Markesinis and Unberath (2002) 770 and BGH 11 December 1984, NJW 1985, 1078. See also Stoll, *Handeln auf eigene Gefahr* (1961), 272.   [31] BGH 9 February 1988, NJW 1988, 1588.
[32] BGH 19 May 1967, VersR 1967, 801: the owner of a hotel is liable for the damage of a guest who fell in an unprotected shaft of a cellar next to the hotel.
[33] RG 2 July 1915, RGZ 87, 128 ('... weil er dort nichts zu suchen habe').
[34] BGH 18 October 1988, JZ 1989, 249 = VersR 1989, 155 ('Eine derartige Warnung ist viel zu undifferenziert, um auf die besondere Gefahr, wie sie sich hier verwirklicht hat, hinzuweisen. Hier

a public swimming pool had taken extensive and appropriate measures to prevent accidents with a 46 m long water slide, the BGH held that it had fulfilled its safety duty.[35]

Once people are on the premises proper measures have to be taken to protect their safety, also taking into account the vulnerability of elderly visitors. After a German Advent celebration an older lady broke her hip when she fell on her way to a coach on an unlit and unpaved car park. The BGH decided that the operator of the car park owed a safety duty (*Verkehrspflicht*) to prevent health risks for the visitors of the celebration, not only at the place of the celebration but also on their way to the car park, because it could have been expected that a number of elderly people would visit the celebration.[36]

As regards children, the main rule is to prevent risks rather than to warn of them. Outside the shower area of a swimming pool there was a small slide made of wired glass which was intended to transport clothes and keep them dry. When a girl climbed it and slid down it, the slide broke under her weight and she was severely injured. The BGH decided that the operator had breached its duty of care because the slide was at the wrong place (children were able to climb it) and it was made of the wrong material. The operator had to prevent this risk, particularly because there was no supervision in the shower area.[37]

If it is not possible to take physical measures to prevent the risk, children have to be warned at their own level of knowledge and understanding (see also nr 807-3). At a shunting yard, which was accessible to children, goods wagons stood under a charged overhead wire. Children were warned against climbing onto the roofs of the wagons (this was rather easy given the circumstances) by a warning sign with a thunderbolt (*Blitzpfeil*). The BGH deemed this to be insufficient and required warning signs with, for instance, pictograms that preclude any possible misunderstanding (*unmißverständlich*) about the possible risk of a fatal electrical surge.[38]

Visitors who suffer damage on roads, premises, or grounds can file a claim not only on the basis of tort law (§ 823 BGB) but sometimes also on the basis of breach of contract. The latter way can be advantageous as regards compensation for pure economic loss as well as for third parties. When a mother and daughter

---

hätten (...) wirksame Schutzmaßnahmen ergriffen und zumindest für Kinder einprägsamere Warnschilder aufgestellt werden müssen.'). See also BGH 11 February 1969, VersR 1969, 517: duty of the owner of a ground in order to protect children against the risks from the ruin of a building.

[35] BGH 3 February 2004, NJW 2004, 1449, ETL 2004, 318 (Fedtke).

[36] BGH 21 November 1989, NJW 1990, 905 = VersR 1990, 211, 756. The same duty was owed by the organizer of the celebration.

[37] BGH 21 February 1978, VersR 1978, 561. According to the BGH the girl's contributory negligence was at least 50 per cent.

[38] BGH 14 March 1995, NJW 1995, 2631. Due to decisions like BGH 10 October 1989, VersR 1990, 913, the railway operator could not know this safety duty (*Verkehrpflicht*) and was thus not liable on the basis of negligence (§ 823 BGB) (nr 810-2). However, it was strictly liable on the basis of art. 1 HaftpflG (nr 405-2) but by then strict liability did not provide for damages for pain and suffering.

visited a self-service store the daughter allegedly slipped on a vegetable leaf, fell and was injured. The BGH decided that she was entitled to claim damages for economic loss and prospective damage under the contract her mother entered into with the store (nr 713).[39]

1504 England

1504-1 *Statutory duties: Occupiers' Liability Acts*

English law contains various specific rules as regards liability for damage caused on premises, grounds, and roads.[40] Claims can be based on negligence (nr 503), private nuisance (nr 1413-2), public nuisance (nr 1504-2), the *Rule in Rylands v Fletcher* (nr 1414-2), and breach of statutory duty. As regards the latter the most important examples are the Defective Premises Act 1972, the Occupiers' Liability Act 1957, the Occupiers' Liability Act 1984, and the Highway Act 1980 (see about the latter Act nr 1507).

According to s. 1(1) of the Defective Premises Act 1972, builders, sub-contractors, and architects who take on work for or in connection with the provision of a dwelling (whether the dwelling is provided by the erection or by the conversion or enlargement of a building) owe a duty to third parties to see that the work which they take on is done in a workmanlike or, as the case may be, professional manner, with proper materials and so that, as regards that work, the dwelling will be fit for habitation when completed. This rule is said to be stricter than in negligence.[41]

The Occupiers' Liability Acts apply to damage which someone suffers on someone else's premises. Premises include the movables which are on the premises. Section 1(3)(a) speaks about the '. . . control over any fixed or movable structure, including any vessel, vehicle or aircraft.' One may also think of smaller movables like for instance a ladder.[42]

It depends on the circumstances of the case who can be considered to be the occupier. In this respect the rules of property law are not relevant. According to s. 1(2) of the Occupiers' Liability Act 1957 the relevant question is who occupies or has control over the premises. Factual control is generally considered to be decisive but this is not always the case: for example, a building contractor is

---

[39] BGH 28 January 1976, BGHZ 66, 51 = NJW 1976, 712 = JZ 1976, 776 = VersR 1976, 589, about which Markesinis and Unberath (2002), 789–793. Apart from the third party effect, the issue at stake here was that it was unclear when exactly the contract was concluded. The BGH said that this should not matter and therefore held that even if there had not been a full-fledged contract there would be a precontractual relationship (*vorvertragliches Schuldverhältnis*). Both issues are now codified in § 311 BGB.
[40] The leading work is still P.M. North, *Occupiers' Liability* (London: Butterworths, 1971).
[41] Markesinis and Deakin (2003), 355–356.   [42] *Wheeler v Copas* [1981] 3 All ER 405.

regarded as an occupier but a decorator is not.[43] 'The foundation of occupier's liability is occupational control, ie control associated with and arising from presence in and use of or activity in the premises.'[44] In this respect, the definition of occupier is comparable to that of the French *gardien* within article 1384 al. 1 CC (nr 303-3).[45]

The rules in the Occupiers' Liability Acts are based on negligence and the applicable standard does not really differ from the duty of care in the framework of the tort of negligence. Also the burden of proof is still with the claimant. Section 2(2) of the Occupiers' Liability Act 1957 describes the occupier's duty as follows:

The common duty of care is a duty to take such care as in all the circumstances of the case is reasonable to see that the visitor will be reasonably safe in using the premises for the purposes for which he is invited or permitted by the occupier to be there.

This duty focuses on the safety of the visitor rather than on that of the premises.[46]

It is required that the risk arising on the premises was '. . . due to the state of the premises or to things done or omitted to be done on them.'[47] This was at stake in a case about a man who suffered serious injuries when he dived into a lake at the defendant's country park and hit his head on the sandy bottom. Because of the various risks, the responsible borough had issued a swimming ban for the lake and had enforced it by distributing leaflet warnings and employing rangers. A majority of the House of Lords held that '. . . the only risk arose out of what [the claimant] chose to do and not out of the state of the premises.'[48] This interpretation leads to an all or nothing approach: if it had been established that the occupier had breached its duty, contributory negligence of the claimant could have led to a more subtle solution. According to Oliphant, the House of Lords's approach pre-empts the truly important questions: '. . . whether the defendant acted reasonably and whether and to what extent the accident can be attributed to the claimant's own conduct.'[49]

Section 2(3) holds that '. . . an occupier must be prepared for children to be less careful than adults'. Already in 1913 Hamilton J held:

The child must take the place as he finds it and take care of himself; but how can he take care of himself? If his injury is not to go without legal remedy altogether by reason of his failure to use a diligence which he could not possibly have possessed, the owner of the close might be practically bound to see that the wandering child is as safe as in a nursery.[50]

---

[43] Winfield and Jolowicz (2002), para. 9.4; Markesinis and Deakin (2003), 331–333.
[44] Lord Pearson in *Wheat v Lacon & Co Ltd* [1966] AC 552, 589.
[45] Von Bar (1998), N 363.
[46] Markesinis and Deakin (2003), 337; Winfield and Jolowicz (2002), para. 9.8.
[47] S. 1(1) of the Occupier's Liability Act 1957 and s. 1(1)(a) of the Occupier's Liability Act 1984.
[48] *Tomlinson v Congleton Borough Council* [2003] UKHL 47, 1 AC 46, ETL 2003, 132 (Oliphant). [49] Ken Oliphant, ETL 2003, 134.
[50] Hamilton LJ in *Latham v R Johnson & Nephew Ltd* [1913] 1 KB 398.

More generally Lord Fraser said that '... the duty will tend to be higher in a question with a very young or very old person than in the question with a normally active and intelligent adult or adolescent'.[51]

The occupier owes a duty of care to visitors; these are persons who have an implicit or explicit permission to enter. One may think of the guest of a hotel, the customer in a shop, and the visitors of recreation areas. The onus of proof about the permission is on the visitor. Canvassers are not visitors if they have passed a sign with: 'no canvassers, hawkers or circulars'.[52] Sometimes the occupier has to protect the visitor against the violence of a third party.[53]

If someone is not a visitor, he will be considered to be a trespasser. The common law did not provide for a general duty towards trespassers[54] but the Occupiers' Liability Act 1984 does. According to section 1(3), the occupier only owes the duty if

(a) he is aware of the danger or has reasonable grounds to believe that it exists; (b) he knows or has reasonable grounds to believe that the other is in the vicinity of the danger concerned or that he may come into the vicinity of the danger (...); and (c) the risk is one against which, in all the circumstances of the case, he may reasonably be expected to offer the other some protection.

All in all, the required level of care towards a trespasser is only slightly lower than towards a visitor. One difference is that it is easier to discharge the duty of care to trespassers by warnings and prohibitions than to visitors.[55] Another important difference is that the occupier's duty towards trespassers only concerns personal injury and not property damage.[56]

In a case prior to the Occupiers' Liability Act 1984, Lord Reid said in *British Railways Board v Herrington*:

Normally the common law applies an objective test (...). If a person chooses to assume a relationship with members of the public, say by setting out to drive a car or to erect a building fronting a highway, the law requires him to conduct himself as a reasonable man with adequate skill, knowledge and resources would do (...). But an occupier does not voluntarily assume a relationship with trespassers. By trespassing they force a 'neighbour' relationship on him. When they do so he must act in a humane

---

[51] *McGinlay or Titchener v BR Board* [1983] 1 WLR 1427, 1432–1433. See furthermore *Glasgow Corporation v Taylor* [1922] 1 AC 44. Winfield and Jolowicz (2002), para. 9.7; Markesinis and Deakin (2003), 337–339.

[52] Winfield and Jolowicz (2002), para. 9.6; Markesinis and Deakin (2003), 337.

[53] *Cunningham v Reading Football Club Ltd*, The Times 22 March 1991, about which nr 1506-5.

[54] See, however, *British Railways Board v Herrington* [1972] AC 877, in which the idea of 'a duty of common humanity' was introduced but the scope of this duty was far from clear.

[55] This follows from the difference between s. 2(4)(a) of the Occupiers' Liability Act 1957 and s. 1(5) of the Occupiers' Liability Act 1984.

[56] S. 1(1) of the Occupiers' Liability Act 1984. Winfield and Jolowicz (2002), para. 9.7 en 9.24; Markesinis and Deakin (2003), 334–335.

manner—that is not asking too much of him—but I do not see why he should be required to do more.[57]

1504-2 *Public nuisance*

As has been pointed out, a public nuisance consists of an interference with a public or common right, such as an obstruction of the highway. It requires that the claimant has suffered special damage, which means that the damage is not related to general inconveniences: the damage has to be distinct from that of the general public.

Public nuisance only covers cases in which someone suffers damage while outside the premises. One may think of someone who, outside a butcher's shop, slips on a piece of fat which came from the shop,[58] someone who is injured by snow falling from a roof[59] and a passer-by who is injured by a collapsing house.[60] If someone suffers damage while *inside* the building he has to base his claim on the tort of negligence or the Occupiers' Liability Acts because in such a case there is no infringement of a common right.[61]

According to Markesinis and Deakin, a claim for special damages based on public nuisance requires negligent conduct though negligence is presumed and it is up to the defendant to prove that he did not act negligently.[62] In *Wringe v Cohen*, a case about premises partly collapsing because of want of repair, the Court of Appeal held that the defendant was liable unless the collapse occurred through the act of a trespasser or by a secret and unobservable operation of nature.[63] This decision does not differ strongly from what would have been decided under the German § 836–838 BGB (nr 1503-1).[64]

Liability based on public nuisance for falling *natural* projections (for example a branch from a tree) seems to be less strict. In such a case it needs to be established that the occupier knew or should have known of the defect that caused the collapse. *Noble v Harrison* was about a vehicle that was damaged when a branch of a tree growing on the defendant's land and overhanging a highway suddenly broke. The mere fact that the branch overhung the highway did not constitute a nuisance because it did not obstruct free passage. The break appeared to be caused by a latent defect which was not discoverable by reasonable and careful inspection. On the basis of a negligence test, the defendant was held not liable because he had not created the danger and there was neither actual nor implied knowledge of the break.[65]

---

[57] Lord Reid in *British Railways Board v Herrington* [1972] AC 877, 898–899.
[58] *Dollman v Hillman* [1941] 1 All ER 355.
[59] *Slate v Worthington Cash Stores Ltd* [1941] 1 KB 488 (CA).
[60] *Mint v Good* [1951] 1 KB 517.   [61] Fleming (1998), 461–462.
[62] Markesinis and Deakin (2003), 490.   [63] *Wringe v Cohen* [1940] 1 KB 229.
[64] See also von Bar (1998), N 269.
[65] *Noble v Harrison* [1926] 2 KB 332; *Caminer v Northern and London Investment Trust Ltd* [1951] AC 88 (HL).

B NEGLIGENCE AND STRICT LIABILITY

1505 Relation between negligence and strict liability

It follows from the overview above that strict liability rules generally have a rather limited scope of application. The English tort of public nuisance, the German § 836–838, and the French article 1386 CC provide for rules regarding (partly) collapsing buildings. In France this is a strict liability, whereas in Germany this is a liability for rebuttable negligence. The same goes for England although in certain circumstances it is up to the claimant to prove negligence. Moreover, the English rule only applies to persons who were outside the collapsing building.

Considering the limited scope of these rules, the general rules for fault liability remain of great importance. One may not only think of the restrictions as to the way the damage occurs but also as regards the protected interests. For instance, § 836–838 BGB only protect against death, personal injury, and property damage. Pure economic loss has to be recovered on the basis of other provisions like § 823 II (breach of a statutory duty), § 826 (intentional infliction of damage *contra bonos mores*), or breach of contract (nr 713).

From a practical point of view, it is conceivable that the strictly liable person is not able to pay damages, for instance because he does not have liability insurance, his liability exceeds the insured maximum amount, or the insurer does not pay at all, for instance in cases of undisclosed information or a *claims made* coverage. In such a case it is important to see whether another person can also be liable for the damage on the basis of fault.

Apart from collapsing buildings, English and German law apply rules of fault liability whereas in France in most other cases strict liability rules apply. The differences in this respect should not be overestimated. The most important difference is that, in strict liability rules, the onus of proof will be on the defendant, whereas in fault cases it will be on the claimant. A French case was about a child that fell from an escalator in a hotel and was injured. The *Cour de cassation* decided on the basis of article 1384 al. 1 (strict liability for things) that the custodian (*gardien*) of the escalator (the operator of the hotel) was liable for the damage unless he could prove *force majeure*, in the sense that the accident was neither caused by the escalator's operation nor that the accident could have been foreseen or avoided by the hotel.[66] If such a case had been decided on the basis of fault, the burden of proof would have been on the claimant. He has to prove intentional or negligent conduct of the hotel operator, for instance bad maintenance of the escalator, and that the accident could have been foreseen or avoided by the hotel.

---

[66] Civ. 2e 2 April 1997, D. 1997. IR. 105 ('...que l'accident avait une cause étrangère au fonctionnement de l'escalator et révêtait à l'égard de l'hôtel un caractère imprévisible et irrésistible').

However, in more striking cases the claimant's burden of proof may be mitigated by the courts by accepting *prima facie* evidence and applying the *res ipsa loquitur* principle. One may think of a chimney pot falling off a roof, a hot water tank exploding, or a pothole in the road. If a strict liability rule applies, the responsible person will generally be liable unless he can prove *force majeure*, a comparable defence, or contributory negligence. If a fault rule applies, it is basically for the claimant to prove that the defendant knew of the danger or the defect. In these kinds of cases, the courts will often be inclined to conclude that the sudden defect or danger is an indication of a lack of maintenance. It will then for the present assume negligence and give the defendant the opportunity to make clear or at least plausible that he has fulfilled his duty of care as regards design, checking, and maintenance of the premises, grounds, or roads. If the principle of *res ipsa loquitur* is applied, this will come close to the German rules of § 836–838 BGB (nr 1503-1).

1506 Common issues in negligence and strict liability

1506-1 *Liable person*

The rules of stricter liability explicitly indicate the liable person. In France (article 1386) and England (public nuisance) this is the owner, whereas in Germany it is the possessor. The latter is mostly, though not always, also the owner.

If liability is based on a general rule (in France a general strict rule and in the other countries a general fault rule), the potentially liable person is established on the basis of the circumstances of the case. This means that the liable person is the one who has the factual, and to a certain extent, legal control over the premises, grounds, or roads. In France this is the *gardien*, in Germany the *Verkehrspflichtige*, and in England the *occupier*.

In Germany it has been inimitably stated that the *Verkehrspflichtige* has *die Verantwortung für einen räumlich-gegenständlichen Herrschaftsbereich*, ie is responsible for the space within his powers of control.[67] A safety duty rests on the person who, by virtue of legal or factual authority, has the factual and legal potential to autonomously take the required safety measures at the premises, grounds, or roads.[68]

In the French strict liability rule for things (article 1384 al. 1), the custodian (*le gardien*) also has to be determined on a factual basis. This implies that it is decisive who, at the moment of the accident, has the use, control, and direction over the thing (*l'usage, le contrôle et la direction*, nr 303-3).

---

[67] Larenz-Canaris (1994) § 76 III 1, 400.
[68] BGH 30 April 1953, BGHZ 9, 373; BGH 15 June 1954, BGHZ 14, 83 = NJW 1954, 1403; BGH 29 November 1983, NJW 1984, 801. Münchener Kommentar-Wagner (2004), § 823 N 225: 'Unabdingbare Voraussetzung ist (...) die tatsächliche und rechtliche Möglichkeit zur Gefahrsteuerung im konkreten Einzelfall.'

The English Occupiers' Liability Act 1957 provides that the person who occupies or has control over the premises is the liable person (s. 1(3)). Who this person is, is also dependent on the circumstances of the case.

In all jurisdictions it is required that the supervisor has authority over the place and the possibility of improving its safety, which means that he is not just entitled but also obliged to take precautionary measures. This factual approach implies that supervisor can be the owner, the long lease-holder, the tenant, the lessee, and the administrator. It also implies that there can be more than one supervisor at the same time. Particularly at a building site complicated situations are conceivable: duties to take safety measures can be divided or converge between the inspector, the building contractor, the owner, or the subcontractors.[69]

Children generally will not qualify as supervisor and hence will not owe a safety duty to visitors. Though they might factually be able to take precautionary measures, they will generally not be obliged to do so.[70] The reason is that children do not have authority with regard to the premises, and that they are not, or only to a certain extent, able to improve its safety. This does not rule out that a child can be liable for the damage he actively causes to other people on 'his or her' premises, grounds, or roads. Moreover, rules of strict liability usually apply regardless of the liable person's age. If the child owns a building, the stricter rule of liability will apply. If this were different, it would be easy to circumvent the rules of stricter liability.

According to German law the owner or tenant can transfer his safety duty (*Verkehrspflicht*) to a third party. In this case, the safety duty of the owner or tenant is reduced to the duty to appoint an appropriate third party and to supervise him. The BGH takes the view that the first obligor is not liable for the negligence of the delegate.[71] Most authors do not agree with this and argue that this wrongly implies that the insolvency risk of the third party is to be borne by the victim and not by the owner or the tenant.[72] In other jurisdictions such a transfer does not seem to be possible, at least not in the sense that the person who owes the duty can prevent liability towards the victim. This means that a transfer can be effective between the parties involved (it can have 'internal' effect) but not between the liable persons and the victim (no 'external' effect').

1506-2 *Character of the premises*

The character of the premises or the ground can influence the extent of precautionary measures to be taken by the supervisor. For instance in Germany, the

---

[69] BGH 19 December 1984, NJW 1985, 1078.
[70] See for instance HR 22 November 1974, NJ 1975, 149, comm. GJS (Breadman). See also nr 1702-1.
[71] BGH 25 October 1951, BGHZ 4, 1 = NJW 1952, 418; BGH 19 October 1988, NJW-RR 1989, 394; Münchener Kommentar-Wagner (2004), § 823 N 288–295.
[72] See for example Kötz-Wagner (2001), N 238–239.

visitor to a private ground or building is not entitled to expect the same safety as on public grounds or in a public building.[73] This point of view is related to the element of the character of the conduct, in the framework of negligence (nr 807).

If premises and grounds are intended to be used for the performance of certain activities (such as sports or games) or if they are intended to be visited by a lot of people (such as stadiums), this has to be taken into account in the design and the layout of the premises or grounds. In such cases the effectiveness of safety measures is greater since more people benefit from them. An example is an English case about doors in a corridor of a municipal school containing simple glass panes. When a 12-year-old girl tried to stop a swaying door the breaking glass severely injured her hand. The court decided that the school had acted negligently by not putting safety glass in the windows.[74] This is now the common standard, and it makes sense because all users of the building benefit from this measure.

The safety of the premises or roads is not only to be improved by physical measures but also by people supervising the premises, grounds, and roads. This is usually expensive because it has to be done by paid personnel. This, however, does not rule out that intensive investigation can be required if more visitors can benefit from it One may think of premises where many visitors are to be expected, such as shops, stadiums, and roads (nr 807-1).[75]

It is common knowledge that a person is less attentive if he is a member of a group. Therefore, people behave less intelligently in company than when they are alone. If a supervisor knows that his premises or grounds will be visited by groups, he will have to take into account that warnings will be less effective to inform the groups about certain risks. In such circumstances it will be often preferable to eliminate risks rather than to restrict them (nr 807-2).[76]

The premises' character can imply that the risk does not need to be taken away but that it is sufficient if the supervisor warns about it in an effective way. This is, for instance, the case in historic (listed) buildings: the nature of the building can be an obstacle for a duty to remove the risk, particularly if this would harm the ancient character of the building. One may think of narrow stairs, treacherous steps, and low ceilings. Normally the supervisor will have a duty to remove the risk by physically changing the potentially dangerous situation. But if the particular part of the building is of historic value, this value can be taken into account, which means that the supervisor can confine himself to warning visitors in a clear and effective way.

[73] BGH 7 November 1967, VersR 1968, 68.
[74] *Reffell v Surrey County Council* [1964] 1 WLR 358.
[75] See about the duty of department stores to take precautionary measures to prevent slippery floors: BGH 11 March 1986, NJW 1986, 2757 = VersR 1986, 765 and BGH 5 July 1994, NJW 1994, 2617. See also BGH 28 February 1966, VersR 1966, 684: strong demands may be required of the owner of a building in which many tenants live.
[76] Münchener Kommentar-Wagner (2004), § 823 N 257 ff.

One may for instance think of old gravestones in churchyards. The supervisor of the church is not obliged to take these gravestones away, and it can be argued that he does not even have a duty to warn. It is also debatable whether a church is always obliged to take care to have good lighting. When someone tripped in a semi-lit French church, the court denied the church's liability, considering that the special character of the place justified the twilight and that more attentiveness can be required from the visitor.[77] So, the court allowed the church's twilight and admonished the stumbling visitor to mend his ways.

The character of a scenic area can also be an objection to removing the risk in order to let nature be nature. Generally, the scenic area's supervisor is not obliged to remove the risk but he can confine himself to warning about the risk in a clear and effective way. Such a duty to warn will particularly exist if he has special knowledge of a risk, whereas it can be expected that the visitor will not have that knowledge.

What goes for scenic areas does not always go for parks in cities and villages, where fewer objections exist to remove risks. An old English case was about a 7-year-old boy, who picked berries in a park. They looked like harmless cherries, he ate them and was poisoned, as a consequence of which he died. The court held the park's supervisors liable because they breached their *occupier's duty* to warn about the risk.[78] A century later it seems to be more appropriate to decide that a warning was not sufficient and that the supervisor was obliged to take the bush away. This would not noticeably affect the value of the park. More generally it could be argued that poisonous plants, bushes, or trees are not allowed in gardens, green areas, parks, and recreation areas because the risk that man or animal will suffer harm from them is too high. Exceptions could be made for botanical gardens in which warnings will be sufficient, and as regards plants spontaneously springing up, such as toadstools.

The required safety level of premises is not only determined by its character but also by the local circumstances. For instance, in areas in which snow is a regular winter feature, constructional provisions can be required in order to prevent layers of snow and ice falling off the roof. In France this duty, for instance, does not apply to buildings in Paris because it seldom snows in Paris and thus investments in constructional provisions will not be balanced by the magnitude of the risk.[79]

1506-3 *Unauthorized visitors*

It goes without saying that liability of the supervisor of premises, grounds, and roads primarily aims to protect authorized visitors, ie those persons who are

---

[77] Civ. 2e 19 July 1966, JCP 1967. 15228, comm. Dejean de la Bathie, Gaz. Pal. 1966. II. 222 ('... la nature particulière des lieux justifie la pénombre; celle-ci imposait, de plus, une vigilance de la victime.') [78] *Glasgow Corporation v Taylor* [1922] 1 AC 44. [79] Civ. 1re 9 June 1975, JCP 1977. 18544 (1re espèce).

explicitly or implicitly allowed by the supervisor to enter. The question of whether this is the case will also depend on the character of the premises. Everyone is entitled to use a road, unless this is forbidden, but no one will be allowed to enter a house, unless he has explicitly been invited by the supervisor. It will be clear that the scope of the supervisor's liability is not to protect the burglar, but the key question is where to put the boundaries.[80]

In many cases the supervisor can confine himself to prohibit entry to a road, grounds, or a building. Sometimes such a ban follows from the character of the premises, for instance if it is a house. If someone disregards a ban to enter, French law considers his conduct as amounting to 100 per cent contributory negligence, whereas German law will, in principle, hold that the supervisor has discharged his duties. This implies that the unauthorized visitor has deprived himself of the protection provided by tort law and that he has to bear the harmful consequences of the risks on or in the premises. English law seems to be more claimant-friendly, under certain circumstances imposing on the occupier a duty to trespassers to prevent them from harm (nr 1504-1).

In most cases, however, it is not sufficient for a supervisor to just prohibit entering the premises or grounds. In order to prevent mistakes by potential visitors, the ban to enter must be sufficiently visible and clear, in such a way that it should not be possible for a reasonable visitor to make a mistake. This means that the visitor will only be considered as unauthorized if he has entered the premises against his better judgment.

Secondly, a ban will generally be insufficient if the risk is too big or if it is unknown to the public. In such a case the reason for the ban needs to be specifically indicated. If the risks are too high and the character of the premises allows it, the supervisor should go further by making it virtually impossible to enter the premises.

Finally, supervisors have to take into account that bans to enter are usually not effective against children's investigating and adventurous nature. Hence, young visitors are generally qualified as unauthorized only if the entrance of the premises was child-proof. If proper closure of the site is not possible, either for financial reasons or because of the character of the premises, the supervisor can confine himself to a ban to enter, provided the ban is accompanied with a sufficiently clear and penetrating warning for children.

1506-4 *Negligent visitors*

In the framework of fault liability, it has been pointed out that one has to take into account that other people do not always behave carefully, and that it can be important to prevent people from suffering damage because of their own negligence (nr 807-4). This goes particularly for the supervisor of premises and grounds.

---

[80] Kötz-Wagner (1998), N 250.

The starting point is that the supervisor has to remove the risks the visitor does not need to expect.[81] The mirror of this starting point is that the supervisor does not have to warn of or remove risks which are known to visitors or which are easily recognizable and visible.[82] As regards the latter one may think of the possibility of falling off a staircase, even when all safety measures are met. The supervisor of the staircase does not owe a duty to remove this risk or to warn for it, provided the stairs are even and there is a proper railing.

Taking into account a visitor's imprudence is particularly important when people are expected to be less attentive. This is for instance the case in a restaurant or a pub where visitors are under the influence of alcohol and can therefore act foolishly or be absent-minded.[83] The same goes for drunken passengers, such as in an American case about a drunken passenger who was put out of the train at a station where high steep stairs led to the street. The train guard accompanied the passenger halfway down the stairs and left him there. When the passenger tried to descend to street level he fell and was injured. The railway was held liable for the injuries because it had not accompanied the drunken passenger until he had reached a safer place outside the premises of the railway station.[84]

Special care has to be taken towards children, as is for instance explicitly provided in England by s. 2(3)(a) of the Occupiers' Liability Act. A supervisor has to be prepared for children to be rash, impulsive, and less careful than adults. For instance, the supervisor of a children's playground has to take measures in order to prevent children from impulsively crossing the adjacent road.[85] A boarding school ought to know that children around the age of 12 are not always able to resist the temptation to use a stair's handrail as a slide. It cannot confine itself to giving warnings but it has to take away the temptation, for instance by covering the handrail with rough material.[86]

Particularly in swimming pools, children's impulsiveness is an important issue. The operator of pools and baths has to mark deep and shallow parts clearly, particularly in respect of children.[87] A simple ban from diving is insufficient if the shallowness of the water is not clearly indicated.[88] However, if this is the case the swimming pool supervisor has complied with its duty of care. Hence, the operator of a swimming pool was not liable for the damage of a 15-year-old boy

[81] BGH 19 May 1978, VersR 1978, 739 = NJW 1978, 1629. See also BGH 23 October 1984, NJW 1985, 620 = VersR 1985, 64, with regard to the duty of the operator of a ski lift to protect falling skiers against the iron pillars of the lift; see about this decision nr 810-2.
[82] BGH 19 May 1978, VersR 1978, 739 = NJW 1978, 1629.
[83] HR 5 November 1965, NJ 1966, 136, comm. GJS (cellar-flap).
[84] *Black v New York* (1907) 79 NE 797.
[85] BGH 21 April 1977, VersR 1977, 817. See also *Carmarthenshire County Council v Lewis* [1956] AC 549, about which nr 1604.
[86] BGH 11 March 1980, NJW 1980, 1745. According to OLG Celle 6 July 1983, MDR 1983, 933, this duty is not owed to adult persons.
[87] BGH 18 October 1988, VersR 1989, 155 = JZ 1989, 249, about which nr 1503-2. All legal systems (including that of the EU) have statutory provisions on the safety of swimming pools and baths.   [88] BGH 16 February 1982, VersR 1982, 492 (Raft).

who broke his neck after diving steeply downwards at a place where the water was only 90 centimetres deep when this was sufficiently clearly indicated. The BGH considered that the operator was not obliged to take into account foolish and extremely imprudent conduct (*ganz unvernünftiges und äußerst leichtfertiges Verhalten*) of young people.[89]

It goes without saying that an imprudent visitor may be faced with the supervisor's defence that the visitor does not have a right to full compensation because of contributory negligence (nr 1212).

1506-5 *Protection of visitors against each other*

Not only is the supervisor obliged to supervise the safety of his premises and ground but he may also have to supervise the conduct of the visitors, for instance in swimming pools and stadiums.[90] The aim of this rule is to protect the visitors not only against their own imprudence (nr 1506-4) but also against the imprudence of other visitors.

If many people can be expected to attend an event and there is a reasonable risk that an accident will occur, the supervisor is at least bound to have first aid available; in swimming pools rescuers and respirators are also required.[91] Even if the supervisor is not liable for the accident—for instance someone gets cramp during swimming, or one visitor is injured by another for which the supervisor is not to blame—he is in principle liable if first aid is not available in time and as a consequence the victim suffers more damage.

Duties to protect visitors against other visitors' imprudence apply, for instance, to organizers of professional soccer games and other mass meetings. In such cases stadiums ought to have tested evacuation plans available and, in case of emergency, exits must be opened immediately.[92] Generally, sporting associations have regulations applying to the safety of visitors of stadiums; the breach of such a regulation can be an indication for negligence.

Under certain circumstances the supervisor may even owe a duty to protect visitors against criminal acts of other visitors, provided the supervisor knew of the risk or ought to have known of it. During an English soccer game hooligans dislodged pieces of concrete and threw them at the police. Such an incident had already happened before. The club was held liable because it had breached its duty of care towards the policemen and women.[93]

If a supervisor neither knew nor ought to have known that visitors were going to commit criminal acts on his premises, he will not be liable towards the injured visitor (nr 810-2). This is for instance the case when suddenly and unexpectedly

---

[89] BGH 22 October 1980, VersR 1980, 863 = NJW 1980, 1159.
[90] BGH 18 October 1988, VersR 1989, 155 = JZ 1989, 249, about which nr 1503-2.
[91] Münchener Kommentar-Wagner (2004), § 823 N 482.
[92] *Alcock v Chief Constable of South Yorkshire* [1992] 1 AC 310, about which nr 1211.
[93] *Cunningham v Reading Football Club Ltd*, The Times 22 March 1991.

a fight breaks out in a usually quiet café. In such a case the operator is not liable for the harmful consequences if, for instance, a visitor is stabbed with a knife by another visitor.[94]

Generally, the supervisor's duty to protect against criminal behaviour will be with regard to personal injury rather than property damage. A German case was about a guard who was held personally liable for damage caused by the theft during his duty of a fur, valued at DM 60,000 (€30,500).[95] Yet, the BGH rejected a general duty to protect another person's property against theft or damage. This difference can also be explained by considering that in personal injury cases the burden of precautionary measures will be more easily set off by the risk than in cases of property damage.

An infamous example as to what level of care may be expected from organizers of big events as regards criminal behaviour is the Monica Seles case. Tennis player Monica Seles was attacked at a tournament in Hamburg in 1993. During an interval between two games a man stabbed her in the back with a knife. Later he told the police that he could not accept that Seles had a higher ATP ranking than his favourite Steffi Graf. The attack interrupted Seles' tennis career for some years. She filed a claim for more than DM 24 million (€12.25 million) against the tournament organizer but the local court in Hamburg dismissed the claim. It established that until 1993 a tennis player had never been attacked during a comparable tournament. It also established that the organizer did not have to know of the risk since it was not obvious at that time.[96] Since 1993, safety measures have been increased: the players' chairs are at a greater distance from the stands and during breaks ball boys and girls face the audience.

Much better known is the risk that before, during, and after soccer matches conflicts may arise between supporters of the contesting clubs. As regards this risk the supervisor has to take adequate precautionary measures. An example of how things can go wrong is the Heyzel drama, during the European Cup final in 1985 between Liverpool and Juventus in the Brussels' Heyzel Stadium, causing the death of many Juventus fans. The Brussels Court of Appeal decided that the organizer of the match, the Belgian Football Association, had breached its safety duty towards the spectators. It had permitted the match to be played in a stadium that was unfit for the number of spectators, it had insufficiently taken into account the risk that supporters of both clubs could enter each other's sections of the stands, and it did not inform authorities about the increased risk of the match.[97]

---

[94] KG 22 December 1970, VersR 1972, 157.

[95] BGH 16 June 1987, NJW 1987, 2510 = VersR 1988, 34: 'Eine allgemeine Rechtspflicht, fremdes Eigentum gegen Gefahren zu schützen und vor Diebstahl oder Beschädigung zu bewahren, besteht nicht'. In the same sense already: BGH 28 April 1953, BGHZ 9, 301 = NJW 1953, 1180. See also *Deyong v Shenburn* [1946] 1 KB 236: the employer does not have a duty to protect the employee's property against theft.   [96] LG Hamburg 19 December 1996, NJW 1997, 2606.

[97] Hof Brussel 26 June 1990, RGAR 1991, no 11.757. In the same decision it was held that the police (*Rijkswacht*) acted negligently because a police officer who was on the premises did not take action, although the situation in the stadium should definitely have alarmed him.

C ROADS

1507 England: Highways Act 1980

Liability for highways is intertwined with liability of public bodies (nr 1804). The topic is, however, dealt with here, because it is structurally more linked to immovable objects, thus the object for which one is liable, than to the person who is liable.

In English law liability of the highway authority can be based on the torts of negligence, public nuisance (nr 1500-0), and breach of statutory duty. The latter duties can be found mainly in the Highways Act 1980.[98] The Act does not hold rules of strict liability but it imposes on the highway authority a negligence liability with a reversed burden of proof.

Section 41(1) of the Highways Act 1980 holds a general duty for the highway authority to maintain the highway. Section 58(1) provides that if a highway authority has failed to maintain the highway and damage occurs, it may not only invoke the defence of contributory negligence but it may also prove that it had taken such care as in all the circumstances was reasonably required to secure that the part of the highway to which the action relates was not dangerous to traffic.

For the purposes of a defence under s. 58(1), the court shall in particular have regard to:

(a) the character of the highway, and the traffic which was reasonably expected to use it; (b) the standard of maintenance appropriate for a highway of that character and used by such traffic; (c) the state of repair in which a reasonable person would have expected to find the highway; (d) whether the highway authority knew, or could reasonably have been expected to know, that the condition of the part of the highway to which the action relates was likely to cause danger to users of the highway; (e) where the highway authority could not reasonably have been expected to repair that part of the highway before the cause of the action arose, what warning notices of its condition had been displayed.[99]

In practice the highway authority's duty of care focuses on the question of whether the road is sufficiently safe. If the road user is able to prove that this was not the case, the onus of proof shifts to the highway authority, which may prove that it performed its duties with due care or that it established priorities in a proper way, given its financial means.[100] The level of care of the highway authority should not be related to the model road user but to the ordinary driver who is inclined to make a mistake (see also nr 1506-4).[101] The Highways Act

---

[98] Winfield and Jolowicz (2002), para. 14.42; Fleming (1998), 484–488; Markesinis and Deakin (2003), 492.
[99] See also Winfield and Jolowicz (2002), 14.42; Markesinis and Deakin (2003), 492.
[100] *Haydon v Kent County Council* [1978] QB 343.
[101] *Rider v Rider* [1973] QB 505; *Tarrant v Rowlands* [1979] RTR 144. Winfield and Jolowicz (2002), para. 14.44.

does not govern all kinds of harmful incidents on the highway. For instance, the responsibility for well-functioning traffic lights cannot be based on the Highways Act but has to be based on the tort of negligence.[102] Also, the highway authority's duty only relates to the physical condition of the road and not to the painting of warning markings on it.[103]

According to s. 41(1)(1A) the highway authority also has to ensure, so far as is reasonably practicable, that safe passage along a highway is not endangered by snow or ice. This provision reversed the House of Lords' decision in *Goodes v East Sussex County Council* that the highway authority's duty did not extend to gritting or salting the road to prevent the accumulation of ice or the removal of snow.[104]

A very important case in this respect is *Stovin v Wise*.[105] Mr Stovin was injured when his motorcycle collided with Mrs Wise's car. Mrs Wise's view of approaching traffic had been obstructed by a raised bank of earth adjacent to the road. The highway authority's duty to maintain the highway did not apply here because the highway as such was in good order.[106] Though s. 79 of the Highways Act 1980 provides the highway authority with the statutory *power* to require landowners to remove dangerous obstructions to the view of road users, the question is whether the authority was *obliged* to do so. The House of Lords decided that this was not the case, even though the authority a year before the accident had started to take action by writing to the landowner but had then not taken further action. In his leading speech Lord Hoffman said that in such a case of non-exercise of a statutory power the authority would only be liable if it would have been irrational not to have exercised the power. He concluded '. . . that the question of whether anything should be done about the junction was at all times firmly within the area of the [highway authority's] discretion.' This issue is strongly connected to liability for omissions (nr 808), particularly of public bodies and will be more thoroughly analysed in nr 1804.

Another illustration of the reluctant approach towards liability of highway authorities is *Gorringe v Calderdale Metropolitan Borough Council*. Mrs Gorringe, driving too fast on a country road, reached the crest of a rise and then braked sharply, probably because she thought a bus coming towards her was on her side of the road. She skidded, collided head-on with the bus, and suffered severe injuries. She claimed that the highway authority should have provided a warning by painting the word 'SLOW' on the road surface on the approach to the crest. The House of Lords unanimously held that the highway authority's duty to maintain did not include the painting of warning markings. Probably concerned

---

[102] *Lavis v Kent CC* [1992] 90 LGR 425.
[103] *Gorringe v Calderdale Metropolitan Borough Council* [2004] UKHL 15, [2004] 1 WLR 1057, [2004] 2 All ER 326, ETL 2004, 234 (Oliphant); see below.
[104] *Goodes v East Sussex County Council* [2000] 1 WLR 1356.
[105] *Stovin v Wise* [1996] AC 923.
[106] It would have been a case of public nuisance by the owner of the adjacent land if parts of the bank of earth had slid onto the highway (nr 1504-2).

by what is called the 'compensation culture', their Lordships strongly shifted the responsibility from the highway authority to the road user. Lord Rodger of Earlsferry said: 'By insisting that drivers always look out for dangers themselves and not rely on others, the common law supports the overall policy of promoting road safety.'[107]

Finally, constructors can also have a duty of care towards road users. This duty is not based on the Highways Act 1980 but on the tort of negligence. For example, in *Haley v London Electricity Board*, the court established that the number of visually handicapped people using the pavement unaccompanied is sufficiently high to take into account when determining the character of precautionary measures to indicate construction work.[108]

1508 France: *Droit administratif*

In France the applicable liability regime for roads depends on the question whether the road is a private or a public one. Liability for private roads is governed by article 1384 al. 1 CC but most roads are publicly owned and in these cases liability is governed by administrative law (*droit administratif*). Claims are decided by administrative courts and in highest resort by the *Conseil d'Etat* (State Council) (nr 301-3). The administrative courts have developed a full fledged liability regime for public authorities, ranging from negligence (*responsabilité pour faute*) to strict liability (*responsabilité sans faute*). See about the French regime of administrative liability nr 1802.[109]

As regards liability for highways, administrative law imposes a liability for rebuttable negligence. The public highway authority is liable for damage caused by a lack of maintenance of the road (*défaut d'entretien normal*) unless it proves that it has maintained the road in a proper way.[110] This regime is less strict than the regime of article 1384 al. 1. Examples are pieces falling down from a balustrade at the Paris Opéra and a defective traffic signal installation at the entrance of a one-way road.[111] The assumption of negligent maintenance for the highway authority even applies if a driver makes an abnormal use of the road. This was for example the case when a driver used a towpath without having an authorization to do so.[112]

---

[107] *Gorringe v Calderdale Metropolitan Borough Council* [2004] UKHL 15, [2004] 1 WLR 1057, 2 All ER [2004] 326, ETL 2004, 234 (Oliphant), §82 per Lord Rodger of Earlsferry. See for a similar policy approach *Tomlinson v Congleton Borough Council* [2003] UKHL 47, 1 AC 46, ETL 2003, 132 (Oliphant), about which nr 1504-1.

[108] *Haley v London Electricity Board* [1965] AC 778, about which nr 806-2.

[109] René Chapus, *Droit administratif général*, 3rd edn. (Paris: Montchrestien, 1987), nr 1204 ff.; Jean Rivero and Jean Waline, *Droit administratif*, 17th edn. (Paris: Dalloz, 1998), nr 271 ff.

[110] Chapus (1987), nr 1256; Rivero and Waline (1998), nr 313.

[111] CE 24 April 1963, AJDA 1963, 570, 3e esp. (*Dme Abelson*); CE 5 October 1966, AJDA 1967, 115, 3e esp., comm. De Laubadère (*Del Carlo*).

[112] CE 30 October 1964, Rec. CE 1964, 506 (*Piquet*).

Another important duty of the highway authority is to warn of dangerous situations. Mme Palouller skidded with her car because of dung on a local road and collided with another car. It was established that dung on this road was not an exceptional feature and the *Conseil d'État* decided that the highway authority was liable for the damage because it should have warned road users.[113] The same applies, for example, in cases of a bend in the road, slipperiness, and road construction work.[114]

The highway authority does not need to warn of sudden and unexpected dangers such as heavy rain or oil on the road. However, if an accident happens, and the authority knows about it or ought to have known about it, it immediately has to take measures to prevent further damage. If nevertheless an accident occurs, the highway authority is liable, unless it did not have sufficient time to take precautionary measures. For example, the *Conseil d'État* decided that the authority was not liable for damage caused by a manhole cover that had come loose because the accident took place that same night.[115] However, the authority was liable for the damage a woman suffered when she fell on the icy stairs of a pedestrian tunnel. This happened at 10.15am and the *Conseil d'État* decided that by then the authority should have cleared the stairs because the tunnel was in frequent use.[116]

If in normal weather a tree falls onto the road, the *Conseil d'État* holds that the authority is liable for the damage caused if a driver collides with the tree, unless it proves that it was not visible from the outside of the tree that it was in a bad condition.[117] This is different if a road sign collapses and lands on the road. In such a case the authority is strictly liable for the damage caused and it has no defence.[118]

1509 Germany: *Straßenverkehrssicherungspflichten*

In Germany liability for roads can be based on violation of a statutory rule or the breach of a safety duty (*Verkehrssicherungspflicht*) (see nr 1503-2), particularly a safety duty as regards road (*Straßenverkehrssicherungspflicht*).

The responsible bodies for the safety of public roads are generally the lands and the municipalities. The safety of federal motorways (*Bundesautobahnen*) is the responsibility of the federal state. Though this is thus a liability of public bodies, the content of the safety duty remains the same: in these cases liability for violation of a *Verkehrspflicht* (§ 823 BGB) and for violation of an official duty (§ 839 BGB) coincide.[119] See about § 839 nr 1803-2.

---

[113] CE 23 September 1988, RTD pub. 1989, 543.
[114] CE 6 March 1985, RTD pub. 1985, 53; CE 24 October 1984, RTD pub. 1985, 61; CE 4 March 1988, RTD pub. 1989, 29.   [115] CE 20 February 1985, RTD pub. 1985, 78.
[116] CE 21 November 1984, RTD pub. 1985, 50.
[117] CE 25 November 1987, RTD pub. 1988, 22.
[118] CE 24 April 1985, RTD pub. 1986, 39.
[119] Münchener Kommentar-Wagner (2004), § 823 N 409–410. The BGH holds that in cases of the violation of a road safety duty the subsidiary clause of § 839 I 2 does not apply (this is

The *Verkehrspflichtige* is obliged to avoid risks for road users, as far as is feasible and can be required. It is compelled to take such measures of which the benefits in terms of prevention of future damage are not out of proportion in relation to the costs. In this respect the character of the road can be relevant in order to establish the acceptable risks: busier roads can require greater and more costly precautionary measures than quiet country roads.[120] Also, road users in the new lands (*Bundesländer*) in former East Germany have to reckon with a generally less good road surface than in the old *Bundesländer*.[121]

The supervisor of a road is also obliged to base its safety measures on the fact that road users will not always drive carefully. It does not have to take into account the most careful or the most imprudent road user; on the contrary, it has to prevent accidents which are caused by obvious mistakes by road users. Hence, the focus needs to be on the average (*durchschnittliche*) road user.[122]

The extent of the duty to maintain depends partially on the financial means of the supervisor of the road. This implies that the supervisor has some space to establish priorities, such as giving precedence to roads of greater importance. The supervisor's capacity with regard to its duty to maintain is called the capacity to achieve (*Leistungsfähigkeit*).[123]

This can be well illustrated with the duty to sprinkle salt or gravel on snowy or icy streets.[124] In accordance with the way in which safety duties and road safety duties are generally established, the duty to clear the streets and the duty to sprinkle salt or gravel depend on the character, use, and danger of the road on the one hand and on what can economically be required from the *Verkehrssicherungs-pflichtigen*.[125] The case law distinguishes between roads inside and outside built-up areas. Outside this area only particularly dangerous spots need to be sprinkled, such as bridges.[126] This does not go for cycle-tracks and footpaths because in such wintry weather one does not expect to come across cyclists and pedestrians in these circumstances.[127] Inside such areas the duty concerns the most important roads and to sprinkle at the most dangerous spots, ie where cars brake or change direction.[128]

---

particularly of importance for recourse claims of private and social insurers): BGH 12 July 1979, BGHZ 75, 134 = NJW 1979, 2043; BGH 11 June 1992, BGHZ 118, 368 = NJW 1992, 2476; BGH 18 November 1993, VersR 1994, 618.

[120] Münchener Kommentar-Wagner (2004), § 823 N 416 and 418.

[121] LG Bautzen 25 August 1998, DAR 1999, 26. See however also LG Halle 15 May 1998, DAR 1999, 28: even in the new *Bundesländer* a road user does not have to expect a 12 cm (5 inch) deep hole in the surface of the road.

[122] BGH 26 March 1981, NJW 1981, 2120; BGH 24 January 2002, VersR 2002, 1040. Münchener Kommentar-Wagner (2004), § 823 N 417.

[123] BGH 5 July 1990, BGHZ 112, 74 = NJW 1991, 33; BGH 20 December 1990, VersR 1991, 665; BGH 1 July 1993, NJW 1993, 2802.

[124] Münchener Kommentar-Wagner (2004), § 823 N 426–433.

[125] BGH 5 July 1990, BGHZ 112, 74 = NJW 1991, 33; BGH 1 July 1993, NJW 1993, 2802.

[126] BGH 1 October 1959, BGHZ 31, 73 = NJW 1960, 32; BGH 21 February 1972, NJW 1972, 903.   [127] BGH 20 October 1994, VersR 1995, 721.

[128] BGH 5 July 1990, BGHZ 112, 74 = NJW 1991, 33; BGH 1 October 1959, BGHZ 31, 73 = NJW 1960, 32; BGH 20 December 1009, VersR 1991, 665.

Apart from the highway authority, other parties can owe road users a duty to take care for the safety of the road, for example the constructor who performs work on the road. Furthermore the owner of land adjacent to the road can owe a duty of care towards road users in order to maintain the trees which are on his land.[129]

1510 Comparative observations

In all jurisdictions liability for the safety of roads is mainly liability of public bodies because most roads are owned by the state or by local governments. Liability for roads, therefore, is a foreshadowing of the general problem of the liability of public bodies. In France the matter is dealt with in the framework of administrative law, containing a full-fledged liability system developed by the administrative courts, whereas in Germany and England civil law remedies are provided.

The road supervisor's standard of care does not differ substantially between the jurisdictions. France explicitly holds a liability for rebuttable negligence, whereas in Germany and England the road user has to prove negligence but the courts will accommodate him in his burden of proof. In this respect the difference between France on the one hand, and Germany and England on the other, should not be overestimated. A more important difference is that in England the highway authority's statutory duties are limited to the maintenance of the road whereas in France and Germany the duties more generally extend to safety of the road and may include, for example, warning notices and signs.

Hence, the fact that road supervisors are generally public bodies does not as such lead to a lower standard of care as regards road safety. In this respect this is not an ordinary branch of liability for public bodies. As with private parties, road supervisors need to balance the risk with the costs of removing or limiting this risk. Roads do not need to be completely safe but the road supervisor needs to avert risks which road users do not have to expect. It has to take responsibility for a safe road design, for removing avoidable risks, and for warning properly for inevitable risks.

The limited resources of road supervisor are particularly taken into account in cases of snow and ice on the road. In such cases the supervisor's duty to clear the road depends on the importance of the road and the costs, effort, and time needed to take precautionary measures. Also here, it is a matter of balancing the risks of slipperiness and the costs of removing ice and snow or sprinkling salt or gravel. In this respect it is relevant that slipperiness caused by snow is a visible and known risk for road users.

---

[129] BGH 30 October 1973, MDR 1974, 217.

Although in establishing the standard of care for road supervisors their limited financial resources are sometimes taken into account, this is only remotely related to the so-called margin of discretion (nr 1810). Road supervisors need to have a proper plan as to how to set priorities in case of snow and ice and to carry out that plan properly. The German and French case law is well developed in this respect. This is not so much the case in England although there does not seem to be a valid climatological reason for this difference.

An important commonality is that the road supervisors have to take into consideration that not all road users take sufficient care and that they are inclined to make mistakes. This point of view plays an important role in establishing negligence generally (nr 807-4) and its relevance was also pointed out in the framework of the duty of the supervisor of premises and grounds (nr 1506-4). The basic view is that a road supervisor needs to take the average road user (*ordinary driver, durchschnittlicher Verkehrsteilnehmer*) rather than the careful or prudent driver as a benchmark for taking precautionary measures and placing warning signs. However, in England this point of view is put in doubt by the latest case law of the House of Lords (nr 1507).

D CONCLUDING REMARKS

1511 Comparative observations

Liability for damage caused by immovable objects shows a rather patchy picture. There are similarities between French and German law as regards the rules applying to liability for damage caused by collapsing buildings, but the French rule is strict and the German rule implies liability for rebuttable negligence. There are also similarities between the English Occupier's Liability and the German *Verkehrspflichten* but the English level of care to be observed by the *occupier* is somewhat lower and less extensive than that of the *Verkehrspflichtige* in Germany. Hence, the level of liability differs strongly: from strict to fault liability with all shades between. Also, the fields of application of the various rules differ substantially. This makes it hard to find a European common core.

The legal systems also differ on various other levels. An important issue is to which level the supervisor needs to take into account a visitor's imprudence. In many cases the rule of contributory negligence enables an intermediate solution in the sense that the supervisor is held liable but that the visitor's contributory negligence leads to a reduction of his right to compensation. However, recent English case law seems to be less tolerant as regards the visitor's conduct, in certain cases holding his negligence to be the only cause of the accident, and leaving him without compensation (nr 1504-1 and 1507). In this respect, English law strikes a slightly different balance between the supervisor's and the visitor's responsibilities. In comparison with French and German law it puts a stronger emphasisis on the visitor's own responsibility to be vigilant when visiting other people's premises.

Furthermore, differences exist as regards unauthorized (adult) visitors or trespassers. French law holds the supervisor (custodian) in principle liable, but attributes 100 per cent contributory negligence to the trespasser. German law takes the view that the supervisor (*Verkehrspflichtige*) either does not owe the trespasser a safety duty or that he has discharged his duties, provided he has sufficiently indicated that entering is not allowed. Under these circumstances the defence of contributory negligence is not relevant any more. English law, on the contrary, acknowledges a duty of the occupier towards trespassers: this duty is only slightly lower than towards a visitor. The difference from French and German law is mitigated by the fact that the latter legal systems apply a somewhat narrower concept of trespasser.

The liable person is generally the person who has the factual control over the immovable object but in rules of strict liability it is generally the person who is the owner or the possessor. These latter rules particularly concern the constructive safety of the building. It would make sense to hold the owner or possessor liable for the constructive safety of the building and the factual controller for the safety of the daily use of the building. However, such a distinction will not be always easy to make and as such it is not carried through in the legal systems.

The draft ECC proposes in Article 3:202 a special liability rule for insufficiently safe immovable objects. This provision runs as follows:

A person who independently exercises control over an immovable and has it for their own use is accountable for the causation of personal injury and consequential loss, loss within Article 2:202 [loss suffered by third parties as a result of another's personal injury or death], and for loss resulting from property damage by a state of the immovable which does not ensure such safety as a person in or near the immovable is entitled to expect having regard to the circumstances including (a) the nature of the immovable, (b) the access to the immovable, and (c) the cost of avoiding the immovable being in that state.

This rule is not very strict since the latter three circumstances are similar to the ones to be taken into account in fault liability (nr 806–809). The only requirement that would be abolished is the foreseeability of the damage. It remains to be seen whether such a rule would be consistently applied in each legal system, given the current divergence between the systems which has been pointed out in this chapter.

16

Liability for Other Persons

A INTRODUCTION

1601 Overview

An advertisement in an American newspaper once told the reader: 'Can't sue the person who hurt you? Don't sulk. Hire a personal-injury lawyer and sue someone else.'[1] If the person who actually caused the damage is not a sufficiently solvent debtor, if he is untraceable or does not have sufficient liability insurance coverage, liability of the actual wrongdoer will not help the claimant. Hence, the latter will look for other possibly liable persons, particularly those who had to supervise the actual wrongdoer.[2]

In a number of cases the legal systems hold specific rules as regards liability for others. Often these rules are strict and sometimes they provide a liability for rebuttable negligence. In other cases, no specific liability rule exists, which means that liability has to be established on the basis of negligent conduct which is to be proved by the claimant. Also these latter cases can be considered as liability for others.[3] This means that the topic of this chapter is broader than what in the common law is known as 'vicarious liability' which is primarily strict for the supervisor (in practice the employer).

Negligence-based liability for others is directly related to the issue of liability for omissions. Liability for omissions is generally accepted if the defendant has a special relationship with the place of the accident, with the object that played a role in the occurrence of the damage that was caused, with the potential victim or with the potential tortfeasor (nr 802-2). In this chapter the latter special relationship is at stake: the obligation to supervise another person follows from the special relationship someone has with the person who actually caused the

---

[1] See Jean Stapleton, 'Duty of Care: Peripheral Parties and Alternative Opportunities for Deterrence', *LQR*, 111 (1995), 301.

[2] See on liability for damage caused by other persons: Zweigert-Kötz, *Introduction to Comparative Law* (1998), 629–645; von Bar (1998), N 131–205; J. Spier (ed.), *Unification of Tort Law: Liability for Damage Caused by Others* (The Hague-London-New York: Kluwer Law International, 2003).

[3] This also makes sense considering the gradual difference between strict and negligence liability (nr 1005).

damage. In some legal systems this obligation is governed by strict liability, in others by negligence liability with or without a reversed burden of proof.

Generally, the duty to control and to interfere requires the authority to do so. This means for instance that a passenger does not have a duty to supervise the driver. But sometimes the strings are tightened:

> If the owner was a passenger in his own vehicle at the time of the accident, liability has been justified by imputing to him a "right to control" the manner of driving. Even against absent owners recourse is now frequently available to traffic victims, either on the basis of widespread statutory vicarious liability or an extended notion of agency whenever the driver was not solely engaged on purposes of his own. This development is of course primarily attributable to the desire to tap the owner's insurance policy.[4]

A duty to supervise is generally more easily accepted in cases of death, personal injury, and property loss than in cases of pure economic loss, particularly in English law.[5]

Special rules as regards liability for damage caused by others only apply to supervisors of young children and to employers. Liability of other supervisors has to be based on the general rules of fault liability. In such cases it is more difficult for the victim to prove the relevant facts and therefore negligence. One may think of prisoners and people in psychiatric hospitals causing damage to other persons (nr 1605). Another example is the liability of regulators (watchdogs) for negligently supervising companies in their area of competence. This liability is considered to be liability of public bodies; see nr 1801.

There are several goals to be achieved with the rules of liability for other persons. The main goal is to protect third parties against insolvency of the actual tortfeasor: the child or the employee. To a certain extent the rules also protect the child and employee against the financial consequences following from their negligent conduct since these consequences can be devastating for both of them. Additionally, the rules channel the costs of the activity to the person who benefits from it; this goes particularly for employer's liability. Finally, liability for others serves a preventive function by placing liability on the person who is best positioned to prevent the harm from arising. This generally also makes him the cheapest cost avoider (nr 1607-2).

These strict liability rules for damage caused by other persons' conduct are mostly created by the legislator and they have not been subject to change since the late 19th century. The strict rules which were created by the courts are *vicarious liability* in England (nr 1606-4) and the French general strict liability for persons in 1991, which affects all supervisors of minors and of persons with a mental or physical shortcoming (nr 305).

⁴ Fleming (1998), 171. Such a duty can also apply against the driver if he is younger or less experienced: see *Harper v Adams* (1976) VR 44 (FC).
⁵ Winfield and Jolowicz (2002), para. 5.23. See *Yuen Kun Yeu v Attorney-General of Hong Kong* [1988] AC 175, about which Van Gerven (2000), 369–371; *Davis v Radcliffe* [1990] 1 WLR 321; *Banque Keyser Ullman SA v Skandia (UK) Insurance Co Ltd* [1990] 1 QB 665.

B CHILDREN AND MENTALLY DISABLED PERSONS

1602 Liability of parents

1602-1 *France*

The general rule of strict liability for persons has been discussed in nr 305. This rule also envisages liability for damage caused by children and mentally disabled persons. However, the regime is not confined to such persons. Nevertheless, the possibilities of the judge-made strict liability rule for persons can be of great importance in case children or mentally disabled persons cause damage to third parties.

Article 1384 al. 4 holds the father and the mother jointly and severally liable for the damage caused by their minor child living with them and of whom they have the custody, unless they can prove an external cause or contributory negligence of the victim. The provision only applies to parents of a minor child, under 18 years of age, who lives with them in their home and over whom they exercise their parental rights.[6] Article 1384 al. 4 neither applies to grandparents and other family members nor to the tutor.[7] However, the latter might be liable on the basis of the general rule of strict liability for persons (nr 305).[8]

Several facts can trigger the parents' strict liability. Firstly, the child can cause damage by committing a *faute*. In this respect it is sufficient if it has committed an unlawful act (*un acte objectivement illicite*). It is not required that the child could be blamed for its conduct: the parents will also be liable if the child did not know how to behave or was not capable of refraining from its behaviour. See about subjective aspects of negligence nr 811. Secondly, the parents can also be liable if the damage is a result of the fact of a thing (*fait de la chose*) of which the child is custodian (*gardien*) (nr 303-3).[9]

Thirdly, in 1984 the *Cour de cassation* held that it is sufficient for parental liability that the child's conduct was the direct cause of the damage the victim had suffered (*un acte qui soit la cause directe du dommage invoqué par la victime*).[10]

---

[6] Terré-Simler-Lequette (2002), nr 819–821; Carbonnier (1998), § 237, 428–430.

[7] Civ. 2e 25 January 1995, D. 1995. 232, comm. Delebecque.

[8] Crim. 10 October 1996, D. 1997. 309, comm. Huyette, JCP 1997. II. 22833; Viney-Jourdain (1998), nr 874.

[9] Civ. 2e 10 February 1966, D. 1966. 332: 'Si la responsabilité du père suppose que celle de l'enfant ait été établie, la loi ne distingue pas entre les causes qui ont pu donner naissance à la responsabilité de l'enfant.'

[10] Civ. 2e 16 July 1969, RTD civ. 1970, 575, obs. Durry; Civ. 2e 10 February 1966, D. 1966. 332, JCP 1968. II. 15506, comm. Plancquéel; Ass. plén. 9 May 1984, JCP 1984. II. 20255, comm. Dejean de la Bathie, D. 1984. 525, comm. Chabas, RTD civ. 1984, 509, obs. Huet (Fullenwarth); Civ. 13 April 1992, Bull. civ. II, no 122.

Despite fierce criticism by many authors, the *Cour de cassation* has confirmed the rule more than once. One of the cases was about a boy who was injured during an improvised rugby match: another boy fell onto him after he had tackled him. The parents of the boy who caused the damage were held liable for the directly caused damage, even though the minor had not committed a *faute*.[11] This case law has brought the parental liability rule for damage caused by minors close to the liability rule for the custodian for damage caused by a thing (nr 303).[12] It shows the determination of the *Cour de cassation* to develop very general and broad principles of strict liability, wandering away from liability for someone else's negligence to liability for someone else's harmful conduct. The case law is a powerful illustration of the French fondness of *grands principes* (nr 608-3).

Until 1997 the parents could avoid liability by proving that the damage was not caused by a surveillance failure (*faute de surveillance*) or by an education failure (*faute d'éducation*). This defence was rather easy to establish with respect to older children.[13] However, in 1997 the *Cour de cassation* substantially restricted the parents' defences to an external cause and contributory negligence of the victim.[14] The case was about a 12-year-old boy racing across a main road with his bicycle and causing a collision, as the consequence of which a motor-cyclist was injured. The latter claimed damages from the boy's father on the basis of article 1384 al. 4. The *Cour de cassation* decided that only an external cause or contributory negligence could relieve the father from liability: it was not necessary to examine whether there was a lack of supervision on the part of the father.

With this decision the *Cour de cassation* aligned the defence of article 1384 al. 4 with the rule it had created in 1991 as regards strict liability for persons in general (nr 305). The court's decision has had radical consequences for the liability of parents for damage caused by their older minor children. Formerly, in most cases parents could escape liability because, in principle, it was not required to keep a close watch on older children. The new rule holds parents liable in most cases. Hence, the legislator has obliged parents to take a liability insurance policy.[15]

---

[11] Ass. plén. 13 December 2002, D. 2003. 231, comm. Jourdain, ETL 2002, 199 (Brun) and the comparative case comments in *ERPL* 11 (2003) 5, 691–751. In the same sense Civ. 2e 10 May 2001, Bull. civ. II, no 96, D. 2001, D. 2851, comm. Tournafond, JCP 2001. II. 10613, note Mouly, JCP 2001. I. 124, no 20, obs. Viney.

[12] It remains to be seen whether this neutral approach can always be maintained since also in the framework of art. 1384 al. 1 it is sometimes relevant whether the *chose* 'acted' normally; see nr 303-2.

[13] Terré-Simler-Lequette (2002), nr 822; Carbonnier (2000), § 237, 409.

[14] Civ. 2e 19 February 1997, D. 1997. 265, comm. Jourdain, JCP 1997, II. 22848, comm. Viney, RTD civ. 1997, 668 (Bertrand): '… seule la force majeure ou la faute de la victime pouvait exonérer le père de la responsabilité de plein droit encourue du fait des dommages causés par son fils mineur habitant avec lui.' See the comparative case comments in *ERPL* 7/4 (1999), 481–504; Van Gerven (2000), 520.

[15] Carbonnier (2000), § 241, 436; Viney-Jourdain (1998), nr 789-14.

1602-2 *Germany*

§ 832 BGB imposes liability on anyone who is bound by law or by contract to supervise other persons because of their minority or their physical or mental condition. However, the supervisor's liability is not strict: he is liable for the injury that person wrongfully inflicts upon a third party, unless he proves that he complied with his supervisory duty or that the injury would also have occurred if that duty had been satisfied, ie, that his own negligence was not causal for the injury. In this section the emphasis will be on parental liability. Liability for negligent supervision of mentally and physically handicapped persons will be dealt with in nr 1605.

The victim has to prove that the minor acted unlawfully (*rechtswidrig*); intention or negligence (*Verschulden*) is not required.[16] This means that the supervisor can be liable despite the fact the minor did not know the danger or could not behave in a different way because of his young age (nr 813-3). If the victim cannot prove that the child caused the damage in an unlawful way, the supervisor is not liable. In such a case it is irrelevant whether the supervisor complied with his supervisory duties.[17]

If the child has acted unlawfully, the supervisor has to prove that he has supervised and educated the child in a proper way. More generally, the level of supervision depends on the influence that education has had on the child.[18] The extent of the supervision depends on the age, the nature, and the character of the child and of what can be required of a supervisor in the circumstances of the case.[19] According to §626 II BGB the parent has to take into account the growing capacity and need of the child to act independently and with responsibility.[20] The older the child grows, the more responsibility it will have (nr 813-3) and the less supervision is necessary, unless the child has given reason to decide otherwise. For example, a child that tends to commit mischievous or criminal acts must be supervised more closely.[21]

If parents leave the supervision of their child to another person, their own duty to supervise will be limited but they have to make sure that this other person is suitable for the task.[22] In this respect, there is a parallel with the transfer of a safety duty (*Verkehrspflicht*); see nr 1506-1.

The younger the child, the more difficult it will be for a supervisor to prove he acted with due care. The courts require a detailed report from the supervisor

---

[16] BGH 1 February 1966, FamRZ 1966, 228.
[17] Kötz-Wagner (2001), N 330; the same rule applies with regard to § 831 (employer's liability): see nr 1606-1.   [18] BGH 10 July 1984, NJW 1984, 2574.
[19] BGH 19 January 1993, FamRZ 1993, 666, 667.
[20] BGH 10 July 1984, NJW 1984, 2574.   [21] BGH 19 January 1984, NJW 1985, 677.
[22] Münchener Kommentar-Wagner (2004), § 832 N 4.

as to what he has done to prevent the child's conduct. As regards children under the age of 6, the courts require permanent supervision. The use of dangerous things, such as bows and arrows, has to be prohibited and parents have to carefully supervise the compliance with this ban. With regard to older children, supervisors have to make sure that the child is able to handle risks in a safe way.[23] If a child between 7 and 10 years of age causes damage while riding a bicycle, the parents have to prove that they have taught the child about the traffic rules and that they have shown it the risks of cycling.[24] There is a tendency to not always require to keep children away from risks, because teaching children how to handle risks is considered to be the best way to avoid damage.[25]

If the parents are not liable, the victim is entitled to file a claim against the child on the basis of the equitable liability rule of § 829 BGB, for which non-liability of the parents is a prerequisite (nr 813-3).

1602-3 *England*

English law does not possess a special rule as regards parental liability. This means that liability of parents for damage caused by their children has to be based on the tort of negligence (nr 503). However, this requires a duty of care of the parent towards the person who suffered the damage. The problem is that this would be an affirmative duty, and English law is generally not very fond of such duties (nr 808-1). However, it is established that parents do indeed have a duty to supervise their children in order to protect third parties.

There are few English cases to illustrate parental liability and its impact. *Carmarthenshire County Council v Lewis* is often mentioned but this concerns liability of a school for damage caused by one of its pupils (nr 1506-4).

The authority is therefore not English but Australian:[26] *Smith v Leurs* of 1945 in which Dixon J said:

It is . . . exceptional to find in the law a duty to control another's actions to prevent harm to strangers. The general rule is that one man is under no duty of controlling another to prevent his doing damage to a third. There are, however, special relations, which are the source of a duty of this nature. It appears now to be recognised that it is incumbent upon a parent who maintains control over a young child to take reasonable care so to exercise that control as to avoid conduct on his part exposing the person or property of others to unreasonable danger. Parental control, where it exists, must be exercised with due care to prevent the child inflicting intentional damage on others or causing damage by conduct involving unreasonable risk of injury to others.[27]

---

[23] Deutsch-Ahrens (2002), N 334.
[24] BGH 10 October 1967, NJW 1968, 249; BGH 11 June 1968, NJW 1968, 1672.
[25] BGH 6 April 1976, NJW 1976, 1684.
[26] See more generally about the relations between the common law systems nr 501-2.
[27] Dixon J in *Smith v Leurs* (1945) 70 CLR 256, 261–262.

1603 Liability of other supervisors over children

Persons other than parents can also be responsible for supervising children; this particularly concerns liability of teachers for pupils.

In Germany someone who is contractually obliged to supervise persons, for instance the leader of a crèche,[28] is liable for damage caused by the child unless he proves that he did not supervise the child negligently (§ 832 II). The quality of supervisor can follow from statutory provisions, mainly parents and custodians, and from a contract. Hence, this provision for instance applies to nurseries, nannies, and to neighbours and relations taking care of young children. Particularly for the latter, this provision is considered to be a discouragement to take on supervisory tasks as regards children.[29] Nannies will be protected by their position as employee of the parents; the latter will be generally liable for insufficient supervision by their employee-nanny (§ 831 BGB, nr 1606-1). Teachers are not supervisors in the sense of § 832. Their liability is governed by § 839 if they teach at a state-funded school, and by § 823 if they teach at a private school.[30] In state-funded schools a first party injuries insurance scheme applies which provides compensation regardless of fault.[31]

In France a supervisor of minors may be liable on the basis of the general strict liability rule for persons, which holds him liable unless he can prove an external cause or contributory negligence (nr 305). It is yet unclear whether this new French regime also applies to teachers. Initially, teachers' liability (*les instituteurs*) on the basis of article 1384 al. 6 was the same as that of parents (nr 1602-1). But the legislator changed this regime in favour of the teachers. This happened in 1899 after the suicide of teacher Leblanc, who was ruined by a liability resting on him by virtue of his position. Since that time a distinction has been made between private schools on the one hand, and public schools and other private schools having an association-contract with the State, on the other. In the latter category, teachers are not personally liable towards the victim because these schools can neither select nor limit the number of their pupils. Teachers at private schools can be liable, but the victim has to prove a *faute* of the teacher which means he has insufficiently educated or supervised his pupil. There has to be a relationship between the education and the damage, and the pupil has to be under the teacher's supervision at the time he caused the damage.[32] In all cases the teacher's liability will give rise to the vicarious liability of its (public or private) employer (nr 1606-3).

[28] BGH 2 July 1968, NJW 1968, 1874.   [29] Von Bar (1998), N 158.
[30] BGH 15 March 1954, BGHZ 13, 25 = NJW 1954, 874; Münchener Kommentar-Wagner (2004), § 832 N 12.
[31] § 539 I no 14 Reichsversicherungsordnung; von Bar (1998), N 163.
[32] Carbonnier (2000), § 239, 433–435; Le Tourneau (2004), nr 7591–7654.

French case law provides an example of a case in which a very high level of care was required. A schoolboy was injured when a pair of scissors sticking out of a case was thrown into his face by another pupil. The court considered it to be a *faute* of the departing teacher to leave the 15-year-old pupils and not to wait for the teacher who was giving the next lesson. Such a seamless change of teachers can be especially required if the class in question gave reason to assume that it needed constant supervision.[33] Unfortunately, the court did not answer the question as to how this could be organized if each teacher has to wait for the other.

English law does not have a special rule as regards liability for children. The burden of proof for negligent conduct is on the claimant. *Carmarthenshire County Council v Lewis* is a good example. A child jumping from a schoolyard onto a busy road caused a driver to swerve to avoid the child. He collided with a lamppost and died. The school was held liable for the damage to his next of kin because it had not erected a fence which could have prevented children from getting into the street too easily.[34] A comparable decision can be found in Germany, in which the BGH held that the operator of a children's playground is under a duty to surround it with a fence to protect children against impulsively crossing an adjacent public road.[35] This case illustrates the link between liability of the supervisor of a child and that of the supervisor of premises on or in which children are to be expected (nr 1506-4). Another example is *Dorset Yacht Co v Home Office* in which a community home (Borstal) was held liable for damage caused to boats by Borstal boys who were on the run as the consequence of a failure to supervise.[36]

In all jurisdictions, liability of schools can generally be based on vicarious liability for insufficient supervision by the teacher as the school's employee. In this respect the private school's liability for damage caused by its pupils converges with the employer's liability (nr 1606–1607) and the public school's liability with that of public bodies (nr 1802–1804). In both cases it has to be established that the teacher acted negligently by not sufficiently supervising the child. The general rule in this respect is that the teacher has to take the measures as may be required from a good supervisor in order to prevent harm to third parties caused by the conduct of its pupils. The court has to take into account the age and character of the child, its interests, and the requirements of school life.

[33] Civ. 1er 20 December 1982, Bull. civ. I, no 369, D. 1983. IR. 131, RTD civ. 1984, 544, obs. G. Durry.
[34] *Carmarthenshire County Council v Lewis* (1956) AC 549. See also *Rich v LCC* [1953] 1 WLR 895; *Wray v Essex CC* [1936] 3 All ER 97; *Portelance v Trustees* (1962) 32 DLR (2d) 337; Winfield and Jolowicz (2002), para. 5.23.
[35] BGH 21 April 1977, VersR 1977, 817.
[36] *Dorset Yacht Co v Home Office* [1970] AC 1004, about which also nr 503-2.

1604 Comparative observations

It has been said that children are not just a blessing but also a nuisance. As far as they are a nuisance to third parties, national legal systems take different approaches as regards the possibilities of redress. In tort law the claimant generally has two possibilities to recover damage: from the child and from its parents.[37]

Claiming damages from the child itself is not always very worthwhile, particularly in Germany and England where a child is not liable if its conduct did not fall below the standard of its age group (nr 813). In France the child's conduct is judged in an objective way, which means that it is compared to that of an adult person. This is a more beneficial approach for the claimant but it may lead to harsh results for the child since it has to meet standards of conduct which it cannot meet because of its age. Even if a child is liable, it might be troublesome to recover damages, unless the child's liability is covered under its parents'. liability insurance policy.

Hence, from a claimant's perspective there will be a considerable number of situations in which it is important to find another liable person from whom compensation can be obtained. It follows from the foregoing that parental liability regimes vary from strict liability with a restricted *force majeure* defence in France, via a negligence liability with a reversed burden of proof in Germany, to a liability for proven negligence in England. As regards younger children, German law is in practice closer to French than to English law since German parents or supervisors have to meet high standards as to the supervision of younger children. As regards older children, German law is closer to English than to French law, since in such cases in Germany and England parents and supervisors are more easily exculpated, while in France the parents are always strictly liable. Moreover, in Germany failures in properly educating the child can lead to liability, whereas in England only the lack of supervision can do this. The former rule may but does not necessarily give rise to a tendency to go in the direction of strict liability.[38]

In this respect it is interesting to note the solution adopted in the Dutch Civil Code (*Burgerlijk Wetboek*). Article 6:164 BW holds that a child under the age of 14 is never liable for its own unlawful conduct. In lieu of the child, the parent or custodian is liable if the child's conduct, provided it would have been performed by an adult person, can be qualified as an imputable unlawful act (article 6:169(1) BW). This rule replaces the child's liability by that of the parents or custodian. It avoids liability of the child and the harsh judgments which in France are necessary

[37] Von Bar (1998), N 131–165; Peter H.M. Rambach, *Die deliktische Haftung Minderjähriger und ihrer Eltern im französischen, belgischen und deutschen Deliktsrecht* (Antwerp: Maklu, 1994).
[38] Von Bar (1998), N 143.

to protect the victim in a reasonable way and puts the burden of liability on the parents who are responsible for raising the child and caring for it.[39]

The question of which of the parents is liable depends on the liability regime. In the strict regime in France, the parents are both jointly and severally liable, unless they can prove *force majeure*. In Germany and England liability depends on the question of whether the parent can prove he had been sufficiently careful in supervising the child, and in Germany this also applies in cases of educational negligence. The latter implies the only possibility of holding an 'absent' parent liable for damage caused by the child. In fact, liability for lack of supervision does not reflect the responsibility both parents have towards their children. Moreover, such a rule generally burdens the mother, since in most cases she will be the one who looks after the child, and this is in fact discriminatory. It would be advisable to hold both parents jointly and severally liable if one of them has failed to properly supervise the child.[40]

Parents are not liable for all damage caused by their child. In Germany the child's conduct needs to be unlawful (*widerrechtlich*), ie its conduct would fulfil a *Tatbestand* in the sense of for example § 823, ie infringing a right or violating a statutory rule. It is not required that the child knew about the risk or ought to have known about it. Neither is it necessary that the child could have behaved in a different way (nr 1602-2). Though English law is not clear on this point, it seems to be obvious that only damage caused by the child's objectively negligent conduct can give rise to parental liability. The parental duty to supervise the child is not aimed at preventing a child's conduct that does not involve unreasonable risk of injury to others (nr 1602-3). French courts do not require that the child's conduct was *illicite* but only that it was the direct cause of the victim's damage (nr 1602-1).

All in all, the child's liability is not a prerequisite of parental liability. This makes sense inasmuch as liability of parents aims to compensate the damage for

---

[39] The ECC and the PETL have not adopted this recent Dutch solution but have opted for a solution that comes close to the German rule. Art. 3:104 ECC:

(1) Parents or other persons obliged by law to provide parental care for a person under fourteen years of age are accountable for the causation of legally relevant damage where that person under age caused the damage by conduct that would constitute negligence if it were the conduct of an adult. (2) An institution or other body obliged to supervise a person is accountable for the causation of legally relevant damage suffered by a third party when: (a) the damage is personal injury, loss within Article 2:202 or damage to property; (b) the person whom the institution or other body is obliged to supervise caused that damage intentionally or negligently or, in the case of a person under eighteen, by conduct, that would constitute intention or negligence if it were the conduct of an adult; and (c) the person whom they are obliged to supervise is a person likely to cause damage of that type. (3) However, a person is not accountable under this Article for the causation of damage if that person shows that there was no defective supervision of the person causing the damage.

Art. 6:101 PETL: 'A person in charge of another who is a minor or subject to mental disability is liable for damage caused by the other unless the person in charge shows that he has conformed to the required standard of conduct in supervision.'

[40] See also von Bar (1998), N 144.

which a child is not liable. In fact, however, parental liability is not a supplement for all situations in which the child is not liable. In France the child's liability is based on a comparison of its conduct with that of an adult, or on the strict liability following from article 1384 al. 1 (nr 813-2) and the parents' liability is strict. This gives the claimant two favourable chances to get compensation for his loss. In England the child's liability is based on a comparison of its conduct with a child of its age and the parents' liability is one for proven negligence, giving the claimant two less favourable opportunities. Germany takes an intermediate position. This shows that parental liability is not just intended to compensate the lack of the child's liability but that it has a standing of its own, reflecting the parents' responsibility for damage caused by their children.

1605 Supervising mentally disabled persons

The life of disabled persons, particularly those with serious mental problems, is nowadays organized by granting them more freedom of movement than used to be the case some decades ago. On the one hand this is due to want of (public) money to provide them with proper accommodation, and on the other to modern therapeutic views. How happily the twain have met.[41]

Liability of mentally disabled persons shows many similarities with liability of the child (nr 813). In both cases it is problematic to hold the person liable for damage, and in both cases the victim may look to see whether a supervisor is liable. The dilemma to be solved is also comparable. On the one hand, it can be harsh to impose liability on a mentally disabled person, particularly if the reasoning is that they did not comply with standards even though it is clear that they were not able to meet these standards. On the other hand, it is not desirable to let the loss lie where it falls just because it is caused by wrongful conduct of a disabled person.

English law applies a subjective test to mentally disabled persons, though this only happens in strong cases, and supervisors are liable if the victim can prove negligent supervision. In Germany reluctance exists as to the liability of a mentally disabled person but in many cases an additional liability in equity can be established; persons who are statutorily or contractually obliged to supervise are liable for damage caused by the supervised person unless they can prove that their supervision was not negligent. France holds an explicit statutory provision in which a *trouble mental* is no defence against liability; supervisors are strictly liable for damage caused by their pupils (nr 813).

If liability of supervisors of mentally disabled persons, for example hospitals, asylums, and relatives, is based on negligence they are under a duty to take reasonable care in order to prevent a person under their supervision from causing

---

[41] Terré-Simler-Lequette (2002), nr 850.

damage to third parties. This is the case in England and Germany, in the latter country with a reversed burden of proof on the basis of § 832. The extent of this duty is determined on one hand by the risks the patient causes to other people, taking into account the character of his disorder, and by the burden of taking precautionary measures on the other (nr 805).[42] As regards the amount of precautionary measures, one may also think of the fundamental rights of the supervised person, such as his freedom of movement (Article 5 ECHR and Article 9 ICCPR) and the requirements of his medical treatment.

Liability based on negligence also assumes that the risk caused by the patient is known or ought to have known by the supervisor (nr 810). In this respect the professional status of a supervisor can play an important role to impute psychiatric knowledge on the supervisor (nr 812).

In France a strict liability rule applies in these cases. This avoids the complicated balance between the level of supervision on the one hand, and the interests of the child on the other. On the other hand, in individual cases such a strict liability rule may lead to results which are not always entirely satisfactory. But this is not an unusual price for having a rule of strict liability.

C EMPLOYEES

1606 National rules

1606-1 *Germany: § 831 BGB*

According to § 831 BGB anyone who has employed another person for a task (*zu einer Verrichtung bestellt hat*) is liable for the injury unlawfully caused by that other person in the accomplishment of the task. However, the employer's liability is not strict. He possesses two defences: firstly, he is not liable if he proves that he has exercised reasonable care in the selection of the employee and in the procurement of tools and the supervision of the employee. Secondly, he is not liable if the injury would also have been caused if he had taken such reasonable care. Hence, § 831 implies a negligence liability with a reversed burden of proof. The courts generally require the employer to act with a high level of care which, in fact, causes § 831 in its application to be close to a rule of strict liability.[43]

---

[42] See for Germany Münchener Kommentar-Wagner (2004), § 832, N 36 with reference to BGH 19 January 1984 NJW 1985, 677, 678.

[43] BGH 8 March 1951, BGHZ 1, 248; Münchener Kommentar-Wagener (2004), § 831 N 27–43; Kötz-Wagner (2001), N 282–283.

§ 831 describes the employer as the *Geschäftsherr*. The employee is a subordinate who is dependent on the instructions of the *Geschäftsherr*. Employees include senior officials and executives but generally exclude employed commercial representatives because of their autonomy.[44] Even independent contractors and traders can be *Verrichtungsgehilfe* if they are dependent on the instructions of the *Geschäftsherr*.[45]

The employee must have committed a *Tatbestand* in the sense of, for example, § 823 I and II BGB. The fulfilment of such a *Tatbestand* implies unlawfulness (*Rechtswidrigkeit*); see nr 402. Generally, it is sufficient that the employee's conduct can be considered to be the adequate cause of the damage but if the employee has acted with due care the employer is not liable. In such a case the employer's defences do not need any further discussion, let alone decision.[46] Since § 831 does not require the employee's *Verschulden*, his liability is not necessary to establish the employer's liability. But if the employee has *Verschulden* and is liable, he will be jointly and severally liable with the employer (§ 840).

The employee's conduct has to fall within the scope of his duty (*in Ausführung der Verrichtung*) which means that there has to be an immediate relationship between the activity he has been instructed to perform and the act causing the damage. The courts interpret this relationship in a broad sense.[47] For example, it is sufficient to invoke application of § 831 if a driver causes an accident with his employer's excavator even when he had neither a licence to use it on the public highway, nor a driver's licence, and his employer had explicitly instructed him to only transport the excavator on a low loader.[48] The same can go for an intentional crime if the employee's work has given him the opportunity for the act, for example when a luggage office employee at a railway station steals a suitcase which had been deposited with him.[49]

An exception is the position of the employer of a larger company, who can confine himself to proving that he acted with due care in choosing the manager responsible for selecting personnel. He does not have to prove that he acted with due care in selecting the personnel himself. This is the so-called decentralized exoneration (*dezentralisierter Entlastungsbeweis*).[50]

If the employer has paid damages to the victim, he only has a right of recourse against the employee if the latter has acted intentionally or with gross negligence.

[44] BGH 30 June 1966, BGHZ 45, 311 = NJW 1966, 1807 = JZ 1966, 645 = VersR 1966, 959, about which Van Gerven (2000), 496–497 and Markesinis and Unberath (2002), 772–773; BGH 25 February 1988, BGHZ 103, 298 = NJW 1988, 1380.

[45] Münchener Kommentar-Wagner (2004), § 831 N 10.

[46] BGH 2 October 1979, NJW 1980, 392; Kötz-Wagner (2001), N 279.

[47] BGH 30 October 1967, BGHZ 49, 19, 23 = NJW 1968, 391 = VersR 1968, 92, about which Markesinis and Unberath (2002), 755–758; BGH 6 October 1970, NJW 1971, 31 = VersR 1970, 1157, about which Markesinis and Unberath (2002), 758–760; Kötz-Wagner (2001), N 276.   [48] BGH 20 September 1966, VersR 1966, 1074.

[49] BGH 9 May 1957, BGHZ 24, 188.

[50] BGH 25 October 1951, BGHZ 4, 1 = NJW 1952, 418, about which Markesinis and Unberath (2002), 775–776.

The employee has a right of recourse against the employer if he himself is sued and did not act intentionally.[51]

1606-2 *Germany: bypasses for § 831 BGB*

The employer's possibilities of escaping liability under § 831 BGB were generally considered to be too broad. Courts and legal authors have expressed their discontent with the provision, arguing that it should not be relevant whether the employer has exercised due care as regards choice, direction, and supervision of the employee. Meanwhile, the courts looked for other ways to reach reasonable results. In the words of von Bar: 'A self-confident judiciary does not indefinitely embrace the obvious misjudgements of its legislature.'[52]

Firstly, § 31 is applied if the employer is a legal body. This provision runs as follows:

> The association is liable for the damage caused to a third party by the board of directors, a member of the board or another representative appointed in accordance with the articles of association, through a course of conduct that was taken in execution of the tasks entrusted to it or him and that was such as to give rise to liability.[53]

The rule does not establish liability for others but liability for what is considered to be the legal body's own conduct. The case law has extended the provision by also applying it to persons exercising management functions within large organisations, such as branch directors and heads of department. The BGH has decided that it is sufficient '. . . that the representative is charged, through the general operational guidelines and practices of the business in question, with the autonomous execution of the legal person's significant and essential functions.'[54]

Secondly, employer's liability can also be based on § 823. This is the case if the employer has negligently failed to organize his business in a proper way. This is called organizational negligence (*Organisationsverschulden*). The employer's duty to organize his business properly is a non-delegable duty: he cannot leave the organization in the hands of managers or other persons in the organization. If he nonetheless does so and things go wrong, it is assumed that he has organized his business in a negligent way and he will be liable for the consequential damage. Generally, the duty obliges the employer to organize and supervise the management and the activities of his employees in such a way as, in the circumstances of the case, is required with respect to preventing damage to third parties.[55] For

---

[51] Kötz-Wagner (2004), N 299; BAG 27 September 1994, ZIP 1994, 1712.
[52] Von Bar (1998), N 179; see also Münchener Kommentar-Wagner (2004), § 831 N 2–6.
[53] Translation from Van Gerven (2000), 487.
[54] BGH 30 October 1967, BGHZ 49, 19, 21 = NJW 1968, 391 = VersR 1968, 92. Translation from Van Gerven (2000), 488; see also Markesinis and Unberath (2002), 755–758.
[55] BGH 13 May 1955, BGHZ 17, 214; BGH 9 February 1960, BGHZ 32, 53, 59; BGH 20 April 1971, NJW 1971, 1313 = VersR 1971, 741, about which Markesinis and Unberath (2002), 766–769; Kötz-Wagner, (2001), N 292; Münchener Kommentar-Wagner (2004), § 831 N 39;

example, a tour operator was held liable for negligently not ensuring the safety of a hotel building at Gran Canaria. It was established that for this reason the operator had breached its *Verkehrspflicht* and had to pay for the damage of one of the guests who was injured when he fell off the balcony of his apartment on the upper floor of the hotel when the balustrade's wooden railing broke off.[56]

Thirdly, even if the employer can exonerate himself from liability under § 831, he has to indemnify the employee if the latter is personally liable for the damage caused. This is the case if he did not only act unlawfully but he also had *Verschulden*. This duty to indemnify can even exist where the employee acted with gross negligence.[57] This rule is intended for the protection of the employee but its consequence is that, in the end, the employer has to pay for the damage wrongfully and negligently caused by his employee. Moreover, the company's liability insurance generally covers the employee's liability.[58] This means that if the employee is liable, the claimant in most cases will find a solvent debtor.[59]

Fourthly, the courts have applied the contractual rule of strict liability for damage caused by others (§ 278 BGB) in a broad way, by creating accessory contractual obligations as regards safety and information and by extending the protective scope of contractual obligations to identifiable third parties (*Vertrag mit Schutzwirkung zugunsten Dritter*) (nr 713). This interpretation is for instance applied in the so-called *Department store* cases, in one of which the BGH held that store staff are obliged to examine the floor for objects which do not belong there and it is up to the department store to prove that this obligation was fulfilled.[60] As Kötz writes, it is astonishing how audaciously bridges can be constructed in order to avoid tort law and to reach the promised land of contract law.[61]

Finally, in specific circumstances special rules of strict liability apply to employers. Such a rule can, for instance, be found in § 3 Liability Act (*Haftpflichtgesetz*), holding that the operator is liable if, in the operating of a mine, a quarry, a factory, or during excavation, damage occurs as a consequence

---

Münchener Kommentar-Wagner (2004), § 823 N 370–371; Gert Brüggemeier, 'Organisationshaftung', *AcP* 191, (1991), 33 ff.

[56] BGH 25 February 1988, BGHZ 103, 298.

[57] BAG 12 October 1989, NJW 1990, 468 (banana skin).

[58] Deutsch-Ahrens (2002), N 328; Kötz-Wagner (2004), N 300.

[59] Münchener Kommentar-Wagner (2004), § 831 N3.

[60] BGH 26 September 1961, NJW 1962, 31. See also RG 7 December 1911, RGZ 78, 239 (linoleum); RG 10 February 1930, RGZ 127, 218 (Gas fitter); BGH 28 January 1976, BGHZ 66, 51 = NJW 1976, 776 = JZ 1976, 776, note Kreuzer (vegetable leaf). See more generally about safety duties as regards premises nr 1503-2. See about contractual obligations to protect third parties also nr 713.

[61] Kötz-Wagner (2004), N 298:

Indessen wird jeder, der noch nicht gänzlich betriebsblind geworden ist, sich ein gewisses Staunen darüber nicht versagen können, wie verwegen mittlerweile die Brücken konstruiert werden, mit deren Hilfe die Rechtssprechung deliktsrechtliche Fallabwicklung zu vermeiden und das gelobte Land des Vertragsrechts zu erreichen sucht.

of a fault of a person in charge. The operator does not have the defences of § 831.[62]

1606-3 *France*

French law holds employers (*commettants*) and principals (*maîtres*) strictly liable for damage caused by a *faute* of their employees (*préposés*) and servants (*domestiques*) committed in the course of the functions for which they are employed (article 1384 al. 5).[63] Employers and principals are strictly liable without any defence whatsoever apart from the victim's contributory negligence. Liability of principals dates from the time that servants lived with their masters but this is no longer required for the principal's liability.

Article 1384 al. 5 creates a strict liability regime for situations in which someone carries out activities as someone else's subordinate. A contract between the two is not required. The courts are inclined to a broad interpretation, and the rule has even been applied to situations where someone renders a friendly and gratuitous service to another. However, the employer-employee relationship has to be real and cannot result from a situation of pure appearance. If someone willingly allows the appearance of a subordination relationship, liability has to be based on article 1382.[64]

The employer's and principal's liability requires a *faute* of the employee as well as damage and causation (article 1382). This implies that the employee also needs to be personally liable for the damage he caused. According to article 489-2 CC a *faute* can be established even if the employee suffered from a mental disorder (nr 800). It has been argued that a *faute* should not be a requirement for liability, and that a causal connection between the employee's conduct and the damage should be sufficient, but this has not yet been followed by the *Cour de cassation*.[65] This clearly contrasts with the position the court has taken in cases of parental liability (nr 1602-1).

Finally, an important requirement is the necessary relationship between the employee's conduct and his job. This requirement is subject to a lively case law and a fierce debate in the legal literature.[66] The leading judgment in this area was handed down in 1988 by the *Assemblée plénière* of the *Cour de cassation*, opting for a broad interpretation of the requirement. The case was about a travelling insurance salesman working for insurance company La Cité, selling financial

---

[62] Kötz-Wagner (2004), N 269.

[63] Art. 1384 al. 5: '... les maîtres et les commettants, du dommage causé par leurs domestiques et préposés dans les functions auxquelles ils les ont employés'.

[64] Crim. 15 February 1972, D. 1972. 368, JCP 1972. II. 17159, about which Van Gerven (2000), 490.

[65] Terré-Simler-Lequette (2002), nr 833; Viney-Jourdain (1998), nr 807. See also Ass. plén. 13 December 2002, D. 2003. 231, comm. Jourdain, ETL 2002, 199 (Brun), about which nr 1603-1.

[66] Terré-Simler-Lequette (2002), nr 834–835; Viney-Jourdain (1998), nr 797–805; Van Gerven (2000), 502 ff.

products to an elderly woman. He fraudulently kept more than half of the woman's payments for himself. The woman sued the salesman and the insurance company for damages. The *Cour de cassation* held that the salesman had acted within his functions and it provided the following rule: '...the employer (*commettant*) can be exonerated only if the employee (*préposé*) acted outside the functions for which he was employed, without authorisation, and for purposes foreign to the tasks entrusted to him'.[67] These three cumulative requirements are hard to prove for the employer.

If the above-mentioned requirements are met the employer is strictly liable. The victim's contributory negligence is his only defence. Sufficient supervision or care in choosing his employee does not preserve him from liability because his liability is irrebuttable (*responsabilité de plein droit*).[68]

Article 1384 al. 5 requires that the employee is liable on the basis of article 1382. This implies that employer and employee are jointly and severally liable. If the employer has paid damages to the victim he has, in principle, a right of recourse against the employee. However, the *Cour de cassation* has consistently reduced the employer's possibilities for recourse. In 1993 it decided that recourse was only possible if the employee committed a *faute personnel.*[69] It was not exactly clear what has to be understood by this requirement. Probably, the *Cour de cassation* intended to bring the regime of article 1384 al. 5 closer to the state liability for their civil servants' conduct. In the latter system recourse is, in principle, only possible if the civil servant acted maliciously or with gross negligence (nr 1802-2). Later the *Cour de cassation* ruled that the employee is not personally liable if he did not exceed the limits of the task he was commissioned to do by the employer.[70] Finally, in 2001 the *Cour de cassation*'s *Assemblée plénière* held that the employee is only personally liable if he acted intentionally.[71]

It has since long been recognized in French law that a legal body (*une personne morale*) can commit a *faute* by his organ.[72] An organ is a person who represents the will of the legal body and acts in its name (*qui veut et agit en son nom*), such that his conduct is to be identified with the legal body.[73] It can be liable for acts by organs legally entitled to take decisions, as well as for acts committed in the name and for the account of the legal body. The latter means that the legal body can still be liable if the organ has transgressed its powers.[74] A legal body can also

---

[67] Ass. plén. 19 May 1988, D. 1988. 513, comm. Larroumet, Gaz. Pal. 1988, 640, about which Van Gerven (2000), 501–502 from which the translation is derived.
[68] Viney-Jourdain (1998), nr 809; Le Tourneau (2004), nr 7492.
[69] Com. 12 October 1993, D. 1994. 124, comm. Viney.
[70] Ass. plén. 25 February 2000, JCP 2000. II. 10295 (*Costedoat c. Girard et autres*).
[71] Ass. plén. 14 December 2001, D. 2002. 1230, comm. Julien.
[72] Civ. 15 January 1872, DP 1872. 1. 165; Civ. 2e 17 July 1967, Gaz. Pal. 1967. 2. 235, comm. Blaevoet; Crim. 5 April 1965, Gaz. Pal. 1965. 2. 36; Civ. 2e 17 March 1993, D. 1993. IR. 89.
[73] Terré-Simler-Lequette (2002), nr 725; Le Tourneau (2004), nr 1371: 'La faute commise par un organe de la personne morale, c'est-à-dire par une personne qui veut et agit en son nom, est une faute de la personne morale.' [74] Le Tourneau (2004), nr 1373.

be liable through the acts of its representatives (*représentant*, aritical 121-2 *Code penal*). A regular employee is supposed to be not a representative, but an appointed employee with delegated powers (*salarié titulaire d'une delegation de pouvoirs*).[75] Some time before holding the same for employees, the *Cour de cassation* held in 1997 that an organ or representative could not be held personally liable if he had acted within the limits of his function.[76] Generally, the *Cour de cassation* does not seem to bother much about the identity or status of the human agents involved in the harmful act.[77]

1606-4 *England*

In England the employer is strictly liable for damage caused to third parties by his employee. This liability for other people's conduct is called vicarious liability.[78] There are three requirements: the author of the damage has to be an employee, he must have committed a tort, and this must have happened 'in the course of the employment'. Once these requirements are met, the employer is liable: he cannot escape liability by arguing that he did not act negligently: his liability is strict.[79]

Firstly, the employer is only vicariously liable for a tort of an employee and not for a tort of an independent contractor.[80] However, the employer can be liable for a tort committed by an independent contractor if he has authorized it or if he has breached his own non-delegable duty to supervise that due care was exercised.[81] Vicarious liability does not require a labour contract. What is decisive is the level of independence with which the work is carried out, who determines the working hours, and who has control over the work. In practice, it can be difficult to distinguish one from the other, particularly in cases where someone works more or less independently but mainly for the benefit of, and

---

[75] Le Tourneau (2004), nr 1365.

[76] Civ. 2e 19 February 1997, Bull. civ. II, no 53; JCP 1997, 4070, no 25, obs. Viney, RTD civ. 1998, 688, obs. Jourdain.

[77] Suzanne Galand-Carval, 'Comparative Report on Liability for Damage Caused by Others (Part I)', in J. Spier (ed.), *Liability for Damage Caused by Others* (The Hague, London, New York: Kluwer Law International, 2003), 294.

[78] Von Bar (1998), N 337, rightly argues that this expression is inappropriate because true vicarious liability is liability by agency and employer's liability does not replace but supplement the employee's liability.

[79] *Stavely Iron & Chemical Co Ltd v Jones* [1956] AC 627 (HL); *Imperial Chemical Industries v Shatwell* [1965] AC 656 (HL). Markesinis and Deakin (2003), 571–597; Winfield and Jolowicz (2002), paras 20.1–20.21.

[80] *D & F Estates Ltd v Church Commissioners for England* [1989] AC 177, 208 per Lord Bridge: 'It is trite law that the employer of an independent contractor is, in general, not liable for the negligence or other torts committed by the contractor in the course of the execution of the work.'

[81] E. McKendrick, 'Vicarious Liability and Independent Contractors—A Re-Examination', *Mod LR*, 53 (1990), 770 ff. Markesinis and Deakin (2003), 597–599; Winfield and Jolowicz (2002), para. 20.21.

under the direction of, a principal.[82] For example, it was decided that the master of a hunt can be liable for wrongful conduct by hunt members when the latter hunt outside the marked hunt area.[83]

Secondly, the employee must have committed a tort. This can concern the torts of negligence, trespass, conversion, or any other tort. Hence, liability of the employee is a prerequisite for the employer's vicarious liability. This implies that employer and employee will be jointly and severally liable for the damage of the victim. Though the employer is entitled to recover paid damages from the negligent employee,[84] in practice this only happens in cases of collusion or wilful misconduct of the employee. This is due to a gentlemen's agreement between employer's liability insurers not to seek contribution from employees.[85] If the employee is not liable, the employer cannot be vicariously liable. However, he can be liable on the basis of negligence by engaging an incompetent servant or for not having a proper system of work.[86]

Thirdly, the employee must have committed the tort in the course or 'scope' of his employment. English courts and writers have grappled with the formulation of this requirement. The best known test on scope of employment is that which was set out by Salmond: an act is deemed to be in the course of employment 'if it is either (1) a wrongful act authorised by the master, or (2) a wrongful and unauthorised mode of doing some act authorised by the master'.[87] Recent case law has substituted this test with an equally opaque criterion: an employer is now considered to be liable in respect of those of the employee's act which had a 'close connection' with the employment.[88]

The question of scope of employment is essentially one of fact, and the casuism of English courts has resisted all attempts of systemization. Indeed, one judge has commented that '... the large body of case law ... is notable for one thing, its inconsistency very often with an immediately preceding case'.[89] Courts have experimented with a number of factors, for example, whether there was implied authority for the employee to commit the act,[90] or whether (in fraud cases) he enjoyed ostensible authority to act from his employer.[91] On the other hand, the employee's personal motive for performing the act is not conclusive either way: for example, an employer has been held to be vicariously liable where his employee committed the tort in an attempt to defend his business property;[92]

---

[82] *Honeywill and Stein Ltd v Larkin Brothers Ltd* [1934] 1 KB 191; *Lee v Chung* [1990] 2 AC 374, about which Van Gerven (2000), 492–494.

[83] *League Against Cruel Sports Ltd v Scott* [1986] QB 240.

[84] *Lister v Romford Ice and Cold Storage Co* [1957] AC 555 (HL).

[85] Markesinis and Deakin (2003), 595–597; Winfield and Jolowicz (2002), para. 20.18.

[86] See for instance *Stavely Iron & Chemical Co Ltd v Jones* [1956] AC 627 (HL).

[87] Salmond and Heuston (1996), 443.   [88] *Lister v Hesley Hall* [2002] 1 AC 215.

[89] *Harrison v Michelin Tyre Co Ltd* [1985] 1 All ER 918, 920, per Comyn J.

[90] *Poland v Parr & Sons* [1927] 1 KB 236, 240.

[91] *Lloyd v Grace, Smith & Co* [1912] AC 716; see also Winfield and Jolowicz (2002), nr 20.17.

[92] *Poland v Parr & Sons* [1927] 1 KB 236, 240.

but also in the case where his employee was a lorry driver who lit a cigarette at a petrol station.[93] It is also interesting to note the impact of human rights in this area: for example, it has been decided that 'course of employment' should be construed widely in cases of racial discrimination so as to give the imposition of liability an educative or exemplary effect.[94]

The consensus among legal writers remains realistic as to the function of the scope of duty test: 'The underlying idea is that the injury done by the servant must involve a risk sufficiently inherent in or characteristic of the employer's business that it is just to make him bear the loss.'[95] Put another way: '. . . one is tempted to suggest that the courts tend to expand the notion of "course of employment" if by doing so they are serving better an "important purpose" '.[96] The English 'test' for scope of employment thus masks an approach to liability which is essentially policy-oriented.

Employer's liability has to be distinguished from liability for the corporation's own conduct. For the latter it is decisive whether the legal person committed a tort by virtue of a natural person representing 'the directing mind and will of the corporation'.[97] This circle of natural persons is confined to the central governing authority of a company entrusted with the exercise of the powers of the company and does not, for example, include a branch manager.[98] In such a case the employer's vicarious liability will provide the answer to the liability question.

1607 Comparative observations

1607-1 *General remarks*

Damage caused by an employee is not always easily recoverable from him, since generally he will not be insured or have the financial means to pay compensation. Hence, all legal systems contain special regimes for the liability of the employer for damage caused by his employee.[99] These rules mainly date from the 19th and early 20th century. Despite major changes in the way commercial and industrial activities are organized, these liability rules have hardly changed. They have appeared to be flexible enough to cope with current issues. The ECC and the PETL hold similar provisions.[100]

---

[93] *Century Insurance Company Ltd v Northern Ireland Transport* [1942] AC 509.
[94] *Jones v Tower Boot Co Ltd* [1997] ICR 254; see also Markesinis and Deakin (2003), 585–86.
[95] Winfield and Jolowicz (2002), nr 20.9.   [96] Markesinis and Deakin (2003), 583.
[97] *Lennard's Carrying Company Ltd v Asiatic Petroleum Company Ltd* [1915] AC 705; Winfield and Jolowicz (2002), para. 24.22.   [98] *Tesco Supermarkets Ltd v Nattrass* [1972] AC 153.
[99] Protection of the employee also depends on the restrictions to the employer's right of recourse against the employee.
[100] Art. 3:201(1) ECC:
A person who employs or similarly engages another, is accountable for the causation of legally relevant damage suffered by a third person when the person employed or engaged (a) caused the

In line with these developments is Article 288(4) EC, providing that in case of non-contractual liability, the Community shall, in accordance with the general principles common to the laws of the Member States, make good any damage caused by its institutions or by its servants in the performance of their duties. The latter words are the basis for the Community's liability for damage caused by its servants.[101]

In addition to rules regarding liability for employees, rules as regards liability of the legal body itself have been developed. All three legal systems comprise rules as regards this liability, which is generally related to conduct by persons in the corporation who have a central and leading management function. A difference in application is, for example, that in Germany the conduct of branch managers qualifies for this liability but in England it does not.

There are thus various rules on the basis of which an organization (in the form of a legal body) can be liable for damage caused by persons related to this business, either for its 'own conduct' or for the conduct of its subordinates. Sometimes it will not even be clear who exactly the person was who committed the harmful conduct. However, there is a strong tendency that it is not necessary to identify the employee as long as it is clear that it was a defendant's employee.[102] This comes close to the German *Organisationsverschulden* (organizational fault), although this tenet is generally applied as a means of repair and not as an overall principle.

The developments thus go in the direction that an organization or business is liable for damage unlawfully caused by conduct (individualized or not) that can be reasonably attributed to, or identified with, the organization or business. The emphasis has shifted from the employee's individual conduct to the organization's conduct. This development runs parallel with the growing complexity nowadays of organizations and businesses.

Legally, unlawful conduct is attributed to the legal or natural person that runs the organization or business. However, current business organization is often characterized by the use of a complex structure of many legal persons. A subsequent question would then be how the law deals with this phenomenon, and how conduct of one legal person can be identified with that of another. From a legal point of view there are currently strong arguments against such identification, but from a factual or organizational point of view the answer seems to be less obvious.

---

damage in the course of employment or engagement, and (b) caused the damage intentionally or negligently, or is otherwise accountable for the causation of the damage.

Art. 6:102(1) PETL is more concise: 'A person is liable for damage caused by his auxiliaries acting within the scope of their functions provided that they violated the required standard of conduct.'

[101] See for example ECJ 8 October 1986, Joined Cases 169/83 and 136/84, ECR 1986, 2801 (*Leussink and Others v Commission*), about which nr 1210.

[102] Suzanne Galand-Carval, in J. Spier (ed.), *Liability for Damage Caused by Others* (The Hague, London, New York: Kluwer Law International, 2003), 303.

1607-2 *Rationales*

The rationale of the employer's liability for damage caused by his employee has, for example, been expressed by Lord Pearce:

The doctrine of vicarious liability has not grown from any very clear, logical or legal principle but from social convenience and rough justice. The master having (presumably for his own benefit) employed the servant, and being (presumably) better able to make good the damage which may occasionally result from the arrangement, is answerable to the world at large for all the torts committed by his servant within the scope of it.[103]

Hence, strict liability is justified for the loss caused in activities carried out in the course of business. In this respect, the rationale for employer's liability does not differ substantially from his liability for damage caused by his defective products or his harmful waste (nr 1401). Businesses and organizations should pay their way.

Initially, these rules were designed to protect the claimant against the employee's insolvency. In the course of time, however, the discussion has shifted to the protection of the employee. The basic idea in this respect is that it is considered to be unfair to let an employee pay for the damage he causes while carrying out activities for the benefit of the employer.[104]

In most cases employer and employee are jointly liable for the damage caused by the employee. This may be different if the employee is not liable because he caused the damage under the influence of a mental illness, but this will be the exception rather than the rule.[105] At the end of the day the question arises who of them has to bear the loss. The rationale for the employer's external liability (businesses and organizations should pay their way) also justifies that the employee is, in principal, exempted from liability. Moreover, an employee runs a substantial risk to be liable for damage he has caused in the course of his employment. This could be disastrous if his employer is not able to pay the damages due to insolvency. Such a liability can only be justified if the employee acted intentionally or with gross negligence or if he has a sufficient liability insurance coverage. Hence, the best balance would be that the employee is only liable, and the employer only has a right of recourse, if the employee acted intentionally or with gross negligence.

This, however, is far from a general principle in the national systems. Only the French *Cour de cassation* has taken the step to exclude the employee's personal liability where he acted within the limits of his task. In Germany the employee is fully liable towards third parties (this is one of the ways in which the defective German rule on employer's liability is repaired, nr 1606-2) but he will be insured by his employer, he will have a right of recourse against his employer, or both. In

---

[103] *Imperial Chemical Industries Ltd v Shatwell* [1965] AC 656, 685–686 (HL).
[104] Compare BAG 27 September 1994, ZIP 1994, 1712.
[105] This can be the case in Germany and England; see nr 1606-1 and 1606-4.

England third party liability of the employee is considered to be a breach of contract between employer and employee, making the latter liable to the former.[106] Though in practice the employer's insurer will only take recourse against the employee with the employer's consent, this does not always put the employee in a safe position.

1607-3 *Conditions*

Though employer's liability is strict from the employer's point of view, it is fault liability from a victim's point of view: basically he has to prove the employee's negligent or improper conduct.

Generally, it is considered to be sufficient for the employer's liability that the employee has caused damage by his negligent conduct in the course of his employment. In England and France, and in Community law, the employer has no defence whatsoever once these requirements have been established: employer's liability is strict. § 831 BGB holds a negligence liability with a reversed burden of proof. Besides this rule the courts apply additional rules which lead to results not very different from those reached in countries with a strict liability regime.

For whom is the 'employer' liable? The way companies are organized has been subject to change in the course of the last decades and it is still changing. Work relations are getting more flexible, non-core business activities are being outsourced to other companies, and more people work on a freelance basis or they work from home. This has complicated the distinction between employees and independent contractors. In his famous speech in *Donoghue v Stevenson* Lord Atkin asked: 'Who is my neighbour?' (nr 503-1). In current labour relations employers may ask: 'Who is my employee?'

The systems are unanimous in that the liability rules only apply to relationships of subordination and not to relationships with independent contractors. If the tortfeasor worked independently, the other party to the contract can only be liable on the basis of his own fault or on the contract implying safety duties to third parties.[107] However, if the tortfeasor was a subordinate the master can be strictly liable (England and France) or liable for rebuttable negligence (Germany). The often quoted English test is from Cooke J, and his considerations do not differ much from what goes for the other legal systems in this respect:

The fundamental test to be applied is this: 'Is the person who has engaged himself to perform these services performing them as a person in business on his own account?' If the answer to that question is 'yes', then the contract is a contract for services. If the answer is 'no', then the contract is a contract of service .... The most that can be said is that control will no doubt always have to be considered, although it can no longer be regarded as the sole determining factor; and that factors which may be of importance are such matters as whether the man performing the services provides his own equipment,

---

[106] *Lister v Romford Ice and Cold Storage Co Ltd* [1957] AC 555 (HL).
[107] Von Bar (1998), N 200–201 and 353, with further references.

whether he hires his own helpers, what degree of financial risk he takes, what degree of responsibility for investment and management he has, and whether and how far he has an opportunity of profiting from sound management in the performance of his task.[108]

In other words one may look who controls, supervises the risk and is the best insurer.[109]

The general view is that someone is subordinate if he is bound to follow instructions from someone else. This implies that the other has the authority to give instructions. These instructions do not have to be detailed. For example, a hospital can be liable for damage caused by its employee doctors because it has the right to give instructions, if only as regards their working hours.[110] A clergyman in a church can also be considered to be a subordinate for whose unlawful conduct, for example sexual abuse, the church can be liable. In a *spiritual* sense, the clergyman may be considered to be a worker in his Employer's vineyard (Matthew 20:1–16). In a *legal* sense, however, his earthly employer is the church. For the time being, the legal criterion must be decisive.[111]

The special rule also applies outside employment situations. Generally, the emphasis is not on the legal criterion of 'employment' but rather on the more factual criterion of subordination or—which is the flipside of this coin—on the authority of the master to give instructions. This means that 'employer's' liability may also apply outside labour relations. France and Germany seem to go a small step further in this respect than England, by also applying the rule if someone carries out a gratuitous task for a neighbour or a friend. If he causes damage to a third party, the neighbour or the friend is strictly liable (France) or liable for rebuttable negligence (Germany).[112]

The employee's conduct has to be sufficiently related to the employee's tasks. This is undisputed in all legal systems but it is acknowledged that in practice it can be difficult to establish whether such a relation exists. Hence, in all legal systems a lot of case law can be found on this subject. The fact that the employer must have had control over the work does, of course, not imply that it is required that the employer ordered or allowed the negligent conduct. Also, if an employee acts contrary to clear instructions from the employer, the employee's conduct is generally sufficiently related to the employee's task: the instructions are evidence for this relationship. This was, for instance, decided in England when a milkman allowed children to help him to deliver which was contrary to his instructions.[113]

[108] Cooke J in *Market Investigations Ltd v Minister of Social Security* [1969] 2 QB 173 at 184.
[109] See Kötz-Wagner (2004), N 273 quoting von Caemmerer: '...ein guter Test zu prüfen, wer eigentlich das Risiko organisatorisch beherrscht und überblickt und wirtschaftlich der richtige Versicherungsnehmer ist'. [110] Von Bar (1998), N 191 with further references.
[111] See also Civ. 2e 6 February 2003, Bull. civ. II, no 28, ETL 2003, 159 (Lafay, Moréteau and Pellerin-Rugliano).
[112] Suzanne Galand-Carval, 'Comparative Report on Liability for Damage Caused by Others (Part I)', in J. Spier (ed.), *Unification of Tort Law: Liability for Damage Caused by Others* (The Hague, London, New York: Kluwer Law International, 2003), 300.
[113] *Rose v Plenty* [1976] 1 WLR 141.

Difficult cases are those in which the employee caused the damage by his intentional or criminal conduct. This conduct (fighting, killing, theft) does not necessarily fall outside the scope of the employer's liability, particularly if the risk of committing a crime is enhanced by the work or by the way the work was organized. An example is an English case about a bouncer at Flamingo's Nightclub in south-east London who, after a fight with a customer, went home, returned with a knife and attacked another customer in the street causing him severe injuries. The nightclub, whose owner encouraged bouncers to be aggressive in ejecting customers, was held vicariously liable for the damage caused.[114] France probably takes the most vigorous position by solely requiring an objective link between the employee's act and the work. This requirement is generally satisfied if the act took place during working hours. This implies that, for example, a company employing office cleaners will be liable for long distance telephone calls made by a cleaner from one of the client's offices, and that the employer of a painter, asked to repaint the kitchen of a manor house, will be liable for the damage caused to the housemaid who is raped by the painter.[115]

[114] *Mattis v Pollock* [2003] EWCA 887, [2003] 1 WLR 2158. See also *Dyer v Munday* [1895] 1 QB 742 and Robert Weekes, 'Vicarious Liability for Violent Employees', *CamLJ*, 63 (2004) 53–63.
[115] Suzanne Galand-Carval, 'Comparative Report on Liability for Damage Caused by Others (Part I)', in J. Spier (ed.), *Unification of Tort Law: Liability for Damage Caused by Others* (The Hague, London, New York: Kluwer Law International, 2003), 300–302.

17

Liability in Emergency Cases

1701 Pure omissions: emergency cases

The issue of liability for omissions was dealt with in nr 808 and 1301. It appeared that all jurisdictions have struggled with this issue one way or another. Though English law has more reluctantly than French and German law, they have all acknowledged the existence of affirmative duties, the breach of which can give rise to a claim in damages. This can particularly be the case if someone has a special relationship with the movable object with which the damage is caused (Chapter 14), with the place where the accident occurred (Chapter 15), with the person causing the damage (Chapter 16), or with the person deserving protection (nr 808-2).

This chapter deals with the question of whether there is a basis for liability for an omission if no such relationship exists. This issue is about what is called 'liability for pure omissions' and it mainly occurs in emergency situations in which someone needs to be rescued. The question is: can such a situation bring two persons in such proximity that this creates a special relationship between them?

The seminal example in this respect is the parable of the Good Samaritan (Luke 10:29–37) which tells us about a man who was on his way from Jerusalem to Jericho when he was robbed, wounded, and left half dead. A priest came down and when he saw the man he passed by on the other side. A Levite who was also on his way to Jericho saw the man and also passed by on the other side. Finally, a Samaritan came down and when he saw the man he had compassion on him, he went to him, bound up his wounds, set him on his beast, brought him to an inn, and took care of him. This parable illustrates the question at stake in this chapter, which is whether someone owes a duty to rescue to someone who is in peril.[1]

All legal systems are reluctant in acknowledging that a moral duty to rescue can turn into a legal duty to do so. English law does not acknowledge a general

---

[1] See extensively Jeroen Kortmann, *Altruism in Private Law. Liability for Nonfeasance and Negotiorum Gestio* (Oxford: Oxford University Press, 2005); and J.M. Smits, *The Good Samaritan in European Private Law. On the Perils of Principles and a Programme for the Future* (Deventer: Kluwer, 2000); F.J.M. Feldbrugge, 'Good and Bad Samaritans, A Comparative Survey of Criminal Law Provisions Concerning Failure to Rescue', *AJCL* 14 (1967), 630–657; Michael A. Menlowe and Alexander McCall Smith, *The Duty to Rescue. The Jurisprudence of Aid* (Aldershot: Dartmouth, 1993).

criminal duty to rescue, not even when someone else's life is in danger, neither does it hold a civil duty to rescue (nr 1702-3). German law does hold a criminal duty to rescue but the violation of such a rule does not give rise to a claim *in civilibus* because it is not a *Schutzgesetz* in the sense of § 823 II (nr 1702-2). French law also holds a criminal duty to rescue and the violation of this rule amounts to a *faute* in the sense of article 1382 CC (nr 1702-1).

After an overview of the national rules as regards liability for pure omissions (1702), the circumstances will be considered under which a duty to rescue would be reasonable (nr 1703-1). Subsequently, the level of care to be maintained by the rescuer, as well as his right to compensation if he has suffered damage himself, will be briefly touched upon (nr 1703-2 and 1703-3).

1702 National rules

1702-1 *France*

French law does not clearly distinguish between acts and omissions, and affirmative duties are generally recognized by the courts. In many of such cases a strict liability rule applies (nr 1301). Liability for damage caused by pure omissions is also conceivable but in exceptional cases only. In such a case it is required that the defendant intentionally did not act or was aware of the consequences.[2]

Civil liability for pure omissions is based on the criminal liability provision of article 223-6 New Penal Code (*Nouveau Code pénal*) which has replaced article 63 old Penal Code. This provision holds someone criminally liable if he voluntarily does not provide help to someone who is in peril whilst he is able to provide such help without risk for himself or other persons, either by his own action or by getting help by other persons. He can be punished with five years imprisonment or a €75,000 fine.[3]

As has been pointed out (nr 302-1), a criminal offence implies a civil *faute* in the sense of article 1382 CC. Hence, violation of the above mentioned criminal provision implies civil liability for the damage caused.[4] The *Cour de cassation* is,

---

[2] Terré-Simler-Lequette (2002), nr 721. In the same sense Aubry and Rau-Dejean de la Bathie (1989), nr 38; Carbonnier (2000), § 221, 402–403. See Civ. 2e 18 January 1963, JCP 1963. II. 13316, comm. C. Blaevoet; Civ. 2e 18 October 1962, Bull. civ. II, no 288, p. 201; Civ. 2e 22 May 1968, D. 1968. Somm. 102; Civ. 2e 9 November 1971, D. 1972. 75.

[3] Art. 223-6:

Quiconque pouvant empêcher par son action immédiate, sans risque pour lui ou pour les tiers, soit un crime, soit un délit contre l'intégrité corporelle de la personne s'abstient volontairement de le faire est puni de cinq ans d'emprisonnement et de 75,000 euros d'amende. Sera puni des mêmes peines quiconque s'abstient volontairement de porter à un personne en péril l'assistance que, sans risque pour lui ou pour les tiers, il pouvait lui prêter soit par son action personnelle, soit en provoquant un secours.

[4] Crim. 16 March 1972, D. 1972, 394, comm. Costa, JCP 1973. II. 17474, comm. Moret. Terré-Simler-Lequette (2002), nr 721; Aubry and Rau-Dejean de la Bathie (1989), nr 36.

however, somewhat cautious in drawing this conclusion.[5] For example, if someone stays inactive while he sees another person in danger, he is only liable if he intentionally refuses to provide help.[6] Furthermore, no liability exists if the potential rescuer did not understand there was an emergency situation or if he was not able to provide effective assistance.[7]

An example is a case about a person who walked on thin ice, fell through and nearly drowned. Another person tried to rescue him by handing him an iron bar to cling to but his father-in-law had walked away from the scene refusing to assist in the rescue The father-in-law was held liable and had to pay his son-in-law 25,000 francs.[8]

The test to be applied to the defendant is subjective *(appréciation 'in concreto')* which means that the personal knowledge and abilities of the defendant are decisive (nr 811-1). A duty to rescue is generally not owed by children.[9]

1702-2 *Germany*

According to German law an omission *(eine bloße oder reine Unterlassung)* can only be unlawful *(rechtswidrig)* if someone owed a duty to act towards the victim and this act would have prevented the damage. Such a duty will generally be a safety duty *(Verkehrspflicht)*, which presupposes a special relationship of the person who owes the duty with a movable or immovable object, with the tortfeasor or with the victim (nr 804-2).[10]

Without such a special relationship liability is hard to establish. A general criminal duty to rescue can be found in § 323c *Strafgesetzbuch* (Penal Code) *(Unterlassene Hilfeleistung)*. According to this provision someone can be liable to punishment if he does not render assistance in case of an accident, common danger, or an emergency, although this assistance was needed and could be rendered by him under the circumstances without a substantial risk for his own safety or breach of other important duties. He can face imprisonment of up to one year.[11]

---

[5] Civ. 2e 9 July 1969, Bull. civ. II, no 238, 172; Carbonnier (2000), § 230, 416–417 mentions the difficult position of physicians who do not provide help after a (phone) call for help: see Crim. 21 July 1954, D. 1954. 224, Crim. 20 February 1958, D. 1958, 534; Crim. 17 February 1972, D. 1972. 325. [6] Aubry and Rau-Dejean de la Bathie (1989), nr 38.

[7] Carbonnier (2000), § 230, 416; see for instance Versailles 26 June 1989, D. 1989, IR. 247: it was taken into account that someone was in a stress situation.

[8] Tribunal Correctionnel d'Aix 27 March 1947, D. 1947. 304.

[9] Civ. 2e 17 February 1982, Gaz. Pal. 1982. 2. 554, comm. Chabas (no children's *faute* if they do not interfere if another child throws a lighter into a fire); Civ. 2e 19 April 1985, Gaz. Pal. 1986. 1. Somm. 252, obs. Chabas (no children's *faute* if they allow their companion to set a straw stack on fire).

[10] See also BGH 19 November 1971, BGHZ 57, 245; BGH 5 July 1973, BGHZ 61, 118; BGH 19 February 1975, BGHZ 64, 46; BGH 14 February 1978, BGHZ 71, 86.

[11] § 323c StGB:

Wer bei Unglücksfällen oder gemeiner Gefahr oder Not nicht Hilfe leistet, obwohl dies erforderlich und in den Umständen nach zuzumeten, insbesondere ohne erhebliche eigene Gefahr und ohne Verletzung anderer wichtiger Pflichten möglich ist, wird mit Freiheitsstrafe bis zu einem Jahr oder mit Geldstrafe bestraft.

See also § 138 StGB (not notifying the police about a possible crime).

As has been pointed out (nr 903), violation of a statutory rule that aims to protect the claimant leads to civil liability on the basis of § 823 II BGB (*Schutzgesetz*). Though it is likely that the legislator intended this provision to protect individuals, the current majority opinion is that the criminal duty to provide help to someone in peril (§ 323c StGB) does not aim to protect the person in danger or his next of kin, but only society as a whole. It is argued that it cannot reasonably be the aim of the rule that the person who did not prevent the crime or the accident is liable in the same way as the offender or the direct tortfeasor. The purport of the threat of punishment is not the warrant of individual help for the benefit of certain persons, but the citizen's duty (*ein staatsbürgerlicher Pflicht*) to assist to preserve the public order and safety in extremely dangerous situations.[12] Another argument is that the assistance provided need not be successful to escape criminal liability. Thus, if first aid fails and the person still dies, the duty under § 323c StGB could be satisfied. The aim is not the successful rescue of the injured, but to require people to show a minimum of solidarity. Hence, liability for pure omissions cannot be based on § 823 II BGB although a minority of the legal authors do consider § 323c and § 138 StGB to be *Schutzgesetze*, statutory rules for the protection of the individual.[13]

An alternative basis for liability for pure omissions is § 826 BGB: intentional infliction of damage contrary to ethical principles (*contra bonos mores: vorsätzliche sittenwidrige Schädigung*: nr 402-4). To establish intention (*Vorsatz*) it is sufficient if the tortfeasor was aware of his harmful conduct; it is not necessary that his intention was to cause damage (nr 802-2). It is assumed that not interfering in an emergency situation is conduct *contra bonos mores* in special circumstances only. One may think of danger to the life of a person who is in trouble, or to prevent a serious road traffic accident if this is possible without much effort.[14]

1702-3 *England*

English law has grappled and still grapples with liability for omissions. In the course of time English law has acknowledged a number of categories of cases in which such an affirmative duty exists, particularly if there is a special relationship with the premises where the danger occurs or with the person whose conduct needs to be controlled, either for his own safety or for that of others. One may think of the relationship between employer and employee, driver and passenger, occupier and visitors, or parent and child.[15]

---

[12] Wilhelm Dütz, 'Zur privatrechtlichen Bedeutung unterlassener Hilfeleisung (§ 330c StGB)', *NJW* 1970, 1822 ff.

[13] See for example, Larenz-Canaris (1994), 441.

[14] Dütz, NJW 1970, 1826.

[15] Fleming (1998), 163–164; Markesinis and Deakin (2003), 151–152. See for instance about the duty of care towards a fire fighter: *Ogwo v Taylor* [1987] 3 All ER 961. In most American states professional rescuers do not have a right to compensation for physical damage on the basis of the fireman's rule; see for instance *Krauth v Geller* (1960) 157 A 2d 129.

If no such relationship exists, a duty of care cannot be established. Only in situations of purest nonfeasance, does our modern law continue to disclaim any general duty of care.[16] This means that, '... where the plaintiff is endangered from a source quite unconnected with the defendant, the latter is not required to come to his assistance, although it is in his power to remove the peril with little effort (*"easy rescue"*).'[17]

This implies that a doctor, who coincidentally passes the spot of an accident, may refuse to help the injured person.[18] An expert swimmer may stay on the bank and watch another person drown. An American case was about someone who hired a canoe to a drunken person who was clearly not able to handle it properly and safely. The man canoed away, capsized, and shouted for help for half an hour. The boat hirer heard the shouting and saw the problem but did not take action, and consequently his customer drowned. The court decided that the boat hirer was not liable for the relatives' damage since he did not owe his customer a duty of care.[19]

Markesinis and Deakin consider it possible that the English judge will follow this decision but that it is also conceivable that the relationship between the boat hirer and his customer can be seen as a relationship giving rise to a duty to rescue.[20] In this respect reference can be made to the *Ogopogo* case in which it was held that a boat owner owes a duty of rescue towards a passenger who has fallen overboard.[21]

The common law position has been fiercely criticized by Markesinis and Deakin:

The hostility of the common law to the concept of affirmative duties in tort is long-standing, the product, it has been said, of 'values of an era in which private selfishness was elevated to the rank of a public virtue'. Though the socio-economic environment is changing, there are few signs that the courts are currently prepared to abandon their unwillingness to treat omissions like acts.[22]

Fleming also cherished hope that liability for pure omissions would play a role in common law in the near future:

Nor is it altogether idle to entertain the hope that the demands of elementary civilised conduct will yet be reinforced by legal sanctions, if nothing more onerous than a simple

[16] Fleming (1998), 164. See also Lord Goff in *Smith v Littlewoods Organization Ltd* [1987] 2 AC 241, 271: '... the common law does not impose liability for what are called pure omissions'. See about this case Van Gerven (2000), 291–296.

[17] Fleming (1998), 164. See also Markesinis and Deakin (2003), 151–152.

[18] It can be concluded from *Barnett v Chelsea and Kensington Hospital* [1969] 1 QB 428 that the Emergency Department of a hospital owes a duty to someone in a medical emergency situation: see Markesinis and Deakin (2003), 150–151.   [19] *Osterlind v Hill* (1928) 160 NE 301.

[20] Markesinis and Deakin (2003), 150–151.

[21] *Horsley v MacLaren (The Ogopogo)* [1971] 2 Lloyd's Rep. 410.

[22] Markesinis and Deakin (2003), 149. See also B.S. Markesinis, 'Negligence, Nuisance and Affirmative Duties of Action', *LQR*, 105 (1989),104–124; Winfield and Jolowicz (2002), para. 5.19 ff.; Fleming (1998), 163.

warning would suffice to safeguard a fellow-being from imminent peril to life and limb, like alerting a blind person or even a trespasser about to walk over a precipice.[23]

However, in 1996 the House of Lords strongly confirmed the English position in *Stovin v Wise*. Lord Nicholls said:

The recognised legal position is that the bystander does not owe the drowning child or the heedless pedestrian a duty to take steps to save him. Something more is required than being a bystander. There must be some additional reason why it is fair and reasonable that one person should be regarded as his brother's keeper and have legal obligations in that regard. When this additional reason exists, there is said to be sufficient proximity. That is the customary label.[24]

This principle goes not only for the duty to rescue but also for the duty to warn of dangerous situations. In the words of Lord Keith of Kinkel there is no negligence '... on the part of one who sees another about to walk over a cliff with his head in the air, and forbears to shout a warning.'[25]

1703 Duty to rescue

1703-1 *When does a duty to rescue exist?*

All legal systems are very reluctant in accepting liability for pure omissions, particularly in rescue cases, whereas English law does not accept such liability at all.

Provided that a general denial of liability in cases of pure omissions is unsatisfactory, the key issue is to find the standard as to when someone should be liable in such cases. It is enticing to give way to one's feelings or to conclude liability on moral grounds. Such a reaction would not do justice to the character and function of tort law. Moreover, one should be aware that there are also other instruments to react to omissions, such as criminal law or moral disapproval.

In order to find a useful and appropriate standard it is necessary to refer to nr 808-2 where the justification for affirmative duties, more particularly the responsibility of supervisors of premises, movable objects, tortfeasors, and victims, was found in the circumstance that supervisors possess knowledge of the risk and the ability to avoid it while the potential victim has less knowledge or ability as regards these risks, and often does not have knowledge or ability at all. This implies that in cases of pure omissions a duty to warn, to assist, or to rescue can only exist if at least the following cumulative requirements are met:

a. Someone has specific knowledge of a dangerous situation in which specific third persons can suffer serious mental or physical harm or can be killed.

---

[23] Fleming (1998), 166.
[24] *Stovin v Wise* [1996] 3 All ER 801 at 807. See also the speech of Lord Hoffmann, cited in nr 808-1.   [25] *Yuen Kun Yeu v Attorney General of Hong Kong* [1988] AC 175, 192.

This restriction to serious harm is crucial since everybody is confronted on a daily basis with many dangerous situations, particularly as regards property damage. It would be much too burdensome to require intervention in all such situations.

b. He has the capacity and ability to prevent or to put an end to the dangerous situation by providing aid, assistance, or asking others to do so.

In this respect it should be taken into account that socio-psychological research has revealed that passiveness in such a situation is the rule rather than the exception, particularly if one is aware of the presence of other potential rescuers. This is know as the bystander effect or the Genovese syndrome. This can be a factor to determine whether someone is capable to provide the required assistance. An infamous case to illustrate the latter is a sociological study about the fate of Kitty Genovese who came home from work around 3am and was attacked and killed by someone before she could enter her home. The noise of her screaming was heard by 38 persons. A subsequent *New York Times* article bore the headline: 'Thirty-Eight who saw Murder Didn't call the police'. This article was factually incorrect since none of the neighbours could have witnessed the entire attack, but the incorrect story became an example of the bystander effect.[26]

c. The possible restriction or prevention of the risk outweighs the burden of precautionary measures, ie the risks run during assistance or rescue, or for instance reprisals from the underworld in cases of informing the police about a crime.

d. He knows and is aware that the potential victim does not possess the knowledge of the serious risk or the ability to rescue himself, and that he is not able either to ask other persons to provide help. This restriction follows from the idea that most people are well suited to protect their own interests. Only if there is a clear gap between the two persons as regards knowledge and ability, can a duty to assist or rescue be established.

If these requirements are met it can be concluded that a duty is justified by the special relationship between the two persons. In such a case the relationship was not previously there but it is born from the emergency situation.

Things will be different as regards professional rescuers. Professionals like the police, ambulance services, fire brigades, rescue services, and a hospital's Accident and Emergency department, are generally obliged to provide help and assistance on the basis of a statute or unwritten law.[27]

1703-2 *Rescuer's standard of care*

Once someone has started to provide assistance two other questions arise. Firstly, what is the level of care to be maintained towards the person to be rescued?

---

[26] J.M. Darley and B. Latané, 'Bystander Intervention in Emergencies: Diffusion of Responsibility', *Journal of Personality and Social Psychology*, 8 (1968), 377–383.

[27] See also the *Osman* and *Kilic* cases in the framework of Article 2 ECHR as regards the police's duty to rescue as regards unidentified persons (nr 1807-2).

Secondly, does the rescuer have a right to compensation towards the rescued or his next of kin for his expenses and the damage he has possibly suffered? The lower the required level of care and the bigger the chance to get compensation, the more reasonable it is to require someone to provide assistance. See about the right to compersation nr 1703-3.

As regards the level of care it is important to distinguish between professional and non-professional help. It seems to be reasonable not to require a high level of care from a non-professional rescuer: '... rescuers will not normally be held to a high *standard* of care; but in a case of an egregious failure to act, the prior existence of a duty leaves open the possibility of a liability.'[28] It is submitted that the personal knowledge and abilities of such a rescuer are to be taken into account when establishing due care in the circumstances of the case (nr 811-1). The bottom line is that the rescuer is only liable if the victim's position has deteriorated due to the rescuer's intervention.[29] A low level of care for volunteers is necessary to avoid

... that the good Samaritan who tries to help may find himself mulcted in damages, while the priest and the Levite who pass by on the other side go on their cheerful way rejoicing. It has been pointed out often enough that this in fact operates as a real, and serious, deterrent to the giving of needed aid.[30]

In Germany the rules regarding *Geschäftsführung ohne Auftrag* (agency without authority: § 677ff BGB) are of relevance. He, who is taking care for another person's affairs without being obliged to do so, has to run the affairs in the interest of the other person (§ 677).[31] However, if the affairs involve averting an urgent danger that threatens the other person, the agent is only liable for intention and gross negligence (§ 680).[32]

Things are different if help is provided by a professional, like the police, ambulance of services, fire brigades, rescue services, and a hospital's Accident and Emergency department. They are generally able to prepare themselves for emergency situations which as such do not occur unexpectedly. In principle, it can be required that standard procedures are to be followed faithfully, even under time pressure. However, mistakes will not always establish liability since

[28] Markesinis and Deakin (2003), 152.
[29] Markesinis and Deakin (2003), 151–152; Fleming (1998), 164–165; Dobbs II (2001), § 318, 859–860. See also *East Suffolk Rivers Catchments Board v Kent* [1941] AC 74; Lord Diplock in *Home Office v Dorset Yacht Co Ltd* [1970] AC 1004, 1060; Lord Bridge of Harwich in *Curran v Northern Ireland Co-Ownership Housing Association Ltd* [1987] 2 WLR 1043; *Quinn v Hill* (1957) VLR 439; *Goldman v Hargrave* [1967] 1 AC 645.
[30] Prosser and Keeton (1984), 378; Dobbs I (2001), § 227, 579.
[31] § 677 BGB: 'Wer ein Geschäft für einen anderen besorgt, ohne von ihm beauftragt oder ihm gegenüber sonst dazu berechtigt zu sein, hat das Geschäft so zu führen, wie das Interesse des Geschäftsherrn mit Rücksicht auf dessen wirklichen oder mutmaßlichen Willen es erfordert.'
[32] § 680 BGB: 'Bezweckt die Geschäftsführung die Abwendung einer dem Geschäftsherrn drohenden dringenden Gefahr, so hat der Geschäftsführer nur Vorsatz und grobe Fahrlässigkeit zu vertreten.'

an emergency situation may require quick and split second decisions about diagnosis and therapy. Hindsight knowledge should not be used to impose liability in such cases.

1703-3 *Rescuer's right to compensation*

The basis for a claim for compensation for the rescuer's expenses and the possible damage he has suffered can be a tort law claim if the rescued had caused the dangerous situation himself.[33] If this is not the case, the rescuer will have to rely on a different source of obligations: *negotiorum gestio*, in France *gestion d'affaire d'autrui* and in Germany *Geschäftsführung ohne Auftrag*.

Article 1375 CC grants the *gérant* (manager) a right to indemnification and to reimbursement of all the useful and necessary expenses against the *maître* (principal). This includes the loss suffered during the rescue operation but not a salary.[34] See in a different setting the rescue case in which a public authority was held liable for the damage of the rescuer on the basis of the equality principle (nr 1802-3).[35]

§ 683 BGB provides that the *Geschäftsführer* (manager) may demand reimbursement of his expenses from the *Geschäftsherr* (principal). An example is a driver who swerved to avoid a child and suffered severe injuries. She was entitled to recover her loss under the heading of *Geschäftsführung ohne Auftrag*.[36] Compensation may also include a salary for the professional rescuer.[37] No right to compensation exists if the 'rescuer' does not have a sound reason to interfere. For example, if a bank is being robbed and someone tries to disarm one of the robbers, he does not have a claim against the bank if he is shot. Disarming a robber may be a heroic act but it is disproportional to put one's life in danger to only prevent a financial loss. This is also why banks have instructed their personnel not to endanger themselves to defend cash tills.[38]

English law does not hold a general rule in this respect; it does not have a doctrine of *negotiorum gestio*. A general rule does not exist and a rescuer will be in great uncertainty whether or not to be able to claim damages, though in specific cases damages may be awarded, particularly if the rescued person intentionally or negligently created the dangerous situation.[39] In this respect reference can be made to *Carmarthenshire County Council v Lewis*, concerning a lorry driver swerving to avoid the child: in this case the school (local authority) was held

---

[33] Von Bar (2000), N 512–513.
[34] Civ. 28 January 1988, D. 1989. 405; Civ. 16 November 1955, JCP 1956. II. 9087; Com. 15 December 1992, Bull. civ. IV. 415.
[35] CE 29 September 1970, in Brown and Bell (1998), 195 (*Commune de Batz-sur-Mer c. Tesson*). In the same vein CE 9 October 1970 Rec CE 1970, 565 (*Gaillard*).
[36] BGH 27 November 1962, BGHZ 38, 270.
[37] Münchener Kommentar-Seiler (1997), § 683 N 24.
[38] Von Bar (1998), N 512 with reference to OLG Karlsruhe 23 March 1977, VersR 1977, 936.
[39] See for an overview Kortmann, *Altruism in Private Law* (2005), 111 ff.

liable for not taking precautionary measures to prevent the child from running onto the street.[40]

Given the above-mentioned rules, English law provides the most powerful deterrence for interveners and rescuers: it does not oblige someone to intervene, even if someone's life is in danger. If he decides to (voluntarily) come to someone's rescue, it is doubtful whether he will have a right to compensation for the costs he spent and the damage he suffered. French and German law on the other hand provide a civil law duty to rescue but in very special circumstances only. If someone has intervened, either voluntarily or compulsorily, he has a right to have his costs reimbursed and his damage compensated.

---

[40] *Carmarthenshire County Council v Lewis* [1956] AC 549, about which nr 1506-4.

18

Liability of Public Authorities

A INTRODUCTION

1801 Overview

Liability of public authorities, for example national and local governments and regulators, is currently one of the most discussed and most complicated areas of the law and differs in a number of ways from liability of individuals and companies.[1]

Firstly, liability of public authorities is not always governed by tort law. In France liability consists in principle of a two-track system that combines private law and administrative law (*droit administrative*) but the emphasis is on the latter. Germany also provides a two-track system but here liability of public authorities is generally considered as a private and not as a public law affair. English law is purely tort law orientated: it does not hold special administrative liability rules: torts apply to private individuals and bodies as well as public authorities.

Secondly, there is a relationship between judicial review of public authorities' decisions on one hand, and the claim for damages on the other. If a decision is annulled in judicial review this can be an indication for the public authority's unlawful or negligent conduct. This, however, concerns only part of the cases. In other cases the harm is already done and annulment of the decision will be of no use to the harmed citizen, or a decision has not been taken at all. In these latter cases the only redress can be found in an action for damages.

---

[1] See *inter alia* Walter van Gerven, *Casebook on Torts*, (Oxford: Hart Publishing, 2000), 358–394; Donal Nolan, 'Suing the State: Governmental Liability in Comparative Perspective', *Mod LR*, 67 (2004), 843–859; B.S. Markesinis, J.-B. Auby, D. Coester-Waltjen and S.F. Deakin, *Tortious Liability of Statutory Bodies: A Comparative and Economic Analysis of Five English Cases*, (Oxford: Hart Publishing, 1999) Georges Vandersanden and Marianne Dony, *La responsabilité des états membres en cas de violation du droit communautaire: études de droit communautaire et de droit national comparé*, (Brussels: Établissement Émile Bruylant, 1997); J.S. Bell and A.W. Bradley (eds.), *Governmental Liability: A Comparative Study*, (London: BIICL; 1991); Duncan Fairgrieve, *State Liability in Tort, A Comparative Law Study*, (Oxford: Oxford University Press, 2003); Duncan Fairgrieve, Mads Andenas and John Bell (eds.), *Tort Liability of Public Authorities in Comparative Perspective*, (London: BIICL, 2002); Carol Harlow, *State Liability: Tort Law and Beyond*, (Oxford: Oxford University Press, 2004).

Finally, when assessing liability of public authorities or reviewing a public authority's decision, the court has to take into consideration that authorities enjoy a certain freedom to develop their own policy. For example, public authorities decide how to enforce health and safety rules, how to look after the well-being of children in vulnerable families, or how to prevent crime. If policy issues are at stake, courts are more reluctant to scrutinize a public body's conduct. The courts are ever mindful of the separation of powers principle and they hesitate to embark upon a merits-based review of the exercise of executive power. All three systems have grappled with this problem but they deal with it in different ways.

In establishing liability of public authorities, courts have to steer between not hampering good government, on the one hand, and correcting bad government, on the other. Until the 1990s the aspect of 'not hampering good government' has been strongly emphasized by the English House of Lords. In many cases it rejected a duty of care of public authorities because such a duty was deemed to be not fair, just, and reasonable (nr 1804). The reasons for this position were manifold: that tort law could cut across the statutory system; that the authority's task was a delicate one and the authority's organization complicated; and that liability risks could lead to defensive tactics and to vexatious complaints. Moreover, it was considered that statutes often provide for other remedies such as complaint and investigation procedures.[2]

These concerns do not seem to be very convincing if the French approach is taken into consideration. French law rather generously provides damages, not only for negligent governmental conduct but also, on a general basis, for lawful acts. The latter is in fact a kind of strict liability (nr 1802-3). Despite this higher burden of liability, French public authorities do not seem to show an excess of defensive tactics nor do French citizens seem to be inclined to file vexatious complaints. Hence, liability of public authorities is not about the feasibility of this liability (as is suggested by the considerations of the House of Lords) but about its (un)desirability.

For a long time the principle that 'the King can do no wrong' has been a basis for a (limited) immunity of public authorities. Particularly on the continent such immunities to liability are now hardly accepted any more. For example, the French *Conseil constitutionnel* has held that a complete immunity of a public official from liability is unconstitutional.[3] Immunity to liability implies full freedom to act and this could endanger interests which are worthwhile protecting. Particularly the ECtHR has developed a body of case law regarding what contracting States are supposed to do in order to protect their citizens against the infringement of their fundamental rights. States do not only have to refrain from certain conduct but the Court has also imposed positive obligations on the State

[2] *X (Minors) v Bedfordshire County Council* [1995] 2 AC 633.
[3] Cons. Const. 28 July 1989, (Commission des opérations de bourse), in Brown and Bell (1998), 202.

in this respect (nr 1807–1808). This is an important countervailing power against the public authority's freedom to act.

In creating a comprehensive system of Community liability the ECJ has set up minimum standards to which the Member States and the Community institutions must comply (nr 205). Although the system as such is impressive, there are some doubts as to whether its application really sets an effective minimum (nr 206). For example, despite the principle of Community liability the ECJ has allowed the liability immunity of the German supervisor of the banking system (nr 905-2).

Section B will set out the different approaches of liability of public authorities in the national states and in Community tort law. In section C the case law of the European Court of Human Rights will illustrate the minimum standards for States to take care for the protection of their citizens' fundamental rights.

It is worth mentioning that the draft ECC and the PETL do not deal with liability of public authorities, at least not as far as they are exercising public powers. See explicitly Article 7:202 ECC: 'This Book does not govern the liability of a person or body arising from the exercise or omission to exercise public law functions or from performing duties during court proceedings.' This reflects the fact that the national laws in these areas do not only differ considerably (if only because of the division between civil or public law) but also that opinions about liability of public authorities diverge strongly and that these seem hard to reconcile.[4]

B NATIONAL LEGAL SYSTEMS

1802 France

1802-1 *Administrative liability*

In France liability of public authorities is not governed by the Civil Code but by administrative law. The competent courts are not the civil courts and the *Cour de cassation* but the administrative courts and the *Conseil d'État* as the highest appeal court (nr 301-3). The development of a system of administrative liability which enjoys real autonomy is the result of a strict application of the principle of separation of powers (which is of constitutional value in French law).[5] One of

---

[4] All legal systems hold compensation schemes set up by the State in order to compensate people for damage they suffer regardless of any liability. One may think of compensation funds for the victims of crime, about which also Directive 2004/80/EC of 29 April 2004 relating to compensation to crime victims. The number and scope of application of these funds vary considerably between the legal systems. They are only occasionally referred to in this book.

[5] See loi des 16 et 24 août 1790.

the odd consequences of the division between civil and administrative liability is that the applicable law for medical negligence depends on the question of whether the patient was treated in a State hospital or in a private clinic.

The principle of administrative liability was established in the famous *Blanco* decision in 1873. Agnes Blanco was hit by a wagon crossing the street between different parts of a state-owned tobacco factory in Bordeaux. The *Tribunal des Conflits* held:

Considering that the liability which may fall upon the state for damage caused to individuals by the act of persons which it employs in the public service cannot be governed by the principles which are laid down in the Civil Code for relations between one individual and another (. . .): that it has its own special rules which vary according to the needs of the service and the necessity to reconcile the rights of the state with private rights.[6]

In the same case it was decided that claims for compensation from public authorities have to be brought before an administrative court. In a later case it was decided that this principle applies to all public authorities. This means that French law has two laws of tort, the one private and the other public or administrative.[7]

On the basis of this division of tasks the *Conseil d'État* has built a complete body of case law as regards administrative liability in addition to the system of civil liability which has been developed by the *Cour de cassation*. Traditionally, the administrative courts were not extremely generous to claimants, which may not be entirely surprising with the judge called *juge administrateur* and a *Conseil d'État* sitting in the *Palais Royale*. This was particularly the case in the area of medical liability (for damage suffered in a public hospital), the law of damages, and it still is in the area of liability for public roads as opposed to liability for private roads (nr 1508). However, this reluctant position has changed over the years and the administrative courts have now become important protectors of citizens' rights against public authorities, particularly by acknowledging fundamental rights for the protection of citizens and by developing strict liability for public authorities, on the basis of the equality principle in many areas including that of damage caused by medical treatment.

Given the absence of a legislative code containing generalized, abstract principles of liability, French administrative tort law is essentially case law based. In search of inspiration needed to develop its own principles, the *Conseil d'Etat* has thus looked towards the decisions of the *Conseil constitutionnel* (by which it is formally bound in law) as well as the case law of the *Cour de cassation* (which has only a *de facto* persuasive value).

---

[6] TC 8 February 1873 (Blanco), in Brown and Bell (1998), 183. The *Tribunal des Conflits* was set up to resolve problems as regards the division of competences between the *Conseil d'État* and the *Cour de cassation*.   [7] Brown and Bell (1998), 183.

In respect of the first of these, the *Conseil constitutionnel* has effectively constitutionalised the principle contained in article 1382 CC[8] and, in order to preserve its *effet utile*, has decided that the claimant must further be given a fair opportunity to make his claim.[9] The second relationship, between the *Conseil d'Etat* and the *Cour de cassation*, has also contributed significantly to the development of administrative tort law. It is generally considered to be in the interests of harmonization and legal certainty (from the victim's perspective) that the *Conseil d'Etat* chooses to align its case law with that of the *Cour de cassation*. On transversal issues which are of common relevance to both public and private tort law, it is not unusual for the *Conseil d'Etat* to transpose a rule of private tort law to *droit administratif*, via the concept of a *principe général du droit* (general principle of law). For example, the possibility for a claimant to recover damages for injury to feelings;[10] the transmission of a victim's action in tort to his inheritors;[11] and the possibility for a person to sue in respect of the death of her unmarried partner.[12] However, the *Conseil d'Etat* adopts a cherry-picking attitude to 'borrowing' private law principles: it does so only on an *ad hoc* and discretionary basis, as and when it considers that this would be opportune, and only after due consideration of the likely impact of the application of the private law rule on State action (and especially public services).[13]

Usually, three categories of administrative liability of public authorities are being distinguished. Firstly, liability can be based on a *faute* (nr 1802-2). Secondly, liability can follow from the application of the equality principle (*égalité devant les charges publiques*) (nr 1802-3). Thirdly, various statutory rules provide the right for persons to obtain damages from compensation funds in certain extraordinary situations. One may think of riots, war damage, and criminal injuries, but such compensation systems also exist as regards school accidents and accidents arising from public works. These latter provisions are also based on the equality principle and strictly speaking they are no liability rules.[14] However, it is considered to be part of the State's *responsabilité* which is also the French word for liability.

1802-2 *Liability based on fault*

A public body can be liable for damage caused by its *faute*. In this sense the French judiciary has designed a system analogous to the civil liability system of article 1382 CC (nr 300).

[8] Cons. const. 9 November 1999, JCP 2000. I. 280, no 1, obs. Viney; see Le Tourneau (2004) nr 192.
[9] Cons. const. 13 December 1985, Rec. cons. const., 78.
[10] CE, 24 November 1961 (Letisserand), Rec. CE, 1961, 661, GAJA.
[11] CE, 29 March 2000 (Assistance publique-Hopitaux de Paris), D. 2000. 563, comm. Bourrel; JCP 2000. II. 10360, comm. Derrien.
[12] CE comm. 3 March 1978 (Dame Muësser), Rec CE, 1978, 116.
[13] CE 22 July 1992 (Dépt du Var) in the conclusions of B. de Froment.
[14] Brown and Bell (1998), 184.

An important distinction exists between a *faute personnelle* and a *faute de service publique* (a public service-related *faute*). A *faute personnelle* is a *faute* that can be attributed personally to an administrator of the public body but cannot be linked with the public service. A *faute de service publique* is a *faute* linked with the public service. It can be committed by an individual administrator but also by the impersonal bureaucracy if the *faute* cannot be individualized.[15] In principle, a claim for damage caused by a *faute personnelle* has to be filed in a civil court, whereas a claim for damage caused by *faute de service publique* has to be filed in an administrative court.

The distinction between a public-service-related *faute* and a personal *faute* resembles, but is not identical with, the question of whether the *faute* was committed in the course of the employment (nr 1606-3). A *faute* can be linked with the public service if the public service has provided the conditions of the fault. An official's personal *faute* can be a service-related *faute* at the same time.[16] Various examples can illustrate this.

A tanker driver made a detour to his home village with a petrol tanker and crashed into the wall of a house. It was decided not only that he committed a personal *faute* but also that the *faute* was service related. Hence, the State was liable for the damage caused.[17] The decision was different in the case of a customs officer, in uniform but off duty, who killed someone with his service revolver. This was regarded to be a *faute personnelle* only and not a *faute de service de publique*. Hence, the State was not liable for the damage caused.[18] A final example is a case about someone who left a post office via the staff entrance because the public entrance had been prematurely closed. Two post office employees did not confine themselves to politely asking what he was doing but assaulted him and broke his leg. The *Conseil d'État* decided there were two distinct *fautes*: the premature closing was a *faute de service* and the unwarranted violence of the officials was a *faute personnelle*. It concluded that this combination of *fautes* (*cumul*) had caused the visitor's damage. Hence, he could claim full damages from the State and did not need to depend on the financial means of the officials.[19]

To a great extent the standard to establish a *faute de service publique* is similar to that of a *faute* in the sense of article 1382 CC. Usually a simple *faute objective* (nr 300) is sufficient for liability but in a number of cases the case law requires a *faute lourde* (gross negligence). Whether this is the case depends on the problems with which the particular public service has to deal. Generally, a *faute lourde* is required for damage caused by a particularly difficult or sensitive task, such as the

[15] TC 30 July 1873 (*Pelletier*), in Brown and Bell (1998), 186; TC 29 February 1908 (*Feutry*), in Brown and Bell (1998), 185.
[16] CE 26 July 1918 (*Lemonnier*), in Brown and Bell (1998), 187; CE 18 November 1949 (*Mimeur, Defaux, Besthelsemer*), JCP 1950. II. 5286.
[17] CE 19 November 1949 (*Mimeur, Defaux, Besthelsemer*), in Brown and Bell (1998), 187.
[18] CE 23 June 1954 (*Litzler*), in Brown and Bell (1998), 188.
[19] CE 3 February 1911 (*Anguet*), in Brown and Bell (1998), 186.

police,[20] the tax authorities,[21] and supervisory or regulatory authorities.[22] Hence, in matters of discretion, the public authority can be liable provided it acted with gross negligence. Previously, gross negligence was also required for a *faute* committed in a public hospital, but since 1992 simple medical negligence is sufficient for liability.[23]

Liability immunities are not popular with the *Conseil d'Etat*. When the legislator had excluded liability of the administration for the loss of ordinary mail in the Code of Posts and Telecommunications (by then state company activities), the *Conseil d'Etat* interpreted this exclusion as inapplicable to cases of *faute lourde* (gross negligence).[24] Hence, the administration of the by then state owned post company was held liable for a misdirected letter which caused someone to miss the opportunity to sit in an examination.[25] More generally, the *Conseil constitutionnel* has ruled that a complete immunity of a public official from liability is unconstitutional.[26]

This implies that French law was already in line with the developments in European law that started with the *Francovich* case (nr 1805). It was for instance decided that insurance brokers were in principle entitled to damages where they had paid VAT under a French law which wrongly implemented the Sixth VAT EC Directive.[27]

1802-3 *Liability based on risk: the equality principle*

Whereas French civil tort law is characterized by its emphasis on strict liability it is not surprising that public tort law has also been influenced by this phenomenon. This basis for strict liability in French administrative law is the principle of 'equality before public burdens' (*égalité devant les charges publiques*) as stated in Article 13 of the Declaration of the Rights of Man and of the Citizen (1789). This principle has since then been specified in a number of statutory provisions. Particularly in the second part of the 20th century, the *Conseil d'État* has built a general principle of liability without fault. This case law can also play a role in situations in which the public authority enjoys a margin of discretion. In such a case there may be no liability for *faute* but the public authority can be liable on the basis of strict liability.

The idea behind the principle is that the State acts in the interest of the entire community. If an activity of the State causes disproportional damage to one or

[20] CE 20 October 1972, AJDA 1972. 597.
[21] CE 27 July 1990, AJDA 1991. 53 (*Bourgeous*), comm. Richer, in which it was also decided that a simple fault is sufficient when damage is caused in the implementation of routine tax matters.
[22] CE 24 January 1964, Leb. 1964. 43: state liable for wrongful supervision over banks; CE 29 December 1978, D. 1979. 278 (*Darmont*), comm. Vasseur.
[23] CE 10 April 1992 (*Epoux V*), in Brown and Bell, (1998), 191.
[24] CE 24 April 1981 (*Secrétaire d'Etat Aux Postes c. Mme Doublet*), in Brown and Bell (1998), 201.
[25] CE 22 January 1986 (*Grellier*), in Brown and Bell (1998), 201.
[26] Cons. const. 28 July 1989 (*Commission des operations de bourse*), in Brown and Bell (1998), 202.
[27] CE 30 October 1996 (*Cabinet Revert et Badelon*), in Brown and Bell (1998), 191.

more particular citizens, it has to compensate them in order to avoid the public burdens to weigh more heavily on some than on others. It is not required that the State acted unlawfully. This principle is an expression of community thinking and solidarity, as opposed to the prevailing individualized thinking in English law (nr 1804), and is one of the more striking aspects of French administrative law. Unlike fault liability which is based upon an abnormal *fait generateur* (the conduct of the administration), strict liability is based upon an abnormal damage.[28] Here we are witnessing what is probably the biggest gap between the English and the continental way of thinking in providing redress for damage.

The cases in which public authorities had to pay damages on the basis of the equality principle are manifold.[29] Firstly, people who suffer damage from *dangerous operations* carried out or allowed by the State can claim damages from the State.[30] One of the leading cases was about the explosion of a large dump of grenades which was installed by the State in a residential area in Saint-Denis on the outskirts of Paris in 1915. This explosion caused considerable loss of life and damage to property. The *Conseil d'Etat* did not base the State's liability on fault but on risk, holding that the State had introduced an abnormal risk in a residential area by installing this munitions dump.[31] The principle is also applied when an innocent person is shot by the police when pursuing a criminal[32] and when a prisoner escapes and commits a crime.[33]

Secondly, the State can be liable to people suffering damage when they *assist in public service*. Public service men and women, including volunteers, are entitled to compensation for injuries they suffer on active service or in training.[34] The most striking case is about the widow of a man who drowned while trying to rescue a child swept out to the sea. There was no lifeguard on the beach at that place and time but the local authority had a public duty to prevent accidents. Even though the man had taken on a public service on a voluntary basis, the widow's claim for damages was awarded.[35] For the award of such a claim it is required that the help was urgently necessary and the provided help was useful and expedient.[36] This

---

[28] Le Tourneau (2004), nr 460.

[29] Le Tourneau (2004), nr 458–508; Brown and Bell (1998), 194–200.

[30] Le Tourneau (2004), nr 464–474.

[31] CE 28 March 1919, Rec. CE 1919, 329 (*Regnault-Desroziers*). Brown and Bell (1998), 195, suggest comparing this case with the narrow application of the *Rule in Rylands v Fletcher* by the House of Lords in *Read v Lyons* [1947] AC 156 (nr 1414-2).

[32] CE 24 June 1949, Rec. CE, 1949, 307 (*Lecomte* and *Daramy*).

[33] CE 9 April 1987 (*Garde des Sceaux c. Banque Populaire de la Région Economique de Strasbourg*), in Brown and Bell (1998), 196. See also CE 27 March 1985 (*Henry*) in Brown and Bell (1998), 197, in which it was held that there was no causal link because the prisoner committed the crime six months after he failed to return to prison from home leave.

[34] CE 22 November 1946, D. 1947. 375, comm. Blaevoet (*Commune de Saint-Priest-la-Plaine*); CE 27 July 1990 (*Bridet et al.*), Brown and Bell (1998), 195,

[35] CE 29 September 1970 (*Commune de Batz-sur-Mer c. Tesson*), in Brown and Bell (1998), 195. See about liability for rescue actions also nr 1702–1703.

[36] CE 9 October 1970, Rec. CE, 1970, 565 (*Gaillard*): a surgeon contracted HIV while operating in a public hospital and was awarded damages by the State on the basis of strict liability.

liability category is related to the liability of the employer towards his employee which has been a no-fault compensation system since the end of the 19th century. See also nr 303-1 about the history of the general strict liability rule for things.

Thirdly, abnormal burdens suffered in the public interest can give rise to a claim against the State, particularly if for reasons of public policy the authorities decide not to enforce the law.[37] The first landmark decision dates from 1923 and is about Mr Couitéas, who received a declaration from the court that he was the owner of land in southern Tunisia. His request to the police to help him evicting the nomadic occupiers from his land was dismissed because the police feared serious disorder. The *Conseil d'Etat* did not go into the correctness of the dismissal but held that Couitéas had to bear an abnormal burden in the public interest. In order to protect the principle of equality he was compensated for his special sacrifice.[38] This case law was also applied in favour of British company Sealink, that could not ferry passengers to Britain over a busy bank holiday as the consequence of an illegal blockade in the French port of Calais, which was not removed by the authorities. Sealink's loss was deemed to be specific compared to other port users because of the character of the trade and the timing of the blockade.[39] One could guess that it is not so likely that English law will be as generous for a French ferry facing an illegal blockade in an English port.[40]

Finally, the State can be liable for damage caused by legislation if this unequally imposes a sacrifice on an individual or a company.[41] This happened for the first time in 1938 in the *Fleurette* case. The legislator had issued a statute allowing the use of the word 'cream' only if the product contained real cream. As a consequence, the dairy company *La Fleurette* had to discontinue the marketing of its artificial cream. The *Conseil d'Etat* held that it was not the legislator's intention to impose an unequal burden upon the claimant and awarded *La Fleurette's* claim: it was the only company that went out of business because of the legislative measure.[42] Later, the applied test became less generous for affected individuals since it has to be established that the legislator has not implicitly or

---

[37] Le Tourneau (2004), nr 499–508.
[38] CE 30 November 1923, Rec. CE 1923, 789 (*Couitéas*):

...le gouvernement a le devoir d'apprécier les conditions de cette exécution et de refuser le concours de la force armée, tant qu'il estime qu'il y a danger pour l'ordre et la sécurité, le prejudice qui résulte de ce refus ne saurait, s'il excède une certaine durée, être une charge incombant normalement à l'intéressé, et qu'il appartient au juge de déterminer la limite à partir de laquelle il doit être supporter par la collectivité.

[39] CE 22 June 1984 (*Sealink UK Ltd*); in Brown and Bell (1998), 198.
[40] See also ECJ 9 December 1997, Case 265/95, ECR I-6959 (*Commission v France*), about the so-called 'strawberry war' in which the ECJ held that insufficient action by the French government against road blockades by French farmers was an infringement of Article 30 EC (free movement of goods), even though it had compensated the victims of the blockades on the basis of the *Couitéas* case law. See nr 1805-2.   [41] Le Tourneau (2004), nr 495–498.
[42] CE 14 January 1938, Rec. CE, 1938, 25 (*SA des produits latiers La Fleurette*). This case law is also applied to specific damage suffered because of the entering into force of a treaty: CE 30 March 1966, Rec. CE, 1966, 257 (*Compagnie générale d'énergie radioélectrique*).

explicitly excluded the possibility of compensation.[43] Nowadays, in many cases the legislator himself provides for compensation in the enacted law and this has resulted in the equality principle in this category to be less applied by the courts.[44]

1803 Germany

1803-1 *Introduction*

The basis for liability of public authorities in Germany is the combination of § 839 BGB and Article 34 *Grundgesetz* (Basic Law).[45] The first provision (civil law) holds the civil servant personally liable for the damage he causes by breaching his official duty and the second provision (public law) shifts this liability to the State, provided the civil servant exercised sovereign power. In principle, this means that the State and not the civil servant is liable towards the claimant.[46]

Contrary to the French model and similarly to the English, in Germany the civil courts adjudicate claims against public authorities. The difference with England is that Germany does have an administrative judiciary, and cases against public bodies would normally be filed before the administrative courts. However, Article 34 *Grundgesetz* stipulates an exception to that general rule for cases involving liability of public bodies. This exception reflects the traditional allocation of competences and the 19th century idea that administrative courts would be too close to the State being itself a party in such cases.

Liability of the State can also be based on strict liability in a similar way as is the case in France on the basis of the principle of *égalité devant les charges publiques*. There is no statutory basis for this liability, it is rather based on custom which goes back to 18th century Prussian law.[47] The rule is that the individual (*Sonderopfer*, special victim), who by public law constraint which infringes the equality rule and for the benefit of the general interest has to face a special burden, has the right to a fair compensation.[48] For example, a woman contracted syphilis and was statutorily obliged to get medical treatment. As a

[43] Le Tourneau (2004), nr 497; see for example CE 23 September 1988, Rec. CE, 470, D. 1989. 267, note Moulin (*Martin et Société Michel Martin*).   [44] Brown and Bell (1998), 200.
[45] See on German state liability for example Gert Brüggemeier, 'Governmental or State Liability in Germany', in Duncan Fairgrieve, Mads Andenas and John Bell (eds.), *Tort Liability of Public Authorities in Comparative Perspective*, (London BIICL, 2002), 571–581. Fritz Ossenbühl, *Staatshaftungsrecht*, 5th edn., (Munich: Beck, 1998); Bernd Tremml and Michael Karger, *Der Amtshaftungsprozess*, 2nd edn. (Munich: Vahlen, 2004).
[46] Special liability rules apply to judges (§ 839 II: *Spruchrichteprivileg*), who are only liable for misfeasance amounting to a crime and expert witnesses (§ 839a: *Sachverständigenprivileg*) who are only liable for intentional or grossly negligent conduct.
[47] Fritz Ossenbühl, Staatshaftungsrecht, 5th edn., (Munich: Beck, 1998), p. 124 ff. with further references.   [48] Münchener Kommentar-Papier (2004), § 839 N 57.

consequence of this treatment she got paraplegia. The BGH held that these facts amounted to a right to compensation on the basis of the *Sonderopfer* principle.[49] Following Article 2 II GG the rule only applies to infringements of life, health, bodily integrity, and personal freedom. Other claims can only be based on the expropriation provision in Article 14 *Grundgesetz*, which is considered to be a special constitutional application of the general customary rule.[50]

The principle has lost some of its independent importance, because in many statutes compensation rules have been enacted, such as in case of vaccinations, emergencies, and for prosecutions which later appear to be without ground. The *Sonderopfer* rule is subsidiary to these statutory compensation rules, as it is subsidiary to other compensation systems such as social security claims or claims based on the infringement of the provisions of the ECHR.[51]

1803-2 *Civil servant's personal liability (§ 839 BGB)*

§ 839 holds that an official (*Beamter*) is liable for the damage he causes by intentionally or negligently breaching his official duty (*Amtspflicht*) towards a third party.[52] For the purposes of liability matters, an official is considered to be someone who carries out a public function (*öffentliches Amt*). This includes all activities in which public interests are observed.[53] The legal position of the person working for this public service is not relevant: also someone who is working on the basis of a private law contract (*Angestellte*) is considered to be an official in the sense of § 839. The same goes for soldiers, mayors, and parliamentarians.[54]

The most important civil servant's duty is the duty to abide by the law: this follows from Article 20 III GG.[55] Many other and more specific official duties have been laid down in treaties, community law, statutes, and regulations. Also, if a civil servant infringes one of the provisions of § 823 ff. BGB and thus acts unlawfully, this will usually amount to the breach of his official duty (*Amtspflichtverletzung*), unless he can rely on specific public law grounds of justification.[56] An unlawful infringement in one of the protected rights of § 823 I assumes a causal link between the breach and the loss. It is then up to the civil

---

[49] BGH 26 September 1957, BGHZ 25, 238, 242 = NJW 1957, 1924.
[50] Münchener Kommentar-Papier (2004), § 839 N 57.
[51] BGH 16 February 1956, BGHZ 20, 81, 83 = NJW 1956, 825; BGH 31 January 1966, BGHZ 45, 58, 80 = NJW 1966, 1021, 1027; Ossenbühl., *Staatshaftungsrecht* (1998), 141 ff; Münchener Kommentar-Papier (2004), § 839 N 59–60.
[52] 'Verletzt ein Beamter vorsätzlich oder fahrlässig die ihm einem Dritten gegenüber obliegende Amtspflicht, so hat er dem Dritten den daraus entstehenden Schaden zu ersetzen.'
[53] BGH 21 June 1951, BGHZ 2, 350 = NJW 1951, 919; BGH 9 January 1961, VersR 1961, 262.
[54] Münchener Kommentar-Papier (2004), § 839 N 131.
[55] 'Die Gesetzgebung ist an die verfassungsmäßige Ordnung, die vollziehende Gewalt und die Rechtsprechung sind an Gesetz und Recht gebunden' (The legislature is bound to the constitutional order, the executive and the judiciary are bound to statutes and law).
[56] Münchener Kommentar-Papier (2004), § 839 N 191–211; BGH 16 June 1977, BGHZ 69, 128, about which Van Gerven (2000), 372–374.

servant to prove that the loss would also have occurred if he had not acted negligently. This rule of evidence is comparable to the rule that applies to the breach of a safety duty (*Verkehrspflicht*) providing that the breach indicates a causal relation with the harm (nr 1107-1).

Important official duties follow from the unwritten general principles of administrative law, such as the principle of respecting legitimate expectations, the principle of equal treatment, the principle of proportionality (*Grundsatz der Verhältnismäßigkeit*), and the duty to provide correct information (*Auskunfts- und Aufklärungsplicht*). The principle of equal treatment includes the concept of *Selbstbindung der Verwaltung*, ie if the administration has adopted a certain practice, eg used its discretion in a particular way over time, it may not depart from this practice without good reason. An infringement of the principle of equal treatment is fairly often established, and this is an important reason why decisions that would normally be considered legal can become illegal. The principle of proportionality may be the most important principle and the reason for which most decisions or laws are declared illegal or unconstitutional.[57]

The aim of the official duty has to be the protection of an individual or a member of an identifiable class of persons. The claimant cannot invoke provisions that only protect general interests. This is the so-called requirement of the *Drittbezogenheit der Amtspflicht* (the official duty has to be owed to a third person).[58] This requirement is easily fulfilled if the official has infringed a subjective public right or one of the § 823 rights of a third person. In many cases, however, the scope of the official duty (*Schutzzweck der Amtspflicht*) is decisive, and this scope needs to be established on the basis of the provisions regulating this duty or the specific character of the official's work.[59] This exercise is comparable to that in the framework of § 823 II BGB as regards the scope of protection of a violated statutory rule (nr 903).[60] The requirement of *Drittbezogenheit* has been illustrated with the *Peter Paul* case. The key issue in *Peter Paul* was that the bank supervisor discharges its duties in the general interests and that he does not owe individual depositors a duty: his duty is not *drittbezogen*. In *Brasserie du Pêcheur*, the ECJ held that this requirement is incompatible with Community law in cases of a sufficiently serious breach of a rule conferring rights on individuals (nr 905-2).

Provided the breached official duty is owed to a third person, § 839 does not contain restrictions as to the character of the harmed interests.[61] This means that a civil servant can also be liable for causing pure economic loss. This is an important difference with § 823 I requiring the infringement of a limited number of rights, such as life, health, body, and property (nr 402-3).

[57] Münchener Kommentar-Papier (2004), § 839 N 212–222.
[58] Münchener Kommentar-Papier (2004), § 839 N 227–275.
[59] BGH 29 March 1971, BGHZ 56, 40 = NJW 1971, 1172.
[60] BGH 25 September 1990, NJW 1991, 292; Deutsch-Ahrens (2002), N 344.
[61] BGH 12 June 1986, VersR 1986, 1084.

As regards the civil servant's negligence, an objective test is applied: the civil servant has to act according to what can be expected from a duty-abiding average civil servant (*pflichtgetreue Durchschnittsbeamte*), not from an ideal and perfect prototype civil servant (*ideal vollkommene Musterexemplar*).[62] A civil servant has to have or gain the legal knowledge which is required in his function[63] but if a statutory provision is not entirely clear a wrong interpretation is not necessarily negligent.[64]

The application of the objective test has been accompanied by a development of de-individualizing the fault requirement. Though § 839 focuses on an individual civil servant committing an unlawful act against a third party, in many cases it is not particularly the individual but rather the organization as such (the public body) that breaches an official duty. If a third party suffers damage by a collegial body (*Kollegialorgane*), and the victim is not able to prove which civil servant has breached his duty, the courts have constructed a joint act (*Gesamtverhalten*) to enable liability of a public body for breach of an official duty.[65] A similar issue was at stake in the framework of employer's liability as regards organizational negligence (*Organisationsverschulden*) of an enterprise under § 823 I BGB (nr 1606-2). Brüggemeier has argued that the unlawfulness of the public act needs to replace the conventional element of breach of the official duty:

> It really does not matter any longer whether a public servant within the hierarchical structure of the governmental body personally committed a wrongful act. It is rather the question whether the respective governmental action was a violation of the public law rule governing the external relationship between the governmental body and the affected private individual or enterprise.[66]

If the civil servant acted negligently and not intentionally, his liability has a subsidiary character: he is only liable if the claimant cannot obtain compensation from other persons (§ 839 I 2).[67] This includes payments by the claimant's insurers, for instance for medical expenses and lost income. Neither is the claimant entitled to compensation if he intentionally or negligently failed to use his possibilities as regards judicial review in order to avoid damage (§ 839 III). These provisions were intended to protect individual civil servants, but considering the role of Article 34 GG (nr 1803-4) they have lost their protective purpose as a privilege of the employee. Though the BGH has strongly limited

---

[62] Deutsch-Ahrens (2002), N 348; BGH 15 December 1958, VersR 1959, 385; RG 29 June 1937, RGZ 156, 34.

[63] BGH 20 February 1992, BGHZ 117, 240 = NJW 1992. 3229; BGH 1 July 1993, NJW 1993, 3065.   [64] BGH 23 March 1959, BGHZ 30, 19 = NJW 1959, 1219.

[65] Münchener Kommentar-Papier (2004), § 839 N 292.

[66] Gert Brüggemeier, 'Governmental or State Liability in Germany', in *Tort Liability of Public Authorities in Comparative Perspective* (2002), 575.

[67] 'Fällt dem Beamten nur Fahrlässigkeit zur Last, so kann er nur dann in Anspruch genommen werden, wenn der Verletzte nicht auf andere Weise Ersatz zu erlangen vermag.'

the scope of the subsidiarity rule it has never put the rule's validity as such into question.[68]

1803-3 *Discretion*

The civil servant and the public body generally possess a margin of discretion (*Ermessensfreiheit*). This freedom to decide means that, in a certain situation described by a legal norm, more than one decision can be the correct and legally justified one. An example would be that police powers in the Police Acts of the *Länder* are usually phrased so as to allow *Ermessen* (discretion whether to act or not). It is at the discretion of the policeman to decide to stop a cyclist riding through a pedestrian zone, but he can also decide not to do so for various reasons.

Until the 1970s the case law allowed the official a broad margin of discretion in case of policy decisions. It only amounted to a breach of the official duty if the official's discretionary conduct was faulty to such a high degree that it could not be brought into line with a properly functioning administration (*ordnungsgemäße Verwaltung*).[69] This standard was considered to be too narrow, and in 1979 the BGH held that discretionary decisions can also be unlawful if the threshold of abuse is not yet passed as well as if evident faulty conduct does not lie.[70] The current approach is consonant with that of the public law test which means that discretion is limited in various ways.[71]

Firstly, the official has to take the decision in accordance with his official duty. This means that the decision has to be taken on the basis of objective and relevant considerations, free from arbitrariness, in accordance with the scope of the law.[72] This includes the official's obligation to interfere with citizens' interests only with the proper, necessary and proportional means.[73] The official also has to observe the equality principle which implies that he has to follow a consistent policy (*Selbstbindung der Verwaltung*). If the administration has developed a steady policy in a certain area, the equality principle implies that in similar cases the administration is bound to its own policy from which it cannot depart without an objective reason.[74] Secondly, the official acts unlawfully if he transgresses the limits of his discretion (*Ermessen*), for example, if he exceeds

---

[68] Ossenbühl, *Staatshaftungsrecht* (1998), 79 with further references. Münchener Kommentar-Papier (2004), § 839 N 300–320.

[69] See for example BGHZ 4, 302, 313 = NJW 1952, 583, 584: '... wenn die Fehlerhaftigkeit der beanstandeten Maßnahme sich jedem sachlichen Beurteiler ohne weiteres aufdrängt, so daß die Maßnahme unter keinem möglichen Gesichtspunkt den Erfordernissen einer ordnungsgemäßen Verwaltung genügt.'   [70] BGH 15 February 1979, BGHZ 74, 144, 156.

[71] BVerwG 18 August 1960, BVerwGE 11, 95, 97; Münchener Kommentar-Papier (2004), § 839 N 198.

[72] BverfG 22 May 1962, BVerfGE 14, 105, 114. BGH 15 February 1979, BGHZ 74, 144, 156.

[73] BGH 27 October 1955, BGHZ 18, 366, 368 = NJW 1956, 57; BGH 29 April 1993, BGHZ 122, 268 = NJW 1993, 2927.

[74] BGH 30 November 1982, VersR 1983, 242; BGH 12 July 1979, BGHZ 75, 120, 124 = NJW 1979, 1879; RG 12 March 1937, RGZ 154, 167; Münchener Kommentar-Papier (2004), § 839 N 220–221.

the range of discretion in imposing a certain amount as a fine (*Ermessensüberschreitung*). Thirdly, the official also acts unlawfully if he does not use his discretion and should have done so (*Ermessensunterschreitung*). Finally, he can abuse his discretionary freedom if, for example, he takes an otherwise correct decision for the wrong reasons such as personal dislike (*Ermessensmissbrauch*).[75]

Of particular importance are cases in which discretion is shrunk or reduced to zero (*Ermessensschrumpfung auf Null* or *Ermessensreduzierung auf Null*).[76] These are cases in which there usually is discretion, but only one particular decision is the correct one in the specific case. This can, for instance, be the case if there is a severe nuisance or a high safety risk. The way the official interferes may then again involve a certain degree of discretion.[77] An example would be that a police officer *must* stop a suicide bomber; he cannot choose not to do so as is the case with the cyclist. The way to stop the bomber will then to a certain extent be up to the police officer to decide.

As regards enforcement agencies, including police and prosecutors, the BGH has ruled that their measures should not be reviewed on the basis of their legality but on the basis of the question whether they were justifiable from an *ex ante* point of view.[78]

1803-4 *State liability (Article 34* Grundgesetz)

In most situations the personal liability of the civil servant will be shifted to the State or the relevant public body. This shift is not based on § 839 BGB but on Article 34 I GG which reads: 'If someone, in the exercise of a public office entrusted to him, breaches his official duty towards a third person, responsibility will lie in principle with the State or the governmental body he is serving.'[79] In principle, the shift applies to all those who are officials in the sense of § 839 (nr 1803-2).

However, regardless of the formal function of the wrongdoer (public worker, public employee, civil servant), the shift only takes place if the official has caused damage in exercising a public law function (*öffentlichrechtlicher Tätigkeit*, also indicated as *hoheitrechtlicher* or *öffentlichrechtlicher Gewalt*).[80] This may imply that also the liability of someone who is not an official in the sense of § 839

[75] BGH 21 May 1992, BGHZ 118, 263, 271.
[76] BGH 21 May 1992, BGHZ 118, 263, 271; BGH 15 February 1979, BGHZ 74, 144, 156; Münchener Kommentar-Papier (2004), § 839 216.
[77] BVerwG 18 August 1960, BVerwGE 11, 24; Münchener Kommentar-Papier (2004), § 839 N 198. [78] BGH 23 October 2003, VersR 2003, 332, ETL 2004, 314 (Fedtke).
[79] Gert Brüggemeier, 'Governmental or State Liability in Germany', in *Tort Liability of Public Authorities in Comparative Perspective* (2002), 573. The original text runs as follows: 'Verletzt jemand in Ausübung eines ihm anvertrauten öffentlichen Amtes die ihm einem Dritten gegenüber obliegende Amtspflicht, so trifft die Verantwortlichkeit grundsätzlich den Staat oder die Körperschaft, in deren Dienst er steht.'
[80] BGH 15 May 1951, BGHZ 4, 10, 45–46; Münchener Kommentar-Papier (2004), § 839 N 143.

can be shifted to the State, provided he exercised public powers. Liability will not be shifted if only private law interests of the public employer are served, for example buying goods. Also, state-owned hospitals do not carry out tasks in a public law function. In such cases liability can be based on § 839 (civil servant), § 823 (non-civil servant), and § 831 (public body in its 'private market transactions'). See about this latter provision nr 1606-1.

In order to answer the question of whether the official exercised a public law function, the legal form of the administrative activity and not the character of the activity is decisive. The answer raises lots of difficulties, particularly in areas in which the public body may choose between private and public law possibilities to exercise its public duties. It is not surprising that this has created fertile ground for developing various theories to help in finding the right answer.[81] If liability is shifted to the State it has no right of recourse against the civil servant unless the latter caused the damage intentionally or with gross negligence.[82]

A good illustration of the legal framework of § 839 BGB and Article 34 I GG is the case in which a travel company filed a claim against the State for damage caused by actions of air-traffic controllers (public servants) who wanted to put pressure on working conditions negotiations. These actions caused considerable aviation disruptions over almost half a year, and this affected the travel company. The BGH held that the controllers exercised sovereign power of the State (Article 34 GG), and that the scope of their duty was not only to ensure safety but also to ensure the quick and efficient flow of air traffic. The BGH decided that the air-traffic controllers had infringed the travel company's right to business (*Recht am Gewerbebetrieb*). This liability of the civil servants which was based on § 839 was shifted to the State following Article 34 GG.[83]

Another example is the claim of the father of a police officer who committed suicide after being bullied by her superior officer. The father's claim against the officer personally was dismissed because the discriminatory treatment was intrinsically connected to the working relationship between the police officers. In such a case, a personal claim is only possible if the damaging event is so far removed from the professional activity that application of the rules of personal liability is justified. In this case only the State was liable: the officer caused the damage when exercising sovereign power in the sense of Article 34 GG and his liability was therefore shifted to the State.[84] In this case this is a somewhat awkward outcome, but as a rule it makes sense to protect civil servants from liability for damage caused in the exercise of their official duties.

---

[81] Ossenbühl, *Staatshaftungsrecht* (1998), 27; Münchener Kommentar-Papier (2004), § 839, N 144–190. [82] Münchener Kommentar-Papier (2004), § 839, N 370–371.

[83] BGH 16 June 1977, BGHZ 69, 128, about which Van Gerven (2000), 372–374. Liability for damage caused by labour disputes will generally be based on § 826 (voluntary act *contra bonos mores*, see nr 402-4), particularly if the rules related to fair labour disputes have not been observed: see BGH 31 January 1978, BGHZ 70, 277.

[84] BGH 1 August 2002, ZfS 2002, 517, ETL 2002, 224 (Fedtke).

The current system of liability of public authorities is broadly considered to be unsatisfactory. It was fundamentally reorganized by the State Liability Act of 1981[85] but the Federal Constitutional Court (*Bundesverfassungsgericht*) declared the Act unconstitutional in 1982. According to the Court the German Federal Legislator by then did not have the necessary competence to enact such a law. This competence was with the *Länder*, some of which had instituted the procedures before the BVerfG.[86] Though in the meantime the federal government has got this competence, no new initiative has been undertaken in this respect.

1804 England

1804-1 *Introduction*

For a long time the maxim that 'The King can do no wrong' provided public authorities in the United Kingdom with immunity to liability. It was only in the Crown Proceedings Act 1947 that liability of the Crown and other public authorities was introduced. However, this did not imply that English law got a system of administrative liability.[87] Liability of public authorities can only be based on private law torts like negligence, breach of statutory duty, and misfeasance in a public office.[88] There is no direct link between administrative law and tort law: a decision which is declared invalid in public law terms and becomes subject to judicial review does not for this reason become civilly actionable in damages.[89]

While State liability in tort may essentially be *modelled* on the private law rules, it becomes necessary to adopt a nuanced *application* of these rules in view of the specificity of the mission of public bodies.

For example, in the tort of negligence an important role is played by the discretion public authorities enjoy in matters of policy. It is generally accepted that it is necessary to leave public authorities a margin of discretion in order to avoid hampering good government. This generally sets a high threshold for liability because in many cases the existence of a duty of care is denied on this basis: imposing a duty of care on a public authority would not be fair, just, and reasonable. In other torts, discretion does not play a role, but here other control mechanisms keep public authority liability within limits: one may think of the requirement of intention in the tort of malicious prosecution (nr 504-1), the

---

[85] Bundesgesetzblatt I 1981, 553.

[86] BVerfG 19 October 1982, BVerfGE 61, 149 = NJW 1983, 25.

[87] See about liability of public bodies in English law John Bell, 'The Law of England and Wales', in John Bell and Anthony W. Bradley, *Governmental Liability: A Comparative Study*, (London, 1991), 17–44; S. Arrowsmith, *Civil Liability and Public Authorities*, Winteringham 1992; Duncan Fairgrieve, *State Liability in Tort, A Comparative Law Study*, (Oxford, 2003).

[88] Other possible torts are breach of contract, false imprisonment and malicious prosecution (nr 504-1).   [89] Winfield and Jolowicz (2002), para. 5.37.

requirement of bad faith in the tort of misfeasance in a public office (nr 1804-5), and the requirement of a conferment of a private right of action in the tort of breach of statutory duty (nr 902).

As regards the latter tort, many claims have been brought for breach of statutory duties concerning child protection, education, and other matters of social welfare. In many of these cases the claim was denied because it was established that it was not Parliament's intention to confer a civil right of action.[90] Hence, most of these cases were decided on the basis of the tort of negligence.

Discussion in this section will focus on the torts of negligence and misfeasance in public office.

1804-2 *Tort of negligence: duty of care, discretion, and justiciability*

The tort of negligence requires a duty of care, the breach of this duty, and consequential damage (nr 503). Establishing a public authority's duty of care generally does not give rise to serious problems or restrictions if personal injury or property damage has been actively caused and no discretionary issues are at stake. Most cases in which a duty of care is disputed are therefore omission cases, particularly about the question of whether a public authority is under a duty of care to make use of its statutory powers.

Generally, in order to establish a duty of care the three *Caparo* requirements have to be met: the harm needs to have been foreseeable, sufficient proximity between claimant and defendant has to be established, and it has to be 'just, fair, and reasonable' to impose a duty of care (nr 714-1). Particular problems arise as regards the conditions of 'proximity' and 'just, fair, and reasonable' and how they relate to issues of discretion and justiciability (this section). A further issue relates to the compatibility of English case law under this test with Article 6 of the European Convention on Human Rights (nr 1804-3).

As stated by Lord Wilberforce in *Anns v Merton London Borough Council*, the problem for the court is ' . . . to define the circumstances in which the law should impose over and above, or perhaps alongside, these public-law powers and duties, a duty in private law towards individuals so that they may sue for damages in a civil court'.[91] Although case law in this area is muddled and often sets tests which are circular, it is nevertheless possible to discern a number of factors used by the courts when deciding upon the existence of a common law duty of care.

---

[90] Winfield and Jolowicz (2002), para. 7.2. See *X v Bedfordshire County Council* [1995] 2 AC 633; *Barrett v Enfield London Borough Council* [2001] 2 AC 550, about which Van Gerven (2000), 363–366; *Phelps v Hillingdon London Borough Council* [2001] 2 AC 619. An Act that does confer a private right of action is the Highways Act 1980 as regards the liability of the highway authority; see nr 1507.

[91] *Anns v Merton London Borough Council* [1978] AC 728, 748, per Lord Wilberforce.

(a) A central criterion which has been proposed by the courts involves distinguishing between so-called *policy* and *operational* decisions.[92] Put simply, '... the more operational a power or duty may be, the easier it is to superimpose on it a common law duty of care'.[93] Although this test seems simple enough, the real problem lies in classing the conduct of the public defendant as a decision of policy or otherwise. A decision can be said to be one of policy if it concerns '... social policy, the allocation of finite financial resources between the different calls made upon [the public authority] or ... the balance between pursuing desirable social aims as against the risk to the public inherent in so doing.'[94] But the distinction between policy and operation is not sharp, and operational decisions may also contain policy aspects. Indeed it has been admitted overtly by one Law Lord that '... it is probably a distinction of degree',[95] whereas another has described it as '... an inadequate tool with which to discover whether it is inappropriate to impose a duty of care or not'.[96] Academics assume that there is no real distinction to be made because in reality there is a continuum[97]. The unpredictability of case law only illustrates this point: for example, allowing youth offenders to gain work experience outside of the detention centre is a policy decision,[98] whereas the inspection under the Public Health Act 1936 is deemed 'heavily operational'.[99] However, even once a court has decided upon the qualification of the defendant's decision as being one of policy or operation, this is not conclusive:

> ... the fact that the decision under attack is capable of being described as having been of a policy character does not in itself render the case unsuitable for judicial decision, but that it is necessary to weigh and analyse all the relevant considerations in considering whether it is appropriate that a court should adjudicate on the negligence alleged.[100]

To discover what 'all the relevant considerations' may be, it is helpful to look at the approaches adopted in case law.

(b) Firstly, several cases have suggested a test which operates in a negative manner, in the form of an exception of 'non-justiciability'.[101] This has been held to preclude the existence of a duty of care at common law in relation to decisions made in the course of a police investigation;[102] those made in processing a

---

[92] Markesinis and Deakin (2003), 384 ff.
[93] *Anns v Merton London Borough Council* [1978] AC 728, 754, per Lord Wilberforce.
[94] Lord Browne-Wilkinson, cited in Markesinis and Deakin (2003), 392.
[95] *Anns v Merton London Borough Council* [1978] AC 728, 754, per Lord Wilberforce.
[96] *Stovin v Wise* [1996], 3 All ER 801, 826, per Lord Hoffmann.
[97] Winfield and Jolowicz (2002), para. 5.38; Bailey and Bowman, 'The Policy/Operational Dichotomy—A Cuckoo in the Nest', *ComLJ*, (1986), 430.
[98] *Home Office v Dorset Yacht Co* [1970] AC 1004
[99] *Anns v Merton London Borough Council* [1978] AC 728, 753.
[100] *Barrett v Enfield London Borough Council* [2001] 2 AC 550, 581, per Lord Hutton.
[101] Markesinis and Deakin (2003), 392.
[102] *Hill v Chief Constable of West Yorkshire* [1989] AC 53.

prosecution;[103] or in respect of child protection orders;[104] or the decision of a Health and Safety inspector to order the temporary closure of a business.[105] However, the test is circular, the tautology being self-evident: there will be no duty of care and the courts will not adjudicate on the claim of negligence if the conduct of the defendant is related to a matter which is . . . not justiciable!

(c) Next, although it is widely accepted in principle that some regard should also be paid to the statutory context, it is unclear precisely *how* this is relevant.[106] Whereas some Law Lords have considered that Parliament must have intended to confer a private law right of action for a breach of statutory duty,[107] other decisions have adopted a more purposive approach. Under the latter, a common law duty of care does exist, but its scope is defined by the finality set out in the statute. For example, a statutory power which is conferred upon a local council in the interests of health and safety of home occupiers and their families cannot found an action by a construction company to sue for financial loss.[108]

(d) Another consideration is the coexistence of tort law with judicial review, which is a distinct public law procedure allowing individuals to challenge the actions of administrative bodies. A 'public law duty to act' is a prerequisite to a private law duty of care. It is considered essential here that private law be deferential to public law criteria, so that the latter are not undermined by the former.[109] If discretionary issues are involved, a public authority's conduct can only be challenged in public law if the exercise of public functions was illegal (*ultra vires*), if it was affected by impropriety (taking into account irrelevant matters when reaching the decision), or if it was irrational. In practice this latter test plays the most prominent role of the three. It refers to the so-called *Wednesbury* test: a public body acts irrationally if its decision was so unreasonable that no reasonable body would have taken it.[110] It is assumed that the threshold provided by this test is not as high as it used to be and that elements of proportionality may also play a role, particularly in human rights cases.[111] However, the judiciary is still inclined to keep its distance from the administrator and to leave it a margin of discretion.[112] An important case in this respect is *Stovin v Wise* about a road accident caused by poor visibility at a junction

---

[103] *Elguzouli-Daf v Commissioner of Police of the Metropolis and Another* [1995] QB 335.

[104] *X v Bedfordshire County Council* [1995] 2 AC 633.

[105] *Harris v Evans* [1998] 1 WLR 1285.   [106] Markesinis and Deakin (2003), 387–391.

[107] *Caparo Industries plc v Dickman* [1989] QB 653, 714, per O'Connor and Oliver LLJ; see also the majority in *Stovin v Wise* [1996] AC 923.

[108] *Governors of the Peabody Donation Fund v Sir Lindsay Parkinson & Co* [1985] AC 210.

[109] Markesinis and Deakin (2003), 398.

[110] *Associated Provincial Picture Houses Ltd v Wednesbury Corporation* [1948] 1 KB 223. Winfield and Jolowicz (2002), para. 5.37.

[111] Winfield and Jolowicz (2002), para. 5.37, with reference to *R (Daly) v Home Secretary* [2001] 2 WLR 1622.

[112] Winfield and Jolowicz (2002), para. 5.37, as regards human rights aspects referring to *R (Daly) v Home Secretary* [2001] 2 WLR 1622.

because of an obstruction that had not been removed by the local authority for more than a year (nr 1507). The House of Lords held that, in principle, a statutory authority to act cannot be turned into a common law duty of care. This can only be the case if two conditions are met: it is irrational not to exercise the power (this refers to the *Wednesbury* test), and there are exceptional grounds for holding that the policy of the statute requires compensation to be paid to persons who suffer loss because the power was not exercised.[113]

(e) Finally, it is worth noting that an authority is more likely to incur liability if it had voluntarily assumed responsibility towards the claimant.[114] For example, courts have admitted the existence of a duty of care where a police authority had agreed to preserve the anonymity of informants;[115] where officers had failed in their duty to keep a detainee on suicide watch;[116] and where an ambulance service had agreed to respond to an emergency call.[117]

Neither the content of these 'factors' nor their precise interaction are settled in English law. There has been no decisive House of Lords case where Law Lords have unanimously set down clear and definitive criteria for applying the duty of care test to public bodies.

1804-3 *Tort of negligence and Article 6 ECHR: from Osman to Z*

The application by the English courts of the duty of care in the tort of negligence was put under high pressure in the *Osman* case. The decision of the ECtHR in 1998 brought the English legal world in turmoil. However, the subsequent decision of the Court in *Z v United Kingdom* brought this *Osmania* to an end (this section). Nevertheless in a psychological rather than a legal way *Osman* still seems to have impact (nr 1804-4).

A teacher was initially attached to his pupil Ahmet Osman (aged 14) but later started to threaten him. After a stone was thrown through the window of the Osman's home the police failed to arrest the teacher. Sometime later, he killed Ahmet's father and severely injured Ahmet and his mother. They claimed damages from the police for negligently failing to prevent the teacher from carrying out his plans.

The authority for this case was the House of Lords' decision in *Hill*, about a 20-year-old student who was murdered by the notorious Yorkshire Ripper. The relatives' claim for negligent acting by the police was dismissed. Firstly,

---

[113] *Stovin v Wise* [1996] AC 923, [1996] 3 All ER 801.
[114] Markesinis and Deakin (2003), 393–394.
[115] *Swinney v Chief Constable of Northumbria Police Force* [1997] QB 464.
[116] *Reeves v Commissioner of Police of the Metropolis* [1998] 2 WLR 401.
[117] *Kent v Griffiths* [2000] 2 WLR 1158.

because there was no special relationship between the police and the potential victim or between the police and the wrongdoer (the student was not an individualized target). Secondly, for the sake of public policy it would not be fair, just, and reasonable to impose upon the police a duty of care as regards criminal investigation.[118] In *Osman* the Court of Appeal held that there was sufficient proximity because the family was exposed to a much greater risk than the general public and the police knew both the teacher and the boy. However, the Osman's claim was struck out for the policy reasons given in *Hill*.

Before the European Court of Human Rights the Osmans called upon the violation of, *inter alia*, Article 6 ECHR: the right to a fair trial or access to justice.[119] The Court considered that the right of access to justice can be restricted, but it considered the decision in *Hill* not to be proportionate, since it acted as a

... watertight defence to the police and it was impossible to prise open an immunity which the police enjoy from civil suit in respect of their acts and omissions in the investigation and suppression of crime. The Court would observe that the application of the rule in this manner without further enquiry into the existence of competing public interest considerations only serves to confer a blanket immunity on the police for their acts and omissions during the investigation and suppression of crime and amounts to an unjustifiable restriction on an applicants' right to have a determination on the merits of his or her claim against the police in deserving cases.[120]

According to the Court the requirement of the duty of care—as applied by the House of Lords—worked as an exclusionary rule: though the aim of the rule was legitimate, the principle of proportionality was not satisfied and it concluded that Article 6 had been infringed.[121] On an equitable basis the Court awarded each of the applicants the sum of £10,000 (€14,000).

In later cases, however, the ECtHR retreated from its *Osman* decision, most remarkably in the so-called *Z* case. Before the English courts this case was known as *X v Bedfordshire*: five youngsters claimed damages for personal injury arising out of breach of statutory duty and negligence by the defendant local authority. The claimants alleged they were neglected and abused by their parents

[118] *Hill v Chief Constable of West Yorkshire* [1989] AC 53. See in the same sense *K v Secretary of State for the Home Department*, [2002] EWCA 775 (CA), ETL 2002, 154 (Oliphant).
[119] See nr 1800 about the alleged violation of Art. 2. It is only since the entering into force of the Human Rights Act 1998, in 2000, that claimants are allowed to invoke fundamental rights of the European Convention on Human Rights before the national court. Previously, a claimant had to go to Strasbourg to file a complaint against the United Kingdom (see nr 501-3).
[120] ECtHR 28 October 1998, Case 87/1997 (*Osman v United Kingdom*), § 150–151. See also Tony Weir, 'Down Hill—All the Way?', *CamLJ* (1999), 4–7.
[121] Markesinis and Deakin (1999), 148, wrote that this decision gave '... a serious and, arguably, well-deserved blow to the use of the notion of duty of care as a device for stopping all claims of damages directed against public bodies in general (...) irrespective of any countervailing arguments that may exist in favour of the plaintiff's position.'

and that the authority had failed to exercise its statutory duties to take measures to protect them from harm. The House of Lords held that, even if *Wednesbury* unreasonableness could be established (nr 1804-2 sub. d); it would not be fair, just, and reasonable to impose a duty of care on the local authority towards children in respect of whom it was discharging statutory welfare functions.[122]

The youngsters appealed to the ECtHR. Unlike *Osman* the Court did not consider this decision to be a violation of Article 6:

> ... the Court is not persuaded that the House of Lords' decision that, as a matter of law, there was no duty of care in the applicants' case may be characterised as either an exclusionary rule or an immunity which deprived them of access to a court. As Lord Browne-Wilkinson explained in his leading speech, the House of Lords was concerned with the issue whether a novel category of negligence, that is a category of cases in which a duty of care had not previously been held to exist, should be developed by the courts in their law-making role under the common law (...). The House of Lords, *after weighing in the balance the competing considerations of public policy*, decided not to extend liability in negligence into a new area. In so doing, it circumscribed the range of liability under tort law.[123]

To put it broadly: according to the ECtHR the matter was about substantive law and not about a procedural barrier (the access to justice of Article 6). What was in fact incompatible with Article 6 in *Osman* was not so much the substantial result that there was no duty of care owed by the police, but rather the use of the strike-out procedure which prematurely denied the claimant a right to trial without adequate consideration of the actual merits of his case. The House of Lords now considers that a rule (such as the duty of care in negligence) can be made ECHR-proof by arguing that the rule is a *substantive* limitation on the right to sue and not a *procedural* bar.[124] The problem is, however, that a substantive limitation in fact amounts to a procedural bar. For, as it as always been, where there is no writ (remedy), there is no right (nr 502-1).[125]

---

[122] *X (Minors) v Bedfordshire County Council* [1995] 2 AC 633. See for the policy considerations underlying this decision particularly Lord Browne-Wilkinson at 749–750. Reference was made to *Yuen Kun Yeu v Att.-Gen. of Hong Kong* [1988] AC 175, about which Van Gerven (2000), 369–370 and *Hill v Chief Constable of West Yorkshire* [1989] AC 53.

[123] ECtHR 10 May 2001, Case 29392/95 (*Z v United Kingdom*), para. 96 (emphasis added). See about this case with further references: Jane Wright, 'The Retreat From Osman: Z v United Kingdom in the European Court of Human Rights and Beyond', in Duncan Fairgrieve, Mads Andenas and John Bell (eds.), *Tort Liability of Public Authorities in Comparative Perspective*, (London: BIICL, 2002), 55–80. See also ECtHR 10 May 2001, Case No 28945/95 (*TP and KM v United Kingdom*).

[124] See *Matthews v Ministry of Defence* [2003] UKHL 2003, 4, ETL 2003, 124 (Oliphant).

[125] See for example the partly dissenting opinion of judges Thomassen, Casadevall and Kovler in ECtHR 10 May 2001, Case 29392/95 (*Z v United Kingdom*): ' ... the notion of "access to a court" under Article 6 guarantees not only that the applicants have their claims brought before the courts, but implies also the right to have these claims examined on the basis of the facts before the courts and to have them decided on'.

1804-4 *Tort of negligence: recent developments*

In the wake of the ECtHR cases of *Osman* and *Z* against the United Kingdom
(nr 1804-3), concurring with the entering into force of the Human Rights Act in
2000, the House of Lords deals scrupulously with human rights matters. Lord
Bingham of Cornhill has commented that

...the question does arise whether the law of tort should evolve, analogically and
incrementally, so as to fashion appropriate remedies to contemporary problems or
whether it should remain essentially static, making only such changes as are forced upon
it, leaving difficult and, in human terms, very important problems to be swept up by the
Convention. I prefer evolution.[126]

However, a couple of cases illustrate that his opinion is not representative for the
development of English law in this sector.

Barrett v London Borough Council was about a claimant who had been in the
care of the local authority from a young age. He alleged that the authority was
negligent in failing to arrange his adoption, organizing inappropriate placements
with foster parents, and obtaining psychiatric treatment. The House of Lords
held that a duty of care should not be ruled out in this context but that the case
had to be looked at on its own facts and in the light of the statutory context.
Indeed, the wording is less reluctant than in *Bedfordshire*[127] but there is an
important difference in policy weight. In *Bedfordshire* a local authority had to
decide whether or not to take a child into its care, whereas in *Barrett* the
authority had the child in its care and the question was about the provided level
of care. The former kind of decision involves a stronger policy element and this
could justify a more reluctant approach.

In *Phelps v Hillingdon London Borough Council* a school was held vicariously
liable for the failure of its employees to provide for a pupil with special educational
needs for late observing dyslexia.[128] This decision used the vehicle of vicarious
liability to bypass the decision in *X v Bedfordshire* where it had been held that
employees of a local authority did not owe a duty directly to members of the public
but only to their employer.[129] These acts and omissions of individual employees
were thought not to present any fatal conflict with the statutory framework.[130]

W v Essex County Council was about parents that had fostered a child on an
assurance that he was not a known sexual abuser when, to the knowledge of the

---

[126] *JD v East Berkshire Community Health NHS Trust and others* [2005] UKHL 23, nr 3 and 50
per Lord Bingham of Cornhill.

[127] *X (Minors) v Bedfordshire County Council* [1995] 2 AC 633.

[128] *Phelps v Hillingdon London Borough Council* [2001] 2 AC 619. The claim for breach of a
statutory duty following from the Education Acts was dismissed.

[129] *X (Minors) v Bedfordshire County Council* [1995] 2 AC 633, 766. The Court of Appeal
interpreted this very restrictively in *Phelps v Hillingdon London Borough Council* [1999] 1 WLR
500, 522 (CA) but was overruled by the House of Lords.

[130] Winfield and Jolowicz (2002), para. 5.39.

local authority, he was. During his placement he sexually abused their children. The trial judge struck out the parents' claims but not those of the children. The Court of Appeal unanimously upheld the judge's decision as regards the parents' claim and by a majority upheld his decision on the children's claim. The House of Lords unanimously allowed the parents' appeal, holding that a duty of care towards the parents and a breach of that duty were not unarguable. The parents' claim could go to trial to be judged on the basis of its merits.[131]

Finally, in *JD v East Berkshire Community NHS Trust* a daughter complained that her father was denied access to her because of (unfounded) suspicions of sexual abuse. The Court of Appeal held that the House of Lords' decision in *Bedfordshire* could not survive the Human Rights Act, introducing Article 8 ECHR into English law (the right to respect for family life).[132] Hence, it was no longer legitimate to rule that '... as a matter of law, no common law duty of care is owed to a child in relation to the investigation of suspected child abuse'.[133] The Court of Appeal decided that the daughter's claim for damages could proceed to trial.

Conversely, the claims from *parents* were struck out because the Court of Appeal thought their position to be 'very different' since there would always be potential conflicts with the child's interests.[134] This argument was refuted by Lord Bingham: 'The professional is not required to be right, but only to be reasonably skilful and careful. If such skill and care are required in relation to the child, there is no reason why this consideration should preclude a duty to the parent.'[135] Lord Bingham dismissed all policy arguments against a duty of care his noble and learned friend Lord Browne-Wilkinson had put forward one decade earlier in *Bedfordshire* and concluded to allow the appeal (§ 31ff) (see in more detail about this discussion nr 1800). However, his speech was not followed by the other Law Lords. For similar reasons as the Court of Appeal the other Law Lords argued that social workers do not owe parents a duty as regards accusations of child abuse. The parents' appeal was dismissed.[136]

It may be questioned whether this result sits easily with that reached in the *W* case where the parents' claims were allowed in respect of damage caused to their

---

[131] *W v Essex County Council* [2001] 2 AC 592, 598.

[132] *D v East Berkshire Community NHS Trust* [2003] EWCA Civ. 1151, ETL 2003, 115 (Oliphant). In this respect also the fact that ECtHR 10 May 2001, Case 29392/95 (*Z v United Kingdom*) found that Article 3 had been violated must have played a role; see nr 1800. This is one of the few instances in legal history of the Court of Appeal 'overruling' the House of Lords.

[133] *D v East Berkshire Community NHS Trust and others* [2003] EWCA Civ. 1151, ETL 2003, 115 (Oliphant), § 84.

[134] *D v East Berkshire Community NHS Trust and others* [2003] EWCA Civ. 1151, ETL 2003, 115 (Oliphant), § 86.

[135] *JD v East Berkshire Community Health NHS Trust and others* [2005] UKHL 23, nr 3 per Lord Bingham of Cornhill. See also ECtHR 10 May 2001, Case 28945/95 (*TP and KM v United Kingdom*) and *L v Reading Borough Council* [2001] 1 WLR 1575.

[136] Lord Nicholls of Birkenhead, nr 77, argued that it would be strange to acknowledge a duty of care whereas in criminal investigations in such a case no action for negligence lies; see also *Calveley v Chief Constable of the Merseyside Police* [1989] 1 AC 1228, 1238 per Lord Bridge of Harwich.

children (see above). Also, the English position as regards the rights of parents in these situations, strongly contrasts with France and Germany where such claims are generally allowed.[137]

1804-5 *Misfeasance in a public office*

In addition to the tort of negligence, another tort provides an opportunity to hold a public body liable for damages. Misfeasance in a public office is a tort about abuse of power which had been asleep for many years but was kissed awake by the House of Lords in the second part of the 20th century and played an important role in the *Three Rivers* cases.[138] These cases were about clients of the collapsed Bank of Credit and Commerce International (BCCI) suing the Bank of England for improper supervision causing loss to over 6,000 depositors. The claim based on breach of Community law (breach of statutory duty) failed because it was established that the European legislation at stake did not confer rights on individuals (nr 902 and 905). Also, the claim based on negligence had to be dismissed because s. 1(4) of the Banking Act 1987 precluded such a claim. Hence, the claimants took the tort of misfeasance in a public office as their last resort.[139]

The tort requires an unauthorized act by a person holding public office who acted in bad faith. Bad faith means that the person either had the purpose of causing harm to the claimant, or was aware that his act would probably cause damage of the type in fact suffered by the claimant, or that he was consciously indifferent to that risk.[140] In *Three Rivers II* the majority of the House of Lords held that the question of whether the pleaded particulars could be established could not be determined on the pleadings but required the case to go to trial.[141]

The tort also requires that the misfeasance took place in the public office which means that malicious acts in someone's private capacity do not fall within the scope of this tort. The tort applies to a public authority exercising non-exclusive public body functions: 'It is not the nature or origin of the power which

[137] B.S. Markesinis, J.-B. Auby, D. Coester-Waltjen and S.F. Deakin, *Tortious Liability of Statutory Bodies; A Comparative and Economic Analysis of Five English cases* (Oxford, 1999), 15–20; Martina Künnecke, 'National Report on Germany' and Duncan Fairgrieve, 'Child Welfare and State Liability in France' in Duncan Fairgrieve and Sara Green, *Child Abuse Tort Claims against Public Bodies: A Comparative Law View* (2004), 58–71 and 179–197.

[138] Perhaps the 20th century wake up kiss for this tort came from the Privy Council which in *Dunlop v Woollahra Municipal Council* [1982] AC 158, had considered the tort to be well-established. See Mads Andenas and Duncan Fairgrieve, 'Misfeasance in Public Office, Governmental Liability and European Influences' *ICLQ*, 51 (2002), 757.

[139] *Three Rivers District Council v Bank of England (Three Rivers I)* [2000] 2 WLR 1220; *Three Rivers District Council v Bank of England (Three Rivers II)* [2001] UKHL 16.

[140] Winfield and Jolowicz (2002), para. 7.18.

[141] *Three Rivers District Council v Governor and Company of the Bank of England (Three Rivers II)* [2001] UKHL 16. The trial collapsed when the creditors withdrew their claim for lack of perspective to win the case, Financial Times, 3 November, 2005.

matters. Whatever its nature or origin, the power may be exercised only for the public good. It is the office on which everything depends.'[142] This means that the tort also applies to a misfeasance by a public body in the framework of a contract.[143]

Misfeasance in a public office does not provide a very likely basis for liability of public authorities. Apart from the fact that it does not apply to acts of the legislator, the public officer's bad faith will be very hard to prove, and it remains to be seen whether this downside will be outweighed by the advantages that the claimant does not have to have a civil right of action (as is required by the tort of breach of statutory duty) or that there does not have to be sufficient proximity between claimant and defendant (as is required by the tort of negligence).[144]

Considering the foregoing, it is not surprising that the ECJ has held that this basis of liability is not compatible with Community law. In *Brasserie and Factortame* the Court held:

> . . . any condition that may be imposed by English law on State liability requiring proof of misfeasance in public office, such an abuse of power being inconceivable in the case of the legislature, is also such as in practice to make it impossible or extremely difficult to obtain effective reparation for loss or damage resulting from a breach of Community law where the breach is attributable to the national legislature.[145]

Although the ECJ concentrates on the liability of the legislature which was at stake in *Factortame*, it may be taken on the basis of the ECJ's wording, that the misfeasance tort is also incompatible with Community law in case of liability for acts of the administration.

C COMMUNITY LAW

1805 Sufficiently serious breach

1805-1 *Relevant factors*

Liability for breach of community law, be it by a Community institution, a Member State, or an individual, is subject to three requirements: (i) the rule of

---

[142] Nourse LJ in *Jones v Swansea CC* [1989] 3 All ER 162, 186.

[143] Winfield and Jolowicz (2002), para. 7.20.

[144] One of the few successful claims on the basis of this tort was against the corporate officer of the House of Commons for unequally treating tenders for a construction contract concerning the new Parliament building: *Harmon Facades Ltd v The Corporate Officer of the House of Commons* (1999) 67 Construction Law Reports 1; *Harmon Facades Ltd v The Corporate Officer of the House of Commons (No 2)* (2000) 72 Construction Law Reports 21.

[145] ECJ 5 March 1996, Joined cases C-46/93 and C-48/93, ECR 1996, I-1029 (*Brasserie du Pêcheur and Factortame III*), para. 73.

law infringed must be intended to confer rights on individuals; (ii) the breach must be sufficiently serious; and (iii) there must be a direct causal link between the breach of the obligation resting on the State and the damage sustained by the injured parties (nr 206).[146] The first requirement of the conferment of rights was dealt with in nr 905, whereas the third requirement of consequential damage has been touched upon in nr 1106 and 1205. This section will look in more detail at the requirement of sufficiently serious breach.

It has long been unclear what was required to establish a sufficiently serious breach, either by a Community institution or a Member State. At last, in *Bergaderm*, the ECJ held that the content of the requirement does not depend on the form of the contested measure (be it legislative or administrative) or its content (general or specific). What is decisive is the margin of discretion the Community institution or the Member States enjoys. This led the Court to two different categories of cases: (i) in case the Community institution or the Member State has a reduced or no margin of discretion, the mere infringement of Community law may do for a sufficiently serious breach; (ii) if the Community institution or the Member State has a wide margin of discretion, a sufficiently serious breach depends on the circumstances of the case.[147]

Here, the Court referred to *Brasserie du Pêcheur* and *Factortame* in which the ECJ mentioned the following (not limitative) circumstances:

... the clarity and precision of the rule breached, the measure of discretion left by that rule to the national or Community authorities, whether the infringement and the damage caused was intentional or involuntary, whether any error of law was excusable or inexcusable, the fact that the position taken by a Community institution may have contributed towards the omission, and the adoption or retention of national measures or practices contrary to Community law.[148]

---

[146] ECJ 4 July 2000, Case 352/98, ECR 2000, I-5291 (*Laboratoires Pharmaceutiques Bergaderm SA and Goupil v Commission*).

[147] In ECJ 2 December 1971, Case 5/71, ECR 1971, 975 (*Zuckerfabrik Schöppenstedt v Council*) provided a specific test for damage caused by a Community institution disposing of a wide margin of discretion, particularly acts of the Community legislature. This *Schöppenstedt* test contained three elements: (i) a superior rule of law (ii) that aims to protect individuals (iii) must have been breached sufficiently flagrantly. These requirements have been unified with Member State liability in *Bergaderm*. The sufficiently flagrantly breach of a superior rule of law that aims to protect individuals has now become the sufficiently serious breach of a rule of law intended to confer rights on individuals: ECJ 4 July 2000, Case 352/98, ECR 2000, I-5291 (*Laboratoires Pharmaceutiques Bergaderm SA and Goupil v Commission*), para. 62. The margin of discretion and not the character of the contested measure (legislative or administrative) is decisive for the sufficiently seriousness test.

[148] ECJ 5 March 1996, Joined cases C-46/93 and C-48/93, ECR 1996, I-1029 (*Brasserie du Pêcheur and Factortame III*), para. 56. See also ECJ 26 March 1996, Case C-392–93, ECR 1996, I-1631 (*R v HM Treasury, ex parte British Telecommunications*); ECJ 17 October 1996, Case 283, 291 and 292/94, ECR 1996, I-5063 (*Denkavit International v Bundesamt für Finanzen*); ECJ 24 September 1998, Case C-319/96 ECR 1998 I-5255 (*Brinkmann Tabakfabriken*). In these cases the breach of Community law was considered to be not sufficiently serious. See also Craig and De Búrca (2003), 555.

However, *Haim*, handed down on the same day as *Bergaderm*, may cause confusion. In *Bergaderm* and *Haim* the ECJ held that the mere infringement of a rule of Community law *may* do for liability in case of reduced or no margin of discretion.[149] Does this mean that it is not necessarily the case? Indeed, in *Haim* the Court also held that ' . . . a mere infringement of Community law by a Member State may, but not necessarily, constitute a sufficiently serious breach'. In order ' . . . to determine whether such an infringement of Community law constitutes a sufficiently serious breach, a national court hearing a claim for reparation must take account of all the factors which characterize the situation before it.'[150]

This means that in all cases of liability for breach of Community law, regardless of whether the State or the Community institution has a margin of discretion, the *Brasserie du Pêcheur* and *Factortame* circumstances catalogue has to be applied.

1805-2 *Application*

Since *Haim*, Member State liability is solely based on a fault-related balancing of the circumstances of the case. What does this mean for the strict liability for late implementing a Directive? In *Francovich* and *Dillenkofer* the ECJ held that exceeding an appointed term amounts to a sufficiently serious breach of Community law.[151] In such a situation a Member State does not have a margin of discretion. According to *Brasserie du Pêcheur* and *Factortame* this is also the case if the breach of Community law ' . . . has persisted despite a judgment finding the infringement in question to be established, or a preliminary ruling or settled case-law of the Court on the matter from which it is clear that the conduct in question constituted an infringement'.[152] *Haim* has cast doubt on the sustainability of this case law, since in this case the ECJ held that a national court always

---

[149] See also ECJ 8 February 2003, Case C-312/00, ECR 2003, I-11355 (*Commission v Camar and Tico*), para. 54; ECJ 23 August 2003, Case C-472/00, ECR 2003, I-7541 (*Commission v Fresh Marine*), para. 261; ECJ 12 July 2005, Case C-198/03 P (*Commission v CEVA and Pfizer*), para. 65.

[150] ECJ 4 July 2000, Case C-424/97, ECR 2000, I-5123 (*Salomone Haim v Kassenzahnärztliche Vereinigung Nordrhein*), paras 41–42. See also ECJ 28 June 2001, Case C-118/00, ECR 2001, I-5063 (*Larsy v INASTI*). The ECJ's reasoning looks circular: (i) *Bergaderm* and *Haim* hold that in case of no or a reduced margin of discretion a mere infringement may do; (ii) *Haim* holds that whether a mere infringement constitutes a sufficiently serious breach depends on the *Brasserie* circumstances of the case; and (iii) one of the *Brasserie* circumstances is the measure of discretion left by the breached rule . . .

[151] ECJ 19 November 1991, Joined cases C-6/90 and C-9/90, ECR 1991, I-5357 (*Francovich and Bonifaci v Italy*); ECJ 8 October 1996, Joined cases C-178/94, C-179/94, C-188/94, C-189/94 and C-190/94, ECR 1996, I-4845 (*Dillenkofer and Others v Germany*). Member States have a broad margin of discretion in choosing *how* they implement a Directive into national law. See for instance ECJ 26 March 1996, Case C-392/93 ECR 1996, I-1631 (*British Telecommunications*) and ECJ 17 October 1996, Joined cases C-283/94, C-291/94 and C-292/94, ECR 1996, I-5063 (*Denkavit*).

[152] ECJ 5 March 1996, Joined cases C-46/93 and C-48/93, ECR 1996, I-1029 (*Brasserie du Pêcheur and Factortame III*), para. 57.

has to take all factors into account in order to establish a sufficiently serious breach. Although in practice this will not often amount to a different outcome, the possibilities for the Member States to escape liability in such cases are enhanced by the ECJ's case law.

In this respect, one may think of a situation such as the *Brinkmann* case of 1998. The case was about the fact that Denmark had not implemented an EC Directive. In principle, this was a sufficiently serious breach of Community law. However, the Court decided that, for two independent reasons, Denmark was not liable. Firstly, the Danish authorities had immediately applied the provisions of the Directive; for that reason there was no direct causal link between the damage and the breach of Community law.[153] Secondly, the Court decided that Community law was not sufficiently breached, taking into consideration the degree of clarity and precision of the relevant provisions:

... the interpretation given by the Danish authorities to the relevant definitions was not manifestly contrary to the wording of the Second Directive or in particular to the aim pursued by it (...). That being so, it is of little importance that the authorities refused to suspend the decision, since Community law does not require that, in a case such as this, the national authorities should suspend the operation of a decision adopted in application of a provision which was open to a number of perfectly tenable interpretations.[154]

More generally, it can be feared that the element of 'the clarity and precision of the rule breached' will be a powerful tool in the hands of Member States in order to escape liability since it can be argued that Community legislation is generally not very well known for its clarity and precision. The effectiveness of the action for damages for breach of Community law thus also depends on the quality of the Community legislation.

Of importance as regards a Member State's margin of discretion in Community law matters is also the ECJ decision in the so-called *Strawberry war* case about the limits of discretion of a Member State in order to fulfil its Community obligations. The case was about the passivity of the French authorities in face of violent acts committed by farmers and protesters against agricultural products from other Member States. Lorries were intercepted, their loads destroyed, the drivers intimidated, and supermarkets selling non-French products were threatened and their goods on display were damaged. These acts took place on a regular basis for about a decade and as from 1993 the campaign was particularly directed at strawberries from Spain.

The ECJ considered that Article 30 EC requires Member States not merely to abstain from adopting measures constituting an obstacle to trade but also, in

[153] ECJ 24 September 1998, Case C-319/96 ECR 1998 I-5255 (*Brinkmann Tabakfabriken*), para. 29. See also ECJ 15 June 1999, Case C-140/97, ECR 1999, I-3499 (*Rechberger*).
[154] ECJ 24 September 1998, Case C-319/96 ECR 1998 I-5255 (*Brinkmann Tabakfabriken*), para. 32. These considerations of the ECJ can also be linked to the fact that the Member States have a margin of discretion in the way they implemented the Directive.

conjunction with Article 5 EC, to take all necessary and appropriate measures to ensure that that fundamental freedom is respected on their territory. In this respect Member States unquestionably enjoy a margin of discretion in determining what measures are most appropriate to eliminate barriers to the importation of products in a given situation (paras 32–33). However, the Court, while not discounting the difficulties faced by the authorities in dealing with the situations, could not but find that, having regard to the frequency and seriousness of the incidents, the measures adopted by the French Government were manifestly inadequate to ensure freedom of intra-Community trade in agricultural products on its territory (para. 52). The fact that France had assumed responsibility for the losses caused to the victims on the basis of strict liability (see the *Couitéas* case law cited under nr 1802-3), was rejected by the ECJ as an argument to escape Community obligations.[155]

1805-3 *Terminology and comparison*

The terminology 'sufficiently serious breach' was introduced in *Brasserie*, the case in which the ECJ linked Member State liability with the Community liability following from Article 288 EC (nr 205-2). As regards the 'older' liability of Community institutions on the basis of Article 288, the ECJ initially used the words 'sufficiently flagrant breach' and 'manifest breach'. In *Bergaderm* the Court unified the terminology by requiring a sufficiently serious breach also in cases of liability of a Community Institution.[156]

The previous terminology of manifest breach is also known in the international law concept of state responsibility. In this area of the law, state sovereignty is the predominant principle and therefore the margin of discretion of the national state is considered to be wide. This implies a reluctant approach to liability and this is reflected in the terminology of the manifest breach. It is questionable whether this link to an international law concept is appropriate, since it repudiates the fact that Community law differs from international law in that, in the European treaties, the national states have sacrificed aspects of their sovereignty to the Community, at the same time making themselves subject to the authority of the Community. Hence, the international law concept of manifest breach (and hence, sufficiently serious breach) is not a suitable requirement for Community liability, apart from the fact that this concept does not sit well with Community liability of individuals (nr 205-3).

The requirement of a 'sufficiently serious breach of Community law' is still the most confusing element of the Community liability system and it raises lots of questions, regrettably even after more than dozens of cases in which the Court could have clarified its goals and means. The confusion is partly due to

[155] ECJ 9 December 1997, Case 265/95, ECR 1997, I-6959 (*Commission v France*).
[156] ECJ 4 July 2000, Case 352/98, ECR 2000, I-5291 (*Laboratoires Pharmaceutiques Bergaderm SA and Goupil v Commission*).

the fact that the ECJ does not use 'neutral' words like breach or unlawfulness but requires the breach to be *sufficiently serious*. The English terminology wrongly suggests a rather high threshold for liability for breach of Community law than the other languages which only require the breach to be sufficiently *qualified*.[157] One thing the ECJ's case law has made clear is that a sufficiently serious breach does not imply intention or gross negligence on the part of the defendant. Neither does it mean a marginal unreasonableness test.

It would have been preferable to apply a terminology which simply requires a 'breach' in stead of a 'sufficiently serious breach' in order to establish Community liability. This does not rule out that if, in the circumstances of the case, a Member State or Community institution has a margin of discretion, this has to be taken into account when establishing such a breach. Van Gerven rightly stated that it would have been possible to find a

... comprehensive common principle, to be applied regardless of discretion, by using the test of 'a reasonable authority acting under similar circumstances' as a general standard to establish the wrongfulness of a public authority's conduct. Whereby the words 'under similar circumstances' would then include, among other circumstances, the more or less discretionary nature of the competences attributed to the authority concerned.[158]

The ECJ has been keen to avoid confusion by stressing that 'sufficiently serious breach' does not mean or imply 'fault'. This latter concept has various meanings in the Member States (nr 604), and this is why the ECJ has embarked on developing its own Community law terminology. Certainly,

... certain objective and subjective factors connected with the concept of fault under a national legal system may well be relevant for the purpose of determining whether or not a given breach of Community law is serious (...). The obligation to make reparation for loss or damage caused to individuals cannot, however, depend upon a condition based on any concept of fault going beyond that of a sufficiently serious breach of Community law. Imposition of such a supplementary condition would be tantamount to calling in question the right to reparation founded on the Community legal order.[159]

Hence, Community liability does not depend ' ... on the existence of intentional fault or negligence on the part of the organ of the State to which the infringement is attributable', except where the serious breach factors include such an element.[160]

---

[157] In French it is required that ' ... la violation soit suffisamment caractérisée' and in German that ' ... der Verstoß hinreichend qualifiziert ist'.

[158] Walter van Gerven, 'A Common European Law in the Area of Tort Law', in Duncan Fairgrieve, Mads Andenas and John Bell (eds.), *Tort Liability of Public Authorities in Comparative Perspective*, (London, 2002), 136. In the same sense for instance John Bell, 'Governmental Liability in Tort', *National Journal of Constitutional Law* 1996, 96–97.   [159] *Brasserie du Pêcheur*, paras 76–79.

[160] ECJ 8 October 1996, Joined cases C-178/94, C-179/94, C-188/94, C-189/94 and C-190/94, ECR 1996, I-4845 (*Dillenkofer and Others v Germany*), para. 28; in the same sense *Brasserie*, paras 56, 78 and 79.

Although the terminology is different, the technique is similar. In *Brasserie du Pêcheur* and *Factortame* the ECJ has adopted a multifaceted breach concept. Such an approach is inevitable considering it needs to provide flexibility and elasticity to enable application in a wide variety of situations. This is the same function as the standard of conduct in negligence liability in general. In fact, also the negligence standard is not so much a real standard as an agenda of aspects which the courts may, but not necessarily will, address (nr 816), just like the *Brasserie de Pêcheur* and *Factortame* circumstances catalogue.

1806 Liability for lawful acts and specific damage

On the threshold of the 21st century the ECJ has given a long awaited indication about a general rule for liability for damage caused by a lawful act of a Community institution.[161] This may as such be an interesting decision but the proof of the pudding is also here in the eating: it remains to be seen whether a rule of liability for lawful acts will really lead to decisions to award compensation or whether it is only another nice flag on the *Francovich* building.

In *Dorsch Consult* the ECJ stated that,

... such liability can be incurred only if the damage alleged, if deemed to constitute a 'still subsisting injury', affects a particular circle of economic operators in a disproportionate manner by comparison with others (unusual damage) and exceeds the limits of the economic risks inherent in operating in the sector concerned (special damage), without the legislative measure that gave rise to the alleged damage being justified by a general economic interest.[162]

The ECJ thus acknowledged the possibility of a claim for damage caused by a lawful act of a Community institution on the basis of Article 288 s. 2.

The case was filed against the Commission by a German engineering office, Dorsch Consult, which had had long-term contracts with the Iraqi government since the 1970s. It suffered damage because of the issuing by the Council of an embargo on trade with Iraq in 1990, following the Iraqi invasion of Kuwait (which ultimately led to the 1991 Gulf war). Dorsch Consult claimed that the Community legislature was under an obligation to compensate operators affected and that the failure to do so rendered the Community liable under Article 288 s. 2 EC. The CFI first considered the conditions under which such

---

[161] The ECJ thus followed Recommendation No. R (84) 15, of the Committee of Ministers of the Council of Europe (ie not the European Union), relating to public liability, that recommends a rule in all Member States as regards the right to compensation on the basis of the equality principle: Council of Europe, Recommendations to Member States 1984, (Strasbourg, 1985).

[162] CFI 28 April 1998, Case T-184/95, ECR 1998, II-688 (*Dorsch Consult v Council*), para. 80. With reference to ECJ 29 September 1987, Case 81/86, ECR 1987, 3677 (*De Boer Buizen v Council and Commission*); ECJ 13 June 1972, Cases 9 and 11/71, ECR 1972, 391 (*Compagnie d'Approvisionnement and Grands Moulins de Paris v Commission*); ECJ 6 December 1984, Case 59/83, ECR 1984, 4057 (*Biovilac v EEC*).

a claim could be awarded: apart from the general requirements (the damage has to be real and there has to be a causal link between the act and the damage), it also has to be established that the damage is 'unusual' and 'special'.[163] However, given the circumstances of the case, the CFI rejected the claim of the applicants,[164] a judgment which was upheld by the ECJ. The latter court considered that

> ... the Community cannot incur non-contractual liability in respect of a lawful act, as in the present case, unless the three conditions referred to in the two preceding paragraphs, namely the reality of the damage allegedly suffered, the causal link between it and the act on the part of the Community institutions, and the unusual and special nature of that damage, are all fulfilled.[165]

The claim was rejected because the ECJ concluded that the applicant was not able to prove the requirements for liability.

The acknowledgement of the principle is one step; its application is another. It does not seem to be very likely that the European Courts will be generous in applying the principle. It is, however, hoped that the European compromise between the legal principles of the Member States is not found, in that the principle is acknowledged (with a *révérence* to France) but that it is not applied (with a curtsy to England).

The requirement that the damage has to be 'unusual' and 'special' is no novelty, since it also appeared in the older case law as regards liability for damage caused by discretionary acts of a Community institution. In such a case it was not only required to prove a sufficiently serious breach, causation, and damage but also that the contested measure (i) had affected a limited and clearly defined group of individuals and (ii) that the damage has exceeded the bounds of the economic risks inherent in the business activity in the sector concerned.[166] In *Biovilac* the Court held that ' ... an action for damages brought under Article [288] of the Treaty for unlawful legislative action cannot succeed unless the

---

[163] ECJ 13 June 1972, Joined cases 9/71 and 11/71, ECR 1972, 391. paras 45 and 46 (*Compagnie d'Approvisionnement and Grands Moulins de Paris v Commission*); ECJ 6 December 1984, Case 59/83, ECR 1984, 4057, para. 28 (*Biovilac v EEC*); ECJ 24 June 1986, Case 267/82, ECR 1986, 1907, para. 33 (*Développement SA and Clemessy*); ECJ 29 September 1987, Case 81/86, ECR 1987, 3677, paras 16 and 17 (*De Boer Buizen v Council and Commission*). See also the similar requirement in English law for the tort of public nuisance (nr 1504-2).

[164] CFI 28 April 1998, Case-T 184/95, ECR 1998, II-688 (*Dorsch Consult v Council*).

[165] ECJ 15 June 2000, Case C-237/98, ECR 2001, I-4549 (*Dorsch Consult v Council*). The CFI still shows reluctance as regards the conclusion that the ECJ has acknowledged the principle of liability for lawful acts: see, for example, CFI 15 June 2002, Case T-170/00, ECR 2002, II-515 (*Förde Reederei v Council and Commission*), para. 56

[166] ECJ 25 May 1978, Joined case 83 and 94/76 4, 15 and 40/77, ECR 1978, 1209, 1234 (*Bayerische HNL and Others v Council and Commission*); ECJ 4 October 1979, Case 238/78, ECR 1979, 2955 (*Ireks-Arkady v Council and Commission*); ECJ 4 October 1979, Joined cases 261 and 262/78, ECR 1979, 3045 (*Interquell Stärke-Chemie v Council and Commission*); ECJ 4 October 1979, Joined cases 241, 242 and 245–250/78, ECR 1979, 3017 (*DGV v Council and Commission*); ECJ 4 October 1979, Joined cases 64 and 113/76, 167 and 239/78, 27, 28 and 45/79, ECR 1979, 3091 (*Dumortier Frères v Council*).

damage alleged by the applicants exceeds the limits of the economic risks inherent in operating in the sector concerned.'[167] And in the *Mulder* case the Court considered that, '... in order for the Community to incur non-contractual liability, the damage alleged must go beyond the bounds of the normal economic risks inherent on the activities in the sector concerned.'[168]

In *HNL* the matter of specific damage played a role in the question of whether there was a sufficiently serious breach. The case was about a Council Regulation on the compulsory purchase of skimmed-milk powder for use in feeding stuffs. The ECJ decided that this Regulation was void on the basis that the purchase price of skimmed-milk powder was fixed at a level which was so much higher than that of the substances it replaced that it amounted to a discriminatory distribution of the cost burden between the various agricultural sectors, contrary to what is now Article 34(3) EC. This is very much a reasoning based on the equality principle. The Court, however, dismissed the applicant's claim. Firstly, it held that it could not be established that the Council had manifestly and gravely disregarded the limits on the exercise of its powers. Secondly, there was no specific damage since the contested measure affected all buyers of feeding stuffs containing protein and that the effect of the Regulation on the price of the feeding stuffs was small.[169] In other words, one agricultural sector had suffered more than others but within this sector the pain was limited.

This approach was rather odd since it has long been generally accepted that specific damage is a requirement for liability for lawful acts, and that it cannot be applied if the hurdle of unlawfulness has already been taken. Either the conduct is unlawful, which implies that all consequential damage within the scope of the violated rule is recoverable, or the conduct is lawful, which implies that only specific damage can be compensated. After *Brasserie du Pêcheur* and *Bergaderm* it can be taken that specific damage is no longer required for liability for damage caused by a Member State's or a Community institution's unlawful conduct.[170]

---

[167] ECJ 6 December 1984, case 59/83, Rep. 4057, 4081 (*Biovilac v EEC*).
[168] ECJ 19 May 1992, Joined Cases C-104/89 and C-37/90, ECR 1992, I-3061 (*Mulder v Council and Commission*).
[169] ECJ 25 May 1978, Joined Case 83 and 94/76 4, 15 and 40/77, ECR 1978, 1209, 1234 (*Bayerische HNL and Others v Council and Commission*); however, in the second *Mulder* case the large number of claimants was no obstacle for establishing liability. The case was about a Community Regulation, which precluded many farmers from being qualified for a milk quota. It was held that this Regulation violated the farmers' legitimate expectations and this was not justified by higher public interests: ECJ 19 May 1992, Joined cases C-104/89 and C-37/90, ECR 1992, I-3061 (*Mulder and Others v Council and Commission (Mulder)*), about which Van Gerven (2000), 902–906.
[170] ECJ 4 July 2000, Case 352/98, ECR 2000, I-5291 (*Laboratoires Pharmaceutique Bergaderm SA and Gouplin v Commission*), paras 42–44. In the same sense for example Wurmnest, *Grundzüge eines europäisches Haftungsrecht* (2003), 222.

D EUROPEAN CONVENTION ON HUMAN RIGHTS

1807 The right to life: Article 2 ECHR

1807-1 *Introduction*

The European Convention on Human Rights and the European Court of Human Rights have substantially contributed to a 'minimum' as regards liability of public authorities. This 'minimum' is that Contracting States are obliged to respect fundamental rights. In the framework of this book these are particularly the right to life (Article 2, nr 1807), the right to physical integrity and health (Article 3, nr 1808) access to justice (Article 6, nr 1804-3), and the right to privacy, family life and home (Article 8, nr 705-5, 1413-5 and 1808-2).

Article 2 ECHR protects the right to life against infringements by a Contracting State and runs as follows:

1. Everyone's right to life shall be protected by law. No one shall be deprived of his life intentionally save in the execution of a sentence of a court following his conviction of a crime for which this penalty is provided by law.
2. Deprivation of life shall not be regarded as inflicted in contravention of this article when it results from the use of force which is no more than absolutely necessary:
    a. in defence of any person from unlawful violence;
    b. in order to effect a lawful arrest or to prevent the escape of a person lawfully detained;
    c. in action lawfully taken for the purpose of quelling a riot or insurrection.

Article 2 not only obliges the State to refrain from the intentional and unlawful taking of life but the European Court of Human Rights holds that it also obliges States to prevent danger they caused themselves and to prevent real and immediate dangers for someone's life caused by other people.[171] These are the so-called positive obligations to actively protect citizens' lives. These positive obligations are pivotal in the recent development of the Court's case law, and they have provided a minimum standard of care for public authorities, particularly in the area of health and safety.[172] Three aspects can be distinguished as regards Article 2.

Firstly, the State owes a duty to take precautionary measures if the authorities know or ought to know about a *real and imminent danger* for someone's life; see nr 1807-2.

---

[171] ECtHR 28 March 2000, Case 22492/93 (*Kilic v Turkey*), § 65.
[172] See Alastair Mowbray, *The Development of Positive Obligations under the European Convention on Human Rights by the European Court of Human Rights*, (Oxford: Hart, 2004).

Secondly, the State owes an obligation to *provide information* about serious health threats; see nr 1808-2.

Finally, if a person has died as the consequence of violence or if someone alleges that he has been tortured, humiliated, or has suffered inhumane treatment or punishment (see Article 3), Article 2 obliges the authorities of the state to *investigate* the case.

Where the events in issue lie wholly, or in large part, within the exclusive knowledge of the authorities, as for example in the case of persons within their control in custody, strong presumptions of fact will arise in respect of injuries and death which occur. Indeed, the burden of proof may be regarded as resting on the authorities to provide a satisfactory and convincing explanation.[173]

If individuals have been killed as a result of the use of force by the authorities, the essential purpose of such investigation is

... to secure the effective implementation of the domestic laws which protect the right to life and, in those cases involving State agents or bodies, to ensure their accountability for deaths occurring under their responsibility. What form of investigation will achieve those purposes may vary in different circumstances. However, whatever mode is employed, the authorities must act of their own motion, once the matter has come to their attention. They cannot leave it to the initiative of the next of kin either to lodge a formal complaint or to take responsibility for the conduct of any investigative procedures.[174]

In *Kelly and others v United Kingdom* the Court considered that investigations ought to be independent, effective and prompt. In this case the next-of-kin of nine men killed in 1987 during a British security force operation in Northern Ireland alleged that their relatives had been unjustifiably killed and that there had been no effective investigation into the circumstances of their death. The Court found a number of shortcomings, such as a lack of independence of the investigating police officers from the security forces involved in the incident, a lack of public scrutiny, and a lack of information to the victims' families of the reasons for the decision not to prosecute any soldier. Also, the inquest proceedings did not commence promptly and were not pursued with reasonable expedition. The Court held that the United Kingdom authorities had thus violated Article 2 and awarded, on the basis of Article 41, each applicant a sum of £10,000 for non-pecuniary loss.[175]

[173] ECtHR 4 May 2001, Case 30054/96 (*Kelly and others v United Kingdom*), § 92; ECtHR 27 June 2000, Case 21986/93 (*Salman v Turkey*), § 100. See also ECtHR 27 September 1995, Case 18984/91 (*McCann and others v United Kingdom*).

[174] ECtHR 4 May 2001, Case 30054/96 (*Kelly and others v United Kingdom*), § 94; ECtHR 27 September 1995, Case 18984/91 (*McCann and others v United Kingdom*), § 161; ECtHR 19 February 1998, Case 22729/93 (*Kaya v Turkey*), § 105.

[175] ECtHR 4 May 2001, Case 30054/96 (*Kelly and others v United Kingdom*), § 94–98, 136 and 161–165. See also ECtHR 27 July 1998, Case 21593/93 (*Güleç v Turkey*), § 81–82; ECtHR 19 February 1998, Case 22729/93 (*Kaya v Turkey*), § 87; ECtHR 2 September 1998, Case 22495/93 (*Yaşa v Turkey*).

1807-2 *Protection against imminent life-threatening danger*

A second positive obligation following from Article 2 is the State's obligation to take precautionary measures if the authorities know or ought to know about a real and imminent danger for someone's life. Three cases are of particular importance in this respect: *Osman, Kilic* and *Öneryildiz.* The main requirements in this case law are that the authorities knew or ought to have known about the threat for a specific person but that an obligation to take precautionary measures must be interpreted in a way which does not impose an impossible or disproportionate burden on the authorities. It is not required that the precautionary measures would have prevented the risk; it can be sufficient that the risk would only have be reduced (compare nr 807-2).

The *Osman* case was about a boy who was harassed by his teacher, the latter in the end using violence, killing the boy's father and injuring the boy and his mother. The Court of Appeal dismissed the Osman's claim against the police for not timely tracking down the teacher. It held that it would not be fair, just, and reasonable to impose a duty of care on the police in investigation matters, thus following the House of Lords' precedent in *Hill* (nr 1804-2). The Osmans went to Strasbourg and invoked, *inter alia*, an infringement of Article 2, particularly the violation of the authorities' positive obligation to take preventive operational measures to protect an individual against imminent life-threatening danger.[176] The Court pointed out that such an obligation must be interpreted in a way which does not impose an impossible or disproportionate burden on the authorities, and that a violation of this obligation can only be established if

... the authorities knew or ought to have known at the time of the existence of a real and immediate risk to the life of an identified individual or individuals from the criminal acts of a third party and that they failed to take measures within the scope of their powers which, judged reasonably, might have been expected to avoid that risk.[177]

The Court concluded that in this case there was no violation of Article 2 since '... the applicants have failed to point to any decisive stage in the sequence of the events leading up to the tragic shooting when it could be said that the police knew or ought to have known that the lives of the Osman family were at real and immediate risk from [the teacher].'[178] In *Kilic v Turkey* the Court considered that the knowledge requirement was satisfied. This case was about Kemal Kilic, a journalist who worked for the

---

[176] ECtHR 28 October 1998, Case 87/1997 (*Osman v United Kingdom*). See nr 1804-3 about the decision of the Court in this case on Article 6.

[177] ECtHR 28 October 1998, Case 87/1997 (*Osman v United Kingdom*), § 116.

[178] ECtHR 28 October 1998, Case 87/1997 (*Osman v United Kingdom*), § 121. This conclusion came as a surprise since the teacher had told a police officer before his action that he was going to do 'a sort of Hungerford', referring to August 1987, when a lone gunman went on the rampage through a sleepy English town, shooting dead 15 people and wounding 14 others, before turning the gun on himself. See the Court of Appeal decision in *Osman v Ferguson* [1993] 4 All ER 344.

Turkish Kurdish oriented Özgür Gündem newspaper and who had been subjected to death threats. He had pleaded for help from the authorities and was murdered later. The Court considered that a range of preventive measures could have been taken to minimize the risk but that the authorities had denied that there was any risk at all. The Court awarded £15,000 (€25,000) for non-pecuniary loss to be paid to his heirs (para. 105).[179]

Öneryildiz was about people who lived in a zone surrounding a rubbish tip in illegally built dwellings in the neighbourhood of Istanbul, also known as the slums of Ümraniye. The accommodation was tolerated by the authorities though they knew that experts had concluded that the Ümraniye tip exposed humans, animals, and the environment to every form of danger. On 28 April 1993 a methane explosion occurred at the site. Thirty-nine people died, including nine members of the family of the applicant, Maşalla Öneryildiz. The Grand Chamber of the Court concluded that the Turkish authorities

... at several levels knew or ought to have known that there was a real and immediate risk to a number of persons living near the Ümraniye municipal rubbish tip. They consequently had a positive obligation under Article 2 of the Convention to take such preventive operational measures as were necessary and sufficient to protect those individuals (...), especially as they themselves had set up the site and authorised its operation, which gave rise to the risk in question.[180]

According to the Court the Turkish authorities had failed to take those necessary urgent measures.

The Court rejected the Government's argument, comparable to the contributory negligence defence (nr 1212), that the applicant had acted illegally in settling by the rubbish tip.[181] It held that the authorities had acknowledged the existence of the slums and the way of life of the citizens, that they had provided them with public services and had levied council tax. Accordingly, the Government could not maintain that they were absolved of responsibility on account of the victim's negligence or lack of foresight.[182]

As regards the remedy, the Court considered that the applicants undoubtedly suffered loss as a result of the violations found and that there was a clear causal link between the violations and the pecuniary damage alleged. The Court awarded Öneryildiz €29,000 for pecuniary loss (including legal costs) and €33,750 for non-pecuniary loss. The same amount for non-pecuniary loss was awarded to his three surviving adult sons.[183]

---

[179] ECtHR 28 March 2000, Case 22492/93 (*Kilic v Turkey*).
[180] ECtHR 30 November 2004, Case 48939/99 (*Öneryildiz v Turkey*), § 101.
[181] With reference to ECtHR 18 January 2001, Case 27238/95 (*Chapham v United Kingdom*).
[182] ECtHR 30 November 2004, Case 48939/99 (*Öneryildiz v Turkey*), § 105–106.
[183] ECtHR 30 November 2004, Case 48939/99 (*Öneryildiz v Turkey*), § 171–175.

It can be concluded from the foregoing that States have a margin of appreciation and that a violation of Article 2 will be established in specific circumstances only. The Court described the background of this reluctance in *Osman*:

Bearing in mind the difficulties involved in policing modern societies, the unpredictability of human conduct and the operational choices which must be made in terms of priorities and resources, such an obligation must be interpreted in a way which does not impose an impossible or disproportionate burden on the authorities. Accordingly, not every claimed risk to life can entail for the authorities a Convention requirement to take operational measures to prevent that risk from materialising.[184]

In other words, public authorities have a margin of discretion but this does not exclude their possible liability. They are bound to comply with feasible and proportionate obligations to protect citizens against imminent life-threatening danger.

1808 The right to physical integrity and health

1808-1 *Article 3 ECHR*

Article 3 explicitly protects the right to bodily integrity against injury caused by torture, inhuman or degrading treatment, or punishment. This does not only apply to active misfeasance by public authorities or civil servants, for example in prisons. Similar to Article 2 the Court has developed positive obligations for a Contracting State to protect its citizens' physical integrity and health.

An important example of a breach of Article 3 is *X v Bedfordshire* before the House of Lords, and the same case under the name *Z v United Kingdom* before the European Court of Human Rights.[185] This case was about a failure of local authorities to take neglected and abused children into care (see nr 1804-3 for the facts of this case and the childrens' claim based on Article 6 ECHR). The ECtHR established a violation of Article 3, considering that there was

... no dispute in the present case that the neglect and abuse suffered by the four child applicants reached the threshold of inhuman and degrading treatment (...). This treatment was brought to the local authority's attention, at the earliest in October 1987. It was under a statutory duty to protect the children and had a range of powers available to them, including removal from their home. The children were however only taken into emergency care, at the insistence of the mother, on 30 April 1992. (...). The Court acknowledges the difficult and sensitive decisions facing social services and the important countervailing principle of respecting and preserving family life. The present case however leaves no doubt as to the failure of the system to protect these child applicants from serious, long-term neglect and abuse. Accordingly, there has been a violation of art 3 of the Convention.[186]

---

[184] ECtHR 28 October 1998, Case 87/1997 (*Osman v United Kingdom*).
[185] ECtHR 10 May 2001, Case 29392/95 (*Z v United Kingdom*).
[186] ECtHR 10 May 2001, Case 29392/95 (*Z v United Kingdom*), paras 74–75.

The Court also found (para. 111) that in this case

... the applicants did not have available to them an appropriate means of obtaining a determination of their allegations that the local authority failed to protect them from inhuman and degrading treatment and the possibility of obtaining an enforceable award of compensation for the damage suffered thereby. Consequently, they were not afforded an effective remedy in respect of the breach of art 3 and there has, accordingly, been a violation of art 13 of the Convention.

This Article provides that everyone '... whose rights and freedoms as set forth in the Convention are violated shall have an effective remedy before a national authority notwithstanding that the violation has been committed by persons acting in an official capacity.' On the basis of Article 41, the Court afforded just satisfaction to the claimants by awarding substantial amounts of compensation for pecuniary loss of up to £50,000 (para. 113 ff).

Similar to the positive obligation following from Article 2 the Court requires that the public authority knew or ought to have known about the risk to the citizens' health or physical integrity. Also, the Court is prepared to take into account the difficult and sensitive decisions to be made by public authorities and the important countervailing principle of respecting and preserving family life. However, this does not exclude the duty to protect the citizens' health and physical integrity.

The Court awarded damages to the applicants on the basis of Article 41 ECHR. For pecuniary loss, consisting of future medical costs (particularly psychological help) and for loss of employment opportunities the awards ranged from £4,000 (€5,700) to £50,000 (€72,000) (para. 127). For non-pecuniary loss all applicants were awarded a sum of £32,000 (€46,000), mainly for suffering because of psychiatric illness (para. 128).

1808-2 *Articles 2 and 8 ECHR*

As regards the protection of physical integrity and health Articles 2 and 8 ECHR can also play a role. The Court has derived from Article 2 (nr 1807-1) that public authorities owe a duty to provide the public with adequate information about serious health risks. *LCB v United Kingdom* was a case about soldiers who had been exposed to radioactivity. As a consequence of this exposure, many children of those soldiers suffered from leukaemia. On the basis of Article 2 ECHR the Court held that authorities are generally obliged to provide adequate information if they know that someone is exposed to radiation and as a consequence of this runs an actual health risk. In this case, however, the Court did not find a violation of Article 2.[187]

In *Öneryildiz* (nr 1807-2) the Chamber of the Court generalized this decision by stating that such a duty to inform exists if (a) the information about the specific risk was not directly available to the applicant and (b) the information in question could

---

[187] ECtHR 9 June 1998, Case 23413/94 (*LCB v United Kingdom*), § 38.

not have been imparted to the public other than by action by the authorities which were in possession of that information. In this case the information provided by the authorities would have enabled the applicant to assess the serious dangers for himself and his family in continuing to live in the vicinity of the rubbish tip.[188]

Article 8 ECHR protects the right to private life (nr 705-5) and home (nr 1413-5). The scope of this provision includes the protection of a person's physical and psychological integrity. Article 8 is also a sound basis for a claim for failing to provide information about health risks. An example is *Guerra v Italy*. This case was about people living close to a factory that emitted toxic substances. They alleged that the authorities had failed to provide information enabling them to assess the risks to their health if they continued living there. The Court concluded that this was a violation of Article 8. The applicants were not obliged to prove causation, ie that the neighbours would have moved away if they had known of the risk. The Court held that the applicants undoubtedly suffered non-pecuniary loss and awarded each of them ITL 10,000,000 (€5,150).[189] This means that, if national law inadequately protects the physical well-being of an individual, a claim can be filed on the basis of both Article 3 and Article 8.[190]

Articles 2, 3 and 8 are very much intertwined but the main difference is that the obligation following from Article 2 envisages situations in which the life of persons is at stake, whereas the obligations based on Article 3 and 8 are related to situations that can endanger health but are not directly life threatening.

E CONCLUDING REMARKS

1809 The issue of public authority liability

It could be argued that a public authority can be liable if it does not act with the care one may expect from a reasonable acting public authority given the circumstances of the case.[191] In this way liability of public bodies does not look much different from that of private bodies and individuals. However,

---

[188] ECtHR 18 June 2002, Case 48939/99 (*Öneryildiz v Turkey*), § 85–88 with reference to ECtHR 9 June 1998, Case 23413/94 (*LCB v United Kingdom*), § 40–41.

[189] ECtHR 19 February 1998, Case 14967/89 (*Guerra v Italy*).

[190] In ECtHR 26 March 1985, Case 8978/80 (*X and Y v The Netherlands*) the Court found a violation of Article 8 (a rapist could not be prosecuted where the victim was a minor and mentally handicapped) and did not go into the violation of Article 3. In ECtHR 10 May 2001, Case 29392/95 (*Z v United Kingdom*), about which nr 1808-1, the Court found a violation of Article 3 and did not consider the complaint based on Article 8.

[191] In this sense for instance Walter van Gerven, 'A Common European Law in the Area of Tort Law', in Duncan Fairgrieve, Mads Andenas and John Bell (eds.), *Tort Liability of Public Authorities in Comparative Perspective* (London: BIICL, 2002), 136; see also his 'Bridging the Unbridgeable: Community and National Tort Laws After Francovich and Brasserie', *ICLQ*, 45 (1996), 507–544, at 521.

throughout the legal systems the question of liability of public authorities is answered in very different ways. Although all systems acknowledge liability in cases of actively caused damage, the main issue is whether a public authority can be liable for not taking action where it could have prevented or limited the damage. Hence, the discussion in this chapter mainly focused on liability for public authorities' omissions. Various arguments have been put forward against liability in such situations.[192]

Firstly, the task of a public authority can be extraordinarily delicate. It may need to tread a fine line between taking action or not, to take it neither too soon nor too late. Though this is undoubtedly true, it is a standard function for any professional to assess what may be a fraught and difficult situation. One may especially think of doctors having to cope with similar conflicts; they do not have a privileged position in tort law but in their cases this is generally not a reason for not requiring the exercise of reasonable skill and care in the task. 'The professional is not required to be right, but only to be reasonably skilful and careful.[193] Hence, this delicacy argument is not convincing for excluding liability.'

Secondly, public authorities might adopt a defensive approach if they are faced with the risk of being held liable. This assertion, however, does not seem to be evidence-based and is also unfair towards public authorities and the professionals working there. In making choices they are driven by many other considerations than just potential liability. 'To describe awareness of a legal duty as having an "insidious effect" on the mind of a potential defendant is to undermine the foundation of the law of professional negligence'.[194] Moreover, in *Z v United Kingdom* the ECtHR explicitly rejected the argument that potential liability would lead to a defensive approach by public authorities (nr 1808-1).

Thirdly, other remedies may be available such as recourse to statutory appeal mechanisms, judicial review, compensation by funds for victims of crime, and Ombudsman schemes. However, in many cases these remedies may be less effective to solve the claimant's problem than an action for damages. The other remedies can particularly be insufficient to satisfy the requirement of Article 13 ECHR that everyone whose rights and freedoms are violated shall have an effective remedy before a national authority (nr 1202-6). Also in Community law an effective remedy is considered to be pivotal: in its *Francovich* case law the ECJ has put strong emphasis on the importance of a right to damages for the full effectiveness of Community law. A claim for damages is likely to be more effective than other remedies and in many cases it is probably the only effective

---

[192] See for this discussion also and in particular the refutation in *JD v East Berkshire Community Health NHS Trust and Others* [2005] UKHL 23, nr 31–36, per Lord Bingham of Cornhill of the arguments against liability of public authorities put forward by Lord Browne-Wilkinson in *X (Minors) v Bedfordshire County Council* [1995] 2 AC 633.

[193] *JD v East Berkshire Community Health Trust and Others* [2005] UKHL 23, para. 32, per Lord Bingham of Cornhill.

[194] *JD v East Berkshire Community Health NHS Trust and Others* [2005] UKHL 23, para. 33, per Lord Bingham of Cornhill.

remedy. More generally, infringing the rights of citizens should not be cheaper than respecting them.

Finally, perhaps the most fundamental policy reason to exclude public authorities' liability is that it can cut across the statutory system and raise problems of ascertaining and allocating responsibility. This argument is related to the principle of the separation of powers: judiciary, legislature, and executive are considered to have different responsibilities. This is a basic principle in each Member State. One of the consequences of this principle is that political questions have to be answered by the executive and the legislator and not by the judiciary. It is considered not to be the task of the judge to review the desirability of choices made by executive and legislator. Since legislative acts often imply a stronger policy element than administrative (executive) acts, the judicial role as regards legislative acts is generally smaller than as regards administrative acts.

In many, if not all, Member States the conditions for liability for legislative action are appreciably different from those concerning administrative action. Often proof of some degree of wrongful conduct is all that is required in the case of administrative authorities. (...). The liability of the legislative authorities, however, is governed by stricter rules, with in particular a requirement of unusual and specific damage, or is quite simply non-existent.[195]

This illustrates the importance of the issue of discretion in liability of public authorities.

1810 Inevitability and limits of discretion

The key issue in liability of a public authority is the fact that in many cases it is considered to have a margin of discretion if it deals with policy-related issues. If this is the case the courts do not establish liability by applying a full-fledged negligence test but they use a more reluctant test. In France a serious fault (*faute lourde*) is required, whereas in Germany the public authority has to use its discretion in a proper way. In Community law, discretion is a factor to be taken into account although it is not yet quite clear in which way this needs to be done and what the limits of discretion are. In England the discussion is still very much at a basic level, where public bodies' decisions in which policy issues are involved are often deemed to be not justiciable at all.

The discretion issue is complicated by the fact that public bodies' conduct cannot be divided into policy matters and non-policy matters. It is rather a matter of more or less policy. This implies that the level of court's reluctance will

---

[195] Advocate-General Darmon, before ECJ 13 March 1992, Case C-282/90, ECR 1992, I-1937, 1958, para. 43 (*Vreugdenhil v Commission (Vreugdenhil II)*).

generally correspond with the level of policy involved in the decision: the more policy, the more reluctance in assessing the public authority's conduct. However, even in cases in which policy plays an important role, important limits as to the public authority's discretion apply.[196]

The most important limit in this respect is that policy reasons can never be a ground to infringe human rights. The protection provided by fundamental rights secures a minimum standard of conduct for public authorities, even in matters of pure policy. This development has been strengthened by the creation of positive obligations as regards various provisions in the European Convention on Human Rights (nr 1807-1). Particularly in *López Ostra* (nr 1413-5), *Z*, and *Öneryildiz* (nr 1807-2) human rights have set limits to public authorities' discretion. They have indicated in which situation the public authority's discretion is reduced to zero (in German: a *Ermessensreduzierung auf Null*, nr 1803-3). Certainly, a local authority enjoys a margin of discretion in enforcing environmental law but if the circumstances for a neighbourhood are getting really unhealthy and the authority ought to know this, it has to take action to protect the citizens (*López Ostra*). Certainly, a child protection authority enjoys a margin of discretion but if the circumstances for the child are really serious and the authority ought to know this, it has to take action in order to protect the child (*Z*). Certainly, health and safety authorities enjoy a margin of discretion but if the circumstances are really dangerous and the authority ought to know this, it has to take action in order to protect the potential victims (*Öneryildiz*).

Human rights ensure that even policy-driven conduct of public authorities is subject to scrutiny on a liability level. However, the legal systems are at various stages of infusing their tort law systems with these human rights. Whereas in Germany and France the Constitution has been at the heart of private law and tort law for a long time, it was only on the threshold of this century when the Human Rights Act entered into force that English law allowed claimants to invoke the European Convention on Human Rights before a national court (nr 501-3). For the time being the House of Lords remains cautious when it comes to accepting duties of care for public authorities in matters of policy. After the initial blow of *Osman*, the *Z* case seems to have left space for their Lordships to factually retain important pockets of public authority immunities (nr 1804-4). Even though one should not overestimate the willingness of German and French courts to impose liability for policy-related conduct, the differences with the English approach remain substantial and may be a major obstacle for bringing national tort laws closer to each other.

[196] One may also think of the principles of good governance such as the principle that a public body is not allowed to abuse its power or of the principle that it must not frustrate legitimate expectations.

1811 Strict liability and the equality principle

The necessity to grant public authorities a margin of discretion can leave claimants empty-handed because their damage is not recoverable on the basis of fault liability. This is not always satisfactory, and a way to solve this problem is to create a rule of strict liability for public authorities for the consequences of their lawful conduct. This means that individuals, companies, and organizations who disproportionately suffer from measures taken in the general interest may have a right to compensation for damage which is not deemed to be part of their daily risk of business or life (nr 1802-3 and 1803-1). In France this liability is based on the principle of *égalité devant les charges publiques* and in Germany on the customary *Sonderopfer* rule. The ECJ has also acknowledged the right to compensation for lawful acts, though in practice it has not yet allowed such a claim (nr 1806). England does not acknowledge such a rule of strict liability or for lawful acts.

As has been pointed out, strict liability avoids difficulties created by the tension between the need to compensate the victim and the consequent need of having to set a high level of care that is contrary to the character of the conduct (nr 1004-1). Indeed, this is what a rule of strict liability can avoid in matters of public authority liability, since the rule does not focus on the question of whether the public authority's conduct was correct or incorrect, but on the question of whether citizens are equally treated, ie the focus is on their loss and how this differs from the loss of other citizens. Strict liability is an important tool to shift the loss suffered by a disproportionately affected individual to the collective of taxpayers.

The leading thread running through this book was that there are important differences between France and Germany, on the one hand, and England, on the other as a result of a difference in policy approach in tort law matters (nr 609). These differences have once again been illustrated in this chapter with the more reluctant approach in English law to liability of public authorities in general and the absence of a strict liability rule based on a legal equality principle.

Two lines meet here. Firstly, English tort law is generally reluctant—perhaps even averse—to rules of strict liability (nr 605). Secondly, English tort law has traditionally put a strong emphasis on duties (in this respect: of the government) rather than on rights (in this respect: of the citizens) (nr 610).[196A] A fine illustration of this latter aspect is the fact that citizens are not necessarily left empty-handed if they suffer harm caused by maladministration. Compensation can be obtained by means of so-called *ex gratia* payments by public bodies. These payments are made after investigations of an ombudsman, or on the basis of the public body's internal procedures: particularly since the 1990s public bodies

---

[196A] A third line might be the delicate relationship between legislator and judiciary (nr 501-4). It is thought that the judiciary should not interfere with the legislator's prerogative to provide compensation or not if individuals or groups are disproprotionaly affected.

have set up a 'bewildering' number of compensation schemes.[197] Apart from the fact that this way of providing redress is naturally at odds with the public body's own budget, the more striking matter is that these payments are made without admitting legal liability. Essentially they are paid by the public body's grace. Hence, the basis for payments is a moral duty of the public body rather than an enforceable right of the affected citizen.

It remains a topic for further research as to how deep the differences between the legal systems are rooted in national history, but it is remarkable that countries in which citizens stood up against the crown in historic revolutions take different views in this respect from countries in which this did not happen. However this may be, the Human Rights Act 1998 and its implementation into English law may very well turn out to be such a revolution. It could bring English law closer to French and German legal principles of equality. Whether this will indeed happen is mainly in the hands of the current and future members of the House of Lords, who are called to reconcile the common law traditions with what can be considered to be one of the fruits of the French Revolution.

If it depended on Lord Phillips of Worth Matravers there is reason to believe that legal principles will indeed converge. In his speech in *Marcic v Thames Water Utilities Ltd* he questioned whether a fault-based approach in nuisance would be compatible with Article 8 ECHR (the right to respect for private and family life and home). The case was about the recurring flooding of Marcic's premises because of the overloaded sewers of Thames Water. Lord Phillips, by then Master of the Rolls and since 2005 the Lord Chief Justice, said exactly this:

> ... those who pay to make use of a sewerage system should be charged sufficient to cover the cost of paying compensation to the minority who suffer damage as a consequence of the operation of the system. (...). [W]here an authority carries on an undertaking in the interest of the community as a whole it may have to pay compensation to individuals whose rights are infringed by that undertaking in order to achieve a fair balance between the interests of the individual and the community.[198]

This extract, albeit an *obiter dictum*, is remarkable for two reasons. Firstly, it shows that the discussion on the implementation of human rights is a pivotal one for the development of English tort law, particularly as regards liability of public authorities. Secondly, it illustrates nicely the different approaches of the Master of the Rolls and the House of Lords in the same matter. Whereas the House of Lords limited itself to looking at the case from a fault liability and corrective justice perspective, the Master of the Rolls advocated a strict liability approach based on distributive justice.

---

[197] See about these possibilities for compensation Duncan Fairgrieve, *State Liability in Tort. A Comparative Law Study* (Oxford: Oxford University Press, 2003), 244–251.

[198] *Marcic v Thames Water Utilities Ltd* [2002] 2 WLR 932, 998–999. This was, however, an *obiter dictum*; the Court of Appeal awarded the claim on the basis of nuisance. The High Court had awarded Marcic's claim on the basis of the Human Rights Act. The House of Lords dismissed both the nuisance and the Human Rights Act claim (nr 1413-2).

Although the emphasis in this book has been on the general features of each legal system, it is obvious that there are differences of opinion within the legal systems which sometimes—like in the liability of public authorities in England—interact like tectonic plates. This once again shows the importance of a genuine transboundary discourse on European tort law, ie a discourse from the various policy perspectives rather than from the various national perspectives (nr 609).

Bibliography

LITERATURE CITED IN ABBREVIATED FORM

Aubry and Rau-Dejean de la Bathie (1989)
Charles Aubry, Charles Frédéric Rau, *Droit civil français*, 8th edn. by Noël Dejean de la Bathie (Paris: Librairie Techniques, 1989)

Von Bar (1998)
Christian von Bar, *The Common European Law of Torts*, 1st vol. (Oxford: Oxford University Press, 1998)

Von Bar (2000)
Christian von Bar, *The Common European Law of Torts*, 2nd vol. (Oxford: Oxford University Press, 2000)

Brown and Bell (1998)
Neville Brown and John S. Bell, *French Administrative Law*, 5th edn. (Oxford: Clarendon Press, 1998)

Carbonnier (2000)
Jean Carbonnier, *Droit Civil. Vol. 4: Les Obligations*, 22nd edn. (Paris: Presses Universitaires de France, 2000)

Chapus (1987)
René Chapus, *Droit administratif général*, 3e edn. (Paris: Montchrestien, 1987)

Clerk and Lindsell on Torts (2000)
John Frederic Clerk, William Henry Barber Lindsell and Reginald Walter Michael Dias, *Clerk and Lindsell on Torts*, 18th edn. (London: Sweet & Maxwell, 2000)

Craig and De Búrca (2003)
Paul Craig and Gráinne de Búrca, *EU Law: Text, Cases and Materials*, 3rd edn. (Oxford: Oxford University Press, 2003)

Deutsch-Ahrens (2002)
Erwin Deutsch and Hans-Jürgen Ahrens, *Deliktsrecht*, 4th edn. (Cologne: Heymann, 2002)

Dobbs I (2001)
Dan B. Dobbs, *The Law of Torts* (St. Paul, Minn.: West Group, 2001)

ETL 2002
Helmut Koziol and Barbara C. Steininger (eds.), *European Tort Law 2002* (Vienna, New York: Springer, 2003)

ETL 2003
Helmut Koziol and Barbara C. Steininger (eds.), *European Tort Law 2003* (Vienna, New York: Springer, 2004)

ETL 2004
Helmut Koziol and Barbara C. Steininger (eds.), *European Tort Law 2004* (Vienna, New York: Springer, 2005)

Fleming (1998)
John G. Fleming, *Law of Torts*, 9th edn. (North Ryde: LBC Information Services, 1998)

Van Gerven (2000)
    Walter van Gerven, Jeremy Lever and Pierre Larouche, *Tort Law* (Oxford: Hart, 2000)
Hartkamp, Hesselink and Hondius (eds.) (2004)
    Arthur Hartkamp, Martijn Hesselink and Ewoud Hondius (eds.), *Towards a European Civil Code*, 3rd edn. (The Hague: Kluwer Law International; Nijmegen: Ars Aequi, 2004)
Koch and Koziol (2002)
    Bernhard A. Koch and Helmut Koziol (eds.), *Unification of Tort Law: Strict Liability* (The Hague, London, Boston: Kluwer, 2002)
Kötz-Wagner (2001)
    Hein Kötz and Gerhard Wagner, *Deliktsrecht*, 9th edn. (Neuwied: Luchterhand, 2001)
Larenz (1987)
    Karl Larenz, *Lehrbuch des Schuldrechts. Band 1 Allgemeiner Teil*, 14th edn. (Munich: Beck, 1987)
Larenz-Canaris (1994)
    Karl Larenz, *Lehrbuch des Schuldrechts. Band 2 Besonderer Teil*, 13th edn., 2nd vol. edited by Claus-Wilhelm Canaris (Munich: Beck, 1994)
Markesinis and Deakin (2003)
    Basil S. Markesinis and Simon Deakin, *Markesinis and Deakin's Tort Law* (Oxford: Clarendon, 2003)
Markesinis-Unberath (2002)
    Basil S. Markesinis and Hannes Unberath, *The German Law of Torts: a Comparative Treatise*, 4th edn. (Oxford: Hart, 2002)
Mazeaud-Tunc (1965)
    Henri Mazeaud, Léon Mazeaud and André Tunc, *Traité théorique et pratique de la responsabilité civile: délictuelle et contractuelle*, 3rd vol. (Paris: Montchrestien, 1965)
McGregor on Damages (2003)
    Harvey McGregor, *On Damages*, 17th edn. (London: Sweet & Maxwell, 2003)
Münchener Kommentar-Oetker (2001)
    Münchener Kommentar zum Bürgerlichen Gesetzbuch, Volume 2, Wolfgang Krüger (ed.), Schuldrecht, Allgemeiner Teil § 241–432, FernAbsG, 4th edn. Hartmut Oetker, § 249–254 (Munich: Beck, 2001)
Münchener Kommentar-Grundmann (2003)
    Münchener Kommentar zum Bürgerlichen Gesetzbuch, Volume 2a, Wolfgang Krüger (ed.), Schuldrecht, Allgemeiner Teil § 241–432, 4th edn., Stephan Grundmann, § 276 (Munich: Beck, 2003)
Münchener Kommentar-Seiler (1997)
    Münchener Kommentar zum Bürgerlichen Gesetzbuch, Volume 4, Harm Peter Westermann (ed.), Schuldrecht, Besonderer Teil II (§ 607–704), 3rd edn., Hans Herrmann Seiler, § 683 (Munich: Beck, 1997)
Münchener Kommentar-Wagner (2004)
    Münchener Kommentar zum Bürgerlichen Gesetzbuch, Volume 5, Peter Ulmer (ed.), Schuldrecht, Besonderer Teil III, § 705–853, Partnerschaftsgesellschaftsgesetz, Produkthaftungsgesetz, 4th edn. Gerhard Wagner, Vor § 823–853 and § 823–838 (Munich: Beck, 2004)

Bibliography

Münchener Kommentar-Papier (2004)
  Münchener Kommentar zum Bürgerlichen Gesetzbuch, Volume 5, Peter Ulmer (ed.), Schuldrecht, Besonderer Teil III, §§ 705–853, Partnerschaftsgesellschaftsgesetz, Produkthaftungsgesetz, 4th edn., Hans-Jürgen Papier, § 839 (Munich: Beck, 2004)
Prosser and Keeton (1984)
  William Lloyd Prosser and Page W. Keeton, *Prosser and Keeton on the law of torts*, 5th edn. (St. Paul, Minn.: West Pub. Co., 1984)
Rivero and Waline (1998)
  Jean Rivero and Jean Waline, *Droit administratif*, 17th edn. (Paris: Dalloz, 1998)
Salmond and Heuston (1996)
  Salmond and Heuston on the Law of Torts, 21st edn. edited by Robert Francis V. Heuston and R.A. Buckley (London: Sweet & Maxwell, 1996)
Terré-Simler-Lequette (2002)
  François Terré, Philippe Simler and Yves Lequette, *Droit Civile: Les Obligations*, 8th edn. (Paris: Dalloz, 2002)
Le Tourneau (2004)
  Phillippe Le Tourneau, *Droit de la Responsibalité et des contrats* (Paris: Dalloz, 2004–2005)
Viney, Introduction (1995)
  Geneviève Viney, *Introduction á la responsabilité*, 2nd edn. (Paris: Librairie Générale de Droit et de Jurisprudence, 1995)
Viney-Jourdain (1998)
  Geneviève Viney and Patrice Jourdain, *Les Conditions de la Responsabilité*, 2nd edn. (Paris: Librairie Générale de Droit et de Jurisprudence, 1998)
Weir (2000)
  Tony Weir, *A Casebook on Tort*, 9th edn. (London: Sweet & Maxwell, 2000)
Winfield and Jolowicz (2002)
  Winfield and Jolowicz on Tort, 16th edn. edited by W. H.V. Rogers (London: Sweet & Maxwell, 2002)
Zweigert and Kötz (1998)
  Konrad Zweigert and Hein Kötz, *Introduction to Comparative Law*, 3rd edn. (Oxford: Clarendon Press; New York: Oxford University Press, 1998)

Index

child
  contributory negligence by 1215
  liability for
    comparative observations 1604
    parents, of 1602
    supervisors, of 1603
  parents, liability of
    English law 1602-3
    French law 1602-1
    German law 1602-2
  personal conduct, liability for 813-1
    English tort law, in 813-4
    French tort law, in 813-2
    German tort law, in 813-3
  premises, liability for damage on 1506-4
  premises, safety on
    English law 1504-1
    German law 1503-2
civil law
  common law compared 607-1
  statutory rule, violation of 901
  systematization 607-1
civil partnership
  fatal accident damages 1208
common law
  actions and remedies in 608-2
  around the world 501-2
  binding precedent, doctrine of 501-1
  casebooks, use of 501-5
  cases and precedents, run by 501-1
  civil law compared 607-1
  codified law, and 607-2
  development of 607-1
  statutes, role of 501-1
  statutory rule, violation of 901
  systematization 607-1
  textbooks 501-5
  United States, in 501-2
Community law
  application of 203-2
  breach, liability for 201-1
    Article 288 EC, link with 205-2
    balancing of circumstances 1805-2
    causal link with damage 1805-1
    Community institutions, of 204-5, 205-2
    competition law 205-3
    damages, action for 206
    development of principle 206
    failure to implement Directive 1805-2
    general principles 204-1, 205
    inadequate banking supervision 905-2
    individuals, of 205-3
    individuals, rights conferred on 905-1, 1805-1

  judicial decisions 205-4
  lawful acts, for 1806
  manifest 1805-3
  margin of discretion 1805-2
  Member State, of 205-1
  national courts, decisions of 205-4
  national law
    according to 905-1
    application of 206
    reparations on basis of 205-1
  national legislator, infringement
      stemming from decision
      of 205-4
  relevant factors 1805-1
  requirements for 205-1, 205-4, 206
  rules governing 205-2
  specific damage, for 1806
  sufficiently serious brench 205-1,
      205-4, 1805
  terminology 1805-3
  value of principle 206
case law 204-1
causation in 1106
comparative law, resort to for
      interpretation 201-1
direct effect
  horizontal direct 204-3
  horizontal indirect 204-4
  vertical direct 204-2
Directives
  binding nature of 204-2
  consumer protection 204-1
  failure to implement 1805-2
  timely implementation of 1003-3
  use of 204-2
effectiveness and non discrimination,
      principles of 205-2, 1202-4,
      1217
environmental liability 1415-3
influences on 201-1
legislation 204-1
motor vehicles, insurance of 1405-2
national courts, in 203-2
non discrimination and effectiveness,
      principles of 205-2, 1202-4,
      1217
private enforcement of competition
      law 1217
private law, approach to 611
protected interests 701-2
purposive interpretation 204-4
remedies in 1217
  Community institutions, liability
      of 1202-5
  Member States, liability of 1202-4